大学翻译学研究型系列教材

总主编 张柏然

当代西方翻译理论研究导引

An Introduction to Contemporary Western Translation Theories

韩江洪 编 著

南京大学出版社

当代西方翻译理论探索

上海出版公司

大学本科翻译研究型系列读本
大学翻译学研究型系列教材

顾　问（按首字母排序）

黄国文　中山大学

廖七一　四川外国语学院

潘文国　华东师范大学

王宏印　南开大学

王克非　北京外国语大学

谢天振　上海外国语大学

许　钧　南京大学

仲伟合　广东外语外贸大学

总　序

张柏然

　　到了该为翻译学研究型系列教材说几句话的时候了。两年前的炎炎夏日，南京大学出版社责成笔者总揽主编分别针对高等院校翻译学本科生和研究生学习与研究需求的研究型系列读本和导引。俗话说，独木难撑大厦。于是，笔者便千里相邀"招旧部"，网罗昔日在南大攻读翻译学博士学位的"十八罗汉"各主其事。寒来暑往，光阴荏苒，转眼两年过去了。期间，大家意气奋发，不辞辛劳，借助网络"上天"，躲进书馆"入地"，上下求索，查阅浩瀚的文献经典，进而调动自己的学术积累，披沙拣金，辨正证伪，博采众长，字斟句酌，终于成就了这一本本呈现在读者面前的教材。

　　众所周知，教材乃教学之本和知识之源，亦即体现课程教学理念、教学内容、教学要求，甚至教学模式的知识载体，在教学过程中起着引导教学方向、保证教学质量的作用。改革开放以来，我国各类高校组编、出版的翻译教材逐年递增。我们在中国国家图书馆网站上检索主题名含有"翻译"字段的图书，检索结果显示，1980 至 2009 年间，我国引进、出版相关著作 1800 余种，其中，翻译教材占有很大的比重。近些年来，翻译教材更是突飞猛进。根据有关学者的不完全统计，目前，我国正式出版的翻译教材共有 1000 多种。* 这一变化结束了我国相当长一段时间内翻译教材"一枝独秀"的境地，迎来了"百花齐放"的局面，由此也反映了我国高校翻译教学改革的深化。

　　但是，毋庸讳言，虽然教材的品种繁多，但是真正合手称便的、富有特色的教材仍属凤毛麟角。教材数量增多并不足以表明教学理念的深刻转变。其中大多都具有包打翻译学天下的纯体系冲动，并没有打破我国既往翻译教材编写从某一理论预设出发的本质主义思维模式和几大板块的框架结构。从教材建设看，我国翻译理论教材在概念陈设、模式架构、内容安排上存在着比较严重的雷同化现象。这表明，教材建设需要从根本上加以改进，而如何改则取决于我们有什么样的教学理念。

　　有鉴于此，我们组编了"大学翻译学研究型系列教材"和"大学本科翻译研究型系列读本"这两套系列教材。前者系研究生用书，它包括《中国翻译理论研究导引》、《当代西方翻译理论研究导引》、《当代西方文论与翻译研究导引》、《翻译学方法论研究导引》、《语言学与翻译研究导引》、《文学翻译研究导引》、《汉语典籍英译研究导引》、《英汉口译理论研究导引》、《语料库与翻译研究导引》和《术语翻译研究导引》等 10 册；后者则以本科生为主要读者对象，它包括《翻译概论读本》、《文化翻译读本》、《文学翻译读本》、《商务英语翻译读本》、《法律英语翻译读本》、《传媒英语翻译读本》、《科技英语翻译读本》、《英汉口译读本》、《英汉比较与翻译读本》和《翻译资源与工具读本》等 10 册。这两套教材力图综合中西译论、相关学科（如哲学、美学、文学、语

---

* 转引自曾剑平、林敏华：《论翻译教材的问题及编写体系》，《中国科技翻译》，2011 年 11 月。

言学、社会学、文化学、心理学、语料库翻译学等)的吸融性研究以及方法论的多层次研究,结合目前高校翻译教学和研究实践的现状进行创造性整合,编写突出问题型结构和理路的读本和导引,以满足翻译学科本科生和研究生教学与研究的需求。这是深化中国翻译学研究型教材编写与研究的一个重要课题,至今尚未引起翻译理论研究界和教材编写界的足够重视。摆在我们面前的这一课题,基本上还是一片多少有些生荒的地带。因此,我们对这一课题的研究,也就多少带有拓荒性质。这样,不仅大量纷繁的文献经典需要我们去发掘、辨别与整理,中西翻译美学思想发展演变的特点与规律需要我们去探讨,而且研究的对象、范畴和方法等问题,都需要我们进行独立的思考与确定。研究这一课题的困难也就可以想见了。然而,这一课题本身的价值和意义却又变为克服困难的巨大动力,策励着我们不揣浅陋,迎难而上,试图在翻译学研究型教材编写这块土地上,作一些力所能及的垦殖。

这两套研究型系列教材的编纂目的和编纂特色主要体现为:不以知识传授为主要目的,而是培养学生发问、好奇、探索、兴趣,即学习的主动性,逐步实现思维方式和学习方式的转变,引导学生及早进入科学研究阶段;不追求知识的完整性、系统性,突破讲授通史、通论知识的教学模式,引入探究学术问题的教学模式;引进国外教材编写理念,填补国内大学翻译学研究型教材的欠缺;所选论著具有权威性、文献性、可读性与引导性。具体而言,和传统的通史通论教材不同,这两套系列教材是以问题结构章节,这个"问题"既可以是这门课(专业方向)的主要问题,也可以是这门课某个章节的主要问题。在每个章节的安排上,则是先由"导论"说明本章的核心问题,指明获得相关知识的途径;接着,通过选文的导言,直接指向"选文"——涉及的知识面很广的范文,这样对学生的论文写作更有示范性;"选文"之后安排"延伸阅读",以拓展和深化知识;最后,通过"研究实践"或"问题与思考",提供实践方案,进行专业训练,希冀用"问题"牵引学生主动学习。这样的结构方式,突出了教材本身的问题型结构和理路,旨在建构以探索和研究为基础的教与学的人才培养模式,让年轻学子有机会接触最新成就、前沿学术和科学方法;强调通识教育、人文教育与科学教育交融,知识传授与能力培养并重,注重培养学生掌握方法,未来能够应对千变万化的翻译教学与研究的发展和需要。

笔者虽说长期从事翻译教学与研究,但对编写教材尤其是研究型教材还是个新手。这两套翻译学研究型教材之所以能够顺利出版,全有赖各册主编的精诚合作和鼎力相助,全有仗一群尽责敬业的编写和校核人员。特别值得一提的是,在这两套系列教材的最后编辑工作中,南京大学出版社外语编辑室主任董颖和责任编辑裴维维两位女士全力以赴,认真校核,一丝不苟,对保证教材的质量起了尤为重要的作用。在此谨向他(她)们致以衷心的感谢!

总而言之,编写大学翻译学研究型教材还是一项尝试性的研究工程。诚如上面所述,我们在进行这项"多少带有拓荒性质"的尝试时,犹如蹒跚学步的孩童,在这过程中留下些许尴尬,亦属在所难免。作为教材的编撰者,我们衷心希望能听到来自各方的意见和建议,以便日后再版修订,进而发展出更好更多翻译学研究型教材来。

是之为序。

二〇一二年三月二十七日
撰于沪上滴水湖畔临港别屋

前　言

　　20 世纪 80 年代以来,伴随着"西学东渐"的大潮,西方翻译理论陆续被介绍引进到中国。中国翻译界学人运用西方翻译理论来指导自己的翻译研究和翻译实践,大大促进了我国翻译学科的发展和翻译事业的进步。与此同时对西方翻译理论的研究也开展起来,学术成果不断涌现。许多高校的英语语言文学、外国语言学及应用语言学硕士点都开设了"西方翻译理论"、"翻译研究入门"等课程。近年来若干种教授西方翻译理论的教材陆续出版,然而符合我国国情、切合我国英语专业研究生需求的研究型教材极为少见。有的教材只提供西方翻译理论经典论文的内容概述和评介,研究生看不到论文本身,不识其本来面目;有的教材有导引,但只提供经典论文的汉语译文,让读者时有隔靴搔痒、雾里看花的感觉,殊不知此理论已非彼理论也;有的教材按流派或学派选编了未经翻译的经典论文,但没有任何导引。为帮助读者了解当代西方翻译理论的经典,培养读者的研究意识,提高读者开展西方翻译理论研究的能力,编者精选当代西方翻译理论及其研究的学术论文,编写了《当代西方翻译理论研究导引》这本研究性教材。

　　为突显本教材的研究性,编者首先以问题为主题和导向,选择触及翻译学研究重要问题的学术文章,并围绕这些问题设计需要读者深入思考的问题或研究课题。其次,在决定相关学术论文的取舍时,编者重视选文的代表性和经典性。这些文章代表了特定课题研究的较高研究水平,反映了相关研究领域的前沿性研究成果,体现了学界对相关研究课题的当下思考。这些选文可以作为具体研究案例,读者可以通过研读文章掌握相关课题的研究方法及学术论文的写作方法。

　　本书共分十章,分别是"可译性与对等"、"翻译转移"、"多元系统与翻译"、"翻译规范"、"翻译的功能与目的"、"语域与翻译"、"规化和异化"、"文化研究与翻译"、"哲学与翻译"、"翻译研究的跨学科性"。每章由"导论"和"选文"两大部分组成。

　　"导论"部分简要介绍某个问题或主题在当代西方翻译研究界的研究状况,梳理相关研究领域的研究内容、研究路径和代表性研究成果。

　　"选文"部分提供两类学术论文。一类围绕每章主题,以当代西方翻译理论的具体研究内容为依据,每章提供 3～4 篇西方翻译学者撰写的关于该主题的代表性学术论文。这些文章有些选自韦努蒂编的《翻译研究读本》,其他选自近年来国外出版的翻译学专著和学术期刊。另一类紧扣每章主题,每章提供一篇中国翻译学者撰写的学术论文,目的是使研究生读者了解中国学者是如何研究西方学者关于该主题的翻译理论的。这些文章绝大多数均选自近年来国内出版的外语类核心期刊。编者在收录这两类学术论文时,秉承尊重作者的原则,力求保持选文的原汁原味及其完整性。

每篇选文配有"导言"、"延伸阅读"和"问题与思考"。"导言"位于选文的正文之前,介绍所选文章的来源及其主要内容。"延伸阅读"提供了一些专题论文或著作。阅读这些论著,读者可以深化对相关研究课题的认识和理解,从而全面、辩证地分析问题。"问题与思考"提供一些有助于读者理解选文内容的问题或者需要读者进一步探索的问题。

本书在编写过程中得到了南京大学博士生导师张柏然教授和南京大学出版社领导的大力支持,在此表示衷心的感谢。

本书编著者为韩江洪,张淑艳同志也参与并做了部分工作。由于编著者水平有限,书中肯定存在诸多疏漏之处,敬请广大读者批评指正。

韩江洪

目　　录

第一章 可译性与对等

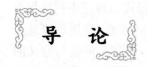

导 论

什么是可译性？可译性是指这样一个范畴：某个语义由一种语言译入另一种语言，无须经历剧烈的变化。雅各布森(Roman Jakobson)赞同可译性，因为在他看来，翻译存在于语言内部、语言之间和不同的符号系统之间。他认为，差异等值是每种语言的基本问题。在词的层面上，某个词的语法意义使其可能很难在目标语中找到一个具有相同语法意义的词来翻译，卡特福德(John C. Catford)认为这种语言差异就其功能来说与对等问题没有什么关联。其他学者注意到单词层面上的不兼容性要么是由源语和目标语文化现象的差异引起的，要么是由于目标语中缺乏称谓源语文化某个特定概念的词。人们普遍认为这种不可译性只是发生于单个词的层面，通常可以在确保保留源语语义特征的前提下通过解释而规避掉。另外，在词的层面上还可以使用补偿等翻译策略来处理这种不可译性。看语言现象是否具有可译性，不能只考虑能否保留其基本的语义特征。隐含意义、搭配意义等语义维度的存在向我们表明，不存在独立于任何语言之外的绝对意义，而可译性只是一个有限概念。此外，诸如寓意之类的文本语境特征，以及双关语、单词游戏和诗学手段等形式特征，在翻译过程中很难保留，这说明意义在很大程度上由具体的文本而产生，因此必须抛弃绝对可译性的概念。可译性概念必须与翻译的每个具体实例或具体行为联系起来考虑，还必须与源语文本类型、翻译目的和译者遵循的翻译原则结合起来加以研究。

对等(equivalence)被许多学者用于描述源语文本和目标语文本或两种更小的语言单位之间关系的本质和相关联的程度。对等在一定意义上是某一语言的语词在不同语言里的对应形式。不过，雅各布森在其名作"On Linguistic Aspects of Translation"(1959)里提出"差异中的对等"(equivalence in difference)这一术语，强调了与对等相关的一些复杂因素。对等涉及的问题很多，对等概念本身也一直处于争议之中。赫曼斯(Theo Hermans)称对等为一个"麻烦的概念"。在英语里，equivalence 一词有多重语义，西方英语世界的学者们对翻译中的对等问题的理解因此也因人而异。有些学者把翻译中的对等与数学中的对等等同起来，认为翻译中的对等不仅具有对称性而且具有可逆性。还有些学者对翻译对等的精确程度要求过高，结果造成其理论缺乏实践指导意义。卡特福德把翻译视为用目标语中对等的语篇材料替换源语的语篇材料，认为翻译的中心任务之一是确定翻译对等的本质和条件。他把翻译对等看做是可量化的，翻译因就是从目标语中所有的潜在的对等表达式中选出最合适的对等语来替换源语中的语项。卡特福德的这一观点反映了他所处时代语言学的局限性。斯内尔-霍恩比(Snell-Hornby)指出，卡特福德的观点其实预设了不同语言之间的对称程度，甚至曲解了翻译的基本问题,因为它把翻译降解为简单的语言练习,忽略了文化、文本和其他情境因素,而恰恰是这些因素在翻译中发挥着重要作用。这种观念导致许多学者以不同的方式进一步划分对等概念,其中最有名的当数奈达(Eugene Nida)的划分:形式对等(formal equivalence)和功能对等(functional equivalence)。

西方学者起初将 equivalence 这一术语引入翻译研究,意在科学地定义翻译,孰料这一术语在使用过程中变得越来越复杂,越来越歧义化。为了摆脱这一困局,有的学者干脆主张翻译研究放弃使用对等概念。赫曼斯就曾批评图里(Gideon Toury)在其翻译规范理论中仍然保留对等观念,因为这会使人忽视翻译的不对等的方面,掩盖了翻译被操纵的实质;而规范概念正好把翻译的不对等方面推向前台。翻译的对等观念完全是虚构和妄想,译文不可能与原文同一。译文的字句不同,意义有异。不仅语言随着翻译变化,而且叙述意图、时间、功能和情景全都随之改变。译者的介入不可避免,无法被清除,除非取消翻译或译文本身。翻译受多种规范的制约,必然是混杂的、不透明的和有差异的。可能在实际翻译中需要对等的观念,但这一观念纯属虚构;某一层次上的对等总是被其他层次上的差异抵消。

本章共选三篇文章。第一篇"On Linguistic Aspects of Translation"研究了等值、可译性等问题,是雅各布森运用语言学方法研究翻译的开先河之作;第二篇"Principles of Correspondence"的作者是奈达,该文较全面地阐发了他本人的动态对等思想;第三篇《关于国外翻译理论的三大核心概念——翻译的实质、可译性和等值》是中国学者蔡毅撰写的,该文较全面地分析了这些核心概念的演变情况及其特点,并在此基础上提出了作者本人的观点。

选 文

选文一 On Linguistic Aspects of Translation

Roman Jakobson

导 言

本文选自韦努蒂(Lawrence Venuti)编的《翻译研究读本》(*The Translation Studies Reader*)。

20 世纪 50 年代以前,西方的翻译研究主要围绕直译、意译等问题展开,且讨论都具有很强的模糊性、主观性。雅各布森秉承了结构主义语言学家索绪尔(Ferdinand de Saussure)有关语言符号能指、所指的划分,认为符号具有任意性。人们习得某个词的语义,不一定要有见过或接触过该词所指事物的认知经验,这一点颇与罗素(Bertrand Russell)的观点相异。语际翻译可以实现信息等值,而在语符单位之间不可能有完全的等值。不同语符之间的等值是语言的根本问题和语言学的主要关注对象。雅各布森是语言共性论者,他认为不同的语言都具有相同的表达力。由于诗歌的语法范畴、词汇形式都传达出特殊的意义,而不同语言间的语法范畴、词汇形式差异很大,因而诗歌是不可译的。本论文从语言学、符号学角度探讨了语言的意义、等值和可译性,其研究具有一定的科学性,开启了语言学派翻译研究的大门。

According to Bertrand Russell, "no one can understand the word 'cheese' unless he has a nonlinguistic acquaintance with cheese."[1] If, however, we follow Russell's fundamental precept and place our "emphasis upon the linguistic aspects of traditional philosophical problems," then we are obliged to state that no one can understand the word "cheese" unless he has an acquaintance with the meaning assigned to this word in the lexical code of English. Any representative of a cheese-less culinary culture will understand the English word "cheese" if he is aware that in this language it means "food made of pressed curds" and if he has at least a linguistic acquaintance with "curds." We never consumed ambrosia or nectar and have only a linguistic acquaintance with the words "ambrosia," "nectar," and "gods"—the name of their mythical users; nonetheless, we understand these words and know in what contexts each of them may be used.

The meaning of the words "cheese," "apple," "nectar," "acquaintance," "but," "mere," and of any word or phrase whatsoever is definitely a linguistic, or to be more precise and less narrow, a semiotic fact. Against those who assign meaning (*signatum*) not to the sign, but to the thing itself, the simplest and truest argument would be that nobody has ever smelled or tasted the meaning of "cheese" or of "apple." There is no *signatum* without *signum*. The meaning of the word "cheese" cannot be inferred from a nonlinguistic acquaintance with cheddar or with camembert without the assistance of the verbal code. An array of linguistic signs is needed to introduce an unfamiliar word. Mere pointing will not teach us whether "cheese" is the name of the given specimen, or of any box of camembert, or of camembert in general or of any cheese, any milk product, any food, any refreshment, or perhaps any box irrespective of contents. Finally, does a word simply name the thing in question, or does it imply a meaning such as offering, sale, prohibition, or malediction? (Pointing actually may mean malediction; in some cultures, particularly in Africa, it is an ominous gesture.)

For us, both as linguists and as ordinary word-users, the meaning of any linguistic sign is its translation into some further, alternative sign, especially a sign "in which it is more fully developed," as Peirce, the deepest inquirer into the essence of signs, insistently stated.[2] The term "bachelor" may be converted into a more explicit designation, "unmarried man," whenever higher explicitness is required. We distinguish three ways of interpreting a verbal sign: It may be translated into other signs of the same language, into another

---

① Bertrand Russell, "Logical Positivism," *Revue Internationale de Philosophie*, Ⅳ (1950), 18; cf. p. 3.

② Cf. John Dewey, "Peirce's Theory of Linguistic Signs, Thought, and Meaning," *The Journal of Philosophy*, ⅩLⅢ (1946), p. 91.

language, or into another, nonverbal system of symbols. These three kinds of translation are to be differently labeled:

(1) Intralingual translation or *rewording* is an interpretation of verbal signs by means of other signs of the same language.

(2) Interlingual translation or *translation proper* is an interpretation of verbal signs by means of some other language.

(3) Intersemiotic translation or *transmutation* is an interpretation of verbal signs by means of signs of nonverbal sign systems.

The intralingual translation of a word uses either another, more or less synonymous, word or resorts to a circumlocution. Yet synonymy, as a rule, is not complete equivalence: For example, "every celibate is a bachelor, but not every bachelor is a celibate." A word or an idiomatic phrase-word, briefly a code-unit of the highest level, may be fully interpreted only by means of an equivalent combination of code-units, i. e. , a message referring to this code-unit: "Every bachelor is an unmarried man, and every unmarried man is a bachelor," or "every celibate is bound not to marry, and everyone who is bound not to marry is a celibate."

Likewise, on the level of interlingual translation, there is ordinarily no full equivalence between code-units, while messages may serve as adequate interpretations of alien code-units or messages. The English word "cheese" cannot be completely identified with its standard Russian heteronym "сыр," because cottage cheese is a cheese but not a сыр. Russians say: принеси сыру и творогу "bring cheese and [sic] cottage cheese." In standard Russian, the food made of pressed curds is called сыр only if ferment is used.

Most frequently, however, translation from one language into another substitutes messages in one language not for separate code-units but for entire messages in some other language. Such a translation is a reported speech; the translator recodes and transmits a message received from another source. Thus translation involves two equivalent messages in two different codes.

Equivalence in difference is the cardinal problem of language and the pivotal concern of linguistics. Like any receiver of verbal messages, the linguist acts as their interpreter. No linguistic specimen may be interpreted by the science of language without a translation of its signs into other signs of the same system or into signs of another system. Any comparison of two languages implies an examination of their mutual translatability; widespread practice of interlingual communication, particularly translating activities, must be kept under constant scrutiny by linguistic science. It is difficult to overestimate the urgent need for and the theoretical and practical significance of differential bilingual dictionaries with careful comparative definition of all the corresponding units in their intention and extension. Likewise differential bilingual grammars should define what unifies and what differentiates the two languages in their selection and delimitation of grammatical concepts.

Both the practice and the theory of translation abound with intricacies, and from time to time attempts are made to sever the Gordian knot by proclaiming the dogma of untranslatability. "Mr. Everyman, the natural logician," vividly imagined by B. L. Whorf, is supposed to have arrived at the following bit of reasoning: "Facts are unlike to speakers whose language background provides for unlike formulation of them."[1] In the first years of the Russian revolution there were fanatic visionaries who argued in Soviet periodicals for a radical revision of traditional language and particularly for the weeding out of such misleading expressions as "sunrise" or "sunset." Yet we still use this Ptolemaic imagery without implying a rejection of Copernican doctrine, and we can easily transform our customary talk about the rising and setting sun into a picture of the earth's rotation simply because any sign is translatable into a sign in which it appears to us more fully developed and precise.

A faculty of speaking a given language implies a faculty of talking about this language. Such a "metalinguistic" operation permits revision and redefinition of the vocabulary used. The complementarity of both levels—object-language and metalanguage—was brought out by Niels Bohr: All well-defined experimental evidence must be expressed in ordinary language, "in which the practical use of every word stands in complementary relation to attempts of its strict definition."[2]

All cognitive experience and its classification is conveyable in any existing language. Whenever there is deficiency, terminology may be qualified and amplified by loan-words or loan-translations, neologisms or semantic shifts, and finally, by circumlocutions. Thus in the newborn literary language of the Northeast Siberian Chukchees, "screw" is rendered as "rotating nail," "steel" as "hard iron," "tin" as "thin iron," "chalk" as "writing soap," "watch" as "hammering heart." Even seemingly contradictory circumlocutions, like "electrical horse-car" (зпектрическая конка), the first Russian name of the horseless street car, or "flying steamship" (*jena paragot*), the Koryak term for the airplane, simply designate the electrical analogue of the horse-car and the flying analogue of the steamer and do not impede communication, just as there is no semantic "noise" and disturbance in the double oxymoron-"cold beef-and-pork hot dog."

No lack of grammatical device in the language translated into makes impossible a literal translation of the entire conceptual information contained in the original. The traditional conjunctions "and," "or" are now supplemented by a new connective—"and/or"—which was discussed a few years ago in the witty book *Federal Prose—How to Write in and/or for Washington*.[3] Of these three conjunctions, only the latter occurs in one of the Samoyed languages.[4] Despite these differences in the inventory of conjunctions, all three varieties of messages observed in "federal prose" may be distinctly translated both into traditional

① Benjamin Lee Whorf, *Language, Thought, and Reality* (Cambridge, Mass., 1956), p. 235.

② Niels Bohr, "On the Notions of Causality and Complementarity," *Dialectica*, I (1948), 317f.

③ James R. Masterson and Wendell Brooks Phillips, *Federal Prose* (Chapel Hill, N. C., 1948), p. 40f.

④ Cf. Knut Bergsland, "Finsk-ugrisk og almen språkvitenskap," *Norsk Tidskrift for Sprogvidenskap*, XV (1949), 374f.

English and into this Samoyed language. Federal prose: (1) John and Peter, (2) John or Peter, (3) John and/or Peter will come. Traditional English: (3) John and Peter or one of them will come. Samoyed: John and/or Peter both will come, (2) John and/or Peter, one of them will come.

If some grammatical category is absent in a given language, its meaning may be translated into this language by lexical means. Dual forms like Old Russian? Para are translated with the help of the numeral: "two brothers." It is more difficult to remain faithful to the original when we translate into a language provided with a certain grammatical category from a language devoid of such a category. When translating the English sentence "She has brothers" into a language which discriminates dual and plural, we are compelled either to make our own choice between two statements "She has two brothers"—"She has more than two" or to leave the decision to the listener and say: "She has either two or more than two brothers." Again in translating from a language without grammatical number into English one is obliged to select one of the two possibilities—"brother" or "brothers" or to confront the receiver of this message with a two-choice situation: "She has either one or more than one brother."

As Boas neatly observed, the grammatical pattern of a language (as opposed to its lexical stock) determines those aspects of each experience that must be expressed in the given language: "We have to choose between these aspects, and one or the other must be chosen."[1] In order to translate accurately the English sentence "I hired a worker," a Russian needs supplementary information, whether this action was completed or not and whether the worker was a man or a woman, because he must make his choice between a verb of completive or noncompletive aspect—нанял or нанимал—and between a masculine and feminine noun—работника or работницу. If I ask the utterer of the English sentence whether the worker was male or female, my question may be judged irrelevant or indiscreet, whereas in the Russian version of this sentence an answer to this question is obligatory. On the other hand, whatever the choice of Russian grammatical forms to translate the quoted English message, the translation will give no answer to the question of whether I "hired" or "have hired" the worker, or whether he/she was an indefinite or definite worker ("a" or "the"). Because the information required by the English and Russian grammatical pattern is unlike, we face quite different sets of two-choice situations; therefore a chain of translations of one and the same isolated sentence from English into Russian and vice versa could entirely deprive such a message of its initial content. The Geneva linguist S. Karcevski used to compare such a gradual loss with a circular series of unfavorable currency transactions. But evidently the richer the context of a message, the smaller the loss of information.

Languages differ essentially in what they *must* convey and not in what they *may* convey. Each verb of a given language imperatively raises a set of specific yes-or-no questions, as for instance: Is the narrated event conceived with or without reference to its completion? Is the narrated event presented as prior to the speech event or not? Naturally the attention of native

---

① Franz Boas, "Language," *General Anthropology* (Boston, 1938), pp. 132f.

speakers and listeners will be constantly focused on such items as are compulsory in their verbal code.

In its cognitive function, language is minimally dependent on the grammatical pattern because the definition of our experience stands in complementary relation to metalinguistic operations—the cognitive level of language not only admits but directly requires receding interpretation, i. e. , translation. Any assumption of ineffable or untranslatable cognitive data would be a contradiction in terms. But in jest, in dreams, in magic, briefly, in what one would call everyday verbal mythology and in poetry above all, the grammatical categories carry a high semantic import. In these conditions, the question of translation becomes much more entangled and controversial.

Even such a category as grammatical gender, often cited as merely formal, plays a great role in the mythological attitudes of a speech community. In Russian the feminine cannot designate a male person, nor the masculine specify a female. Ways of personifying or metaphorically interpreting inanimate nouns are prompted by their gender. A test in the Moscow Psychological Institute (1915) showed that Russians, prone to personify the weekdays, consistently represented Monday, Tuesday, and Thursday as males and Wednesday, Friday, and Saturday as females, without realizing that this distribution was due to the masculine gender of the first three names (понедельник, вторник, четверг) as against the feminine gender of the others (среда, пятница, суббога). The fact that the word for Friday is masculine in some Slavic languages and feminine in others is reflected in the folk traditions of the corresponding peoples, which differ in their Friday ritual. The widespread Russian superstition that a fallen knife presages a male guest and a fallen fork a female one is determined by the masculine gender of нож "knife" and the feminine of вилка "fork" in Russian. In Slavic and other languages where "day" is masculine and "night" feminine, day is represented by poets as the lover of night. The Russian painter Repin was baffled as to why Sin had been depicted as a woman by German artists: He did not realize that "sin" is feminine in German (*die Sünde*), but masculine in Russian (грех). Likewise a Russian child, while reading a translation of German tales, was astounded to find that Death, obviously a woman (Russian смерть, fem.), was pictured as an old man (German *der Tod*, masc.). *My Sister Life*, the title of a book of poems by Boris Pasternak, is quite natural in Russian, where "life" is feminine жизнь, but was enough to reduce to despair the Czech poet Josef Hora in his attempt to translate these poems, since in Czech this noun is masculine *zivot*.

What was the initial question which arose in Slavic literature at its very beginning? Curiously enough, the translator's difficulty in preserving the symbolism of genders, and the cognitive irrelevance of this difficulty, appears to be the main topic of the earliest Slavic original work, the preface to the first translation of the *Evangeliarium*, made in the early 1860's by the founder of Slavic letters and liturgy, Constantine the Philosopher, and recently restored and interpreted by A. Vaillant. ①"Greek, when translated into another language, cannot always be reproduced identically, and that happens to each language being translated," the Slavic apostle states. "Masculine nouns as ποταμός 'river' and αστήρ 'star' in Greek, are feminine in another language as рѣка and звѣзда in Slavic." According to Vaillant's commentary, this divergence effaces the symbolic identification of the rivers with demons and of the stars with angels in the Slavic translation of two of Matthew's verses (7:25 and 2:9). But to this poetic obstacle, Saint Constantine resolutely opposes the precept of Dionysius the Areopagite, who called for chief attention to the cognitive values (силѣ разуму) and not to the words themselves.

In poetry, verbal equations become a constructive principle of the text. Syntactic and morphological categories, roots, and affixes, phonemes and their components (distinctive features)—in short, any constituents of the verbal code—are confronted, juxtaposed, brought into contiguous relation according to the principle of similarity and contrast and carry their own autonomous signification. Phonemic similarity is sensed as semantic relationship. The pun, or to use a more erudite, and perhaps more precise term—paronomasia, reigns over poetic art, and whether its rule is absolute or limited, poetry by definition is untranslatable. Only creative transposition is possible: either intralingual transposition—from one poetic shape into another, or interlingual transposition—from one language into another, or finally intersemiotic transposition—from one system of signs into another, e. g. , from verbal art into music, dance, cinema, or painting.

If we were to translate into English the traditional formula *Traduttore, traditore* as "the translator is a betrayer," we would deprive the Italian rhyming epigram of all its paronomastic value. Hence a cognitive attitude would compel us to change this aphorism into a more explicit statement and to answer the questions: Translator of what messages? Betrayer of what values?

【延伸阅读】

[1] Catford, J. C. (1965). *A Linguistic Theory of Translation*. London: OUP.

[2] Malpas, J. E. (1989). The Intertranslatibility of Natural Languages. *Synthèse*, 78 (3), 233 - 264.

[3] Toury, G. (1980). *In search of a Theory of Translation*. Tel Aviv: The Porter Institute for Poetics and Semiotics.

[4] Wilss, W. (1982). *The Science of Translation: Problems and Methods*. Tübingen: Gunter Narr Verlag.

【问题与思考】

1. 雅各布森是站在符号学的立场上讨论翻译问题的吗? 为什么?

---

① André Vaillant, "Le Préface de l'Évangeliaire vieux-slave," *Revue des ÉtudesSlaves*, XXIV (1948), 5f.

2. 雅各布森如何看待语言意义的本质和对等的本质？

3. 为什么雅各布森认为只有诗歌是不可译的？

4. 如何理解雅各布森的观点"语言的关键区别在于它们必须表达的东西，而不在于它们可以表达的东西"？

5. 如何理解雅各布森提出的概念"创造性转换"（creative transportation）？

选文二　Principles of Correspondence

Eugene Nida

导　言

本文较全面地阐发了奈达的动态对等思想。文章认为，语言之间不存在绝对的对应，为了确立不同的对应原则，必须辨别翻译的不同类型。而辨别翻译类型须考虑三种要素：信息的性质、原文作者的目的或译文译者的目的、读者类型。他在分析译语文化和源语文化关系的基础上，提出翻译的两种基本导向，亦即两条翻译标准：形式对等和动态对等。制约形式对等翻译的原则是：翻译以原文为中心，尽可能地重现原文信息的形式和内容。制约动态对等翻译的原则是：译者应重视接受者的反应，其注意力不完全集中于原文的信息。动态对等原则在《圣经》翻译中起到很大的指导作用，在翻译一些以传达信息为主的文本类型时也能使用。然而它过于强调译文的交际性和易懂性，因此也存在一定的局限，如果应用于文学翻译，有可能导致风格的失落和文学性的削弱。

Since no two languages are identical, either in the meanings given to corresponding symbols or in the ways in which such symbols are arranged in phrases and sentences, it stands to reason that there can be no absolute correspondence between languages. Hence there can be no fully exact translations. The total impact of a translation may be reasonably close to the original, but there can be no identity in detail. Constance B. West (1932, p. 344) clearly states the problem: "Whoever takes upon himself to translate contracts a debt; to discharge it, he must pay not with the same money, but the same sum." One must not imagine that the process of translation can avoid a certain degree of interpretation by the translator. In fact, as D. G. Rossetti stated in 1874 (Fang, 1953), "A translation remains perhaps the most direct form of commentary."

Different types of translations

No statement of the principles of correspondence in translating can be complete without recognizing the many different types of translations (Phillips, 1959). Traditionally, we have tended to think in terms of free or paraphrastic translations as contrasted with close or literal ones. Actually, there are many more grades of translating than these extremes imply. There are, for example, such ultraliteral translations as interlinears; while others involve highly concordant relationships, e. g. the same source-language word is always translated by one—and only one-receptor—language word. Still others may be quite devoid of artificial restrictions in form, but nevertheless may be over traditional and even ar-chaizing. Some translations aim at very close formal and semantic correspondence, but are generously supplied with notes and commentary. Many are not so much concerned with giving information as with creating in the reader something of the same mood as was conveyed by the original.

Differences in translations can generally be accounted for by three basic factors in translating: (1) the nature of the message, (2) the purpose or purposes of the author and, by proxy, of the translator, and (3) the type of audience.

Messages differ primarily in the degree to which content or form is the dominant consideration. Of course, the content of a message can never be completely abstracted from the form, and form is nothing apart from content; but in some messages the content is of primary consideration, and in others the form must be given a higher priority. For example, in the Sermon on the Mount, despite certain important stylistic qualities, the importance of the message far exceeds considerations of form. On the other hand, some of the acrostic poems of the Old Testament are obviously designed to fit a very strict formal "strait jacket." But even the contents of a message may differ widely in applicability to the receptor-language audience. For example, the folk tale of the Bauré Indians of Bolivia, about a giant who led the animals in a symbolic dance, is interesting to an English-speaking audience, but to them it has not the same relevance as the Sermon on the Mount. And even the Bauré Indians themselves recognize the Sermon on the Mount as more significant than their favorite "how-it-happened" story. At the same time, of course, the Sermon on the Mount has greater relevance to these Indians than have some passages in Leviticus.

In poetry there is obviously a greater focus of attention upon formal elements than one normally finds in prose. Not that content is necessarily sacrificed in translation of a poem, but the content is necessarily constricted into certain formal molds. Only rarely can one reproduce both content and form in a translation, and hence in general the form is usually sacrificed for the sake of the content. On the other hand, a lyric poem translated as prose is not an adequate equivalent of the original. Though it may reproduce the conceptual content, it falls far short of reproducing the emotional intensity and flavor. However, the translating of some types of poetry by prose may be dictated by important cultural considerations. For example, Homer's epic poetry reproduced in English poetic form usually seems to us antique and queer—with nothing of the liveliness and spontaneity characteristic of Homer's style. One reason is that we are not accustomed to having stories told to us in poetic form. In our Western European tradition such epics are related in prose. For this reason E. V. Rieu chose prose rather than poetry as the more appropriate medium by which to render *The Iliad* and *The Odyssey*.

The particular purposes of the translator are also important factors indictating the type of translation. Of course, it is assumed that the translator has purposes generally similar to, or at least compatible with, those of the original author, but this is not necessarily so. For example, a San Blas story-teller is interested only in amusing his audience, but an ethnographer who sets about translating such stories may be much more concerned in giving his audience an insight into San Blas personality structure. Since, however, the purposes of the translator are the primary ones to be considered in studying the types of translation which result, the principal purposes that underlie the choice of one or another way to render a particular message are important.

The primary purpose of the translator may be information as to both content and form. One intended type of response to such an informative type of translation is largely cognitive, e. g. an ethnographer's translation of texts from informants, or a philosopher's translation of Heidegger. A largely informative translation may, on the other hand, be designed to elicit an emotional response of pleasure from the reader or listener.

A translator's purposes may involve much more than information. He may, for example, want to suggest a particular type of behaviour by means of a translation. Under such circumstances he is likely to aim at full intelligibility, and to make certain minor adjustments in detail so that the reader may understand the full implications of the message for his own circumstances. In such a situation a translator is not content to have receptors say, "This is intelligible to us." Rather, he is looking for some such response as, "This is meaningful for us." In terms of Bible translating, the people might understand a phrase such as "to change one's mind about sin" as meaning "repentance." But if the indigenous way of talking about repentance is "spit on the ground in front of," as in Shilluk,① spoken in the Sudan, the translator will obviously aim at the more meaningful idiom. On a similar basis, "white as snow" may be rendered as "white as egret feathers," if the people of the receptor language are not acquainted with snow but speak of anything very white by this phrase.

A still greater degree of adaptation is likely to occur in a translation which has an imperative purpose. Here the translator feels constrained not merely to suggest a possible line of behavior, but to make such an action explicit and compelling. He is not content to translate in such a way that the people are likely to understand; rather, he insists that the translation must be so clear that no one can possibly misunderstand.

In addition to the different types of messages and the diverse purposes of translators, one must also consider the extent to which prospective audiences differ both in decoding

---

① This idiom is based upon the requirement that plaintiffs and defendants spit on the ground in front of each other when a case has been finally tried and punishment meted out. The spitting indicates that all is forgiven and that the accusations can never be brought into court again.

ability and in potential interest.

Decoding ability in any language involves at least four principal levels: (1) the capacity of children, whose vocabulary and cultural experience are limited; (2) the double-standard capacity of new literates, who can decode oral messages with facility but whose ability to decode written messages is limited; (3) the capacity of the average literate adult, who can handle both oral and written messages with relative ease; and (4) the unusually high capacity of specialists (doctors, theologians, philosophers, scientists, etc.), when they are decoding messages within their own area of specialization. Obviously a translation designed for children cannot be the same as one prepared for specialists, nor can a translation for children be the same as one for a newly literate adult.

Prospective audiences differ not only in decoding ability, but perhaps even more in their interests. For example, a translation designed to stimulate reading for pleasure will be quite different from one intended for a person anxious to learn how to assemble a complicated machine. Moreover, a translator of African myths for persons who simply want to satisfy their curiosity about strange peoples and places will produce a different piece of work from one who renders these same myths in a form acceptable to linguists, who are more interested in the linguistic structure underlying the translation than in cultural novelty.

Two basic orientations in translating

Since "there are, properly speaking, no such things as identical equivalents" (Belloc, 1931 and 1931a, p. 37), one must in translating seek to find the closest possible equivalent. However, there are fundamentally two different types of equivalence: one which may be called formal and another which is primarily dynamic.

Formal equivalence focuses attention on the message itself, in both form and content. In such a translation one is concerned with such correspondences as poetry to poetry, sentence to sentence, and concept to concept. Viewed from this formal orientation, one is concerned that the message in the receptor language should match as closely as possible the different elements in the source language. This means, for example, that the message in the receptor culture is constantly compared with the message in the source culture to determine standards of accuracy and correctness.

The type of translation which most completely typifies this structural equivalence might be called a "gloss translation," in which the translator attempts to reproduce as literally and meaningfully as possible the form and content of the original. Such a translation might be a rendering of some Medieval French text into English, intended for students of certain aspects of early French literature not requiring a knowledge of the original language of the text. Their needs call for a relatively close approximation to the structure of the early French text, both as to form (e. g. syntax and idioms) and content (e. g. themes and concepts). Such a translation would require numerous footnotes in order to make the text fully comprehensible.

A gloss translation of this type is designed to permit the reader to identify himself as fully as possible with a person in the source-language context, and to understand as much as he can of the customs, manner of thought, and means of expression. For example, a phrase such as "holy kiss" (Romans 16:16) in a gloss translation would be rendered literally, and would probably be supplemented with a footnote explaining that this was a customary method of greeting in New Testament times.

In contrast, a translation which attempts to produce a dynamic rather than a formal equivalence is based upon "the principle of equivalent effect" (Rieu & Phillips, 1954). In such a translation one is not so concerned with matching the receptor-language message with the source-language message, but with the dynamic relationship, that the relationship between receptor and message should be substantially the same as that which existed between the original receptors and the message.

A translation of dynamic equivalence aims at complete naturalness of expression, and tries to relate the receptor to modes of behavior relevant within the context of his own culture; it does not insist that he understand the cultural patterns of the source-language context in order to comprehend the message. Of course, there are varying degrees of such dynamic-equivalence translations. One of the modern English translations which, perhaps more than any other, seeks for equivalent effect is J. B. Phillips' rendering of the New Testament. In Romans 16:16 he quite naturally translates "greet one another with a holy kiss" as "give one another a hearty handshake all around."

Between the two poles of translating (i. e. between strict formal equivalence and complete dynamic equivalence) there are a number of intervening grades, representing various acceptable standards of literary translating. During the past fifty years, however, there has been a marked shift of emphasis from the formal to the dynamic dimension. A recent summary of opinion on translating by literary artists, publishers, educators, and professional translators indicates clearly that the present direction is toward increasing emphasis on dynamic equivalences (Cary, 1959).

Linguistic and cultural distance

In any discussion of equivalences, whether structural or dynamic, one must always bear in mind three different types of relatedness, as determined by the linguistic and cultural distance between the codes used to convey the messages. In some instances, for example, a translation may involve comparatively closely related languages and cultures, e. g. translations from Frisian into English, or from Hebrew into Arabic. On the other hand, the languages may not be related, even though the cultures are closely parallel, e. g. as in translations from German into Hungarian, or from Swedish into Finnish (German and Swedish are Indo-European languages, while Hungarian and Finnish belong to the Finno-Ugrian family). In still other instances a translation may involve not only differences of linguistic affiliation but also highly diverse cultures, e. g. English into Zulu, or Greek into Javanese. ①

Where the linguistic and cultural distances between source and receptor codes are least, one should expect to encounter the least number of serious problems, but as a matter of fact if languages are too closely related one is likely to be badly deceived by the superficial similarities, with the result that translations done under these circumstances are often quite poor. One of the serious dangers consists of so-called "false friends," i. e. borrowed or cognate words which seem to be equivalent but are not always so, e. g. English *demand* and French *demander*, English *ignore* and Spanish *ignorar*, English *virtue* and Latin *virtus*, and English *deacon* and Greek *diakonos*.

When the cultures are related but the languages are quite different, the translator is called upon to make a good many formal shifts in the translation. However, the cultural similarities in such instances usually provide a series of parallelisms of content that make the translation proportionately much less difficult than when both languages and cultures are disparate. In fact, differences between cultures cause many more severe complications for the translator than do differences in language structure.

Definitions of translating

Definitions of proper translating are almost as numerous and varied as the persons who have undertaken to discuss the subject. This diversity is in a sense quite understandable; for there are vast differences in the materials translated, in the purposes of the publication, and in the needs of the prospective audience. Moreover, live languages are constantly changing and stylistic preferences undergo continual modification. Thus a translation acceptable in one period is often quite unacceptable at a later time.

A number of significant and relatively comprehensive definitions of translation have been offered. Procházka (Garvin, 1955, p. 111ff.) defines a good translation in terms of certain requirements which must be made of the translator, namely: (1) "He must understand the original word thematically and stylistically;" (2) "he must overcome the differences between the two linguistic structures;" and (3) "he must reconstruct the stylistic structures of the original work in his translation."

In a description of proper translation of poetry, Jackson Mathews (1959, p. 67) states: "One thing seems clear: To translate a poem whole is to compose another poem. A whole translation will be faithful to the *matter*, and it will 'approximate the form' of the original; and it will have a life of its own, which is the voice of the translator." Richmond Lattimore

---

① We also encounter certain rare situations in which the languages are related but the cultures are quite disparate. For example, in the case of Hindi and English one is dealing with two languages from the same language family, but the cultures in question are very different. In such instances, the languages are also likely to be so distantly related as to make their linguistic affiliation a matter of minor consequence.

(1959, in Brower, 1959, p. 56) deals with the same basic problem of translating poetry. He describes the fundamental principles in terms of the way in which Greek poetry should be translated, namely: "To make from the Greek poem a poem in English which, while giving a high minimum of meaning of the Greek, is still a new English poem, which would not be the kind of poem it is if it were not translating the Greek which it translates."

No proper definition of translation can avoid some of the basic difficulties. Especially in the rendering of poetry, the tension between form and content and the conflict between formal and dynamic equivalences are always acutely present. However, it seems to be increasingly recognized that adherence to the letter may indeed kill the spirit. William A. Cooper (1928, p. 484) deals with this problem rather realistically in his article on "Translating Goethe's Poems," in which he says: "If the language of the original employs word formations that give rise to insurmountable difficulties of direct translation, and figures of speech wholly foreign, and hence incomprehensible in the other tongue, it is better to cling to the spirit of the poem and clothe it in language and figures entirely free from awkwardness of speech and obscurity of picture. This might be called a translation from culture to culture."

It must be recognized that in translating poetry there are very special problems involved, for the form of expression (rhythm, meter, assonance, etc.) is essential to communicating the spirit of the message to the audience. But all translating, whether of poetry or prose, must be concerned also with the response of the receptor; hence the ultimate purpose of the translation, in terms of its impact upon its intended audience, is a fundamental factor in any evaluation of translations. This reason underlies Leonard Forster's definition (1958, p. 6) of a good translation as "one which fulfills the same purpose in the new language as the original did in the language in which it was written."

The resolution of the conflict between literalness of form and equivalence of response seems increasingly to favor the latter, especially in the translating of poetic materials. C. W. Orr (1941, p. 318), for example, describes translating as somewhat equivalent to painting, for, as he says, "The painter does not reproduce every detail of the landscape"—he selects what seems best to him. Likewise for the translator, "It is the spirit, not only the letter, that he seeks to embody in his own version." Oliver Edwards (1957, p. 13) echoes the same point of view: "We expect approximate truth in a translation ... What we want to have is the truest possible *feel* of the original. The characters, the situations, the reflections must come to us as they were in the author's mind and heart, not necessarily precisely as he had them on his lips."

It is one thing, however, to produce a generalized definition of translating, whether of poetry or prose; it is often quite another to describe in some detail the significant characteristics of an adequate translation. This fact Savory (1957, pp. 49 - 50) highlights by contrasting diametrically opposed opinions on a dozen important principles of translating. However, though some dissenting voices can be found on virtually all proposals as to what translating should consist of, there are several significant features of translating on which many of the most competent judges are increasingly in agreement.

Ezra Pound (1954, p. 273) states the case for translations making sense by declaring for "more sense and less syntax." But as early as 1789 George Campbell (1789, p. 445ff.) argued that translation should not be characterized by "obscure sense." E. E. Milligan (1957) also argues for sense rather than words, for he points out that unless a translation communicates, i. e. makes sense to the receptor, it has not justified its existence.

In addition to making sense, translations must also convey the "spirit and manner" of the original (Campbell, 1789, p. 445ff.). For the Bible translator, this means that the individual style of the various writers of the Scriptures should be reflected as far as possible (ibid. , p. 547). The same sentiment is clearly expressed by Ruth M. Underhill (1938, p. 16) in her treatment of certain problems of translating magic incantations of the Papago Indians of southern Arizona: "One can hope to make the translation exact only in spirit, not in letter." Francis Storr (1909) goes so far as to classify translators into "the li-teralist and the spiritualist schools," and in doing so takes his stand on the Biblical text, "The letter killeth but the spirit giveth life." As evidence for his thesis, Storr cites the difference between the Authorized Version, which he contends represents the spirit, and the English Revised Version, which sticks to the letter, with the result that the translation lacks a *Sprachgefühl*. The absence of literary stylists on the English Revised Committee was, however, corrected in the New English Bible (New Testament, 1961), in which one entire panel was composed of persons with special sensitivity to and competence in English style.

Closely related to the requirement of sensitivity to the style of the original is the need for a "natural and easy" form of expression in the language into which one is translating (Campbell, 1789, p. 445ff.). Max Beerbohm (1903, p. 75) considers that the cardinal fault of many who translate plays into English is the failure to be natural in expression; in fact, they make the reader "acutely conscious that their work is a translation ... For the most part, their ingenuity consists in finding phrases that could not possibly be used by the average Englishman." Goodspeed (1945, p. 8) echoes the same sentiment with respect to Bible translating by declaring that: "The best translation is not one that keeps forever before the reader's mind the fact that this is a translation, not an original English composition, but one that makes the reader forget that it is a translation at all and makes him feel that he is looking into the ancient writer's mind, as he would into that of a contemporary. This is, indeed, no light matter to undertake or to execute, but it is, nevertheless, the task of any serious translator." J. B. Phillips (1953, p. 53) confirms the same viewpoint when he declares that: "The test of a real translation is that it should not read like translation at all." His second principle of translating re-enforces the first, namely a translation into English should avoid "translator's English."

It must be recognized, however, that it is not easy to produce a completely natural translation, especially if the original writing is good literature, precisely because truly good writing intimately reflects and effectively exploits the total idiomatic capacities and special genius of the language in which the writing is done. A translator must therefore not only contend with the special difficulties resulting from such an effective exploitation of the total resources of the source language, but also seek to produce something relatively equivalent in the receptor language. In fact, Justin O'Brien (1959, p. 81) quotes Raymond Guérin to the effect that: "The most convincing criterion of the quality of a work is the fact that it can only be translated with difficulty, for if it passes readily into another language without losing its essence, then it must have no particular essence or at least not one of the rarest."

An easy and natural style in translating, despite the extreme difficulties of producing it—especially when translating an original of high quality—is nevertheless essential to producing in the ultimate receptors a response similar to that of the original receptors. In one way or another this principle of "similar response" has been widely held and effectively stated by a number of specialists in the field of translating. Even though Matthew Arnold (1861, as quoted in Savory, 1957, p. 45) himself rejected in actual practice the principle of "similar response," he at least seems to have thought he was producing a similar response, for he declares that: "A translation should affect us in the same way as the original may be supposed to have affected its first hearers." Despite Arnold's objection to some of the freer translations done by others, he was at least strongly opposed to the literalist views of such persons as F. W. Newman (1861, p. xiv). Jowett (1891), on the other hand, comes somewhat closer to a present-day conception of "similar response" in stating that: "An English translation ought to be idiomatic and interesting, not only to the scholar, but to the learned reader ... The translator ... seeks to produce on his reader an impression similar or nearly similar to that produced by the original."

Souter (1920, p. 7) expresses essentially this same view in stating that: "Our ideal in translation is to produce on the minds of our readers as nearly as possible the same effect as was produced by the original on its readers," and R. A. Knox (1957, p. 5) insists that a translation should be "read with the same interest and enjoyment which a reading of the original would have afforded."

In dealing with translating from an essentially linguistic point of view, Procházka (in Garvin, 1955) re-enforces this same viewpoint, namely, that "the translation should make the same resultant impression on the reader as the original does on its reader."

If a translation is to meet the four basic requirements of (1) making sense, (2) conveying the spirit and manner of the original, (3) having a natural and easy form of expression, and (4) producing a similar response, it is obvious that at certain points the conflict between content and form (or meaning and manner) will be acute, and that one or the other must give way. In general, translators are agreed that, when there is no happy compromise, meaning must have priority over style (Tancock, 1958, p. 29). What one must attempt, however, is an effective blend of "matter and manner," for these two aspects of any message are inseparably united. Adherence to content, without consideration of form, usually results in a flat mediocrity, with nothing of the sparkle and charm of the original. On the other hand, sacrifice of meaning for the sake of reproducing the style may produce only an impression, and fail to communicate the message. The form, however, may be changed more radically than the content and still be substantially equivalent in its effect upon the receptor. Accordingly, correspondence in meaning must have priority over correspondence in style. However, this assigning of priorities must never be done in a purely mechanical fashion, for what is ultimately required, especially in the translation of poetry, is "a re-creation, not a reproduction" (Lattimore, in Brower, 1959, p. 55).

Any survey of opinions on translating serves to confirm the fact that definitions or descriptions of translating are not served by deterministic rules; rather, they depend on probabilistic rules. One cannot, therefore, state that a particular translation is good or bad without taking into consideration a myriad of factors, which in turn must be weighted in a number of different ways, with appreciably different answers. Hence there will always be a variety of valid answers to the question, "Is this a good translation?"

Principles governing a translation oriented toward formal equivalence

In order to understand somewhat more fully the characteristics of different types of translations, it is important to analyze in more detail the principles that govern a translation which attempts to reproduce a formal equivalence. Such a formal-equivalence (or F-E) translation is basically source-oriented; that is, it is designed to reveal as much as possible of the form and content of the original message.

In doing so, an F-E translation attempts to reproduce several formal elements, including: (1) grammatical units, (2) consistency in word usage, and (3) meanings in terms of the source context. The reproduction of grammatical units may consist in: (1) translating nouns by nouns, verbs by verbs, etc. ; (2) keeping all phrases and sentences intact (i. e. not splitting up and readjusting the units); and (3) preserving all formal indicators, e. g. marks of punctuation, paragraph breaks, and poetic indentation.

In attempting to reproduce consistency in word usage, an F-E translation usually aims at so-called concordance of terminology; that is, it always renders a particular term in the source-language document by the corresponding term in the receptor document. Such a principle may, of course, be pushed to an absurd extent, with the result being relatively meaningless strings of words, as in some passages of the so-called Concordant Version of the New Testament. On the other hand, a certain degree of concordance may be highly desirable in certain types of F-E translating. For example, a reader of Plato's Dialogues in English may prefer rigid consistency in the rendering of key terms (as in Jowett's translation), so that he may have some comprehension of the way in which Plato uses certain word symbols to develop his philosophical system. An F-E translation may also make use of brackets, parentheses, or even italics (as in the King James Bible) for words added to make sense in the translation, but missing in the original document.

In order to reproduce meanings in terms of the source context, an F-E translation normally attempts not to make adjustments in idioms, but rather to reproduce such expressions more or less literally, so that the reader may be able to perceive something of the way in which the original document employed local cultural elements to convey meanings.

In many instances, however, one simply cannot reproduce certain formal elements of the source message. For example, there may be puns, chiasmic orders of words, instances of assonance, or acrostic features of line-initial sounds which completely defy equivalent rendering. In such instances one must employ certain types of marginal notes, if the feature in question merits an explanation. In some rare instances one does light upon a roughly equivalent pun or play on words. For example, in translating the Hebrew text of Genesis 2:23, in which the Hebrew word *isshah* "woman" is derived from *ish* "man," it is possible to use a corresponding English pair, *woman* and *man*. However, such formal correspondences are obviously rare, for languages generally differ radically in both content and form.

A consistent F-E translation will obviously contain much that is not readily intelligible to the average reader. One must therefore usually supplement such translations with marginal notes, not only to explain some of the formal features which could not be adequately represented, but also to make intelligible some of the formal equivalents employed, for such expressions may have significance only in terms of the source language or culture.

Some types of strictly F-E translations, e. g. interlinear renderings and completely concordant translations, are of limited value; others are of great value. For example, translations of foreign-language texts prepared especially for linguists rarely attempt anything but close F-E renderings. In such translations the wording is usually quite literal, and even the segments are often numbered so that the corresponding units may be readily compared.

From what has been said directly and indirectly about F-E translations in preceding sections, it might be supposed that such translations are categorically ruled out. To the contrary, they are often perfectly valid translations of certain types of messages for certain types of audiences. The relative value and effectiveness of particular types of translations for particular audiences pose another question, and must not be confused with a description of the nature of various kinds of translations. At this point we are concerned only with their essential features, not with their evaluation.

Principles governing translations oriented toward dynamic equivalence

In contrast with formal-equivalence translations others are oriented toward dynamic equivalence. In such a translation the focus of attention is directed, not so much toward the source message, as toward the receptor response. A dynamic-equivalence (or D-E) translation may be described as one concerning which a bilingual and bicultural person can justifiably say, "That is just the way we would say it. " It is important to realize, however, that a D-E translation is not merely another message which is more or less similar to that of the source. It is a translation, and as such must clearly reflect the meaning and intent of the source.

One way of defining a D-E translation is to describe it as "the closest natural equivalent to the source-language message." This type of definition contains three essential terms: (1) *equivalent*, which points toward the source-language message, (2) *natural*, which points toward the receptor language, and (3) *closest*, which binds the two orientations together on the basis of the highest degree of approximation.

However, since a D-E translation is directed primarily toward equivalence of response rather than equivalence of form, it is important to define more fully the implications of the word *natural* as applied to such translations. Basically, the word *natural* is applicable to three areas of the communication process; for a *natural* rendering must fit (1) the receptor language and culture as a whole, (2) the context of the particular message, and (3) the receptor-language audience.

The conformance of a translation to the receptor language and culture as a whole is an essential ingredient in any stylistically acceptable rendering. Actually this quality of linguistic appropriateness is usually noticeable only when it is absent. In a natural translation, therefore, those features which would mar it are conspicuous by their absence. J. H. Frere (1820, p. 481) has described such a quality by stating, "the language of translation ought, we think ... be a pure, impalpable and invisible element, the medium of thought and feeling and nothing more; it ought never to attract attention to itself ... All importations from foreign languages ... are ... to be avoided. " Such an adjustment to the receptor language and culture must result in a translation that bears no obvious trace of foreign origin, so that, as G. A. Black (1936, p. 50) describes James Thomson's translations of Heine, such renderings are "a reproduction of the original, such as Heine himself, if master of the English language, would have given. "

A natural translation involves two principal areas of adaptation, namely, grammar and lexicon. In general the grammatical modifications can be made the more readily, since many grammatical changes are dictated by the obligatory structures of the receptor language. That is to say, one is obliged to make such adjustments as shifting word order, using verbs in place of nouns, and substituting nouns for pronouns. The lexical structure of the source message is less readily adjusted to the semantic requirements of the receptor language, for instead of obvious rules to be followed, there are numerous alternative possibilities. There are in general three lexical levels to be considered: (1) terms for which there are readily available parallels, e. g. *river*, *tree*, *stone*, *knife*, etc. ; (2) terms which identify culturally different objects, but with somewhat similar functions, e. g. *book*, which in English means an object with pages bound together into a unit, but which, in New Testament times, meant a long parchment or papyrus rolled up in the form of a scroll; and (3) terms which identify cultural specialties, e. g. *synagogue*, *homer*, *ephah*, *cherubim*, and *jubilee*, to cite only a few from the Bible. Usually the first set of terms involves no problem. In the second set of terms several confusions can arise; hence one must either use another term which reflects the form of the referent, though not the equivalent function, or which identifies the equivalent function at the expense of formal identity. In translating terms of the third class certain "foreign associations" can rarely be avoided. No translation that attempts to bridge a wide cultural gap can hope to eliminate all traces of the foreign setting. For example, in Bible translating it is quite impossible to remove such foreign "objects" as *Pharisees*, *Sadducees*, *Solomon's temple*, *cities of refuge*, or such Biblical themes as *anointing*, *adulterous generation*, *living sacrifice*, and *Lamb of God*, for these expressions are deeply imbedded in the very thought structure of the message.

It is also inevitable that when source and receptor languages represent very different cultures there should be many basic themes and accounts which cannot be "naturalized" by the process of translating. For example, the Jivaro Indians of Ecuador certainly do not understand 1 Corinthians 11:14, "Does not nature teach us that for a man to wear long hair is a dishonor to him?", for in general Jivaro men let their hair grow long, while Jivaro adult women usually cut theirs rather close. Similarly, in many areas of West Africa the behavior of Jesus' disciples in spreading leaves and branches in his way as he rode into Jerusalem is regarded as reprehensible; for in accordance with West African custom the path to be walked on or ridden over by a chief is scrupulously cleaned of all litter, and anyone who throws a branch in such a person's way is guilty of grievous insult. Nevertheless, these cultural discrepancies offer less difficulty than might be imagined, especially if footnotes are used to point out the basis for the cultural diversity; for all people recognize that other peoples behave differently from themselves.

Naturalness of expression in the receptor language is essentially a problem of co-suitability—but on several levels, of which the most important are as follows: (1) word classes (e. g. if there is no noun for "love" one must often say "God loves" instead of "God is love"); (2) grammatical categories (in some languages so-called predicate nominatives must agree in number with the subject, so that "the two shall be one" cannot be said, and accordingly, one must say "the two persons shall act just as though they were one person"); (3) semantic classes (swear words in one language may be based upon the perverted use of divine names, but in another language may be primarily excremental and anatomical); (4) discourse types (some languages may require direct quotation and others indirect); and (5) cultural contexts (in some societies the New Testament practice of sitting down to teach seems strange, if not unbecoming).

In addition to being appropriate to the receptor language and culture, a natural translation must be in accordance with the context of the particular message. The problems are thus not restricted to gross grammatical and lexical features, but may also involve such detailed matters as intonation and sentence rhythm (Pound, 1954, p. 298). The trouble is that, "Fettered to mere words, the translator loses the spirit of the original author" (Manchester, 1951, p. 68).

A truly natural translation can in some respects be described more easily in terms of what it avoids than in what it actually states; for it is the presence of serious anomalies, avoided in a successful translation, which immediately strike the reader as being out of place in the context. For example, crude vulgarities in a supposedly dignified type of discourse are inappropriate, and as a result are certainly not natural. But vulgarities are much less of a problem than slang or colloquialisms. Stanley Newman (1955) deals with this problem of levels of vocabulary in his analysis of sacred and slang language in Zuñi, and points out that a term such as *melika*, related to English *American*, is not appropriate for the religious atmosphere of the kiva. Rather, one must speak of Americans by means of a Zuñi expression meaning, literally, "broad-hats." For the Zuñis, uttering *melika* in a kiva ceremony would be as out of place as bringing a radio into such a meeting.

Onomatopoeic expressions are considered equivalent to slang by the speakers of some languages. In some languages in Africa, e. g., certain highly imitative expressions (sometimes called ideophones) have been ruled out as inappropriate to the dignified context of the Bible. Undoubtedly the critical attitudes of some missionary translators toward such vivid, but highly colloquial, forms of expression have contributed to the feeling of many Africans that such words are inappropriate in Biblical contexts. In some languages, however, such onomatopoeic usages are not only highly developed, but are regarded as essential and becoming in any type of discourse. For example, Waiwai, a language of British Guiana, uses such expressions with great frequency, and without them one can scarcely communicate the emotional tone of the message, for they provide the basic signals for understanding the speaker's attitude toward the events he narrates.

Some translators are successful in avoiding vulgarisms and slang, but fall into the error of making a relatively straightforward message in the source language sound like a complicated legal document in the receptor language by trying too hard to be completely unambiguous; as a result such a translator spins out his definitions in long, technical phrases. In such a translation little is left of the grace and naturalness of the original.

Anachronisms are another means of violating the co-suitability of message and context. For example, a Bible translation into English which used "iron oxide" in place of "rust" would be technically correct, but certainly anachronistic. On the other hand, to translate "heavens and earth" by "universe" in Genesis 1:1 is not so radical a departure as one might think, for the people of the ancient world had a highly developed concept of an organized system comprising the "heavens and the earth," and hence "universe" is not inappropriate. Anachronisms involve two types of errors: (1) using contemporary words which falsify life at historically different periods, e. g. translating "demon possessed" as "mentally distressed," and (2) using old-fashioned language in the receptor language and hence giving an impression of unreality.

Appropriateness of the message within the context is not merely a matter of the referential content of the words. The total impression of a message consists not merely in the objects, events, abstractions, and relationships symbolized by the words, but also in the stylistic selection and arrangement of such symbols. Moreover, the standards of stylistic acceptability for various types of discourse differ radically from language to language. What is entirely appropriate in Spanish, for example, may turn out to be quite unacceptable "purple prose" in English, and the English prose we admire as dignified and effective often seems in Spanish to be colorless, insipid, and flat. Many Spanish literary artists take delight in the flowery elegance of their language, while most English writers prefer bold realism, precision, and movement.

It is essential not only that a translation avoid certain obvious failures to adjust the message to the context, but also that it incorporate certain positive elements of style which provide the proper emotional tone for the discourse. This emotional tone must accurately reflect the point of view of the author. Thus such elements as sarcasm, irony, or whimsical interest must all be accurately reflected in a D-E translation. Furthermore, it is essential that each participant introduced into the message be accurately represented. That is to say, individuals must be properly characterized by the appropriate selection and arrangement of words, so that such features as social class or geographical dialect will be immediately evident. Moreover, each character must be permitted to have the same kind of individuality and personality as the author himself gave them in the original message.

A third element in the naturalness of a D-E translation is the extent to which the message fits the receptor-language audience. This appropriateness must be judged on the basis of the level of experience and the capacity for decoding, if one is to aim at any real dynamic equivalence. On the other hand, one is not always sure how the original audience responded or were supposed to respond. Bible translators, for example, have often made quite a point of the fact that the language of the New Testament was Koine Greek, the language of "the man in the street," and hence a translation should speak to the man in the street. The truth of the matter is that many New Testament messages were not directed primarily to the man in the street, but to the man in the congregation. For this reason, such expressions as "Abba Father," *Maranatha*, and "baptized into Christ" could be used with reasonable expectation that they would be understood.

A translation which aims at dynamic equivalence inevitably involves a number of formal adjustments, for one cannot have his formal cake and eat it dynamically too. Something must give! In general, this limitation involves three principal areas: (1) special literary forms, (2) semantically exocentric expressions, and (3) intraorganismic meanings.

The translating of poetry obviously involves more adjustments in literary form than does prose, for rhythmic forms differ far more radically in form, and hence in esthetic appeal. As a result, certain rhythmic patterns must often be substituted for others, as when Greek dactylic hexameter is translated in iambic pentameter. Moreover, some of the most acceptable translating of rhymed verse is accomplished by substituting free verse. In Bible translating the usual procedure is to attempt a kind of dignified prose where the original employs poetry, since, in general, Biblical content is regarded as much more important than Biblical form.

When semantically exocentric phrases in the source language are meaningless or misleading if translated literally into the receptor language, one is obliged to make some adjustments in a D-E translation. For example, the Semitic idiom "gird up the loins of your mind" may mean nothing more than "put a belt around the hips of your thoughts" if translated literally. Under such circumstances one must change from an exocentric to an endocentric type of expression, e. g. "get ready in your thinking." Moreover, an idiom may not be merely meaningless, but may even convey quite the wrong meaning, in which case it must also be modified. Often, for example, a simile may be substituted for the original metaphor, e. g. "sons of thunder" may become "men like thunder."

Intraorganismic meanings suffer most in the process of translating, for they depend so largely upon the total cultural context of the language in which they are used, and hence are not readily transferable to other language-culture contexts. In the New Testament, for example, the word *tapeinos*, usually translated as "humble" or "lowly" in English, had very definite emotive connotations in the Greek world, where it carried the pejorative meanings of "low," "humiliated," "degraded," "mean" and "base." However, the Christians, who came principally from the lower strata of society, adopted as a symbol of an important Christian virtue this very term, which had been used derisively of the lower classes. Translations of the New Testament into English cannot expect to carry all the latent emotive meanings in the Greek word. Similarly, such translations as "anointed," "Messiah," and "Christ" cannot do full justice to the Greek *Christos*, which had associations intimately linked with the hopes and aspirations of the early Judeo-Christian community. Such emotive elements of meaning need not be related solely to terms of theological import. They apply to all levels of vocabulary. In French, for example, there is no term quite equivalent to English *home*, in contrast with *house*, and in English nothing quite like French *foyer*, which in many respect is like English *home*, but also means "hearth" and "fireside" as well as "focus" and "salon of a theater." Emotively, the English word *"home"* is close to French *foyer*, but referentially *home* is usually equivalent to *maison*, *habitation*, and *chez* (followed by an appropriate pronoun).

【延伸阅读】

[1] Catford, J. C. (1965). *A Linguistic Theory of Translation*. London: OUP.

[2] Hermans, T. (1995). Toury's Empiricism Version One: Review of Gideon Toury's *In Search of a Theory of Translation*. *The Translator*, 1 (2), 215 – 223.

[3] Ivir, V. (1981). Formal Correspondence vs. Translation Equivalence Revisited. *Poetics Today*, 2(4), 51 – 59.

[4] Newmark, P. (1981). *Approaches to Translation*. Oxford and New York: Pergamon.

[5] Nida, E. A. (1995). Dynamic Equivalence in Translating. In Sin-Wai Chan & D. E. Pollard (eds.), *An Encyclopaedia of Translation: Chinese-English, English-Chinese* (pp. 223 – 230). Hong Kong: The Chinese University Press.

[6] Nida，E. A. and Charles，R. T. (1969/1982). *The Theory and Practice of Translation*. Leiden：E. J. Brill.

【问题与思考】

1. 概念 correspondence 与概念 equivalence 有何异同？

2. 几十年来"对等"概念在西方可谓众说纷纭，围绕对等问题的争论更是不断，为什么会有这样的争论？

3. 试比较奈达的 dynamic/formal equivalence 和纽马克的 semantic/communicative translation 的异同。

4. 奈达的动态对等原则是否适用于指导广告翻译、科技翻译和文学翻译？为什么？

5. 奈达的翻译理论与信息论有何关联？

选文三 关于国外翻译理论的三大核心概念
——翻译的实质、可译性和等值

蔡 毅

导 言

本文发表于《中国翻译》1995 年第 6 期。

翻译的实质、可译性和等值是西方翻译理论的三大核心概念。本文较全面地分析了这些核心概念的演变情况及其特点，并在此基础上提出了作者本人的观点。

国外翻译理论有三大核心概念，即翻译的实质（定义）、可译性和等值。三者相互交织，互为前提，被视为决定翻译战略以及评价翻译质量的理论依据，因此成为各国翻译理论家反复论述的课题。我们研究国外翻译理论，必须全面了解这些核心概念的演变情况及其特点，取其精华，为我所用。

一

翻译的实质回答"究竟什么是翻译"这一问题。翻译同其他语言活动相比，有哪些重要的典型特征？

在这个问题上，国外翻译理论界随着时间的推移，不断改变提法，增添了新的内容。但是基本上可以分为以下四类：

第一类是早期的提法，以奥廷格为代表。他认为："可以把翻译定义为：将符号改变为另外的符号。如果原文表达某种意义,那么我们往往要求它的代替物也表达同样的意义,或(更现实些)尽可能地表达同样的意义。保留不变意义是从一种自然语言译为另一种自然语言的核心问题。"

把翻译归结为符号的转变显然是过于简单化了。奥廷格提出的定义受到了科勒的批评:"奥廷格关于翻译的定义反映了 20 世纪 50—60 年代提出自动化翻译的热情,但对寻找出发语和译语单位之间对应物的问题估计不足。"

第二类提法以费道罗夫和温特为代表,他们在翻译的定义中加上了"忠实"、"全面"、"等值"等要求。

费道罗夫说:"翻译是用一种语言手段忠实、全面地表达另一种语言表达的东西。(传达的忠实和全面是翻译区别于转述、简述以及各种改写之所在。)"

温特提出:"翻译是将论释我们周围世界某部分的说法用尽可能等值的说法来代替。"(按:这里包括语言内部翻译。)

奈达和泰伯也使用了类似的提法:"翻译是接受语复制源语信息的最近似的自然等值物,首先是在意义方面,其次是在文体方面的等值物。"

第三类提法以卡特福德、巴尔胡达罗夫、威尔斯等人为代表,明确翻译的对象是话语。

卡特福德指出:"翻译可以定义为:将一种语言(出发语)的话语材料用另外一种语言的等值话语予以替代。"

巴尔胡达罗夫说:"翻译是将一种语言的言语产物(话语)在保持内容,即意义不变的情况下改变为另外一种语言的言语产物的过程。"

威尔斯指出:"翻译是将源语话语变为尽可能等值的译语话语的过程。"

从这类定义中可以清楚地看到一门新兴的语言学科——话语语言学的某些论点已为翻译理论所接受。正是在这样的背景下费道罗夫于 1983 年也为翻译的定义增加了新的内容:"翻译是将一种语言(源语)的言语产物用另外一种语言(译语)予以再现。"

第四类以什维采尔为代表,在翻译的定义中又增加了"文化"的内容:"翻译是单向双相的语际和文化际交际过程。在此过程中,在对原话语进行有针对性(翻译)分析的基础上,创造另一种语言和文化介质中代替原话语的次生话语。

这个过程的目的是传达原话语的交际效果,但因两种语言、两种文化、两种交际情景的不同,局部有变化。"

什维采尔认为,翻译定义的变化在很大程度上反映了翻译学发展的逻辑。

对此实难苟同。

首先,应当把"翻译的定义"与"对翻译质量的要求"区别开来,这两者属于不同的范畴。"忠实"、"全面"、"等值"等是对翻译质量的要求,把它们纳入"翻译的定义"未必恰当。因为有各式各样的翻译:有全译,有节译;有意译,有直译;有优质翻译,有劣质翻译等。初学翻译的人其翻译质量未必都能达到"忠实"、"全面"、"等值"。

其次,翻译理论可以侧重研究话语的翻译,但翻译的对象并不仅限于话语。双语词典词条中提供的是词、短语和例句及其译文,而不是(也不可能是)话语及其译文。但双语词典还是可以称做翻译词典而不是其他。研究专有名词的翻译问题不一定都要通过话语才能说清。对音译和意译的选择也不一定都要通过话语来论证。总之,把翻译的定义界定为话语的语际转变是片面的。

最后,定义应当言简意赅,一目了然。过于烦琐会使人望而生畏,感到茫然而无所适从。

总之,是否可廓清多余和局限,言简意赅地将翻译的定义概括为:"将一种语言传达的信息用另外一种语言传达出来"?

这里所谓的信息,其内涵是多方面的,包括:意义、思想内容、感情、修辞、文体、风格、文化及形式等。

二

在人类历史上,不同民族的交往,包括口头的和笔头的,是客观存在,特别是在文明社会中,以文字形式记载下来的翻译成果比比皆是。然而某些语言学家,包括翻译理论家却一而再,再而三地论证可译性或不可译性。

对可译性持否定态度的语言学家中,德国的洪堡可算是个代表人物。他于 1796 年 7 月 23 日给友人的一封信中写道:"对我来说每次翻译都是一次企图解决无法完成的任务的尝试。因为每个译者都必然会被两大暗礁中的一个碰得头破血流:或是过分拘泥于原文而损害本民族的味道和语言,或是过分拘泥于本民族的特色而损害原文。要找出某种折中的方案,不仅困难,而且干脆就是不可能的。"

洪堡之所以对可译性持这样的观点,是因为他认为,语言是表达民族精神的形式,语言的个性是民族精神的特性所决定的,不同的语言彼此是没有共约性的。

以魏斯格尔伯为代表的新洪堡学派对洪堡的上述思想作了进一步的发展。他认为,语言形成"中间世界",人类透过"中间世界"认识现实。各种语言特有的语义场中对语言内容的划分不同。这证明,每种母语都含有"该语言集团特有的中间世界",形成其世界图像。

依照上述理论,不可译性是由语言的本性本身所决定的,是语言学的一个普遍公理。

切斯诺科夫在评价新洪堡学派对语言与思维关系的理论时指出:"新洪堡学派的哲学是主观唯心主义的实证主义哲学。它形而上学地夸大了语言在认识过程中的能动性。"

把语言与思维等同起来的倾向表现得更为明显的是以沃尔夫为代表的语言相关论学派。他们认为,操用非印欧语的民族思维中有一种与操用印欧语民族逻辑不同的特殊逻辑方式。因为逻辑形式(思想逻辑方式)同语义形式(语义结构)是不可分的。

其实,人的逻辑方式基本上是相同的。因为"思想、逻辑方式源于人的认识本性,它是由人认识活动的需要,由实践的需要所决定的。所以语言结构的特点并不能改变思想逻辑方式。"

但这仅仅是问题的一个方面,涉及的仅仅是语言的表达方式。作为可译性的理论依据,还有更重要的一面,涉及的是语言的表达对象,即内容,那就是各民族历史地经历过相同或类似的现实,具有标志这些现实的语义共相。这是可译性的前提的前提。

当然,不同民族的语言中除了语义共相之外,还存在着语义差异。但是这些差异对于翻译来说并不是不可克服的障碍,因为任何一种语言的描述潜力都是无限的。通过语言接触和环境接触还可以淡化,甚至排除语义差异。把外语译为母语可以丰富母语的词汇和表达方式。

这里需要指出的是,有人认为具有无限描述能力的语言仅限于"发达"语言。例如,费道罗夫在论证可译性时曾写道:"每种高度发达的语言都是一种强有力的手段,足以传达用另一种语言的手段表达的与形式相统一的内容。"(注:费道罗夫在 1983 年《翻译概论基础》一书的第 4 版中对此作了纠正。)言外之意就是"不发达"语言则不可能做到这一点。这种观点是完全错误的。实际上语言是不应有"发达"与"不发达"之分的。巴尔胡达罗夫说得好:"任何一种语言都能够描述其使用者所碰到或将碰到的任何实物、概念和情景。使用某种'原始'语言的集团,只要知道了某种实物、技术设备、政治制度、科学概念等,他们的语言中立刻就会出现标志这些实物和概念的相应词语。"科勒也说:"如果说每种语言都能表达所指的一切,那么,从原则上说,某种语言所表达的一切都能被译为另外一种语言。"

这就是说,可译性原则应适用于任何两种语言之间。

然而,可译性是就整体而言。在翻译过程中往往不可避免地会有所损失。

卡德说:"源语的任何话语都能在保持理性信息内容(注:平时所谓的'所指功能')不变的情况下用译语的话语所替代。至于内容等其他要素(表情感情负荷、艺术审美价值、受一定语言集体语言特征制约的语用负荷、意义的内涵成分)的传达问题,则需要进一步研究。"

费道罗夫认为,原文的某些要素确实是不可译的。在这里,他指的是违反语言规范的一些现象,主要是方言和行话。

加克说:"洋径浜式语言的传达总是存在着客观困难,就连翻译大师在解决这一问题时,在内容的传达上也不能不有所损失或变动。"

库德拉则提出,在这种情况下"只得借助于各种辅助手段:给以阐释性的翻译,或替换、增补、减略一些东西"。

确实是这样。在传达纯理语言学功能,如文字游戏、双关语、回文诗以及有意义的姓名等时往往就得靠辅助手段,有时甚至得音译。试想,若把我国语言大师赵元任运用 shi 的异声异义字写就的戏作"施氏食狮史"译成外文,不靠辅助手段行吗?

综上所述,关于可译性问题,或许可归结为:① 原则上肯定可译性;② 可译性是个相对的概念。翻译时允许,有时甚至是不可避免地会有所损失或变动,但必须保留原文的主要功能或主要要素。这就涉及国外翻译理论中的另一个核心概念——等值问题。

三

许多国外翻译理论家认为,等值的概念是翻译的重要本质特征之一,它对揭示翻译的实质具有决定性意义。因此随着对翻译定义的变化,对等值也提出了不尽相同的概念。

卡特福德指出:"为了达到翻译等值,必须使出发语和归宿语均符合该情景的功能相关特征。"所谓功能相关特征指的是该情景中话语交际功能的重要特征。他认为等值的决定性(甚至是唯一的)标准是与实物情景相应的语义标志。

奈达为了克服仅仅从语义角度出发看待等值问题的局限性,提出了同形式等值相对立的"能动等值"概念。他把能动等值定义为:"翻译质量,即用接受语传达原文思想内容,使译文接受者的反应与原文接受者的反应基本相同。"这里的所谓反应是指对信息的全面感受,包括对其意思内容、感情等的理解。这也就是说,他在等值的定义中,增添了语用因素。这是完全正确的。但是其中"基本相同"的提法欠妥,是把对翻译质量的理想要求与翻译实践的现实混为一谈了。

耶格尔则提出了交际等值的概念,即"两种话语的交际价值相同,换言之,即两种话语能引起同样的交际效果,也就是,将一定的思想内容传达给收讯人"。

科勒认为,泛泛地对翻译提出等值的要求是没有意义的。明确等值的种类或类型才有实际意义。因此他把等值分为五种。

"(1) 所指等值:保留话语的实物内容(即一般译论著述中所谓的内容不变值);

(2) 内涵等值:选择同义语言手段传达话语的内涵(即所谓的修辞等值);

(3) 文字规范等值:着眼于话语的体裁特征、言语和语言规范(也属于修辞等值);

(4) 语用等值:着眼于收讯人(即所谓交际等值);

(5) 形式等值:传达原文的艺术审美、文字游戏、个人特色等形式特征。"

科勒认为等值是个规范性概念,而不是描述性概念。他提出的五种等值就反映了对翻译的规范性要求。在这一点上,他比奈达提得要明确。

科米萨罗夫将等值划分为五个层次(类型),说它们分别代表译文与原文意思相同的不同程度,即:

"(1) 交际目的层次;

(2) 情景等同层次;

(3) 情景描述方法层次;

(4) 句法结构意义层次;

(5) 文字符号层次。"

其实上述五个层次中,后三者的区别是在句法或形式相似的不同程度上而并不涉及内容的相同的程度。看来他的层次分类并不是源于翻译实践经验。但科米萨罗夫提出等值的必备条件是"保留话语的主导功能"则是正确的。

加克和利文也提出了等值的等级模式,他们把等值划分为三种。

"(1) 形式等值:意义相同,词和形式也相同;

(2) 意思等值:用不同的方法表达同一意义;

(3) 情景等值:用不同的形式和以这些形式表达的不同基本意义(义素)描述同一情景。"

此外,也有人对翻译等值的提法持否定态度,例如,纽马克在《翻译问题探索》一书中指出:"诸如翻译单位、翻译等值、翻译不变值等之类的论题应当摒弃——要么太理论化,要么随机性太强。"

怎样看这个问题呢?

首先,"等值"的提出,实际上是要解决翻译标准,也就是对翻译质量的要求问题。

国外语言学派的翻译理论家们是想借助语言学术语严格界定对翻译质量的要求,以取代一般的"忠实"、"确切"等提法,正如我国翻译理论界探讨"信、达、雅"一样,本身是无可非议的。

为了达到翻译等值,其实提出反对"形式等值"也就够了。奈达的"能动等值"实际上指的是对等值应因地制宜。"能动"是达到等值的手段。其他人提出的等值的种类、层次或类型,实际上是"能动"的具体化,是从不同的侧面阐述对等值要区别对待,因此也有一定的参考价值,尽管有些烦琐。

总之,不能因噎废食,应当肯定对等值问题的探讨。

当然翻译理论的发展有其本身的逻辑。但是它首先应源于翻译实践并服务于指导翻译实践。国外翻译理论的发展中确实存在有"为理论而理论"的偏向,甚至有时"故弄玄虚"。这些都值得我们注意。然而翻译理论是兼有描述性和规范性,而且是以描述性为主的一门科学,因此,有"随机性"是不可避免的。

上述意见极不成熟,衷心希望专家们指正。但愿它们能有利于对翻译理论进行更深入的探讨。

【延伸阅读】

[1] 冯文坤. 论本雅明的"可译性"及关于翻译的哲学思考. 四川师范大学学报:社会科学版,2006(3):110-115.

[2] 韩子满. 翻译等值论探幽. 解放军外国语学院学报,1999(2):68-70.

[3] 蒋林. 西方翻译等值论述评. 中国科技翻译,2005(3):60-62.

[4] 郑海凌. 等值观念与对等理论. 外语学刊,2006(6):83-86.

【问题与思考】

1. 本文作者是如何阐述翻译理论概念的演变情况的?
2. 本文在论证过程中是如何使用归纳法的?
3. 关于这三个核心概念,本文作者是如何提出自己的看法的?

第二章　翻译转移

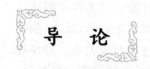

导　论

翻译转移是指从源语出发到目标语的过程中对形式对应的偏离(Catford,1965:73)。法国人韦内(Jean-Paul Vinay)和达贝奈特(Jean Darbelnet)较早开始研究翻译转移,他们描述了翻译中的各种语言变化,提出了七种翻译方法。但他们两人并未使用 shift(转移)一词,最早提出这一术语的是卡特福德,他把翻译转移分为若干类别。源语和目标语在结构上的不对应,导致翻译发生转移,继而引起目标语措辞的调整。卡特福德描述的翻译转移纯属语言范畴,停留在语法和词汇层面,这种转移在翻译过程中在所难免,除非译者有意让译文极端地接近源语结构。但是在任何译本中都有可能存在许多偏离,而它们并非两种语言在形式上的不对应所致。一些译评者不清楚这些偏离背后的动因,笼统地把它们归入错误之列。几乎所有译本都有这种显而易见的"错误",捷克斯洛伐克学者波波维奇(Anton Popovich)注意到了这一事实。他把这些错误一律视为翻译转移,从而大大拓宽了翻译转移概念的外延。在波波维奇看来,那些相对于源语文本来说是新的或者没有出现在合适地方的偏离都是翻译转移。

翻译转移代表了源语文本措辞与译本措辞之间的关系。因此他所谓的翻译转移不仅包括语言现象,而且包括出于文本、文学和文化方面的考量而进行的替换。波波维奇不仅承认不可规避的语言差异的存在,而且也承认译者是在规范的制约下从事翻译工作的,翻译规范影响译者在翻译过程中作出的决定。他认为译者进行翻译转移往往不是因为译者本人缺乏培训或缺少经验,而是因为译者试图尽可能地忠实于源语文本,把源语文本作为一个有机整体全面把握。波波维奇对翻译转移的研究主要基于文学翻译研究之上。与波波维奇相似,还有两名捷克斯洛伐克的翻译学者对文学翻译中的转移作了较为深入的研究,一个是列维(Jiri Levy),另一个是米科(Frantisek Miko)。列维(1969)仔细观察了源语文本的表层结构转换成译语文本的表层结构的各种情况,把文学翻译视为一种再生性、创造性劳动,文学翻译的目的是为了取得对等的美学效果。他还把需要取得对等的文本特征作了分类。列维所做的工作对于他去世前捷克斯洛伐克的翻译理论的发展起到了至关重要的作用,并产生了一些国际影响。他的另一篇论文(1967/2000)把译者的语言选择的渐进性语义转移与游戏理论结合起来进行探讨,也产生了巨大影响。米科(1970:66)主张译者的主要的甚或唯一的目标是在译文中保留源语文本的表达特征或风格。他建议从操作性、形象性、主体性、虚饰、突出和对比等角度研究文学风格。

对翻译转移作出最详尽分析并提出分析模式的是荷兰学者鲁文-兹瓦特(Leuven-Zwart)。她从韦内、达贝奈特和列维提出的语言变化类别入手,将其应用于译本的描述性分析,试图使译本和源语文本的对比具有系统性,并建立一个句子层面上的话语框架。不少学者认为,在翻译转移的各种研究模式中,鲁文-兹瓦特的分析模式是最广泛、最详尽的。图里也对翻译转移问题给予了较多关注。20世纪80年代初,他把充分翻译(adequate translation)作为译本与源语文本对比的不变量,文本要素(texteme)作为对比单位。被作为不变性的对应程度是文本要素层面上的充分性。对比的目的是要确定源语文本与译文间的实际对等相距充分性翻译的最高规范到底有多远。因为强制性转移受规则制约,它们一般不能体现翻译规范的影响,因此不被纳入考量之中。对比过程首先假定对等发生在文本功能层面,然后看源语文本要素和译语文本要素的主要关系是否在文本功能层面。如果在此层面,翻译关系就是充分的,反之,翻译关系就是不充分的,接下来需要做的是要在较低的文本和语言层次上寻找对应关系。翻译规范决定实际的翻译对等在充分性和可接受性之间所处的位置。在图里后来的研究中(1995),翻译转移概念变得不太重要了。

　　本章共选四篇文章。第一篇是Jean-Paul Vinay和Jean Darbelnet撰写的"A Methodology for Translation",该文尽管没有使用"转移"(shift)这个概念,但它是最早讨论翻译转移问题的文献之一。第二篇是J. C. Catford著的"Translation Shifts",明确定义了translation shift概念,并区分了各种转移现象。第三篇"Translation as a Decision Process"的作者是Levy,首次指出了翻译中的"逐渐语义转移"(gradual semantic shifting)现象。第四篇是李德超的《鲁文-兹瓦特论翻译转移的比较》,该文研究了鲁文-兹瓦特关于翻译转移的理论。

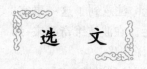

选文一　A Methodology for Translation

Jean-Paul Vinay　Jean Darbelnet

导　言

　　本文选自韦努蒂编《翻译研究读本》。

　　虽然韦内和达贝奈特在论文《翻译的方法》中没有使用"转移"(shift)这个概念,但是他们讨论的内容其实就是翻译转移。两人主要介绍了翻译实践中所要运用的直接翻译(direct translation)和间接翻译(oblique translation),指出弥补"缺无"的翻译方法都是"再创作"的组成部分,译者应根据不同的情况进行应用。论文详细阐述了"借用"、"仿造"、"词类转换"、"调整"、"改编"等翻译技巧,它们也是译者在翻译创作空间中施展发挥的技巧。翻译方法在翻译研究中占有突出地位,它来自翻译实践又可指导翻译实践,是翻译研究的基础。探究韦内和达贝奈特的翻译方法对我们正确认识翻译转移的本质具有重要意义。

At first the different methods or procedures seem to be countless, but they can be condensed to just seven, each one corresponding to a higher degree of complexity. In practice, they may be used either on their own or combined with one or more of the others.

Direct and oblique translation

Generally speaking, translators can choose from two methods of translating, namely direct, or literal translation and oblique translation. In some translation tasks it may be possible to transpose the source language message element by element into the target language, because it is based on either (1) parallel categories, in which case we can speak of structural parallelism, or (2) on parallel concepts, which are the result of metalinguistic parallelisms. But translators may also notice gaps, or "lacunae," in the target language (TL) which must be filled by corresponding elements, so that the overall impression is the same for the two messages.

It may, however, also happen that, because of structural or metalinguistic differences, certain stylistic effects cannot be transposed into the TL without upsetting the syntactic order, or even the lexis. In this case it is understood that more complex methods have to be used which at first may look unusual but which nevertheless can permit translators a strict control over the reliability of their work: These procedures are called oblique translation methods. In the listing which follows, the first three procedures are direct and the others are oblique.

Procedure 1: borrowing

To overcome a lacuna, usually a metalinguistic one (e. g. a new technical process, an unknown concept), borrowing is the simplest of all translation methods. It would not even merit discussion in this context if translators did not occasionally need to use it in order to create a stylistic effect. For instance, in order to introduce the flavour of the source langugae (SL) culture into a translation, foreign terms may be used, e. g. such Russian words as "roubles," "datchas" and "aparatchik," "dollars" and "party" from American English, Mexican Spanish food names "tequila" and "tortillas," and so on. In a story with a typical English setting, an expression such as "the coroner spoke" is probably better translated into French by borrowing the English term "coroner," rather than trying to find a more or less satisfying equivalent title from amongst the French magistrature, e. g. *Le coroner prit la parole.*

Some well-established, mainly older borrowings are so widely used that they are no longer considered as such and have become a part of the respective TL lexicon. Some examples of French borrowings from other languages are *"alcool," "redingote," "paquebot," "acajou,"* etc. In English such words as "menu," "carburetor," "hangar," "chic" and expressions like "déjà vu," "enfant terrible" and "rendez-vous" are no longer considered to be borrowings. Translators are particularly interested in the newer borrowings, even personal ones. It must be remembered that many borrowings enter a language through translation, just like semantic borrowings or faux amis, whose pitfalls translators must carefully avoid.

The decision to borrow a SL word or expression for introducing an element of local colour is a matter of style and consequently of the message.

Procedure 2: calque

A calque is a special kind of borrowing whereby a language borrows an expression form of another, but then translates literally each of its elements. The result is either

(1) a lexical calque, as in the first example, below, i. e. a calque which respects the syntactic structure of the TL, whilst introducing a new mode of expression; or

(2) a structural calque, as in the second example, below, which introduces a new construction into the language, e. g.

English-French calque

| Compliments of the Season! | Compliments de la saison! |
| Science-fiction | Science-fiction |

As with borrowings, there are many fixed calques which, after a period of time, become an integral part of the language. These too, like borrowings, may have undergone a semantic change, turning them into faux amis. Translators are more interested in new calques which can serve to fill a lacuna, without having to use an actual borrowing (cf. "*économiquement faible*," a French calque taken from the German language). In such cases it may be preferable to create a new lexical form using Greek or Latin roots or use conversion (cf. "*l'hypostase*;" Bally, 1944, p. 257 ff.). This would avoid awkward calques, such as:

French calque	*English source*
thérapie occupationnelle	occupational therapy
Banque pour le Commerce et le Développement	Bank for Commerce and Development
les quatre Grands	the four great powers
le Premier Français	The French Premier
Le mariage est une association à cinquante-cinquante.	Matrimony is a fifty-fifty association.
(*LesNouvellesLittéraires*, October 1955)	
l'homme dans la rue	the man in the street
(*Revue des Deux Mondes*, May 1955)	[instead of "l'homme de la rue" or "le Français moyen"]
compagnon de route	fellow-traveller
(*Le Monde*, March 1956)	

La plupart des grandes décisions sur	Most major decisions regarding the
le Proche-Orient ont été prises à un	Near-East were taken when
moment où Sir Winston Churchill	Churchill pretended that the chair
affectait de considérer comme	occupied by France on the inter-
"vide" la "chaise" de la France sur la	national scene was empty.
scène internationale.	[instead of: "la place" or "le fauteuil"]
(*Le Monde*, March 1956)	

Procedure 3: literal translation

Literal, or word for word, translation is the direct transfer of an SL text into a grammatically and idiomatically appropriate TL text in which the translators' task is limited to observing the adherence to the linguistic servitudes of the TL.

I left my spectacles on the table downstairs.	J'ai laissé mes lunettes sur la table en bas.
Where are you?	Où êtes-vous?
This train arrives at Union Station at ten.	Ce train arrive à la gare Centrale à 10 heures.

In principle, a literal translation is a unique solution which is reversible and complete in itself. It is most common when translating between two languages of the same family (e. g. between French and Italian), and even more so when they also share the same culture. If literal translations arise between French and English, it is because common metalinguistic concepts also reveal physical coexistence, i. e. periods of bilingualism, with the conscious or unconscious imitation which attaches to a certain intellectual or political prestige, and such like. They can also be justified by a certain convergence of thought and sometimes of structure, which are certainly present among the European languages (cf. the creation of the definite article, the concepts of culture and civilization), and which have motivated interesting research in General Semantics.

In the preceding methods, translation does not involve any special stylistic procedures. If this were always the case then our present study would lack justification and translation would lack an intellectual challenge since it would be reduced to an unambiguous transfer from SL to TL. The exploration of the possibility of translating scientific texts by machine, as proposed by the many research groups in universities and industry in all major countries, is largely based on the existence of parallel passages in SL and TL texts, corresponding to parallel thought processes which, as would be expected, are particularly frequent in the documentation required in science and technology. The suitability of such texts for automatic translation was recognised as early as 1955 by Locke and Booth. (For current assessments of the scope of applications of machine translation see Hutchins & Somers, 1992; Sager, 1994.)

If, after trying the first three procedures, translators regard a literal translation unacceptable, they must turn to the methods of oblique translation. By unacceptable we mean that the message, when translated literally

(1) gives another meaning, or

(2) has no meaning, or

(3) is structurally impossible, or

(4) does not have a corresponding expression within the metalinguistic experience of the TL, or

(5) has a corresponding expression, but not within the same register.

To clarify these ideas, consider the following examples:

He looked at the map.	Il regarda la carte.
He looked the picture of health.	Il paraissait l'image de la santé.
	Il avait l'air en pleine forme.

While we can translate the first sentence literally, this is impossible for the second, unless we wish to do so for an expressive reason (e. g. in order to characterise an Englishman who does not speak very good conversational French). The first example pair is less specific, since "*carte*" is less specific than "map." But this in no way renders the demonstration invalid.

If translators offer something similar to the second example, above, e. g. "*Il se portait comme un charme*," this indicates that they have aimed at an equivalence of the two messages, something their "neutral" position outside both the TL and the SL enables them to do. Equivalence of messages ultimately relies upon an identity of situations, and it is this alone that allows us to state that the TL may retain certain characteristics of reality that are unknown to the SL.

If there were conceptual dictionaries with bilingual signifiers, translators would only need to look up the appropriate translation under the entry corresponding to the situation identified by the SL message. But such dictionaries do not exist and therefore translators start off with words or units of translation, to which they apply particular procedures with the intention of conveying the desired message. Since the positioning of a word within an utterance has an effect on its meaning, it may well arise that the solution results in a grouping of words that is so far from the original starting point that no dictionary could give it. Given the infinite number of combinations of signifiers alone, it is understandable that dictionaries cannot provide translators with ready-made solutions to all their problems. Only translators can be aware of the totality of the message, which determines their decisions. In the final analysis, it is the message alone, a reflection of the situation, that allows us to judge whether two texts are adequate alternatives.

Procedure 4: transposition

The method called transposition involves replacing one word class with another without changing the meaning of the message. Besides being a special translation procedure, transposition can also be applied within a language. For example, "*Il a annoncé qu'il reviendrait*," can be re-expressed by transposing a subordinate verb with a noun, thus: "*Il a annoncé son retour.*" In contrast to the first expression, which we call the base expression, we refer to the second one as the transposed expression. In translation there are two distinct types of transposition: (1) obligatory transposition, and (2) optional transposition.

The following example has to be translated literally (procedure 3), but must also be transposed (procedure 4)

Dès son lever ...

As soon as he gets up ...

As soon as he gets/got up ...

Dès son lever ...

Dès qu'il se lève ...

In this example, English allows no choice between the two forms, the base form being the only one possible. Inversely, however, when translating back into French, we have the choice between applying a calque or a transposition, because French permits either construction.

In contrast, the two following phrases can both be transposed:

Après qu'il sera revenu ...

Après son retour ...

After he comes back ...

After his return ...

From a stylistic point of view, the base and the transposed expression do not necessarily have the same value. Translators must, therefore, choose to carry out a transposition if the translation thus obtained fits better into the utterance, or allows a particular nuance of style to be retained. Indeed, the transposed form is generally more literary in character.

A special and frequently used case of transposition is that of interchange.

Procedure 5: modulation

Modulation is a variation of the form of the message, obtained by a change in the point of view. This change can be justified when, although a literal, or even transposed, translation results in a grammatically correct utterance, it is considered unsuitable, unidiomatic or awkward in the TL.

As with transposition, we distinguish between free or optional modulations and those that are fixed or obligatory. A classical example of an obligatory modulation is the phrase, "The time when ... " which must be translated as "*Le moment où ... *" The type of modulation which turns a negative SL expression into a positive TL expression is more often than not optional, even though this is closely linked with the structure of each language, e. g.

It is not difficult to show ...

Il est facile de démontrer ...

The difference between fixed and free modulation is one of degree. In the case of fixed modulation, translators with a good knowledge of both languages freely use this method, as they will be aware of the frequency of use, the overall acceptance, and the confirmation provided by a dictionary or grammar of the preferred expression.

Cases of free modulation are single instances not yet fixed and sanctioned by usage, so that the procedure must be carried out anew each time. This, however, is not what qualifies it as optional; when carried out as it should be, the resulting translation should correspond perfectly to the situation indicated by the SL. To illustrate this point, it can be said that the result of a free modulation should lead to a solution that makes the reader exclaim, "Yes, that's exactly what you would say." Free modulation thus tends towards a unique solution, a solution which rests upon a habitual train of thought and which is necessary rather than optional. It is therefore evident that between fixed modulation and free modulation there is but a difference of degree, and that as soon as a free modulation is used often enough, or is felt to offer the only solution (this usually results from the study of bilingual texts, from discussions at a bilingual conference, or from a famous translation which claims recognition due to its literary merit), it may become fixed. However, a free modulation does not actually become fixed until it is referred to in dictionaries and grammars and is regularly taught. A passage not using such a modulation would then be considered inaccurate and rejected. In his M. A. thesis, G. Panneton, from whom we have borrowed the term modulation, correctly anticipated the results of a systematic application of transposition and modulation:

> La transposition correspondrait en traduction à une équation du premier degré,
> la modulation à une équation du second degré, chacune transformant l'équation en
> identité, toutes deux effectuant la résolution appropriée.

(Panneton, 1946)

Procedure 6: equivalence

We have repeatedly stressed that one and the same situation can be rendered by two texts using completely different stylistic and structural methods. In such cases we are dealing with the method which produces equivalent texts. The classical example of equivalence is given by the reaction of an amateur who accidentally hits his finger with a hammer: If he were French his cry of pain would be transcribed as "Aïe!", but if he were English this would be interpreted as "Ouch!". Another striking case of equivalences are the many onomatopoeia of animal sounds, e. g.

cocorico	cock-a-doodle-do
miaou	miaow
hi-han	heehaw

These simple examples illustrate a particular feature of equivalences: More often than not they are of a syntagmatic nature, and affect the whole of the message. As a result, most equivalences are fixed, and belong to a phraseological repertoire of idioms, clichés, proverbs, nominal or adjectival phrases, etc. In general, proverbs are perfect examples of equivalences, e. g.

Il pleut à seaux/des cordes.	It is raining cats and dogs.
Like a bull in a china shop.	Comme un chien dans un jeu de quilles.
Too many cooks spoil the broth.	Deux patrons font chavirer la barque.

The method of creating equivalences is also frequently applied to idioms. For example, "to talk through one's hat" and "as like as two peas" cannot be translated by means of a calque. Yet this is exactly what happens amongst members of so-called bilingual populations, who have permanent contact with two languages but never become fully acquainted with either. It happens, nevertheless, that some of these calques actually become accepted by the other language, especially if they relate to a new field which is likely to become established in the country of the TL. For example, in Canadian French the idiom "to talk through one's hat" has acquired the equivalent "*parler à travers son chapeau.*" But the responsibility of introducing such calques into a perfectly organised language should not fall upon the shoulders of translators: Only writers can take such liberties, and they alone should take credit or blame for success or failure. In translation it is advisable to use traditional forms of expression, because the accusation of using Gallicisms, Anglicisms, Germanisms, Hispanisms, etc. will always be present when a translator attempts to introduce a new calque.

Procedure 7: adaptation

With this seventh method we reach the extreme limit of translation: It is used in those cases where the type of situation being referred to by the SL message is unknown in the TL culture. In such cases translators have to create a new situation that can be considered as being equivalent. Adaptation can, therefore, be described as a special kind of equivalence, a situational equivalence. Let us take the example of an English father who would think nothing of kissing his daughter on the mouth, something which is normal in that culture but which would not be acceptable in a literal rendering into French. Translating, "He kissed his daughter on the mouth" by "*Il embrassa sa fille sur la bouche,*" would introduce into the TL an element which is not present in the SL, where the situation may be that of a loving father returning home and greeting his daughter after a long journey. The French rendering would be a special kind of over translation. A more appropriate translation would be, "*Il serra tendrement sa fille dans ses bras,*" unless, of course, the translator wishes to achieve a cheap effect. Adaptations are particularly frequent in the translation of book and film titles, e. g.

| Trois hommes et un couffin | Three men and a baby. [film] |
| Le grand Meaulnes | The Wanderer. [book title] |

The method of adaptation is well known amongst simultaneous interpreters: There is the story of an interpreter who, having adapted "cricket" into "Tour de France" in a context referring to a particularly popular sport, was put on the spot when the French delegate then thanked the speaker for having referred to such a typically French sport. The interpreter then had to reverse the adaptation and speak of cricket to his English client.

The refusal to make an adaptation is invariably detected within a translation because it affects not only the syntactic structure, but also the development of ideas and how they are represented within the paragraph. Even though translators may produce a perfectly correct text without adaptation, the absence of adaptation may still be noticeable by an indefinable tone, something that does not sound quite right. This is unfortunately the impression given only too often by texts published by international organizations, whose members, either through ignorance or because of a mistaken insistence on literalness, demand translations which are largely based on calques. The result may then turn out to be pure gibberish which has no name in any language, but which René Etiemble quite rightly referred to as "*sabir atlantique*," which is only partly rendered by the equivalent "Mid-Atlantic jargon." Translations cannot be produced simply by creating structural or metalinguistic calques. All the great literary translations were carried out with the implicit knowledge of the methods described in this chapter, as Gide's preface to his translation of *Hamlet* clearly shows. One cannot help wondering, however, if the reason the Americans refused to take the League of Nations seriously was not because many of their documents were un-modulated and un-adapted renderings of original French texts, just as the "*sabir atlantique*" has its roots in ill-digested translations of Anglo-American originals. Here, we touch upon an extremely serious problem, which, unfortunately, lack of space prevents us from discussing further, that of intellectual, cultural, and linguistic changes, which over time can be effected by important documents, school textbooks, journals, film dialogues, etc. , written by translators who are either unable to or who dare not venture into the world of oblique translations. At a time when excessive centralization and lack of respect for cultural differences are driving inter-national organizations into adopting working languages *sui generis* for writing documents which are then hastily translated by overworked and unappreciated translators, there is good reason to be concerned about the prospect that four fifths of the world will have to live on nothing but translations, their intellect being starved by a diet of linguistic pap.

Application of the seven methods

These seven methods are applied to different degrees at the three planes of expression, i. e. lexis, syntactic structure, and message. For example, borrowing may occur at the lexical level—"*bulldozer*," "*réaliser*," and "*stopover*" are French lexical borrowings from English; borrowing also occurs at the level of the message, e. g. "*O. K.*" and "*Five o'clock*." This range of possibilities is illustrated in Table 1, where each procedure is exemplified for each plane of expression.

Table 1 Summary of the seven translation procedures

(Methods in increasing order of difficulty)

	Lexis	*Structures*	*Message*
1 Borrowing	F: *Bulldozer* E: Fuselage	*science-fiction* à la mode	*Five o'Clock Tea* Bon voyage
2 Calque	F: *économiquement faible* E: Normal School (C. E.)	*Lutetia Palace* Governor General	*Compliments de la Saison* Take it or leave it
3 Literal Translation	F: *encre* ↕ E: ink	*Le livre est sur la table.* ↕ The book is on the table.	*Quella heure est-il?* What time is it?
4 Transposition	F: *Expéditeur* ↕ E: From	*Depuis la revalorisation du bois* As timber becomes more valuable	*Défense de fumer* No smoking
5 Modulation	F: *Peu profond* ↕ E: Shallow	*Donnez un peu de votre sang* Give a pint of your blood	*Complet* No vacancies
6 Equivalence	F: (Mil.) ↕ *la soupe* E, UK: (Mil.) Tea E, US: chow	*Comme un chien dans un jeu de quilles* Like a bull in a china shop	*Château de cartes* Hollow triumph
7 Adaptation	F: *Cyclisme* ↕ E, UK: Cricket US: Baseball	*En un clin d'oeil* Before you could say Jack Robinson.	*Bon appétit!* US. Hi!

It is obvious that several of these methods can be used within the same sentence, and that some translations come under a whole complex of methods so that it is difficult to distinguish them; e. g., the translation of "paper weight" by "presse-papiers" is both a fixed transposition and a fixed modulation. Similarly, the translation of PRIVATE (written on a door) by DÉFENSE D'ENTRER is at the same time a transposition, a modulation, and an equivalence. It is a transposition because the adjective "private" is transformed into a nominal expression; a modulation because a statement is converted into a warning (cf. Wet paint: Prenez garde à la peinture, though "peinture fraîche" seems to be gaining ground in French-speaking countries); and finally, it is an equivalence since it is the situation that has been translated, rather than the actual grammatical structure.

【延伸阅读】

[1] Munday, J. (2001). *Introducing Translation Studies*. London: Routledge.

[2] Vinay, J. P. & Darbelnet, J. (1995). *Comparative Stylistics of French and English: A Methodology for Translation*. Amsterdam and Philadelphia, PA: John Benjamins.

【问题与思考】

1. 为什么说韦内和达贝奈特在论文《翻译的方法》中讨论的内容其实就是翻译转移？
2. 如何利用韦内和达贝奈特的理论模式分析中文译本？
3. 韦内和达贝奈特的理论对翻译研究有何指导意义？其理论自身有何不足？

选文二 Translation Shifts

J. C. Catford

导 言

"转移"这一术语最早见于卡特福德的专著《翻译的语言学理论》，其中的"论翻译转移"一章（即本文）着重讨论了这个问题。"转移"的概念最初由卡特福德界定为"偏离从源语到目标语过程中的形式对应"。他的翻译转移理论建立在弗斯（John Rupert Firth）和韩礼德（M. A. K. Halliday）的语言学模式基础之上，并借用了韩礼德的系统语法及其对语言"层次"的分类来说明翻译转移现象。他认为语言是交际性的，在上下文中发挥功能，而且这些功能的发挥需要通过不同的层次（如语音、词形、语法及词汇）和阶级（句子、分句、片语、词及词素等）。卡特福德区分了两种转移：层次转移（level shifts）和范畴转移（category shifts）。层次转移是指一种语言的语法项在翻译时可以转换成另一种语言的词汇项。范畴转移是指"翻译过程中形成的脱离，是在不同阶级之间的自由的转移"。他的转移理论主要涵盖了语法和词汇两个层次，把范畴转移分为单位转移、结构转移、类别转移和系统内转移四个类型。英语和汉语在语言结构上的巨大差异，使许多译者感到翻译工作就像是"戴着脚镣跳舞"。卡特福德的翻译转移理论能使人较充分地了解两种语言在词汇运用、句法结构和表达方式上的内在规律，有助于译者进行诸如词类转换的工作，有利于研究者深化对译本中语言转换的认识，因而值得借鉴。

By "shifts" we mean departures from formal correspondence in the process of going from the SL (source language) to the TL (target language). Two major types of "shifts" occur: *level shifts* (1. 1) and *category shifts* (1. 2).

1. 1 *Level shifts*. By a shift of level we mean that an SL item at one linguistic level has a TL translation equivalent at a different level.

We have already pointed out that translation between the levels of phonology and graphology—or between either of these levels and the levels of grammar and lexis—is impossible. Translation between these levels is absolutely ruled out by our theory, which posits "relationship to the same substance" as the necessary condition of translation equivalence. We are left, then, with shifts from *grammar* to *lexis* and vice-versa as the only possible level shifts in translation; and such shifts are, of course, quite common.

1. 11　Examples of level shifts are sometimes encountered in the translation of the verbal aspects of Russian and English. Both these languages have an aspectual opposition—of very roughly the same type—seen most clearly in the "past" or *preterite* tense: the opposition between Russian *imperfective* and *perfective* (e. g. *pisal* and *napisal*), and between English *simple* and *continuous* (*wrote* and *was writing*).

There is, however, an important difference between the two aspect systems, namely that the *polarity of marking* is not the same. In Russian, the (contextually) marked term in the system is the *perfective*; this explicitly refers to the *uniqueness* or *completion* of the event. The *imperfective* is unmarked—in other words it is relatively neutral in these respects (the event may or may not actually be unique or completed, etc., but at any rate the imperfective is indifferent to these features—does not explicitly refer to this "perfectiveness"). [1]

In English, the (contextually and morphologically) marked term is the *continuous*; this explicitly refers to the development, the *progress*, of the event. The "simple" form is neutral in this respect (the event may or may not actually be in progress, but the simple form does not explicitly refer to this aspect of the event).

We indicate these differences in the following diagram, in which the marked terms in the Russian and English aspect systems are enclosed in rectangles:

Event		
in progress	repeated	unique, completed
pisal	napisal	
was writing		wrote

1. 12　One result of this difference between Russian and English is that Russian *imperfective* (e. g. pisal) is translatable with almost equal frequency by English *simple* (wrote) or *continuous* (was writing). But the *marked* terms (napisal—was writing) are mutually untranslatable.

A Russian writer can create a certain contrastive effect by using an imperfective and then, so to speak, "capping" this by using the (marked) perfective. In such a case, the same effect of explicit, contrastive, reference to *completion* may have to be translated into English by a change of lexical item. The following example [2] shows this:

---

① My attention was first drawn to this difference between English and Russian by Roman Jakobson in a lecture which he gave in London in 1950.

② From *Herzen*, cited by Unbegaun in *Grammaire Russe*, p. 217.

Čto žedelal Bel'tov v prodolženie etix des'ati let? Vse il počti vse. Čto on sdelal? Ničego ili počti ničego.

Here the imperfective, *delal*, is "capped" by the perfectiv *sdelal*. *Delal* can be translated by either *did* or *was doing*—but, since there is no contextual reason to make explicit reference to the *progress* of the event, the former is the better translation. We can thus say "What *did* Beltov *do* ... " The Russian perfective, with its marked insistence on *completion* can cap this effectively: "What did he *do and complete*?" But the English marked term insists on the *progress* of the event, so cannot be used here. ("What *was* he *doing*" is obviously inappropriate.) In English, in this case, we must use a different lexical verb: a *lexical* item which includes reference to completion in its contextual meaning, e. g. *achieve*. [①] The whole passage can thus be translated:

What did Beltov do during these ten years? Everything, or almost everything.
What did he achieve? Nothing, or almost nothing.

1. 13 Cases of more or less incomplete shift from grammar to lexis are quite frequent in translation between other languages. For example, the English: *This text is intended for* ... may have as its French TL equivalent: *Le présent Manuel s'adresse à* ... Here the SL modifier, *This*—a term in a *grammatical* system of deictics—has as its TL equivalent the modifier *Le présent*, an article+a lexical adjective. Such cases are not rare in French, cf. also *This may reach you before I arrive*=Fr. *Il se peut que ce mot vous parvienne avant mon arrivée*. Once again the grammatical item *this* has a partially lexical translation equivalent *ce mot*. [②]

1. 2 *Category shifts.* We referred to *unbounded* and *rank-bound* translation: The first being approximately "normal" or "free" translation in which SL-TL equivalences are set up at whatever rank is appropriate. Usually, but not always, there is sentence-sentence equivalence, [③] but in the course of a text, equivalences may shift up and down the rank-scale, often being established at ranks lower than the sentence. We use the term "rank-bound" translation only to refer to those special cases where equivalence is *deliberately limited* to ranks below the sentence, thus leading to "bad translation"=i. e. translation in which the TL text is either not a normal TL form at all, or is not relatable to the same situational substance as the SL text.

In normal, unbounded, translation, then, translation equivalences may occur between sentences, clauses, groups, words and (though rarely) morphemes. The following is an example where equivalence can be established to some extent right down to morpheme rank:

---

① Another possibility would be "What *did* he *get done*?", but this would be stylistically less satisfactory.

② Examples from Vinay et Darbelnet, *Stylistique comparée du français et de l'anglais*, p. 99.

③ W. Freeman Twaddell has drawn my attention to the fact that in German-English translation, equivalence may be rather frequently established between the German *sentence* and an English unit greater than the sentence, e. g. *paragraph*.

Fr.	SL text	J'ai laissé mes lunettes sur la table
Eng.	TL text	I've left my glasses on the table

Not infrequently, however, one cannot set up simple equal-rank equivalence between SL and TL texts. An SL *group* may have a TL *clause* as its translation equivalent, and so on.

Changes of rank (unit-shifts) are by no means the only changes of this type which occur in translation; there are also changes of *structure*, changes of *class*, changes of *term* in systems, etc. Some of these—particularly *structure-changes*—are even more frequent than rank-changes.

It is changes of these types which we refer to as *category-shifts*. The concept of "category-shift" is necessary in the discussion of translation; but it is clearly meaningless to talk about category-shift unless we assume some degree of formal correspondence between SL and TL; indeed this is the main justification for the recognition of formal correspondence in our theory. Category-shifts are *departures from formal correspondence* in translation.

We give here a brief discussion and illustration of category-shifts, in the order *structure-shifts*, *class-shifts*, *unit-shifts* (rank-changes), *intra-system shifts*.

1. 21　*Structure-shifts*. These are amongst the most frequent category shifts at all ranks in translation; they occur in *phonological* and *graphological* translation as well as in *total translation*.

1. 211　In *grammar*, structure-shifts can occur at all ranks. The following English-Gaelic instance is an example of *clause-structure shift*.

SL text	*John loves Mary*	$=$SPC
TL text	*Tha gradh aig Iain air Mairi*	$=$PSCA

(A rank-bound word-word back-translation of the Gaelic TL text gives us: *Is love at John on Mary.*)

We can regard this as a structure-shift only on the assumption that there is formal correspondence between English and Gaelic. We must posit that the English elements of clause-structure S, P, C, A have formal correspondents S, P, C, A in Gaelic; this assumption appears reasonable, and so entitles us to say that a Gaelic PSCA structure as translation equivalent of English SPC represents a *structure-shift* insofar as it contains different elements.

But the Gaelic clause not only contains different elements—it also places two of these (S and P) in a different sequence. Now, if the sequence $\overrightarrow{SP}$ were the only possible sequence in English (as $\overrightarrow{PS}$ is in Gaelic) we could ignore the *sequence* and, looking only at the particular elements, S and P, say that the English and Gaelic structures were the same as far as *occurrence* in them of S and P was concerned. But sequence *is* relevant in English and we therefore count it as a feature of the structure, and say that, in this respect, too, structure-shift occurs in the translation.

1. 212　Another pair of examples will make this point clearer by contrasting a case where structure-shift occurs with one where it does not.

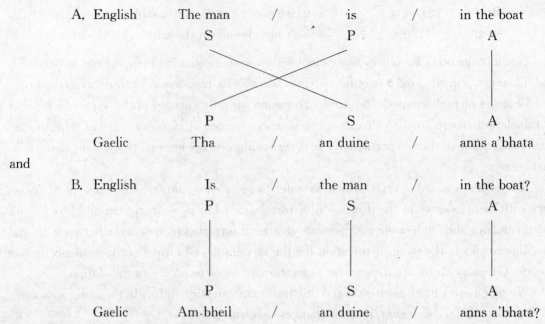

A. English   The man / is / in the boat
        S   P   A

        P   S   A
Gaelic   Tha / an duine / anns a'bhata

and

B. English   Is / the man / in the boat?
        P   S   A

        P   S   A
Gaelic   Am·bheil / an duine / anns a'bhata?

In B, there is complete formal correspondence of clause-structure (no structure-shift); in A, there is a structure-shift at clause-rank.

These two examples, in fact, provide us with a commutation which establishes the following translation equivalences:

A. English ($\overrightarrow{SP}$) Gaelic V^A at P

B. English ($\overleftarrow{SP}$) Gaelic V^I at P

In other words, the Gaelic translation equivalent of the English sequence→of S and P in clause-structure is the occurrence in Gaelic of a verbal group of the class *Affirmative* as exponent of P; the Gaelic translation equivalent of the English sequence ← of S and P in clause-structure is the occurrence in Gaelic of a verbal group of the class *Interrogative* as exponent of P.

These two examples in fact illustrate two different types of translation-shift: In A, there is structure-shift; in B, there is unit-shift, since in this case the Gaelic equivalent of a feature at *clause* rank is the selection of a particular term in a system operating at *group* rank.

1.213 Structure-shifts can be found at other ranks, for example at group rank. In translation between English and French, for instance, there is often a shift from MH (modifier+head) to (M)HQ [(modifier+) head+qualifier], e.g. *A white house* (MH) *Une maison blanche* (MHQ).

1.22 *Class-shifts*. Following Halliday, we define a *class* as "that grouping of members of a given unit which is defined by operation in the structure of the unit next above." Class-shift, then, occurs when the translation equivalent of an SL item is a member of a different class from the original item. Because of the logical dependence of class on structure (of the unit at the rank above) it is clear that structure-shifts usually entail class-shifts, though this may be demonstrable only at a secondary degree of delicacy.

For example, in the example given in 1.213 above (*a white house＝une maison blanche*), the translation equivalent of the English *adjective* "white" is the French adjective "blanche." Insofar as both "white" and "blanche" are exponents of the formally corresponding class *adjective* there is apparently no class-shift. However, at a further degree of delicacy we may recognize two sub-classes of adjectives; those operating at M and those operating at Q in Ngp [Noun group] structure. (Q-adjectives are numerous in French, very rare in English.) Since English "white" is an M-adjective and French "blanche" is a Q-adjective, it is clear that the shift from M to Q entails a class-shift.

In other cases, also exemplified in the translation of Ngps from English to French and vice-versa, class-shifts are more obvious: e. g. Eng. *a medical student＝* Fr. *un étudiant en médecine.* Here the translation equivalent of the adjective *medical*, operating at M, is the adverbial phrase *en médecine*, operating at Q; and the lexical equivalent of the adjective *medical* is the noun *médecine.*

1.23　*Unit-shift.* By unit-shift we mean changes of rank—that is, departures from formal correspondence in which the translation equivalent of a unit at one rank in the SL is a unit at a different rank in the TL.

We have already seen several examples of unit shift in what precedes. A more appropriate term might be "rank-shift," but since this has been assigned a different, technical, meaning within Halliday's theory of grammar we cannot use it here.

1.24　*Intra-system shift.* In a listing of types of translation-shift, such as we gave in 1.2 above, one might expect "system-shift" to occur along with the names of the types of shift affecting the other fundamental categories of grammar-unit, structure and class. There is a good reason for not naming one of our types of shift "system-shift," since this could only mean a departure from formal correspondence in which (a term operating in) one system in the SL has as its translation equivalent (a term operating in) a different—non-corresponding—system in the TL. Clearly, however, such shifts from one *system* to another are always entailed by unit-shift or class-shift. For instance, in example B in 1.212 the Gaelic equivalent of English clause-structure *PS* is shown to be selection of a particular class of Verbal group (V¹). We could say that here there is a system-shift, since PS, a term in a system of clause-classes, is replaced by V¹, a term in a (formally non-corresponding) system of Vgp classes. There is no need to do this, however, since such a shift is already implied by the *unit-shift.*

We use the term *intra-system shift* for those cases where the shift occurs *internally*, within a system; that is, for those cases where SL and TL possess systems which approximately correspond formally as to their constitution, but when translation involves selection of a non-corresponding term in the TL system.

It may, for example, be said that English and French possess formally corresponding systems of *number*. In each language, the system operates in *nominal groups*, and is characterized by concord between the exponents of S and P in clauses and so on. Moreover, in each language, the system is one of two terms—*singular* and *plural*—and these terms may also be regarded as formally corresponding. The exponents of the terms are differently distributed in the two languages—e. g. Eng. *the case/the cases* Fr. *le cas/les cas*—but as terms in a number system *singular* and *plural* correspond formally at least to the extent that in both languages it is the term *plural* which is generally regarded as morphologically marked.

In translation, however, it quite frequently happens that this formal correspondence is departed from, i. e. where the translation equivalent of English *singular* is French *plural* and vice-versa.

e. g.

advice	= des conseils
news	= des nouvelles
lightning	= des éclairs
applause	= des applaudissements
trousers	= le pantalon
the dishes	= la vaisselle
the contents	= le contenu etc. [1]

Again, we might regard English and French as having formally corresponding systems of deictics, particularly *articles*; each may be said to have four articles, *zero*, *definite*, *indefinite* and *partitive*. It is tempting, then, to set up a formal correspondence between the terms of the systems as in this table:

	French	English
Zero	—	—
Definite	le, la, l', les	the
Indefinite	un, une	a, an
Partitive	du, de la, de l', des	some, any

In translation, however, it sometimes happens that the equivalent of an article is not the formally corresponding term in the system:

e. g.

Il est—professeur.	He is *a* teacher.
Il a *la* jambe cassée.	He has *a* broken leg.
L'amour	Love
Du vin	Wine

---

[1] cf. Vinay et Darbelnet, pp. 119 – 123.

In the following table we give the translation-equivalents of French articles found in French texts with English translations. The number of cases in which a French article has an English equivalent at word-rank is 6,958, and the figures given here are percentages; the figure 64.6 against *le* for instance, means that the French definite article (le, la, l', les) has the English definite article as its translation equivalent in 64.6% of its occurrences.[①] By dividing each percentage by 100 we have equivalence-probabilities—thus we may say that, within the limitations stated above, French *le*, etc., will have Eng. *the* as its translation equivalent with probability 65.

French	English				
	zero	the	some	a	(other)
zero	**67.7**	6.1	0.3	11.2	4.6
le	14.2	**64.6**	—	2.4	18.9
du	**51.3**	9.5	11.0	5.9	22.4
un	6.7	5.8	2.2	**70.2**	15.1

It is clear from this table that translation equivalence does not entirely match formal correspondence. The most striking divergence is in the case of the French partitive article, *du*, the most frequent equivalent of which is *zero* and not *some*. This casts doubt on the advisability of setting up *any* formal correspondence between the particular terms of the English and French article-systems.

【延伸阅读】

[1] Catford, J. C. (1965). *A Linguistic Theory of Translation*. London: Oxford University Press.

[2] Delisle, J. (1988). *Translation: An Interpretive Approach*. Ottawa: University of Ottawa Press.

[3] Henry, R. (1984). Points for Inquiry into Total Translation: A review of J. C. Catford's *A Linguistic Theory of Translation*. *Meta*, 29(2), 152-158.

【问题与思考】

1. 为什么卡特福德能提出翻译转移理论？他的理论与当时的语言学理论有何关系？

2. 卡特福德对"翻译转移"(translation shift)概念的界定是否合理？为什么？

3. 卡特福德对翻译转移类型的划分合理性何在？能涵盖所有的翻译转移吗？

4. 能用卡特福德翻译转移理论来分析超出句子层级以上的汉英段落、语篇吗？为什么？

5. 卡特福德的翻译转移理论对翻译研究有何指导意义？

---

① I am indebted to Dr. R. Huddleston for this information.

选文三　Translation as a Decision Process

Jirí Levy

导　言

　　吉里·列维是捷克斯洛伐克学者、当代欧洲翻译研究的突出代表人物之一。其翻译理论代表作有《翻译艺术》(1963)、《文学翻译理论与实践》(1969)和论文《翻译理论对译者有用吗?》(1965)、《翻译即抉择过程》(1967)等。其中《翻译即抉择过程》是其最有影响的作品,列维第一次把维特根斯坦(Ludwig Wittgenstein)的"翻译即语言游戏"的概念用于翻译中,并指出"翻译类似于象棋,接下来的每一步都受到前面所作的抉择的影响"。在《翻译即抉择过程》中,列维借用了博弈论的一些概念到翻译过程中,以此突出翻译文学文本时译者通常作出抉择的特点。他首次指出了翻译中的"逐渐语义转移"(gradual semantic shifting)现象,如原文中单词 A 的一部分意义由译文中的单词 B 表达,但单词 B 的语义范围与 A 不完全一致;单词 A 中的另一部分意义亦可能由译文中的另一个单词 C 表达,同样,C 的语义范围与 A 也不完全一致。在翻译中上述过程反复进行,最终形成了对原文语义的逐渐转移。他还指出,分析特定目标文本中翻译抉择的等级将有助于更清楚地了解"文学作品中各种因素的重要程度"。

From the teleological point of view, translation[①] is a PROCESS OF COMMUNICATION: The objective of translating is to impart the knowledge of the original to the foreign reader. From the point of view of the working situation of the translator at any moment of his work (that is from the pragmatic point of view), translating is a DECISION PROCESS: a series of a certain number of consecutive situations—moves, as in a game—situations imposing on the translator the necessity of choosing among a certain (and very often exactly definable) number of alternatives.

1. A trivial example will show the basic components of a decision problem. Suppose an English translator has to render the title of the play *Der gute Mensch von Sezuan* by Bertold Brecht. He has to decide between two possibilities:

---

① Though by "translation" we mean interlingual translation only, the formal theory expounded here may be applied to all three kinds of translation distinguished by Roman Jakobson: interlingual, intralingual, and intersemiotic (Cp. Roman Jakobson, "On Linguistic Aspects of Translation," in: *Translation*, ed. R. A. Brower, Harvard U. P., 1959, pp. 232-239). Some of the theoretical tenets of this paper have been presented by the present author at the Moscow Symposium on Translation Theory, Feb. 25th—Mar. 2nd 1966.

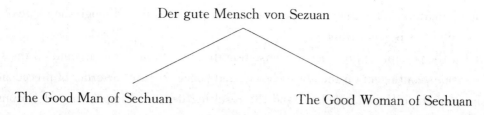

Der gute Mensch von Sezuan

The Good Man of Sechuan   The Good Woman of Sechuan

These are the components of the decision problem:

The SITUATION (i. e., an abstraction of reality, which, in a formalized theory, would be expressed by means of a model): In English, there is no single word equivalent in meaning and stylistic value to the German "Mensch" (since "person" belongs to a different stylistic level); the range of meaning is covered by two words—"man" and "woman."

Instruction I defining the class of possible alternatives: It is necessary to find an English word denoting the class of beings called "homo sapiens."

The PARADIGM, i. e., the class of possible solutions; in our case, the paradigm has two members: man, woman.

Instruction II directing the CHOICE among the alternatives. This instruction is derived from the context; in our case, it is derived from the context of the whole play (macro-context). The two alternatives are not equivalent; the choice is not random but context-bound. Every interpretation has the structure of problem solving: The interpreter has to choose from a class of possible meanings of the word or motif, from different conceptions of a character, of style, or of the author's philosophical views. The choice is more limited ("easier"), if the number of possible alternatives is smaller, or if it is restricted by context.

Once the translator has decided in favour of one of the alternatives, he has predetermined his own choice in a number of subsequent moves: He has predetermined his decisions concerning such technical things as grammatical forms, and such "philosophical" matters as, in our example, the interpretation of the "hero" of the play and the whole manner of its staging. That is to say, he has created the context for a certain number of subsequent decisions, since the process of translating has the form of a GAME WITH COMPLETE INFORMATION—a game in which every succeeding move is influenced by the knowledge of previous decisions and by the situation which resulted from them (e. g., chess, but not card-games). By choosing either the first or the second alternative, the translator has decided to play one of the two possible games; this is a schematic expression of the situation after the first move (alternatives still at the translator's disposal are indicated in complete lines, those eliminated through the first decision in broken lines):

Interpretation Ⅰ   Interpretation Ⅱ

To simplify matters, all decisions are represented in binary form, although the range of theoretical possibilities is 1-n members.

One of the possible approaches to translation theory is to take into account all the subsequent decisions contingent on the given choice, and hence to trace the order of precedence for the solving of the different problems and the resulting degree of importance of various elements in the literary work, when considered from this viewpoint.

The outcome of two different "games" (e. g. of the two series of decisions resulting from the two alternative interpretations of the title of Brecht's play) are two different TRANSLATION VARIANTS; their distance may be measured by the number of differing decisions incorporated in the text.

We are authorized to treat the process of translating in terms of decision problems by the simple fact that this conforms with practical experience. That being so, it should be possible to apply to translation the formal methods of GAME THEORY. No rigorous formalization will be undertaken in the present paper, its aims being restricted to pointing to several noetic premises based on this approach.

The single components of the decision problem will now be discussed in greater detail.

2. Suppose an English translator is to render the German word "Bursche." He may choose from a group of more or less synonymous expressions: boy, fellow, chap, youngster, lad, guy, lark, etc. This is his paradigm, that is, the class of elements complying to a certain instruction, which in this case is a semantic one: "a young man." The paradigm is qualified and circumscribed by this instruction, which we are, therefore, going to denote as a DEFINITIONAL INSTRUCTION. A definitional instruction gives form to the paradigm, and a paradigm is the contents of its definitional instruction. A paradigm is, of course, not a set of completely equivalent elements, but a set ordered according to different criteria (e. g. , stylistic levels, connotative extensions of meaning, etc.); otherwise, no choice would be possible.

Instructions governing the translator's choice from the available alternatives may be termed SELECTIVE INSTRUCTIONS. They may be different in character (in analogy to the definitional instructions): semantic, rhythmical, stylistic, etc.

Selective instructions are in a relation of inclusion to their definitional instructions; there exists between them a relation of a set and its subsets, a system and its subsystems, a class and its members. From the set of alternatives circumscribed by the definitional instruction, a subset is eliminated by the selective instruction, which in turn becomes the definitional instruction of this subset, and so on, till a one-member paradigm is reached:

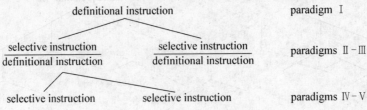

To a system of instructions, a system of paradigms, analogous in pattern, corresponds:

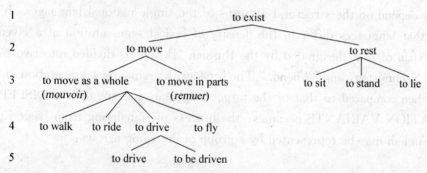

SYSTEM OF INSTRUCTIONS

```
                    "young man"
                  /             \
            "y.m."               "y.m."
          standard             substandard
          /      \             /        \
    "y.m."    "y.m."      "y.m."      "y.m."
   bookish   literary    vulgar     colloquial
```

SYSTEM OF PARADIGMS

```
        boy, fellow, lad, youngster,
            chap, guy, lark
          /                  \
    boy, fellow          chap, guy,
   youngster, lad          lark
     /      \             /      \
 youngster   boy       chap
   lad      fellow    lark, guy
```

The choice of a lexical unit (and of elements of a higher order as well) is governed by such a system of—conscious or unconscious—instructions. They are both objective, dependent on the linguistic material, and subjective, of which the most important are the structure of the translator's memory,[1] his aesthetic standards, etc. The terminal symbol contained in the text could be investigated as to the system of instructions responsible for its occurrence—it is possible to reconstruct the pattern of its genesis, its GENERATIVE PATTERN.

The interpretation by readers of the meanings contained in a text also has the form of a series of moves: The choice of one of the several possible interpretations of a semantic unit (of whatever order) may be represented as a series of decisions from the most general to ever more specific meanings. On this now common semantic theory,[2] the RECOGNOSCATIVE MODEL, i. e., a formalized pattern of interpretation, may be based:

```
1                              to exist
                          /               \
2                  to move                   to rest
                  /       \                 /    |    \
3    to move as a whole  to move in parts  to sit to stand to lie
       (mouvoir)          (remuer)
         /  |  \  \
4   to walk to ride to drive to fly
                    /       \
5              to drive   to be driven
```

The translator, in his system of decisions, may take one step more or less than the author of the original did; cf. the following translation from English into Russian:[3]

His Lordship jumps into a cab, and goes to the railroad.

лорд кью юркнул в извозчичью карегу и приказл везги себя железную дорогу.

① An empirical investigation of the structure of the linguistic memory of translators has been undertaken by the present author (cf. Jiři Levý, *Umění překladu*, Praha, 1963, 91 ff. ; Jiři Levý, "Will Translation Theory be of Use to Translators?", in: *Übersetzen*, Hrsg. R. Italiaander, Frankfurt am Main, 1965, pp. 77 – 82).

② Cp. J. Katz, J. A. Fodor, "The Structure of a Semantic Theory," *Language*, XXXIX (1963), pp. 170 – 210.

③ The example is taken from Я. И. Рецкер "О закономерных соогвегствияхпри переводе на родной яеык," in: *Теория и мемодика уцбцоо иеревода*(Moskva, 1950), pp. 176 – 177.

Here the translator has made two surplus decisions. Since Russian does not dispose of a word of such general meaning as "to go," it was necessary to decide between "to walk, ""to drive," "to ride," and "to fly." The second decision, that between "to drive" and "to be driven," was not necessary.

The translator's decisions may be *necessary* or *unnecessary*, *motivated* or *unmotivated*. The decision is motivated if it is prescribed by context (linguistic or extralinguistic). In our case, both decisions have been motivated by the word "cab; "if there should have been the word "car" in the text, instead of "cab," the second decision would have been unmotivated. Hence four cases are possible:

(1) A necessary and motivated surplus decision.

(2) A necessary and unmotivated surplus decision; here the danger of a misinterpretation is greatest and is reduced only by a search for motivation in ever broader contexts (the whole book, the whole work of the author, the literary conventions of the time etc.).

(3) An unnecessary and motivated surplus decision.

(4) An unnecessary and unmotivated surplus decision; here we are already in the realm of pure arbitrariness and translators' licence.

3. The patterns of instructions and of the corresponding paradigms are dependent on the texture of the MATERIAL in which they are effectuated; in the case of a choice of linguistic means they depend on the structural patterns of the single national languages. It is a notorious fact that languages differ in the density of lexical segmentation of a given semantic field: The span of time designated by the Russian "Behep" is divided into two segments in German—"Nachmittag" and "Abend. " The broader the semantic segmentation in the source language when compared to that of the target language, the greater the DISPERSION OF TRANSLATION VARIANTS becomes; the process of translating from Basic English into Standard English may be represented by a group of diverging arrows:

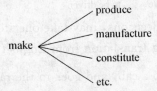

On the contrary, the finer the lexical segmentation of the source language in comparison to that of the target language, the more limited is the dispersion of translation variants; translating from Standard English into Basic English may be represented by converging arrows:

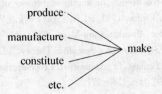

Diverging or *converging* tendencies in choosing the single lexical units (and of course the means of a higher order as well) are operative throughout the process of translating, and they are responsible for the ultimate relation between the source and the target texts. Tendencies operative in the course of decision processes may be observed with great clarity, if the same text passes several times through the process of translation from language A into language B, and back again into A. Of this type were the experiments undertaken by B. van der Pool;[1] A passage taken from an English philosophical treatise was translated into French, back into English, and so on, so that the text finally went through the following process, A—F—A—F—A. Let us interpret the material recorded in Van der Pool's report.

In some cases, even within the limited number of four decisions, 23 alternatives recurred, which may be the symptom of a paradigm limited to a small number of alternatives (limited either by the lexical possibilities of the language or by the verbal ingenuity of the translator):

A　　　　F　　　　A　　　　F　　　　A
tentative—tentative—trials—essais—tentative

The decision process had the following outlines in this case:

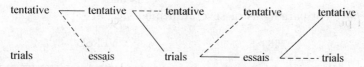

There were cases of converging tendencies whenever the word was being translated from English into French, and of diverging tendencies when the translation was the reverse; this may be interpreted as a symptom of the fact that the paradigm in French was more limited (or even consisted of one member only) than its English counterpart:

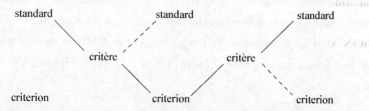

In other cases, where both the source and the target paradigms were rich in expressions of not very clearly defined outlines, translators tended to choose new solutions in every version:

day light—lumière franche—open light—flamme libre—unconfined flame

A gradual semantic shifting takes place in these very frequent cases, due to the fact that one segment of the extension of meaning of word A is expressed by word B of the target language, which again has a semantic range which is not quite identical with that of word A;

---

① B. van der Pool, "An Iterative Translation Test," in: *Information Theory—Third London Symposium* (London, 1956), p. 397ff.

one segment of it is expressed by word C with a different range of meaning again. This is a general model of repeated interpretation and expression (e. g. , a perusal of the text, its translation, the staging of this translation, and its interpretation by the theatre-goer). This is a functional model of pragmatic communication.

Generally speaking, the type of semantic segmentation is dependent not only on the linguistic code, but on the characteristic code of the particular type of literature as well. The word "gooseberry" must be translated by exact equivalents (Stachelbeere, groseille, крыжовник) in prose; in verse also the foreign expressions for "currant," "raspberry," etc. , may be considered to be equivalent, and only pedants could object to Taufer's using "currants" instead of "gooseberries" in his Czech translation of the following lines by S. Schipachev：

> Проходит мимо яблонь,
>
> Смородины густой.

In other words, in prose we are dealing with two groups of paradigms of one member each, standing in a relation of a strict one-to-one correspondence, whereas in verse they coalesce into two equivalent paradigms of several members each：

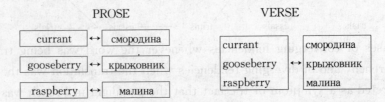

On the syntagmatic level, e. g. , "He departed," "And then off he went," "Lo, see him going off," etc. , may be considered to be equivalent; a line of verse of 10 syllables may therefore be translated in more ways than a prose segment of the same extent. Cf. the seven versions of one line from Shakespeare's *Julius Caesar* found in the MSS of A. W. von Schlegel (and the eighth one by L. Tieck)：[①]

(1) Dein Leben hat von Ehrgefühl gezeugt

(2) Dein Leben zeugte stets von Ehrgefühl

(3) Dein Leben hat gezeigt, du hätst auf Ehre

(4) Dein Leben zeugt von einem Funken Ehre

(5) Ein Sinn für Ehre spricht aus deinem Leben

(6) Du hegtest einen Funken Ehre stets

(7) Du hegtest immer einen Funken Ehre

(8) In deinem Leben war ein Funken Ehre

---

① For the different versions of the line by A. W. von Schlegel see M. Bernays, *Die Entstehungs-geschichte des Schlegelschen Shakespeare* (Leipzig, 1872), p. 239.

Diverging tendencies are undoubtedly at work in translations from less developed languages into more developed ones: It would be interesting to note how widely different are the parallel English (or German, or French, etc.) versions of the poetry of primitive nations. On the contrary, converging tendencies could undoubtedly be traced, e. g., in the translations of the Bible into the primitive languages (this could be quantitatively measured for example by the more limited extent of vocabulary).

Literary texts differing in the density of their semantic segmentation offer analogous phenomena. In most European literatures, there are several parallel translations of Shakespeare differing in their conception, and they are felt to be necessary. With Molière, the dispersion of interpretations is by far not so great. One of the reasons of this fact is undoubtedly the broader segmentation characteristic of the semantic pattern of Shakespeare's work (his characters are complex and incorporate a wide range of possible interpretations), and the minute segmentation of Molière's semantic pattern into elements mostly of one clear meaning: Harpagon incorporates one segment only of the broader semantic range of Shylock. [1]

When considering semantic constructs of a certain complexity, e. g., characters in a play, we have to deal with combinations of a number of instructions, that is to say, we are entering upon the discussion of the SYNTAX OF INSTRUCTIONS.

The rhyming pun from the poem "Das aesthetische Wiesel" by Christian Morgenstern may serve as a very simple example of a combination of instructions (syntagm of instructions):

> Ein Wiesel
> sass auf einem Kiesel
> inmitten Bachgeriesel.

The American translator Max Knight has given five translations of these lines, exposing in this way the paradigm of possible solutions (or more strictly speaking, several members of it):

(1) A weasel
perched on an easel
within a patch of teasel,

(2) A ferret
nibbling a carrot
in a garret,

(3) A mink
sipping a drink
in a kitchen sink,

(4) A hyena
playing a concertina
in an arena,

(5) A lizzard
shaking its gizzard
in a blizzard.

---

① Cp. J. Milnor, "Games Against Nature," in: *Game Theory and Relate Approaches to Social Behavior*, ed. M. Shubik (New York, 1964), 120 ff. On game theory cp. f. ex. D. Blackwell, M. A. Girshick, *Theory of Games and Statistical Decisions* (New York, 1954); Samuel Karlin, *Mathematical Methods and Theory in Games*, *Programming*, *and Economics*, Ⅲ (Reading, Mass., 1959).

The definitional instruction of the paradigm of solutions is a complex one, a combination of the following elementary instructions: (i) the name of an animal; (ii) the object of its activity, rhyming with (i); (iii) the place of this activity, rhyming with (i) and (ii). Each of the three components of the pun has a double semantic function: (1) the denotative "proper" meaning, (2) the function in the pattern of the pun; with each component, function (2) is the definitional instruction of a paradigm, the single elements of which are—among others— the different "proper meanings" used by Knight in his five translations. Every one of the five translations preserves the functions of the three lines in the pun as a whole (definitional instructions), but not the actual meanings of the three motifs (selective instructions). The hierarchy of instructions and of their combinations may be traced on several levels:

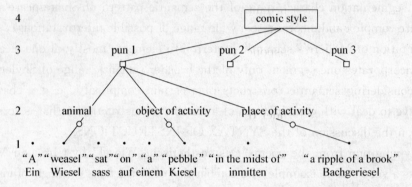

Translation being at the same time an interpretation and a creation, the decision processes operative in it are of two types:

(1) the choice from the elements of the semantic paradigm of the word (or of a more complex semantic construct) in the source text, i. e. , between the possible interpretations of the "meaning" of the text;

(2) the choice from the paradigm of words (verbal constructs) of the target language, which more or less corresponds to the "meaning" chosen under (1), i. e. , "expression of the meaning. "

The decision processes in translation have the structure of a semiotic system, having its semantic aspect (i. e. , a repertory of units defined through their relation to their denotata), and its syntax (i. e. , rules for combining these units—whether by units we mean paradigms or instructions). As all semiotic processes, translation has its PRAGMATIC DIMENSION as well. It will be the aim of the last section of our paper to investigate this aspect of translation.

4. Translation theory tends to be normative, to instruct translators on the OPTIMAL solution; actual translation work, however, is pragmatic; the translator resolves for that one of the possible solutions which promises a maximum of effect with a minimum of effort. That is to say, he intuitively resolves for the so-called MINIMAX STRATEGY.

There can, for example, hardly be any doubt that a verse translation which would preserve in rhymes the vowels of the original, would be—*ceteris paribus*—preferable, since the expressive values of vowels may play a minor part in the whole emotional pattern of the poem. The price a translator would pay for complicating his task in this way would, however, be so great, that modern translators prefer to renounce to it. In a less conspicuous way, the same policy is pursued by translators of prose: They are content to find for their sentence a form which, more or less, expresses all the necessary meanings and stylistic values, though it is probable that, after hours of experimenting and rewriting, a better solution might be found.

Translators, as a rule, adopt a pessimistic strategy, they are anxious to accept those solutions only whose "value"—even in case of the most unfavourable reactions of their readers—does not fall under a certain minimum limit admissible by their linguistic or aesthetic standards. Since the pragmatic aspect of translation work is based on a minimax strategy, it should be possible to exploit corresponding mathematical methods to compute the preferences of the translators (that is to say, the single agents of what is usually called the translators' method). A simple example will show what is meant.

Suppose a translator is to render the English construction "not a little embarrassed" into French. For the sake of simplicity, let him have only two possibilities:

    a. *pas peu embarrassé*,
    b. *très embarrassé*.

These are the outcomes of decision (a):

s—the stylistic trait (understatement) is preserved,

r—the danger is imminent that this construction will be felt by the readers to be an "anglicism."

These are the outcomes of decision (b):

$\bar{s}$—the stylistic trait is not preserved,

$\bar{r}$—there is no danger of the construction being felt to be an anglicism.

The possibilities contained in premise r come into existence according to what are the linguistic standards of the reading public: A certain percentage of purists among them will feel that purity of language has been trespassed upon $/\bar{1}/$, the rest of the readers are going to feel that it is in good French $/1/$. The possible subjective outcomes of both decisions with a greater group of readers may be expressed in the following pay-off matrix:

	NON-PURISTS	PURISTS
(a) *pas peu embarrassé*	v_1: style preserved＋purity of/pres.	v_2: style preserved＋purity of/not pres.
(b) *très embarrassé*	v_3: style not preserved＋purity of/pres.	v_3: style not preserved＋purity of/pres.

The three possible outcomes are:

$$v_1 = s+1 \text{ (style preserved+purity of language preserved)},$$

$$v_2 = s+\overline{1} \text{ (style preserved+purity of language not preserved)},$$

$$v_3 = \overline{s}+1 \text{ (style not preserved+purity of language preserved)}.$$

Among the supposed readers of the translated text, the two categories—purists and non-purists—are represented in a certain proportion, e. g. , 25% non-purists and 75% purists. Then the quantitative interpretation of the matrix is as follows:

	25%	75%
a.	$s+1$	$s+1$
b.	$\overline{s}+1$	$\overline{s}+1$

After decision (b), the value s does not occur at all (0%), neither does the negative value 1. This decision is evidence that the translator valued the preservation of the purity of language higher than the preservation of style ($1 > s$).

After decision (a), value s occurs with 100% of readers, 1 with 25%, and $\overline{1}$ with 75%. For the sake of preservation of value s with 100% of readers, the translator is willing to risk the loss of 1 with 75%, or to agree with an occurrence of 1 in 25% only. The relative utility of the two values for him is:

$$s : 1 \leqslant 1 : 4$$

The degree of importance of a stylistic means for the translator is a relative value measurable in relation to other values only, in the first place to the value ascribed to linguistic purity. To ascertain the relative values ascribed to the two qualities by the translator it would be necessary to ask him the following question (or to find out indirectly, without asking him): What percentage of results $\overline{1}$ (the feeling of the readers that linguistic standards have been violated) are you willing to risk to preserve the stylistic means M? Without making any numerical computations, translators in fact intuitively make guesses concerning the possibilities of the different evaluations by readers.

An investigation into the following problems for example would benefit from the application of minimax procedures (especially if pursued in a more rigorous way than could have been done here):

(1) What degree of utility is ascribed to various stylistic devices and to their preservation in different types of literature (e. g. , prose, poetry, drama, folklore, juvenile literature, etc.)?

(2) What is the relative importance of linguistic standards and of style in different types of literature?

(3) What must have been the assumed quantitative composition of the

audiences to whom translators of different times and of different types of texts addressed their translations? With contemporary translators, the assumptions manifested by their texts could be confronted with results of an empirical analysis of the actual predilections of the audience.

The case we used as our example was a very simple one, and its explicative force was restricted, since we are ignorant of the agents responsible for the outcomes "understatement" or "anglicism" with French readers. The outcomes of decisions may be due to very simple factors, or of one agent only: It will depend, more or less exclusively, on his knowledge or ignorance of the formal conventions of Greek metrics whether, for example, a modern reader will recognize Sapphic metre, or take it for free verse. The situation of a translator deciding whether to preserve Sapphic metre in his translation or choose another can be represented through a simple pay-off matrix:

	"GRECIANS"	"NON-GRECIANS"
SAPPHIC METRE:	will understand the metre	will not understand the metre
OTHER METRE:	will miss the metre	will not miss the metre

Strictly speaking, "will miss the metre" means "will miss the Sapphic metre, if he knows in what measure that particular poem was written." With two types of readers, and two types of decisions, four different aesthetic states are possible, the probability of each of them being the product of the relative frequency of the two solutions in translations of a given time, and of the relative frequency of the two categories of readers. The two pairs of outcomes (will miss the metre—will not miss the metre) are not—as has been evident—exactly antithetical; the statements of the outcomes are simplified.

The suggestions presented here aim at constructing a generative model of translation by means of the methods used in defining decision problems. The establishment of such a model would of course require a much fuller and more rigorous treatment. Once the general formal pattern is established, however, the empirical investigations of the different aspects of translation work could be viewed from a broader and more common perspective.

【延伸阅读】

[1] Miko, F. (1970). La théorie de l'expression et la traduction. In Holmes (ed.), *The Nature of Translation: Essays on the Theory and Practice of Literary Translation* (pp. 61 - 77). The Hague and Paris: Mouton.

[2] Popovié, A. (1970). The Concept "Shift of Expression" in Translation Analysis. In Holmes (ed.), *The Nature of Translation: Essays on the Theory and Practice of Literary Translation*. The Hague and Paris: Mouton.

[3] Toury, G. (1995). *Descriptive Translation Studies and Beyond*. Amsterdam: John

Benjamins.

[4] van Leuven-Zwart, K. M. (1990). Translation and Original：Similarities and Dissimilarities, Ⅱ. *Target*, (2), 69 - 95.

[5] 李德超. 从维内、达贝尔内到图里：翻译转移研究综述. 四川外语学院学报,2005(1)：94 - 99.

【问题与思考】

1. 列维的研究是否属于纯语言视角的翻译研究？为什么？
2. 本论文对翻译转移研究的主要贡献是什么？
3. 从文中的哪些地方可以看出博弈论对作者的影响？简述理由。
4. 列维的理论对翻译研究有何指导意义？为什么？

选文四　鲁文-兹瓦特论翻译转移的比较

李德超

导　言

本文发表于《外国语言文学》2004 年第 4 期。

在翻译转移的种种研究模式中,普遍认为鲁文-兹瓦特的模式是最广泛和最详尽的分析模式。本文讨论了在鲁文-兹瓦特模式中起基础作用的比较模式部分,详细介绍了比较模式对翻译转移的分类及对语义、句法、语用和文体层面的翻译转移的比较和描述。文章认为,鲁文-兹瓦特的比较模式强调对译文和原文进行客观、全面和细致的比较与描写,这恰恰是习惯用朦胧式、直觉式和印象式标准来审视翻译作品的中国传统翻译理论所欠缺的,因而值得我们借鉴。

1　引言

在西方翻译研究传统里,如何准确而全面地描写译文与原文之间的关系一直都是翻译学者孜孜不倦追求的目标。对"翻译转移"(translation shift)的研究也是一种描写译文与原文之间关系的方法,它通过研究"译自源语文本的目标文本中出现的细微的语言变化"(Munday,2001:55)来描述两种文本之间可能出现的种种语言关系,继而在归纳这些关系的基础上来实现对翻译现象的描写。

对"翻译转移"的研究肇始于 20 世纪 50 年代,以韦内和达贝奈特(Vinay & Darbelnet,1958)为代表。随后,雅各布森(Roman Jakobson)在《论翻译的语言学方面》(On Linguistic

Aspect of Translation，1959)一文中亦提到，当遇到无法直接表达的原文的内容时，可采纳语义转移(semantic shift)这种方式来迂回表达(Jakobson，1989:56)，但他主要论述的是翻译的可译性问题，翻译转移并非讨论的重点。以上研究在内容上已属"翻译转移"的范围，但"翻译转移"这个概念却直至 1965 年才由卡特福德(Catford)在《翻译的语言学理论》一书中正式提出。卡特福德运用弗斯(Firth)和韩礼德(Halliday)的语言学理论模式，把翻译转移区分为两种：层次转移(shift of level)和范畴转移(shift of category)。20 世纪 60 年代至 70 年代之间，捷克学者利维(Levy，1967)、米科(Miko，1970)和波波维奇(Popovic，1970)亦对"翻译转移"的类型作出研究，除此之外，他们还述及了"翻译转移"对译文风格的影响。这些早期的对"翻译转移"的研究，从总体上而言，均可视为是一种语言学导向的、基于原文与译文对照的描写翻译的模式。

20 世纪 80 年代以来，对"翻译转移"的研究起了些变化，由原来单一的语言对比转向讨论"翻译转移"对宏观问题的影响，这些问题包括：译者在翻译过程中所受到的限制(constraints)和潜在的翻译规范(norms)(Toury，1980，1995)，译文中的连贯和衔接的实现(Blum-Kulka，1986)以及译文微观结构的转移对其宏观结构的影响和潜在的翻译法则(Leuven-Zwart，1989，1990)等。与前期相比，后期的研究无论在深度还是广度上都更进了一步。

在后期对"翻译转移"的种种研究模式中，普遍认为鲁文-兹瓦特(Leuven-Zwart，1989，1990)的研究模式是最广泛和最详尽的分析模式(Hermans，1999:58；Munday，2001:63)，尤其值得我们注意。鲁文-兹瓦特的模式由比较模式(comparative)和描写模式(descriptive)这两部分组成。比较模式摒弃了早期对"翻译转移"采取的原文与译文直接对比的方法，改为用译素(transeme)与第三比较体(tertium compareationis)——一种独立于原文与译文之外，但具有原文和译文共同意义的理论假设物——进行比较，并在比较的基础上，总结出译文在文本微观结构上发生的种种"翻译转移"种类。而描写模式则根据"翻译转移"在译文中出现的种类和频率来揭示微观层面上的转移对译文宏观结构的影响，并从中总结出具有普遍意义的翻译法则。换句话说，在这两个模式里，比较模式是基础，描写模式相当于起到对比较模式的阐释作用。

尽管鲁文-兹瓦特对"翻译转移"的研究模式在西方译学界具有较大的影响，但据笔者所掌握的资料来看，国内目前尚无对这一模式的详细介绍。囿于篇幅，本文这里亦只能讨论鲁文-兹瓦特研究模式的第一部分——比较模式。比较模式强调对译文和原文进行客观、全面和细致的比较与描写，这恰恰是习惯用朦胧式、直觉式和印象式标准来审视翻译作品的中国传统翻译理论所欠缺的。因此，对比较模式的了解亦有助于我们系统地描述翻译现象，有助于减少翻译研究过程中的主观因素，对现阶段进行的翻译理论的建构具有借鉴和启示意义。

2　译素、元译素及其关系

与早期"翻译转移"的研究模式不同，鲁文-兹瓦特的研究模式专门用于比较和描写"对叙事性文本的整体翻译中出现的转移"(1989:152)。更详细地说，他的研究对象为翻译的小说式叙事性文本(fictional narrative text)。所谓整体性翻译，是指与原文相比较，翻译的文本没有在句子层面以上做出增删(1989:154)，也就是增删的范围不超过一个句子，这与我们通常所说的全译本类似。换句话说，节译、译述或是有删节的翻译作品均不在鲁文-兹瓦特的研究范围之内。比较模式的目的就在于找出发生在文本微观结构(即小于或等于句子)层面上的语义、文体和语用上的转移。

比较之前,首先要确定的是比较的单位。早期对"翻译转移"的研究多以词、短语或句子作为译文与原文的比较单位,但鲁文-兹瓦特认为,作为比较的单位,句子显得太长,而单词和短语又显得太短,均不利于比较,因而需重新定出一个新的可供比较的单位,这个新的单位就是"译素"(transeme)。

按鲁文-兹瓦特的定义,译素是"一个可理解的语篇单位"(1999:155),它可分为事件状态译素(state of affairs transeme)和附属译素(satellite transeme)。事件状态译素由一实义动词或系词(copula)充当的谓词(predicate)和论元(argument)组成,用符号/……/表示;附属译素没有谓词,它可以看做是"事件状态译素的状语的确定或扩充",用符号(……)表示(1999:156)。如例(1)里原文与译文都有两个事件状态译素和一个附属译素,例(2)里原文与译文都各有一个事件状态译素和一个附属译素。

例(1) /There's not enough draft/(up the chimney;)/that's why the fire doesn't burn well. /

(烟囱上)/没有足够的风;//这就是火总烧不旺的原因。/

例(2) (Outside the door,)/a throng of bearded men intermixed with women … /

(在门口,)/一群留胡子的男人和女人混在一起……/

确定比较的单位后,下一步就是确定原文译素与译文译素的共通点(common denominator),也就是这两者之间的共有意义(shared meaning),鲁文-兹瓦特把它称为"元译素"(architranseme),或简称为 ATR。ATR 是独立于原文与译文之外的一种理论上的假设,它相当于起到原文译素与译文译素比较的基点的作用。这与图里早期描述翻译的 AT 模式里所提出的"第三比较体"的作用基本一致(Toury, 1980)。ATR 一般由实词或是共有意义的释义表达。虚词(如介词、连词、代词)不出现在 ATR 之中。鲁文-兹瓦特认为,在实际操作中,确立 ATR 时往往需要借助字典中的解释(1989:157)。见例(3)对 ATR 的确立。

例(3) /She sat up 1 quickly/(in her steamer 2 chair.)

/她(从折叠躺椅 2 上)坐起 1 来。/

ATR1: to rise to a sitting position

ATR2: a portable folding chair

确立原文译素与译文译素之间的 ATR 后,接着就是把这些译素分别与 ATR 对比,以确立它们与 ATR 之间的关系。若译素与 ATR 意义完全吻合,那它们之间的关系就是同义(synonymic)关系。在例(3)中,译文译素(target text transeme,缩写为 ttt)1 与 ATR1 的关系即为同义关系,因为"坐起来"与 to rise to a sitting position 意义一致。

但同样在例(3)中,原文译素(source text transeme,缩写为 stt)1 与 ATR1 却非同义关系,因为 stt1 除具有 ATR1 的意义之外,还强调了动作之快(quickly),而这层意义并没有在 ATR1 中表达出来。换句话说,相对于 stt1,ATR1 的意义更为泛化,这也就是说,stt1 的意义更为具体。这种译素的部分意义与 ATR 重合(或称连接"conjunction"),部分意义与 ATR 不同(或称分离"disjunction")的关系称之为下义(hyponymic)关系。若要判断一个译素是否与 ATR 呈下义关系可借用以下这个公式:"X 是 Y 的一种形式/类别/方式"(X is a form/class/mode of Y),这里 X 指代译素,Y 指代 ATR。只要 X 是 Y 上述三种模式中的一种,那么我们就可以认为 X 与 Y 之间存在着下义关系。

　　概括而言,一个译素(stt 或 ttt)与 ATR 的关系有两种:同义关系或下义关系。确定出单个译素与 ATR 的关系只是比较的基础,我们真正要探讨的是互相对应的 stt 和 ttt 与 ATR 的基本关系,因为只有从它们与 ATR 的关系中我们才能确定 stt 和 ttt 的关系,进而确定翻译中到底发生了哪些类型的转移。但这时已并非难事,因为我们可以根据上述一个译素与 ATR 的两种关系来推导出 stt 或 ttt 与 ATR 可能存在的各种关系。具体而言,这些关系有四种(参见 Leuven-Zwart,1989:159):

　　(1) 当两种译素都与 ATR 保持同义关系,即 stt,ttt 和 ATR 具有"连接"意义时,stt 和 ttt 之间的关系亦为同义关系,这也就意味着在这两种译素之间无翻译转移发生;

　　(2) 当一种译素与 ATR 为同义关系,另一种译素与 ATR 为下义关系时,stt 和 ttt 之间的关系为下义关系,这也就意味着这两种译素之间有翻译转移发生,这种类型的翻译转移称为"调整"(modulation);

　　(3) 当 stt 和 ttt 均与 ATR 保持下义关系时,这两种译素之间的关系为对比(contrast)关系,这时它们之间有翻译转移发生,这种类型的翻译转移称为"修改"(modification);

　　(4) 当 stt 和 ttt 之间不能建立 ATR,即这两种译素之间不存在任何关系时,这时它们之间有翻译转移发生,这种类型的翻译转移称为"转变"(mutation)。

　　在这四种 stt 和 ttt 之间的关系中,显而易见,只有第二、第三和第四种才发生了翻译转移,因而也只有它们才是翻译转移研究的对象。早期翻译转移的研究对象并无严格的区分,通常的观点是只要涉及语言层面上的变异都属于翻译转移研究的范围(如 Vinay & Darbelnet,1958;Catford,1965),这未免显得过于宽泛。鲁文-兹瓦特在研究翻译转移之前先确定了具体的研究范围和研究类型,这就避免了以往翻译转移研究中研究范围不清、研究定义模糊的通病,因而也就更具有科学性和可操作性。

　　发生在微观结构层面的翻译转移有的体现为语义上的转移(semantic shift),有的体现为文体上的转移(stylistic shift),有的体现为语用上的转移(pragmatic shift),有的则同时体现了以上两种甚至三种的转移类型。这也就是说,在发生调整、修改和转变这三种翻译转移类型时可以根据转移的性质(即发生在语义、文体抑或语用层面上)而作出更详尽的划分。而这些对各种转移的详尽的在性质上的划分也就构成了鲁文-兹瓦特比较模式的主要内容。

3　翻译转移类型:调整

　　在"调整"类型的翻译转移中,一种译素与 ATR 为同义关系,另一种译素与 ATR 为下义关系。由于"调整"可以发生在语义层面或是文体层面,因此它又可以细分为语义上的调整和文体上的调整。

3.1　语义调整(semantic modulation)

　　在语义调整中,由于与 ATR 保持下义关系的译素可以是 stt 或 ttt,因此,这种翻译转移类型又可以再细分为两种:如果 stt 与 ATR 呈下义关系,那么这种翻译转移就称为"语义调整/概括化"(modulation/generalization),这是因为原文相对具体、详尽的译素在译文中被相对综合、概括的译素所代替;如果 ttt 与 ATR 呈下义关系,这种翻译转移就称为"语义调整/明确化"(modulation/specification)，这是因为原文的译素被译文的译素表达得更为详尽、更为准确。如在例(3)中，stt2 与 ATR2 即为下义关系，这是因为 stt2 "steamer chair"除表达 ATR2 的 a portable folding chair 这层意义外，它还强调 the chair is of light weight，而 ttt2 "折叠躺椅"与 ATR2 是同义关系，因此，我们可以得出结论：stt2 与 ttt2 之间有翻译转移发生，且这种翻译转移关系属于"语义调整/概括化"。这也就是说，原文相对具体的译素 steamer chair 被转换为译文中相对概括的译素。通过这样的比较，stt 与 ttt 之间的细微翻译转移也就得到了揭示。

3.2 文体调整(stylistic modulation)

"调整"类型的翻译转移亦可以发生在文体层面上，这就是文体调整的由来。但究竟什么才是文体，文体包括哪些成分，学界至今仍众说纷纭。最早对翻译中的文体转换作出详细研究的是捷克语言学家米科(Miko，1970)。他提出对翻译中文体转移的研究可以从"效力性"(operativity)、象似性(iconicity)、主观性(subjectivity)、虚饰(affectation)、突出(prominence)和对比(contrast)这几种范畴着手(Munday，2001：62 - 63)，但他更为关心的是如何在译文中达到对风格的翻译问题。

鲁文-兹瓦特对翻译中文体调整的考察主要采取了莱昂斯(Lyons，1977)对文体所包含的"社会意义"(social meaning)和"表情意义"(expressive meaning)的划分，前者指的是那种"因言者特点的不同而产生的不同的意义"，后者则为"用于建立和维持社会关系的意义"(Leuven-Zwart，1989：162)。具体而言，文体的社会意义包括以下五种因素(Leuven-Zwart，1989：163)：

(1) 语域因素(register element)，如正式与非正式，疏远与亲近，礼貌与粗鲁等语言风格；

(2) 专业因素(professional element)，从中可得知所从事行业的信息；

(3) 时间因素(time element)，即所用语言的时代感，如是古语还是新词；

(4) 文本特定因素(text-specific element)，即具体的文本类型，如小说、书信、童话等；

(5) 文化特定因素(culture-specific element)，即提供有关原文的文化信息还是提供译文的文化信息，也就是通常所说的归化与异化问题。

文体的表情意义则有以下两种因素：

(1) 组合因素(syntagmatic element)，如头韵、押韵、类韵、首语重复、排比等修辞手法；

(2) 聚合因素(paradigmatic element)，如暗喻、转喻、提喻、反说、夸张等修辞手法。鲁文-兹瓦特认为，通过对文体的社会意义或表情意义所包含的这些因素的考察就能揭示翻译转移中的文体调整。例(4)即为一种对翻译中发生在文体的社会意义层面的转移的分析：

例(4) /the chap was married too/

/这位男人也结婚了/

ATR：young man＋to be married

ADstt：stylistic form/variant of "man"

ADttt：0

Stylistic modulation/generalization，register element

在这里，AD 为 Aspect of Disjunction 的缩写，其意义与 shift 类似。ADstt 代表发生在原文译素上的转移，ADttt 为发生在译文译素上的转移。在例(4)中，stt 与 ATR 呈下义关系，因为 chap 除表达 young man 这层语义意义外,还具有一层文体意义,即它是一种口语化的表达法(colloquial usage),但这层意义在 ATR 中却没有表达出来,这就导致了 ADstt 的产生。而 ttt 与 ATR 在这里为同义关系,因而无转移发生,所以 ADttt 的值为 0。这也就是说,在例(4)中 stt 与 ttt 之间有翻译转移发生,这种翻译转移关系发生在文体层面,具体而言是属于由语域因素引起的"文体调整/概括化"。

4　翻译转移类型:修改(modification)

在"修改"类型的翻译转移中,stt 和 ttt 均与 ATR 保持下义关系。与"调整"类型的翻译转移相比,"修改"不仅可以发生在语义和文体层面上,还可以发生在句法层面上。因此,我们可以进一步区分出语义修改、文体修改和句法修改这三种翻译转移形式。

4.1　语义修改(semantic modification)

在"语义修改"这种类型的翻译转移里,无论是 stt 还是 ttt 都与 ATR 在语义上表现出差异,如例(5):

例(5)/this marvel 1 happened(on the 2 lane)/

/这件不可思议的事 1 发生(在 2 小巷里)/

ATR2:narrow road

ADstt2:f/c/m of "narrow road"—in the country, bordered by hedges

ADttt2:f/c/m of "narrow road"—in town;a narrow street

Semantic modification

在例(5)中,stt2 和 ttt2 均为 ATR 的下义,因为无论是原文 lane 还是译文"小巷"都比 ATR "narrow road"的范围小,因此,这就在语义层面上造成了修改。

4.2　文体修改(stylistic modification)

在这种类型的翻译转移中,无论是 stt 还是 ttt 在文体上均与 ATR 不一致。这种不同亦体现在 3.2 中所提及的文体的"社会意义"和"表情意义"所包含的七种因素上。判断一种翻译转移是否属于"文体修改"类型的另一个条件就是 stt 和 ttt 是否都是在同一种文体因素上与 ATR 发生"分离"的。例如,stt 是在时间因素上与 ATR 不同,那么 ttt 亦需在时间因素上与 ATR 不一致,这样才能产生文体修改。见例(6)。

例(6) /Thus the bitterness of a parting was juggled away. /

/这样,离愁别恨变得荡然无存。/

ATR:harsh feeling+separating+disappear

ADstt:stylistic f/v of "disappear"—familiar

ADttt:stylistic f/v of "disappear"—formal

Stylistic modification, register element

在例(6)里,与 ATR 中的 disappear 一词相比,stt 和 ttt 都与之在文体上呈现出一些差异。stt 所用的 juggle away 这个短语比较口语化,属于随意的、非正式的一种表达方式,但 ttt 所用的"荡然无存"却是比较正式的用词,因此 stt 和 ttt 都在语域这个因素上呈现出对 ATR

的背离,也就造成了文体修改这种翻译转移关系。

4.3　句法修改(syntactic modification)

"修改"这种翻译转移除可能发生在语义和文体层面上外,亦可能发生在句法层面。在句法修改里,stt 和 ttt 都在句法层面上与 ATR 发生背离,从而导致翻译转移。但在很多情况下,句法修改相当于一种手段,它最终又会导致译素在语义、文体和语用层面发生转移。因此,对句法修改的探讨往往需要和这三个层面结合在一起。

4.3.1　句法—语义修改(syntactic-semantic modification)

在句法—语义修改里,stt 与 ttt 在句法上的转移直接与语法特征(如时态、人称和数等),或是语法词类(如动词变成名词等),或是语法功能(如原文中的定语从句在译文中变成了状语从句等)联系在一起。换言之,它涵盖了所有发生在语法层面上的翻译转移。在这点上,它与维内和达波内特提出"调换"(transposition)这种翻译过程颇为类似,但涵盖范围较之为大。另外,功能词(即非实词)的增减或意义改变亦属这种类型的翻译转移。以下即为一个句法—语义修改的例子。

例(7)　/My style of cookery caused Joseph's growing indignation. /

　　/我这种烧饭方式让约瑟夫越来越冒火。/

ATR:way of cooking＋result in＋increasing＋anger

ADstt:syntactic form of "anger"—noun

ADttt:syntactic form of "anger"—verb

Syntactic-semantic modification/grammatical class

在例(7)里,stt 表达 ATR 中 anger 之意的为 indignation 这一名词,但 ttt 中却把该词译成"冒火"这一动词形式,这就涉及 stt 和 ttt 中语法类别的改变。又因为这种类型的翻译转移发生在句法—语义层面,因此,这种类型的翻译转移就更为准确地称为"句法—语义修改/语法类别因素",斜杠(/)后表示导致这种翻译转移的原因。

4.3.2　句法—文体修改(syntactic-stylistic modification)

所谓句法—文体修改指的是 stt 与 ttt 在句法层面的转移而导致在文体上的修改。这里,影响文体变化的句法转移主要体现在 stt 和 ttt 表达信息成分(information element)的数量的多寡之上。若 ttt 比 stt 含有更多的信息成分,那它们之间发生的翻译转移就称为"句法—文体修改/明释化(explicitation)";若 stt 中的信息成分比 ttt 多,那么这种翻译转移就称为"句法—文体修改/隐含化(implicitation)"。需要注意的是,无论是 stt 还是 ttt,所多出的信息成分并不表达新的信息,它们表达的还是 ATR 中的意义,只不过用了更多的信息成分(即语言成分)来表达而已。见例(8)。

例(8)　/Laura gave a loud childish sob. /

　　/(宛如一位孩子,)劳拉大声地啜泣起来。/

ATR:proper name＋to sob＋comparison—child

ADstt:syntactic form "comparison"—argument

ADttt:syntactic form "comparison"—satellite

Syntactic-stylistic modification/explicitation

在例(8)里,stt 由一个事件状态译素表达,但 ttt 却把它译成事件状态译素和附属译素的组合。从译素的数量,或称信息成分的数量来看,ttt 较 stt 为多,但 ATR 的意义并不因为 ttt 有较多的信息成分而发生变化。鲁文-兹瓦特把这种类型的翻译转移称为"句法—文体修改/明释化",这是因为 stt 的信息在 ttt 中得到更为明确的阐释的缘故。其实,鲁文-兹瓦特在这里相当于说,如果用于表达一个文本的信息成分越多,那么该文本就能得到更为详尽和明确的表达。

4.3.3 句法—语用修改(syntactic-pragmatic modification)

在句法层面的修改亦可能导致译素在语用上发生变化,因而这种类型的翻译转移鲁文-兹瓦特称之为句法—语用修改。鲁文-兹瓦特认为,具体而言,句法修改对语用上的影响可以表现在言语行为(speech act)、主题/主位意义(thematic meaning)、指称成分(deictic element)或照应成分(anaphoric element)这三个方面。这里,言语行为并非是奥斯汀所说的言语具有的以言指事、以言行事和以言成事这几种行为(Austin, 1959),而是指 stt 与 ttt 之间句式的转换或改变,如把疑问句转换成陈述句,否定句改变成肯定句等;主位意义则主要是指 stt 与 ttt 之间在语态上(即主动语态和被动语态)的转移;指称成分或照应成分上的转移则是指 stt 中的这些成分在 ttt 中没有保留,而改用其他成分代替,典型的例子如把 stt 中的代词译成名词等。见例(9)与例(10)。

例(9) /Must they be hidden by a marquee? /

/是不是要用大帐篷把它们藏起来? /

ATR:must+to hide+protective covering

ADstt:syntactic form of transeme—passive construction

ADttt:syntactic form of transeme—active construction

Syntactic-pragmatic modification/the matic meaning

例(10) A:/Is it true 1? /

B:/When have I told 2 a lie? /

A:/真的吗 1? /

B:/我从不说 2 谎。/

ATR2:negation+lie

ADstt2:syntactic form of transeme—question

ADttt2:syntactic form of transeme—affirmation

Syntactic-pragmatic modification/speech act

例(9)里,stt 的被动语态在 ttt 中转为主动语态,因而属于句法—语用修改类型的翻译转移在"主题意义"范畴的体现;例(10)中,stt 的问句形式在 ttt 中变成了肯定句形式,因此属于句法—语用修改类型的翻译转移在"言语行为"范畴的体现。

上述对这些发生在语用层面的翻译转换的研究不可说不细微,它们在传统翻译研究中往往被忽略或者是当成理所当然的东西,缺乏足够的重视。在翻译实践中,这些往往被列为翻译方法之一而加以教授(国内的如张培基的教材之类),很多译者在翻译时往往都会不假思索地就采取了如改变语态、转变句式等手法。这些在微观结构层面看来并无不妥的翻译方法照鲁文-兹瓦特看来,均是翻译中的转移,且这些翻译中的转移如果具有一定的出现频率和规律的话,那它就会影响译文文本的宏观结构,结果从整个文本的宏观角度来看往往会造成着重点的转移、衔接与连贯之处断裂等现象。

5 翻译转移类型：转变

比较模式中的最后一种翻译转移形式称为"转变"(mutation)，它是由于 stt 与 ttt 之间差别过大，无法建立 ATR 所致。具体分析，在句子层面以内的"转变"又有以下三种形式(Leuven-Zwart，1989：169)：

(1) 增加小句(clause)或短语(phrase)，即增添原文中所没有的成分，如增译、增益；

(2) 删去小句或短语，即删去原文中所含成分，如撮译、缩译等；

(3) 完全改变意义，即删去全部原文内容，完全另起炉灶，如清末民初时所盛行的豪杰译、德莱顿所说的拟作(imitation)等手法。

例(11) /How beautiful the vase was 1，//she thought 2. /

/花瓶多么漂亮啊！/

ATR2：0

stt：she thought

ttt：0

Mutation/deletion

在这例中，原文中的 she thought 这一词组在译文中被删去，因而也就无法比较原文与译文译素以确立 ATR。因为译文删去了原文中的成分，因此这种翻译转移属于"转变/删除"类型。

6 结语

由于篇幅所限，本文只介绍了鲁文-兹瓦特翻译转移研究模式中的基础——比较模式部分。比较模式强调对发生在微观结构上的翻译转移形式进行系统的划分和详尽的描写，为在研究模式中的另一部分——描写模式中进一步解释这种变化因素奠定扎实的语言描写基础。

鲁文-兹瓦特比较模式的优点是很明显的。首先，它是一种至目前为止最系统、最详尽的比较和描写发生在微观层次的翻译转移的方法，并做到了尽量把比较过程中的主观性因素减少到最低限度。这方面最具有代表性的莫过于比较模式在翻译评估(translation assessment)中的运用。长期以来，我们对翻译的评估在很大程度上都流于印象式、直觉式的批评，所根据的往往是从译文中随意摘取的一个或几个译例，而非根据对整篇译文所作的全面比较和描写，因此带有很大程度的主观性和随意性，如国内所盛行的"神似"、"化境"标准正可谓这一方面的典型。这些标准弹性大，模糊且不易掌握，也是往往导致对同一部作品有迥然不同的几种评价的主要原因所在。在西方，对翻译评估作系统研究比较有代表性的有赖斯(Reiss，1971/2000)和豪斯(House，1977，1997)两人。前者把对翻译评估的基础建立于对语篇类型和语篇功能的划分之上，后者则根据语用学理论建立了自己的翻译评估模式。但她们的方法只是突出比较译文某一方面的内容(如语言功能或语用方面)，而忽视了对译文的其他方面，如语义、句法、文体等的综合比较。鲁文-兹瓦特的比较模式则充分顾及了原文和译文在语义、句法、语用和文体这几方面可能出现的翻译转移，并把它们综合归类分析，这样就为翻译评估提供了一个较为客观、全面和可验证(verifiable)的基础，使准确地评估译作成为可能。

其次，与现时翻译研究中的许多"自上而下"(top-down)的研究模式不同，鲁文-兹瓦特的翻译转移研究的比较模式是一种彻头彻尾的"自下而上"(bottom-up)的研究方法。在研究之前，研究者面对的是现实中的具体文学翻译作品(这与 Catford，Vinay & Darblenet 在研究中所用的自己设计的、理想化的翻译例子不同)，在研究过程中研究者通过对语料的一步步分析才得到研究结果。采取这样的研究步骤就能有效地避免在翻译研究过程中常犯的先入为主的错误(如在研究之前已有事先设想好的结论，而研究过程仅限于在语料中寻找与结论相适合的例子来加以证明)，从而保持在研究过程中的客观和中立的立场。

再次，鲁文-兹瓦特的这个模式是用语言学的理论来比较和解释文学翻译作品的一个很好的尝试，它使人看到，语言学翻译理论与文学翻译研究之间并不是如某些学派所认为的那样(如德国的"翻译科学"学派，Snell-Hornby，1995:14)，有着不可逾越的鸿沟。从鲁文-兹瓦特这个比较模式里我们可以看到，强调科学、精确的语言学翻译理论不仅可以运用于非文学翻译作品的比较和研究之中，还能与文学翻译作品的分析很好地结合起来(把语言学翻译理论运用于文学翻译研究之中的尝试可见 Nord，1997)。

当然，这个比较模式也存在着一些不足。最受学者诟病的一点就是这个模式过于复杂和烦琐(Gentzler，1993:137；Munday，2001：66；Hermans，1999:62)。例如，在比较模式中，除三种总的翻译转移类型之外，下面又分 10 种更为具体的转移形式。若算上描写模式中的分类，则共有 37 种。这些种类繁多的分类如未经过专门的学习和研究，很难马上把它们用于实践之中，这就大大降低了模式的可操作性。这似乎也可以解释为什么鲁文-兹瓦特的模式自提出以来在学界颇受好评，但在实际中的运用却不甚多。

另外，虽然鲁文-兹瓦特极力标榜其比较模式的客观性，但仔细研究却并非完全如此。由于比较模式相当复杂，就连她本人都认为如要用该模式从头到尾对一本长篇叙事性文本(如托尔斯泰的《战争与和平》等)进行分析，往往要耗费大量的时间和精力，因而较为可取的做法是选取文本中的部分内容分析。但到底应该选取哪一部分内容才更具有代表性？这就涉及分析者的主观性问题。另外，在 ATR 的确定方面，虽然鲁文-兹瓦特声称可以借助字典，但不可否认，主要还需由分析者决定。鲁文-兹瓦特显然忽略了这些主观成分。

话又说回来，要建立一个完全没有任何主观性的翻译研究模式其实是不可能的。因为观察角度是由研究者所选择，因此，从更广泛的意义上说，自选定研究角度的那一刻起主观性就渗透在研究过程中。既然主观性无法完全摆脱，研究者所需要做的就是在研究过程中尽量减少主观性带来的影响，使研究过程客观且可被重复，而研究结果也可以让他人验证。从这点来看，不可否认，鲁文-兹瓦特的描写模式还是较为客观的，这对缺乏系统的翻译描写模式的我国翻译学界而言，尤其值得借鉴。

【延伸阅读】

[1] 李德超.从维内、达贝尔内到图里:翻译转移研究综述.四川外语学院学报,2005(1):94-99.
[2] 卢晶晶.鲁文·兹瓦特翻译转移比较模式的研究运用.安徽农业大学学报:社会科学版,2008(1):79-83.
[3] 牛宁.范·路文兹瓦特的比较模式以及描写模式.东华大学学报:社会科学版,2009(2):164-168.

【问题与思考】

　　1. 本文是如何分析鲁文-兹瓦特模式中的比较模式部分的？

　　2. 本文作者为什么要对语义、句法、语用和文体层面的翻译转移的比较和描述作详细的介绍？

　　3. 本文对鲁文-兹瓦特翻译转移研究模式的评价是否恰当？为什么？

第三章　多元系统与翻译

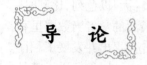

导　论

　　20世纪70年代，以色列特拉维夫大学学者埃文-佐哈尔（Itamar Even-Zohar）在研究希伯来文学的基础上提出了多元系统理论。他的多元系统论的主要来源是俄国形式主义理论。俄国形式主义最早产生于1915年，它强调形式与技巧而不强调题材的表现手法，反对俄国革命前处理叙述材料的传统方式，转而重视艺术语言形式的重要性，逐步影响到当时的各艺术领域。持形式主义观点的文学研究者们不仅仅研究文学的外部联系，而且还研究文学内部的固有的秩序和结构。他们取大量文学作品作为研究素材，从中探求文学形式的特色、结构和原则，把形式作为文学的本质。其主要代表人物有特尼亚诺夫（Jurij Tynjanov）、雅各布森（Roman Jakobson）、埃亨巴乌姆（Boris Ejkhenbaum）等。佐哈尔从他们那里继承了许多有益的思想成分，其中对他后来创立多元系统论意义重大的一个概念就是系统（system）。该术语最早由特尼亚诺夫于1929年给出定义：由相互关联、相互作用的成分构成的多层结构。由于该术语本身的灵活性，特尼亚诺夫能够运用它来解释各个不同层次的现象，不仅能解释个人的作品，而且能解释整个文学传统和体裁，甚至能解释整个社会秩序。此外，他还把文学演变过程称做"系统的变异"。

　　佐哈尔采用形式主义的系统方法有其明确的近期目标，即解决一些与翻译理论和希伯来文学的历史结构相关的问题。他在研究中运用形式主义的思想和方法，并在此基础上创立了多元系统论。在佐哈尔那里，"系统"和"多元系统"很大程度上是同义语。但"多元系统"术语的提出意在强调"系统"概念的动态性质，并试图与传统的索绪尔语言学中带有更多静态含义的"系统"概念区别开来。另外，佐哈尔的"系统"概念的意义也不同于韩礼德功能语法中的"系统"概念。在佐哈尔的理论模式里，"多元系统"（polysystem）表示由许多个互为相关的成分构成的有层次的综合体，它随着其内部成分的互动而不断变化。多元系统可用于解释不同层次的现象，因此某个特定国家的文学可视为更大的社会文化多元系统的一个组成成分，这个更大的社会文化多元系统包含了文学多元系统和艺术、宗教、政治等多元系统。文学不只是被视为文本的集合，而且还被当做制约这些文本的生产、促销和接受的一整套因素。多元系统理论的一个基本观念是，组成特定多元系统的各个层次和子系统在不断地相互竞争，力图占据主要位置。因此在文学多元系统内部，中心和边缘之间总是存在持续的紧张状态，各种不同的文学体裁都力争获得中心的支配地位。

　　虽说佐哈尔创立多元系统概念的初衷是为了解决与翻译相关的一些问题，但他的多元系统理论却很好地解释了翻译学领域具有更一般性质的系统现象。事实上，佐哈尔的大部分作品讨论了翻译文学在某一特定的文学多元系统里所起的作用，以及多元系统理论对翻译研究所具有的较宽泛的理论意义。

多元系统理论问世之后，有些学者指出了该理论存在的一些问题。一些学者提出了新的概念以弥补该理论模式概念之不足。例如，列费维尔（Lefevere，1983）就建议增加终极性（polarity）、时期性（periodicity）和赞助人（patronage）三个概念。根茨勒（Gentzler，1993：122－123）认为，佐哈尔的理论受俄国形式主义的影响太深，多元系统理论需要摆脱一些限制性较强的概念的影响。但总体来说，佐哈尔的多元系统理论对翻译研究的影响巨大，以色列、比利时、荷兰等国的许多学者都从多元系统角度开展对翻译的研究。其中贡献最大的学者当数图里和赫曼斯。图里（1980，1995）强化了佐哈尔的以目标为导向的翻译研究方法，提出并发展了翻译规范论。赫曼斯（1985）在佐哈尔理论的基础上提出了"文学的摆布"（manipulation）说。赫曼斯（1999）指出佐哈尔多元系统理论的局限性在于过多地研究现象、分类及相互关系，而不去研究隐藏在现象背后的原因。赫曼斯把翻译作为一种文化、历史现象来研究，探索翻译的背景及制约因素，寻求新的解释方法。

本章共选三篇论文。第一篇是 Itamar Even-Zohar 撰写的"The Position of Translated Literature Within the Literary Polysystem"，系统地阐发了翻译文学在文学多元系统内部的地位。第二篇"Translation as System"为 Theo Hermans 所著，文章用社会系统论观照翻译，揭示了翻译系统的结构特点和制约因素。第三篇是吴耀武和张建青合写的《佐哈尔多元系统翻译理论的批评性阐释》，对佐哈尔多元系统论的主要特点、影响与局限及其在中国学界的译介情况进行了批评性阐释。

选 文

选文一　The Position of Translated Literature Within the Literary Polysystem

Itamar Even-Zohar

导　言

本文选自韦努蒂编《翻译研究读本》。

在建构翻译理论的时候，通常会遇到许多问题，如翻译文学与文学系统的关系、翻译文学的地位等。"多元系统论"是埃文-佐哈尔提出的说明文学系统行为和演变的理论，本文是埃文-佐哈尔对该理论的系统阐发。本文阐释了一个基本观点，即文学以及文化等社会符号现象都是一个开放式的多元系统，深刻分析了翻译文学在文学多元系统中的中心和边缘的地位转化及成因问题，指出翻译的对策要根据翻译文学的地位而定。多元系统论对翻译研究有重要意义,因为它给定了文学多元系统内翻译所扮演的角色,打破了传统上把翻译文学看做是始终处于边缘地位的观点,解决了翻译文学在整个文学乃至文化中的地位及兴衰原因问题,将一些外围的元素如赞助人、社会条件、经济状况及意识形态制约等都纳入多元系统论的研究范畴,从而将翻译研究推到一个新的发展阶段。

Dedicated to the memory of James S. Holmes—a great student of translation and a dear friend.

I

In spite of the broad recognition among historians of culture of the major role translation has played in the crystallization of national cultures, relatively little research has been carried out so far in this area. As a rule, histories of literatures mention translations when there is no way to avoid them, when dealing with the Middle Ages or the Renaissance, for instance. One might of course find sporadic references to individual literary translations in various other periods, but they are seldom incorporated into the historical account in any coherent way. As a consequence, one hardly gets any idea whatsoever of the function of translated literature for a literature as a whole or of its position within that literature. Moreover, there is no awareness of the possible existence of translated literature as a particular literary system. The prevailing concept is rather that of "translation" or just "translated works" treated on an individual basis. Is there any basis for a different assumption, that is for considering translat-ed literature as a system? Is there the same sort of cultural and verbal network of relations within what seems to be an arbitrary group of translated texts as the one we willingly hypothesize for original literature? What kind of relations might there be among translated works, which are presented as completed facts, imported from other literatures, detached from their home contexts and consequently neutralized from the point of view of center-and-periphery struggles?

My argument is that translated works do correlate in at least two ways: (1) in the way their source texts are selected by the target literature, the principles of selection never being uncorrelatable with the home co-systems of the target literature (to put it in the most cautious way); and (2) in the way they adopt specific norms, behaviors, and policies—in short, in their use of the literary repertoire—which results from their relations with the other home co-systems. These are not confined to the linguistic level only, but are manifest on any selection level as well. Thus, translated literature may possess a repertoire of its own, which to a certain extent could even be exclusive to it. (See Toury, 1985, 1985a.)

It seems that these points make it not only justifiable to talk about translated literature, but rather imperative to do so. I cannot see how any scholarly effort to describe and explain the behavior of the literary polysystem in synchrony and diachrony can advance in an adequate way if that is not recognized. In other words, I conceive of translated literature not only as an integral system within any literary polysystem, but as a most active system within it. But what is its position within the polysystem, and how is this position connected with the nature of its overall repertoire? One would be tempted to deduce from the peripheral position of translated literature in the study of literature that it also permanently occupies a peripheral position in the literary polysystem, but this is by no means the case. Whether translated literature becomes central or peripheral, and whether this position is connected with innovatory ("primary") or conservatory ("secondary") repertoires, depends on the specific constellation of the polysystem under study.

II

To say that translated literature maintains a central position in the literary polysystem means that it participates actively in shaping the center of the polysystem. In such a situation it is by and large an integral part of innovatory forces, and as such likely to be identified with major events in literary history while these are taking place. This implies that in this situation no clear-cut distinction is maintained between "original" and "translated" writings, and that often it is the leading writers (or members of the avant-garde who are about to become leading writers) who produce the most conspicuous or appreciated translations. Moreover, in such a state when new literary models are emerging, translation is likely to become one of the means of elaborating the new repertoire. Through the foreign works, features (both principles and elements) are introduced into the home literature which did not exist there before. These include possibly not only new models of reality to replace the old and established ones that are no longer effective, but a whole range of other features as well, such as a new (poetic) language, or compositional patterns and techniques. It is clear that the very principles of selecting the works to be translated are determined by the situation governing the (home) polysystem: The texts are chosen according to their compatibility with the new approaches and the supposedly innovatory role they may assume within the target literature.

What then are the conditions which give rise to a situation of this kind? It seems to me that three major cases can be discerned, which are basically various manifestations of the same law: (1) When a polysystem has not yet been crystallized, that is to say, when a literature is "young," in the process of being established; (2) when a literature is either "peripheral" (within a large group of correlated literatures) or "weak," or both; and (3) when there are turning points, crises, or literary vacuums in a literature.

In the first case translated literature simply fulfills the need of a younger literature to put into use its newly founded (or renovated) tongue for as many literary types as possible in order to make it serviceable as a literary language and useful for its emerging public. Since a young literature cannot immediately create texts in all types known to its producers, it benefits from the experience of other literatures, and translated literature becomes in this way one of its most important systems. The same holds true for the second instance, that of relatively established literatures whose resources are limited and whose position within a larger literary hierarchy is generally peripheral. As a consequence of this situation, such literatures often do not develop the same full range of literary activities (organized in a variety of systems) observable in adjacent larger literatures (which in consequence may create a feeling that they are indispensable). They may also "lack" a repertoire which is felt to be badly needed vis-à-vis, and in terms of the presence of, that adjacent literature. This lack may then be filled, wholly or partly, by translated literature. For instance, all sorts of peripheral literature may in such cases consist of translated literature. But far more important is the consequence that the ability of such "weak" literatures to initiate innovations is often less than that of the larger and central literatures, with the result that a relation of dependency may be established not only in peripheral systems, but in the very center of these "weak" literatures. (To avoid misunderstanding, I would like to point out that these literatures may rise to a central position in a way analogous to the way this is carried out by peripheral systems within a certain poly system, but this cannot be discussed here.)

Since peripheral literatures in the Western Hemisphere tend more often than not to be identical with the literatures of smaller nations, as unpalatable as this idea may seem to us, we have no choice but to admit that within a group of relatable national literatures, such as the literatures of Europe, hierarchical relations have been established since the very beginnings of these literatures. Within this (macro-)polysystem some literatures have taken peripheral positions, which is only to say that they were often modelled to a large extent upon an exterior literature. For such literatures, translated literature is not only a major channel through which fashionable repertoire is brought home, but also a source of reshuffling and supplying alternatives. Thus, whereas richer or stronger literatures may have the option to adopt novelties from some periphery within their indigenous borders, "weak" literatures in such situations often depend on import alone.

The dynamics within the polysystem creates turning points, that is to say, historical moments where established models are no longer tenable for a younger generation. At such moments, even in central literatures, translated literature may assume a central position. This is all the more true when at a turning point no item in the indigenous stock is taken to be acceptable, as a result of which a literary "vacuum" occurs. In such a vacuum, it is easy for foreign models to infiltrate, and translated literature may consequently assume a central position. Of course, in the case of "weak" literatures or literatures which are in a constant state of impoverishment (lack of literary items existing in a neighbor or accessible foreign literature), this situation is even more overwhelming.

III

Contending that translated literature may maintain a peripheral position means that it constitutes a peripheral system within the polysystem, generally employing secondary models. In such a situation it has no influence on major processes and is modelled according to norms already conventionally established by an already dominant type in the target literature. Translated literature in this case becomes a major factor of conservatism. While the contemporary original literature might go on developing new norms and models, translated literature adheres to norms which have been rejected either recently or long before by the (newly) established center. It no longer maintains positive correlations with original writing.

A highly interesting paradox manifests itself here: Translation, by which new ideas, items, characteristics can be introduced into a literature, becomes a means to preserve traditional taste. This discrepancy between the original central literature and the translated literature may have evolved in a variety of ways, for instance, when translated literature, after having assumed a central position and inserted new items, soon lost contact with the original home literature which went on changing, and thereby became a factor of preservation of unchanged repertoire. Thus, a literature that might have emerged as a revolutionary type may go on existing as an ossified *système d'antan*, often fanatically guarded by the agents of secondary models against even minor changes.

The conditions which enable this second state are of course diametrically opposite to those which give rise to translated literature as a central system: Either there are no major changes in the polysystem or these changes are not effected through the intervention of inter-literary relations materialized in the form of translations.

IV

The hypothesis that translated literature may be either a central or peripheral system does not imply that it is always wholly one or the other. As a system, translated literature is itself stratified, and from the point of view of poly systemic analysis it is often from the vantage point of the central stratum that all relations within the system are observed. This means that while one section of translated literature may assume a central position, another may remain quite peripheral. In the foregoing analysis I pointed out the close relationship between literary contacts and the status of translated literature. This seems to me the major clue to this issue. When there is intense interference, it is the portion of translated literature deriving from a major source literature which is likely to assume a central position. For instance, in the Hebrew literary polysystem between the two world wars literature translated from the Russian assumed an unmistakably central position, while works translated from

English, German, Polish, and other languages assumed an obviously peripheral one. Moreover, since the major and most innovatory translational norms were produced by translations from the Russian, other translated literature adhered to the models and norms elaborated by those translations.

The historical material analyzed so far in terms of polysystemic operations is too limited to provide any far-reaching conclusions about the chances of translated literature to assume a particular position. But work carried out in this field by various other scholars, as well as my own research, indicates that the "normal" position assumed by translated literature tends to be the peripheral one. This should in principle be compatible with theoretical speculation. It may be assumed that in the long run no system can remain in a constant state of weakness, "turning point," or crisis, although the possibility should not be excluded that some polysystems may maintain such states for quite a long time. Moreover, not all polysystems are structured in the same way, and cultures do differ significantly. For instance, it is clear that the French cultural system, French literature naturally included, is much more rigid than most other systems. This, combined with the long traditional central position of French literature within the European context (or within the European macro-polysystem), has caused French translated literature to assume an extremely peripheral position. The state of Anglo-American literature is comparable, while Russian, German, or Scandinavian would seem to show different patterns of behavior in this respect.

V

What consequences may the position taken by translated literature have on translational norms, behaviours, and policies? As I stated above, the distinction between a translated work and an original work in terms of literary behavior is a function of the position assumed by the translated literature at a given time. When it takes a central position, the borderlines are *diffuse*, so that the very category of "translated works" must be extended to semi-and quasi-translations as well. From the point of view of translation theory I think this is a more adequate way of dealing with such phenomena than to reject them on the basis of a static and ahistorical conception of translation. Since translational activity participates, when it assumes a central position, in the process of creating new, primary models, the translator's main concern here is not just to look for ready-made models in his home repertoire into which the source texts would be transferable. Instead, he is prepared in such cases to violate the home conventions. Under such conditions the chances that the translation will be close to the original in terms of adequacy (in other words, a reproduction of the dominant textual relations of the original) are greater than otherwise. Of course, from the point of view of the target literature the adopted translational norms might for a while be too foreign and revolutionary, and if the new trend is defeated in the literary struggle, the translation made according to its conceptions and tastes will never really gain ground. But if the new trend is victorious, the repertoire (code) of translated literature may be enriched and become more flexible. Periods of great change in the home system are in fact the only ones when a translator is prepared to go far beyond the options offered to him by his established home repertoire and is willing to attempt a different treatment of text making. Let us remember that under stable conditions items lacking in a target literature may remain untransferable if the state of the polysystem does not allow innovations. But the process of opening the system gradually brings certain literatures closer and in the longer run enables a situation where the postulates of (translational) adequacy and the realities of equivalence may overlap to a relatively high degree. This is the case of the European literatures, though in some of them the mechanism of rejection has been so strong that the changes I am talking about have occurred on a rather limited scale.

Naturally, when translated literature occupies a peripheral position, it behaves totally differently. Here, the translator's main effort is to concentrate upon finding the best ready-made secondary models for the foreign text, and the result often turns out to be a non-adequate translation or (as I would prefer to put it) a greater discrepancy between the equivalence achieved and the adequacy postulated.

In other words, not only is the socio-literary status of translation dependent upon its position within the polysystem, but the very practice of translation is also strongly subordinated to that position. And even the question of what is a translated work cannot be answered *a priori* in terms of an a-historical out-of-context idealized state; it must be determined on the grounds of the operations governing the polysystem. Seen from this point of view, translation is no longer a phenomenon whose nature and borders are given once and for all, but an activity dependent on the relations within a certain cultural system.

【延伸阅读】

[1] Even-Zohar, I. (1990). *Polysystem Studies*. Tel Aviv: Porter Institute of Poetics and Semiotics. Durham, NC: Duke University Press, special issue of *Poetics Today*, 11 (1).

[2] Gentzler, E. (1993). *Contemporary Translation Theories*. London and New York: Routledge.

[3] Hermans, T. (1985). *The Manipulation of Literature: Studies in Literary Translation*. Beckenham: Croom Helm.

[4] Toury, G. (1980). *In Search of a Theory of Translation*. Tel Aviv: The Porter Institute.

[5] Toury, G. (1995). *Descriptive Translation Studies—And Beyond*. Amsterdam and Philadelphia, PA: John Benjamins.

【问题与思考】

1. 多元系统论从俄国形式主义理论那里受了哪些影响？

2. 佐哈尔认为在三种情形之下，翻译文学在译语文学多元系统中会处于中心地位，你认为他概括得全面吗？为什么？

3. 在本文的末尾，佐哈尔指出"翻译现象的本质和边界并不是一经给出就永远适用的，而是依赖于特定文化系统内部关系的一种活动"，你是如何理解这一观点的？

4. 翻译在我国现阶段的多元系统中地位如何？是居于主要还是次要的地位？近几十年来翻译的地位有无一些显著的变化？请用多元系统论加以分析。

5. 多元系统理论有何缺陷？

选文二 Translation as System (Excerpt)

Theo Hermans

导　言

英国翻译理论家赫曼斯对佐哈尔多元系统论比较推崇，他1999年出版的专著《系统中的翻译》用了较大篇幅解释翻译研究的系统方法，指出了多元系统论的优点与不足。本文节选自该书第十章。本文没有囿于佐哈尔理论的局限，而是引入德国社会学家卢曼(Niklas Luhmann)的社会系统论，用社会系统论观照翻译。本文认为，所有的社会系统都是意义系统：交际信号、解释行为、连接反应，所有这些构成系统并使之运转。对意义处理方式的差异是不同社会系统之间的分水岭。文本没有固定意义，它在各种不同的语境中被赋予意义。一旦选择了某种意义，就意味着同时排斥了所有其他意义。选择受认知性和规范性期待的制约。守护翻译疆界的期待是本质规范，有关内容适当性的期待是调节规范。这些期待构成了翻译社会系统的结构。翻译本身就是社会系统，它具有自我再生性和自我指涉性。本文能拓展和深化读者对翻译系统或翻译多元系统的认识。

As I remarked at the beginning of the previous chapter, there are obvious similarities between Bourdieu and Luhmann. Both have proved prolific, innovative, controversial, and influential well beyond their sociological specialism. Both are primarily concerned with the functioning of modern industrialized society and its subdivisions, including culture. They are relational thinkers, acutely aware of theoretical and methodological issues. Neither has written about translation, but both, Bourdieu more than Luhmann, have in recent years seen their ideas taken up by translation researchers.

The differences between them are no less obvious. If Bourdieu is a sociologist with an anthropological strain, Luhmann is tarred with a system-theoretical brush. Some of Luhmann's writing remains forbiddingly abstract. Luhmann's ideas have also evolved considerably over the years, as he shifted from thinking of systems as means of reducing complexity to an emphasis on self-reproducing and self-referential systems. On the whole Luhmann's outlook, more so than Bourdieu's, is decidedly anti-foundational and constructivist: He sees knowledge and observation as the application of distinctions which are properties of the observing system rather than of the world as such (Laermans, 1997, p. 107). This has brought him close to postmodern and poststructuralist modes of thought (De Berg & Prangel, 1995; *New German Critique*, 1994).

Much of Luhmann's work over the last fifteen years or so has been concerned with large-scale functional systems like the economy, the legal system, politics, education, religion, science and art. The theoretical groundwork for these studies was laid in his *Soziale Systeme* of 1984 (English: Luhmann, 1995a). He has also applied system-theoretical insights to social phenomena such as ecological communication (1989) and protest movements (1996). Attempts to apply Luhmann's concepts in literary and art-historical studies have been made by David Roberts (1992), Dietrich Schwanitz (1990), Niels Werber (1992), Kitty Zijlmans (1990) and others. Siegfried Schmidt's analyses of the literary system in eighteenth-century Germany (Schmidt, 1989, 1991, 1992, 1997) are indebted to Luhmann but add different touches.

In the following pages I will explore some of the ways in which Luhmann's work might be utilized for the study of translation. Some of these reflect my own current interests. Throughout, it will be good to remember J. Herwig-Lempp's remark that the point of working with system concepts is not necessarily to grasp the system as a whole, but to consider an entity in system terms in order to elicit answers to certain questions (in Fokkema, 1991, p. 164). Among such questions could be: How can we conceptualize translation despite its heteronomy? How to account for continuity, diversity and change in concepts and practices of translation? Viewing translation as a social system—or for that matter as a field in Bourdieu's sense—may open up interesting perspectives. Formidable problems are bound to remain, if only because Luhmann's theory of functionally differentiated systems is historically tied to modern industrialized societies; he has had little to say about pre-modern societies. What we may gain from the attempt, however, is a way of conceptualizing translation as simultaneously autonomous and heteronomous, a means of studying disputes over what is or what is not translation, a tool to think about the internal organization and evolution of the social and intellectual space we call translation.

Let me begin by introducing some of the key terms and concepts. Luhmann does not think of social systems as consisting of individuals or collectives. Individuals are made up of physical bodies, which have cells as their constituent parts, and states of consciousness, i. e. psychic systems. The interaction of the biological with the psychic system makes our lives possible. The domain of the social and the interpersonal however requires communication. For Luhmann, social systems consist of communications, in the sense that communications are the elements social systems are made of. All social systems are "sense systems," or "meaning systems" (Luhmann's German term is Sinn systeme): Communicative signals, interpretive acts and connecting responses constitute the system and keep it going. Communications are events, acts, fleeting things which need to be connected over time. The boundaries between social systems are those watersheds where meaning is processed differently on one side as compared with the other.

This can apply to smaller units like families or holiday camps or university departments, or to the large functional systems of society. Luhmann envisages modern industrial society as made up of a number of such "functionally differentiated" social systems, primarily politics, economics, religion, the law, science, the arts, and education. System differentiation consists in the re-introduction of a "system versus environment" boundary within a system. Functional differentiation results in some systems processing certain aspects of reality, thereby leaving other systems free to focus on other aspects. Each can be described as a social system in itself, differentiated from its environment, i. e. the collection of other systems, by the fact that within each system, communications are of a different intensity and quality as compared with the environment. Although the various systems obviously interact and need each other, each system looks at the rest of the world from its own point of view. The legal system, for instance, reads the world in terms of what is lawful and what is not, whereas in the political system power is the measure of things. The main advantage of this decentralized and "decentred" organization of society, in Luhmann's view, is that it makes it easier for society to cope with the world's complexity. Historically this form of societal organization emerged in the West in roughly the seventeenth and eighteenth centuries.

If this is, grossly simplified, the basis on which Luhmann has built his imposing analyses of social systems, the theoretical apparatus has seen various additions and modifications in recent years. In what follows I will take up only some of these, in particular the emphasis on social systems as being self-reproducing (or "autopoietic") and self-referential, and Luhmann's comments on second-order observation.

If we want to see how Luhmann's theory of social systems might be of use to translation studies, there are two fairly obvious, and overlapping, points of entry. One is the work done by the German researcher Andreas Poltermann, the first to apply Luhmann's system-theoretical ideas to literary translation and translation norms. The other is to link the notion of norms with what Luhmann says about expectations. I will explain these two approaches first, and then go on to other questions. These will bear on the possibility of viewing translation in terms of self-reproducing and self-reflexive systems. This latter aspect will lead us back, via a somewhat vertiginous route, to the problematics of description in translation studies.

Expectations structure

Poltermann's essay on "Norms of Literary Translation" (1992) is concerned with norm changes, primarily in Germany, in the context of literature as a differentiated social system in Luhmann's sense. Literature as a "differentiated social system" means that it possesses a degree of autonomy with regard to other systems such as religion, politics, or education. The emergence of literature as a differentiated system with its own function and rules is usually dated to the eighteenth century. The historical process of differentiation is obviously a complex matter (Schmidt 1989 has described it for literature in Germany). As literature abandons, for example, its primary role as an instrument of moral instruction, it no longer wants to be judged by moral criteria but instead lays claim to its own literary or aesthetic rules. Literature begins to concentrate on selective functions like social critique and the production of alternative models of reality. Self-descriptions, in the form of literary criticism and handbooks on poetics, emphasize the unity and difference of the system. The participants in literary communication adopt various social roles, which take account of such things as the overwhelmingly written nature of modern literature, the anonymity of the reading public, and the need for expert critics to mediate between writers and readers.

Among the consequences of these changes for literary translation Poltermann singles out the role of philological renderings, which in the case of theatre translation, for instance, lead to a marked difference between versions destined for the stage and those, like Wilhelm von Humboldt's *Agamemnon* of 1816, intended to be read. The latter thus align themselves with the increasingly written character of literary communication. In passing Poltermann offers an interesting system-theoretical explanation for the fact that the first translations of foreign works tend to stick more closely to domestic genre expectations than subsequent renderings. Meeting genre expectations can be seen as a way of reducing complexity, making "alien" elements easier to handle within the system. The alternative solutions that were not selected, however, continue to lead a virtual existence as "temporalized complexity." In translation criticism and in subsequent translations, which need to legitimize themselves with regard both to existing versions and to the original, the contingency of the first translation is shown up and the temporarily stored complexity of alternative solutions gradually unfolds over time (Poltermann, 1992, p. 19).

Poltermann's account treats literary and translation norms in terms of genre expectations, allowing him to comment on the relevance both of meeting expectations and of confounding them. This way of looking at norms ties in with what was said in the final section of Chapter 6 about focusing on selectivity and exclusion in studying norms. It also accords with Luhmann's view of communication, which itself has phenomenological roots, and possesses elements in common with speech act theory (Luhmann, 1984, p. 191ff. ; Blom, 1997, p. 70ff.).

Luhmann does not conceive of communication in terms of the transmission of a pre-given message. Rather, meaning is construed by the recipient as a result of recognizing selectivity. What is offered acquires meaning against the backdrop of the possibilities that were more or less readily available but were excluded in the event. The element of selection concerns both the enunciation, i. e. the intentional act of utterance, and the information, i. e. the "theme" or the "data" which are highlighted. Because communication takes place at a certain moment in a temporal sequence, in a given context, "understanding" or "making sense" of a communication means being alive not only to its "theme" and "mode of utterance," but also to the selective aspects of both, to their negative foils, the difference between what is included and what is excluded (Luhmann, 1986a, p. 85ff; 1990, p. 12ff.).

It follows that texts and other utterances have no fixed meaning. Recoverable from the semantics of the words, they are invested with meaning in selective, differential contexts. When we look at texts in this way, through their "temporalized semantics" (De Berg, 1990, p. 50), we can probe their significance by asking questions like: How likely, or how new, was this communication in the circumstances? Why this theme, and this mode of transmission, against which set of likely alternatives? What issue or problem is being addressed, and what is occluded? And how does this communication contribute to the establishment of a new context, a new range of possibilities for subsequent communications? Applied to translation: It is part of the meaning of a translation that a particular original was selected from among a range of candidates, that it was selected for translation and not for some other form of importation, recycling or rewriting, and that a particular translating style was selected, one mode of representing the original against other more or less likely, more or less permissible modes.

The reference to "likely" and "permissible" modes reminds us that we are talking about cognitive and normative expectations within a limited range of options. It also allows us to formulate norm concepts in a system-theoretical context. The domain of translation, or the social institution which is termed "translation," has limits, a socially acknowledged boundary differentiating it, sometimes sharply, sometimes only diffusely, from other modes of dealing with anterior discourses. The expectations which police the boundaries of translation are called the "constitutive norms" of translation (see Chapter 6). Breaching them means that the product will not be called "translation," at least not by the group that lays claim to the definition of translation. Within the field of translation we speak of "regulatory norms," expectations concerning what is appropriate with regard to certain types or areas of discourse. These expectations form the structure of the social system of translation, in a sense compatible with Luhmann's terminology. Luhmann holds that whereas communications are the building blocks of social systems, expectations about communications constitute their cement, their structure. Social structures are structures of expectation in an otherwise contingent world (Luhmann, 1984, p. 139, p. 377ff.). Structure here means that some occurrences, and some processes and combinations, are more likely than others.

Luhmann's comments on style are of interest in this respect. Referring to the arts in general, he suggests that style "organizes" the contribution of an individual work to the ongoing production and consumption of art. In this way "[t]he style of a work allows us to recognize what it owes to other works of art and what it means for other, new works of art"

(1990, pp. 196 – 197; 1986, p. 632). By recognizing style, including styles of translating, we establish filiations branching into the past and adjust future expectations. The process, which works by means of contrast as well as parallelism, has multiple orientations. It links the translation we are reading with other texts belonging to the same type or sharing stylistic features, regardless of whether those texts are translations or originals; and it links this particular translation with other translations, whether of the same genre or not. To the extent that in the former case we can speak of translation's external reference and in the latter of its self-reference, we can thus bring into view the idea of translation itself as a social system.

Translation as a social system

We can look upon translation as a recognized social phenomenon, both an intellectual category and a cultural practice. The meaning of the term is codified in dictionaries, fixed by informal as well as professional activities called translation, constantly affirmed by translators' associations and by educational, scholarly, journalistic and other public and private discourses. As was suggested above, it is reasonable also to assume that we bring both cognitive and normative expectations to translation. Both sets of expectations are continually being negotiated, confirmed, adjusted and modified by practising translators and by all who speak about translation.

In this sense we can envisage the world of translation itself as a system, an adaptive, self-regulating, self-reflexive and self-reproducing system in Luhmann's terms. This implies that we account for the simultaneous autonomy and heteronomy of translation, and explore how Luhmann's descriptions of social systems apply to translation. Naturally, the interest of such an exercise lies partly in the excitement of the exploration itself, and partly in the kind of issues it brings to the surface.

If social systems consist of communications, then the elements which build the translation system must be actual translations and statements about translation. The system's temporal dimension, its internal memory, so to speak, reflects the fact that communication generates communication, under the right conditions. A system can only continue to exist if communications connect. We can translate because there are translations which we recognize as translations *and* because, when we translate or speak about translation, we routinely take account of the conditioning factors governing the concepts and practices which count as "translation" in our world. This creates the necessary connectivity and a sufficient "horizon of expectations" to produce further translations and statements about translation. The expectations constitute what Luhmann called the "structure" of the system. These structures, which are themselves the products of communication, in turn fix the conditions for the connectivity of further communications. This, in a nutshell, is the idea of a self-reproducing or "autopoietic" system: Structure and process support each other.

If we regard translation as constituting a functional system, its primary function can be said to consist in producing representations of anterior discourses across semiotic boundaries, and typically that representations can be taken as re-enacting anterior discourses. The system's identity as a separate functional system, its "guiding difference" (Luhmann's term is *Leitdifferenz*), is based on this specific representational role. Some of the practical consequences of this role are profoundly paradoxical. One consequence, for example, is that interlingual translation may need to create an impression of equivalence—an illusion of equivalence, Anthony Pym (1995a) would say—if it is to produce target texts that can serve as replacements of their source texts (see Chapter 7). Another is the fact that the translator, in re-enacting another utterance, does not speak in his or her own name only, which results in translations possessing a hybrid discursive subject, somewhat like direct or indirect quotation (Folkart, 1991; Pym, 1992b; Hermans, 1996b). No doubt an approach employing Bakhtin's notions of dialogism and heteroglossia could take these issues further.

A social system's primary means of differentiation and self-organization is a binary "code," an operational distinction furnishing the ultimate point of orientation for discourse. Science, for Luhmann, uses the "true/false" distinction as its basic code; politics is centred on power; the legal system on legal versus illegal. My suggestion as regards translation would be for the distinction between "valid" or "not valid" as representation. Because the distinction bearing on the validity of the representation marks the system's constitutive difference, it also creates the boundary between the system itself and its environment. In the course of history the terms of this basic "code" can be, and have been, fleshed out in very different ways, in the form of what Luhmann calls "programmes." They take the form of different criteria and preferences, or different poetics of translation, in the way different sets of concrete laws, for example, embody different "programmes" of the legal system. All the normative expectations and codifications of translation can be expressed in these terms. Neoclassical translation as practised by Houdar de la Motte is programmed differently from Hölderlin's literalism. Ezra Pound and Vladimir Nabokov both acknowledge word-for-word and sense-for-sense as divergent but coexisting programmes.

While social systems are open in that they require input from their environment, this input is processed in the system's own terms. Luhmann speaks of "operational closure" in this connection. Churches, for example, interpret the world from a religious point of view. In the case of translation this means that texts and other semiotic constructs are processed with an eye to their "translational" aspects. At the same time, however, translation does not operate in and for itself, but caters for other interests, other systems—hence its heteronomy. Translations enter, and interact with, existing discursive forms and practices. On the whole, we expect translations to defer to the client system's prevailing discourse, although, depending on circumstances, more complex forms of interaction, pliancy and recalcitrance can and will occur. A theoretical account of this form of entanglement or complicity may be found in the notions of "structural coupling" or "resonance" between systems, whereby the norms, criteria and resources of one system are put at the disposal of or forced upon another system, there to be respected or resisted, as the case may be.

Since translation is on the whole less clearly differentiated, less autonomous, than, say, modern art or religion, it is particularly prone to interference. Here we encounter the engine that drives translation and induces change in the social system of translation. Only systems which constantly adapt to their environment can continue to exist—and adaptation can take the form of influencing neighbouring systems. The nature of translation's programmes alters as translational communications respond to all manner of internal and external interference. Connectivity cannot be taken for granted.

In the combination of autonomy and heteronomy, of self-reference and external reference, we can recognize translation's formative role in history. Translation actively contributes to the shaping of cultural and other discourses because, whatever its actual complexion, it possesses a momentum of its own, an internal memory resulting from operational closure. This is what makes translation irreducible, even when it defers to prevailing discourses. The self-reference of translation sees to it that the translative operation never wholly extinguishes a source text's otherness. It is also one of the means to irritate client systems.

To the extent that the translation system has its own momentum, its identity and relative stability as a system, it continually reproduces itself. The way in which translation is maintained and continually modified as a social system governed by particular sets of expectations, determines the way in which we produce and process translations and communicate about them, whether in everyday or in academic conversation, at a translator training institute, in a newspaper review or a translator's preface. Adopting this perspective implies, though, that the term "translation" has no fixed, inherent, immanent meaning. The category "translation," including what I called its representational function, is constantly being reproduced by means of communication. Its semantics changes in this process of reproduction, just as historically its basic code ("valid/not valid as representation") is occupied by different terms, oppositions and values, i. e. by different "programmes." Its durability or stability, as a concept and a practice, stems from its autopoiesis as a system, i. e. from recursive operations of self-production and self-reflexiveness. Our contemporary discourses, including those of translation studies, including the words on this page, are part of that process.

【延伸阅读】

[1] Hermans, T. (1996). The Translator's Voice in Translated Narrative. *Target*, (8), 23 – 48.

[2] Luhmann, N. (1990). *Essays on Self-Reference*. New York: Columbia University Press.

[3] Luhmann, N. (1995). *Social Systems*. John Bednarz, trans. Stanford: Stanford University Press(English).

[4] Pym, A. (1992). Discursive Persons and the Limits of Translation. In B. Lewandowska-

Tomasczyk & M. Thelen（eds.），*Translation and Meaning*（Part 2，pp. 159 - 168）.
Maastricht：Rijkscogeschool Maastricht.

【问题与思考】

1. 多元系统与社会系统有何不同？二者有何关联？
2. 卢曼的社会系统论对翻译有多大的解释力？为什么？
3. 翻译到底是多元系统还是社会系统？或者两者都是？或者两者都不是？为什么？
4. 如何理解作为社会系统的翻译的自我再生性和自我指涉性？
5. 为什么说学习翻译的社会系统论可以拓展和深化我们对翻译系统或翻译多元系统的认识？

选文三　佐哈尔多元系统翻译理论的批评性阐释

吴耀武　张建青

导　言

本文发表于《外语教学》2010 年第 3 期。

本文认为佐哈尔的多元系统论与翻译研究有着密切的关系。文章指出，佐哈尔以多元系统论这一理论假说为基础系统论述了翻译文学在多元系统论中的位置，将翻译文学视为文学多元系统中的子系统，提倡客观描述翻译文学在译语文化中的接受与影响，以期有效揭示制约文学翻译的规范与规律。这就最终把翻译研究引向了文化研究的道路，为翻译研究开拓了一个相当广阔的研究领域。本文对此理论的主要特点、影响与局限及其在中国学界的译介情况进行了批评性阐释。

1　引言

伊塔马·埃文-佐哈尔（Itamar Even-Zohar）是以色列特拉维夫大学文化研究学院教授，著名文化理论家。"他有感于那种孤立地比较译文与原文的传统翻译批评，只反映批评者个人或者其所身处的社会的价值观，不能算是学术活动，而现存的翻译理论均不能作为全面地解释翻译这种复杂的文化现象的框架，于是在俄国形式主义和捷克结构主义的基础上，发展出一套崭新的理论——多元系统论（Polysystem Theory）。"（张南峰，2002：19）这一理论"对翻译研究产生了很大影响，因而（他）被视为'翻译研究学派'的先驱之一"（张南峰，2001：115）。

1979 年，他发表了著名的《多元系统论》（*Polysystem Theory*），后来还有 1990 年、1997 年两个修订版本，前两个版本主要针对文学和翻译研究，最后一个则针对文化研究。所以，多元系统论实际上已从文学理论演变成了一个普通文化理论。它虽常用于文学和翻译研究,但其实是一种普通文化理论,可用来指导任何一种文化现象的整体研究(张南峰,2001:61)。所以严格说来,他是文化理论家而不是翻译理论家(Gentzler,2001/2004:114)。

本文主要就其理论对翻译(文学)研究的影响与意义加以论述和探讨。

2 多元系统论主要内容

佐哈尔主要借鉴了20世纪20年代的俄国形式主义和捷克结构主义,特别是特尼亚诺夫的文学系统理论,从而构建了自己的多元系统论。他指出:在大多数欧洲语言中"系统"一词暗含"僵化的决定论"色彩,指"秩序",而其所用的"系统"这一术语实际完全可以用"关系网络"和"关系性思维"来表述(黄德先,2006:57)。2002年,他又简要概括其多元系统论的主要特点如下:

在系统概念指导之下的研究,重点不再是物质和材料的描述、罗列和分类,而是现象之间的相互关系,因此只需要较少的假说,就能解释各种现象,从而令人类学科发生巨大的变革。但是,为了发展出纯质的系统理论,多样性、冲突、矛盾、变化和时间的推移都被排除在一切系统分析之外;(这样一来)明显异质的现实被简约为同质。多元系统论则尝试改变这种传统,把上述参数纳入其中,令系统概念与异质性和时间的推移完全兼容。(佐哈尔/张南峰,1990/2002:19)

有论者引用佐哈尔的话将多元系统论的主要观点概括为:社会符号系统并非单一的系统,而是多元系统,也就是由若干个不同的系统组成系统……这些系统的地位并不平等,有的处于中心,有的处于边缘。但是多元系统并不是固定不变的。地位不同的系统永远在互相争夺中心位置。任何多元系统都是一个较大的多元系统即整体文化的组成部分,因此必然与整体文化以及整体内的其他多元系统相互关联;同时,它又可能与其他文化中的对应系统共同组成一个大多元系统(mega-或 macro-polysystem)。也就是说,任何一个多元系统里面的转变,都不能孤立地看待,而必须与整体文化甚至世界文化这个人类社会中最大的多元系统中的转变因素联系起来研究(张南峰,2002:19)。

就对翻译研究和文学研究的影响而言,佐哈尔1990年修订版 *Polysystem Theory* 最为重要,也最为系统,集中阐述了其多元系统论。其阐述分两大部分,第一部分分析了现代功能主义中的系统与多元系统,区分了两种理论,即静态系统理论与动态系统理论。第二部分则为"多元系统:过程与程序",也即解释多元系统论视角下进行具体研究的范式。

佐哈尔特别强调指出:多元系统论的原则之一,是绝不以价值判断为准则来预先选择研究对象。这一原则对文学研究尤其重要,因为仍然有人混淆文学批评(criticism)与学术研究(research)(佐哈尔,2002:21)。传统的学术研究把(单一的)系统完全等同于中心阶层(即官方文化,主要体现于标准语言、经典化文学和统治阶级的行为模式),无视各个边缘阶层的存在,或将其视为完全在系统之外(佐哈尔,1990/2002:21)。

3 翻译文学在多元系统论中的位置

以多元系统论为框架的研究,不应以价值判断作为选择研究对象的准则。在这套理论之下,把以前被忽略甚至被排斥的现象纳入研究范围不但成为可能,而且成为全面认识任何一个多元系统的必要条件(Zohar,1990:13)。早在1978年,佐哈尔就特别强调"很有必要将翻译文学纳入文学多元系统,而这点几乎全被忽略。但任何研究文学史的人都无法回避这一重要事实:在特定文学(系统)的共时与历时演进中,翻译(文学)起了十分重要的作用和影响"(Gentzler,2001/2004:116)。其论文《翻译文学在文学多元系统中的位置》(1978/revised 1990)对此提出了不少假说,论述非常系统和集中,也非常经典,对于翻译文学研究极具开拓价值和启发意义。

佐哈尔认为翻译文学既可能处于中心位置,也可能处于边缘位置,如翻译文学处于中心位置,主要有三种可能的情形:① 当一个(文学)多元系统尚未定型,即是说文学的发展尚属"幼嫩",有待确立;② 一种文学(在一组相关的文学的大体系中)处于"边缘"位置,或处于"弱势",或两者皆然;③ 一种文学出现了转折点、危机或文学真空(佐哈尔/庄柔玉,1990/2000:118;Venuti,2000:193-194)。

佐哈尔还特地指出:作为一个系统,翻译文学本身也有层次之分,而就多元系统的分析角度,关系的界定往往是以中心层次为着眼点,来观察系统内的各种关系。这即是说,在某部分翻译文学占据中心位置的同时,另一部分翻译文学可能处于边缘位置。文学之间的接触联系与翻译文学的地位息息相关。当外来文学大规模介入一个文学时,往往是译自重要源语的那一部分才占据中心位置,而不是全部翻译文学都占有同样的位置(佐哈尔/庄柔玉,1990/2000:121)。

最后佐哈尔总结指出:不仅是翻译的社会文学地位取决于它在多元系统内的位置,翻译的实践也完全由此主导。在一个抽离历史现实和社会背景的理想化状态中,我们根本连何谓翻译作品这个基本问题也不能回答,因为这个问题必须视多元系统的运作情况而定。由是观之,翻译其实并非一个本质和界限早已确定的一成不变的现象,而是一种随文化系统内的各种关系而变化的活动(佐哈尔/庄柔玉,1990/2000:123)。

4 贡献与不足

多元系统论对于推进翻译研究贡献巨大:其一,新范式对翻译研究影响深远;其二,推动了翻译研究的文化转向。正如贝克所言:"这一使不进行价值判断成为可能的非精英化、非规约化(描述主义)新范式对于翻译研究带来了深远的影响"(Baker,1998:177)。也如张南峰所论:"多元系统论给翻译研究开辟了一条描述性、面向译语系统的、功能主义的新途径;推动了翻译研究的文化转向,催生了一个跨国界的翻译研究学派"(张南峰,2002:20)。对此研究者多有公论。

但是批评之声也很多。随着时间的推移,国外有些学者已经指出了多元系统论的一些问题。如苏珊·巴斯奈特(Susan Bassnett)认为佐哈尔对文学系统状态的描述有些粗糙;赫曼斯认为佐哈尔对弱小、边缘的评价性陈述并不明晰,对系统演进的描述不仅非常抽象,而且给人决定论的感觉,似乎系统的演进是自主和周期性的;最后,佐哈尔将系统内部的变异完全局限于二元对立的因素,忽略了所有那些模棱两可、混杂不稳定、流动易变和交叉的因素(Hermans,1999:119)。根茨勒列举了对佐哈尔理论的四方面批评:① 试图假定普遍特质的存在,但却建基于很少的证据之上。② 不加批判地采用了形式主义文论框架,保留了形式主义的

"文学性"等诸多概念构建自己复杂的文化系统模式,但这些概念似乎又并不适合这一文化模式,乃至与其相互矛盾;尽管其模式基于历史主义,但佐哈尔仍保留"文学事实"这一基于陌生化形式主义价值系统的概念,这就与他本人宣称的"文学文本具有文化依赖性"相矛盾(Gentzler,2001/2004:121)。③ 倾向于关注抽象的模式而非"社会现实中实际"加诸文本和译者之上的各种制约因素;很少将文本与结合文本生产的"实际制约条件"结合起来研究,仅仅将文本与其假设的结构模式及抽象推论结合;重要的文学外部因素仍然远不在其分析视域。④ 佐哈尔自己的方法论和话语限制了其自身研究范围。(Gentzler,2001/2004:120-123;Munday,2001:111)我国学者也指出:多元系统论只考虑了制约翻译策略选择的客观文化因素,而忽视了作为翻译主体的人的主观能动性,因而不能很好地解释在同一客观的文化背景中可以有两种不同的策略取向的现象。其实,译者翻译策略的选择不仅仅由出发语文化在世界文化大系统里所处的地位决定,同时也深受译者对译语文化主观判定的影响(王东风,2000:2-8)。因而,如果要对佐哈尔多元系统论进行修正、完善,使其具有更大的理论解释力,就需要加进"翻译主体的主观能动性"一"元"(邵璐,2004:43)。

总的来说,佐哈尔和图里的(多元)系统理论帮助翻译研究冲破了某些概念障碍,找到了更好地描述翻译的方法,但是他们的案例研究的主要弱点似乎是没有充分利用这个理论,去研究语言多元系统和文学多元系统与其他多元系统(尤其是政治与意识形态两个系统)之间的相互关系(张南峰,2004:139-140)。对翻译的外部政治的研究者来说,佐哈尔的多元系统论把文化、社会等视为"符号主导的人类交际形式";这意味着它是面向符号学或通讯科学而不是面向行动和社会的……它之所以强调"模式和形式库"这类抽象的概念而不是强调"实际的政治和社会权力关系或者建制、团体之类的实体",似乎正是由于它的符号学根源……但符号只是现实的表面反映,因此问题在于,我们能否透过符号研究来认识符号背后的现实本身,而从社会文化的角度来看,现实才是最关键的。因此对于关注翻译的文化研究的学者而言,这一过于基于社会符号学的理论不可能是最合适的研究途径(张南峰,2004:145)。不过学者们正是受益于佐哈尔多元系统论这些并不完善的假设,并结合自己的研究才对系统概念进行了重要补充,如图里、切斯特曼的翻译规范;赫曼斯的操控理论和列费维尔的翻译改写论等概念。同时佐哈尔本人也对有关批评加以回应,并多次修订自己的理论。这些都进一步完善并发展了多元系统论,推动了翻译研究的迅速发展,翻译研究和学科地位也逐渐因此而牢固确立。

5 多元系统论在中国的批评性接受

佐哈尔的多元系统理论虽然在西方学术界早就引起了相当热烈的反响,但是国内学术界直至 20 世纪 80 年代末对其仍知之甚微。直至 20 世纪 90 年代初,随着我国改革开放政策的实施以及走出国门进行国际学术交流的学者越来越多,才开始有人接触到多元系统理论。

在国内学术界,我国香港、台湾的学者与多元系统理论的接触显然要比大陆学者早,他们在 1994 年即已直接聆听了埃文-佐哈尔的报告,但是令人遗憾的是,佐哈尔的多元系统理论在台港也同样在很长一段时间内"没有引起很大的回响"。在台港,佐哈尔的多元系统理论也要到 20 世纪 90 年代末、21 世纪初才真正引起人们的关注。2001 年第 3 期《中外文学》推出的"多元系统研究专辑"也许可视做这方面的一个标志(谢天振,2003:59-60)。

香港学者张南峰对于多元系统论的系统引进和提倡贡献颇大。2000 年他选编的《西方翻译理论精选》有庄柔玉译的埃文-佐哈尔《翻译文学在文学多元系统中的位置》一文。2002 年《中国翻译》第 4 期载有他精心所译的《多元系统论》，前有埃文-佐哈尔提供的英文摘要和他颇具匠心的译序。这些都大大促进了多元系统论在我国学界的传播与影响。1995 年他的《走出死胡同建立翻译学》提及多元系统论，后他又发表了有关的几篇重头文章，如 2001 年的《从多元系统论的角度看中国翻译研究的过去与未来》、2002 年的《多元系统论批评》和 2004 年的《多元系统翻译研究的前景》，在《多元系统翻译研究的前景》一文中张南峰还提供了自己的"多元系统论精细版"，《多元系统论批评》专门深入探讨了"多元系统论对翻译研究的贡献和其局限性"。这些在 2004 年都收录进其专著《中西译学批评》一书。王宏志教授在其《重释"信达雅"——20 世纪中国翻译研究》（1999）一书的"绪论"中也特别着重介绍过多元系统论，庄柔玉也在《翻译季刊》（2000）上发表《用多元系统研究翻译的意识形态的局限》一文，评论多元系统论。这些都大大促进了多元系统论在我国学界的传播与影响。

20 世纪 90 年代末，国内学者也纷纷关注并应用多元系统论进行翻译研究。其中翻译理论家谢天振的论文集《比较文学与翻译研究》（1994）已经关注了西方翻译研究中的"文化学派"（也称翻译研究派），并提及多元系统论；其专著《译介学》（1999）则有对其较为集中的评介和应用。2003 年他更是发表重要长篇论文《多元系统理论：翻译研究领域的拓展》，对多元系统论高度评价，总结指出它最终"把翻译研究引向了文化研究的道路，为翻译研究开拓了一个相当广阔的研究领域"（谢天振，2003：59）。廖七一教授的《当代西方翻译理论探索》（2000）对于多元系统论也有详细介绍和简要评论。邵璐 2004 年发表的《质疑，解构，颠覆？——论多元系统论的悖谬、误读与误用》、《国内翻译界在多元系统论上的误区》，名虽异内容基本相同。她针对国内误读、误用乃至滥用多元系统论的现象认真反思，分析细致、批评恳切，显示出作者扎实的学风和学术追求的勇气。

6　结束语

黄德先于 2005 年对佐哈尔本人进行了访谈，并将访谈录以"多元系统论释疑"为名发表于 2006 年第 2 期的《中国翻译》。由于多元系统论引起越来越多不同领域的学者高度关注，与此同时我国学者对于多元系统论的贡献和局限性众说纷纭，产生不少的分歧与疑问，对此佐哈尔认真细致地给予回应。因此可以说，多元系统理论一直是一个开放的、动态的、不断进行自我完善的理论体系。

【延伸阅读】

[1] 廖七一. 多元系统. 外国文学，2004(4)：48 - 52.

[2] 谢世坚. 从中国近代翻译文学看多元系统理论的局限性. 四川外语学院学报，2002(4)：103 - 108.

[3] 谢天振. 多元系统理论：翻译研究领域的拓展. 外国语（上海外国语大学学报），2003(4)：59 - 66.

[4] 张齐颜. 论多元系统理论对文学翻译的解释力的不充分性. 四川外语学院学报，2005(1)：100 - 103.

【问题与思考】

1. 本文是如何阐释佐哈尔多元系统理论的？
2. 本文是如何分析佐哈尔多元系统理论的贡献和不足的？
3. 本文是如何研究多元系统理论在中国的接受状况的？这种研究有何普遍意义？

第四章　翻译规范

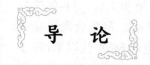

导　论

　　20世纪70年代后期,"翻译研究学派"在以色列和欧洲的一些国家兴起。该学派学者主要研究译本产生的文化背景,以及译本对目标语文化中的文学规范和文化规范所产生的影响。其中探讨翻译规范理论的代表人物有以色列的图里、英国的赫曼斯和荷兰的切斯特曼(Andrew Chesterman)等。

　　第一个系统地研究翻译规范的是图里,此后许多学者都对这个问题作了探讨。图里第一次明确提出翻译是受规范制约的行为。他对翻译规范的关注和研究开始于20世纪70年代他撰写博士论文的时候。他的研究集中在特定的历史时期。他在收集资料的过程中遇到难处:哪些文本应该包括译本,哪些应剔除在外。他发现尽管大部分译本在文字上与原文没有对应关系,但在译语文化里都被视做翻译。他考察了大量关于翻译的定义,最后提出了关于翻译的概念:翻译是由历史社会文化所决定的、由规范制约的行为。他认为规范在翻译行为和翻译过程中处于中心的地位。他就翻译规范的性质、种类、特征和重建规范的途径都作了深入探讨。

　　赫曼斯是另一重要的翻译规范论者,他吸收了图里的规范研究的积极成果,同时也批评了图里规范理论的不足,发展了图里的规范理论。他对翻译规范论的贡献主要有两个方面:第一,系统分析了规范的规定性;第二,由规范概念顺理成章地推导出抛弃对等概念的合理性。赫曼斯认为,规范意味着一定的社会和心理压力。规范通过排除某些选择来约束个人行为,并选择、规定或建议特定行为方式(Hermans,1996;廖七一,2001)。其规定性或者来源于某种社会压力,或者来源于个人认同该规范的态度,或两者兼而有之。规范涵盖常规与法令之间的全部领域,构成一连续体,连续体的一端是常规,另一端为法令,规范与规则位于两端之间。赫曼斯批评图里在其翻译规范理论中仍然保留对等观念,因为这会使人忽视翻译的不对等的方面,掩盖了翻译被操纵的实质;而规范概念正好把翻译的不对等方面推向前台。翻译的对等观念完全是虚构和妄想,译文不可能与原文同一。翻译受多种规范的制约,必然是混杂的、不透明的和有差异的。可能在实际翻译中需要对等的观念,但这一观念纯属虚构;某一层次上的对等总是被其他层次上的差异抵消。

　　切斯特曼是赫尔辛基大学的学者。他把不同时期从不同角度对翻译的不同看法纳入一个更加宏观的框架之下。切斯特曼把规范划分为期待规范(expectancy norms)和专业规范(professional norms)。期待规范是指目标语和社会对译者的期待,比如在可接受性、风格等方面的期待。这些期待部分地受到目标语文化所盛行的种种翻译传统的制约,部分地受到目标语文化中间类似文本类型形式的制约,也受到经济、意识形态等因素的影响。专业规范制约翻译过程中可接受的方法和策略。专业规范也可分为责任规范、交际规范及关系规范。责任规范是道德规范,也即译者接受委托人赋予他的翻译工作的责任。交际规范是一种社会规范,指译者应致力于使参与交际的各方获得最大程度的成功的交际。关系规范是一种语言规范,主要涉及两种语言之间的关系。切斯特曼对翻译规范的研究从本质上讲也是描述性的。他比较注重规范研究在具体翻译活动中的影响,比如:解释翻译者所采用的翻译策略,评价翻译作品,指导翻译教学和培训。

规范研究意义显著,它为我们解释一些翻译现象提供了一个理论框架和工具,对具体的翻译实践有指导意义,拓宽了翻译研究的领域,为人们更深入地思考翻译现象、最终合理解释各种翻译现象打下了基础。翻译规范研究起初只是在文学翻译领域,20世纪80年代以来,许多学者把规范概念运用到自己的语料库研究中,解决他们感兴趣的问题。还有些人把规范概念引入文学翻译范围之外的其他领域,比如同声传译的研究等。

本章共选三篇文章。第一篇是 Gideon Toury 撰写的"The Nature and Role of Norms in Translation",分析了规则、规范和特异倾向的区别,翻译规范的类别、属性,以及重建翻译规范的主要途径。第二篇是 Andrew Chesterman 著的"Translation Norms",对翻译规范作了细致的分类,发展了图里的翻译规范论。第三篇《翻译规范及其研究途径》为廖七一教授所著,研究了图里、切斯特曼、诺德、赫曼斯以及列费维尔等对翻译规范的描述,并在此基础上探讨了翻译规范的特性及研究途径。

选文一　The Nature and Role of Norms in Translation

Gideon Toury

导　言

本文选自韦努蒂编《翻译研究读本》。

图里的描述翻译学特别强调研究两种不同系统中作家、作品、读者及其文学翻译规范之间的关系,对源语和目的语的语用和接受关系,甚至包括出版发行等社会要素之间的关系进行探讨。在《翻译中规范的性质与作用》一文中,图里分析了规则、规范和特异倾向的区别,翻译规范的类别、属性和重建翻译规范的主要途径。他指出翻译是受社会文化规范制约的活动,其社会、文化特点使之不同程度地受到多种因素限制。翻译规范在某种程度上可以说是译者们在两种不同语言、文化、篇章传统规范之间取舍的产物。在翻译过程中,翻译者可受原文及其规范支配,也可受目标语中使用的规范支配。图里1995年出版的专著《描述翻译学及其他》的主要思想在本文中已基本成形。

However highly one may think of Linguistics, Text-Linguistics, Contrastive Textology or Pragmatics and of their explanatory power with respect to translational phenomena, being a translator cannot be reduced to the mere generation of utterances which would be considered "translations" within any of these disciplines. Translation activities should rather be regarded as having cultural significance. Consequently, "translatorship" amounts first and foremost to being able to *play a social role*, i. e., to fulfil a function allotted by a community—to the activity, its practitioners and/or their products—in a way which is deemed appropriate in its own terms of reference. The acquisition of a set of norms for determining the suitability of that kind of behaviour, and for manoeuvring between all the factors which may constrain it, is therefore a prerequisite for becoming a translator within a cultural environment.

The process by which a bilingual speaker may be said to gain recognition in his/her capacity as a translator has hardly been studied so far. [...] In the present chapter the nature of the acquired norms themselves will be addressed, along with their role in directing translation activity in socio-culturally relevant settings. This presentation will be followed by a brief discussion of translational norms as a second-order object of Translation Studies, to be reconstructed and studied within the kind of framework which we are now in the process of sketching. As strictly translational norms can only be applied at the *receiving* end, establishing them is not merely *justified* by a target-oriented approach but should be seen as its very *epitome*.

1　Rules, norms, idiosyncrasies

In its socio-cultural dimension, translation can be described as subject to constraints of several types and varying degree. These extend far beyond the source text; the systemic differences between the languages and textual traditions involved in the act, or even the possibilities and limitations of the cognitive apparatus of the translator as a necessary mediator. In fact, cognition itself is influenced, probably even modified by socio-cultural factors. At any rate, translators performing under different conditions (e. g., translating texts of different kinds, and/or for different audiences) often adopt different strategies, and ultimately come up with markedly different products. Something has obviously changed here, and I very much doubt it that it is the cognitive apparatus as such.

In terms of their potency, socio-cultural constraints have been described along a scale anchored between two extremes: general, relatively absolute *rules*, on the one hand and pure *idiosyncrasies* on the other. Between these two poles lies a vast middle-ground occupied by intersubjective factors commonly designated *norms*. The norms themselves form a graded continuum along the scale: Some are stronger, and hence more rule-like, others are weaker, and hence almost idiosyncratic. The borderlines between the various types of constraints are thus diffuse. Each of the concepts, including the grading itself, is relative too. Thus what is just a favoured mode of behaviour within a heterogeneous group may well acquire much more binding force within a certain (more homogeneous) section thereof, in terms of either human agents (e. g. , translators among texters in general) or types of activity (e. g. , interpreting, or legal translation, within translation at large).

Along the temporal axis, each type of constraint may, and often does move into its neighbouring domain(s) through processes of rise and decline. Thus, mere, whims may catch on and become more and more normative, and norms can gain so much validity that, for all practical purposes, they become as binding as rules; or the other way around, of course. Shifts of validity and force often have to do with changes of *status* within a society. In fact, they can always be described in connection with the notion of norm, especially since, as the process goes on, they are likely to cross its realm, i. e. , actually become norms. The other two types of constraints may even be redefined in terms of norms: rules as "[more] objective," idiosyncrasies as "[more] subjective [or: less intersubjective]" norms.

Sociologists and social psychologists have long regarded norms as the translation of general values or ideas shared by a community—as to what is right and wrong, adequate and inadequate—into performance instructions appropriate for and applicable to particular situations, specifying what is prescribed and forbidden as well as what is tolerated and permitted in a certain behavioural dimension (the famous "square of normativity," which has lately been elaborated on with regard to translation in De Geest, 1992, pp. 38 - 40). Norms are acquired by the individual during his/her socialization and always imply *sanctions*—actual or potential, negative as well as positive. Within the community, norms also serve as criteria according to which actual instances of behaviour are *evaluated*. Obviously, there is a point in assuming the existence of norms only in situations which allow for different kinds of behaviour, on the additional condition that selection among them be nonrandom. [①] Inasmuch as a norm is really active and effective, one can therefore distinguish regularity of behaviour in recurrent situations of the same type, which would render regularities a main source for any *study* of norms as well.

The centrality of the norms is not only metaphorical, then, in terms of their relative position along a postulated continuum of constraints; rather, it is essential: Norms are the key concept and focal point in any attempt to account for the social relevance of activities, because their existence, and the wide range of situations they apply to (with the conformity this implies), are the main factors ensuring the establishment and retention of social order. This holds for cultures too, or for any of the systems constituting them, which are, after all, social institutions *ipso facto*. Of course, behaviour which does *not* conform to prevailing norms is always possible too. Moreover, "non-compliance with a norm in particular instances does not invalidate the norm" (Hermans, 1991, p. 162). At the same time, there would

---

① "The existence of norms is a sine qua non in instances of labelling and regulating; without a norm, all deviations are meaningless and become cases of free variation" (Wexler, 1974, p. 4, n. 1).

normally be a price to pay for opting for any deviant kind of behaviour.

One thing to bear in mind, when setting out to study norm-governed behaviour, is that there is no necessary identity between the norms themselves and any formulation of them in language. Verbal formulations of course reflect *awareness* of the existence of norms as well as of their respective significance. However, they also imply other interests, particularly a desire to *control* behaviour, i. e. , to dictate norms rather than merely account for them. Normative formulations tend to be slanted, then, and should always be taken with a grain of salt.

2 Translation as a norm-governed activity

Translation is a kind of activity which inevitably involves at least two languages and two cultural traditions, i. e. , at least two sets of norm-systems on each level. Thus, the "value" behind it may be described as consisting of two major elements:

(1) being a text in a certain language, and hence occupying a position, or filling in a slot, in the appropriate culture, or in a certain section thereof;

(2) constituting a representation in that language/culture of another, preexisting text in some other language, belonging to some other culture and occupying a definite position within it.

These two types of requirement derive from two sources which—even though the distance between them may vary greatly—are nevertheless always different and therefore often incompatible. Were it not for the regulative capacity of norms, the tensions between the two sources of constraints would have to be resolved on an entirely *individual* basis, and with no clear yardstick to go by. Extreme free variation may well have been the result, which it certainly is not. Rather, translation behaviour within a culture tends to manifest certain *regularities*, one consequence being that even if they are unable to account for deviations in any explicit way, the persons-in-the-culture can often tell when a translator has failed to adhere to sanctioned practices.

It has proven useful and enlightening to regard the basic choice which can be made between requirements of the two different sources as constituting an **initial norm.** Thus, a translator may subject him-/herself either to the original text, with the norms it has realized, or to the norms active in the target culture, or, in that section of it which would host the end product. If the first stance is adopted, the translation will tend to subscribe to the norms of the source text, and through them also to the norms of the source language and culture. This tendency, which has often been characterized as the pursuit of adequate translation,[1] may well entail certain incompatibilities with target norms and practices, especially those lying beyond the mere linguistic ones. If, on the other hand, the second stance is adopted, norms systems of the target culture are triggered and set into motion. Shifts from the source text would be an almost inevitable price. Thus, whereas adherence to source norms determines a translation's adequacy as compared to the source text, subscription to norms originating in the target culture determines its acceptability.

Obviously, even the most adequacy-oriented translation involves shifts from the source text. In fact, the occurrence of shifts has long been acknowledged as a true universal of translation. However, since the need itself to deviate from source-text patterns can always be realized in more than one way, the actual *realization* of so-called obligatory shifts, to the extent that it is non-random, and hence not idiosyncratic, is already truly norm-governed. So is everything that has to do with non-obligatory shifts, which are of course more than just possible in real-life translation: They occur everywhere and tend to constitute the majority of shifting in any single act of human translation, rendering the latter a contributing factor to, as well as the epitome of regularity.

The term "initial norm" should not be overinterpreted, however. Its initiality derives from its superordinance over particular norms which pertain to lower, and therefore more specific levels. The kind of priority postulated here is basically *logical*, and need not coincide with any "real," i. e. , *chronological* order of application. The notion is thus designed to serve first and foremost as an *explanatory tool*. Even if no clear macro-level tendency can be shown, any micro-level decision can still be accounted for in terms of adequacy vs. acceptability. On the other hand, in cases where an overall choice has been made, it is not necessary that every single lower-level decision be made in full accord with it. We are still talking regularities, then, but not necessarily of any absolute type. It is unrealistic to expect absolute regularities anyway, in any behavioural domain.

Actual translation decisions (the results of which the researcher would confront) will necessarily involve some ad hoc combination of, or compromise between the two extremes implied by the initial norm. Still, for theoretical and methodological reasons, it seems wiser to retain the opposition and treat the two poles as distinct in principle: If they are not regarded as having distinct *theoretical* statuses, how would compromises differing in type or in extent be distinguished and accounted for?

Finally, the claim that it is basically a norm-governed type of behaviour applies to translation of all kinds, not only literary, philosophical or biblical translation, which is where most norm-oriented studies have been conducted so far. As has recently been claimed and demonstrated in an all too sketchy exchange of views in *Target* (Shlesinger, 1989; Harris, 1990), similar things can even be said of *conference interpreting*. Needless to say, this does

---

① "An adequate translation is a translation which realizes in the target language the textual relationships of a source text with no breach of its own [basic] linguistic system" (Even-Zohar, 1975, p. 43; my translation).

not mean that the exact same conditions apply to all kinds of translation. In fact, their application in different cultural sectors is precisely one of the aspects that should be submitted to study. In principle, the claim is also valid for every society and historical period, thus offering a framework for historically oriented studies which would also allow for comparison.

3 Translation norms: an overview

Norms can be expected to operate not only in translation of all kinds, but also at every stage in the translating event, and hence to be reflected on every level of its product. It has proven convenient to first distinguish two larger groups of norms applicable to translation: preliminary vs. operational.

Preliminary norms have to do with two main sets of considerations which are often interconnected: those regarding the existence and actual nature of a definite translation policy, and those related to the directness of translation.

Translation policy refers to those factors that govern the choice of text types; or even of individual texts, to be imported through translation into a particular culture/language at a particular point in time. Such a policy will be said to exist inasmuch as the choice is found to be non-random. Different policies may of course apply to different subgroups, in terms of either text-types (e. g. literary vs. non-literary) or human agents and groups thereof (e. g. different publishing houses), and the interface between the two often offers very fertile grounds for policy hunting.

Considerations concerning *directness of translation* involve the threshold of tolerance for translating from languages other than the ultimate source language: Is indirect translation permitted at all? In translating from what source languages/text-types/periods (etc.) is it permitted/prohibited/tolerated/preferred? What are the permitted/prohibited/tolerated/preferred mediating languages? Is there a tendency/obligation to mark a translated work as having been mediated or is this fact ignored/camouflaged/denied? If it is mentioned, is the identity of the mediating language supplied as well? And so on.

Operational norms, in turn, may be conceived of as directing the decisions made during the act of translation itself. They affect the matrix of the text—i. e. , the modes of distributing linguistic material in it—as well as the textual make up and verbal formulation as such. They thus govern—directly or indirectly—the relationships as well that would obtain between the target and source texts, i. e. , what is more likely to remain invariant under transformation and what will change.

So-called *matricial norms* may govern the very *existence* of target-language material intended as a substitute for the corresponding source-language material (and hence the degree of *fullness* of translation), its location in the text (or the form of actual *distribution*), as well as the textual *segmentation*. ① The extent to which omissions, additions, changes of location and manipulations of segmentation are referred to in the translated texts (or around them) may also be determined by norms, even though the one can very well occur without the other.

Obviously, the borderlines between the various matricial phenomena are not clear-cut. For instance, large-scale omissions often entail changes of segmentation as well, especially if the omitted portions have no clear boundaries, or textual-linguistic standing, i. e., if they are not integral sentences, paragraphs or chapters. By the same token, a change of location may often be accounted for as an omission (in one place) compensated by an addition (elsewhere). The decision as to what may have "really" taken place is thus description-bound: What one is after is (more or less cogent) *explanatory hypotheses*, not necessarily "true-to-life" accounts, which one can never be sure of anyway.

Textual-linguistic norms, in turn, govern the selection of material to formulate the target text in, or replace the original textual and linguistic material with. Textual-linguistic norms may either be *general*, and hence apply to translation qua translation, or *particular*, in which case they would pertain to a particular text-type and/or mode of translation only. Some of them may be identical to the norms governing non-translational text-production, but such an identity should never be taken for granted. This is the methodological reason why no study of translation can, or should proceed from the assumption that the later is representative of the target language, or of any overall textual tradition thereof. (And see our discussion of "translation-specific lexical items. ")

It is clear that preliminary norms have both logical and chronological precedence over the operational ones. This is not to say that between the two major groups there are no relationships whatsoever, including mutual influences or even two-way conditioning. However, these relations are by no means fixed and given, and their establishment forms an inseparable part of any study of translation as a norm-governed activity. Nevertheless, we can safely assume at least that the relations which do exist have to do with the initial norm. They might even be found to *intersect* it—another important reason to retain the opposition between "adequacy" and "acceptability" as a basic coordinate system for the formulation of explanatory hypotheses. ②

---

① The claim that principles of segmentation follow *universal* patterns is just a figment of the imagination of some discourse and text theoreticians intent on uncovering as many universal principles as possible. In actual fact, there have been various traditions (or "models") of segmentation, and the differences between them always have implications for translation, whether they are taken to bear on the formulation of the target text or ignored. Even the segmentation of sacred texts such as the Old Testament itself has often been tampered with by its translators, normally in order to bring it closer to *target* cultural habits, and by so doing enhance the translation's acceptability.

② Thus, for instance, in sectors where the pursuit of adequate translation is marginal, it is highly probable that indirect translation would also become common, on occasion even preferred over direct translation. By contrast, a norm which prohibits mediated translation is likely to be connected with a growing proximity to the initial norm of adequacy. Under such circumstances, if indirect translation is still performed, the fact will at least be concealed, if not outright denied.

Operational norms as such may be described as serving as a model, in accordance with which translations come into being, whether involving the norms realized by the source text (i. e. , adequate translation) plus certain modifications or purely target norms, or a particular compromise between the two. Every model supplying performance instructions may be said to act as a *restricting* factor: It opens up certain options while closing others. Consequently, when the first position is fully adopted, the translation can hardly be said to have been made into the target language as a whole. Rather, it is made into a model language, which is at best some part of the former and at worst an artificial, and as such nonexistent variety. ① In this last case, the translation is not really *introduced* into the target culture either, but is *imposed* on it, so to speak. Sure, it may eventually carve a niche for itself in the latter, but there is no initial attempt to accommodate it to any existing "slot. " On the other hand, when the second position is adopted, what a translator is introducing into the target culture (which is indeed what she/he can be described as doing now) is a *version* of the original work, cut to the measure of a preexisting model. (And see our discussion of the opposition between the "translation of literary texts" and "literary translation" as well as the detailed presentation of the Hebrew translation of a German *Schlaraffenland* text.)

The apparent contradiction between any traditional concept of equivalence and the limited model into which a translation has just been claimed to be moulded can only be resolved by postulating that **it is norms that determine the (type and extent of) equivalence manifested by actual translations.** The study of norms thus constitutes a vital step towards establishing just how the functional-relational postulate of equivalence has been realized—whether in one translated text, in the work of a single translator or "school" of translators, in a given historical period, or in any other justifiable selection. ② What this approach entails is a clear wish to retain the notion of equivalence, which various contemporary approaches (e. g. , Hönig & Kussmaul, 1982; Holz-Mänttäri, 1984; Snell-Hornby, 1988) have tried to do without, while introducing one essential change into it: from an ahistorical, largely prescriptive concept to a historical one. Rather than being a single relationship, denoting a recurring type of invariant, it comes to refer to any relation which is found to have characterized translation under a specified set of circumstances.

At the end of a full-fledged study it will probably be found that translational norms, hence the realization of the equivalence postulate, are all, to a large extent, dependent on the

---

① And see, in this connection, Izre'el's "Rationale for Translating Ancient Texts into a Modern Language" (1994). In an attempt to come up with a method for translating an Akkadian myth which would be presented to modern Israeli audiences in an oral performance, he purports to combine a "feeling-of-antiquity" with a "feeling-of-modernity" in a text which would be altogether simple and easily comprehensible by using a host of lexical items of *biblical* Hebrew in *Israeli* Hebrew grammatical and syntactic structures. Whereas "the lexicon... would serve to give an ancient flavor to the text, the grammar would serve to enable modern perception. " It might be added that this is a perfect mirror image of the way Hebrew translators started simulating spoken Hebrew in their texts: Spoken lexical items were inserted in grammatical and syntactic structures which were marked for belonging to the written varieties (Ben-Shahar, 1983), which also meant "new" into "old. "

② See also my discussion of "Equivalence and Non-Equivalence as a Function of Norms" (Toury, 1980, pp. 63 – 70).

position held by translation—the activity as well as its products—in the target culture. An interesting field for study is therefore comparative: the nature of translational norms as compared to those governing non-translational kinds of text-production. In fact, this kind of study is absolutely vital, if translating and translations are to be appropriately contextualized.

4 The multiplicity of translational norms

The difficulties involved in any attempt to account for translational norms should not be underestimated. These, however, lie first and foremost in two features inherent in the very notion of norm, and are therefore not unique to Translation Studies at all: the socio-cultural specificity of norms and their basic instability.

Thus, whatever its exact content, there is absolutely no need for a norm to apply—to the same extent, or at all—to all sectors within a society. Even less necessary, or indeed likely, is it for a norm to apply across cultures. In fact, "sameness" here is a mere coincidence—or else the result of continuous contacts between subsystems within a culture, or between entire cultural systems, and hence a manifestation of interference. (For some general rules of systemic interference see Even-Zohar, 1990, pp. 53 – 72.) Even then, it is often more a matter of apparent than of a genuine identity. After all, significance is only attributed to a norm by the *system* in which it is embedded, and the systems remain different even if instances of external behaviour appear the same.

In addition to their inherent specificity, norms are also unstable, changing entities; not because of any intrinsic flaw but by their very nature as norms. At times, norms change rather quickly; at other times, they are more enduring, and the process may take longer. Either way, substantial changes, in translational norms too, quite often occur within one's life-time.

Of course it is not as if all translators are *passive* in face of these changes. Rather, many of them, through their very activity, help in shaping the process, as do translation criticism, translation ideology (including the one emanating from contemporary academe, often in the guise of theory), and, of course, various norm-setting activities of institutes where, in many societies, translators are now being trained. Wittingly or unwittingly, they all try to interfere with the "natural" course of events and to divert it according to their own preferences. Yet the success of their endeavours is never fully foreseeable. In fact, the relative role of different agents in the overall dynamics of translational norms is still largely a matter of conjecture even for times past, and much more research is needed to clarify it.

Complying with social pressures to constantly adjust one's behaviour to norms that keep changing is of course far from simple, and most people, including translators, initiators of translation activities and the consumers of their products, do so only up to a point. Therefore, it is not all that rare to find side by side in a society three types of competing norms, each having its own followers and a position of its own in the culture at large: the ones that dominate the centre of the system, and hence direct translational behaviour of the so-called *mainstream*, alongside the remnants of *previous* sets of norms and the rudiments of *new* ones, hovering in the periphery. This is why it is possible to speak—and not derogatorily— of being "trendy," "old-fashioned" or "progressive" in translation (or in any single section thereof) as it is in any other behavioural domain.

One's status as a translator may of course be temporary, especially if one fails to adjust to the changing requirements, or does so to an extent which is deemed insufficient. Thus, as changes of norms occur, formerly "progressive" translators may soon find themselves just "trendy," or on occasion as even downright "*passé.*" At the same time, regarding this process as involving a mere alternation of generations can be misleading, especially if generations are directly equated with age groups. While there often are correlations between one's position along the "dated"—"mainstream"—"avant-garde" axis and one's age, these cannot, and should not be taken as inevitable, much less as a starting point and framework for the study of norms in action. Most notably, young people who are in the early phases of their initiation as translators often behave in an extremely epigonic way: They tend to perform according to dated, but still existing norms, the more so if they receive reinforcement from agents holding to dated norms, be they language teachers, editors, or even teachers of translation.

Multiplicity and variation should not be taken to imply that there is no such thing as norms active in translation. They only mean that real-life situations tend to be complex; and this complexity had better be noted rather than ignored, if one is to draw any justifiable conclusions. As already argued, the only viable way out seems to be to contextualize every phenomenon, every item, every text, every act, on the way to allotting the different norms themselves their appropriate position and valence. This is why it is simply unthinkable, from the point of view of the study of translation as a norm-governed activity, for all items to be treated on a par, as if they were of the same systemic position, the same significance, the same level of representativeness of the target culture and its constraints. Unfortunately, such an indiscriminate approach has been all too common, and has often led to a complete blurring of the normative picture, sometimes even to the absurd claim that no norms could be detected at all. The only way to keep that picture in focus is to go beyond the establishment of mere "check-lists" of factors which may occur in a corpus and have the lists *ordered*, for instance with respect to the status of those factors as characterizing "mainstream," "dated" and "avant-garde" activities, respectively.

This immediately suggests a further axis of contextualization, whose necessity has so far only been implied; namely, the *historical* one. After all, a norm can only be marked as "dated" if it was active in a *previous* period, and if, at that time, it had a different, "non-dated" position. By the same token, norm-governed behaviour can prove to have been "avant-garde" only in view of *subsequent* attitudes towards it: An idiosyncrasy which never evolved into something more general can only be described as a norm by extension, so to speak (see Section 1 above). Finally, there is nothing inherently "mainstream" about mainstream behaviour, except when it happens to function as such, which means that it too is time-bound. What I am claiming here, in fact, is that historical contextualization is a must not only for a *diachronic* study, which nobody would contest, but also for *synchronic* studies, which still seems a lot less obvious unless one has accepted the principles of so-called "Dynamic Functionalism" (for which, see the Introduction to Even-Zohar 1990[①] and Sheffy 1992: passim).

Finally, in translation too, *non-normative behaviour* is always a possibility. The price for selecting this option may be as low as a (culturally determined) need to submit the end product to revision. However, it may also be far more severe to the point of taking away one's earned recognition as a translator; which is precisely why non-normative behaviour tends to be the exception, in actual practice. On the other hand, in retrospect, deviant instances of behaviour may be found to have effected *changes* in the very system. This is why they constitute an important field of study, as long as they are regarded as what they have really been and are not put indiscriminately into one basket with all the rest. Implied are intriguing questions such as who is "allowed" by a culture to introduce changes and under what circumstances such changes may be expected to occur and/or be accepted.

5　Studying translational norms

So far we have discussed norms mainly in terms of their activity during a translation event and their effectiveness in the act of translation itself. To be sure, this is precisely where and when translational norms are active. However, what is actually available for observation is not so much the norms themselves, but rather norm-governed instances of behaviour. To be even more precise, more often than not, it is the products of such behaviour. Thus, even when translating is claimed to be studied directly, as is the case with the use of "Thinking-Aloud Protocols," it is only *products* which are available, although products of a different kind and order. Norms are not directly observable, then, which is all the more reason why something should also be said about them in the context of an attempt to *account* for translational behaviour.

---

①　"There is a clear difference between an attempt to account for some major principles which govern a system outside the realm of time, and one which intends to account for how a system operates both 'in principle' and 'in time.' Once the historical aspect is admitted into the functional approach, several implications must be drawn. First, it must be admitted that both synchrony and diachrony are historical, but the exclusive identification of the latter with history is untenable. As a result, synchrony cannot and should not be equated with statics, since at any given moment, more than one diachronic set is operating on the synchronic axis. Therefore, on the one hand a system consists of both synchrony and diachrony; on the other, each of these separately is obviously also a system. Secondly, if the idea of structuredness and systemicity need no longer be identified with homogeneity, a semiotic system can be conceived of as a heterogeneous, open structure. It is, therefore, very rarely a uni-system but is, necessarily, a polysystem" (Even-Zohar, 1990, p. 11).

There are two major sources for a reconstruction of translational norms, textual and extratextual:[①]

(1) **textual**: the translated texts themselves, for all kinds of norms, as well as analytical inventories of translations (i. e., "virtual" texts), for various preliminary norms;

(2) **extratextual**: semi-theoretical or critical formulations, such as prescriptive "theories" of translation, statements made by translators, editors, publishers, and other persons involved in or connected with the activity, critical appraisals of individual translations, or the activity of a translator or "school" of translators, and so forth.

There is a fundamental difference between these two types of source: Texts are *primary* products of norm-regulated behaviour, and can therefore be taken as immediate representations thereof. Normative pronouncements, by contrast, are merely *by*-products of the existence and activity of norms. Like any attempt to formulate a norm, they are partial and biased, and should therefore be treated with every possible circumspection; all the more so since—emanating as they do from interested parties—they are likely to lean toward propaganda and persuasion. There may therefore be gaps, even contradictions, between explicit arguments and demands, on the one hand, and actual behaviour and its results, on the other, due either to subjectivity or naïveté, or even lack of sufficient knowledge on the part of those who produced the formulations. On occasion, a deliberate desire to mislead and deceive may also be involved. Even with respect to the translators themselves, intentions do not necessarily concur with any declaration of intent (which is often put down post factum anyway, when the act has already been completed); and the way those intentions are realized may well constitute a further, third category still.

Yet all these reservations—proper and serious though they may be—should not lead one to abandon semi-theoretical and critical formulations as legitimate sources for the study of norms. In spite of all its faults, this type of source still has its merits, both in itself and as a possible key to the analysis of actual behaviour. At the same time, if the pitfalls inherent in them are to be avoided, normative pronouncements should never be accepted at face value. They should rather be taken as *pre-systematic* and given an explication in such a way as to place them in a narrow and precise framework, lending the resulting explicata the coveted systematic status. While doing so, an attempt should be made to clarify the status of each formulation, however slanted and biased it may be, and uncover the sense in which it was not just accidental; in other words how, in the final analysis, it does reflect the cultural constellation within which, and for whose purposes it was produced. Apart from sheer

---

① Cf. e. g., Vodicka (1964, p. 74), on the possible sources for the study of literary norms, and Wexler (1974, pp. 7 - 9), on the sources for the study of prescriptive intervention ("purism") in language.

speculation, such an explication should involve the comparison of various normative pronouncements to each other, as well as their repeated confrontation with the patterns revealed by [the results of] actual behaviour and the norms reconstructed from them—all this with full consideration for their contextualization. (See a representative case in Weissbrod, 1989.)

It is natural, and very convenient, to commence one's research into translational behaviour by focusing on *isolated* norms pertaining to well-defined behavioural dimensions, be they—and the coupled pairs of replacing and replaced segments representing them—established from the source text's perspective (e. g. , translational replacements of source metaphors) or from the target text's vantage point (e. g. , binomials of near-synonyms as translational replacements). However, translation is intrinsically *multi*-dimensional: The manifold phenomena it presents are tightly interwoven and do not allow for easy isolation, not even for methodical purposes. Therefore, research should never get stuck in the blind alley of the "paradigmatic" phase which would at best yield lists of "normemes," or discrete norms. Rather, it should always proceed to a "syntagmatic" phase, involving the *integration* of normemes pertaining to various problem areas. Accordingly, the student's task can be characterized as an attempt to establish what *relations* there are between norms pertaining to various domains by correlating his/her individual findings and weighing them against each other. Obviously, the thicker the network of relations thus established, the more justified one would be in speaking in terms of a normative *structure* (cf. Jackson, 1960, pp. 149 – 160) or *model*.

This having been said, it should again be noted that a translator's behaviour cannot be expected to be fully systematic. Not only can his/her decision-making be differently motivated in different problem areas, but it can also be unevenly distributed throughout an assignment within a single problem area. Consistency in translational behaviour is thus a *graded* notion which is neither nil (i. e. , total erraticness) nor 1 (i. e. , absolute regularity); its extent should emerge at the end of a study as one of its conclusions, rather than being presupposed.

The American sociologist Jay Jackson suggested a "Return Potential Curve," showing the distribution of approval/disapproval among the members of a social group over a range of behaviour of a certain type as a model for the representation of norms. This model (reproduced as Figure 1) makes it possible to make a gradual distinction between norms in terms of *intensity* (indicated by the height of the curve, its distance from the horizontal axis), the *total range of tolerated behaviour* (that part of the behavioural dimension approved by the group), and the *ratio* of one of these properties of the norm to the others.

One convenient division that can be re-interpreted with the aid of this model is tripartite: [1]

---

[1] Cf. e. g. , Hrushovski's similar division (in Ben-Porat & Hrushovski, 1974, pp. 9-10) and its application to the description of the norms of Hebrew rhyme (in Hrushovski, 1971).

a. **Basic (primary) norms**, more or less mandatory for *all* instances of a certain behaviour (and hence their minimal common denominator). Occupy the apex of the curve. Maximum intensity, minimum latitude of behaviour.

b. **Secondary norms, or tendencies**, determining favourable behaviour. May be predominant in certain *parts* of the group. Therefore common enough, but not mandatory, from the point of view of the group as a whole. Occupy that part of the curve nearest its apex and therefore less intensive than the basic norms but covering a greater range of behaviour.

c. **Tolerated (permitted) behaviour.** Occupies the rest of the "positive" part of the curve (i. e. , that part which lies above the horizontal axis), and therefore of minimal intensity.

"A special group," detachable from (c), seems to be of considerable interest and importance, at least in some behavioural domains:

c′. **Symptomatic devices.** Though these devices may be infrequently used, their occurrence is typical for narrowing segments of the group under study. On the other hand, their absolute *non*-occurrence can be typical of other segments.

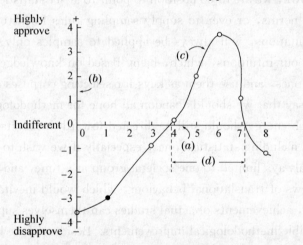

Figure 1 Schematic diagram showing the Return Potential Model for representing norms: (a) a behaviour dimension; (b) an evaluation dimension; (c) a return potential curve, showing the distribution of approval-disapproval among the members of a group over the whole range of behaviour; (d) the range of tolerable or approved behaviour.

Source: Jackson, 1960.

We may, then, safely assume a *distributional* basis for the study of norms: The more frequent a target-text phenomenon, a shift from a (hypothetical) adequate reconstruction of a source text, or a translational relation, the more likely it is to reflect (in this order) a more permitted (tolerated) activity, a stronger tendency, a more basic (obligatory) norm. A second aspect of norms, their *discriminatory capacity*, is thus reciprocal to the first, so that the less frequent a behaviour, the smaller the group it may serve to define. At the same time, the group it does define is not just any group; it is always a sub-group of the one constituted by higher-rank norms. To be sure, even idiosyncrasies (which, in their extreme, constitute groups-of-one) often manifest themselves as personal ways of realizing [more] general attitudes rather than deviations in a completely unexpected direction. [1] Be that as it may, the retrospective establishment of norms is always relative to the section under study, and no automatic upward projection is possible. Any attempt to move in that direction and draw generalizations would require further study, which should be targeted towards that particular end.

Finally, the curve model also enables us to redefine one additional concept: the actual *degree of conformity* manifested by different members of a group to a norm that has already been extracted from a corpus, and hence found relevant to it. This aspect can be defined in terms of the distance from the point of maximum return (in other words, from the curve's apex).

Notwithstanding the points made in the last few paragraphs, the argument for the distributional aspect of the norms should not be pushed too far.

As is so well known, we are in no position to point to strict statistical methods for dealing with translational norms, or even to supply sampling rules for actual research (which, because of human limitations, will always be applied to samples only). At this stage we must be content with our intuitions, which, being based on knowledge and previous experience, are "learned" ones, and use them as keys for selecting corpuses and for hitting upon ideas. This is not to say that we should abandon all hope for methodological improvements. On the contrary: Much energy should still be directed toward the crystallization of systematic research methods, including statistical ones, especially if we wish to transcend the study of norms, which are always limited to one societal group at a time, and move on to the formulation of general laws of translational behaviour, which would inevitably be *probabilistic* in nature. To be sure, achievements of actual studies can themselves supply us with clues as to necessary and possible methodological improvements. Besides, if we hold up research until the most systematic methods have been found, we might never get any research done.

【延伸阅读】

[1] Hermans, T. (1996). Norms and the Determination of Translation: A Theoretical Framework. In R. Alvarez and M. Carmen-Africa Vidal (eds.), *Translation*, *Power*, *Subversion* (pp. 25 – 51). UK: Multilingual Matters Ltd.

[2] Komissarov, V. (1993). Norms in Translation. In P. Zlateva (ed.), *Translation as Social Action: Russian and Bulgarian Perspectives* (pp. 63 – 75). London and New

---

① And see the example of the seemingly idiosyncratic use of Hebrew *ki-xen* as a translational replacement of English "well" in a period when the norm dictates the use of *lu-vexen*.

York：Routledge.

[3] Toury，G.（1995）. *Descriptive Translation Studies—And Beyond*. Amsterdam and Philadelphia，PA：John Benjamins.

[4] 韩江洪. 国外翻译规范研究述评. 解放军外国语学院学报，2004(2)：53－56.

[5] 吴欣欣. 图里翻译规范论评介——读《翻译中规范的性质与作用》. 成才之路，2008：19.

【问题与思考】

1. 图里翻译规范论的来源是什么？佐哈尔的多元系统论对图里有何影响？
2. 图里关于翻译规范的分类有何合理性和不足？
3. 翻译规范是可以重建的吗？试分析图里提出的翻译规范重建途径的有效性。
4. 如何运用图里的翻译规范论指导翻译研究？
5. 描述性翻译理论与规定性翻译理论相比有何异同？

选文二　Translation Norms（Excerpt）

Andrew Chesterman

导　言

本文为切斯特曼专著《翻译模因论》的第三章，论述了翻译规范问题，这也是他对图里的规范论的新发展。他对翻译规范作了细致的分类：社会规范(social norms)、伦理规范(ethical norms)和技术规范(technical norms)。社会规范协调人与人之间的关系；伦理规范指译者应该坚持"明晰、真实、信任和理解"的价值标准；而技术规范之下又分产品规范和生产规范。产品规范又称期待规范，生产规范亦称专业规范，生产规范从属并受制于期待规范。专业规范又可再细分为"责任规范"、"交际规范"和"关系规范"，前两种规范涉及人类所有的交际活动，而第三种规范则涉及文学翻译的核心问题。

3.5.1　Toury's norms

Some norms function as "solutions to problems posed by certain interaction situations" (Ullmann-Margalit, 1977, p. 9; cited by Bartsch, 1987, p. 104). Translation norms are of this type, for they exist to regulate the process whereby communication can take place in a situation where it would otherwise be impossible. The applicability of norm theory to translation studies has been pioneered by Toury, and I shall outline his ideas first. (See also Hermans，1991)

Toury's original interest in the late 1970s (see e. g. 1980, and also 1995) was in literary translation, and his initial framework of norms was set up with that in mind. This framework starts with *preliminary norms*: These have to do with translation policy in a given culture—what works of literature are deemed by publishers and others to be worth translating, and whether or not these can be translated through an intermediate language ("secondary translation"). These are questions of social, cultural and economic policy, perhaps also political policy, and fall outside the main focus of this book. The norms that interest me here are those that come into play after a client has commissioned a translation, those that guide the translator's work itself.

These norms, which "direct actual decisions made during the translation process" (1980, p. 54), Toury calls *operational norms*. Here he includes all the norms that affect the "matrix" of the text, its segmentation and verbal formulation (cf. Toury, 1995, p. 58). They are "textual norms," either generally linguistic/stylistic or specifically literary (determining appropriate genres etc.). In norm-theoretical terms, Toury's operational norms are primarily product norms, regulating the form of a translation as a final product. As such, of course, they also affect the decision-making process, although Toury gives less emphasis to process norms. He does, however, postulate one additional type of norm which he calls the *initial norm*. This has to do with "the translator's basic choice between two polar alternatives" (1980, p. 54), subjecting himself "either to the original text, with its textual relations and the norms expressed by it and contained in it, or to the linguistic and literary norms active in TL [the target language] and in the target literary polysystem, or a certain section of it" (1980, p. 54). The choice of the source language as initial norm leads to a translation that is "adequate," and the choice of target language norms to one that is "acceptable. " (This use of the term "adequate" has been adopted by some scholars but is avoided by others on account of its ambiguity: Still others use "adequate" to mean what Toury means by "acceptable. " I shall henceforth avoid the term.)

3. 5. 2 Expectancy norms

The following analysis of translation norms concerns the area covered by Toury's operational and initial norms, but from a different angle. I start by positing two kinds of translation norms, corresponding quite conventionally to product norms and process norms. I will take the product ones first. Because, as argued above, these product norms are ultimately constituted by the expectancies of the target language readership, I shall call these *expectancy norms*.

Expectancy norms are established by the expectations of readers of a translation (of a given type) concerning what a translation (of this type) should be like. These expectations are partly governed by the prevalent translation tradition in the target culture, and partly by the form of parallel texts (of a similar text-type) in the target language (cf. Hermans,

1991), i. e. by the prevalent scenes and frames in the target culture. They can also be influenced by economic or ideological factors, power relations within and between cultures and the like. They cover a wide range of phenomena. Readers (who may or may not include the client) may have expectations about text-type and discourse conventions, about style and register, about the appropriate degree of grammaticality, about the statistical distribution of text features of all kinds, about collocations, lexical choice, and so on. Hermans (1991, p. 166) puts it this way:

> [T]he "correct" translation ... is the one that fits the correctness notions prevailing in a particular system, i. e. that adopts the solutions regarded as correct for a given communicative situation, as a result of which it is accepted as correct. In other words: When translators do what is expected of them, they will be seen to have done well.

Agreed. However, note that "correct" here does not need to imply the existence of a single correct translation; rather, as "correctness notions," norms can be met in a variety of ways. There is usually more than one way in which translators can do what is expected of them. We might therefore prefer to speak of translations being more or less "appropriate" or "acceptable" or the like. We can thus seek to define a range of possible translations, within which several may be "appropriate." even if some are felt to be better than others.

Expectancy norms thus also allow us to make evaluative judgements about translations. Some translations may conform to expectancy norms more closely than others. In theory, we can distinguish, within the total set of translations in a culture, a fuzzy subset of texts which are felt to conform very closely, prototypically as it were, to the relevant expectancy norms: Such translations tend to assume the status of "norm-models" which in fact embody the norms in question. Other translations, felt to be outside this subset, are still accepted as being translations, albeit not norm-embodying ones. (This distinction will be relevant to the pedagogical aspect of translation studies—see chapter 6.)

For some translationsm, "covert" ones (House, 1981), readers in a given culture at a given time will expect them to be indistinguishable from native, nontranslated texts: A covert translation that is recognized to be "different" from nontranslated, similar (parallel) target-language texts can thus be judged unsatisfactory in some way. (At least, this would be the default judgement on such a translation; there may, of course, be additional factors that would override this judgement—see chapter 5.) Examples of such covert translations might include business letters, advertisements, technical manuals and the like: Translations of such texts typically do not form a category separate from nontranslated target texts of the same type, within the target polysystem.

For other, "overt" translations (in a given culture, at a given time), the target-language expectancies might be different: translations of this type might be felt to occupy a different category or sub-category in the target polysystem, one specifically reserved for translations. Literary translations are one example: When I read Tolstoy in English, I cannot overlook the fact that I know he did not write in English originally; I expect "local colour," Russian forms of address, etc. Another example is interlinear glosses in linguistics texts, which are not even supposed to be fluent or natural but to illustrate the structure of the original. A third would be certain kinds of legal texts, such as those dealing with company law in country A but translated into the language of country B. In short, overt translations tend to be the norm for any text that is particularly closely bound in one way or another to the source culture.

Whether a translation is expected to be overt or covert will also depend partly on the cultural tradition in the target language, including the translation tradition itself. In some cultures, for instance, successfully covert translations may even be treated with suspicion, because readers have come to expect that translations are always overt (i. e. "unnatural") in some way. A translation that is genuinely natural may raise doubts about its accuracy, suspicions that the translator must have been too free.

Expectancy norms are primarily validated in terms of their very existence in the target language community: People do have these expectations about certain kinds of texts, and therefore the norms embodied in these expectations are *de facto* valid. But in some situations these norms are also validated by a norm-authority of some kind, such as a teacher, an examiner, a literary critic reviewing a translation, a translation critic, a publisher's reader, and so on. Within any society, there is usually a subset of members ("experts") who are believed by the rest of the society to have the competence to validate such norms. This authority validation may do no more than confirm a norm that is already acknowledged to exist in the society at large: In this sense, the norm-authorities genuinely "represent" the rest of the society and are presumably trusted by the other members to do so.

But there may be situations where there is a clash between the norms sanctioned by these norm-authorities and the norms accepted and current in the society at large. For instance, the general public may have rather low expectations about the readability of bureaucratic texts (whether translated or not), simply because they have become accustomed to such a quality. But norm-authorities might nevertheless fairly claim that the readability level of such badly written texts did not meet some higher requirement of clarity; further, such criticism might be agreed with by other members of the society when brought to their attention, and pressure might even be brought to bear on writers and/or translators to conform to these higher requirements.

What about translations that deliberately seem to go against expectancy norms? Some literary translators might claim that their intention is precisely to break these norms—recall the discussion of the Logos meme in the previous chapter. (And translations of advertisements sometimes appear deliberately to flout the expectancy norms of the target culture. In such cases, the expectancy norms are broken because of some higher priority: loyalty to some aspect of the form of the source text, for instance, or a particular ideological conviction about the best way to represent the source culture, or the desire to produce a more persuasive text.)

For instance, an advert currently (November 1996) going round Helsinki on the side of a tram, by a Finnish company offering cruises on the Baltic Sea, reads: *Meri Christmas*. Note: This is an advert aimed (primarily) at Finns; they are thus expected to know what the English word *Christmas* means; they obviously know what meri means ("sea"); and they are expected to know the English expression *Merry Christmas*. The wit and the effect of the advertisement thus depend on the English-language proficiency of a Finnish audience, who are not being addressed exclusively in the mother tongue. The bilingual appeal of the ad. suggests also that it is directed particularly at educated Finns; and the fact that it appears on a Helsinki tram indicates that the primary target audience is an urban one. The ad. can thus exploit the fashionable glamour of being, and going, "international."

The effect of such norm-breaking only works because it goes against the expectations of the readers: Here, that Finns can expect to be addressed by other Finns in Finnish. Norm-breaking usages, including norm-breaking translations, are in themselves excellent evidence for the existence of the norms that are being thus broken. However, if, in time, people come to expect that norms will be broken in certain kinds of texts or translations, this expectancy will itself become a norm: the expectancy norm for that kind of text.

Expectancy norms, then, are not static or permanent, nor are they monolithic. They are highly sensitive to text-type—not all text-types are necessarily expected to conform consistently to fluent standard usage—and they are open to modification and change. In this respect, translation theory could benefit by some of the work done in critical linguistics on language awareness: I shall come back to this later (7.8).

3.5.3 Professional norms

The second major category of translation norms is that of process norms: These regulate the translation process itself. From the translator's point of view, these norms are subordinate to the expectancy norms, because they are themselves determined by the expectancy norms: Any process norm is determined by the nature of the end-product which it is designed to lead to.

Where lies the source of these process norms for translation? Recall the point made above, about the existence of norm-authorities in a society. With respect to translation, the norm authorities par excellence are perhaps those members of the society who are deemed to be competent professional translators, whom the society trusts as having this status; and who may further be recognized as competent professionals by other societies also. "Competence" and "professionalism" are thus understood here to be intersubjectively defined: You are competent if you are recognized to be so by people who in turn are recognized by others to be competent to make this judgement; and so on. (Henceforth I shall disregard the existence of non-competent professionals: for "professional" read "competent professional. ")

Professionals are the people who are largely responsible for the original establishment of the expectancy norms, in fact, for the products of their work naturally become the yardsticks by which subsequent translations are assessed by the receiving society. Their translation behaviour, in other words, is accepted to be norm-setting. Conversely, if a translation is accepted as conforming to the relevant expectancy norms, the translator of that text is (qua translator of that text, at least) accepted as being a competent professional. (That is what final diploma exams and the like are about, after all.)

Just as it is possible to distinguish a fuzzy subset of translations which are recognized as conforming especially closely to the expectancy norms (as argued above), so it is equally possible to distinguish (among the total set of people who translate literary or non-literary texts in a given culture) an equally fuzzy subset of translators who are recognized to be competent professionals. It is, then, the translational behaviour of this professional subset from which we derive the process norms of translation. For this reason, I shall call these translation process norms professional norms.

All professional translation norms can, I think, be subsumed under three general higher-order norms. They can be stated in an absolute form, but in real life they naturally tend to be followed only "as far as possible;" moreover, different translation tasks may require ba-lancing acts between different priorities, a point that I overlook here. Note that the following formulations are not prescriptive in the sense that I would be laying down laws for translators to follow. They are descriptive: I hypothesize simply that these are kinds of norms that exist in the culture to which any translator belongs, and that insofar as the translator has internalized them, they help to account for translatorial behaviour. The norms themselves exert a prescriptive pressure—as any norms do. In other words, translators tend to behave as they think they ought to behave, and these norms represent an attempt to capture the nature of this "ought." True, a translator may also have reasons to disregard these norms or to set up particular priorities between them; such translators will feel they "ought" to translate in some different way, they interpret the norms in a way that is different from the majority view. Different interpretations may remain a minority opinion, or they may eventually become the majority view.

I formulate the basis process norms as follows (following Chesterman, 1993c).

(1) The *accountability norm*: A translator should act in such a way that the demands of loyalty are appropriately met with regard to the original writer, the commissioner of the translation, the translator himself or herself, the prospective readership and any other relevant parties.

This is thus an ethical norm, concerning professional standards of integrity and thoroughness. Compare the general language norm of sincerity, mentioned above (3. 3). Translators behave in such a way as to be able to accept responsibility for their translations.

A similar point has been made by Nord (e. g. 1991): She speaks of the translator being "committed" and "responsible," and of loyalty as a moral principle which is indispensable in human communication. (Compare also the ethical norm of the "true interpreter" in Harris, 1990.) Formulated in this way, the norm nevertheless allows for various interpretations concerning which party should be given the primary loyalty in cases of conflict.

(2) The communication norm: A translator should act in such a way as to optimize communication, as required by the situation, between all the parties involved.

This is a social norm, which specifies the translator's role as a communication expert, both as a mediator of the intentions of others and as a communicator in his/her own right. Compare the general communication norm of language, mentioned above (3.3). Note that the norm does not necessarily presuppose a belief in an objectively fixed message, a signified, that must be communicated; the situation may be such that the intended communication is more like a shared sense of linguistic play, or an aesthetic experience. Communication is, after all, a sharing.

Neither the accountability norm nor the communication norm are specific to the translation process; Translation theory merely applies them. But the third higher-order process norm is specific to translation and other rewriting processes: It in fact highlights the difference between these kinds of processes and other communication processes. It can be stated as follows.

(3) The relation norm: A translator should act in such a way that an appropriate relation of relevant similarity is established and maintained between the source text and the target text.

Defined in this way, in terms of a relation between texts, this is therefore a linguistic norm. It accounts for the assumption (argued for above) that equivalence as such is too narrow a concept, because of the wide variety of relations that actually exist between source and target texts. It is up to the translator to decide what kind of relation is appropriate in any given case, according to the text-type, the wishes of the commissioner, the intentions of the original writer, and the assumed needs of the prospective readers. One kind of relation might of course be "equivalence" or "optimal similarity" of some sort. One translation task might require a translation which gave priority to a close formal similarity to the original: legal contracts for instance, which must correspond sentence to sentence. Another might prioritize stylistic similarity: a short story, perhaps a poem. Yet another might highlight the importance of semantic closeness: a scientific or technical article. And another might value similarity of effect above all these: a tourist brochure, an advertisement. Every translation task sets its own profile of "equivalence priorities," and it is part of the translator's job to assess the overall profile that would be appropriate. Simplified binary distinctions (form vs. meaning etc.) are only of limited use in this respect.

But, fundamentally, the question at issue here is broader and more complex. Equivalence (albeit inevitably partial) is only one kind of possible relation: recall the

Wittgensteinian idea of family resemblance, with its infinite variation. In translation, such variation would also cover such parameters as degree of target-culture adaptation considered appropriate, addition or omission of information, relation to accompanying channels (lip movements etc. in film dubbing, melody and pitch in song translations), and so on. The above formulation of the relation norm seeks to capture precisely this potential range of valid family resemblances between source and target text.

These three professional norms are partly validated by norm authorities: other professionals, teachers, critics etc., who are accepted as having norm-giving competence. But, like the expectancy norms, they are also validated by their very existence: That is, to the extent that they are accepted as governing the practice actually followed by such professionals. Furthermore, behaviour which breaks these norms is usually deemed deserving of criticism. This criticism might then be firmly rejected by the translator in question, and thus mark the beginning of an argument about how the appropriate norm should be interpreted. Norms can always be argued about. The point of this chapter is to suggest what the main translation norms are, not to define how they should be universally interpreted.

A final comment: Professional norms of course also govern the way a competent translator reads the source text, before actually translating anything, and the translator's own expectancy norms regarding the source language will affect the comprehension of the source text (cf. Dancette, 1994); however, I shall not discuss this aspect of the overall translation process.

【延伸阅读】

[1] Chesterman, A. (1997). *Memes of Translation*. Amsterdam and Philadelphia, PA: John Benjamins.

[2] Hermans, T. (1999). *Translation in Systems*. Manchester: St Jerome.

[3] Nord, C. (1997). *Translating as a Purposeful Activity: Functionalist Approaches Explained*. Manchester: St Jerome.

[4] Pym, A. (1998). *Method in Translation History*. Manchester: St Jerome.

[5] 韩江洪. 切斯特曼翻译规范论介绍. 外语研究,2004(2):44-47,56.

[6] 韩江洪. 论中国的翻译规范研究. 山东外语教学,2004(6):69-72.

【问题与思考】

1. 与图里的翻译分类相比,切斯特曼对翻译规范的分类有何不同? 为什么?

2. 在翻译过程和翻译产品的描述过程中,翻译规范能起到怎样的作用?

3. 图里和切斯特曼论及的规范是否能够涵盖所有的翻译规范? 你认为是否有一些事实上存在但被他们略而未提的规范?

选文三　翻译规范及其研究途径

廖七一

导　言

本文发表于《外语教学》2009 年第 1 期。

规范是描述性翻译研究中的重要概念。本文通过对规范社会学定义的分析,比较图里、切斯特曼、诺德、赫曼斯以及列费维尔等对翻译规范的描述发现。人们对翻译规范的界定不尽相同,但规范是以某一文化共同体普遍认可和接受为前提,以奖惩为实施手段的社会化行为,具有文化特殊性、不稳定性和矛盾性。翻译文本、相关的副文本和元文本则是描述和考察翻译规范的重要依据。

翻译既然是一种社会化的行为,必然受到社会意识形态和社会习俗的驱动与制约,而意识形态或社会习俗往往给人比较空泛,甚至无所不包的感觉。其实,无论是意识形态、主流诗学或是文化、社会、历史,其对翻译的驱动与制约都必须通过翻译规范这一中介来完成。自从图里提出翻译规范的三分法之后,切斯特曼、赫曼斯、诺德等都对翻译规范进行了比较系统的论述。列费维尔提出的意识形态、诗学和赞助人等概念,也可视为对规范的另一种表述。然而,不同翻译理论家对规范的定义不尽相同,规范涵盖的范围也差别很大,致使翻译规范在应用时显得比较抽象和笼统,甚至出现简单化和浅表化的倾向,主观臆断代替了严密的考证和分析,特别是忽略了规范研究中最重要的文本分析。本文试图从社会规范的视角重新审视翻译规范,比较分析图里、切斯特曼、诺德、列费维尔等对规范的论述,探索研究翻译规范的途径。

1　社会学与规范的定义

从社会学的角度观察,规范是"特定环境中规约和排斥行为的文化现象"(Hechter, 2001:xi),是"约束行为的表述"(statements that regulate behaviour)(Horne, 2001:4),或是"对视为理想的具体行为的口头描述"(ibid.)。也有学者将规范描述为"指导个人行为的规则,由国家之外的第三方通过社会奖惩形式来实施"(Ellickson, 2001:35)。还有学者认为,与法律规范不同,社会规范通常是自然而然地生成而非人为刻意为之(因而起源不太明确),规范不存在书面文本(因而内容与适用规则常常不甚精确),规范的实施则采用非正式的形式(尽管有时奖惩的后果会性命攸关)(Hechter, 2001:xi)。

尽管学者对规范概念的理解还存在一些分歧,但在两个问题上达成了基本一致的认识。一是社会规范的道德强制性(moral imperative),即人们心理上的"应该感"。二是社会期待。就第一点而言,个人被认为应该做出某种行为,不管其对自己的后果如何。就第二点而言,如

果个人偏离社会规范,他必须承担由此产生的后果,并为之付出代价。社会规范可以定义为在群体P中个体行为的规律性R:

(1) R产生于P中成员经常性的交往;

(2) 在P中在几乎所有成员都遵守R的情况下,P中几乎所有成员都希望遵守R;

(3) 在P中几乎每个成员都相信在P中几乎每个其他成员都遵守R;

(4) R是经常性交往中的纳斯平衡(Nash Equilibrium)。(Voss,2001:108)

可以看出,规范是群体中个体自觉遵循的行为模式,并且以群体共同期待和接受为基础。与此同时,学者普遍认为,规范具有排他性(exclusionary)和普遍性(universalistic)。排他性指规范仅适用于某一特定的社区或文化;普遍性则指规范普遍适用于某一特定角色的每个成员(Cook,2001:328)。社会期待决定了行为的"合理性"、"恰当性"或"正确性",正因为如此,社会学家和心理学家一直将正确与错误、适当与不适当这些特定群体的普遍价值或观念转换为特定环境中行为表现的指示,以赏罚作为手段明确规定或禁止社会成员的某些行为。

2　翻译规范

早在20世纪60和70年代,一些翻译研究者开始应用"规范"(norms)的概念来研究翻译。列维(Jiří Levy)认为,翻译是一个决策过程(decision-making process),译者从文本的选择到句子结构、措辞、标点甚至拼写,都面临众多的可能性,而每一个既定的抉择又会影响后续的取舍。从理论上看,所有的抉择均处于"完全可以预测"与"完全无法预测"这两极之间。这种张力正好体现出"译者的权力与责任"(Hermans,1999:73-74)。其后,波波维奇(Anton Popovic)指出,既然抉择既非完全前定的,又非绝对任意的,那么什么原因促使译者作出某一抉择而不是其他? 例如,除了纯粹的主观意愿之外,译者必须面临源语文本和译语文本两套规范或成规(norms and conventions)的制约,翻译实际上就是在上述两套规范制约下的抉择活动。

图里借鉴了列维和波波维奇的观点,从行为主义的角度来探讨规范。他认为,规范是明辨社会行为是否得体的标准,是一种社会文化习得。在翻译中,除了语言的结构规则之外,我们应该着重研究"非强制性"(non-obligatory)的选择。图里称,规范是翻译能力(competence)和翻译实际行为(performance)之间的中介,翻译能力指译者在理论上拥有的所有选择的可能性,而翻译行为则是译者在种种制约因素的影响之下作出的具体抉择(Hermans,1999:74-75)。换言之,规范是"将某一社区共享的普遍价值或观念——如对正确与错误、适当与不适当的观念——转换为适当而且适用于特定情形的行为指南"(Toury,1995:55)。

随后,图里分析了规则(rules)、规范和特异倾向(idiosyncrasies)的区别,称规则是(更)客观的规范,而特异倾向是(更)主观的规范。在实际翻译过程中,译者通常受到三类规范的制约:① 预备规范(preliminary norms)决定待译文本的选择,即翻译政策。在特定历史时期,翻译、模仿、改写有何区别? 目标文化偏爱哪些作家、哪个时代、何种文类或流派的作品? 是用直接翻译或是间接翻译? 即是否允许或接受经过第三国语言的转译? ② 初始规范(initial norms)决定译者对翻译的总体倾向,即倾向于原文本还是倾向于译文文化的读者习惯。图里将这两极称为"充分性"(adequacy)和"可接受性"(acceptability)。③ 操作规范(operational norms)制约实际翻译活动中的抉择。操作规范又细分为——a. 母体规范(matricial norms),

即在宏观结构上制约翻译的原则,例如,是全文翻译还是部分翻译,以及章节、场幕、诗节和段落如何划分等。b. 篇章语言学规范(textual-linguistic norms),即影响文本的微观层次的原则,如句子结构、遣词造句、是否用斜体或大写以示强调等(Hermans,1999:75－76)。

在图里之后,切斯特曼提出了略有区别的翻译规范体系。他认为,规范处于法律(laws)与成规(conventions)之间。强制性的法律是绝对的,客观的。法律由权威机构制定与实施,违反法律将受到相关权威机关惩处。成规代表比规范更弱的习惯;违反成规一般并不会引发批评;成规并不具有约束力,有时仅代表一种偏好(Chesterman,1997:55)。切斯特曼对规范范围的界定显然与图里略有区别。

切斯特曼将翻译规范划分为社会规范(social norms)、道德规范(ethical norms)和技术规范(technical norms)。社会规范协调人与人之间的关系;道德规范指译者应该坚持"晓畅、真实、信任和理解"的价值标准;而技术规范之下又分产品规范和生产规范。产品规范(product norms)又称期待规范,即译作应满足读者对何为翻译的期待;这在很大程度上取决于目标文化主流的翻译传统和相应文本的形式(Chesterman,1997:64)。只有遵循一定标准的译文才可能被"接受为(真正的、恰当的和合法的)翻译"(Hermans,1999:78)。生产规范(process or production norms)制约翻译活动的实践操作,亦称专业规范。生产规范从属并受制于期待规范(Chesterman 1997:67)。生产规范又可细分为"责任规范",这就是道德规范,即满足译文"完整"、"精确"的专业标准;"交际规范",这是交际标准,即发挥协调翻译所涉及各方之间的沟通的作用;以及"关系规范",这是语言标准,即译者根据具体实际决定原文与译文之间"恰当"的相互关系,"等值"或"相似"只是种种关系之一。其关系如下所示。

(1) 产品或期待规范(product norms or expectancy norms)。

(2) 生产或过程规范(production norms or process norms),其中又包括:

① 责任规范(accountability norms);

② 交际规范(communication norms);

③ 关系规范(relation norms)。

显然,切斯特曼在图里的规范理论上又有所扩展,他认为前两种规范,即责任和交际规范,涉及人类社会交际活动的普遍规律,而第三种规范,即关系规范则涉及翻译的特殊关系,是翻译研究的核心问题。

诺德(Nord)根据瑟尔斯(Searles)的言语行为理论(speech act theory)提出了构成成规(constitutive conventions)和调节成规(regulatory conventions),范围似乎比图里和切斯特曼的规范都要广泛。诺德认为,构成成规决定了某一特定文化所接受的对翻译的界定(与改编等其他跨文化文本转换相对)。这些成规的总和构成了"某一特定文化群体中流行的翻译的一般概念,即翻译使用者对实际翻译文本的期待"(Nord,1991:100)。调节成规是支配文本层次之下、处理翻译具体问题普遍接受的形式。诺德的成规理论虽嫌简略,其涵盖范围似乎要宽泛得多,赫曼斯认为其比较明了,有助于认识读者和翻译批评者用以评价翻译的标准。

显然,所谓的"合理"、"正确"或"合适"与否构成了规范的内容;协调社会行为构成了规范的社会功能;奖惩构成了规范的实施方式;而范例则构成了规范的传播方式。从上述对社会规范和翻译规范的分析与论述可以概括出下列特征:第一,各种规范理论涵盖的范围与界限不完全一致。有的包括强制性的法律政令等人们常说的成规;有的仅限定在强制性规定与成规之间;还有的限定在法律法规与个人个性化行为之间。概括起来,规范的范围具有模糊性,起码存在下列四种情况。

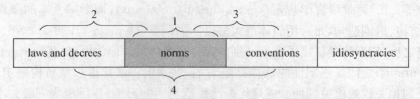

人们对规范所持的观念取决于对翻译理论的理解,即翻译理论是规约性的、描述性的,还是预测性的(Shuttle-Worth & Cowie,2004:113)。第二,规范具有文化特殊性。规范均以特定文化中一定群体的共同期待和共同接受为前提条件,即具有排他性(exclusionary)。适用于一定文化的规范通常并不适用于另一文化。属于某一亚文化的规范也未必适用于该亚文化之外的其他群体。第三,规范具有不稳定性。规范具有历史的特殊性,是一定历史社会的产物。随着时间的推移,旧的规范会因失去赖以生存的社会基础和社会的共同期待而逐渐失去约束力和影响力,而新的规范会取而代之而成为特定文化群体遵循的准则。第四,规范具有矛盾或冲突性。由于社会文化系统的复杂与协调适应性,不同的文化子系统会生成不同的,甚至是相互矛盾的"正确"或"应该"的观念。在同一文化群体中也经常存在彼此冲突的规范。遵守某一规范可能意味着违反另一规范。翻译实际上是"协调众多规范以达到复杂目标的交际活动"(Hermans,1999:166-167)。第五,翻译的历史语境化定义与"对等"或"忠实"并无太大关系。翻译是目的性非常强的人类活动。成功的翻译以满足读者期待,最大限度地完成跨文化交际功能为先决条件。对翻译恰当的定义应该是特定时期特定文化中主流翻译规范和相应翻译典范的建构(Hermans,1999:166)。

3 规范的研究途径

从规范的性质可以看出,规范不仅是个体行为的指南,同时也是对个体行为自由的限制。列费维尔(A. Lefevere)在论述社会文化对翻译的制约的时候,曾经列举出五种限制因素,即赞助人、诗学、话语总体、源语与译语,以及译者意识形态。这五种制约因素实际上是从另一个角度对翻译规范进行表述。切斯特曼就认为,列费维尔的制约因素与翻译规范存在高度的一致性:

赞助人→预备规范

诗学→期待规范

话语总体→期待规范,责任规范

源语与译语→关系规范

译者意识形态→责任规范,交际规范(Chesterman,1997:78-79)

其实,列费维尔的五种制约因素也必须通过行为规范方能付诸实施,即转化为译者具体的翻译行为。图里、诺德、切斯特曼对翻译的分类,列费维尔对意识形态、诗学和赞助人系统的描述,应该说都讨论了特定文化中翻译规范的表现形式和特征。其相互关系可以图示如下:

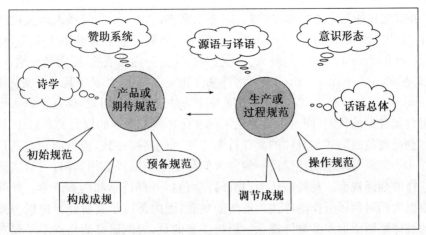

其中：

椭圆形标注——图里的翻译规范；

圆形标注——切斯特曼的翻译规范；

方形标注——诺德的翻译成规；

云形标注——列费维尔的制约因素。

虽然规范是经常性、习惯性的行为模式，但翻译规范本身常常是难以直接观察到的，我们必须从翻译过程和翻译文本中去揭示潜在的规范。概括起来翻译规范主要表现于四个方面：① 为何翻译？② 如何翻译？③ 翻译什么？④ 何为翻译？从另一个角度来看，翻译规范即一个文化或社群对翻译文本的选择、生产、接受和对认可的翻译的观念。

赫曼斯认为，人们有关翻译规范的陈述往往与实际翻译行为有相当大的距离。即便发现了翻译文本中的规律，也未必能揭示译者选择和决定的原因（Hermans，1999：85）。规范研究最重要的根据应该是翻译文本本身；一个被多次翻译的文本所表现出来的差异对揭示翻译规范具有重要意义。其次是相关的副文本（paratexts）和元文本（metatexts）。副文本是译序、译跋、注释等。元文本是独立发表但针对其他文本的文本，包括译者、编者、出版商、读者以及译界的陈述和评论，对译者的讨论与评介，以及其他接受文本资料、理论和实际评述；翻译教科书，由翻译引发的法律纠纷，翻译发行和重印的数据，翻译获奖情况（包括谁获奖，谁颁奖，授奖原因）等（Hermans，1999：85 – 86）。赫曼斯认为，研究翻译规范可以从以下四个方面入手。① 经典化范型及边界案例（canonized models and borderline cases）。经典化范型包括翻译教科书中特别推荐的译作或范例，被重印、收入编选的译作、获奖译作等。这些译作体现了人们对"恰当"或"正确"翻译的认识，是人们效仿的范例。边界案例则指有争议的译作。这些译作体现出人们在区别翻译和其他相关文本，如改写、编写、模仿创作等的时候把握的差异和标准，也就是诺德所谓的翻译的构成成规（constitutive conventions）（Hermans，1999：86）。② 选择与排除（selectivity and exclusion）。根据语言行为理论，言语的意义在很大程度上取决于某一陈述的特定时间和特定场合。在一定的场合必须说什么、决不能说什么、可以说什么或能够说什么具有十分重要的意义。翻译文本、翻译方式、翻译策略等众多可能的选择中，译者刻意回避和排斥的那些选择特别有助于我们发现制约和驱动翻译的"宗教、哲学和教育的标准"（Hermans，1999：87 - 88）。③ 基本态度（discursive stance）。对于源语文化和文本对目的语文化可能产生的影响，不同的文化和社群会持有不同的态度：a. 和睦态度（transdiscursive attitude)。外来文化能与本土文化和睦相处,外来文本的输入不会使译入语文化产生焦虑和惊恐。b. 补足的态度(defective attitude)。外来文化的输入能够弥补本土文化自身的不足。c. 防范态度(defensive attitude)。外来文化会对自我身份构成威胁,因而禁止输入外来文本。d. 帝国主义态度(imperialist attitude)。将外来文化完全归化,并赋予其本土文化视为当然的价值观(Hermans,1999:89)。以上四种态度关注的是意识形态因素,体现了译入语文化的自我形象和对自我身份的认定,同时也反映出不同文化之间不平等的权力关系。④ 符码及注意点。人们对翻译规范的陈述与具体的翻译行为之间可能高度一致,也可能相差甚远。翻译的实践活动并非一定要与理论描述保持一致。人们越是强调翻译必须如何,说明实际上人们并没有遵循这样的翻译规范。赫曼斯认为,翻译诗学包括外部诗学和内部诗学。外部诗学是翻译研究者根据人们对翻译所作的陈述而形成的观念;而内部诗学是研究者根据主流翻译文本所体现出的翻译原则而形成的翻译观念。值得注意的是,规范研究的焦点不是要对翻译本身作出价值判断,而是调查一定社会文化语境中有关翻译的陈述的"评价尺度"(evaluative yard-stick)(Baker,2004:163)。规范或者习惯都不是现实的复制,而只是人为的建构;"翻译研究同其他学科一样,事实不是给定的(given),而是制造的(made)"(Hermans,1999:90)。

4　结语

翻译规范被视为现代翻译研究"绝对必要的概念"(an absolutely essential concept)(Her-mans,1999:165),对不同文化中具体的翻译实践或翻译活动具有比较强的解释力。规范理论从根本上否定了规定性的传统"对等"概念,不是将"对等作为翻译的前提或标准:符合标准的就是翻译,不符合就不是翻译或不是好的翻译";反之"对等只代表译文与原文的一种关系,它随'规范'的变化而变化——不同文化、不同时期可能有不同的'对等'观念"(朱志瑜,2007:xi)。然而,从上面的论述可以看出,目前的规范研究主要基于整体论、系统论、客观主义和宏观的研究理路,将规范视为既定条件,制约并控制处于微观行动的个人。20 世纪 90 年代以后,科尔曼(Coleman)提出了理性选择理论(rational choice theory),并从行为系统、行为结构、行动权力以及社会最优的基本概念出发,将个体行为作为研究规范的基础。理性选择理论不仅要研究社会规范对个体行为的制约与驱动,同时还能揭示个体行为与规范生成、实施和传播的关系,极大地推动了社会规范的研究,同时也为翻译规范开辟了新的研究领域。

【延伸阅读】

[1] 傅勇林. 翻译规范与文化限制:图里对传统语言学与文学藩篱的超越. 外语研究,2001(1):
    68-72.
[2] 韩江洪,张柏然. 国外翻译规范研究述评. 解放军外国语学院学报,2004(2):53-56.
[3] 李德超. 传统翻译观念的逾越:彻斯特曼的翻译规范论. 外国语,2004(4):68-75.

【问题与思考】

1. 本文为什么从社会规范的视角重新审视翻译规范?
2. 本文是如何整合图里、切斯特曼、诺德、列费维尔等对规范的论述的?
3. 研究翻译规范可经由哪些途径? 本文是如何阐述这些途径的?

第五章 翻译的功能与目的

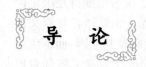

导　论

　　许多语言学家和翻译理论家都曾试图将语言的功能分类。1934 年德国心理学家、语言学家、符号学家布勒(Karl Bühler)在其代表作《语言理论——语言的表征功能》中将语言的语义功能分为三类："表达"(expression)、"再现"(representation)和"感召"(appeal)。雅各布森(1960)在此基础上将语言功能分为六类：表达功能(expressive)、指称功能(referential)、意动功能(conative)、寒暄功能(phatic)、元语言功能(metalingual)和诗学功能(poetic)，其中前三种功能与布勒的分类基本一致。韩礼德(1973)区分了三种宏观功能：意念功能(ideational)、人际功能(interpersonal)和文本功能(textual)。同样是以布勒的划分法为基础，赖斯(Reiss，1976)分出三种文本类型："重内容(content-focused)文本"、"重形式(form-focused)文本"、"重感召(appeal-focused)文本"，后来她又称之为"信息(informative)文本"、"表情(expressive)文本"、"操作(operative)文本"。每一种文本的翻译都要求译者使用相应的翻译技巧和策略。但是有学者指出(Roberts，1992)，很有必要把语言功能与文本功能区别开来。没有一个文本只具有一种功能，所有文本都是多功能的。

　　就译本的功能而言，因为委托或发起一项翻译工作的原因与源语文本创作的起因没有什么关联，译本的功能不一定要与源语文本的功能一致。正是在这个意义上我们可以理解翻译目的论。赖斯和威密尔(Vermeer，1984)认为，译本的功能和目的是决定译者如何决策的关键因素。翻译的目的是一个极为重要的概念。这个目的含三种意义：译者的目的、译文的交际目的和使用某种特殊翻译手段所要达到的目的。根据目的论，所有翻译遵循的首要法则就是"目的法则"：翻译行为所要达到的目的决定整个翻译行为的过程，即结果决定方法。翻译是一种基于源语文本的转换行为，而任何翻译行为都有一定的目的，产生一种结果、一种新的语境或事件。决定翻译目的的最重要因素之一是受众——译文意旨的接受者，他们有自己的文化背景知识、对译文的期待以及交际需求。每一种翻译都指向一定的受众，因此翻译是在"目的语情景中为某种目的及目的受众而生产的语篇"。威密尔认为原文只是为目的受众提供部分或全部信息的源泉。

　　与赖斯和威密尔的翻译目的论一脉相承，曼塔利(Mänttäri，1984)把翻译视为跨文化行为，翻译行为的目标是读者对译文的接受和具体翻译功能的实现。她基于交际理论与行为理论而提出翻译行为理论，目的是为专业翻译情境提供一个模式和指导。翻译行为理论把翻译视为有目的的、重结果的交际活动，把翻译过程视为与文化转换相关联的信息传递综合体(message-transmitter compounds)。曼塔利指出，翻译不是单纯地翻译词语、句子或文本，而是引导意向中的合作,跨越文化障碍,促进功能性的交际。翻译行为理论非常重视为接受人提供一个功能性的交际文本,即在形式和文体上与目的语文化达到功能性适合的目的语文本。

诺德(Nord,1997)在其《翻译中的语篇分析》一书中首次提出"功能加忠诚"概念。当时,曼塔利把文本视为实现交际功能的纯粹工具,认为其固有的价值完全从属于其目的,译者只需对目的环境负责,目的语文本可以完全独立于原文。诺德则认为"没有原文,就没有翻译"。"译者应同时对原文和译文环境负责,对原文信息发送人(或发起人)和目的语读者负责。"根据目的论,译文的目的是译者决定采取何种翻译策略最为重要的标准,译文读者的期待是决定译文目的的主要因素,而目的语文化中的惯例决定译文读者对译文的期待。如果译者对原文做出的改动与目的语文化中的惯例不一致,译者有责任告诉读者其翻译策略及其原因,而不应当欺骗读者。如果译者的传译与原文发送人的期望相悖,译者也有责任向原文发送人解释对原文做了哪些变动,否则就等于误导原文发送人。诺德称这种责任为"忠诚"。功能加忠诚构成了诺德的功能主义方法论的两大基础。她把忠诚原则引入功能主义模式,有助于解决翻译中的激进功能主义问题。

本章共选四篇论文。第一篇论文是 Katharina Reiss 撰写的"Type,Kind and Individuality of Text:Decision Making in Translation"。该文把语言功能划分为三类,在语篇类型学的基础上,细致地分析了翻译过程的步骤,以及语篇类型和体裁对翻译交际中出现的变化所起的作用。第二篇是 Hans J. Vermeer 的"Skopos and Commission in Translational Action"。该文阐发了翻译目的论的要义,突破了赖斯功能对等理论研究的局限,成为功能派翻译理论的核心。第三篇"Translating as a Purposeful Activity:Functionalist Approaches Explained",作者是 Christiane Nord,文章进一步解释了目的论的主要概念和理论。第四篇《翻译目的论及其文本意识的弱化倾向》,为潘平亮所著,论文介绍了目的论产生的时代背景,研究了该理论的优点和弊端。

选文一 Type, Kind and Individuality of Text: Decision Making in Translation

Katharina Reiss

导　言

本文选自韦努蒂编《翻译研究读本》。

赖斯是德国翻译理论家,是德国目的论翻译理论的开创者之一,其翻译理论的核心概念是文本类型及文本功能分析。她早期的著作建基于对等概念之上,但超越了词或句子层次,把语篇视为完成交际和实现对等所在的层次。她的功能研究方法起初目的是要使翻译质量评估系统化。论文《翻译的抉择:类型、体裁及语篇的个性》是她较早期的作品。该文借鉴了卡尔·布勒的做法,把语言功能划分为三类。她把这三种功能与相应的语言维度和语篇类型或交际情境联系起来,研究总结出每种语篇类型的主要特点。她在语篇类型学的基础上,细致地分析了翻译过程的步骤,以及语篇类型和体裁对翻译交际中出现的变化所起的作用。她把翻译过程分为分析阶段和重述阶段。分析阶段要明确原文的功能类型和语篇体裁,然后进行语篇的风格分析。重述阶段是在上一步的基础上组织目标文本的结构。文本功能决定翻译方法、语言和篇章结构。她在后期认识到在翻译中不可能实现真正的对等,对等有时甚至不是人们所期望达到的效果,因此她将研究兴趣转向翻译目的,并与其学生威密尔一起大力倡导翻译目的论。

1　General preliminary remarks

1.1　Interlingual translation may be defined as a bilingual mediated process of communication, which ordinarily aims at the production of a TL [target language] text that is functionally equivalent to an SL text [source language] (2 media: SL and TL+1 medium: the translator, who becomes a secondary sender; thus translating: secondary communication).

1.1.1　The use of two natural languages as well as the employment of the medium of the translator necessarily and naturally result in a change of message during the communicative process. The theoretician of communication, Otto Haseloff (1969), has pointed out that an "ideal" communication is rare even when one single language is employed, because the receiver always brings his own knowledge and his own expectations, which are different from those of the sender. H. F. Plett (1975) calls this factor the "communicative difference." In translating, then, such differences are all the more to be expected. At this point I distinguish between "intentional" and "unintentional" changes affecting the translation.

Unintentional changes may arise from the different language structures as well as from differences in translating competence.

　　Ex. 1　Je suis allée à la gare (French: information about a female person; no information about the means of travel) Ich bin zum Bahnhof gegangen (German: no information about the person; information about the means of travel) = Linguistically conditioned communicative difference.

　　Ex. 2　La France est veuve (Pompidou at the death of de Gaulle) Frankreich ist Witwe—Frankreich ist Witwe geworden—Frankreich ist verwitwet—Frankreich ist verwaist [orphaned] Linguistically conditioned: La France—Witwe [Widow] "Frankreich" is neuter in German. The image of "widow" is odd to a person ignorant of French. "Waise" [orphan] is also neuter; the image of an emotional attachment programmed differently.

Intentional changes frequently occur in translating, if the aims pursued in the translation are different from those of the original; if, besides the language difference of the TL readers, there is a change in the reading circle, etc. Since this will entail a change of function in the act of communication, there is now no attempt any more to strive for a functional equivalence between the SL and the TL text, but for adequacy of the TL reverbalization in accordance with the "foreign function." It follows that, besides a text typology relevant to translating, a translation typology should be worked out.

1.2 Communication comprises linguistic and non-linguistic action.

1.2.1 Written texts and texts put in writing (material for translating purposes) are to be characterized as "one-way communication" (Glinz, 1973). This means, on the one hand, that non-linguistic elements contributing to oral communication (gestures, facial expressions, speed of speech, intonation, etc.) are partly verbalized (=alleviation of the text analy-sis). On the other hand, the text analysis is made more difficult by the limitation of the possibilities of explicit verbalization of such elements as well as by the spatio-temporal separation between addresser and addressee and the lack of feedback during the act of communication; these factors lead, among other reasons, to a variable understanding of a given text.

1.2.2 Action is *intentional behavior in a given situation* (Vermeer, 1972). "Intention" means here speech purpose, speech aim, motive leading to language communication (Lewandowski, 1973, p. 288). Through the intention, verbalized by the author in his text, this text receives a communicative function for the process of communication. In order to be able to establish this intention the translator receives significant assistance if he determines to which text-type and text-variety (relevant for translating) any given text belongs.

Written texts may have single or plural intentions. Plural intentions may be of the same rank and order. Mostly, however, one intention (and, with it, the text function) is dominant:

Ex. 3   C vor o und u und a spricht man immer wie ein k; soll es wie ein c erklingen, lässt man die Cedille springen.

(mnemote-chnical rhyme:

Intention 1—to convey a rule

Intention 2—to facilitate remembering by giving the text an artistic form

Intention 3—to "sweeten" the learning process by giving the text a pleasing form)

Counterexample 3a   Ein Wiesel/sass auf einem Kiesel/inmitten Bachgeriesel
... (Christian Morgenstern)

(Intention 1—the communication of an objective fact

Intention 2—artistic creation to convey an aesthetic impression)

The dominance of intention 2 is established through the text itself: "Das raffinierte Tier/Tat's um des Reimes Willen." Max Knight gives five English versions, and Jiří Levý regards all of them as equivalent (1969, pp. 103 – 104):

A weasel	A ferret	
perched on an easel	nibbling a carrot	
within a patch of teasel	in a garret	etc.

1. 3 Language is (among other factors) a temporal phenomenon and thus subject to the conditions of time. This also applies to language in written texts and therefore to these texts themselves, a factor which is significant for translating.

1. 3. 1 A natural consequence of this fact is, firstly, the necessity of re-translating one and the same SL text, if the TL has changed to such an extent, that the TL version reflecting previous language conditions does not guarantee functional equivalence any more (e. g. , Bible translations, the translations of classical authors).

1. 3. 2 A further consequence of this fact may be the loss of understanding of the original SL text functions, because of a change in the situation, in which the SL text fulfilled its function, and/or because of the impossibility of reconstructing this situation. (e. g. , Caesar, *Commentarii de bello gallico*—electioneering pamphlet＝operative text [see 2. 1. 1 below]. Torn out of its original social context—now a historical report and also translated as such＝informative text; Jonathan Swift, *Gulliver's Travels*—satire on contemporary social ills＝expressive text with an operative secondary function; today only recognizable in this function by the experts specializing in this period; for the ordinary reader (also of the original)—a fantastic adventure tale＝expressive text.)

2　The translating process

Phase of analysis. In order to place a functionally equivalent TL text beside an SL text the translator should clarify the functions of the SL text. This may be done in a three-stage-process, which may, in principle, be carried out either by starting from the smallest textual unit and ending with the text as a whole, or by beginning with the text as a whole and ending with the analysis of the smallest textual unit. For practical as well as for text-theoretical considerations, I have chosen the process of proceeding from the largest to the smallest unit. (In practice, the conscientious translator reads the whole text first to get an impression; from a text-linguistic point of view, the text is nowadays regarded as the primary language sign.) Below, this three-stage process will be presented as a temporal sequence for purely methodological reasons. In practice, the separate stages of analysis dovetail, particularly if the translator is experienced.

2. 1 Total function in the framework of written forms of communication.

2. 1. 1 Establishment of the *"text-type"*—a phenomenon going beyond a single linguistic or cultural context, because the following essentially different forms of written communication may be regarded as being present in every speech community with a culture based on

the written word and also because every author of a text ought to decide in principle on one of the three forms before beginning to formulate his text.

Question: Which basic communicative form is realized in the concrete text with the help of written texts?

(1) The communication of content—informative type

(2) The communication of artistically organized content—expressive type

(3) The communication of content with a persuasive character—operative type

Aids in orientation: semantic as well as pragmatic ones (content and knowledge of the world), for instance, "pre-signals," i. e. , titles or headlines (novel, law, report of an accident, sonnet, strike call, etc.) or "metapropositional expressions" at the beginning of a text (Grosse, 1976) (e. g. , "Herewith I authorize ... " in the case of a general power of attorney, etc.); medium: professional periodicals, pamphlets, the news section of a newspaper, etc.

Use of language:

(1) The particular frequency of words and phrases of evaluation (positive for the addresser or for the cause to which he has committed himself; negative for any obstacle to his commitment), the particular frequency of certain rhetorical figures may, among other factors, lead to the conclusion that the text is operative. Decisive question—Are we dealing with a speech object capable of making an appeal?

(2) "The feature that speech elements are capable of pointing beyond themselves to a significance of the whole" (Grosse, 1976), "the principle of linkage" (rhymes, leit-motifs, parallelisms, rhythm, etc.) and the "transformation of the material of reality" (Mukařovský) may lead to the conclusion that the text belongs to the expressive type.

(3) Should the elements quoted under (1) and (2) be absent, the conclusion may be that the text is informative.

Thus a "rough grid" has been established for the analysis.

2. 1. 2 *Mixed forms*. If we accept the three text types, the informative, expressive and the operative type, as the basic forms of written communication (intercultural), it should be taken into account that these types are not only realized in their "pure" form, that is, that they do not always appear in their "fully realized form;" and it should also be considered that, for a variety of reasons (change in the conventions of a text variety, or if we have to do with plural intentions) the communicative intention and communicative form cannot be unambiguously adapted to each other. In the first case: texts merely appealing to an affirmative attitude of the addressee without intending to trigger off impulses of behavior, e. g. , newspaper articles expressing opinions (no fully realized form of the operative text). In the second case: versified legal texts in the Middle Ages; in order for their content to be acceptable, they had to be presented in verse form＝greater dignity of rhymed language! (Mixed form between informative and expressive text type.)

2.1.3 *Additional types*? Bühler's three functions of the linguistic sign, in analogy to which I have isolated the three main text functions, are extended by Roman Jakobson to include the phatic and the poetic functions. Would both of these functions be suitable to isolate text types relevant to the choice of a translating method? Not so, in my opinion! Related to entire texts and not only to single language elements, the phatic function (=the establishment and maintenance of contact) is realized in all three of the basic forms of communication, i. e., the phatic function does not lead to particulars of the text construction.

For instance,

> Picture postcard from a holiday：informative text with phatic function
> Original birthday poem：expressive text with phatic function
> Memory aid in an advertisement slogan：operative text with phatic function

The phatic function does not arise from the text form, but from the use to which the text is put.

Likewise, the poetic function of the language signs is realized in all three of the basic communicative forms.

> Soccer reportage：informative text, partly with poetic language elements, e. g., "der Mann im fahlgrünen Trikot," "Erstaunlich matt war Hölzenbein, fehlerlos Grabowski, eindrucksvoll Neuberger." (rhetorical triple figure)
> Lyrical poem：expressive text—the poetic function determines the whole text
> Sales promotion：(e. g., in verse form) operative text with elements of poetic language "loan structure" (Hantsch, 1972)

However, in view of the relevancy for translating purposes, an additional type, a "hyper-type," should be isolated as a super-structure for the three basic types：*the multi-medial text type*. The need for this arises from the fact that the translating material does not only consist of "autonomous" written texts, but also, to a large extent, firstly of verbal texts, which, though put down in writing, are presented orally, and, secondly, of verbal texts, which are only part of a larger whole and are phrased with a view to, and in consideration of, the "additional information" supplied by a sign system other than that of language (picture＋text, music and text, gestures, facial expressions, built-up scenery on the stage, slides and text, etc.).

Thus, when the message is verbalized, the multi-medial type possesses its own regularities, which ought to be taken into account in translating, besides—and above—the regularities of the three basic forms of written communication. Therefore I now put this type above the three basic forms, though, formerly, I placed it beside them. However, we should also consider a suggestion made by a research group of the Philips concern, according to which these extra-linguistic conditions should be regarded as the basis for a typology of media relevant to translating.

2.2　The second stage of the analysis aims at the establishment of the *text variety*,

i. e., the classification of a given text according to specifically structured sociocultural patterns of communication belonging to specific language communities. Text variety is still a controversial concept in linguistics. The denotation of text variety as well as that of text type is at present still used for the most variegated textual phenomena. Therefore, I meanwhile define text variety as super-individual acts of speech or writing, which are linked to recurrent actions of communications and in which particular patterns of language and structure have developed because of their recurrence in similar communicative constellations. The *phenomenon* of text variety is not confined to one language. The various kinds of text variety are partly not confined to one language or one culture, but the habits of textualization, the patterns of language and structure often differ from one another to a considerable extent. Hence, the establishment of the text variety is of decisive importance for the translator, so that he may not endanger the functional equivalence of the TL text by naively adopting SL conventions.

Examples:

Es war einmal—textual opening signal in German for fairy tales

In the name of the people—for verdicts

2×4 lines $+ 2 \times 3$ lines—structural pattern for the sonnet

Directions for use in French and German—according to the specific text variety there is a distribution of structures common to both languages.

The passive form and impersonal expressions—conventions in German.

The indefinite pronoun "on" + infinitive phrase—convention in French.

One single example may not always suffice for the establishment of the text variety.

Ex. 4　English death notice

FRANCIS. On Thursday, March 17, Jenny, beloved wife of Tony Francis and mother of Anthony. Service at St. Mary's Church, Elloughton, 9:50 a. m., Tuesday, March 22, followed by cremation. No letters or flowers, please.

The translation into German would be more or less as follows (the italicized words and expressions characterize conventions observed in German).

Am 17. März *verstarb meine* geliebte Frau, *meine* liebe Mutter

JENNY *FRANCIS*

Elloughton *Im Namen der Angehörigen* (or: in tiefer Trauer)

Tony Francis

mit Anthony

Trauergottesdienst: Dienstag, den 22. 3, 9. 50 in St. Marien (Elloughton)

Anschliessend *erfolgt* die Feuerbestattung

Von Kondolenzschreiben und Kranzspenden *bitten wir* höflichst *Abstand zu nehmen.*

2. 3　Third stage of the analysis: the analysis of style (the analysis of a particular textual surface). Now the *text individual* is placed in the foreground. This analysis is of supreme importance, because the translator's "decisive battle" is fought on the level of the text individual, where strategy and tactics are directed by type and variety.

Let style in this connection be understood to mean the ad hoc selection of linguistic signs and of their possibilities of combination supplied by the language system. The use of language in a given SL text is investigated in order to clarify in detail, firstly, what linguistic means are used to realize specific communicative functions, and, secondly, how the text is constructed. This detailed semantic, syntactic and pragmatic analysis is necessary, because, as is well known, not even in one single language do form and function show a 1 : 1 relation. The same phenomenon applies to the relation of SL to TL.

2. 4　At this point I see, as it were, a "juncture" between the first phase of the process of translation, the phase of analysis, and the second phase of the process of translation, the phase of reverbalization, for it is already here that the translator, at any rate the experienced translator, pays heed to possible contrasts.

The detailed semantic, syntactic and pragmatic analysis is carried out in small stages of analysis, proceeding from the word, the syntagma, the phrase, the sentence, the section (paragraph or chapter) up to the level of the entire text.

The process of reverbalization is a linear one constructing the TL text out of words, syntagmas, clauses, sentences, paragraphs, etc. During this process of reverbalization a decision has to be made for each element of the text whether the linguistic signs and sequences of linguistic signs selected in the TL in coordination with a sign form and sign function can guarantee the functional equivalence for which a translator should strive, by due consideration of text variety and text type.

3　Phase of reverbalization

Relevance of the classification of text type and text variety to the translating process.

Thesis: The text type determines the general method of translating; the text variety demands consideration for language and text structure conventions.

3. 1　Normal cases.

If functional equivalence is sought during the process of translation, this means:

(1) If the SL text is written to convey contents, these contents should also be conveyed in the TL text.

Mode of translating—*translation according to the sense and meaning* in order to maintain the invariability of the content. To this end it may be necessary that what is conveyed impli-citly in the SL text should be explicated in the TL and vice versa. This necessity arises, on the one hand, from structural differences in the two languages involved, and, on the other hand, from differences in the collective pragmatics of the two language communities involved.

> Ex. 5a　Vous vous introduisez par l'étroite ouverture *en vous frottant contre ses bords* ... (＝explicit)
>
> Sie *zwängen* sich *durch* die schmale Öffnung (*not* "by rubbing against its walls") (＝implicit)
>
> "durchzwängen" in German contains the image of rubbing against an edge.
>
> Ex. 5b　(after Klaus Rülker) A report by a French press agency about the presidential elections in France—seulement huit départements français votèrent en majorité pour Poher.
>
> Literal translation—Nur acht aller französischen Departements stimmten in ihrer Mehrheit für Poher.
>
> Equivalent translation—Nur acht *der hundert* französischen Departements stimmten in ihrer Mehrheit für Poher.

(2) If the SL text is written in order to convey artistic contents, then the contents in the TL should be conveyed in an analogously artistic organization. Mode of translating—*translating by identification* (not in the sense Goethe uses). The translator identifies with the artistic and creative intention of the SL author in order to maintain the artistic quality of the text.

> Ex. 6　(Ortega y Gasset—*Miseria y Esplendor de la Traducción*) Entreveo que es usted una especie de *último abencerraje*, último superviviente de una fauna desaparecida, puesto que es usted capaz, frente a otro hombre, de creer que es el otro y no usted quien tiene razón.
>
> Literal translation—"eine Art letzter Abencerraje" (without content for the German reader).
>
> Content translation—"eine Art Ausnahmefall" (absence of the artistic components—metaphors and literary allusion).
>
> Functionally equivalent translation—"eine Art letzter Ritter ohne Furcht und Tadel."

(One element of the artistic organization in Ortega's essay is the many verbs and nouns alluding to seafaring, either directly or in a figurative sense, in spite of the fact that the subject has nothing to do with seafaring. This is an indication that he is aware of Jakob Grimm's saying, according to which translating resembles a ship manned to sail the seas, but though it safely carries the goods, it must land at shore with a different soil under a different air. The metaphor is obvious because all the images presented by Ortega on the subject of translation derive from what Schleiermacher, Humboldt and Goethe have said about the problem. Thus, he must have known Grimm's metaphor as well. Hence, the translator is satisfied in choosing as shifted equivalents concepts from seafaring, where there are none in the original, if these are easily available in German. The reason is that at other times, when in the Spanish language the association with "seafaring" is implied, an equivalent German expression is not available—*arribar*＝*ankommen*, instead of *llegar*. This is one of the examples I mean when referring to "the analogy of artistic form. ")

(3) If the SL text is written to convey persuasively structured contents in order to trigger off impulses of behavior, then the contents conveyed in the TL must be capable of triggering off analogous impulses of behavior in the TL reader.

Ex. 7　Black is beautiful

This slogan appearing in English in a German sales promotion could not be retained in the translation into English of a whole sales promoting text, if that text is intended for South African buyers.

Mode of translating—*adaptive translating*. The psychological mechanisms of the use of persuasive language should be adapted to the needs of the new language community.

3. 2　Since form and function of language signs do not show a relation of 1：1, the same SL sequence may be represented in the TL by any other language sequence depending in which text type and text variety they appear and which function they may have to fulfill there.

Ex. 8　El niño lloraba bajo *el agua del bautismo*.

　　Text variety: social news; text type: informative.

　　Das Kind weinte unter dem *Taufwasser*.

Ex. 9　Marcelino lloraba bajo *el agua del bautismo*, como antes callara al advertir *el sabor de la sal*. (Sánchez-Silva, Marcelino, Pan y vino)

　　Text variety: narrative; text type: expressive (parallelisms; rhythm-elements of artistic organization—retained in the TL)

　　Marcelino weinte unter dem *Wasser der Taufe*, wie er zuvor beim *Geschmack des Salzes* geschwiegen hatte.

Ex. 10　*Souvent femme varie*, bien fol est qui s'y fie.

(1) This saying of Francis I is mentioned in a history book.

Text variety: schoolbook; text type: informative.

Frauen ändern sich oft, wer ihnen traut, ist schön dumm.

(2) Mentioned in a drama by Victor Hugo (transl. by Georg Büchner), *Maria Tudor*.

Text variety: drama; text type: expressive.

Ein Weib ändert sich jeden Tag, ein Narr ist, wer ihr trauen mag (several semantic shifts, rhyme and rhythm retained).

(3) Item in an advertisement for wine: "Souvent femme varie. Les vins du Postillon ne varient jamais. " Literary allusion in conjunction with pun-memory aid and the arousal of sympathy in the "connoisseur. " The allusion should be re-programmed.

Text variety: the advertising of products; text type: operative.

Frauenherzen sind trügerisch. Postillon-Weine betrügen nie.

3.3 Problematic cases.

If the three basic forms of communication are not realized in their "pure" form (cf. mixed forms, 2. 1. 2), then the principles of translating for the three basic types serve as aids for a decision in cases of conflict. In principle, the mode of translating for the entire text applies to all text elements, even if they do not belong to the same type as the dominant type.

If, for instance, elements of poetic language are used when content is conveyed (informative type)—the so-called loan structures (Hantsch, 1972)—the translation ought to strive for an analogously poetic form for those elements. However, if this is not possible in the TL without loss of the unity of content and artistic form, then the retention of content is dominant in informative texts and is to be preferred to the maintenance of an artistic form.

> Ex. 11　Nun gibt es freilich moderne Nomaden, für die ein Caravan nur der zweitschönste *Wahn* ist (*Süddeutsche Zeitung*, Streiflicht).
>
> Text variety: newspaper item; text type: informative.

We have here an item referring to an opinion poll among owners of camping places as regards the behavior of German holiday makers. The "Streiflichter" [a newspaper column] in the *Süddeutsche Zeitung* [a newspaper] are often distinguished by an abundance of entertaining puns and other kinds of play with language. At the same time, however, the subject is invariably a topical state of affairs, and the main function of the text is the communication of content. In translation puns and other kinds of play with language will have to be ignored to a great extent so as to keep the content invariant.

If, however, artistically structured contents in a text of the expressive type have to be conveyed and if, during this process, the artistic organization might be harmed by the retention of the same content elements, then the rule applies for expressive texts that the contents may be changed.

> Ex. 12　... une pâquerette, ou une primevère, ou un coucou, ou un bouton d'or ... (Samuel Becket)
> Literally: ... ein Gänse*blümchen*, oder ein Himmels*schlüssel chen*, oder eine *Schlüsselblume* oder eine Butter*blume* ... (invariance of content)
> Elmar Tophoven: ... ein Tausendschönchen, eine Primel, eine Schlüsselblume, eine Butterrose ...

Finally, if, in conveying contents with a persuasive form intended to trigger off impulses of behavior, the unchanged adoption of elements of content or (loaned) elements of artistic structure from the SL texts does not have an operative effect, these elements may be replaced by other elements fulfilling the desired function.

> Ex. 13　Füchse fahren Firestone-Phoenix
> Foxes use Firestone-Phoenix (falsification of association, loss of

alliteration; important elements of the operative use of language)

Pros prefer Firestone-Phoenix (change of content to retain positive association and alliteration)

If operative text elements appear in different text types, then the adapting method of translating also applies to these single elements as long as this is possible without any harm to either the content to be conveyed (in the case of the informative type) or to the artistic organization as a whole (in the case of the expressive text).

3.4 Special cases.

If there is a difference between the original text function and the function of the translation, the text typology relevant to translation as well as the establishment of the given text variety are of no significance at all for the question what mode of translating should be adopted to attain functional equivalence. In that case a *typology of translation* should replace the text typology in order to supply suitable criteria for the mode of translating. As has been mentioned above, in changes of function the aim of the translating process is not anymore the attainment of a functionally TL text, but a TL text possessing a form which is adequate to the "foreign function." The criteria are not to be derived from the question "to what end and for whom has the text been *written*," but from the question "to what end and for whom is the text *translated?*"

> e. g. , a "grammar translation"
>> —Aim of the translation: to examine whether the pupil is acquainted with vocabulary and grammatical structures of the foreign language; translated for the teacher. Regardless of which text type is realized by the SL text, only vocabulary and grammar are considered.
>
> e. g. , interlinear versions
>> —Aim of the translation: the reproduction of the SL text for research purposes; translated for the student ignorant of the SL.
>
> e. g. , summaries of content
>> —Aim of the translation: communication of contents relevant for a certain further use; translated upon somebody's order.

Note

1. Translator's remarks in square brackets.

【延伸阅读】

[1] Halliday, M. (1973). *Explorations in the Functions of Language*. London: Edward Amold.

[2] Jakobson, R. (1960). Closing Statement: Linguistics and Poetics. In T. Sebeok(ed.), *Style in Language* (pp. 350 – 377). Cambridge, MA: MIT Press.

[3] Reiss, K. (2000). *Translation Criticism: Potential and Limitations*. Manchester: St

Jerome and American Bible Society.

[4] Roberts，R. (1992). The Concept of Function in Translation and Its Application to Literary Texts. *Target*，4(1)，1 - 16.

【问题与思考】

1. 赖斯的文本类型分类法与布勒、雅各布森和韩礼德的语言功能分类法有何不同？
2. 文本类型与语篇体裁有何区别？它们与语篇风格有何关系？
3. 分析阶段与重述阶段是两个什么样的阶段？如何看待这两个阶段？
4. 赖斯翻译理论的意义和局限性是什么？

选文二　Skopos and Commission in Translational Action

Hans J. Vermeer

导　言

　　20 世纪 70 年代，功能派翻译理论兴起于德国。翻译目的论是威密尔(Hans J. Vermeer)以"行为理论"为基础创立的翻译理论，是功能翻译理论的核心。它的提出被认为是西方翻译理论研究的重大理论突破，突破了赖斯功能对等理论研究的局限。本文概括了翻译目的论的要义，是一篇重要的译学论文。

　　本文分为"提要"、"目的与翻译"、"反对目的论的观点"和"翻译的委任"四个部分。本文认为翻译是以原文为基础的有目的和有结果的行为，这一行为必须经过协商来完成；翻译必须遵循一系列法则，其中目的法则居于首位。也就是说，译文取决于翻译的目的。此外，翻译还须遵循"语内连贯法则"和"语际连贯法则"。前者指译文必须内部连贯，在译文接受者看来是可理解的，后者指译文与原文之间也应该有连贯性。这三条原则提出后，评判翻译的标准不再是"对等"，而是译本实现预期目标的充分性。威密尔还提出了翻译委任的概念，即应该由译者来决定是否、何时、怎样完成翻译任务。也就是说，译者应该根据不同的翻译目的采用相应的翻译策略，而且有权根据翻译目的决定原文的哪些内容可以保留，哪些需要调整或修改。威密尔认为，翻译中的最高法则应该是"目的法则"。也就是说，翻译的目的不同，翻译时所采取的策略、方法也不同。换言之，翻译的目的决定了翻译的策略和方法。威密尔提出的目的论，将翻译研究从原文中心论的束缚中解脱出来。

This paper is a short sketch of my *skopos* theory (cf. Vermeer, 1978，1983; Reiss & Vermeer, 1984; Vermeer, 1986; Gardt, 1989).

1　Synopsis

The skopos theory is part of a theory of translational action (*translatorisches Handeln*—cf. Holz-Mänttäri, 1984; Vermeer, 1986, pp. 269 – 304, pp. 197 – 246; for the historical background see e. g. Wilss, 1988, p. 28). Translation is seen as the particular variety of translational action which is based on a source text (cf. Holz-Mänttäri, 1984, especially p. 42f; and Nord, 1988, p. 31). (Other varieties would involve e. g. a consultant's information on a regional economic or political situation, etc.)

Any form of translational action, including therefore translation itself, may be conceived as an action, as the name implies. Any action has an aim, a purpose. (This is part of the very definition of an action—see Vermeer, 1986.) The word *skopos*, then, is a technical term for the aim or purpose of a translation (discussed in more detail below). Further: an action leads to a result, a new situation or event, and possibly to a "new" object. Translational action leads to a "target text" (not necessarily a verbal one); translation leads to a *translatum* (i. e. the resulting translated text), as a particular variety of target text.

The aim of any translational action, and the mode in which it is to be realized, are negotiated with the client who commissions the action. A precise specification of aim and mode is essential for the translator. This is of course analogously true of translation proper: Skopos and mode of realization must be adequately defined if the text-translator is to fulfil his task successfully.

The translator is "the" expert in translational action. He is responsible for the performance of the commissioned task, for the final *translatum*. Insofar as the duly specified skopos is defined from the translator's point of view, the source text is a constituent of the commission, and as such the basis for all the hierarchically ordered relevant factors which ultimately determine the *translatum*. (For the text as part of a complex action-in-a-situation see Holz-Mänttäri, 1984; Vermeer, 1986.)

One practical consequence of the skopos theory is a new concept of the status of the source text for a translation, and with it the necessity of working for an increasing awareness of this, both among translators and also the general public.

As regards the translator himself: Experts are called upon in a given situation because they are needed and because they are regarded as experts. It is usually assumed, reasonably enough, that such people "know what it's all about;" they are thus consulted and their views listened to. Being experts, they are trusted to know more about their particular field than outsiders. In some circumstances one may debate with them over the best way of proceeding, until a consensus is reached, or occasionally one may also consult other experts or consider further alternative ways of reaching a given goal. An expert must be able to say—and this implies both knowledge and a duty to use it—what is what. His voice must therefore be respected, he must be "given a say. " The translator is such an expert. It is thus up to him to decide, for instance, what role a source text plays in his translational action. The decisive factor here is the purpose, the skopos, of the communication in a given situation. (Cf. Nord, 1988, p. 9)

2 Skopos and translation

At this point it should be emphasized that the following considerations are not only intended to be valid for complete actions, such as whole texts, but also apply as far as possible to segments of actions, parts of a text [for the term "segment" (*Stück*) see Vermeer, 1970]. The skopos concept can also be used with respect to segments of a *translatum*, where this appears reasonable or necessary. This allows us to state that an action, and hence a text, need not be considered an indivisible whole. (Sub-skopoi are discussed below; cf. also Reiss, 1971, on hybrid texts.)

A source text is usually composed originally for a situation in the source culture; hence its status as "source text," and hence the role of the translator in the process of intercultural communication. This remains true of a source text which has been composed specifically with transcultural communication in mind. In most cases the original author lacks the necessary knowledge of the target culture and its texts. If he did have the requisite knowledge, he would of course compose his text under the conditions of the target culture, in the target language! Language is part of a culture.

It is thus not to be expected that merely "trans-coding" a source text, merely "transposing" it into another language, will result in a serviceable *translatum*. (This view is also supported by recent research in neurophysiology—cf. Bergström, 1989.) As its name implies, the source text is oriented towards, and is in any case bound to, the source culture. The target text, the *translatum*, is oriented towards the target culture, and it is this which ultimately defines its adequacy. It therefore follows that source and target texts may diverge from each other quite considerably, not only in the formulation and distribution of the content but also as regards the goals which are set for each, and in terms of which the arrangement of the content is in fact determined. (There may naturally be other reasons for a reformulation, such as when the target culture verbalizes a given phenomenon in a different way, e. g. in jokes—cf. Broerman, 1984; I return to this topic below.)

It goes without saying that a *translatum* may also have the same function (skopos) as its source text. Yet even in this case the translation process is not merely a "trans-coding" (unless this translation variety is actually intended), since according to a uniform theory of translation a *translatum* of this kind is also primarily oriented, methodologically, towards a target culture situation or situations. Trans-coding, as a procedure which is retrospectively oriented towards the source text, not prospectively towards the target culture, is diametrically opposed to the theory of translational action. (This view does not, however, rule out the possibility that trans-coding can be a legitimate translational skopos itself, oriented prospectively towards the target culture: The decisive criterion is always the skopos.)

To the extent that a translator judges the form and function of a source text to be basically adequate per se as regards the pretermined skopos in the target culture, we can speak of a degree of "intertextual coherence" between target and source text. This notion thus refers to a relation between *translatum* and source text, defined in terms of the skopos. For instance, one legitimate skopos might be an exact imitation of the source text syntax, perhaps to provide target culture readers with information about this syntax. Or an exact imitation of the source text structure, in a literary translation, might serve to create a literary text in the target culture. Why not? The point is that one must know what one is doing, and what the consequences of such action are, e. g. what the effect of a text created in this way will be in the target culture and how much the effect will differ from that of the source text in the source culture. (For a discussion of intertextual coherence and its various types, see Morgenthaler 1980, pp. 138 – 140; for more on Morgenthaler's types of theme and rheme, cf. Gerzymisch-Arbogast, 1987.)

Translating is doing something: "writing a translation," "putting a German text into English," i. e. a form of action. Following Brennenstuhl (1975), Rehbein (1977), Harras (1978, 1983), Lenk (edited volumes from 1977 on), Sager (1982) and others, Vermeer (1986) describes an action as a particular sort of behaviour: For an act of behaviour to be called an action, the person performing it must (potentially) be able to explain *why* he acts as he does although he could have acted otherwise. Furthermore, genuine reasons for actions can always be formulated in terms of aims or statements of goals (as an action "with a good reason", as Harras puts it). This illustrates a point made in another connection by Kaspar (1983, p.139): "In this sense the notion of aim is in the first place the reverse of the notion of cause." (Cf. also Riedl, 1983, p. 159f.) In his *De Inventione* (2.5.18.) Cicero also gives a definition of an action when he speaks of cases where "some disadvantage, or some advantage is neglected in order to gain a greater advantage or avoid a greater disadvantage" (Hubbell, 1976, pp. 181 – 183).

3　Arguments against the skopos theory

Objections that have been raised against the skopos theory fall into two main types.

3.1　Objection (1) maintains that not all *actions* have an aim: Some have "no aim." This is claimed to be the case with literary texts, or at least some of them. Unlike other texts (!), then, such texts are claimed to be "aimless." In fact, the argument is that in certain cases no aim *exists*, not merely that one might not be able explicitly to *state* an aim—the latter situation is sometimes inevitable, owing to human imperfection, but it is irrelevant here. As mentioned above, the point is that an aim must be at least potentially specifiable.

Let us clarify the imprecise expression of actions "having" an aim. It is more accurate to speak of an aim being *attributed* to an action, an author *believing* that he is writing to a given purpose, a reader similarly *believing* that an author has so written. (Clearly, it is possible that the performer of an action, a person affected by it, and an observer, may all have different concepts of the aim of the action. It is also important to distinguish between action, action chain, and action element—cf. Vermeer, 1986.)

Objection (1) can be answered *prima facie* in terms of our very definition of an action: If no aim can be attributed to an action, it can no longer be regarded as an action. (The view that any act of speech is skopos-oriented was already a commonplace in ancient Greece—see Baumhauer 1986, p. 90f.) But it is also worth specifying the key concept of the skopos in more detail here, which we shall do in terms of translation proper as one variety of translational action.

The notion of skopos can in fact be applied in three ways, and thus have three senses: It may refer to

    a. the translation process, and hence the goal of this process;

    b. the translation result, and hence the function of the *translatum*;

    c. the translation mode, and hence the intention of this mode.

Additionally, the skopos may of course also have sub-skopoi.

Objection (1), then, can be answered as follows: If a given act of behaviour has neither goal nor function nor intention, as regards its realization, result or manner, then it is not an action in the technical sense of the word.

If it is nevertheless claimed that literature "has no purpose," this presumably means that the creation of literature includes individual moments to which no goal, no function or intention can be attributed, in the sense sketched above.

For instance, assume that a neat rhyme suddenly comes into one's mind. (This is surely not an action, technically speaking.) One then writes it down. (Surely an action, since the rhyme could have been left unrecorded.) One continues writing until a sonnet is produced. (An action, since the writer could have chosen to do something else, unless the power of inspiration was simply irresistible, which I consider a mere myth.)

If we accept that the process of creating poetry also includes its publication (and maybe even negotiations for remuneration), then it becomes clear that such behaviour as a whole does indeed constitute an action. Schiller and Shakespeare undoubtedly took into account the possible reactions of their public as they wrote, as indeed anyone would; must we actually denounce such behaviour (conscious, and hence purposeful), because it was in part perhaps motivated by such base desires as fame and money?

Our basic argument must therefore remain intact: Even the creation of literature involves purposeful action.

Furthermore, it need not necessarily be the case that the writer is actually conscious of his purpose at the moment of writing—hence the qualification (above) that it must be "potentially" possible to establish a purpose.

One recent variant of objection (1) is the claim that a text can only be called "literature" if it is art, and art has no purpose and no intention. So a work which did have a goal or intention would not be art. This seems a bit hard on literature, to say the least! In my view it would be simpler to concede that art, and hence also literature, can be assigned an intention (and without exception too). The objection seems to be based on a misunderstanding. Nowadays it is extremely questionable whether there is, or has even been, an art with no purpose. Cf. Busch (1987, p. 7):

> Every work of art establishes its meaning aesthetically [...] The aesthetic can of course serve many different functions, but it may also be in itself the function of the work of art.

Busch points out repeatedly that an object does not "have" a function, but that a function is attributed or assigned to an object, according to the situation.

And when Goethe acknowledges that he has to work hard to achieve the correct rhythm for a poem, this too shows that even for him the creation of poetry was not merely a matter of inspiration:

> Oftmals hab'ich auch schon in ihren Armen gedichtet, Und des Hexameters Mass leise mit fingernder Hand Ihr auf dem Rücken gezählt.
>
> (*Römische Elegien* 1.5.)
>
> [Often have I composed poems even in her arms, counting the hexameter's beat softly with fingering hand, there on the back of the beloved.]

Even the well-known "*l'art pour l'art*" movement ("art for art's sake") must be understood as implying an intention: namely, the intention to create art that exists for its own sake and *thereby* differs from other art. Intentionality in this sense is already apparent in the expression itself. [Cf. also Herding (1987, p. 689), who argues that the art-for-art's-sake movement was "a kind of defiant opposition" against idealism—i. e. it did indeed have a purpose.]

3.2　Objection (2) is a particular variant of the first objection. It maintains that not every *translation* can be assigned a purpose, an intention; i. e. there are translations that are not goal-oriented. (Here we are taking "translation" in its traditional sense, for "translation" with no skopos would by definition not be a translation at all, in the present theory. This does not rule out the possibility that a "translation" may be done retrospectively, treating the source text as the "measure of all things;" but this would only be a translation in the sense of the present theory if the skopos was explicitly to translate in this way.)

This objection too is usually made with reference to literature, and to this extent we have already dealt with it under objection(1): It can scarcely be claimed that literary translation takes place perforce, by the kiss of the muse. Yet there are three specifications of objection (2) that merit further discussion.

a. The claim that the translator does not have any *specific* goal, function or intention in mind: he just translates "what is in the source text."

b. The claim that a specific goal, function or intention would restrict the translation possibilities, and hence limit the range of interpretation of the target text in comparison to that of the source text.

c. The claim that the translator has no specific addressee or set of addressees in mind.

Let us consider each of these in turn.

a. Advertising texts are supposed to advertise; the more successful the advertisement is, the better the text evidently is. Instructions for use are supposed to describe how an apparatus is to be assembled, handled and maintained; the more smoothly this is done, the better the instructions evidently are. Newspaper reports and their translations also have a purpose: to inform the recipient, at least; the translation thus has to be comprehensible, in the right sense, to the expected readership, i. e. the set of addressees. There is no question that such "pragmatic texts" must be goal-oriented, and so are their translations.

It might be said that the postulate of "fidelity" to the source text requires that e. g. a news item should be translated "as it was in the original." But this too is a goal in itself. Indeed, it is by definition probably the goal that most literary translators traditionally set themselves. (On the ambiguity of the notion "fidelity," see Vermeer, 1983, pp. 89 – 130.)

It is sometimes even claimed that the very duty of a translator forbids him from doing anything else than stick to the source text; whether anyone might eventually be able to do anything with the translation or it is not the translator's business. The present theory of translational action has a much wider conception of the translator's task, including matters of ethics and the translator's accountability.

b. The argument that assigning a skopos to every literary text restricts its possibilities of interpretation can be answered as follows. A given skopos may of course rule out certain interpretations because they are not part of the translation goal; but one possible goal (skopos) would certainly be precisely to preserve the breadth of interpretation of the source text. (Cf. also Vermeer, 1983: A translation realizes something "different," not something "more" or "less;" for translation as the realization of *one* possible interpretation, see Vermeer, 1986.) How far such a skopos is in fact realizable is not the point here.

c. It is true that in many cases a text-producer, and hence also a translator, is not thinking of a specific addressee (in the sense of: John Smith) or set of addressees (in the sense of: the members of the social democrat party). In other cases, however, the addressee(s) may indeed be precisely specified. Ultimately even a communication "to the world" has a set of addressees. As long as one believes that one is expressing oneself in a "comprehensible" way, and as long as one assumes, albeit unconsciously, that people have widely varying levels of intelligence and education, then one must in fact be orienting oneself towards a certain restricted group of addressees; not necessarily consciously—but unconsciously. One surely often uses one's own (self-evaluated) level as an implicit criterion [the addressees are (almost) as intelligent as one is oneself ...]. Recall also the discussions about the best way of formulating news items for radio and television, so that as many recipients as possible will understand.

The problem, then, is not that there is no set of addressees, but that it is an indeterminate, fuzzy set. But it certainly exists, vague in outline but clearly present. And the clarity or otherwise of the concept is not specified by the skopos theory. A fruitful line of research might be to explore the extent to which a group of recipients can be replaced by a "type" of recipient. In many cases such an addressee-type may be much more clearly envisaged, more or less consciously, than is assumed by advocates of the claim that translations lack specific addressees. (Cf. also Morgenthaler, 1980, p. 94 on the possibility of determining a "diffuse public" more closely; on indeterminacy as a general cultural problem see Quine, 1960.)

The set of addressees can also be determined indirectly: For example, if a publisher specializing in a particular range of publications commissions a translation, a knowledge of what this range is will give the translator a good idea of the intended addressee group (cf. Heinold et al., 1987, pp. 33 – 36).

3.3　Objection (2) can also be interpreted in another way. In text linguistics and literary theory a distinction is often made between text as potential and text as realization. If the skopos theory maintains that every text has a given goal, function or intention, and also an assumed set of addressees, objection (2) can be understood as claiming that this applies to text as realization; for a text is also potential in the "supersummative" sense (Paepcke, 1979, p. 97), in that it can be used in different situations with different addressees and different functions. Agreed; but when a text is actually composed, this is nevertheless done with respect to an assumed function (or small set of functions) etc. The skopos theory does not deny that the same text might be used later (also) in ways that had not been foreseen originally. It is well known that a *translatum* is a text "in its own right" (Holz-Mänttäri et al., 1986, p. 5), with its own potential of use: a point overlooked by Wilss (1988, p. 48). For this reason not even potential texts can be set up with no particular goal or addressee—at least not in any adequate, practical or significant way.

This brings us back again to the problem of the "functional constancy" between source and target text: Holz-Mänttäri (1988) rightly insists that functional constancy, properly understood, is the exception rather than the rule. Of relevance to the above objections in general is also her following comment (ibid. , p. 7):

> Where is the neuralgic point at which translation practice and theory so often diverge? In my view it is precisely where texts are lifted out of their environment for comparative purpos-es, whereby their process aspect is ignored. A dead anatomical specimen does not evade the clutches of the dissecting knife, to be sure, but such a procedure only increases the risk that findings will be interpreted in a way that is translationally irrelevant.

3.4　I have agreed that *one* legitimate skopos is maximally faithful imitation of the original, as commonly in literary translation. True translation, with an adequate skopos, does not mean that the translator *must* adapt to the customs and usage of the target culture, only that he *can* so adapt. This aspect of the skopos theory has been repeatedly misunderstood. (Perhaps it is one of those insights which do not spread like wildfire but must first be hushed up and then fought over bitterly, before they become accepted as self-evident—cf. Riedl, 1983, p. 147.)

What we have is in fact a "hare-and-tortoise" theory (Klaus Mudersbach, personal communication): The skopos is always (already) there, at once, whether the translation is an assimilating one or deliberately marked or whatever. What the skopos states is that one must translate, consciously and consistently, in accordance with some principle respecting the target text. The theory does not state what the principle is: This must be decided separately in each specific case. An optimally faithful rendering of a source text, in the sense of a transcoding, is thus one perfectly legitimate goal. The skopos theory merely states that the translator should be aware that *some* goal exists, and that any given goal is only one among many possible ones. (How many goals are actually realizable is another matter. We might assume that in at least some cases the number of realizable goals is one only.) The important point is that a given source text does not have one correct or best translation only (Vermeer, 1979, 1983, pp. 62 – 88).

We can maintain, then, that every reception or production of a text can at least retrospectively be assigned a skopos, as can every translation, by an observer or literary scholar etc. ; and also that every action is guided by a skopos. If we now turn this argument around we can postulate *a priori* that translation—because it is an action—always presupposes a skopos and is directed by a skopos. It follows that every translation commission should explicitly or implicitly contain a statement of skopos in order to be carried out at all. Every translation presupposes a commission, even though it may be set by the translator to himself (*I will translate this keeping close to the original* ...). "A" statement of skopos implies that it is not necessarily identical with the skopos attributed to the source text: There are cases where such identity is not possible.

4　The translation commission

Someone who translates undertakes to do so as a matter of deliberate choice (I exclude the possibility of translating under hypnosis), or because he is required to do so. One translates as a result of either one's own initiative or someone else's: In both cases, that is, one acts in accordance with a "commission" (*Auftrag*).

Let us define a commission as the instruction, given by oneself or by someone else, to carry out a given action—here: to translate. (Throughout the present article translation is taken to include interpretation.)

Nowadays, in practice, commissions are normally given explicitly (*Please translate the accompanying text*), although seldom with respect to the ultimate purpose of the text. In real life, the specification of purpose, addressees etc. is usually sufficiently apparent from the commission situation itself: Unless otherwise indicated, it will be assumed in our culture that for instance a technical article about some astronomical discovery is to be translated as a technical article for astronomers, and the actual place of publication is regarded as irrelevant; or if a company wants a business letter translated, the natural assumption is that the letter will be used by the company in question (and in most cases the translator will already be sufficiently familiar with the company's own in-house style, etc.). To the extent that these assumptions are valid, it can be maintained that any translation is carried out according to a skopos. In the absence of a specification, we can still often speak of an implicit (or implied) skopos. It nevertheless seems appropriate to stress here the necessity for a change of attitude among many translators and clients: As far as possible, detailed information concerning the skopos should always be given.

With the exception *of forces majeures*—or indeed even including them, according to the conception of "commission" (cf. the role of so-called inspiration in the case of biblical texts)—the above definition, with the associated arguments, allows us to state that every translation is based on a commission.

A commission comprises (or should comprise) as much detailed information as possible on the following: (1) the goal, i. e. a specification of the aim of the commission (cf. the scheme of specification factors in Nord, 1988, p. 170); (2) the conditions under which the intended goal should be attained (naturally including practical matters such as deadline and fee). The statement of goal and the conditions should be explicitly negotiated between the client (commissioner) and the translator, for the client may occasionally have an imprecise or even false picture of the way a text might be received in the target culture. Here the translator should be able to make argumentative suggestions. A commission can (and should) only be binding and conclusive, and accepted as such by the translator, if the conditions are clear enough. (I am aware that this requirement involves a degree of wishful thinking; yet it is something to strive for.) Cf. Holz Mänttäri, 1984, p. 91f, p. 113; Nord, 1988, p. 9, p. 284, note 4.

The translator is the expert in translational action (Holz-Mänttäri, 1984, 1985); as an expert he is therefore responsible for deciding whether, when, how, etc. , a translation can be realized (the Lasswell formula is relevant here—see Lasswell, 1964, p. 37; Vermeer, 1986, p. 197 and references there). The *realizability* of a commission depends on the circumstances of the target culture, not on those of the source culture. What is dependent on the source culture is the source text. A commission is only indirectly dependent on the source culture to the extent that a translation, by definition, must involve a source text. One might say that the realizability of a commission depends on the relation between the target culture and the source text; yet this would only be a special case of the general dependence on the target culture: a special case, that is, insofar as the commission is basically independent of the source text function. If the discrepancy is too great, however, no translation is possible—at most a rewritten text or the like. We shall not discuss this here. But it should be noted that a target culture generally offers a wide range of potential, including e. g. possible extension through the adoption of phenomena from other cultures. How far this is possible depends on the target culture. (For this kind of adoption see e. g. Toury, 1980.)

I have been arguing—I hope plausibly—that every translation can and must be assigned a skopos. This idea can now be linked with the concept of commission: It is precisely by means of the commission that the skopos is assigned. (Recall that a translator may also set his own commission.)

If a commission cannot be realized, or at least not optimally, because the client is not familiar with the conditions of the target culture, or does not accept them, the competent translator (as an expert in intercultural action, since translational action is a particular kind of intercultural action) must enter into negotiations with the client in order to establish what kind of "optimal" translation can be guaranteed under the circumstances. We shall not attempt to define "optimal" here—it is presumably a supra-individual concept. We are simply using the term to designate one of the best translations possible in the given circumstances, one of those that best realize the goal in question. Besides, "optimal" is clearly also a relative term: "Optimal under certain circumstances" may mean "as good as possible in view of the resources available" or "in view of the wishes of the client," etc. —and always only in the opinion of the translator, and/or of the recipient, etc. The translator, as the expert, decides in a given situation whether to accept a commission or not, under what circumstances, and whether it needs to be modified.

The skopos of a translation is therefore the goal or purpose, defined by the commission and if necessary adjusted by the translator. In order for the skopos to be defined precisely, the commission must thus be as specific as possible (Holz-Mänttäri, 1984). If the commission is specific enough, after possible adjustment by the translator himself, the decision can then be taken about *how* to translate optimally, i. e. what kind of changes will be necessary in the *translatum* with respect to the source text.

This concept of the commission thus leads to the same result as the skopos theory outlined above: A *translatum* is primarily determined by its skopos or its commission, accepted by the translator as being adequate to the goal of the action. As we have argued, a *translatum* is not *ipso facto* a "faithful" imitation of the source text. "Fidelity" to the source text (whatever the interpretation or definition of fidelity) is one possible and legitimate skopos or commission. Formulated in this way, neither skopos nor commission are new concepts as such—both simply make explicit something which has always existed. Yet they do specify something that has hitherto either been implicitly put into practice more unconsciously than consciously, or else been neglected or even rejected altogether: That is, the fact that one translates according to a particular purpose, which implies translating in a certain manner, without giving way freely to every impulse; the fact that there must always be a clearly defined goal. The two concepts also serve to relativize a viewpoint that has often been seen as the only valid one: that a source text should be translated "as literally as possible."

Neglecting to specify the commission or the skopos has one fatal consequence: There has been little agreement to date about the best method of translating a given text. In the context of the skopos or the commission this must now be possible, at least as regards the macro-strategy. (As regards individual text elements we still know too little about the functioning of the brain, and hence of culture and language, to be able to rely on much more than intuition when choosing between different variants which may appear to the individual translator to be equally possible and appropriate in a given case, however specific the skopos.) The skopos can also help to determine whether the source text needs to be "translated," "paraphrased" or completely "re-edited." Such strategies lead to terminologically different varieties of translational action, each based on a defined skopos which is itself based on a specified commission.

The skopos theory thus in no way claims that a translated text should *ipso facto* conform to the target culture behaviour or expectations, that a translation must always "adapt" to the target culture. This is just one possibility: The theory equally well accommodates the opposite type of translation, deliberately marked, with the intention of expressing source-culture features by target-culture means. Everything between these two extremes is likewise possible, including hybrid cases. To know what the point of a translation is, to be conscious of the action—that is the goal of the skopos theory. The theory campaigns against the belief that there is no aim (in any sense whatever), that translation is a purposeless activity.

Are we not just making a lot of fuss about nothing, then? No, insofar as the following claims are justified: (1) The theory makes explicit and conscious something that is too often denied; (2) the skopos, which is (or should be) defined in the commission, expands the possibilities of translation, increases the range of possible translation strategies, and releases the translator from the corset of an enforced—and hence often meaningless—literalness; and (3) it incorporates and enlarges the accountability of the translator, in that his translation must function in such a way that the given goal is attained. This accountability in fact lies at the very heart of the theory: What we are talking about is no less than the ethos of the translator.

By way of conclusion, here is a final example illustrating the importance of the skopos or commission.

An old French textbook had a piece about a lawsuit concerning an inheritance of considerable value. Someone had bequeathed a certain sum to two nephews. The will had been folded when the ink was still wet, so that a number of small ink-blots had appeared in the text. In one place, the text could read either as *deux* "two" or *d'eux* "of them." The lawsuit was about whether the sentence in question read *à chacun deux cent mille francs* "to each, two hundred thousand francs," or *à chacun d'eux cent mille francs* "to each of them, one hundred thousand francs. " Assume that the case was being heard in, say, a German court of law, and that a translation of the will was required. The skopos (and commission) would obviously be to translate in a "documentary" way, so that the judge would understand the ambiguity. The translator might for instance provide a note or comment to the effect that two readings were possible at the point in question, according to whether the apostrophe was interpreted as an inkblot or not, and explain them (rather as I have done here). —Now assume a different context, where the same story occurs as a minor incident in a novel. In this case a translator will surely not wish to interrupt the flow of the narrative with an explanatory comment, but rather try to find a target language solution with a similar kind of effect, e. g. perhaps introducing an ambiguity concerning the presence or absence of a crucial comma, so that 2000, 00 francs might be interpreted either as 2000 or as 200000 francs. Here the story is being used "instrumentally;" the translation does not need to reproduce every detail, but aims at an equivalent effect. The two different solutions are equally possible and attainable because each conforms to a different skopos. And this is precisely the point of the example: One does not translate a source text in a void, as it were, but always according to a given skopos or commission.

The above example also illustrates the fact that any change of skopos from source to target text, or between different translations, gives rise to a separate target text, e. g. as regards its text variety. [On text varieties (*Textsorten*), see Reiss & Vermeer, 1984; but cf. also Gardt's (1987, p. 555) observation that translation strategies are bound to text varieties only "in a strictly limited way. "] The source text does not determine the variety of the target text, nor does the text variety determine *ipso facto* the form of the target text (the text variety does not determine the skopos, either); rather, it is the skopos of the translation that also determines the appropriate text variety. A "text variety," in the sense of a classificatory sign of a *translatum*, is thus a consequence of the skopos, and thereby secondary to it. In a given culture it is the skopos that determines which text variety a *translatum* should conform to.

For example:

An epic is usually defined as a long narrative poem telling of heroic deeds. But Homer's *Odyssey* has also been translated into a novel—its text variety has thus changed from epic to novel, because of a particular skopos. [Cf. Schadewaldt's (1958) translation into German, and the reasons he gives there for this change; also see Vermeer, 1983, pp. 89 – 130.]

【延伸阅读】

[1] Nord, C. (1997). *Translating as a Purposeful Activity*: *Functionalist Approaches Explained*. Manchester: St. Jerome Publishing.

[2] Schäffner, C. (1998). Skopos Theory. In M. Baker (ed.), *Routledge Encyclopedia of Translation Studies*. London and New York: Routledge.

【问题与思考】

1. 威密尔的目的论与赖斯的文本类型理论有何关联？
2. 如何正确理解翻译中的委任？你同意威密尔关于委任的所有观点吗？为什么？
3. 你认为威密尔对反目的论的观点的驳斥有说服力吗？请陈述理由。
4. 目的法则似乎与忠实法则差异很大，翻译时译者应何去何从？为什么？
5. 威密尔翻译目的论有何不足？为什么？

选文三 Translating as a Purposeful Activity：Functionalist Approaches Explained（Excerpt）

Christiane Nord

导 言

　　本文节选自德国功能主义翻译学派代表人物克里斯蒂安·诺德(Christiane Nord)的著作《目的性行为——析功能翻译理论》(*Translating as a Purposeful Activity：Functionalist Approaches Explained*)中的第三章"Basic Aspects of Skopostheorie"。该书用通俗易懂的语言和大量的实例全面介绍了德国功能翻译学派的理论。贯穿全书的一条主线便是威密尔的目的论，也就是该书的第三章——本篇选文的主要内容。

　　目的论就是将 Skopos 概念运用到翻译中的理论，它的核心观点是：决定翻译过程的最主要因素是整体翻译行为的目的。选文从两个角度介绍了目的论的基本概念：威密尔的"一般理论"和赖斯的"具体理论"。文章阐述了"一般理论"中的 Skopos、目标、目的、意图、功能和翻译纲要等概念，对目标与目的、意图与功能加以区分，并详细介绍了翻译纲要对翻译行为的目的起到的作用。文章分析了威密尔对"一致"所下的定义，包括"篇际一致"(intertextual coherence)和"篇内一致"(intratextual coherence)，继而讨论了威密尔理论中"文化"的概念。文章剖析了"具体理论"中的合适(adequacy)与对等(equivalence)的概念，并详细介绍了文本分类及其作用。

　　本文对目的论主要概念和理论的进一步解释，有助于人们更好地理解和接受目的论。

The theory of action outlined in the previous chapter provides the foundation for Hans J. Vermeer's general theory of translation, which he calls *Skopostheorie*. In addition to the works mentioned earlier (Vermeer，1978，1983，1986a) the theory is explained in detail in the book co-authored by Vermeer and Reiss in 1984. The first part of this book presents Vermeer's general or "basic theory" (pp. 6 - 121)，which is then made compatible with various translation traditions in the "specific theories" part written by Reiss (pp. 122 – 219). There is nevertheless a certain discrepancy between the two parts of the book, largely due to the fact that Reiss tried to adjust her text-bound approach, originally based on equivalence theory, to Vermeer's action-oriented approach.

In the following sections we will take a closer look at some of the basic concepts presented in the book, placing particular emphasis on the relationship between the general theory (Vermeer) and the specific theories (Reiss). The first three sections will deal with Vermeer's concepts of Skopos, coherence and culture, while the two remaining sections explain Reiss's concepts of adequacy vs. equivalence and the role of her text-typology within the frame of a functional approach to translation.

Skopos, aim, purpose, intention, function and translation brief

Skopos is a Greek word for "purpose." According to *Skopostheorie* (the theory that applies the notion of *Skopos* to translation), the prime principle determining any translation process is the purpose (*Skopos*) of the overall translational action. This fits in with intentionality being part of the very definition of any action.

To say that an action is intentional is to presuppose the existence of free will and a choice between at least two possible forms of behaviour. One form of behaviour is nevertheless held to be more appropriate than the other in order to attain the intended goal or purpose (*Skopos*). As Vermeer puts it, quoting Hubbell's translation of Cicero's De inventione, "genuine reasons for actions can always be formulated in terms of aims or statements of goals" (1989b, p. 176). In his De inventione (2. 5. 18), Cicero defines actions when he speaks of cases where "some disadvantage," or some advantage is neglected in order to gain a greater advantage or avoid a greater disadvantage (cit. Vermeer, 1989b, p. 176).

We can distinguish between three possible kinds of purpose in the field of translation: the general purpose aimed at by the translator in the translation process (perhaps "to earn a living"), the communicative purpose aimed at by the target text in the target situation (perhaps "to instruct the reader") and the purpose aimed at by a particular translation strategy or procedure (for example, "to translate literally in order to show the structural particularities of the source language") (cf. Vermeer, 1989a, p. 100). Nevertheless, the term *Skopos* usually refers to the purpose of the target text.

Apart from the term *Skopos*, Vermeer uses the related words aim, purpose, intention and function. We find a distinction between aim and purpose in Vermeer, 1990, p. 93ff:

> "Aim" (Ziel) is defined as the final result an agent intends to achieve by means of an action (cf. Vermeer, 1986a, p. 239). For example, a person may learn Chinese in order to read Li T'ai-po in the original (Vermeer, 1989a, p. 93).

> "Purpose" (Zweck) is defined as a provisional stage in the process of attaining an aim. Aim and purpose are thus relative concepts. For example, somebody goes

out to buy a Basque grammar (purpose 1) in order to learn the language (purpose 2) in order to be able to translate Basque short stories (purpose 3) in order to make Basque literature known to other language communities (aim) (example adapted from Vermeer 1989a, p. 94).

"Function" (Funktion) refers to what a text means or is intended to mean from the receiver's point of view, whereas the aim is the purpose for which it is needed or supposed to be needed (cf. Vermeer, 1989a, p. 95).

"Intention" (Intention or Absicht) is conceived as an "aim-oriented plan of action" (Vermeer, [1978] 1983, p. 41) on the part of both the sender and the receiver, pointing toward an appropriate way of producing or understanding the text (cf. Vermeer, 1986a, p. 414). The term intention is also equated with function of the action (Reiss & Vermeer, 1984, p. 98).

In order to avoid this conceptual confusion, I have proposed a basic distinction between intention and function (Nord, [1988], 1991, p. 47f). "Intention" is defined from the viewpoint of the sender, who wants to achieve a certain purpose with the text. Yet the best of intentions do not guarantee a perfect result, particularly in cases where the situations of the sender and the receiver differ considerably. In accordance with the model of text-bound interaction, the receivers use the text with a certain function, depending on their own expectations, needs, previous knowledge and situational conditions. In an ideal situation the sender's intention will find its aim, in which case intention and function would be analogous or even identical.

This distinction is particularly useful in translation, where the sender and receiver by definition belong to different cultural and situational settings. Because of this separation of sender and receiver, intention and function may have to be analyzed from two different angles.

Vermeer briefly discusses my distinction but does not take it up (cf. Vermeer, 1989a, p. 94f). As a general rule he considers the teleological concepts aim, purpose, intention and function to be equivalent (cf. Reiss & Vermeer, 1984, p. 96), subsuming them under the generic concept of Skopos.

The top-ranking-rule for any translation is thus the "Skopos rule," which says that a translational action is determined by its Skopos; that is, "the end justifies the means" (Reiss & Vermeer, 1984, p. 101). Vermeer explains the skopos rule in the following way.

Each text is produced for a given purpose and should serve this purpose. The Skopos rule thus reads as follows: translate/interpret/speak/write in a way that enables your text/translation to function in the situation in which it is used and with the people who want to use it and precisely in the way they want it to function. (Vermeer, 1989a, p. 20; my translation)

Most translational actions allow a variety of Skopoi, which may be related to each other in a hierarchical order. The translator should be able to justify (begründen) their choice of a particular Skopos in a given translational situation.

This rule is intended to solve the eternal dilemmas of free vs. faithful translation, dynamic vs. formal equivalence, good interpreters vs. slavish translators, and so on. It means that the Skopos of a particular translation task may require a "free" or a "faithful" translation, or anything between these two extremes, depending on the purpose for which the translation is needed. What it does not mean is that a good translation should *ipso facto* conform or adapt to target-culture behaviour or expectations, although the concept is often misunderstood in this way.

This misunderstanding may be due to a subsequent rule that, in a more sociological way, states that the Skopos can be described as a "variable of the receiver" (Reiss & Vermeer, 1984, p. 101). This means that the receiver, or rather the addressee, is the main factor determimng the target-text Skopos. What it does not mean, however, is that this strictly excludes philological or literal or even word-for-word translations. There are many cases where relative literalism is precisely what the receiver (or the Client or the user) needs, for example in the translation of a marriage certificate or driver's license, foreign legal texts for comparative purposes or direct quotations in newspaper reports. As Vermeer puts it,

> what the Skopos states is that one must translate, consciously and consistently, in accordance with some principle respecting the target text. The theory does not state what the principle is: This must be decided separately in each specific case. (1989b, p. 182)

Now, the question is who decides what the principle is. Yet the answer is fairly obvious. As we have mentioned above, translation is normally done "by assignment." A client needs a text for a particular purpose and calls upon the translator for a translation, thus acting as the initiator of the translation process. In an ideal case, the client would give as many details as possible about the purpose, explaining the addressees, time, place, occasion and medium of the intended communication and the function the text is intended to have. This information would constitute an explicit translation brief (*Übersetzungsauftrag*).

Here we have to clarify a translation problem. The German word *Übersetzungsaufirag* may be translated literally as either translation commission or translation assignment. We find both terms used in works by (mostly German) functionalist translation scholars writing in English or translated into English. Vermeer (1989b) uses the term commission, whereas Pöchhacker (1995, p. 34) and Kussmaul (1995, p. 7 et passim) speak of assignment. Nord has even introduced a third term, translating instructions, "because it highlights the pedagogical aspect" ([1988] 1991, p. 8, note 3). However, in a recent study Janet Fraser uses the term brief (1995, p. 73), which seems to express very aptly what is meant by *Übersetzungsauftrag*. It implicitly compares the translator with a barrister who has received the basic information and instructions but is then free (as the responsible expert) to carry out those instructions as they see fit. In the present book we will thus use the term translation brief wherever appropriate.

The translation brief specifies what kind of translation is needed. This is why the initiator or the person playing the role of initiator (who might also be the translator) actually decides on the translation *Skopos*, even though the brief as such may not be explicit about the conditions.

Evidently, the *Skopos* often has to be negotiated between the client and the translator, especially when the client has only a vague or even incorrect idea of what kind of text is needed for the situation in question. Clients do not normally bother to give the translator an explicit translation brief, not being experts in intercultural communication, they often do not know that a good brief spells a better translation.

Note that the translation brief does not tell the translator how to go about their translating job, what translation strategy to use, or what translation type to choose. These decisions depend entirely on the translator's responsibility and competence. If the client and the translator disagree as to what kind of target text would serve the intended purpose best, the translator may either refuse the assignment (and starve) or refuse any responsibility for the function of the target text and simply do what the client asks for.

In many cases, of course, an experienced translator is able to infer the *Skopos* from the translational situation itself. As Vermeer puts it,

> unless otherwise indicated, it will be assumed in our culture that for instance a technical article about some astronomical discovery is to be translated as a technical article for astronomers [...] or if a company wants a business letter translated, the natural assumption is that the letter will be used by the company in question (and in most cases the translator will already be sufficiently familiar with the company's own in-house style, etc.). (Vermeer, 1989b, p. 183)

This is what I would call a "conventional assignment," since it is based on the general assumption that, in a particular culture community at a given time, certain types of text are normally translated by certain types of translation. Katharina Reiss's correlation between text type and translation method (1971, 1976) is based precisely on this assumption.

This leads us to another, more specific aspect of *Skopostheorie*, namely the relationship between the source and target texts within a functionalist framework.

Intertextual and intratextual coherence

In terms of *Skopostheorie*, the viability of the brief depends on the circumstances of the target culture, not on the source culture. Since we have defined translation as a translational action involving a source text, the source is usually part of the brief. In terms of action theory, however, the agents (sender, receiver, initiator, translator) play the most important parts and it is problematic to speak of "the source text" unless we really only mean source language words or sentence structures. The meaning or function of a text is not something inherent in the linguistic signs; it cannot simply be extracted by anyone who knows the code. A text is made meaningful by its receiver and for its receiver. Different receivers (or even the same receiver at different times) find different meanings in the same linguistic material offered by the text. We might even say that a "text" is as many texts as there are receivers (cf. Nord, 1992b, p. 91).

This dynamic concept of text meaning and function is common enough in modern theories of literary reception (*Rezeptionsästhetik*). Vermeer sums it up by saying that any text is just an "offer of information" (cf. Vermeer, 1982) from which each receiver selects the items they find interesting and important. Applying this concept to translation, we could say that a target text is an offer of information formulated by a translator in a target culture and language about an offer of information formulated by someone else in the source culture and language (cf. Reiss & Vermeer, 1984, p. 67ff).

This concept does not allow us to speak of the meaning of the source text being transferred to the target receivers. Guided by the translation brief, the translator selects certain items from the source-language offer of information (originally meant for source-culture addressees) and processes them in order to form a new offer of information in the target language, from which the target-culture addressees can in turn select what they consider to be meaningful in their own situation. In these terms, the translation process is irreversible.

What the translator can do, and should do, is to produce a text that is at least likely to be meaningful to target-culture receivers. In Vermeer's terms, the target text should conform to the standard of "intratextual coherence"(Reiss & Vermeer, 1984, p. 109ff). This means the receiver should be able to understand it; it should make sense in the communicative situation and culture in which it is received (cf. Pöchhacker, 1995, p. 34). A communicative interaction can only be regarded as successful if the receivers interpret it as being sufficiently coherent with their situation. Accordingly, another important rule of *Skopostheorie*, the "coherence rule," specifies that a translation should be acceptable in a sense that it is coherent with the receivers' situation (Reiss & Vermeer, 1984, p. 113). Being "coherent with" is synonymous with being "part of" the receiver's situation (cf. Vermeer [1978], 1983, p. 54).

However, since a translation is an offer of information about a preceding offer of information, it is expected to bear some kind of relationship with the corresponding source text. Vermeer calls this relationship "intertextual coherence" or "fidelity." This is postulated as a further principle, referred to as the "fidelity rule" (Reiss & Vermeer, 1984, p. 114). Again, as in the case of the *Skopos* rule, the important point is that intertextual coherence should exist between source and target text, while the form it takes depends both on the translator's interpretation of the source text and on the translation *Skopos*. One possible kind of intertextual coherence could be a maximally faithful imitation of the source text. As Vermeer points out, this may be the form expected in literary translation:

> It might be said that the postulate of "fidelity" to the source text requires that e. g. a news item should be translated "as it was in the original. " But this too is a goal in itself. Indeed, it is by definition probably the goal that most literary translators traditionally set themselves. (1989b, p. 179f)

Intertextual coherence is considered subordinate to intratextual coherence, and both are subordinate to the Skopos rule. If the Skopos requires a change of function, the standard will no longer be intertextual coherence with the source text but adequacy or appropriateness with regard to the Skopos (Reiss & Vermeer, 1984, p. 139). And if the Skopos demands intratextual incoherence (as in the theatre of the absurd), the standard of intratextual coherence is no longer valid.

Note that the Skopos concept is applicable not only to entire texts but also to text segments or "in-texts" such as examples, footnotes or citations (Nord [1988], 1991, p. 102). The Skopos or sub-Skopos of such smaller units may be different from that of other segments or the text as a whole.

The concept of culture and culture-specificity

Vermeer's concept of culture is based on Göhring's definition, which is in turn based on the concept cited from Goodenough in the previous chapter (cf. Vermeer, 1986a, p. 178):

> Culture is whatever one has to know, master or feel in order to judge whether or not a particular form of behaviour shown by members of a community in their various roles conforms to general expectations, and in order to behave in this community in accordance with general expectations unless one is prepared to bear the consequences of unaccepted behaviour. (Göhring, 1978, p. 10; my translation)

Vermeer places special emphasis on the following features of the definition: its dynamic qualities (focusing on human action and behaviour), its comprehensiveness (conceiving culture as a complex system determining any human action or behaviour, including language) and the fact that it may be used as a starting point for a descriptive as well as explicative or prescriptive approach to culture-specificity (cf. Vermeer, 1986a, p. 179). Vermeer's own definition focuses even more on norms and conventions as the main features of a culture. For him, a culture is

> the entire setting of norms and conventions an individual as a member of his society must know in order to be "like everybody" or to be able to be different from everybody. (Vermeer, 1987a, p. 28)

According to Vermeer, every cultural phenomenon is assigned a position in a complex system of values, it is "evaluated." And every individual is an element in a system of spacetime coordinates. If this is accepted, transcultural action or communication across culture barriers has to take account of cultural differences with regard to behaviour, evaluation and communicative situations (cf. Vermeer, 1990b, p. 29).

Cultural features have been termed "culturemes" (Vermeer, 1983a, p. 8). A cultureme is a social phenomenon of a culture X that is regarded as relevant by the members of this culture and, when compared with a corresponding social phenomenon in a culture Y, is found to be specific to culture X. "Corresponding" here means that the two phenomena are comparable under certain definable conditions (cf. Vermeer & Witte, 1990, p. 137). For example, they may be different in form but similar in function (as in trains vs. cars vs. bicycles) or vice versa (for example, "to have coffee" in England in the morning vs. "tomar un café" in Spain after dinner vs. "Kaffeetrinken" in Germany in the afternoon).

A culture-specific phenomenon is thus one that is found to exist in a particular form or function in only one of the two cultures being compared. This does not mean that the phenomenon exists only in that particular culture. The same phenomenon might be observable in cultures other than the two in question.

Translating means comparing cultures. Translators interpret sourceculture phenomena in the light of their own culture-specific knowledge of that culture, from either the inside or the outside, depending on whether the translation is from or into the translator's native language-and-culture. A foreign culture can only be perceived by means of comparison with our own culture, the culture of our primary enculturation (cf. Witte, 1987, p. 119). There can be no neutral standpoint for comparison. Everything we observe as being different from our own culture is, for us, specific to the other culture. The concepts of our own culture will thus be the touchstones for the perception of otherness. Further, our attention tends to focus on phenomena that are either different from our own culture (where we had expected similarity) or similar to our own culture (where difference had been expected).

If every action is to be seen in the context of a specific culture, this applies to translation as well. We may thus assume there are various culture-specific concepts of what constitutes translation or a translational action. This point will be taken up in the next chapter.

Adequacy and equivalence

When presenting an offer of information the source-text author takes account of the presumed interests, expectations, knowledge and situational constraints of the source-culture addressees. Even if a source text is produced specifically for translation purposes it may be assumed that the author has some kind of source-culture addressees in mind, since source-culture text producers by definition lack all the necessary knowledge of the target culture. If they didn't, they would probably compose the target text themselves, in the target language (cf. Vermeer, 1989b, p. 175).

In the case of a translation, the translator is a real receiver of the source text who then proceeds to inform another audience, located in a situation under target-culture conditions, about the offer of information made by the source text. The translator offers this new audience a target text whose composition is, of course, guided by the translator's assumptions about their needs, expectations, previous knowledge, and so on. These assumptions will obviously be different from those made by the original author, because sourcetext addressees and target-text addressees belong to different cultures and language communities. This means the translator cannot offer the same amount and kind of information as the source-text producer. What the translator does is offering another kind of information in another form (cf. Reiss & Vermeer, 1984, p. 123).

This view of the translator's task directly challenges the traditional concept of equivalence as a constitutive feature of translation. But does it negate equivalence entirely? A certain answer may be found in the work of Reiss. After discussing several definitions of equivalence, Reiss does not completely abandon the concept; instead, she relates it to the superordinate concept of adequacy (Adäquatheit) (Reiss & Vermeer, 1984, p. 124).

We should note here that Reiss's concept of "adequacy" is almost the opposite of other uses of the term. Toury, for instance, points out that "adherence to source norms determines a translation's adequacy as compared to the source text" (1995, p. 56; emphasis in the original). He also cites the following definition by Even-Zohar:

> An adequate translation is a translation which realizes in the target language the textual relationships of a source text with no breach of its own [basic] linguistic system. (Even-Zohar, 1975, p. 43; Toury's translation)

Like Adäquatheit in German, adequacy describes a quality with regard to a particular standard, as in "I hope you will prove adequate to the job." This is the sense that Reiss makes use of. Within the framework of Skopostheorie, "adequacy" refers to the qualities of a target text with regard to the translation brief: The translation should be "adequate to" the reqirements of the brief. It is a dynamic concept related to the process of translational action and referring to the "goal-oriented selection of signs that are considered appropriate for the communicative purpose defined in the translation assignment" (Reiss, [1983] 1989, p. 163).

"Equivalence," on the other hand, is a static, result-oriented concept describing a relationship of "equal communicative value" between two texts or, on lower ranks, between words, phrases, sentences, syntactic structures and so on. In this context "value" refers to meaning, stylistic connotations or communicative effect. Reiss ([1983] 1989, p. 163) makes a distinction between the concept of equivalence used in comparative linguistics (which studies langues or language-systems) and the notion of textual equivalence used in translation studies (which focuses on parole or speech acts). Paroleorientation means the translator has to take account of the way linguistic signs are used by communicative agents in culture-bound situations. For example, equivalence at word rank does not imply textual equivalence, nor does equivalence at text rank automatically lead to lexical or syntactic equivalence. The

Skopos of the translation determines the form of equivalence required for an adequate translation.

Example: For a word-for-word translation, where the purpose is a faithful reproduction of the words and structures of the source text, the translator chooses, one by one, the target-language words and structures corresponding exactly to those of the source-language with regard to meaning and, if possible, style. This is an adequate translation, which requires equivalence only on the ranks of words and syntactic structures. (cf. Reiss [1983]1989, p. 162)

For Reiss, the generic concept is adequacy, not equivalence. Equivalence may be one possible aim when translating but it is not held to be a translation principle valid once and for all (cf. Reiss & Vermeer, 1984, p. 146). Equivalence is by no means the kind of general normative defining quality we find expressed in definitions like Koller's:

> Translation can be understood as the result of a text-reprocessing activity, by means of which a source-language text is transposed into a target-language text. Between the resulting text in L2 (the target-language text) and the source text in L1 (the source-language text) there exists a relationship which can be designated as a translational, or equivalence relation. (1995, p. 196)

In *skopostheorie*, equivalence means adequacy to a *Skopos* that requires that the target text serve the same communicative function or functions as the source text, thus preserving "invariance of function between source and target text" (cf. Reiss & Vermeer, 1984, p. 140 and Vermeer's concept of fidelity or intertextual coherence, outlined above). That is, the concept of equivalence is reduced to "functional equivalence" on the text level of what Reiss refers to as "communicative translation." Reiss ([1983] 1989, p. 166) gives the following example.

> *Source text*: Is life worth living? —It depends upon the liver!
> *French translation*: La vie, vaut-elle la peine? —C'est une question de foi(e)!
> *German translation*: Ist das Leben lebenswert? —Das hängt von den leberwerten ab.

The French and German translations can be considered functional equivalents of the English original because they are apt to fulfil the same communicative function (a play on words) in their respective culture communities. The pun is based on the structural properties of each language: homonymy in the case of liver in English, homophony between foi (faith) and foie (liver) in French, and similarity of form between lebenswert (worthliving) and Leberwerte (liver count) in German. Equivalence here is thus not at word level.

The role of text classifications

Having seen the source text "dethroned" and regarded as a mere "offer of information" or the translator's "raw material" (Vermeer, 1987b, p. 541), one might be surprised to find that one of the specific theories in Reiss and Vermeer's 1984 book is Katharina Reiss's theory of text types. This has to be appreciated in connection with Reiss's concept of a specific translation type referred to as "communicative translation," which we have just seen associated with a certain notion of equivalence.

According to Reiss, text typologies help the translator specify the appropriate hierarchy of equivalence levels needed for a particular translation *Skopos* (cf. Reiss & Vermeer, 1984, p. 156). Like several other German linguists and translation scholars, Reiss ([1977] 1989, p. 105) distinguishes between two forms of text categorization, which are located on different levels of abstraction: On the one hand, text types (Texttypen) are classified according to the dominant communicative function (basically informative, expressive or operative); on the other, text genres or varieties (Textsorten) are classified according to linguistic characteristics or conventions (like those of reference books, lectures, satires or advertisements).

Reiss's text typology, first published in 1968—1969, is based on the "organon model" of language functions proposed by the German psychologist Karl Bühler in 1934. The typology will be briefly summarized in the following paragraphs (for more details see Nord, 1996b, p. 82ff).

In informative texts the main function is to inform the reader about objects and phenomena in the real world. The choice of linguistic and stylistic forms is subordinate to this function. Since the typology is assumed to be universal, this applies to both the source and the target cultures. In a translation where both the source and the target texts are of the informative type, the translator should attempt to give a correct and complete representation of the source text's content and should be guided, in terms of stylistic choices, by the dominant norms of the target language and culture. As Reiss points out in a more recent description of her typology ([1977] 1989, p. 108), the informative type is also taken to include "purely phatic communication, where the actual information value is zero and the message is the communication process itself."

In *expressive* texts the informative aspect is complemented or even overruled by an aesthetic component. The stylistic choices made by the author contribute to the meaning of the text, producing an aesthetic effect on the reader. This effect has to be taken into account in translation. If the target text is meant to belong to the same category as the source (which, for example, is not the case in bilingual editions of poetry) the translator of an expressive text should attempt to produce an analogous stylistic effect. In this case, stylistic choices in translation are naturally guided by those made in the source text.

In operative texts both content and form are subordinate to the extralinguistic effect that the text is designed to achieve. The translating of operative texts into operative texts should be guided by the overall aim of bringing about the same reaction in the audience, although this might involve changing the content and/or stylistic features of the original.

In her first publications on text typology and translation, Reiss established a general correlation between text type and translation method. Within the framework of Skopostheorie, however, this correlation is restricted to the special case of functional invariance between source and target text. Nevertheless, Reiss's comments on the divergent relationships between content, form and effect in the three text types may also be useful in cases calling for functional change, since any kind of target text may be seen as representing a particular text type. Text-type classifications sharpen the translator's awareness of linguistic markers of communicative function and functional translation units.

Each text type is assumed to include various text genres, but one text genre (such as letters) does not necessarily correlate with just one text type: A love letter may be of the expressive type, a business letter would be informative, whereas a letter requesting help would belong to the operative type. Since text genres are characterized by conventional features, their classification plays an important role in functional translation. The importance of conventions will be discussed in greater detail in the next chapter.

【延伸阅读】

[1] Nord, C. (1997). *Translating as a Purposeful Activity*. Manchester: St Jerome Publishing.

【问题与思考】

1. 到底应该如何区分下面一组概念:Skopos, aim, purpose, intention?
2. 篇际一致与篇内一致有何实质性的不同?
3. 合适与对等有何不同? 区分这对概念有什么意义?
4. 诺德是如何看待文本分类的作用的?

选文四　翻译目的论及其文本意识的弱化倾向

潘平亮

导　言

本文发表于《上海翻译》2006 年第 1 期。

翻译目的论是从译文视角进行翻译研究的一种解构主义的理论模式,它以译文功能为取向,注重翻译的实用性。本文介绍了目的论产生的时代背景,指出它在反拨传统翻译理论中"文本中心论"方面的积极作用,并同时论述了其自身文本意识的弱化倾向。

1　目的论产生的背景

自巴特从"话语"的视角撼动了作者的文本中心地位开始,到他宣布"作者的死亡"(方生,1999:90),再到 20 世纪 60 年代接受美学和读者反应批评文论思想正式在欧洲登上历史舞台,这一系例事件标志着以"读者为中心"的"接受美学向整个西方批评发动冲击"。(金元浦,1998:3)这是姚斯、伊瑟尔等一批文论家开辟的时代新风,它也为翻译目的论的诞生提供了肥沃的土壤。从译文角度、从翻译的实用功能来进行翻译理论建构与翻译实践(最初是翻译培训)探索就成了几代翻译目的论倡导者的一条研究主线。

凯瑟琳娜·赖斯(Katharina Reiss)在 1971 年出版的 *Possibilities and Limitations in Translation Criticism* 一书中首次提出了功能派理论。她认为在实践中出于翻译具体要求(translation brief)(包括翻译的发起人要求、译者的目的和译文读者的要求与期待等)的需要,译文可能与原文的功能不同,译者应该优先考虑译文的功能特征而不是对等原则。(Nord,2001:前言)后来,其学生威密尔(Vermeer)在她的理论基础上创立了翻译目的论(Skopostheorie),进一步把翻译从源语的奴役中解放出来,摆脱传统翻译中的"文本中心论"。他认为:"仅仅语言学不能帮助我们(翻译),因为其一翻译不仅仅甚至不主要是一个语言学的过程;其二语言学还没有找到有效的方法来解决翻译中的问题。因此我们要把目光投向其他领域。"(Nord,2001:10)他目光投向的是宏观的后现代文化语境,尤其是译语文化的传统、习惯以及规范等诸多社会因素,也是每个具体翻译功能实现的必不可少的要素。之后,贾斯塔·赫兹·曼塔利(Justa Holz Manttari)把翻译直接定义为"翻译目的性行为",即翻译是"为取得某一特定目的而进行的复杂活动"。因而,翻译往往是译者从原作提供的诸多信息中进行选择性翻译;同时,翻译是文化比较,译者总是根据自己的特定文化知识来阐释"他者",这没有中间立场;"每个行为都是特定文化情境中的行为,翻译也不例外"(Nord,2001:34)。这实际上是把翻译看做具体的文化语境中的行为,而不是结构主义翻译家们所认为的"真空中的行为",翻译中的每一个决定都是在具体语境中作出的。因而,目的论主张文化的相对性,而不同于语言学翻译研究中强调文化的普遍一致性。诺德(Nord)是德国功能派的主要倡导者,她对目的论理论既继承又发展,提出了主要是针对文学文本翻译的"功能 plus 忠诚"的原则,一定程度上减少了人们对目的论功用主义的批评,扩大了其影响。

2　目的论对"文本中心论"的反拨

"文本中心论"是新批评文论的核心观点。新批评文论家兰色姆首先提出:应该建立文本中心论(胡经之,1998:200)。他们认为:"文学的本体即作品,作品本身是文学活动的本源与目的,作家的创作从作品中来,又回到作品中去。"(胡经之,1998:203)因此,文学作品就成了"自存自足的实体,无需外界的一切给予"。(同上)我们看到"文本中心论"的倡导者们用"作品"这一术语,不同于后结构主义文论家们所使用的"文本",表明了他们对作者"主宰"其创作的高度认可;因而,新批评文论家们只对作品本身关注,在一定程度上反映了他们诗学研究的特点,但是像韦勒克、沃伦、李维斯等人明确反对文学的社会性、文化性、经验性,而同时忽略作品与作品的历史联系和现实联系,其不足也是显而易见的(胡经之,1998:222)。

"文本中心论"的思想在翻译中一直体现为原作的"主宰"地位和译文的从属地位以及译者的奴仆形象。在漫漫几千年的翻译长河中,自经文的翻译发端,翻译便要"案本而传",与原作"亦步亦趋"。中国古代译经高僧释道安提出的"五失本"、"三不易"以及唐玄奘的"五不翻"(马祖毅,1998:36-37)等理论和《七十子希腊文本》的问世以及廷代尔因出版《新约》而被焚烧(谭载喜,2000:17,101)的事实无不反映出其时下的人们把原作奉为神明,对其顶礼膜拜。"忠实"的标准就是基于原文本神圣不可亵渎的地位而提出来的判断译文优劣的最高标准。虽然翻译家们时有"文"、"质"之争,但"忠实"的标准始终与翻译似影随形。

"等值论"是现当代"义本中心论"的代名词。它是雅各布森最先在翻译领域引入的术语,他的"On Linguistic Aspects of Translation"一文中生造的"差异对等"(equivalence in difference)一词,结果成了现当代翻译的关键词(Wilss, 2001:138)。其后,众多翻译家争相引用和阐述:卡特福德认为翻译是"将一种语言(源语)组成的材料替换成等值的另一种语言(译语)的成文材料"(黄忠廉,2000:10)。巴尔胡达罗夫给翻译下的定义是"翻译是把一种语言的言语产物在保持内容也就是意义不变的情况下改变为另一种语言的言语产物的过程"(巴尔胡达罗夫,1985:4-10)。这两位语言学大师俨然都是等值论"天条"的忠实守护者。而奈达,这位语言学派翻译研究的集大成者,将翻译等值定义为:所谓等值,就是译文读者能够像原文读者那样去理解和欣赏原文(Nida, 2001:87)。这是他从"形式对等"过渡到"功能对等"的翻译理论,其中已有"功能主义"的萌芽,但可惜他没有朝"功能主义"方向进一步发展,而是仍然偏重"对等"概念并为此而总结出一整套核心句式(kernel sentence)以对应翻译不同语言的句式,这使得"等值论"一直成为结构主义语言学范式翻译研究的桎梏。

"等值论"反映了结构主义语言学的翻译观,它蕴含了这样的预设前提:语言在表达上的普遍性及其对客观世界的"镜像反映";作者意图的"先在性";译者的全真模仿与表达及其文化价值观上的中立性;特别是译语、源语文化语境的无差异性即文化的普遍一致性。而这些前提在我们从语言哲学和后现代文化语境视角来重新加以审视时,发现它们都难以立足:语言的"表征危机"已在语言哲学的论证中一目了然——语言并非一面"镜子",能够对现存客观世界作出"镜像反映",语言具有不及物性和自足性;作者"意图"的先在性已为接受美学和读者反应文论的"意图谬误"说所论证;而译者的绝对中立的"忠实"表达不论在其伦理道德上还是在其语言能力上都难以得到保证;更为重要的是"文化普遍性"的误判已为我们的时代所匡正——突显文化身份以及包孕政治、宗教、意识形态等诸多因素的权力话语已成为后现代文化语境的主题。正如詹姆逊在《政治无意识》一书的开篇所说:"本书将论证对文学文本进行政治阐释的优越性。它不把政治视角作为某种增补的方法,不是作为当今流行的其他阐释方法……的选择性补充,而是作为一切阅读和一切阐释的绝对视界"(谢少波,1999:43)。因而,文本的自足性遇到了极大的挑战,诸多文本外部因素的介入对"文本中心论"进行了有力的解构。功能主义翻译论就是从译者的目的性和译文的实用性,以及文化的相对性入手,指出翻译的每一个决定并非都是原文本的厘定,而是具体语境与情境的产物,即目的论的翻译要求的具体厘定。这是对结构主义语言学范式下"文本中心论"的最有力的反拨。

赖斯首先提出了"翻译要求"这一术语,她认为译文要注重其功能。由于翻译要求的不同,在有些时候要求译文与原文有不同的功能。这个翻译要求,源于其培训基地中对培训学员翻译习作的具体指导,包括顾客的要求、译文的具体功能、译文读者的期待视野等(Nord, 2001:60)。在实际翻译中,还包括把关人(gate-keeper)以及出版地对新闻出版的审查等,渗透着一个社会经济、文化和政治的诸多因素。同时,目的论认为"文本是一个提供信息的信息源,读者从中选择感兴趣的或重要的信息"。因而,"原文不再是译者翻译首先或是首要考虑的标准,它只是译者选取信息时诸多因素中的一个"(Nord,2001:31,25)。而信息选择的重要依据是"语际连贯从属于语内的连贯,而它们都从属于目的原则"(Nord,2001:32-33)。由此,我们推断译文自身的功能性要比它对原文的忠实性更为重要。这样的译文 Reiss 称之为"称职的翻译"(adequate translation),因为它是对目的论中的"翻译要求"的"称职",与"等值论"中的"对等"不同。前者是动态的、共识论的,表现为对翻译要求的实现效果,即译文功能是否有效实现;而后者是静态的、符合论的,即以与原文相对照的结果为判断的标准。因而,以译语为倾向的目的论就从翻译研究的另一极入手,推翻了原文本的"中心"地位,树起了译文和译者的"中心"地位。

无独有偶,在目的论颠覆"文本中心论"的同时,图里也在世界的另一角进行着类似的研究。他在《描述翻译学及其他》一书中说,"威密尔目的论的提出几乎和我转向译语倾向的研究同时开始。这是学术趋势的有趣变化,特别是在我们彼此之间很长时间内都不了解对方工作的情况下"(Toury,2001:25)。这是 20 世纪 70 年代后"源语倾向"的翻译研究达到顶峰之后的两股反拨潮流,只可惜人们对描述翻译学这一分支未予足够重视(Toury,2001:出版前言)。而翻译目的论却在德国继而在世界范围内被人们所接受。但显而易见,目的论在树立新中心的同时,必然忽视前"中心"的地位与功能,出现另一个极端,即原文本意识的弱化倾向。

3 目的论原文本意识的弱化表现

相对于传统翻译理论重视翻译内部研究来说,目的论更注重翻译的外部研究。翻译发起人、译者的目的、翻译具体语境的设定、译文服务对象的考虑以及译文所处的宏观语境都形成了对原文本"唯我独尊"的挑战和解构。这是一种后结构主义的翻译观。它尊重社会文化语境的相对性和译文的具体语境的可理解性,运用相应的翻译策略,以达到翻译的目的;但它对原文本的"尊重"却大大降低。我们试从目的论研究者对文本功能的分类、对翻译要求的倚重、语内连贯优于语际连贯原则以及对译者角色的界定等几个方面来论证其原文本意识的弱化倾向。

Reiss 认为文本类型的分类可以帮助译者确定为某一特定的翻译目的而需要的相应对等程度(Nord,2001:37)。她将文本分为两个层次:一层是根据交际功能而划分的文本类型,包括信息型、表达型和祈使型;另一层是根据语言特征或表达习惯而划分的文体,包括文献体、演讲体、讽刺体和广告体。信息文本的主要功能是让读者了解现实世界的事物和现象,其语言和文体要从属于目的;在信息文本中,功能是最主要的,词汇和文体的选择是次要的,如寒暄、一些旅游景点的介绍等就属于信息文本,达到应有的交际效果就是成功的翻译。表达性文本中美学成分是主要的,译者要为读者创造美感,因而译文要有与原文类似的文体效果,多数文学文本的翻译便是如此。祈使性文本内容和文体都从属于文本要达到的言外效果,如广告宣传等。我们不妨看一则广告实例的翻译,从中体会为实现广告功能而对其文体的改变:

Butlin's—the right choice.

Don't labour the point, or be conservative in your choice, or liberal with your money. Come to Butlin's for the real party.

Great Party Ahead.

这是旅游公司利用各政党之间的竞争为自己做的广告。广告中的 labour, conservative, liberal 是英国三大政党的名字，而 labour the point, be conservative, be liberal with money 分别可以译为：详尽说明，在作选择时保守，大手大脚地花钱。很显然，这则双关英文广告在汉语中起不到它应有的效果，但用排比的句式可以达到预期的功能：

布特林旅游公司——您的正确选择。

不要劳烦讲个没完，

不要保守，也别犹豫，

不要放任自由地乱花钱。

到布特林旅游公司，参加实实在在的聚会吧。

盛大的聚会正等着你！

实际上，一个文本包括多种文体，一个文体也不只限于一个文本；由于文体有着特定的语言表达习惯，所以它们的分类对功能翻译起很大作用，即为了实现不同的翻译功能可以采用不同的文体或是文本，而不一定局限于原文本或文体了。在奈达的《圣经》翻译中不乏把"雪白"译成 as white as goose feather 的译例。

不过，相对文本功能的翻译策略只是实现翻译目的的第一步。实际上，目的论最重要的翻译策略是具体情况具体分析，即每个翻译都有自己的具体要求，这个具体要求的设定者是顾客。顾客为翻译情境提供各种可能的细节：如译文的受众、时间、空间、场合、交际媒体以及文本要达到的功能（Nord，2001：30）。目的论首要考虑的是翻译要求，而不是原文本。Reiss 认为在现实生活语境中，有时候对等是不可能实现的，甚至是不可取的。她列举的情形之一就是译文要取得与原文不一样的目的或功能时，如把莎士比亚的散文作品译成话剧，其翻译必然要注意到话剧的舞台效果，如语句的相对简短和口语化。另一情形是当译文面向与原文不同的读者群时，要改变译文的功能。如为孩子们译的《格利佛游记》（Gulliver's Travel）与以宗教、伦理或者商业为目的而进行意识形态改编的译本就不可能一样；儿童版的《格利佛游记》语言活泼，充满好奇的悬念，而改编版的游记是让成人看的，掺杂着各种意识形态的说教。所以，要重视译文功能的实现。

在译文本形成过程中，目的论研究者认为语内连贯原则优于语际连贯原则。"语际连贯原则或称'忠实'原则，是建立在译者对原文阐释和译文的功能基础之上的，且它从属于语内连贯原则，并共同隶属于目的（功能）原则。"（Nord，2001：32－33）换言之，在功能翻译过程中，译者要谨遵语内连贯原则：在交际情境和读者文化语境中读者能够理解译文，就像有些学者所说的译本"读起来不像译文"，以保证实现其功能；至于原文本，目的论只把它看做译文所要依托的语句、结构而已；原文本的功能由接受者来确定，正所谓"有多少个读者就有多少个文本"（Nord，2001：31）。接受者从原文本这个"信源"中挑选重要的、感兴趣的信息。在中国译界享有盛誉的翻译理论家严复就是以"翻译图强"为己任，用其华丽、文雅的桐城体译介了《天演论》、《原富》等一批旨在让国人奋发图强的名著，在译文中还特别阐发他认为重要的信息，如达尔文进化论、马尔萨斯人口论等。他用流畅的译笔来完成翻译所应担当的历史功能。他的同乡、《巴黎茶花女遗事》的译者林纾更"以华文之典料，写欧人之性情，曲曲以赴，煞费匠心。好语穿珠，哀感顽艳。读者但见马克之花魂，亚猛之泪渍，小仲马之文心，冷红生之笔意，一时都活，为之欲叹观止"（邹振环，1996：123）。如此优美的文字、生动的画面，竟出于一个不识英文半字的翻译者之手实在是翻译史上的奇迹；这个成就不得不归功于译者深厚的文学功底和他在语内连贯上的高超技巧。尽管翻译界对严、林的"忠实"颇有微词，但谁又能否认他们的译文功能得到了完美的实现呢？

由此看来，翻译的成功并非要把原文本置于神圣、高不可攀的地位。这直接导致了功能派文本意识的弱化。威密尔在其目的论中就进一步提出了"颠覆原文"的口号："原文的语言特征和文体特征不再是衡量译文的唯一标准。"（Nord，2001：119）至此，在传统翻译中成为判断译文标准的神圣不可侵犯的原文一下子"连降两级"，位于翻译目的和译文（自身连贯）的双重关照之下了。这个目的论文本观的执行者是译者。

根据目的性行为理论，行动者（信息发送者、接收者、发起人、译者）起至关重要的作用。译者是原文的真正接受者，是他把原文传递给另外一批读者。他所提供的译文是他对其读者的需求、期待、前知识等进行预设的产物；这个预设与原作者的假定必然不同，其原因在于其各自文化语境的迥异。因而，译者不会为他的读者提供和源语读者同质、同量的信息；也就是说译文是另一种形式表达出来的另一种信息。它不仅是原文的另外包装，其内部组装也可能不尽一样了。目的论的译者在翻译活动中实际上担当着"电影导演"或"乐队指挥"的角色（Nord，2001：85）。正是从这个意义上，有人批评目的论（功能主义）是一种改写理论，功能主义的译者是原文本的"背叛者"（Nord，2001：121）。

纽马克和科勒尔（Koller）对目的论的文本意识弱化倾向给予了尖锐的批评。纽马克指责功能主义过分简单化，只注重信息而牺牲意义的丰富性，损害了原文本的权威性。他认为："一个文本的语言越重要，翻译就要越贴近，其文化成分的翻译也要越贴切。"他还声称："我不会去颠覆原文……我会非常看重它。好的语言我在翻译中准确地传达它；瑕疵的语言我也会如实地呈现它。"（Nord，2001：120 - 121）当然，这种指责还是以语言学为理论依据，但就文学文本的翻译来说纽马克的批评还是有一定的警示作用。科勒尔也坚持译文与原文存在翻译的或是对等的关系，主张把等值要求分成等级即分为"重写式翻译"和"对等式翻译"；功能主义的翻译被认为是阐释或改写的"重写式翻译"，而不属于"专门的翻译"（translation proper）即"对等式翻译"。这实际上还是以"等值论"为判断标准。我们认为这种划分在实际操作中恐怕很难分清：难道一个译者只有在拿经典名著时才在做真正的翻译，而在接受广告、旅游介绍等文本时就不是在做翻译吗？

Nord 就文学文本翻译提出了"功能 plus 忠诚"的翻译原则。"忠诚"是指译者的伦理道德观，不同于传统翻译研究中的"忠实"。它的含义有两层，既对原文又对译文，对原文是指尊重作者，对译文是指不欺骗读者。这是 Nord 就人们对功能主义的批评作出的回应，同时也避免了可能极端的功能主义倾向。

4　余论

目的论作为一种解构主义的翻译视角，为翻译学研究提供了新的宏观认知模式，对于我们克服纯粹的文本认知模式起到了积极的反拨作用。它重视从社会学角度理解文本，承认文化的相对性，对于译者翻译"意识"而非仅仅翻译技能的培养起到了开拓的作用，深化了译者对文本的认知，从而使翻译研究具有了更深的维度。目的论具有广阔的实用性，它注重文本类型的特点，这有助于提高译者对交际功能和功能的翻译单位的语言标志的意识，提高翻译的效率。

但是,目的论偏重于译文功能的研究,为译文效果而进行有目的的"改写",大大弱化了原文本的功能,有可能跌入"为翻译而翻译"的功用主义陷阱,偏离翻译研究应循的轨道。因此,在实践翻译目的论的同时,不可忽视翻译本体论的坚持与研究。

【延伸阅读】

[1] 卞建华. 功能主义目的论在中国的引进、应用与研究(1987—2005). 解放军外国语学院学报,2006(5):82-88.

[2] 王建斌. 泰山北斗一代通儒——缅怀德国功能派翻译理论创始人汉斯·费梅尔教授. 中国翻译,2010(3):80-83.

[3] 仲伟合. 德国的功能派翻译理论. 中国翻译,1999(3):47-49.

【问题与思考】

1. 本文对目的论产生背景的分析有何特点?
2. 为什么说目的论是对"文本中心论"的反拨?
3. 目的论原文本意识弱化的原因是什么? 本文是如何分析的?

第六章　语域与翻译

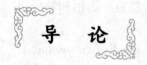

导　论

　　语域分析,即对语言变异的研究,可以追溯到韩礼德、莫今沓西(McIntosh)和斯垂文斯(Strevens)对"语域"一词的定义(1964:87):"语言随着其功能的变化而变化。语言在不同的情境之下会有不同。按照用途区别开来的语言变体就是语域。"韩礼德等语言学家们指出:"语域是由与多种情景特征——特别是指语场、语旨和语式的意义——相联系的语言特征构成的。"也就是说,语言特征的情景因素可归纳为三个参数(variables),即语场(field)、语旨(tenor)和语式(mode)。语场指的是正在发生的事情,包括语言发生的环境、谈话的话题以及参与讲话者的整个活动(如政治、科技和家庭事务等);语旨指参与讲话者之间的角色关系,包括他们的社会地位以及说话者的态度和想要实施的意图等,体现在语篇中就是指语言的正式程度(如亲密体和随便体等,实际是双方关系的反映);语式指的是语言的交际渠道以及语言所要达到的功能,包括修辞方式,可分为书面语体和口语体、正式语体和非正式语体等。从韩礼德对语境要素的归纳可以看出,他是从实际使用语言的过程来观察语境的,这三个因素之间是相互联系的。如规模较大的学术会议这一话语范围决定了它必然是以口语方式进行的,而会议所使用的语言就应该是正式的,甚至是学究气很浓的语体。语域的这三种因素相互作用的结果规定,语域的这三个组成部分中任何一项的改变都会引起所交流的意义的变化,从而引起语言的变异,产生不同类型的语域。如商业通信和亲朋好友之间的通信虽然都属于书面交际,但由于通信双方的关系不同(即语旨的差异),后者的交际更接近口语体。

　　通常情况下,语言学理论首先被应用语言学接受之后,才会被翻译研究界承认并接纳。但这种时间上的滞后性规律并不适用于语域理论。语域理论刚一问世,马上便引起翻译理论家的关注,并被应用于翻译研究当中,出现了一批研究成果,代表了翻译"科学"阶段性发展水平(Gregory, 1980)。翻译研究中的语域分析一般集中于两个维度:一个维度与语言使用者(user)有关,重视方言意义;另一维度与语言的使用(use)相关,重视语域本身。与使用者相关的变异包括说话人地理、历史、社会背景因素和个人语型意义因素等。与语言使用相关的变异包含信息建构的各个方面如语场、语旨和语式等。这两个维度都很重要,但相对来说,翻译理论家们更加注重研究与语言使用相关的变异。确定语域属籍(register membership)被认为是翻译成功的先决条件。

　　朱莉安·豪斯(Juliane House)是较早把语域概念应用到翻译研究中的学者,尤其注重语域在翻译质量评估中的作用。她认为翻译质量评估必须考虑语域。语场、语旨、语式参数的组合,可能影响语篇的词汇选择、传递方式和样式。不同语言中的语域在特定的情形下可能有所变化,翻译质量评估也应该注意到这种表面上对等而实际上不对等的情形,双语对照文本中经常有这样的情况发生。豪斯的翻译质量评估模式以语域对等程度为衡量标准。哈蒂姆和梅森(Hatim & Mason)在把韩礼德的包括语域分析在内的语言学理论用于翻译研究方面用力最勤。他们把翻译置于其发生时所处的社会文化语境之下,视翻译活动为特殊的交际事件。他们认为,分析语篇语境的交际因素应该从语域入手,语域分析是处理话语交际过程非常重要的组成部分,因为语域决定了交际的内容、交际双方的关系和交际的方式。作为交际事件,翻译活动具有交际、语用和符号三个层面。语域分析不能仅限于交际层面,要兼顾语用和符号层面,努力实现交际、语用与符号的三方互动。

本章共选三篇论文。第一篇是 Juliane House 撰写的 "Translation Quality Assessment: Linguistic Description versus Social Evaluation",作者从语域入手,提出了翻译评估的功能语用模式,强调了使用文化过滤器的重要性。第二篇 "The Translator as Communicator" 的作者是 Basil Hatim 和 Ian Mason,他们从与语言使用者相关的范畴出发探讨语域变化,讨论了文学翻译中的语域属籍问题。第三篇是司显柱著的《朱莉安·豪斯的"翻译质量评估模式"批评》,该文介绍了豪斯的翻译质量评估模式,重点分析、阐释了其背后的理论依据,批评了存在的不足之处。

选 文

选文一　Translation Quality Assessment: Linguistic Description versus Social Evaluation

Juliane House

导　言

本文 2001 年刊载于国际译学期刊 *Meta*(XLⅥ:243 - 257)。

本文首先介绍了三种现存的翻译评估方法,它们都是学者们基于对意义(meaning)和翻译本质的不同认识提出来的。然后作者提出了翻译评估的功能语用模式,强调了使用文化过滤器的重要性,指出了翻译评估中语言分析与社会价值判断的区别。豪斯的评估模式从语域入手,从语域决定(语言)形式,而形式表达意义/功能的角度分析译文是否在概念和人际意义上与原文对等或偏离。为此,她把原文和译文分成八个语域维度(dimensions)进行比较。通过对原文语域与形式的分析和互照,把握其功能/意义,秉循同样的方法分析译文,如此自然可以发现和确定译文是否与原文功能对等或偏离。豪斯对翻译对等所要做到的功能相符的基本标准是:译文文本与原文文本不仅应该功能相符,并且要运用对等的语域维度方式去获得这些功能,分析原文文本和译文文本时,要看她所提出的那个模式的八个维度是否两两相符,是否用同样的方法获得同样的功能。两者相符程度越高,翻译质量越好。因此译文文本的最终质量判断包括对上述语域里的每个维度不匹配程度的陈述,即对隐性错误(在语域维度上的错误)和显性错误(词语的所指意义与原文不对等或不符合目的语系统规范)的数量及类型的描述。

Introduction

How do we know when a translation is good? This simple question lies at the heart of all concerns with translation criticism. But not only that, in trying to assess the quality of a translation one also addresses the heart of any theory of translation, i. e. , the crucial question of the nature of translation or, more specifically, the nature of the relationship between a source text and its translation text. Given that translation is essentially an operation in which the meaning of linguistic units is to be kept equivalent across languages, one can distinguish at least three different views of meaning, each of which leads to different conceptions of translation evaluation. In a mentalist view of meaning as a concept residing in language users' heads, translation is likely to be intuitive and interpretative. If meaning is seen as developing in, and resulting from, an externally observable reaction, translation evaluation is likely to involve response-based methods. And if meaning is seen as emerging from larger textual stretches of language in use, involving both context and (situational and cultural) context surrounding individual linguistic units, a discourse approach is likely to be used in evaluating a translation.

In this paper I want to first elaborate briefly on these three approaches to translation evaluation; secondly, I will present my own views on the matter, and thirdly and most importantly, I will discuss the often blurred distinction between linguistic description and social evaluation.

1　Translation evaluation in different schools of thought

1. 1　Mentalist views

Subjective and intuitive evaluations of a translation have been undertaken since time immemorial by writers, philosophers, and many others, consisting more often than not of global judgements such as "the translation does justice to the original" or "the tone of the original is lost in the translation" and so forth. In a newer guise, such intuitive assessments are being propagated by neo-hermeneutic translation scholars who regard translation as an individual creative act depending exclusively on subjective interpretation and transfer decisions, artistic-literary intuitions and interpretive skills and knowledge. Texts have no core meanings at all, rather their meanings change depending on individual speakers' positions. I will not elaborate here my critique of the hermeneutic position (but see the recent lucid discussion by Bühler, 1998), suffice to say that such a relativising stance, and especially the relativisation of "content" and "meaning" is particularly inappropriate for the evaluative business of making argued statements about when, how and why a translation is good.

1.2 Response-based approaches

1.2.1 Behavioristic views

As opposed to subjective-intuitive approaches to translation evaluation, the behaviorist view aims at a more "scientific" way of evaluating translations dismissing the translator's mental actions as belonging to some in principle unknowable "black box." This tradition, influenced by American structuralism and behaviorism, is most famously associated with Nida's (1964) pioneering work. Nida took readers' reactions to a translation as the main yardstick for assessing a translation's quality, positing global behavioral criteria, such as intelligibility and informativeness and stating that a "good" translation is one leading to "equivalence of response"—a concept clearly linked to his principle of "dynamic equivalence of translation," i. e. , that the manner in which receptors of a translation respond to the translation should be "equivalent" to the manner in which the source text's receptors respond to the original. Nida operationalized this equivalence as comprising equal "informativeness" and "intelligibility." Assuming that it is true that a "good" translation should elicit a response equivalent to the response to its original, we must immediately ask whether it is possible to measure an "equivalent response," let alone "informativeness" or "intelligibility." If these phenomena cannot be measured, it is useless to postulate them as criteria for translation evaluation. And indeed, even the most imaginative tests designed to establish verifiable, observable responses a translation presumably evokes—using for instance reading aloud techniques, various close and rating procedures—have ultimately failed to provide the desired results, because they were unable to capture such a complex phenomenon as the "quality of a translation." Further, the source text is largely ignored in all these methods, which means that nothing can be said about the relationship between original and translation, nor about whether a translation is in fact a translation and not another secondary text derived via a different textual operation.

1.2.2 Functionalistic, "skopos"-related approach

Adherents of this approach (cf. Reiss & Vermeer, 1988) claim that it is the "skopos" or purpose of a translation that is of overriding importance in judging a translation's quality. The way target culture norms are heeded or flouted by a translation is the crucial yardstick in evaluating a translation. It is the translator or more frequently the translation brief he is given by the person (s) commissioning the translation that decides on the function the translation is to fulfil in its new environment. The notion of "function," critical in this theory, is, however, never made explicit, let alone operationalized in any satisfactory way. It seems to be something very similar to the real-world effect of a text. How exactly one is to go about determining the (relative) equivalence and adequacy of a translation, let alone how exactly one is to go about determining the linguistic realization of the "skopos" of a translation, is not clear. Most importantly, however, it naturally follows from the crucial role assigned to the "purpose" of a translation that the original is reduced to a simple "offer of information," with the word "offer" making it immediately clear that this "information" can freely be accepted or rejected as the translator sees fit. But since any translation is simultaneously bound to its source text and to the presuppositions and conditions governing its reception in the new environment, Skopos theory cannot be said to be an adequate theory when it comes to tackling the evaluation of a translation in its fundamental bidirectionality.

1.3 Text and discourse based approaches

1.3.1 Literature-oriented approaches: descriptive translation studies

This approach is oriented squarely towards the translation text: A translation is evaluated predominantly in terms of its forms and functions inside the system of the receiving culture and literature (cf. Toury, 1995). The original is of subordinate importance, the main focus—retrospective from translation to original—being "actual translations," and the textual phenomena that have come to be known in the target culture as translations.

The idea is to first of all attempt to "neutrally" describe the characteristics of that text as they are perceived on the basis of native (receptor) culture members' knowledge of comparable texts in the same genre. However, if one aims at judging a particular text which is plainly not an "independent," "new" product of one culture only, such a retrospective focus seems peculiarly inappropriate for making valid statements about how and why a translation qua translation is as it is. While the solid empirical-descriptive work and the emphasis put on contextualization at the microlevel of the reception situation and the macrolevel of the receiving culture at large, as well as the inclusion of both a "longitudinal" (temporal, diachronic) and a (synchronic) systemic perspective (considering the polysystemic relations into which the translation enters with other texts in the receiving cultural system), is certainly commendable, the approach does fail to provide criteria for judging the merits and weaknesses of a particular "case." In other words, how are we to judge whether one text is a translation and another one not? And what are the criteria for judging merits and weaknesses of a given "translation text?"

1.3.2 Post-modernist and deconstructionist thinking

Scholars belonging to this approach (cf. e. g. Venuti, 1995) try to critically examine translation practices from a psycho-philosophical and socio-political stance in an attempt to unmask unequal power relations, which may appear as a certain skewing in the translation. In a plea for making translations (and especially translators as their "creators") "visible" and for revealing ideological and institutional manipulations, proponents of this approach aim to make politically pertinent (and "correct") statements about the relationship between features of the original text and the translation text. They focus on the hidden forces shaping both the process of selecting what gets translated in the first place and the procedures that result in the ways original texts are bent and twisted in the interests of powerful individuals and groups "pulling strings" when choosing texts for translation and adopting particular strategies of re-textualization. This is certainly a worthwhile undertaking, especially when it comes to explaining the influence translators can exert through their translation on the receiving national literature and its canon. Further, the application of currently influential lines of thinking such as post-colonial theory (Robinson, 1997) or feminist theory (von Flotow, 1997) to translation may not be uninteresting in itself. However, if comparative analyses of original and translation focus primarily on the shifts and skewings stemming from ideologically motivated manipulations, and if an agenda is given priority which stresses the theoretical, critical and textual means by which translations can be studied as loci of difference, one wonders how one can ever differentiate between a translation and any other text that may result from a textual operation which can no longer claim to be in a translation relationship with an original text.

1.3.3　Linguistically-oriented approaches

Pioneering linguistic work in translation evaluation includes the programmatic suggestions by Catford (1965), the early Reiss (1971), Wilss (1974), Koller (1979) and the translation scholars of the Leipzig school. In this early work, however, no specific procedures for assessing the quality of a translation were offered. In more recent times, several linguistically oriented works on translation such as by Baker (1992), Doherty (1993), Hatim and Mason (1997), Hickey (1998), Gerzymisch-Arbogast and Mudersbach (1998) and Steiner (1998) have made valuable contributions to evaluating a translation by the very fact that all these authors—although not directly concerned with translation quality assessment—widened the scope of translation studies to include concerns with linguistics, pragmatics, sociolinguistics, stylistics and discourse analysis.

Linguistic approaches take the relationship between source and translation text seriously, but they differ in their capacity to provide detailed procedures for analysis and evaluation. Most promising are approaches which explicitly take account of the interconnectedness of context and text because the inextricable link between language and the real world is both definitive in meaning making and in translation. Such a view of translation as re-contextualization is the line taken by myself in a functional-pragmatic evaluation model first developed some 25 years ago and recently revised (House, 1981, 1997).

2　A functional-pragmatic model of translation evaluation

2.1　An analytic framework for analysing and comparing original and translation texts

The assessment model (House, 1997) is based on Hallidayan systemic-functional theory, but also draws eclectically on Prague school ideas, speech act theory, pragmatics, discourse analysis and corpus-based distinctions between spoken and written language. It provides for the analysis and comparison of an original and its translation on three different levels: the levels of Language/Text, Register (Field, Mode and Tenor) and Genre. One of the basic concepts underpinning the model is "translation equivalence"—a concept clearly reflected in conventional everyday understanding of translation, i. e. , the average "normal," i. e. , non-professionally trained person thinks of translation as a text that is some sort of "representation" or "reproduction" of another text originally produced in another language, with the "reproduction" being of comparable value, i. e. , equivalent. (This is the result of an informal interview study I conducted with 30 native speakers of German support staff as well as medical and economics students at the university of Hamburg). Over and above its role as a concept constitutive of translation, "equivalence" is the fundamental criterion of translation quality. In an attempt to make "a case for linguistics in translation theory," Ivir expresses the inherent relativity of the equivalence relation very well: "Equivalence is ... relative and not absolute ... it emerges from the context of situation as defined by the interplay of (many different factors) and has no existence outside that context, and in particular it is not stipulated in advance by an algorithm for the conversion of linguistic units of L1 into linguistic units of L2" (1996, p. 155).

It is obvious that equivalence cannot be linked to formal, syntactic and lexical similarities alone because any two linguistic items in two different languages are multiply ambiguous, and because languages cut up reality in different ways. Further, language use is notoriously indirect necessitate inferencing to various degrees. This is why functional, pragmatic equivalence—a concept which has been accepted in contrastive linguistics for a long time—is the type of equivalence which is most appropriate for describing relations between original and translation. And it is this type of equivalence which is used in the functional pragmatic model suggested by House (1997), where it is related to the preservation of "meaning" across two different languages and cultures. Three aspects of that "meaning" are particularly important for translation: a semantic, a pragmatic and a textual aspect, and translation is viewed as the recontextualization of a text in L1 by a semantically and pragmatically equivalent text in L2. As a first requirement for this equivalence, it is posited that a translation text have a **function** equivalent to that of its original which—consisting of an ideational and an interpersonal functional component—is defined pragmatically as the application or use of the text in a particular context of situation, the basic idea being that "text" and "context of situation" should not be viewed as separate entities, rather the context of situation in which the text unfolds is encapsulated in the text through a systematic relationship between the social environment on the one hand and the functional organization of language on the other. The text must therefore refer to the particular situation enveloping it, and for this a way must be found for breaking down the broad notion of "context of situation" into manageable parts, i. e. , particular features of the context of situation or "situational dimensions:" for instance "Field," "Mode" and "Tenor."

Field captures social activity, subject matter or topic, including differentiations of degrees of generality, specificity or "granularity" in lexical items according to rubrics of specialized, general and popular. Tenor refers to the nature of the participants, the addresser and the addressees, and the relationship between them in terms of social power and social distance, as well as degree of emotional charge. Included here are the text producer's temporal, geographical and social provenance as well as his intellectual, emotional or affective stance (his "personal viewpoint") vis a vis the content she is portraying. Further, Tenor captures "social attitude," i. e. different styles (formal, consultative and informal). Mode refers to both the channel—spoken or written (which can be "simple," i. e. , "written to be read" or "complex," e. g. "written to be spoken as if not written"), and the degree to which potential or real participation is allowed for between writer and reader. Participation can be "simple," i. e. , a monologue with no addressee participation built into the text, or "complex" with various addressee—involving linguistic mechanisms characterizing the text. In taking account of (linguistically documentable) differences in texts between the spoken and written medium, reference is made to the empirically established (corpus-based) oral-literate dimensions hypothesized by Biber (1988). Biber suggests dimensions along which linguistic choices may reflect medium, i. e. , involved vs. informational text production; explicit vs. situation-dependent reference; abstract vs. non-abstract presentation of information.

The type of linguistic-textual analysis in which linguistic features discovered in the original and the translation correlated with the categories Field, Tenor, Mode does not, however directly lead to a statement of the individual textual function. Rather, the concept of "Genre" is incorporated into the analytic scheme, "in between," as it were, the register categories Field, Tenor, Mode, and the textual function. Genre thus enables one to refer any single textual exemplar to the class of texts with which it shares a common purpose. The category of Genre is useful for the analysis and evaluation process because, although Register (Field, Tenor, Mode) descriptions are useful for accessing the relationship between text and context, they are basically limited to capturing individual features on the linguistic surface. In order to characterize "deeper" textual structures and patterns, a different conceptualization is needed. This is attempted via the use of "Genre." While register captures the connection between texts and their "microcontext," Genre connects texts with the "macrocontext" of the linguistic and cultural community in which texts are embedded. Register and Genre are both semiotic systems realized by language such that the relationship between Genre,

Register and language/text is one between semiotic planes which relate to one another in a Hjelmslevian "content-expression" type, i. e. , the Genre is the content plane of Register, and the Register is the expression plane of Genre. Register in turn is the content plane of language, with language being the expression plane of Register.

The analytic model is displayed in Figure 1:

INDIVIDUAL TEXTUAL FUNCTION

REGISTER		GENRE
FIELD	TENOR	MODE
Subject matter	participant relationship and social action	medium
	author's provenance and stance	simple/complex
	participation	
	social role relationship	simple/complex
	social attitude	

LANGUAGE/TEXT

Figure 1   A scheme for analysing and comparing original and translation texts

Taken together, the analysis yields a textual profile characterizing the individual textual function. Whether and how this textual function can in fact be maintained, depends, however, on the type of translation sought for the original. I distinguish between two types: overt and covert translation, which I will briefly describe in the following section.

2.2   Two types of translation: overt and covert translation

The distinction between an "Overt Translation" and a "Covert Translation" goes back at least to Friedrich Schleiermacher's famous distinction between "verfremdende" and "einbürgernde" Übersetzungen, which has had many imitators using different terms. What sets the Overt-Covert distinction apart from other similar distinctions and concepts is the fact that it is integrated into a coherent theory of translation criticism, inside which the origin and function of the two types of translation are consistently described and explained. Translation involves text transfer across time and space, and whenever texts move, they also shift frames and discourse worlds. "Frame" is a psychological concept and it is thus, in a sense, the psychological pendant to the more "socially" conceived concept of context, delimiting a class of messages or meaningful actions. A frame often operates unconsciously as an explanatory principle, i. e. , any message that defines a frame gives the receiver instructions in his interpretation of the message included in the frame. Similarly, the notion of a "discourse world" refers to a superordinate structure for interpreting meaning in a certain way just as a locutionary act acquires an illocutionary value by reference to an operant discourse world.

Applying the concepts of frame and discourse world to overt and covert translation, we can say that an overtly translated text is embedded in a new speech event, which also gives it a new frame. An overt translation is a case of "language mention" (as opposed to "language use"). Relating the concept of "overt translation" to the four-tiered analytical model (Function—Genre—Register—Language/Text), we can state that an original and its overt translation are to be equivalent at the level of Language/Text and Register as well as Genre. At the level of the individual textual function, functional equivalence, while still possible, is of a different nature: It can be described as enabling access to the function the original has in its discourse world or frame. As this access is to be realized in a different language and takes place in the target linguistic and cultural community, a switch in discourse world and frame becomes necessary, i. e. , the translation is differently framed, it operates in its own frame and its own discourse world, and can thus reach at best second-level functional equivalence. As this type of equivalence is, however, achieved though equivalence at the levels of Language/Text, Register and Genre, the original's frame and discourse world are co-activated, such that members of the target culture may "eavesdrop," as it were, i. e. , be enabled to appreciate the original textual function, albeit at a distance. In overt translation, the work of the translator is important and visible. Since it is the translator's task to give target culture members access to the original text and its cultural impact on source culture members, the translator puts target culture members in a position to observe and/or judge this text "from outside. "

In covert translation, which is a case of "language use," the translator must attempt to re-create an equivalent speech event. Consequently, the function of a covert translation is to reproduce in the target text the function the original has in its frame and discourse world. A covert translation operates therefore quite "overtly" in the frame and discourse world provided by the target culture, with no attempt being made to co-activate the discourse world in which the original unfolded. Covert translation is thus at the same time psycholinguistically less complex and more deceptive than overt translation. Since true functional equivalence is aimed at, the original may be manipulated at the levels of Language/Text and Register via the use of a "cultural filter. " The result may be a very real distance from the original. While the original and its covert translation need thus not be equivalent at the levels of Language/Text and Register, they must be equivalent at the levels of Genre and the Individual Textual Function. Schematically, the theoretical distinction between overt and covert translation can be displayed as follows:

Figure 2　The dimension of overt-covert translation

Level	Is strict equivalence the translational goal?	
	Overt Translation	Covert Translation
Primary level function	No	YES
Secondary level function	YES	N/A
Genre	YES	YES
Register	YES	NO
Language/Text	YES	NO

In evaluating a translation, it is thus essential that the fundamental differences between overt and covert translation be taken into account. These two types of translation make qualitatively different demands on translation criticism. The difficulty of evaluating an overt translation is generally reduced in that considerations of cultural filtering can be omitted. Overt translations are "more straightforward," as the original can be "taken over unfiltered," as it were. In evaluating covert translations, the translation assessor has to consider the application of a "cultural filter" in order to be able to differentiate between a covert translation and a covert version.

2. 3 The concept and function of a cultural filter

The concept of a "cultural filter" is a means of capturing socio-cultural differences in shared conventions of behavior and communication, preferred rhetorical styles and expectation norms in the two speech communities. These differences should not be left to individual intuition but should be based on empirical cross-cultural research. Given the goal of achieving functional equivalence in a covert translation, assumptions of cultural difference should be carefully examined before interventions in the original's meaning structure is undertaken. The unmarked assumption is one of cultural compatibility, unless there is evidence to the contrary. To take an example, in the case of the German and anglophone linguistic and cultural communities the concept of cultural filter has been given some substance through a number of empirical contrastive-pragmatic analyses, in which anglophone and German communicative priorities along a set of hypothesized dimensions were hypothesized. Converging evidence from a number of cross-cultural German-English studies conducted with different data, subjects and methodologies suggests that there are German preferences for rhetorical styles and conventions of communicative behavior which differ from Anglophone ones along a set of dimensions, among them directness, content focus, explicitness and routine-reliance. (cf. House, 1996, 1998).

Given the distinction between overt and covert translation, it is obvious that cultural transfer is only possible in the case of overt translation, where cultural items are transported from L1 to L2 acting as a sort of "Verfremdung." In covert translation, however, there is no cultural transfer, but only a sort of "cultural compensation" for L1 cultural phenomena in L2 with the means of L2.

In speaking of a "cultural filter," we need to know, of course, what we mean by "culture." Given widespread postmodernist critiques of culture as an untenable idealization and as something outdatedly relating to the nation state of the nineteenth century, is it today still possible to talk of "the culture" of a language community? Has not the extension of culture to modern complex societies brought about a complexification and problematisation of "culture" which renders it useless as a methodological and conceptual entity? Should we therefore not follow the argumentation by Holliday (1999) who suggested substituting "non-essentialist," "non-reified," "small cultures" for "culture?" Obviously there is no such thing as a stable social group untouched by outside influences and group and personal idiosyncracies, and obviously it is wrong to assume a monolithic unified culture of which all differentness is idealized and cancelled out. Nevertheless, modernist relativation has in practice never yet led to its logical conclusion: The annihilation of research concerned with culture, nor has it prevented researchers from describing cultures as interpretive devices for understanding emergent behavior. Further, we cannot ignore the experiences reported by "ordinary" members of a speech community, when they perceive members of another cultural group as behaving "differently" in particular situated discourse events.

2.4   Distinguishing between different types of translations and versions

Over and above distinguishing between covert and overt translation in translation criticism, it is necessary to make another theoretical distinction: between a translation and a version. This distinction is important in view of recent widespread attempts to indiscriminately view intentionally non-equivalent "versions" as translations—even though the new text may have a function different from the original text's function. Producing a version results from a deliberate turning away from the original, a re-evaluation and often renunciation of the original. Versions are "freed" to become their own original, particularly in contexts where only intentions of clients and product specifications count, i. e. , in highly practice-oriented, mostly technical translation activities, in which considerations of equivalence would only stand in the way of achieving client satisfaction and consumer service. While functionally equivalent covert translations may certainly look like new creations, it is still true that they would not have come into existence if there had not been an original text. And it is important to stress that despite the seemingly cavalier manner with which a translator may have dealt with linguistic correspondences at the word, group and sentence levels (i. e. , below the levels of text and discourse), in a covert translation, her actions must be viewed as being subservient to producing correspondences that, each in their different ways, contribute to the overall functional equivalence of the entire translation to its original. This is what makes a translation a translation. It is only when new purposes are superimposed on the translation that a new product, i. e. , a version results.

Overt versions are produced in two cases: Firstly, whenever a special function is overtly added to a translation text. e. g. to reach a particular audience, as in special editions for children or second language learners with the resultant omissions, additions, simplifications or different accentuations of certain aspects of the original, or popularisations of specialist works designed for the lay public, and secondly, when the "translation" is given a special added purpose. Examples are interlingual versions, resumes and abstracts.

A covert version results whenever the translator—in order to preserve the function of the source text—has applied a cultural filter randomly manipulating the original.

In discussing different types of translations and versions, I do not want to imply, however, that a particular text may be adequately translated in only one particular way. For instance, the assumption that a particular text necessitates either a covert or an overt translation clearly does not hold in any simple way: Any text may, for a specific purpose, require an overt translation, i. e. , it may be viewed as a text of an "independent value" of its own, e. g. when its author has become, in the course of time, a distinguished figure, in which case the original text acquires the status of a sacrosanct document.

Further, while contrastive pragmatics has certainly made important contributions to assessing covert translations in a non-arbitrary way, it remains a challenge to assess the adequateness of applications of a cultural filter. Given the dynamic nature of socio-cultural and communicative norms and the way research necessarily lags behind, translation critics will have to struggle to remain abreast of new developments if they want to be able to fairly judge the appropriateness of changes through the application of a cultural filter in a translation between two given languages. One important new development that affects many social contexts today is the increasing importance of the English language.

3　English as a global lingua franca in cultural (non) filtering

With globalisation and internationalisation characterizing much of our life today, there is a concomitant rise in the demand for texts which are simultaneously meant for recipients in many different communities. In other words, ever more texts are needed that are either translated covertly or produced immediately as "parallel texts" in different languages. Until recently translators and text producers tended to routinely apply a cultural filter with which differences in culture-conditioned expectation norms and stylistic conventions were taken into account. However, due to the impact of English as a global lingua franca this situation may now be in a process of change leading to a conflict in translational processes between culture specificity and universality in textual norms and conventions, with "universality" really standing for North European /North American Anglo-Saxon norms. It is this hypothesized change in global translation conventions which has in fact motivated a research project which is presently being conducted in Hamburg inside a larger research undertaking (a Sonderforschungsbereich "Mehrsprachigkeit" funded by the *Deutsche Forschungsgemeinschaft*). Our main hypothesis in this project is that, instead of using a cultural filter in covert translations or parallel text production, increasingly many culturally universal (or rather culturally neutral translation) texts are created, and a species of "hybrid text" results, which is in reality a carrier of anglophone cultural norms "invading" other linguistic and cultual communities rendering, for example, German texts less content-focused, more interpersonally oriented, more emotionally involved, more situation-dependent and more concrete, to use Biber's (1988) dimensions of orality vs. writtenness in text production, than was the case before.

While the influence of the English language in the area of lexis has long been acknowledged and bemoaned by many linguistic "purists" in Germany and France, anglophone influence at the levels of syntax, pragmatics and discourse has hardly been researched. Rules of discourse, conventions of textualisation and communicative preferences tend to remain hidden, operating stealthily at a deeper level of consciousness and thus presenting a particular challenge for translation evaluation.

In the Hamburg project which examines the influence of English as a lingua franca on covert translations into German (and later into French and Spanish), we are trying out a multi-method approach to translation evaluation, a method which goes beyond the procedure suggested in the assessment model by House (1997). As detailed above, this evaluation model provides for detailed qualitative case-study assessments of the quality of a translation. Just as the much maligned notion of equivalence cannot be taken to provide general guidelines for the translation process, because equivalence derives from the interaction of a particular text and a particular context, so the case-study approach adopted in the functional pragmatic evaluation model forbids any facile generalization, simply because the achievement of functional equivalence varies from translation to translation. In the case of covert translation, for example, equivalence must be achieved via the assessment of the specific communicative environments of the two texts and their linguistic correlates. The communicative environments of original and translation must therefore be compared in each individual case, and it is only through amassing evidence of similar textual exemplars that we can approximate generalizations. In order to validate both the hypothesized cross-cultural dimensions that substantiate the cultural filter and the results of the linguistic analysis, introspective methods may be used with which one may tap the translation process. While the evaluation of a translation is primarily product-based it can thus be supplemented or "triangulated" by process-oriented work. Other ways of triangulating the primary analyses include interviews with commissioners of the translation, with editors and other persons involved in the making of a translation. In addition, background documentation, as well as comparisons of translations of the same original into different languages and comparisons of parallel texts and "monolingual" texts belonging to the same Genre can be taken into account. A further extension of the qualitative case-study approach consists of the use of computerized parallel and translation corpora suitable for quantitative analyses.

4　Linguistic description versus social evaluation in translation criticism

In translation criticism it is important to be maximally aware of the difference between (linguistic) analysis and (social) judgement. In other words, a distinction must be made between describing and explaining linguistic features of the original text and comparing them with the relevant linguistic features of the translation text on the one hand and judging "how good a translation" is on the other hand. Instead of taking the complex psychological categories of translation receptors' intuitions, feelings, beliefs or the (equally vague) effect of a translation as a cornerstone for translation criticism, the functional-pragmatic approach outlined in the above model focuses on texts (validated by introspective accounts of their production). Such an approach, however, cannot ultimately enable the evaluator to pass judgements on what is a "good" or a "bad" translation. Judgements of the quality of a translation depend on a large variety of factors that enter into any social evaluative statement. Critical in the case of translation evaluation is the fact that evaluative judgements emanate from the analytic, comparative process of translation criticism, i. e. , it is the linguistic analysis which provides grounds for arguing an evaluative judgement.

As mentioned above, the choice of an overt or a covert translation depends not on the text alone, or on the translator's subjective interpretation of the text, but also on the reasons for the translation, the implied readers, on a variety of publishing and marketing policies, i. e. , on factors which clearly have nothing to do with translation as a **linguistic** procedure because these are social factors which concern human agents as well as socio-cultural, political or ideological constraints and which—in the reality of translation practice—turn out to be often more influential than linguistic considerations or the professional competence of the translator herself. However, it must be stressed that despite all these "external" influences, translation is at its core a linguistic-textual phenomenon, and it can be legitimately described, analysed and evaluated as such. It is for this reason that I would argue that the primary concern of translation criticism should be linguistic-textual analysis and comparison, and any consideration of social factors—if it is divorced from textual analysis—must be of secondary relevance in a scientific discipline such as translation studies. Linguistic description and explanation must not be confused with evaluative assertions made solely on the basis of social, political, ethical or individual grounds. It seems imperative to emphasize this distinction given the current climate in which the criteria of scientific validity and reliability are often usurped by criteria such as social acceptability, political correctness, vague emotional commitment or fleeting zeitgeist tastes. If we take translation seriously as an object of scientific inquiry, translation must be seen first and foremost for what it is, namely a phenomenon in its own right: a linguistic-textual operation. And the nature of translation as a linguistic-textual operation should not be confused with issues such as what the translation is for, what it should, might, or must be for.

In approaches to translation criticism such as those squarely oriented towards the purpose and effect of a translation in a new cultural environment, it is unfortunately often the case that no clear line is drawn between translations and other (non-equivalence oriented) multilingual textual operations. One way out of this conceptual (and methodological) confusion seems to be to make a clear distinction between a translation and a version, a distinction which can, as I have tried to show above, only be made if one posits functional equivalence as an incontrovertible criterion for translation.

Translation quality is a problematical concept if it is taken to involve individual and externally motivated value judgement alone. Obviously, passing any "final judgement" on the quality of a translation that fulfills the demands of scientific objectivity is very difficult indeed. However, this should not lead us to assume that translation criticism as a field of inquiry is worthless. As an evaluator one will always be forced to flexibly move from a macro-analytical focus to a micro-analytical one, from considerations of ideology, function, genre, register, to the communicative value of individual linguistic items. In taking such a multi-perspectival viewpoint, a responsible translation critic will arrive at a position where he or she can give a probabilistic reconstruction of the translator's choices, and with the support of the translator's own "voice," be able to throw some light on his or her decison processes in as objective a manner as possible. That this is an extremely complex undertaking which, in the end, yields but approximative outcomes, should not detract us from its usefulness. It is the task of the translation critic to work out, as far as possible, for each individual case, exactly where and with what types of consequences and (possibly) for which reasons (parts of) translated texts are what they are in relation to their "primary texts." Such a modest goal might guard the translation evaluator against making both prescriptive, apodictic and global judgements (of the "good" vs. "bad type") that are not intersubjectively verifiable.

In the field of translation criticism, it is unfortunately often the case, that the difference between linguistic analysis and value judgement is ignored when one talks about the quality of a translation. While it is true that both a linguistic and a judgemental component are implicit in translation evaluation, I would caution against mixing them up. I would also caution against using the evaluative component in isolation from the linguistic one.

Translation criticism, like language itself, has two basic functions, an ideational function and an interpersonal function. These two functions have their counterpart in two different methodological steps. The first and, in my estimation, the primary one, refers to linguistic-textual analysis, description, explanation, and comparison, and it is based on empirical research and on professional knowledge of linguistic structures and norms of language use. The second step refers to value judgements, social, interpersonal and ethical questions of socio-political and socio-psychological relevance, ideological stance or individual persuasion. Without the first, the second is useless, in other words, to judge is easy, to understand less so. In other words, in translation criticism we have to make explicit the grounds for our judgement basing it on a theoretically sound and argued set of intersubjectively verifiable set of procedures. A detailed analysis of the "hows" and the "whys" of a translated text (i. e. , its linguistic forms and functions) in comparison with the original from which it is derived, is the descriptive foundation for any valid, and argued assessment of whether, how, and to what degree a given translation can be taken to be (more or less) adequate. Clearly, this means recognizing the inevitable subjective part of any translation assessment by a human evaluator. However, this recognition does not invalidate the objective part of the assessment, it merely reinforces its necessity. Making a distinction between empirically motivated linguistic description and socially conditioned grounds for evaluating a translation, as I have tried to do in this paper, may lead us one step further towards solving the puzzling complexity of human translation.

【延伸阅读】

[1] Eggins, S. (1994). *An Introduction to Systemic Functional Linguistics*. London: Pinter.

[2] Gutt, E. (1991). *Translation and Relevance: Cognition and Context*. Oxford: Blackwell; Manchester: St Jerome.

[3] Halliday, M. A. K. (1994). *An Introduction to Functional Grammar* (2nd ed.). London: Arnold.

[4] House, J. (1997). *Translation Quality Assessment: A Model Revisited*. Germany: Gunter Narr Verlag Tubingen.

[5] 司显柱,朱莉安·豪斯的"翻译质量评估模式"批评. 外语教学,2005(5):79-84.

【问题与思考】

1. 豪斯的语域观与韩礼德的语域观有何异同?
2. 语域在翻译评估中有何作用?
3. 豪斯在本文中设置了八个语域维度,这种设置是否合理? 为什么?
4. 如何评价豪斯翻译质量评估模式中语域的地位?

选文二 The Translator as Communicator (Excerpt)

Basil Hatim Ian Mason

导 言

　　巴兹尔·哈蒂姆是英语和阿拉伯语翻译专家、翻译理论家,长期执教于英国赫里奥特-沃特大学。伊恩·梅森与哈蒂姆是同事,长期从事翻译研究及教学。两人合著有《话语与译者》和《作为交际者的译者》。本文选自《作为交际者的译者》(*The Translator as Communicator*)第六章"Register Membership in Literary Translating"。

　　本文从与语言使用者相关的范畴入手探讨语域变化,讨论文学翻译中的语域属籍问题。作者以肖伯纳戏剧《卖花女》的阿拉伯语翻译为例,研究了语域中的静态性与动态性、个人言语方式的意义、个人言语方式的语用特点和文学作品人物的态度意义。作者特别注重在翻译过程中实现源语文本的概念功能和人际功能,并把话语的符号层面纳入他们的分析模式中来。他们认为个人言语方式和方言都行使符号功能。本文对语域和语旨的分析都考虑到了个人言语方式。在作者看来,译者必须分析某一特定语旨层面上的个人言语方式,注意人物个人言语方式的重现性和功能性,对个人言语方式的变化及其意图要有清醒的认识。《卖花女》中人物的伦敦佬方言的语音、词汇和句法特点为许多英国观众所熟悉,操这种方言的人通常被认为受教育程度不高。本文认为剧本原作中特定人物伦敦佬言语方式的系统重现是值得译者关注的对象。这种方言的独特性和内涵,任何目标语文化都不大可能很容易地复制。另外,目标语文学体裁习俗会对翻译进行干预。该剧的阿拉伯语译者一般会采用正式的、古典的风格,因为人们认为它是唯一一种适合阿拉伯语文学的风格。以往的语域研究只是围绕语场、语旨、语式三个层面展开,哈蒂姆和梅森的语域研究引入了符号学和语用学相关原理,因而取得了突破。

The common thread which, we suggested in Chapter 1, unites all types of translating, including literary and non-literary translating, is by now familiar to the reader. Differences in the prominence of particular features, procedures and translator focus in different translation tasks cannot and should not be overlooked. But, from the perspective of a view of textuality which holds that the structure and texture of texts is subject to higher-order contextual requirements, the differences have to be seen in the light of the register-based, pragmatic and semiotic features which determine the communicative potential of all utterances.

The field to be investigated in this chapter is literary translating and aspects of literary expression. At the same time, we shall concentrate on one particular domain of context, namely **register** membership, through the analysis of an instance of register variation. In discussing literary language in terms of use-and user-related categories of register variation, issues of common concern to literary and non-literary translating will emerge and contribute to our broad view of a unified text strategy. From this perspective, our discussion will encompass both semiotics and pragmatics, which will be seen to work in harness with register in shaping the actual structure and texture of texts.

The translation of idiolect and tenor

The translation problem tackled in this chapter relates generally to the techniques adopted in handling literary discourse. In this domain of translating, however, a common concern of both literary and non-literary translators will emerge. It has to do with user-related aspects of the message such as idiolect and use-related categories such as **tenor.** By idiolect we understand the individual's distinctive and motivated way of using language at a given level of formality or tenor. To demonstrate the validity of this approach to a common problem in translation (i. e. informal, idiolectal use of language), we take a literary text (Shaw's *Pygmalion*) and focus on the way translators have dealt with the Flower Girl's idiolectal use of tagged statements such as *I'm a good girl*, *I am*, and the general informality characteristic of the tenor of a dialect such as Cockney English.

What we hope to show in this exercise, then, is that features of idiolect or tenor are not the exclusive preserve of one variety rather than another (e. g. spoken, non-literary language), but have wider currency across domains of language use as varied as literature and factual reporting. More specifically, we intend to show that, preoccupied with surface manifestations, some translators of *Pygmalion* have not been entirely successful in tackling subtle aspects of discoursal meaning. In the case of Arabic—a language from which we wish initially to illustrate success or failure in establishing translation adequacy—the straightforward and rather static approach to the entire play has been to opt for a high and a low variety of the language to relay formal and informal tenor respectively, dealing rather casually with idiolectal meaning as not being particularly noteworthy. With some exceptions, this procedure is not untypical of the way translation problems of this kind are tackled in other languages.

In this discussion, we shall also address some wider issues. Contextual categories such as tenor, although universal in the sense that every language in the world is bound to possess some sort of scale of formality, are in fact language-specific when it comes to (1) the way the formal-informal distinction is operationally perceived (i. e. where to draw the line between formal and informal), and (2) the way formality or informality is linguistically realized (i. e. the options selected in the actual production of texts). Categories such as tenor thus become a problem in translation between languages in which the formal-informal distinction does not operate in the same way.

Idiolectal use: the translator's options

Let us now consider Shaw's *Pygmalion* as a source text and reflect on the kind of translation procedures which might be adopted in Arabic to handle formality. At the disposal of the translator, there would be many language varieties and a fundamental choice to be made between the classical and one of the vernaculars (Moroccan, Egyptian, etc.). Broadly speaking, the following options are possible. Translators may opt for the classical variety throughout (hypothetical version 1), one of the vernaculars throughout (version 2) or one of the vernaculars for less formal speech and the classical for more formal speech (version 3).

Leaving aside the thorny issue of whether the translation is intended to be read or to be performed, version 1 would most certainly be well received, as classical Arabic is felt by many to be the only variety compatible with the written mode in fields such as creative literature. But this solution is surely far from satisfactory as it cannot possibly reflect source text variation in tenor and idiolectal use. Version 2 no doubt goes some way towards preserving this variation, but also remains lacking in consistency as far as general translation strategy is concerned: How informal should a source text utterance be to be marked as such within the vernacular, and which vernacular is to be chosen? Version 3 shares some of the problems of inconsistency suffered by version 2 but would also attract much louder criticism not only from the classical Arabic language establishment who would decry this abuse, but also from those whose vernacular happens to be used for informal speech.

In fact, the Arabic version of *Pygmalion* which we have consulted adopts a solution of the type of version 3 above: a combination of classical and vernacular to render the formal and informal parts of the text. But, as we shall demonstrate in the following critique, none of the three types of approach seems adequately to address the real issues. The problem is that a scale of categories (of formality in this case) which works for English is naively imposed on languages in which it may not necessarily be applicable. In the context of Arabic, to borrow the scale of formality from English and use it uncritically would inevitably entail the erroneous assumption that categories such as classical/vernacular always correlate with standard/non-standard English, on the one hand, and with formal/informal speech, on the other. What is suspect in this kind of approach to language variation is not only the unconstrained positing of correlations, but also, and perhaps more significantly, the perpetuation of the notion that varieties such as RP and cockney or classical and vernacular Arabic are mere catalogues of static features, to be called up mechanistically with little or no regard for what is actually going on in communication.

Towards a more workable solution

As will become clearer in the course of the following discussion, simple solutions to complex problems such as dialectal fluctuation in Shaw's *Pygmalion* invariably run the risk of glossing over a basic text linguistic principle governing language variation in general. This is the requirement that, whatever options are selected to uphold the register membership of a text, they should always be adequately motivated. Register is a configuration of features which reflect the ways in which a given language user puts his or her language to use in a purposeful manner. This intentionality acquires its communicative thrust when intertextuality comes into play and utterances become signs (socio-textual/rhetorical or socio-cultural/semantic) —cf. Chapter 2, where these notions are explained.

We are all familiar with the way advertisers, for example, take meticulous care in their choice of what kind of speaker or professional activity is appropriate to given settings for selling certain products. It would indeed be bizarre if a speaker of southern British English were used to sell the traditional qualities of Yorkshire bitter or if a strongly-marked regional accent were used to sell pharmaceutical products. Advertising copy-writers make sure that this does not happen. What is involved here is precisely an advertiser's attempt at being, perhaps intuitively, in tune with the way texts develop in natural settings. A given register thus takes us beyond the geographical provenance of, say, the beer drinker or the consumer of pharmaceutical products to questions of identity (i. e. self-image). Register consequently carries all kinds of intended meanings and thus functions as the repository of signs, whose range of semantic as well as rhetorical values is intuitively recognized by all textually competent speakers of a language.

To illustrate this notion of "motivation" from a well-known literary text, let us consider the following example from Eugene Ionesco's play, *The Lesson*. The play is about the interaction between a professor and his 18-year-old pupil. The interactive dynamic hinges on the way the professor and the pupil behave towards each other at the start of their encounter and how they end up behaving. The nervousness and diffidence of the professor is contrasted with the dynamism and liveliness of the girl in the beginning. Gradually attitudes are reversed and a powerful climax ensues.

Simpson (1989) analyses this reversal from the perspective of politeness theory (cf. Chapter 5) and traces the professor's movement (as shall we with that of *Pygmalion*'s Flower Girl) from utterances such as "You are … er … I suppose you really are … er … the new pupil?" to "Be quiet. Sit where you are. Don't interrupt." Hesitancy or confidence are aspects of behaviour which find expression in actual patterns of language use. These tend to be both recurrent and functional and must therefore be heeded as such by readers or translators. The need to be aware of variation and of the underlying motivations becomes even more urgent in domains such as literary analysis or literary translation, where some of the most elliptic or opaque forms of utterance (and hence the easiest to overlook) come to occupy a crucial position in the literary work, serving as important clues in the portrayal of a certain scene or persona.

The static and the dynamic in register specification

Registers, then, have a pragmatic and a semiotic meaning potential. We can see this potential in terms of the marked vs. unmarked use of language referred to in Chapters 1 and 2. As we have shown in the analysis of a number of texts so far, a register feature, like any other instance of language use, may be seen as unmarked when expectations are upheld and when the text world is unproblematic and retrieved without difficulty (i. e. maximally stable): Lawyers speak like lawyers, scientists like scientists, and so on. Markedness, on the other hand, arises when expectations are defied, and when lawyers' language, for example, is borrowed and used to best effect by, say, an anguished housewife, resentful of the deplorably indifferent attitude of the police (see Sample 3. 11 in Chapter 3) or indeed by a politician, relaying a particularly detached, coldblooded attitude towards some humanitarian issue (see Sample 11. 3 in Chapter 11). In these highly dynamic uses of language, communicative stability has been gradually removed, intentions are blurred and intertextuality is less than straightforward.

Let us return to *Pygmalion*. In dealing with this play, translators would be confronted with similar dynamic uses of language. Firstly, they would have to account for a number of register features intended to relay special effects and which go beyond established, unmarked characteristics. To be fully appreciated, such features must first be seen against the background of some unmarked "norm" and then within the wider perspective of pragmatic action and semiotic interaction. In both these domains, intended actions and conventional signs can and often do display remarkably high levels of dynamism. To explain these adequately, we have to detect the rhetorical purposes which they serve (in the text), the attitudinal meanings they express (in discourse) and the social activity they perform (in genre).

Register, then, is not always a neutral category. The more creative the text is, the more dynamic language use must be. In order to illustrate this, we shall, in the following discussion of literary translation, merge values yielded by tenor with idiolectal use of language. With the use and user of language implicated in this way, we shall seek to show that the preservation of these aspects of the construction of meaning is not only crucial but is also a concern for both the language user and the literary critic.

Idiolectal meaning

Within register, the "user" dimension includes variation due to geographical, temporal, social and idiolectal factors. Of particular interest to the translation assessment exercise conducted in this study is idiolectal/tenor variation. Idiolectal meaning enjoys a special status within the dialectal spectrum. An idiolect subsumes features from all of the other aspects of variation and, before developing as an idiolect, has its origin in straightforward dialectal use of language envisaged along geographical, historical, or social lines. For example, the Flower Girl's idiolectal use of the peculiar form of tagging (*I'm a good girl, I am*) is undoubtedly shared by many speakers and bears traces of Cockney English, a London dialect spoken by a particular class of people at a particular stage in time.

In this way, idiolect incorporates those features which make up the individuality of a speaker or writer. Now, this varies in scope from what may be described as a person's idiosyncratic way of speaking (a favourite expression, a quaint pronunciation of particular words, the over-use of certain syntactic structures and so on) to more collectively shared sets of features that single out entire groups of users and set them apart from the rest in certain respects (e. g. the tagging feature to be discussed here or frequent use of the "posh" pronoun "one"). Another equally attractive feature of idiolects is that, contrary to common belief, they are not peripheral. They are in fact systematic, their use is often linked to the purpose of utterances and they are frequently found to carry wider sociocultural significance. It is the task of the translator to identify and preserve the purposefulness behind the use of these seemingly individualistic mannerisms.

In classifying idiolects, it is particularly useful to make a distinction, on the one hand, between the transient and the durable (along what we shall call the "recurrence" continuum) and, on the other hand, between functional and nonfunctional (the "functionality" continuum). The two axes overlap in the sense that, if idiolectal occurrences happen to be short-lived, they will also tend to be a functional (a category which would include instances of the person-or group-oriented idiosyncrasies discussed above). But it is recurrent and functional idiolectal features which are by far the more interesting as carriers of both pragmatic and semiotic meanings. In actual texts, these tend to recur systematically and, in so doing, consistently relay a variety of rhetorical values which have to be properly appreciated for the overall effect to be preserved.

For example, like the professor's um's and ah's referred to above, the far-from-logical over-use of the connector *on the other hand* by the miser in the musical *The Fiddler on the Roof* is an instance of a functional feature of idiolect. This recurs systematically and, every time it is uttered, it serves more or less the same rhetorical function that is crucial for making sense of both the character and the plot. It is this sense of idiolectal meaning which will preoccupy us in the remainder of this discussion. But a brief summary of our position regarding the scope of idiolectal usage may now be in order. We assume that, to attain the status of genuine idiolectal variation, and thus become a noteworthy object of the translator's attention, idiosyncrasies must first display systematic recurrence in the speech behaviour of a given individual or group. Impermanence renders this kind of variation a one-off aberration and diminishes the returns which language users hope to obtain from a closer scrutiny of texts. An important corollary to this principle of recurrence is that it is only when shown to be employed for a specific purpose that idiolects become truly functional and, therefore, an essential part of the repertoire of meanings at the disposal of the text user.

The flower girl and functionally-motivated idiolectal meaning

We begin our illustration by presenting (Sample 6.1) some representative examples of the use of "tagging" in the linguistic performance of Shaw's Eliza Dolittle.

Sample 6.1

(a) THE FLOWER GIRL (*subsiding into a brooding melancholy over her basket and talking very low-spiritedly to herself*) I'm a good girl, I am. [p. 24]

(b) THE FLOWER GIRL (*still nursing her sense of injury*) Ain't no call to meddle with me, he ain't, [p. 24]

(c) THE FLOWER GIRL (*resenting the reaction*) He's no gentleman, he ain't, to interfere with a poor girl. [p. 25]

(d) THE FLOWER GIRL (*rising in desperation*) You ought to be stuffed with nails, you ought. [p. 28]

(e) ELIZA (*protesting extremely*) Ah-ah-ah-ah-ow-ow-oo-oo!!! I ain't dirty: I washed my face and hands afore I come, I did. [p. 41]

This particular form of pseudo-emphasis occurs regularly in the speech of Eliza on her way to becoming what Higgins wants her to be. Under the watchful eye of the Professor, however, the form tends to disappear gradually, reappearing infrequently and only when the reader needs to be reminded of Eliza's linguistic and social past. This rules out the possibility that the peculiar form of emphasis is merely an accidental feature of dialect and encourages us as audience or readers to enquire into the motivation behind its use. Of course, a number of critical theories could be put forward in an attempt to account for this occurrence. But whatever theory one is to subscribe to, it must be able to explain the tagging, its emergence and disappearance in terms of Shaw's attempt subtly to transform Eliza and shift the power dynamic between her and others. In this kind of explanation, it is important to note, from the perspective of translation, that we have not remained prisoners of core register theory but have gone beyond this into the pragmatics of the communicative act as something intended and not as a mere dialectal reflex.

The pragmatics of idiolect

Judging by mainstream solutions to problems of idiolectal meaning in translation, we are inclined to think that, in comparison to other communicative variables, features of idiolect are given fairly low priority by translators when dealing with utterances such as those in Sample 6. 1. As noted earlier, idiolectal meanings have always been located on the periphery of language variation and domains such as geographical or historical variation in language use have always proved somehow more worthy of attention by dialectologists, linguists and, for that matter, translators.

In the analysis and translation of variation in language use, the three aspects of field, mode and tenor are usually given careful attention. Sometimes, however, this may be based on a rather superficial conception of what, say, field of discourse implies. Thus, notions such as subject matter, casual speech and so on, which hardly capture the intricacies involved, tend to be at the top of the register analyst's checklist. The utterances in Sample 6. 1 above would be classified along these lines and some vernacular form would be selected by the translator in the hope that, not being a standard form of language use, the vernacular would take care of the user and use dimensions of the source text (dialect, informality, etc.).

In looking at actual versions of *Pygmalion* in various languages, we soon discover that our criticisms of translations which adopt monolithic solutions such as Standard English＝high variety and cockney＝low variety are not justified in all respects. In the case of the Arabic version, for example, the translator has perceived the functionality of the tags, as can be seen from the following

Figure 6. 1   Idiolect in the Arabic version

Form	Variety	Function
(a) *ummal* (Lit, "or what!")	Egypt. Ar.	defiant
(b) *inta malak* ("what's wrong with you")	Egypt. Ar.	defiant
(c) *abadan* ("never")	Egypt. Ar.	defiant
(d) *tihish hash* ("stuffed fully")	Egypt. Ar.	defiant
(e) *waalahi ghasalthum kuwayyis khalis* ("By God, I washed them thoroughly")	Egypt. Ar.	defiant

Figure 6.2 Idiolect in French, Catalan and Portuguese versions

Form	Variety	Function
FRENCH Il n'a pas le droit de se mêler de mes affaires, il n'a pas le droit.	standard	emphatic
CAT Pro aisòs no és motiu perfer-me la llesca.	low social dialect[1]	defiant
PORT No tinha nada que se meter na'nha bida!	geographical	defiant

summary of our findings in the case of the Arabic version as in Figure 6.1 and Figure 6.2 shows solutions adopted in some other translations of the play for the problem represented by *Ain't no call to meddle with me*, *he ain't*.

Two points may be made about the translator's attempt to preserve in Arabic Eliza's peculiar use of emphasis. First, although easy to overlook, the minutiae of Eliza's idiolectal use of tags have all been noticed and relayed. Second, some form of dialect is opted for in rendering the entire performance of Eliza, a decision which is not altogether inappropriate. The success of the translations under study remains relative, however. A number of questions can be posed at this stage regarding the translator's text strategy. For example, did the translator make a serious attempt at formally preserving the sense of recurrence by opting for one and the same form to translate each instance (a)—(e) in Sample 6.1 or were variants preferred? And, whatever the option taken, is the ultimate effect which cumulatively builds up through Eliza's performance properly relayed?

Judgements of this kind involve issues that are semiotic in essence. Utterances need to be seen as signs in constant interaction with each other and governed by intertextual conventions. Register membership and pragmatic purposes remain dormant unless and until they are placed within a wider socio-cultural perspective, involving sign systems as means of signification.

To proceed, we need to clear up a matter we have so far taken for granted. This is the literary-critical issue of what Shaw actually intended to say (or do with his words) through Eliza's use of the tags. As we have pointed out above, defiance is the reading which generally comes through in the translations consulted, a reading which we find not altogether inappropriate. However, going by the textual evidence, we would suggest that, if it is "defiance," then this must be the kind of defiance that emanates from utter frustration; that is, it is ultimately reducible to a cry from someone trapped. Consider, for example, Shaw's directions when introducing the various utterances where tagging occurs: *subsiding into a brooding melancholy over her basket*, *and talking very low-spiritedly to herself*; *still nursing her sense of injury*, and so on.

Contextually, on the other hand, Eliza cannot plausibly be seen as "defiant," given that this form of tagging emerges in the early stages of her linguistic development only to disappear altogether as she "matures" linguistically and ideologically. Rather, what Eliza is more likely to be doing is betraying a tremendous lack of self-confidence, desperately seeking assurance for almost every statement she makes. It is this uncertainty, combined with an acute sense of failure that characterizes the power relations at work in her interaction with the outside world.

Here, the intentionality involved in the way Shaw willed Eliza to be has gone beyond the individual speech acts uttered in relative isolation from each other, in the same way as it has gone beyond the formal features of register attached to the various modes of use encountered. Complex systems of inference and presupposition, together with a variety of cultural assumptions and conventions are crucial to the intricate network of relations developed throughout the play. These surround what Eliza has to say and reflect the ways in which a given culture constructs and partitions reality.

Preserving the function of Eliza's idiolectal use may thus have to be informed by the "human" or "socio-geographical" criterion, rather than a purely "locational" one (Catford 1965, pp. 87 – 88). The translation of *Pygmalion* must therefore seek to bring out Eliza's socio-linguistic "stigma," a communicative slant which, incidentally, should not necessarily entail opting for a particular regional variety and could as effectively be relayed through simply modifying the standard itself. By the same token, and remarking in general on the entire performance by Eliza, the user's status could adequately be reflected not primarily through phonological features but through a deliberate manipulation of the grammar or the lexis to relay the necessary ideological thrust.

We now have the beginnings of an answer to one of the two questions put earlier, concerning the cumulative values to be relayed. Rather than defiance, Eliza is more likely, from a position of weakness, to be displaying her powerlessness, albeit resentfully. Once this crucial value is identified, the remaining task for the translator is to ensure that consistency is established and maintained. We would suggest in the case of the Arabic version, for example, that *ummal* (which was chosen by the translator in one instance) will serve this purpose adequately throughout.

Attitudinal meanings in the flower girl's performance

In terms of genre analysis, Eliza may be said to operate within the constraints of a recognizable genre—a conventionalized "form of text" which reflects the functions and goals involved in a particular "social occasion," as well as the purposes of the participants in them (Kress, 1985). To master the genre, Eliza could thus be presumed to have internalized a set of norms as part of her ability to communicate. Criteria for an adequate translation must therefore involve relaying the hurt feelings of a woman suspected unjustly of some social ill such as prostitution. Also relayed should be the agony of a woman protesting her innocence in such a situation, knowing full well that her voice is simply not loud enough to be heard or heeded either by a good-for-nothing father, or by those who perpetuate an inequitable social structure which has put her in the gutter in the first place. Emphatic tags relaying defiance, as in the Arabic translation, would simply fail to relay all of this and instead present an entirely different genre structure: It is not one of protesting one's innocence, but of protesting, full stop. Nor is it the cry of the downtrodden but of the powerful, the "cocky," the "cheeky."

In all of this, attitudinal meanings are prominent. The ideological stance emanating from such a confident genre in the translation would not be the one intended in the source text: A different discourse to the one originally used emerges, a different mode of thinking and talking. Like the "committed" discourse of the feminist, for example, what should be relayed is the subdued discourse of the powerless. This is the cultural code (Barthes, 1970) or the ideological statement made by the likes of Eliza, expressing itself through a variety of key terms and syntactic devices. In short, hesitancy is a discoursal feature that characterizes Eliza's use of the tags. But, in the various translations consulted, this reading is consistently blurred by the use of the defiant or emphatic tagging. Instead, we are given a more self-assured tone, sparking off the wrong intertextuality.

Discourse and genre values, however, are too diffuse to be readily amenable to structured modes of expression. These various signals, which can give rise to sometimes conflicting readings, have to be accounted for by reference to a more stable framework. This is provided by the unit "text," which imposes order on the open-endedness of discoursal meanings. Within the model of discourse processing advocated here, a textual structure is one in which communicative intentions are made mutually relevant in the service of a given rhetorical purpose (cf. Beaugrande & Dressler, 1981; Werlich, 1976). To illustrate how texts become units in which problems are resolved, let us consider one of the statements made by Eliza:

> I'm a good girl, I am.

Here, the passage from *I'm a good girl* to the tag *I am* indicates that a problem is encountered. This problem may best be seen in terms of the tension between Eliza's past, her "here and now" and her future aspirations. The conflict has to be resolved one way or another, and this may account for the style-switching from statement to tag syntagmatically and from a tag proper to the particular tag used here, paradigmatically. This configuration, together with intentionality, constitutes the mechanism by which texture is created and made to serve particular discoursal attitudes and particular genre structures.

In sum, the occurrence of tagging in *Pygmalion* is a textual phenomenon which has to be handled in translation by ensuring that the characteristics of use and user, intentionality and semiotic interaction are reflected. It is the latter characteristic of texts which is perhaps the most crucial. The use of tags by Eliza can be related intertextually to any one or all of the following.

(a) Similar tag occurrences in the immediate textual environment, for example,

> ELIZA (*rising reluctantly and suspiciously*) You're a great bully, you are ... I never asked to go to Bucknam Palace, I didn't. I was never in trouble with the

police, not me. I'm a good girl.

(b) Similar occurrences of tagging in the distant textual environment, for example, *I'm a good girl*, echoing the earlier occurrence *I'm a good girl*, *I am* (p. 24).

(c) Similar tag occurrences that lie completely outside the present textual environment (immediate or distant), as in the use of similar tagging in cockney.

(d) Utterances which in one form or another relay a similar meaning to that intended by The Flower Girl (e. g. by the "oppressed" and the "victimized," in the discourse of "stigma" and "hesitancy").

(e) Utterances which in one way or another point to the social occasion in question (e. g. the genre of feeble defiance and wounded feelings of someone who is unable to stand up to the bully).

(f) Utterances which in one way or another recall any of the above contexts only to contradict it, parody it, etc. For example,

ELIZA (*shaking hands with him*) Colonel Pickering, is it not?

In effect, Eliza's idiolect in *Pygmalion* acquires mythical dimensions almost akin to those of a fully-fledged persona. At one level of semiotic analysis, the entire performance of Eliza could be considered as one "huge" sign that is made operational by the "smaller" signs included within it. Like all semiotic constructs, emphatic tagging in Eliza's performance comes into being at an early stage in the play, acts on and interacts with the textual and extra-textual environment, changes and then dies away. Using a set of sign relationships [of the nature of (a)—(e) in Sample 6. 1], Shaw intends idiolectal tagging to relay feelings of stigma. But this gradually gives way to a more defiant Eliza. When it fully comes to fruition, defiance no longer attracts the usual tag signs which were once the mode of expressing injured feelings, but becomes more forceful through the use of "proper" tags and indeed tag-free English.

In conclusion, neither the Arabic version of *Pygmalion*, nor the other versions consulted, have fully upheld this dynamic fluctuation which builds on intended meanings and intertextual potential. Yet if communication in translation is to succeed, due heed must be paid to relaying intentional and intertextual diversity of the kind discussed here.

【延伸阅读】

[1] Hatim, B., Mason, I. (1990). *Discourse and the Translator*. London & New York: Longman.

[2] Hatim, B., Mason, I. (1997). *The Translator as Communicator*. London & New York: Routledge.

【问题与思考】

1. 从本文中能看出语用学和符号学对作者有哪些影响？

2.《卖花女》原作的阿拉伯语译本在对语域的处理上存在的主要问题是什么？

3. 如何看待个人言语方式在语域研究中的重要性？为什么？

4. 本文作者是如何正确理解《卖花女》中卖花女行为的态度意义的？

5. 本文对我们继续研究语域与翻译有哪些启发？

选文三　朱莉安·豪斯的"翻译质量评估模式"批评

司显柱

导　言

本文发表于《外语教学》2005 年第 3 期。

本文认为朱莉安·豪斯的《翻译质量评估模式》(*A Model of Translation Quality Assessment*)(1981)及其修订本《翻译质量评估——修订的模式》(*Translation Quality Assessment：A Model Revisited*)(1997)，依据系统功能语言学、语篇分析等理论，拥有比较完整的参数体系，步骤上遵循一定的程序，并适度引入定量的方法，是国际翻译批评界第一个具有完整的理论和实证的翻译质量评估模式。本文在介绍这一模式的同时，重点分析、阐释了其背后的理论依据，批评了存在的不足之处：参数设置不够合理，运行步骤有待优化。杰勒德·麦卡莱斯特(Mcalester，2000：231)概括翻译评估的研究发展现状时指出，迄今为止只有两本专门研究翻译评估的著作，一是朱莉安·豪斯的《翻译质量评估模式》(1981)及其修订本《翻译质量评估——修订的模式》(1997)，二是凯瑟琳娜·赖斯的《翻译批评：前景与局限》(*Translation Criticism：Prospects and Limitations*)(2000)。对这两部著作，国内亦有人著文评述。前者如张春柏(2002)，后者如屠国元、王飞虹(2003)，但主要是介绍，鲜有批评。本文主要介绍和评论豪斯的评估模式(包括初版和修订版)。

一、豪斯模式述介

对翻译质量进行评估首先要依赖一定的标准，而标准的确立又取决于对翻译本质的认识，即对翻译的定义。可以说，不同的翻译观产生不同的翻译标准、不同的翻译策略和方法，也因此导致不同的翻译质量概念和翻译评估方法。由于问题的极其复杂性，以及研究者的认知水平和切入视角的差别，对以上问题的回答，可谓见仁见智。这一点，豪斯是了然于心的，如在1997 年的修订版和 2001 年关于翻译评估的论文里，她均清楚地阐述了上述观点，认为翻译质量评估的关键问题是对翻译本质的认识。如果是翻译研究中的新阐释学派，认为意义来自语言使用者，文本根本就没有核心意义，那么就会把翻译看成是直觉的、阐释的；如果是翻译研究的行为/反应/功能主义者,则翻译评估就会把读者反应和目的语文化规范作为主要的依据,而严重忽略原文文本;如果是描述性翻译研究、后现代主义和解构主义以及以语言学为主的翻译学派,就会利用独立语言单位所包含的语境或者话语分析的方法(以文本和话语为基础的方法)去进行翻译评估(参见 House,1997:1-23;2001)。

不过,在该书的初版(即 1977 年版,它是作者 1976 年通过的博士论文的正式出版;第二版即 1981 年版与初版相比除了在文字上有少许修改外在内容上几乎没有差别——见作者 1997 年版前言)中,她并没有将以上思想付诸文字,而是直接给出自己对该问题的见解:翻译的实质在于"意义"在从一种语言转移到另一种语言时保持不变。而这里的意义包含三个方面的基本内容,即语义的(semantic)、语用的(pragmatic)和语篇的(textual)(House,1977:25)。所以翻译是用语义和语用对等的译语文本代替源语文本。(Translation is the replacement of a text in the source language by a semantically and pragmatically equivalent text in the target language.)(House,1977:30)。因此在这样的翻译定义下,对译文质量的判断,就是看译文是否在上述三种意义上与原文对等。

从翻译评估研究的视角看,上述关于翻译的定义有三点值得我们特别注意:一是"意义",二是"语篇/文本",三是"对等"。下面分别阐述。

先谈"意义"。

"意义"的三个方面,即语义、语用和语篇对翻译都特别重要。不过,三类意义中,由于语言的语篇意义是一种基于语言内部的,对语言所传递的信息的组织意义(Halliday,1994:33-36),作用是辅助前两种意义的实现,换言之是一种言内意义(司显柱,2004b),所以对译文质量的判断只消看译文语篇的概念意义和人际意义是否和原文对等(House,1977:37)〔在前述她给出的翻译定义中,她用的是"语义的"、"语用的"和"语篇的"术语,但在其评估模式和对收入书中的译文语料的质量评估中,她把前两种"语义的"和"语用的"提法分别换成了"概念意义"和"人际意义",即用的是韩礼德功能语言学关于语言三种元功能/意义的术语。事实上这里的语义和语用意义就是功能语言学里的概念和人际意义,正如她在再版中所承认的,她的翻译质量评估模式的主要理论基础就是功能语言学(House,1997:118),尽管在初版里并未明确提及〕。这一思想贯穿于她旨在检验自己提出的翻译质量评估模式而对精心选择的八种文本的语言—情景—功能分析及其译文的质量判断过程中。

再说"语篇/文本"。这里要区分与文本直接相关的几种"意义/功能"。

一是语篇意义,英文叫 Textual Meaning,在功能语言学看来,它是构成语言三位一体的三种元功能或意义的其中之一(根据功能语言学,语言的上述三种意义是由语言的三种元功能体现的,因此两者是互为指代的。所以在以下的论述中,"意义"和"功能"的所指是同一的)。其作用,如前所述,是对语言表达的概念和人际意义的组织。

二是文本意义/功能与语言意义/功能是不同角度的同一所指。我们知道,语言使用的实际存在形式是语篇/文本。正如彭宣维(2000:225)所说的那样,语言是以语篇为代表的,正如语言是由言语表现的一样,文本所表现出的功能就是对语言作为一种系统所具有的功能的验证、折射或反映。因此,在这个意义上,文本功能与语言功能是同一的(不言而喻,这个层面的文本/语篇功能,与前述构成语言三种元功能之一的语篇功能不可同日而语,后者只是组成前者内涵的"三分天下有其一"。换个说法,如果把等同于语言功能的语篇功能看做上义词的话,那么作为语言元功能一部分的语篇功能则是下义词。名称虽同,所指却相异)。

三是文本类型学意义上的文本功能/意义。

豪斯关于翻译的定义及其评估模式的建立都是基于文本的,而非,比如,孤立的句子,所以要实现译文对原文在功能上的对等,不仅意味着包括语义和语用意义在内的语言功能相符,还要求文本功能对等。换言之,要建立达到功能对等的评估模型,就要考虑译文与原文的语言功能和文本功能。

那么何为文本的功能呢? 为了阐述豪斯的模式,搞清楚文本功能这一概念的内涵以及与语言功能的关系,我们不能不讨论一下所谓文本类型学、翻译类型学以及翻译策略等问题。这里我们有必要简单涉及一下翻译批评研究领域的另一专著——赖斯的《翻译批评:前景与局限》。

诚如朱志瑜(2004)所指出的,赖斯的著作《翻译批评:前景与局限》试图为翻译批评提出一套客观的标准,建构总体框架,形成一个可以自动调节的幅度和范围。这个框架应适用面广,评估力强。其理论架构的核心是文本类型学,其背后则是德国心理学家、语言学家布勒的语言功能理论。根据布勒的《语言理论》,他将语言的语意功能分为三类:"再现"(representation)、"表达"(expression)和"感染"(appeal)(Bühler,1990:35)。再现功能:对事物而言,语言符号客观地再现事物,符号与事物之间是"暗指"(symbol)关系,语言指涉的是事物。表达功能:对发送者而言,语言符号主观地表达发送者的内心状态,符号与发送者之间是"暗含"(symptom)的关系,语言包含的是发送者的感情。感染功能:对接受者而言,语言符号感动、影响接受者的内心感受或外在行动,符号与接受者之间是"暗示"(signal)的关系,语言指示的是接受者的行动。

赖斯以布勒的三种语言功能为基础,分出三种文本类型:"重内容(content-focused)文本"、"重形式(form-focused)文本"、"重感染(appeal-focused)文本"(Reiss,1971/2000:24-38),后来,她分别称之为"信息(informative)文本"、"表情(expressive)文本"、"感染(operative)文本"(Reiss,1989:109)。

由此我们可以看出,文本类型取决于文本功能,而文本功能是建立在语言功能之上的(House,1977:35)。

但是语言功能与文本功能又不完全是一回事。从前面关于文本功能内涵的第二种阐述,我们可以把语言功能和文本功能的关系类比为语言(langue)与言语(parole)的关系:一是抽象的,一是具体的。文本,作为语言的具体使用,是语言使用者对语言系统里词汇、语法资源等的有机操纵,即选词连句、组句成篇的结果;而文本功能/意义的呈现则是依赖于其各级组成单位,如词组、小句、句群等表达的意义依循一定逻辑方式的合成。不同的文本,之所以其(文本)功能不同,或因其所组成部分的语言的概念和人际意义的不同,或因对其基本相同的组成部分的意义的配置(由语言的语篇功能来完成)的不同,或因两者兼而有之——组成部分如各个小句的语言意义和对其的组织都不同所致。语言功能,按照功能语言学的论述,只有三种:概念、人际和语篇,而且这三种功能是三位一体的,对其重要性的认识是一视同仁的。但对文本来说,从集合的意义上来看,正如对作为一种系统的语言在功能上可以抽象、归纳出前面的三种元功能一样,同样可以把文本归纳、抽象出三种功能:"再现"、"表达"和"感染"(布勒关于语言——实质上是言语/文本的三种功能划分是从语言所表达的"言外内容"的角度阐述的,自然没有涉及语言内部机制的"语篇功能"。这样,它与功能语言学的三种元功能的对应关系为,布勒所概括的三种语言功能中,其中的"再现功能"基本上对应于功能语言学所归纳的概念功能,而"表达"和"感染"功能则包含在人际功能之内），而且任一文本，作为对语言系统的使用，必然一方面表现出上述三种语言功能（概念、人际和语篇），另一方面，肯定也同样呈现出"再现"、"表达"和"感染"等多种功能，即功能不是单一的。但由于文本组成部分及其组织上的上述三种不同情形，对某一具体文本而言，总有以某一功能/意义（"再现"、"表达"或"感染"）为主导的问题(Reiss,1989:111)。我们把文本的这种主导功能称做文本类型学意义上的文本功能，上述赖斯关于不同文本类型的划分也正是在此意义上操作的。显而易见，这种意义上的文本功能虽是由语言功能支撑的，但不是完全等同的，它更多的是对语言概念和人际功能中某一种功能的强调和突出。

将以上这个文本分类法应用到翻译上，就形成了不同的翻译策略：根据文本目的和性质，信息文本要求"直接、完整地传递源语文本的概念内容"；表情文本传达"源语文本内容概念的艺术形式"；感染文本再造"文本形式以直接达到预期的（接受者）反应"(Reiss,1989:109)，其重点分别为"内容"、"形式"、"效果"。

这样，对不同文本类型的翻译来讲，语言功能和文本功能就会表现出不同的关系：对信息文本而言，一般只要在微观层面如小句实现了概念和人际意义等语言功能的对等转换，整个译文文本也基本实现了与原文文本功能的对等，即语言功能和文本功能基本上是统一的；但对于如感染文本的翻译，为追求译文文本对原文文本功能的对等——相同或类似的言后效果(perlocutionary effect)，往往要实施豪斯称之的"文化过滤"——表现在文字层面上即对包括原文的篇章结构、表达方式等作出调整，增、删、合、并和改变说法等，连带地，微观层面，如词组、句子的概念意义等语言功能就常常不能保持对原文的一致，这样一来，语言功能和文本功能就不完全统一了。由此，在我们看来，这就是为什么赖斯在谈论翻译批评时特别突出了对文本类型、翻译类型和翻译策略等概念的阐述；这就是为什么豪斯的翻译质量评估模式要将语言功能和文本功能并置为功能对等的参数——如果语言功能与文本功能能够完全一致的话，就只需提其一了。

最后讲"对等"。

对等的概念是与跨语言意义(meaning)的保存相关联的。豪斯把对等当做翻译质量评估的基本标准。"意义"的三个方面即语义、语用和文本对翻译都重要。豪斯认为文本意义（即文本类型学意义上的文本的主导功能或意义）的重要性在以前的翻译评估中一直受到忽视，而它正是获得翻译对等的关键之一[赖斯认为，翻译中最重要的变量就是原文文本所属的文本类型，因为它决定了译者后面的所有选择，翻译就是要保证这些文本类型不变。豪斯也持相同的看法。(House,1997:115)当然，实际的翻译，常常基于不同的原因，译文的文本功能时与原文不同，比如《格列佛游记》属讽刺文学，原有感染（警世或劝世）功能，而在译文中通常当做表情文本对待(Reiss,1989:114;2000:162)]。

那么如何把握、判断译文在语言功能上是否与原文对等呢？

豪斯的思路是从语境入手，从语境决定（语言）形式，而从形式表达意义/功能的角度分析译文是否在概念和人际意义上与原文对等或偏离。为此，她把原文和译文分成八个语境维度(dimensions)进行比较，这八个维度分别是(House,1977:42)：

语言使用者的维度 Dimensions of Language User	所处地域 Geographical Origin
	社会阶层 Social Class
	所处时代 Time

语言使用的维度
Dimensions of Language Use

语言媒介 Medium（simple/complex）

介入程度 Participation（simple/complex）

社会职能 Social Role Relationship

社会态度 Social Attitude

话题范畴 Province

语境决定形式，同时又是由形式建构的，而形式表示意义（Tompson，1996/2000：10）。通过对原文语境与形式的分析和互照，把握其功能/意义；秉循同样的方法分析译文，如此自然可以发现和确定译文是否与原文功能对等或偏离。因此假如译文在某个语境维度上与原文没有不匹配现象，就可判定译文文本在此维度上令人满意了，相应地表现为措辞上的适切和功能/意义上的对等（也可以反过来说，译文体现出与原文同样适切的措辞和对等的功能/意义，也自然建构了与原文相应的语境维度）。换言之，豪斯对翻译对等所要做到的功能相符的基本标准是：译文文本与原文文本不仅应该功能相符，并且要运用对等的语境维度方式去获得这些功能，分析原文文本和译文文本时，要看她所提出那个模式的八个维度是否两两相符，是否用同样的方法获得同样的功能。两者相符程度越高，翻译质量越好。因此译文文本的最终质量判断包括对上述语境里的每个维度不匹配程度的陈述，即对隐性错误（在语境维度上的错误）和显性错误（词语的所指意义与原文不对等或不符合目的语系统规范）的数量及类型的描述。由于该模式建立在详细的原文/本分析的基础上，因此被称为以源语文本为取向的模式（source text-based studies/source-oriented model）（House，1997：159）。

另一方面，既然文本功能是判定译文是否与原文对等的另一关键，所以在作出对译文质量的整体评价时，当然必须考虑所译语篇的类型，即体裁。一般说来，基于功能与语篇类型的关系，文本可以划分为概念意义主导型和人际意义主导型两类（House，1977：67）。鉴于不同类别语篇的主要功能不同，对之翻译的要求与重点也自然有别，翻译评估时理应根据所译语篇的类型，即是重在传达概念意义，如科研论文，还是着眼于人际功能，如文学、广告。在考察译文对原文在概念和人际意义参数上的偏离总数的同时，还必须视语篇类型对两种不同类别的意义/功能偏离对译文语篇整体质量/功效的影响大小设定权重，即对于重在传达概念意义的语篇，译文在概念意义上的偏离对译文质量的影响要大于在人际意义上的偏离对译文造成的伤害；反之，亦然。

以上系对豪斯模式的简单介绍和阐释，下面开展批评。

二、对豪斯模式的批评

（一）语篇/文本层面的参数设置及运行环节上的缺陷

虽然豪斯的翻译评估是立足于语篇、文本的，但在评估模式建构中，参数设置不够合理，运行步骤有待优化。

语篇，作为语言交际的存在形式，虽然是静止的成品——记录在纸面上的文本，但其背后却是语言交际涉及的各种因素的流动，并对语篇的编码与解码产生巨大的影响，这种影响表现在语篇的层面就是语篇之所以为语篇的语篇属性（Textuality）（司显柱，2004a）。Neubert（1992：70）将这种语篇属性具体化为七个方面：意向性、可接受性、情景性、信息性、互文性、连贯性和衔接性。仔细研究可以发现,上述反映语言交际所涉因素的七种语篇属性或者说参数,其实包括了两大方面的内容:一是语篇实体与外部因素的关系,如意向性、情景性等;二是语篇实体本身的组织,如连贯和衔接。

豪斯在建构其评估模式时,客观地说确实对语篇予以了相当的重视。这既表现在从文本外部因素——八个语境维度对语言编码的影响来分析译文的得体与否和功能上是否与原文对等;也体现在从语篇的内部关系即衔接、连贯的视角分析译文中的各个句子表达的语义,语用意义的组织是否妥当,从而帮助实现了对原文的概念和人际意义的对等转换。但是同样也在这两个方面存在不足。

就前者来说,语境参数设置虽然有八个之多,但彼此之间不少是重合的,所涉及的内容便未超出语域的语场、语旨和语式范围。这样便产生了两大问题:一方面,从模式的可操作性角度考量,参数设立不宜过多,尤其是不必设立虽然视角不同但反映的内容却大同小异的参数。以此观之,不难看出作者从语言使用者视角所设立的上述几个参数,由于其反映的内容也基本同样可以在语言使用维度上所设立的参数上反映出来(可参见下文对这几个参数内容的阐述),所以可以略去。而且就语言使用的参数本身还可以做进一步的合并和简化,如,可以将"社会角色关系"和"社会态度"合并,因为两者谈论的内容都是关于人际意义的范畴;而"介入程度"的内容,事实上业已被"方式"所包含,似看不出单独"立项"的必要性。这样,我们就可以把反映语言交际情景的参数简化为:交际方式、交际参与者之间的社会关系和态度,以及交际范围/领域,而这三个参数就是语域分析的三个变项,即语式、语旨和语场[有鉴于此,在1997年的修订版中她将上述参数统一在语场、语旨和语式之下,但仍然保留了先前的八个参数(House,1997:108),这便未解决参数设置烦琐的问题];另一方面,语域只是语境的一种,并未涵盖影响语言交际七种主要因素的全部,比如模式未对影响译文编码的重要因素——反映文化语境的体裁和译文读者予以考虑,所以该设立的参数又未列入[不过在修订版中,她认识到这点,明确把体裁作为一个参数纳入评估模式(House,1997:108),但她以将翻译本身与翻译的用途要区分为由把介入译文重构的要素——读者对象仍不纳入评估模式的做法(House,1997:165),是难以令人信服的,因此这方面虽有改进,但仍不彻底]。

就后者来讲,在以句子作为分析和描写单位评估其是否与原文的对应物在概念和人际意义上对等时,该模式虽然注意到了语篇的连贯和衔接,但总体上说其对译文质量的判断基本上是囿于组成语篇的微观成分——句子,整个评估框架是单向度的"自下而上"。尽管在实际的翻译评估中,尤其对象所涉对象是语言和文化十分接近的英德语言作品间的翻译的质量评估,常有的情形是,无论是只从微观上,还是宏观和微观上并进,在结果上,其得出的对译文质量的结论或许并无什么大的差别,但从方法论的角度审视显然不足为训。因为,尽管语篇的整体功能或意义的实现有赖于其组成部分,但是根据心理语言学中格式塔理论,对事物的整体认识毕竟不能完全依赖于对其各个组成部分的分析而获得——"整体要大于部分之和"(沈家煊,1999)。毕竟语篇的整体意义是依赖于其组成部分,按一定的方式编织而成,而非简单的累加,即中国传统文章学所归纳的"总文理,统首尾,定与夺,合涯际,弥纶一篇,使杂而不越"(《文心雕龙》)。即便是英德语言之间的翻译,对其实际的操作也时常不能完全限于原文的微观层面而字比句次,而必须根据所译文本类型在目的语里的相应结构要求(互文性)作出变通。对此,Nord(1991:19)在谈到英德语言间的翻译时就曾指出,"所有指示性语篇,如操作指令、使用说明或食谱,都有某种典型的句法结构"。因此开展翻译质量的评估实有必要从本体论的高度,从反映语言交际所涉基本因素的成篇属性等多个层面审查整个译文文本和其组成部分是否与原文对等或偏离。

另外，一个科学、完整和具有操作性的评估模式的建构，不仅要涵盖所有必要的参数，而且还必须有明确的运行步骤和环节。在我们看来，既然所要建立的模式是基于文本的，是要对译文文本的整体质量作出评估，而文本的整体意义实现既依赖于其组成的各个部分的意义，又不是其各部分的简单之和，所以，评估模式的建构至少要分三步：第一步，在微观层面上，即构成整体语篇的基本单元，也即小句层面上，从形式、功能、情景互动的角度，揭示和描写原文与译文小句的概念与人际意义以发现哪些译文句子对原文发生了"偏离"；第二步，在宏观层面，站在整个语篇的高度，从反映语言交际因素的语篇属性视角对前述微观层面所描写的各种"偏离"予以分类梳理和作出价值判断——排除从宏观视野看对译文质量未造成伤害的偏离个案；第三步，根据第二步对译文质量的价值判断再对第一步的统计数量进行修正，如此统计的偏离值才是判定译文多大程度上和原文"对等"或者说"忠实"的依据。但豪斯模式，无论是本身还是运用语料对其作实证的过程中基本上没有第二和第三环节，而显得不尽合理和操作性不足。

（二）缺乏分析和发掘文本意义/功能的参数

如前所述，为对译文是否与原文的意义/功能对等作出描写和判断，作者分别从语言使用者和语言使用的角度，从情景和语言关系的视角，设立了反映语篇的概念和人际意义的情景参数。从使用者的角度，涉及了所处地域、社会阶层和所处时代三项情景参数。所处地域关乎何种语言或方言，社会地位则决定是书面还是口语，而所处时代因素与语言的关系则表现在是当代语言还是古语等。从语言使用的角度，与语言使用相关的情景参数共立了五项：方式，书面还是口头；介入程度，当面还是背场，一人还是多人；社会角色关系，交际所涉方社会地位如何，平等还是不平等；社会态度，亲密还是疏远；领域（话题），宗教还是政治等。

显而易见，从情景与语言关系的角度来看，不同的情景必然决定了不同的言语编码特征，这些特征或在措辞、句式和成篇特征的所有维度，或在其中的一部分上有所体现。由于情景与语言之间存在着这样的对应关系，因此，对编码方来说，只有了解交际情景，才可望生成与情景一致、适切的言语/语篇；反过来，从解码方角度来看，通过对所读语篇、所听话语言辞特征的分析也能基本把握所涉交际事件里的各种情景。同理，从评估的视角来看，自然可以根据情景与语言特征的匹配与否对语篇的质量——编码的适切性作出高低上下的评价。不难看出，研究情景与语言的关系根本上是服务于如何有效地使用语言进行交际，宗旨是使编码出的语篇/话语发挥出其应有的功能。而语篇功能，或曰文本功能，如前所述，是由语言功能支撑的；而语言功能，又可归纳、概括为语义的和语用的，或者说概念的和人际意义/功能两块。因此分析情景与语言（形式）是否对应事实上也就是据此判断语言使用者所要表达的概念和人际意义是否成功实现，进而判断译文文本功能与原文文本功能是否对等——当然，如前所述，语言功能的对等并不总是意味着文本功能的自动对等，如对感染类文本的翻译，为实现文本功能的对等有时反而要在某些语言层面偏离原文才行。虽然说两者不总是同一的，但前者是后者的基础委实是不容置疑的——比如，对于人际功能主导型语篇，表情类和感染类文本的翻译，根据前面关于翻译类型的论述，这两类语篇/文本翻译的焦点分别是"发送者"和"感染"的对象——"接受者"，因此翻译是"重形式的"、"重感染的"，而不是"重内容的"。所以为实现基于形式的和感染的文本功能的对等而有时不得不容忍在语言概念功能上的偏离，即不是"重内容的"，但根本上说，这样的偏离是局部的，而非全局的；是从属的，而非主导的。能设想不追求概念功能对等而实现译文对原文的"重作者的"和"重读者的"文本功能吗？试想：如果大范围的，比如对文本里大多数的句子都允许甚至鼓励在概念意义上偏离原文以追求或形式的，或感染/反应的对等，译文面貌因此与原文相差十万八千里，那么这样的翻译还能叫翻译吗？在描写译学那里，它或许可以仍称为翻译，但在前面豪斯关于翻译定义的框架下，怕是没有叫做翻译的资格的。豪斯之所以把语言功能与文本功能对等并置为译文质量的参数，道理也正在于此。

因此，不能以人际功能主导型语篇的翻译是"重形式的"、"重感染的"而错误地认定可以不重视内容的忠实。与"重内容的"概念主导型语篇的翻译相比，差异只是在程度而已！同样，对"重内容的"概念主导型语篇的翻译也同样不能忽视对人际意义的传递——尽管对其关注与重视的程度可能没有与"重形式的"、"重感染的"语篇类型那样高，同样，差异也只在程度而已。所以，译文对原文在语言功能上的对等是实现三类语篇/文本功能（主旨）的——形式的、感染的、内容的——共同诉求与基础。

不过，问题是，读者，更具体地说，译文质量评估者，面对译文和原文文本时，有无有效提取语言的概念和人际意义的途径呢？显然，上述关于情景与语言特征的阐述并不能完全解决这样的问题——它们主要的作用在于帮助我们判断文本是否充分、适切地传达了交际者所要表达的意义，但并不能完全解决我们对文本的意义或发挥的功能的识别和发掘。为了从文本里识别和挖掘上述两种意义，我们需要一些参数或某种分析工具。如果没有这样的工具或者说参数，面对文本，我们实难较为全面、系统地发掘文本的概念和人际意义。自然从翻译评估的角度就难以对译文的质量作出较为全面、系统的评价。遗憾的是作者并未给我们提供这样一个工具（系统功能语言学关于体现语言元功能的词汇—语法系统——及物性、语气和主位系统就可以帮助评估者解决上述问题，可是作者尽管在修订版里明确声称其理论基础是韩礼德的系统功能语言学，却不去使用体现语言元功能的词汇—语法系统来分析、把握和对比原文、译文的功能/意义，委实令人费解！）。作者没有提供一个对文本里的上述意义进行观察和描写的参数，这样一来，对于译文和原文概念和人际意义的识别与判断，大家只能根据自己的习惯、倾向和悟性，各有侧重，也自然各有遗漏了，因此难免较多的主观性和缺乏系统性。

三、结束语

尽管存在上述种种不足，但从文章第一部分对该模式内容的介绍和背后理据的阐述不难看出，该模式在理论上有据可依（如系统功能语言理论、语篇分析等），拥有比较完整的参数体系，步骤上遵循一定的程序，并适度引入定量的方法，确实具有较强的系统性、科学性。更难能可贵的是，至少根据我们所掌握的文献来看，这是国际翻译批评界第一个具有完整的理论和实证的翻译质量评估模式——赖斯虽早豪斯几年写出翻译批评的专著，但她并未提出一套完整的评估模式来，因此，意义就更非同寻常。事实上，由于翻译批评与评估所涉因素极其复杂，所以在豪斯之后，虽然不乏对其问题的探索，但总的说来，人们在这一领域迄今所取得的成就仍十分有限，尤其在建构翻译质量评估模式方面目前仍无人能出其右。这一方面突显要建立一个具有较为系统、全面和科学的译文质量评估模式的难度，另一方面也进一步昭示豪斯模式业已取得了相当的高度。作为第一个系统、全面的翻译质量评估模式，其开拓性的历史性地位是否定不了的。我们今天对豪斯模式展开学术批评，根本宗旨还是希冀在其基础上，站在前人的

.肩膀上,推进对翻译质量的评估模式研究。

【延伸阅读】

[1] 吕桂. 系统功能语言学翻译质量评估模式的实证与反思. 外语研究,2010(2):64 - 69.

[2] 司显柱. 论功能语言学视角的翻译质量评估模式研究. 外语教学,2004(4):45 - 50.

[3] 司显柱. 功能语言学视角的翻译质量评估模式——兼评《孔乙己》英译本的翻译质量. 解放军外国语学院学报,2005(5):60 - 65.

[4] 武光军. 当代中西翻译质量评估模式的进展、元评估及发展方向. 外语研究,2007(4):73 - 79.

【问题与思考】

1. 本文是如何述介豪斯的翻译质量评估模式的?

2. 本文是如何对豪斯的翻译质量评估模式展开批评的?

3. 本文对我们研究西方翻译理论有何启发意义?

第七章　归化和异化

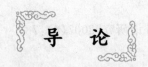

　　作为翻译策略,归化在西方至少在古罗马帝国时期就开始实施了。翻译是征服的一种形式。贺拉斯等拉丁语诗人把希腊语文本翻译成拉丁语文本。拉丁语译者不仅删除了文化专有词,而且把希腊诗人的名字换成了他们自己的名字,使得译本看上去不像译本,而像是用拉丁语创作的文本。

　　归化策略在英法翻译史中尤其是近代早期都是影响最大的翻译策略。无论是拟译文本的选择还是翻译方法的采用,归化策略都要求遵循目标语文学经典。翻译中使用归化策略有时是出于经济利益的考虑,但这种考虑常常受到文化和政治发展状况的限制。意大利作家翁贝托·艾柯(Umberto Eco)的小说《玫瑰的名字》的英文译本曾获巨大成功,这引得美国出版商们在国际图书博览会上争相购买类似外国图书的翻译权。但译本成功的最主要原因是,艾柯的叙事风格是美国读者所熟悉并喜闻乐见的。

　　归化策略常常被西方国家用来为具体的国家事务服务。威廉·琼斯(William Jones)是亚细亚协会的主席、东印度公司的代理总督,他把 *Institutes of Hindu Law* (1799)由印度语译成英语,以便增强英国殖民统治的有效性。他在译文中把印度人的形象塑造成为民族文化的不可靠的阐释者(Niranjana, 1992)。对于奈达来说,归化策略有助于完成基督教传教使命。作为许多传播《圣经》的机构的翻译顾问,他负责监督了好几个《圣经》英文译本的翻译,这些译本的共同特点是让读者去接受美国文化所推崇的行为模式。

　　在西方,翻译的异化策略首先是由德国人提出来的,德国浪漫主义时期的哲学家和神学家施莱尔马赫(Friedrich Schleiermacher)起到了决定性作用。在他 1813 年做的关于翻译方法的演讲中,施莱尔马赫认为只有两种翻译方法,“译者要么尽量不打扰原文作者,让读者靠近作者,要么尽量不打扰读者,让作者靠近读者”(Venuti, 1995:12 - 20)。施莱尔马赫承认大多数翻译都是归化翻译,这种翻译把外国文本简约到目标语文化价值标准,是种族中心主义的翻译策略。但他主张采用异化翻译策略,强调在翻译过程中保留外国文本的异质因素,给目标读者带来一种新异的阅读体验。

　　法国翻译理论家贝尔曼(Antoine Berman)把施莱尔马赫的观点视为翻译伦理,在他看来这种翻译伦理把译本作为一个场所,文化他者在这个场所不是被消除,而是得到充分的展示。贝尔曼《异域的体验:德国浪漫派的文化及翻译》(*The Experience of the Foreign: Culture and Translation in Romantic Germany*, 1992)以及他后来写的一篇文章《翻译和对异类的审判》(“Translation and the Trial of the Foreign”)论述了西方文化对“非我族类”的异域他者的同化过程。

贝尔曼的研究对美国学者韦努蒂的异化翻译理论产生了直接影响。韦努蒂认为翻译的异化策略非常理想(highly desirable),它能够抑制翻译中的民族中心主义的暴力。异化策略是一种不通顺的翻译风格,旨在通过突出源语文本的外国身份并使其摆脱目标语文化的意识形态的支配,使译者的存在变得可见而不是隐身,韦努蒂又称之为"阻抗式翻译"(resistancy)。虽然韦努蒂主张异化翻译,但他对其中的一些矛盾因素了然于胸:异化翻译是一个主观的、相对意义上的术语,它仍然牵涉某种归化,因为异化翻译毕竟是为目标语文化而翻译,它必须依赖处于支配地位的目标语文化价值才能使自己显而易见。然而韦努蒂还是要为异化翻译辩护。"在阐释外国文本时,异化翻译的确像归化翻译那样有所偏好,但异化翻译倾向于夸示偏好而不是掩饰偏好"(1995:34)。韦努蒂(1999)认为,归化和异化是两个具有探索性的概念,创立这两个概念的目的在于促进对问题的思考和研究而不是要制造新的二元对立。

本章共选三篇文章。第一篇是 Antoine Berman 撰写的"Translation and the Trials of the Foreign",阐述了译者在翻译过程中应尽量避免的 12 种变形倾向。第二篇是 Lawrence Venuti 著的"The Translator's Invisibility——A History of Translation",分析了施莱尔马赫异化翻译思想的主要内容。第三篇《重新解读韦努蒂的异化翻译理论——兼与郭建中教授商榷》,为蒋骁华、张景华所著,探讨了与韦努蒂的异化翻译理论相关的一些基本问题。

 选 文

选文一 Translation and the Trials of the Foreign

Antoine Berman

导 言

本文选自韦努蒂编《翻译研究读本》。

安托瓦纳·贝尔曼是法国后结构主义翻译批评学家。他的后结构主义翻译理论成果对翻译研究产生了巨大的影响,在全球掀起了解构主义大潮。他也成为翻译文化转向的领军人物。

作为翻译批评家的贝尔曼,在本文中质疑以归化为主的传统结构主义翻译批评标准,认为语言学派过分注重翻译的工具性,而无视翻译的文学性。这使得译者不得不为了迎合译入语及其文化,按照归化的标准,把原文扭曲变形(deform),使洋味尽失。而这种归化的翻译模式也是基于种族中心主义之上的一种翻译模式。在贝尔曼看来,这是失败的翻译(bad translation)。这种翻译不光归化原文,而且是在可译性的借口之下,系统地否定原文的异

域文化。所以贝尔曼倡导"异化"(foreignizing)的翻译策略。贝尔曼认为翻译是异域的审判。这种审判通过向读者展示异域的文化和语言,建立起原文与译语之间的联系,这也是翻译的力量所在。所以好的翻译应该尊重原文与译文在文化和语言上的差别,并通过能够充分展示这种差异的两种语言的对应(correspondence)来表达原文的核心意义。

作者提出了译者在翻译活动中的 12 种变形倾向以解释译者是如何去求同而去异的,作为译者在翻译过程中就可以尽量避免这 12 种变形倾向而达到丰富译入语文化的目的。本文的观点对美国翻译理论家韦努蒂产生了很大的影响,正是他于 2000 年把本文译介到英语世界。

The general theme of my essay will be *translation as the trial of the foreign* (*comme épreuve de l'étranger*). "Trial of the foreign" is the expression that Heidegger uses to define one pole of poetic experience in Hölderlin (*Die Erfahrung des Fremden*). Now, in the poet, this trial is essentially enacted by translation, by his version of Sophocles, which is in fact the last "work" Hölderlin published before descending into madness. In its own time, this translation was considered a prime manifestation of his madness. Yet today we view it as one of the great moments of western translation: Not only because it gives us rare access to the Greek tragic Word, but because while giving us access to this Word, it reveals the veiled essence of every translation.

Translation is the "trial of the foreign." But in a double sense. In the first place, it establishes a relationship between the Self-Same (*Propre*) and the Foreign by aiming to open up the foreign work to us in its utter foreignness. Hölderlin reveals the strangeness of the Greek tragic Word, whereas most "classic" translations tend to attenuate or cancel it. In the second place, translation is a trial *for the Foreign as well*, since the foreign work is uprooted from its own *language-ground* (*sol-de-langue*). And this trial, often an exile, can also exhibit the most singular power of the translating act: to reveal the foreign work's most original kernel, its most deeply buried, most self-same, but equally the most "distant" from itself. Hölderlin discerns in Sophocles' work—in its language—two opposed principles: On the one hand, the immediate violence of the tragic Word, what he calls the "fire of heaven," and on the other, "holy sobriety," i. e. , the rationality that comes to contain and mask this violence. For Hölderlin, translating first and foremost means liberating the violence repressed in the work through a series of *intensifications* in the translating language—in other words, accentuating its strangeness. Paradoxically, this accentuation is the only way of giving us access to it. Alain addressed the topic of translation in one of his remarks on literature:

I have this idea that one can always translate a poet—English, Latin, or Greek—exactly word for word, without adding anything, preserving the very order of the words, until at last you find the meter, even the rhymes. I have rarely pushed the experiment that far; it takes time, I mean, a few months, plus uncommon patience. The first draft resembles a mosaic of barbarisms; the bits are badly joined; they are cemented together, but not in harmony. A forcefulness, a flash, a certain violence remains, no doubt more than necessary. It's more English than the English text, more Greek than the Greek, more Latin than the Latin [...]

(Alain, 1934, pp. 56 - 57)

Thanks to such translation, the language of the original shakes with all its liberated might the translating language. In an article devoted to Pierre Klossowski's translation of the *Aeneid*, Michel Foucault distinguishes between two methods of translation:

> It is quite necessary to admit that two kinds of translations exist; they do not have the same function or the same nature. In one, something (meaning, aesthetic value) must remain identical, and it is given passage into another language; these translations are good when they go "from like to same" [...] And then there are translations that hurl one language against another [...] taking the original text for a projectile and treating the translating language like a target. Their task is not to lead a meaning back to itself or anywhere else; but to use the translated language to derail the translating language.

(Foucault, 1969, p. 30)

Doesn't this distinction simply correspond to the great split that divides the entire field of translation, separating so-called "literary" translations (in the broad sense) from "non-literary" translations (technical, scientific, advertising, etc.)? Whereas the latter perform only a semantic transfer and deal with texts that entertain a relation of exteriority or instrumentality to their language, the former are concerned with *works*, that is to say texts so bound to their language that the translating act inevitably becomes a manipulation of signifiers, where two languages enter into various forms of collision and somehow *couple*. This is undeniable, but not taken seriously. A superficial glance at the history of translation suffices to show that, in the literary domain, everything transpires as if the second type of translation came to usurp and conceal the first type. As if it were suddenly driven to the margins of exception and heresy. As if translation, far from being the trials of the Foreign, were rather its negation, its acclimation, its "naturalization. " As if its most individual essence were radically repressed. Hence, the necessity for reflection on the properly *ethical* aim of the translating act (receiving the Foreign as Foreign). Hence, the necessity for an analysis that shows how (and why) this aim has, from time immemorial (although not always), been skewed, perverted and assimilated to something other than itself, such as the play of hypertextual transformations.

The analytic of translation

I propose to examine briefly the system of textual deformation that operates in every translation and prevents it from being a "trial of the foreign. " I shall call this examination *the analytic of translation*. Analytic in two senses of the term: a detailed analysis of the deforming system, and therefore an analysis in the Cartesian sense, but also in the psychoanalytic sense, insofar as the system is largely unconscious, present as a series of tendencies or *forces* that cause translation to deviate from its essential aim. The analytic of translation is consequently designed to discover these forces and to show where in the text they are practiced—somewhat as Bachelard, with his "psychoanalysis" of the scientific spirit, wanted to show how the materialist imagination confused and derailed the objective aim of the natural sciences.

Before presenting the detailed examination of the deforming forces, I shall make several remarks. First, the analysis proposed here is provisional: It is formulated on the basis of my experience as a translator (primarily of Latin American literature into French). To be systematic, it requires the input of translators from other domains (other languages and works), as well as linguists, "poeticians" and ... psychoanalysts, since the deforming forces constitute so many censures and resistances.

This *negative* analytic should be extended by a *positive* counterpart, an analysis of operations which have always limited the deformation, although in an intuitive and unsystematic way. These operations constitute a sort of counter-system destined to neutralize, or attenuate, the negative tendencies. The negative and positive analytics will in turn enable a *critique of translations* that is neither simply descriptive nor simply normative.

The negative analytic is primarily concerned with ethnocentric, annexationist translations and hypertextual translations (pastiche, imitation, adaptation, free rewriting), where the play of deforming forces is freely exercised. Every translator is inescapably exposed to this play of forces, even if he (or she) is animated by another aim. More: These unconscious forces form part of the translator's *being*, determining the *desire* to translate. It is illusory to think that the translator can be freed merely by becoming aware of them. The translator's practice must submit to analysis if the unconscious is to be neutralized. It is by yielding to the "controls" (in the psychoanalytic sense) that translators can hope to free themselves from the system of deformation that burdens their practice. This system is the internalized expression of a two-millennium-old tradition, as well as the ethnocentric structure of every culture, every language; it is less a crude system than a "cultivated language." Only languages that are "cultivated" translate, but they are also the ones that put up the strongest resistance to the ruckus of translation. They censor. You see what a psychoanalytic approach to language and linguistic systems can contribute to a "translatology." This approach must also be the work of analysts themselves, since they experience translation as an essential dimension of psychoanalysis.

A final point: The focus below will be the deforming tendencies that intervene in the domain of literary prose—the novel and the essay.

Literary prose collects, reassembles, and intermingles the polylingual space of a community. It mobilizes and activates the totality of "languages" that coexist in any language.

This can be seen in Balzac, Proust, Joyce, Faulkner, Augusto Antonio Roa Bastos, Joao Guimarães Rosa, Carlo Emilio Gadda, etc. Hence, from a *formal* point of view, the language-based cosmos that is prose, especially the novel, is characterized by a certain *shapelessness*, which results from the enormous brew of languages and linguistic systems that operate in the work. This is also characteristic of canonical works, *la grande prose*.

Traditionally, this shapelessness has been described negatively, that is, within the horizon of poetry. Herman Broch, for example, remarks of the novel that "in contrast to poetry, it is not a producer, but a consumer of style. [...] It applies itself with much less intensity to the duty of looking like a work of art. Balzac is of greater weight than Flaubert, the formless Thomas Wolfe more than the artistic Thornton Wilder. The novel does not submit, like proper poetry, to the criteria of art" (Broch, 1966, p. 68).

In effect, the masterworks of prose are characterized by a kind of "bad writing," a certain "lack of control" in their texture. This can be seen in Rabelais, Cervantes, Montaigne, Saint-Simon, Sterne, Jean Paul Richter, Balzac, Zola, Tolstoy, Dostoevsky.

The lack of control derives from the enormous linguistic mass that the prose writer must squeeze into the work—at the risk of making it formally explode. The more totalizing the writer's aim, the more obvious the loss of control, whether in the proliferation, the swelling of the text, or in works where the most scrupulous attention is paid to form, as in Joyce, Broch, or Proust. Prose, in its multiplicity and rhythmic flow, can never be entirely mastered. And this "bad writing" is rich. This is the consequence of its polylingualism. *Don Quixote*, for example, gathers into itself the plurality of Spanish "languages" during its epoch, from popular proverbial speech (Sancho) to the conventions of chivalric and pastoral romances. Here the languages are intertwined and mutually ironized.

The Babelian proliferation of languages in novels pose specific difficulties for translation. If one of the principal problems of poetic translation is to respect the polysemy of the poem (cf. Shakespeare's *Sonnets*), then the principal problem of translating the novel is to respect its *shapeless polylogic* and avoid an arbitrary homogenization.

Insofar as the novel is considered a lower form of literature than poetry, the deformations of translation are more accepted in prose, when they do not pass unperceived. For they operate on points that do not immediately reveal themselves. It is easy to detect how a poem by Hölderlin has been massacred. It isn't so easy to see what was done to a novel by Kafka or Faulkner, especially if the translation seems "good." The deforming system functions here in complete tranquillity. This is why it is urgent to elaborate an analytic for the translation of novels.

This analytic sets out to locate several deforming tendencies. They form a systematic whole. I shall mention twelve here. There may be more: some combine with or derive from others; some are well known. And some may appear relevant only to French "classicizing" translation. But in fact they bear on all translating, at least in the western tradition. They can be found just as often in English translators as in Spanish or German, although certain tendencies may be more accentuated in one linguistic-cultural space than in others. Here are the twelve tendencies in question:

(1) Rationalization

(2) Clarification

(3) Expansion

(4) Ennoblement and popularization

(5) Qualitative impoverishment

(6) Quantitative impoverishment

(7) The destruction of rhythms

(8) The destruction of underlying networks of signification

(9) The destruction of linguistic patternings

(10) The destruction of vernacular networks or their exoticization

(11) The destruction of expressions and idioms

(12) The effacement of the superimposition of languages

Rationalization

This bears primarily on the syntactical structures of the original, starting with that most meaningful and changeable element in a prose text: *punctuation*. Rationalization recomposes sentences and the sequence of sentences, rearranging them according to a certain idea of discursive *order*. Wherever the sentence structure is relatively free (i. e. , wherever it doesn't answer to a specific idea of order), it risks a rationalizing contraction. This is visible, for instance, in the fundamental hostility with which the French greet repetition, the proliferation of relative clauses and participles, long sentences or sentences without verbs—all elements essential to prose.

Thus, Marc Chapiro, the French translator of the *Brothers Karamazov*, writes:

> The original heaviness of Dostoevsky's style poses an almost insoluble problem to the translator. It was impossible to reproduce the bushy undergrowth of his sentences, despite the richness of their content.
>
> (cited by Meschonnic, 1973, p. 317)

This signifies, quite openly, that the cause of rationalization has been adopted. As we have seen, the essence of prose includes a "bushy undergrowth. " Moreover, every formal excess curdles novelistic prose, whose "imperfection" is a condition of its existence. The signifying shapelessness indicates that prose plunges into the depths, the strata, the polylogism of language. Rationalization destroys all that.

It annihilates another element of prose: *its drive toward concreteness*. Rationalization means abstraction. Prose is centered on the concrete and even tends to render concrete the numerous abstract elements bobbing in its flood (Proust, Montaigne). Rationalization makes the original pass from concrete to abstract, not only by reordering the sentence structure, but—for example—by translating verbs into substantives, by choosing the more general of two substantives, etc. Yves Bonnefoy revealed this process with Shakespeare's work.

This rationalization/abstraction is all the more pernicious in that it is not *total*. It doesn't mean to be. It is content to *reverse* the relations which prevail in the original between formal and informal, ordered and disorderly, abstract and concrete. This conversion is typical of ethnocentric translation: It causes the work to undergo a change of *sign*, of *status*—and seemingly without changing form and meaning.

To sum up: Rationalization deforms the original by *reversing* its basic tendency.

Clarification

This is a corollary of rationalization which particularly concerns the level of "clarity" perceptible in words and their meanings. Where the original has no problem moving in the *indefinite*, our literary language tends to impose the definite. When the Argentine novelist Roberto Arlt writes: "y los excesos eran desplazados por desmedimientos de esperanza" (the excesses were displaced by the excessiveness of hope; Arlt, 1981, p. 37), French does not tolerate a literal rendering because everywhere, in this passage from *Los Siete Locos*, excess is *still* in question. French asks: An excess of what?

The same goes for Dostoevsky. Chapiro writes: "To render the suggestions of a Russian sentence, it is often necessary to complete it" (cited by Meschonnic, 1973, pp. 317–318).

Clarification seems to be an obvious principle to many translators and authors. Thus, the American poet Galway Kinnell writes: "The translation should be a little clearer than the original" (cited by Gresset, 1983, p. 519).

Of course, clarification is inherent in translation, to the extent that every translation comprises some degree of explicitation. But that can signify two very different things:

(1) The explicitation can be the manifestation of something that is not apparent, but concealed or repressed, in the original. Translation, by virtue of its own movement, puts into play this element. Heidegger alludes to the point for philosophy: "In translation, the work of thinking is transposed into the spirit of another language and so undergoes an inevitable transformation. But this transformation can be fecund, because it shines a new light on the fundamental position of the question" (Heidegger, 1968, p. 10).

The power of illumination, of *manifestation*, (1) as I indicated apropos Hölderlin, is the supreme power of translation. But in a negative sense, (2) explicitation aims to render "clear" what does not wish to be clear in the original. The movement from polysemy to monosemy is a mode of clarification. Paraphrastic or explicative translation is another. And that leads us to the third tendency.

Expansion

Every translation tends to be longer than the original. George Steiner said that translation is "inflationist." This is the consequence, in part, of the two previous tendencies. Rationalizing and clarifying require expansion, an *unfolding* of what, in the original, is "folded." Now, from the viewpoint of the text, this expansion can be qualified as "empty." It can coexist quite well with diverse quantitative forms of impoverishment. I mean that *the addition adds nothing*, that it augments only the gross mass of text, without augmenting its way of speaking or signifying. The addition is no more than babble designed to muffle the work's own voice. Explicitations may render the text more "clear," but they actually obscure *its own mode of clarity*. The expansion is, moreover, a stretching, a slackening, which impairs the rhythmic flow of the work. It is often called "overtranslation," a typical case of which is Armel Guerne's translation of *Moby Dick* (1954). Expanded, the majestic, oceanic novel becomes bloated and uselessly titanic. In this case, expansion aggravates the initial shapelessness of the work, causing it to change from a shapeless plenitude to a shapeless void or hollow. In German, the *Fragments* of Novalis possess a very special brevity, a brevity that contains an infinity of meanings and somehow renders them "long," but vertically, like wells. Translated by the same Guerne (1973), they are lengthened immoderately and simultaneously flattened. Expansion flattens, horizontalizing what is essentially deep and vertical in Novalis.

Ennoblement

This marks the culminating point of "classic" translation. In poetry, it is "poetization." In prose, it is rather a "rhetorization." Alain alludes to this process (with English poetry):

> If a translator attempts a poem by Shelley into French, he will first spread it out, following the practice of our poets who are mostly a bit too oratorical. Setting up the rules of public declamation as his standard, he will insert their thats and whichs, syntactical barriers that weigh upon and prevent—if I can put it this way— the substantial words from biting each other. I don't disdain this art of articulation ... But in the end it isn't the English art of speaking, so clenched and compact, brilliant, precise and strongly enigmatic.
>
> (Alain, 1934, p. 56)

Rhetorization consists in producing "elegant" sentences, while utilizing the source text, so to speak, as *raw material*. Thus the ennoblement is only a rewriting, a "stylistic exercise" based on—and at the expense of—the original. This procedure is active in the literary field, but also in the human sciences, where it produces texts that are "readable," "brilliant," rid of their original clumsiness and complexity so as to enhance the "meaning." This type of re-writing thinks itself justified in recovering the rhetorical elements inherent in all prose—but in order to banalize them and assign them a predominant place. These elements—in Rous-seau, Balzac, Hugo, Melville, Proust, etc.—restore a certain "orality," and this orality ef-fectively possesses its own norms of nobility—those of "good speaking," which may be popu-lar or "cultivated." But good speaking in the original has nothing to do with the "rhetorical elegance" extolled by the *rewriting* that ennobles. In fact, the latter simultaneously annihi-lates both oral rhetoric and formless polylogic (see above).

The logical opposite of ennoblement—or its counterpart—occurs in passages judged too "popular": blind recourse to a pseudo-slang which *popularizes* the original, or to a "spoken" language which reflects only a *confusion between oral and spoken*. The degenerate coarse-ness of pseudo-slang betrays rural fluency as well as the strict code of urban dialects.

Qualitative impoverishment

This refers to the replacement of terms, expressions and figures in the original with terms, expressions and figures that lack their sonorous richness or, correspondingly, their signifying or "iconic" richness. A term is iconic when, in relation to its referent, it "creates an image," enabling a perception of resemblance. Spitzer alludes to this iconicity: "A word that denotes facetiousness, or the play of words, easily behaves in a whimsical manner—just as in every language worldwide, the terms that denote the butterfly change in a kaleidoscopic manner" (Spitzer, 1970, p. 51).

This does not mean that the word "butterfly" objectively resembles "a butterfly," but that in its sonorous, physical substance, in its density as a word, we feel that it possesses something of the butterfly's butterfly existence. Prose and poetry produce, in their own pe-culiar ways, what can be called *surfaces of iconicity*.

When translating the Peruvian *chuchumeca* with *pute* (whore), the meaning can certain-ly be rendered, but none of the word's phonetic-signifying truth. The same goes for every term that is commonly qualified with *savoureux* (spicy), *dru* (robust), *vif* (vivid), *coloré* (colorful), etc., epithets that all refer to the iconic physicality of the sign. And when this practice of replacement, which is most often unconscious, is applied to an entire work, to the whole of its iconic surface, it decisively effaces a good portion of its signifying process and mode of expression—what makes a work *speak* to us.

Quantitative impoverishment

This refers to a lexical loss. Every work in prose presents a certain *proliferation* of sig-nifiers and signifying chains. Great novelistic prose is "abundant." These signifiers can be described as *unfixed*, especially as a signified may have a multiplicity of signifiers. For the signified *visage* (face) Arlt employs *semblante*, *rostro* and *cara* without justifying a particular choice in a particular sentence. The essential thing is that *visage* is marked as an important *reality* in his work by the use of three signifiers. The translation that does not respect this multiplicity renders the "visage" of an unrecognizable work. There is a loss, then, since the translation contains *fewer* signifiers than the original. The translation that attends to the lexical texture of the work, to its mode of lexicality—enlarges it. This loss perfectly coexists with an increase of the gross quantity or mass of the text with expansion. For expansion consists in adding articles and relatives (*le*, *la*, *les*, *qui*, *que*), explicative and decorative signifiers that have nothing to do with the lexical texture of the original. The translating results in a text that is at once *poorer* and *longer*. Moreover, the expansion often works to mask the quantitative loss.

The destruction of rhythms

I shall pass rapidly over this aspect, however fundamental it may be. The novel is not less rhythmic than poetry. It even comprises a multiplicity of rhythms. Since the entire bulk of the novel is thus in movement, it is fortunately difficult for translation to destroy this rhythmic movement. This explains why even a great but badly translated novel continues to transport us. Poetry and theater are more fragile. Yet the deforming translation can considerably affect the rhythm—for example, through an arbitrary revision of the punctuation. Michel Gresset (1983) shows how a translation of Faulkner destroys his distinctive rhythm: Where the original included only *four* marks of punctuation, the translation uses *twenty-two*, eighteen of which are commas!

The destruction of underlying networks of signification

The literary work contains a hidden dimension, an "underlying" text, where certain signifiers correspond and link up, forming all sorts of networks beneath the "surface" of the text itself—the manifest text, presented for reading. It is this *subtext* that carries the network of word-obsessions. These underlying chains constitute one aspect of the rhythm and signifying process of the text. After long intervals certain words may recur, certain kinds of substantives that constitute a particular network, whether through their resemblance or their aim, their "aspect." In Arlt you find words that witness the presence of an obsession, an intimacy, a particular perception, although distributed rather far from each other—sometimes in different chapters—and without a context that justifies or calls for their use. Hence, the following series of *augmentatives*:

portalón	*alón*	*jaulón*	*portón*	*gigantón*	*callejón*
gate	wing	cage	door/entrance	giant	lane/alley

which establishes a network:

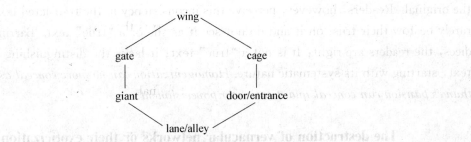

This simple network shows that the signifiers in themselves have no particular value, that what *makes sense* is their linkage, which in fact signals a most important dimension of the work. Now, all of these signifers are *augmentatives*, appropriately enough, as Arlt's novel *Los Siete Locos* contains a certain *dimension of augmentation*: gates, wings, cages, entrances, giants, alleys acquire the inordinate size they have in nocturnal dreams. If such networks are not transmitted, a signifying process in the text is destroyed.

The misreading of these networks corresponds to the treatment given to *groupings of major signifiers* in a work, such as those that organize its mode of expression. To sketch out a visual domain, for example, an author might employ certain verbs, adjectives and substantives, and *not others*. V. A. Goldsmidt studies the words that Freud did *not use* or *avoided* where they might be expected. Needless to say, translators have often inserted them.

The destruction of linguistic patterning

The systematic nature of the text goes beyond the level of signifiers, metaphors, etc.; it extends to the type of sentences, the sentence constructions employed. Such patternings may include the use of time or the recourse to a certain kind of subordination (Gresset cites Faulkner's "because"). Spitzer studies the patterning system in Racine and Proust, although he still calls it "style." Rationalization, clarification, expansion, etc. destroy the systematic nature of the text by introducing elements that are excluded by its essential system. Hence, a curious consequence: When the translated text is more "homogeneous" than the original (possessing more "style" in the ordinary sense), it is equally more *incoherent* and, in a certain way, more heterogeneous, more *inconsistent*. It is a *patchwork* of the different kinds of writing employed by the translator (like combining ennoblement with popularization where the original cultivates an orality). This applies as well to the position of the translator, who basically resorts to every reading possible in translating the original. Thus, a translation always risks appearing *homogeneous and incoherent* at the same time, as Meschonnic has shown with the translation of Paul Celan. A carefully conducted textual analysis of an original and its translation demonstrates that the writing-of-the-translation, the-discourse-of-the-translation is *asystematic*, like the work of a neophyte which is rejected by readers at publishing houses from the very first page. Except that, in the case of translation, this asystematic nature is not apparent and in fact is concealed by what still remains of the linguistic patterings in the original. Readers, however, perceive this inconsistency in the translated text, since they rarely bestow their trust on it and do not see it as the or a "true" text. Barring any prejudices, the readers are right: It is not a "true" text; it lacks the distinguishing features of a text, starting with its systematic nature. *Homogenization can no more conceal asystematicity than expansion can conceal quantitative impoverishment.*

The destruction of vernacular networks or their exoticization

This domain is essential because all great prose is rooted in the vernacular language. "If French doesn't work," wrote Montaigne, "Gascon will!" (cited by Mounin, 1955, p. 38).

In the first place, the polylogic aim of prose inevitably includes a plurality of vernacular elements.

In the second place, the tendency toward concreteness in prose necessarily includes these elements, because the vernacular language is by its very nature more physical, more iconic than "cultivated" language. The Picard "bibloteux" is more expressive than the French "livresque" (bookish). The Old French "sorcelage" is richer than "sorcellerie" (sorcery), the Antillais "dérespecter" more expressive than "manquer de respect" (to lack respect).

In the third place, prose often aims explicitly to recapture the orality of vernacular. In the twentieth century, this is the case with a good part—with *the* good part—of such literatures as Latin American, Italian, Russian, and North American.

The effacement of vernaculars is thus a very serious injury to the textuality of prose works. It may be a question of effacing diminutives in Spanish, Portuguese, German or Russian; or it may involve replacing verbs by nominal constructions, verbs of action by verbs with substantives (the Peruvian "alagunarse," s'enlaguner, becomes the flat-footed "se transformer en lagune," "to be transformed into a lagoon"). Vernacular signifiers may be transposed, like "porte ño," which becomes "inhabitant of Buenos Aires."

The traditional method of preserving vernaculars is to *exoticize* them. Exoticization can take two forms. First, a typographical procedure (italics) is used to isolate what does not exist in the original. Then, more insidiously, it is "added" to be "more authentic," emphasizing the vernacular according to a certain stereotype of it (as in the popular woodcut illustrations published by Épinal). Such are Mardrus's over-Arabizing translations of the *Thousand and One Nights* and the *Song of Songs*.

Exoticization may join up again with popularization by striving to render a foreign vernacular with a local one, using Parisian slang to translate the *lunfardo* of Buenos Aires, the Normandy dialect to translate the language of the Andes or Abruzzese. Unfortunately, a vernacular clings tightly to its soil and completely resists any direct translating into another vernacular. *Translation can occur only between "cultivated" languages.* An exoticization that turns the foreign from abroad into the foreign at home winds up merely ridiculing the original.

The destruction of expressions and idioms

Prose abounds in images, expressions, figures, proverbs, etc. which derive in part from the vernacular. Most convey a meaning or experience that readily finds a parallel image, expression, figure, or proverb in other languages.

Here are two idioms from Conrad's novel *Typhoon*:

> He did not care a tinker's curse
>
> Damme, if this ship isn't worse than Bedlam!

Compare these two idioms with Gide's amazingly literal version:

> Il s'en fichait comme du juron d'un étameur
>
> (He didn't give a tinker's curse)
>
> Que diable m'emporte si l'on ne se croirait pas à Bedlam!
>
> (The Devil take me if I didn't think I was in Bedlam!)

(cited by Meerschen, 1982, p. 80)

The first can easily be rendered into comparable French idioms, like "il s'en fichait comme de l'an quarante, comme d'une guigne, etc.," and the second invites the replacement of "Bedlam," which is incomprehensible to the French reader, by "Charenton" (Bedlam being a famous English insane asylum). Now it is evident that even if the meaning is identical, replacing an idiom by its "equivalent" is an ethnocentrism. Repeated on a large scale (this is always the case with a novel), the practice will result in the absurdity whereby the characters in *Typhoon* express themselves with a network of French images. The points I signal here with one or two examples must always be multiplied by five or six thousand. To play with "equivalence" is to attack the discourse of the foreign work. Of course, a proverb may have its equivalents in other languages, but ... these equivalents do not *translate* it. To translate is not to search for equivalences. The desire to replace ignores, furthermore, the existence in us of a *proverb consciousness* which immediately detects, in a new proverb, the brother of an authentic one: the world of our proverbs is thus augmented and enriched (Larbaud, 1946).

The effacement of the superimposition of languages

The superimposition of languages in a novel involves the relation between dialect and a common language, a koine, or the coexistence, in the heart of a text, of two or more koine. The first case is illustrated by the novels of Gadda and Günter Grass, by Valle-Inclan's *Tirano Banderas*, where his Spanish from Spain is decked out with diverse Latin American Spanishes, by the work of Guimarães·Rosa, where classic Portuguese interpenetrates with the dialects of the Brazilian interior. The second case is illustrated by José Maria Arguedas and Roa Bastos, where Spanish is modified profoundly (syntactically) by two other languages from oral cultures: Quechua and Guarani. And there is finally—the limit case—Joyce's *Finnegans Wake* and its sixteen agglutinated languages.

In these two cases, the superimposition of languages is threatened by translation. The relation of tension and integration that exists in the original between the vernacular language and the koine, between the underlying language and the surface language, etc. tends to be effaced. How to preserve the Guarani-Spanish tension in Roa Bastos? Or the relation between Spanish from Spain and the Latin American Spanishes in *Tirano Banderas*? The French translator of this work has not confronted the problem; the French text is completely homogeneous. The same goes for the translation of Mario de Andrade's *Macumaïma*, where the deep vernacular roots of the work are suppressed (which does not happen in the Spanish version of this Brazilian text).

This is the central problem posed by translating novels—a problem that demands maximum reflection from the translator. Every novelistic work is characterized by linguistic superimpositions, even if they include sociolects, idiolects, etc. The novel, said Bakhtin, assembles a *heterology* or diversity of discursive types, a *heteroglossia* or diversity of languages, and a *heterophony* or diversity of voices (Bakhtin, 1982, p. 89). Thomas Mann's novel *The Magic Mountain* offers a fascinating example of heteroglossia, which the translator, Maurice Betz, was able to preserve: the dialogues between the "heroes," Hans Castorp and Madame Chauchat. In the original, both communicate in French, and the fascinating thing is that the young German's French is not *the same* as the young Russian woman's. In the translation, these two varieties of French are in turn framed by the translator's French. Maurice Betz let Thomas Mann's German resonate in his translation to such an extent that the three kinds of French can be distinguished, and each possesses its specific foreignness. This is the sort of success—not quite impossible, certainly difficult—to which every translator of a novel ought to aspire.

The analytic of translation broadly sketched here must be carefully distinguished from the study of "norms"—literary, social, cultural, etc.—which partly govern the translating act in every society. These "norms," which vary historically, never specifically concern translation; they apply, in fact, to any writing practice whatsoever. The analytic, in contrast, focuses on the universals of deformation inherent in translating as such. It is obvious that in specific periods and cultures these universals overlap with the system of norms that govern writing: Think only of the neoclassical period and its "belles infidèles." Yet this coincidence is fleeting. In the twentieth century, we no longer submit to neoclassical norms, but the universals of deformation are not any less in force. They even enter into conflict with the new norms governing writing and translation.

At the same time, however, the deforming tendencies analyzed above are not ahistorical. They are rather historical in an original sense. They refer back to the figure of translation based on Greek thought in the West or more precisely, Platonism. The "figure of translation" is understood here as the form in which translation is deployed and appears to itself, before any explicit theory. From its very beginnings, western translation has been an embellishing restitution of meaning, based on the typically Platonic separation between spirit and letter, sense and word, content and form, the sensible and the non-sensible. When it is affirmed today that translation (including non-literary translation) must produce a "clear" and "elegant" text (even if the original does not possess these qualities), the affirmation assumes the Platonic figure of translating, even if unconsciously. All the tendencies noted in the analytic lead to the same result: the production of a text that is more "clear," more "elegant," more "fluent," more "pure" than the original. They are the destruction of the letter in favor of meaning.

Nevertheless, this Platonic figure of translation is not something "false" that can be criticized theoretically or ideologically. For it sets up as an absolute only one essential possibility of translating, which is precisely the restitution of meaning. All translation is, and must be, the restitution of meaning.

The problem is knowing whether this is the unique and ultimate task of translation or whether its task is something else again. The analytic of translation, insofar as the analysis of properly deforming tendencies bears on the translator, does in fact presuppose another figure of translating, which must necessarily be called literal translation. Here "literal" means: attached to the letter (of works). Labor on the letter in translation is more originary than restitution of meaning. It is through this labor that translation, on the one hand, restores the particular signifying process of works (which is more than their meaning) and, on the other hand, transforms the translating language. Translation stimulated the fashioning and refashioning of the great western languages only because it labored on the letter and profoundly modified the translating language. As simple restitution of meaning, translation could never have played this formative role.

Consequently, the essential aim of the analytic of translation is to highlight this other essence of translating, which, although never recognized, endowed it with historical effectiveness in every domain where it was practiced.

【延伸阅读】

[1] Berman, A. (1992). *The Experience of the Foreign: Culture and Translation in Romantic Germany*. S. Heyvaert, trans. Albany: State University of New York.

[2] 许钧,袁筱一. 当代法国翻译理论. 武汉:湖北教育出版社,2001.

【问题与思考】

1. 论文标题"翻译及对异化的考验"中的"考验"的含义是什么?
2. 贝尔曼是如何看待归化和异化的?
3. 如何正确理解贝尔曼提出的"负面解析"(negative analytic)?
4. 你认为贝尔曼提出的12种翻译变形倾向能概括所有的变形倾向吗? 为什么?
5. 贝尔曼的翻译理论对我们作翻译研究有何指导意义?

选文二　The Translator's Invisibility
—A History of Translation (Excerpt)

Lawrence Venuti

导　言

　　劳伦斯·韦努蒂是美籍意大利翻译家和翻译理论家,他多年受解构主义的影响和文学批评的训练,既擅长文学翻译实践,又精于翻译理论,是异化翻译策略的积极倡导者。本文节选自他的代表作《译者的隐身———一部翻译史》(*The Translator's Invisibility—A History of Translation*) 第三章"Nation"。

　　本文回顾了 19 世纪初异化翻译在德国兴起的历史。1813 年,施莱尔马赫在一篇关于翻译的不同方法的演讲中指出了两种翻译方法:译者要么尽可能不去打扰作者,而让读者向作者靠拢;要么尽可能不去打扰读者,而让作者向读者靠拢。施莱尔马赫支持前一种方法,即异化翻译方法。施莱尔马赫的演讲被看做异化翻译兴起的标志。从本文中我们可以领略施莱尔马赫翻译思想主旨,了解他支持异化翻译方法的缘由以及异化翻译的特点、本质、意义和操作途径等。

> The translator who attaches himself closely to his original more or less abandons the originality of his nation, and so a third comes into existence, and the taste of the multitude must first be shaped towards it.
>
> 　　　　　(Johann Wolfgang yon Goethe, translated by André Lefevere)

The search for alternatives to fluent translation leads to theories and practices that aim to signify the foreignness of the foreign text. At the turn of the nineteenth century, foreignizing translation lacked cultural capital in English, but it was very active in the formation of another national culture—German. In 1813, during the Napoleonic wars, Friedrich Schleiermacher's lecture "Ueber die verschiedenen Methoden des Uebersetzens" ("On the Diffe- rent Methods of Translating") viewed translation as an important practice in the Prussian nationalist movement: It could enrich the German language by developing an elite literature and thus enable German culture to realize its historical destiny of global domination. And yet, surprisingly, Schleiermacher proposed this nationalist agenda by theorizing translation as the locus of cultural difference, not the homogeneity that his ideological configuration might imply, and that, in various, historically specific forms, has long prevailed in English-language translation, British and American. Schleiermacher's translation theory rested on a chauvinistic condescension toward foreign cultures, a sense of their ultimate inferiority to German-language culture, but also on an antichauvinistic respect for their differences, a sense that German-language culture is inferior and therefore must attend to them if it is to develop.

These contradictory tendencies are peculiar to the vernacular nationalist movements that swept through Europe during the early nineteenth century, and they indicate that Schleiermacher's translation theory can be detached from the ideological purpose it was intended to serve and be put to other uses. The central contradiction of vernacular nationalist movements is that they are at once made possible and vulnerable by language. As Benedict Anderson has observed, "seen as both a *historical* fatality and as a community imagined through language, the nation presents itself as simultaneously open and closed" because "language is not an instrument of exclusion: In principle, anyone can learn any language" (Anderson, 1991, p. 134, p. 146). Language forms the particular solidarity that is the basis of the nation, but the openness of any language to new uses allows nationalist narratives to be rewritten—especially when this language is the target of translations that are foreignizing, most interested in the cultural difference of the foreign text.

If, as Schleiermacher believed, a foreignizing translation method can be useful in building a national culture, forging a foreign-based cultural identity for a linguistic community about to achieve political autonomy, it can also undermine any concept of nation by challenging cultural canons, disciplinary boundaries, and national values in the target language. This is borne out by the English translation controversy that pitted Francis Newman's foreignized *Iliad* (Newman, 1856) against Matthew Arnold's Oxford lectures "On Translating Homer" (1860): Newman's theory of foreignization requires the development of translation strategies that deviate from Victorian standards of transparent discourse, but also from an Arnoldian concept of the national culture that favors an academic elite. The following genealogy reconstructs a foreignizing translation tradition, partly German, partly English, examines the specific cultural situations in which this tradition took shape, and evaluates its usefulness in combating domesticating translation in the present.

I

For Schleiermacher, "the genuine translator" is a writer

> who wants to bring those two completely separated persons, his author and his reader, truly together, and who would like to bring the latter to an understanding and enjoyment of the former as correct and complete as possible without inviting him to leave the sphere of his mother tongue.

(Lefevere, 1977, p. 74)

Antoine Berman has called attention to the hermeneutical paradigm introduced here, the emphasis on translation as an object of textual interpretation and a means of interpersonal communication, "a method of intersubjective encounter" ("un processus de rencontre intersubjectif") (Berman, 1984, p. 235). And this makes communication the criterion by which methodological choices are validated and authentic translation distinguished from inauthentic. Schleiermacher in fact finds only two methods of effecting the domestic reader's understanding of the foreign author: "Either the translator leaves the author in peace, as much as possible, and moves the reader towards him; or he leaves the reader in peace, as much as possible, and moves the author towards him" (p. 74). Schleiermacher privileges the first method, making the target-language reader travel abroad, and he describes the authentic translator's "aim" in social terms, with translation offering an understanding of the foreign text that is not merely ethnocentric, but relative to a specific social group.

> The translator must therefore take as his aim to give his reader the same image and the same delight which the reading of the work in the original language would afford any reader educated in such a way that we call him, in the better sense of the word, the lover and the expert ("Leibhaber und Kenner/amateur et connaisseur"), the type of reader who is familiar with the foreign language while it yet always remains foreign to him: He no longer has to think every single part in his mother tongue, as schoolboys do, before he can grasp the whole, but he is still conscious of the difference between that language and his mother tongue, even where he enjoys the beauty of the foreign work in total peace.
>
> (Lefevere, 1977, p. 76)

The translator aims to preserve the linguistic and cultural difference of the foreign text, but only as it is perceived in the translation by a limited readership, an educated elite. This means, first, that translation is always ethnocentric: Even when a translated text contains discursive peculiarities designed to imitate a foreign text, even when the translation seems, in Schleiermacher's (English translator's) words, "bent towards a foreign likeness" (pp. 78 – 79); "zu einer fremden Aehnlichkeit hinübergebogen" (p. 227), it never escapes the hierarchy of cultural values inscribed in the target language. These values mediate every move in the translation and every target-language reader's response to it, including the perception of what is domestic or foreign: André Lefevere's English version—"bent toward a foreign likeness"—domesticates Schleiermacher's German by submitting its syntax to the dominant fluent strategy, whereas "toward a foreign likeness bent," a discursive peculiarity that resists fluency by marking the English translation as archaic for the contemporary Anglo-American reader, foreignizes English by bending it toward the German syntax. Interestingly, to imitate the German this closely is not to be more faithful to it, but to be more English, that is, consistent with an English syntactical inversion that is now archaic.

Schleiermacher's theory anticipates these observations. He was keenly aware that translation strategies are situated in specific cultural formations where discourses are canonized or marginalized, circulating in relations of domination and exclusion. Thus, the translation method that cultivates discursive peculiarities to imitate the foreignness of the foreign text "cannot thrive equally well in all languages, but only in those which are not the captives of too strict a bond of classical expression outside of which all is reprehensible;" the ideal site for this method is "languages which are freer, in which innovations and deviations are tolerated to a greater extent, in such a way that their accumulation may, under certain circumstances, generate a certain characteristic mode of expression" (pp. 79 - 80). This linguistic and cultural freedom is complexly determined: Not only is it defined against the "bonded languages" of other national cultures, but the "innovations and deviations" of foreignizing translation are defined against the norm set by other translation discourses in the target-language culture. And since Schleiermacher's advocacy of the foreignizing method was also an advocacy of discourses specific to an educated elite, he was investing this limited social group with considerable cultural authority, going so far as to assign it a precise social function—to "generate a certain characteristic mode of expression,""developing a national language," "influencing the whole evolution of a culture" (pp. 80 - 81); "die gesammte Geiste sentwikkelung" (p. 231). Here it becomes clear that Schleiermacher was enlisting his privileged translation method in a cultural political agenda: An educated elite controls the formation of a national culture by refining its language through foreignizing translations.

Schleiermacher's lecture permits a much more detailed social and historical specification of this agenda. He concludes with some explicit references to "we Germans," remarking that "our nation," "because of its respect for what is foreign and its mediating nature"(p. 88); "seiner vermittelnden Natur" (p. 243), uniquely satisfies the "two conditions" necessary for foreignizing translation to thrive,namely "that understanding foreign works should be a thing known and desired and that the native language should be allowed a certain flexibility" (p. 81). This is the understanding of foreign works sought by educated "Germans" like Schleiermacher, a university professor and minister in the Reformed church, who feels that the German language possesses the "flexibility" to support foreignizing translation since it is undeveloped, lacking a definite "mode of expression," not yet "bonded" to the "classical," a "partial mother tongue:" "our language, because we exercise it less owing to our Nordic sluggishness, can thrive in all its freshness and completely develop its own power only through the most many-sided contacts with what is foreign" (p. 88). Since the category "foreign" here is determined by the educated, Schleiermacher is using translation to mark out a dominant space for a bourgeois minority in early nineteenth-century German culture.

As Albert Ward observes of this period,

> literature was [...] a predominantly bourgeois art, but it was only a small part
> of this section of the community that responded most readily to the classical writers
> of the great age of German literature. [...] Writers like Goethe and Schiller found
> their public in the Honoratioren of the large towns, in the university-trained professional men, the ministers of religion, teachers, doctors, and lawyers, in what
> might be termed the elite of middle-class society. "High literature" was then even
> more than now a thing for a small group of scholars.

(Ward, 1974, p. 128)

Ward demonstrates the cultural and economic marginality of German "literature," both classical and romantic, by referring to sizes of editions and sales figures amid some striking testimonies from contemporaries in the publishing industry:

> Karl Preusker, who came to Leipzig as a bookseller's apprentice in 1805, names in his autobiography the authors most in demand at that time; the most classical (as we understand the term today) of the authors on his list is Zschokke, "whereas the works of Schiller and Goethe were sold in only meagre quantities."
>
> (ibid., p. 132)

Schleiermacher, who associated with the leading German romantics, briefly shared a Berlin apartment with Friedrich Schlegel, and contributed to the Schlegel brothers' small-circulation journal, *the Athenaeum*, was entirely in agreement with Goethe when developing his theory of foreignizing translation. In an essay on "Wieland's brotherly memory" published in February of 1813, four months before Schleiermacher's lecture, Goethe wrote:

> There are two maxims in translation: one requires that the author of a foreign nation be brought across to us in such a way that we can look on him as ours; the other requires that we should go across to what is foreign and adapt ourselves to its conditions, its use of language, its peculiarities. The advantages of both are sufficiently known to educated people through perfect examples. Our friend, who looked for the middle way in this, too, tried to reconcile both, but as a man of feeling and taste he preferred the first maxim when in doubt.
>
> (Lefevere, 1977, p. 39)

In siding with this "feeling and taste" for "what is foreign," Schleiermacher was valorizing an elite bourgeois cultural discourse of literary refinement against the larger, more heterogeneous culture of the middle and working classes. "The average middle-class reader," Ward points out, "wanted works which were within his own experience and range of emotion, reflecting his own interests and not conflicting with the demands of his morality" (Ward, 1974, p. 133). Whereas Schleiermacher's lecture on translation is quite scholarly in citing only Greek and Latin writing (Plato, Cicero, Tacitus, Grotius, and Leibniz), the wider middle-class readership favored Gothic tales, chivalric romances, realistic novels both sentimental and didactic, biographies of exemplary men, travel literature. This audience was reading translations as well, but the greatest percentage consisted of translations from French and English novels, including the work of Choderlos de Laclos and Richardson. Schleiermacher himself had translated Plato, while other romantics—Voss, August Wilhelm Schlegel, Hölderlin —translated Homer, Sophocles, Dante, and Shakespeare. They were very much aware that they were translating for a relatively narrow audience, even a coterie, and like Schleiermacher, they saw this social fact as a value that improved their "literature" and endowed it with cultural authority. Friedrich Schlegel boasted that "[readers] are forever complaining that German authors write for such a small circle, often in fact for themselves as a group. I find this a good thing. German literature gains more and more in spirit and character because of it" (Ward, 1974, p. 191, p. n. 46).

Schlegel's comment shows that this is not only a bourgeois, but a nationalist concept of literature—"German." And Schleiermacher's theory of foreignizing translation reveals a similar ideological configuration: It is also pitched against a German nobility that was not literary and had long lain under French cultural domination. Aristocratic culture eschewed scholarly research and wide reading in past and contemporary literature; "the few courts which did take an active interest in literary affairs," Ward notes, "were characterized by a predominantly bourgeois atmosphere" (Ward, 1974, p. 128). In aristocratic education, "the accent was on languages, particularly French, and often to such an extent that many noblemen could express themselves better in that language than in their mother tongue" (ibid., p. 123). In a letter from 1757, the aesthetician and dramatist Johann Christoph Gottsched described an audience with Frederick II, during which he informed the Prussian king of the serious threat to literary culture posed by the Gallicized nobility.

> When I said that German writers did not receive sufficient encouragement, as the aristocracy and the courts spoke too much French and understood too little German to be able to grasp and appreciate fully anything written in German, he said: That is true, for I haven't read no German book since my youth, and je parle comme un cocher, but I am an old fellow of forty-six and have no time for such things.
>
> (ibid., p. 190n.)

Some fifty years later, Schleiermacher's lecture on translation engages in the cultural struggle for a German literature with an equally bold criticism of Frederick II. Schleiermacher represents the king, however, not as Gottsched's anti-intellectual oaf, but as a German intellect limited by his utter dependence on French:

> Our great king received all his finer and higher thoughts in a foreign language, which he had most intimately appropriated for this field. He was incapable of producing in German the literature and philosophy he produced in French. It is to be deplored that the great preference for England which dominated a part of the family could not have taken the direction of familiarizing him from childhood on with the English language, whose last goldenage was then in bloom, and which is so much closer to German. But we may hope that he would have preferred to produce literature and philosophy in Latin, rather than in French, if he had enjoyed a strict scholarly education.
>
> (Lefevere, 1977, p. 83)

Here the vernacular nationalism in Schleiermacher's cultural politics becomes more evident: The king is taken to task not so much because he is not "scholarly" (he is in fact portrayed as being genuinely interested in "literature and philosophy"), but because he doesn't write in German, or in a language "closer to German" than French. Whereas Gottsched seems to be lamenting the dearth of literary patronage ("sufficient encouragement") because the Prussian aristocracy is Francophone, Schleiermacher is more concerned about the unequal cultural production in German and French: "He was incapable of producing in German."

Schleiermacher's criticism of the king is a nationalist protest against French domination in Germany, and it is consistent with his intense activity in the Prussian movement for German unification during the Napoleonic wars. As Jerry Dawson makes clear, the war between France and Prussia in 1806, with the resulting collapse of the Prussian armies and the humiliating peace terms dictated to Prussia by Napoleon, proved to be the final factor needed to turn [Schleiermacher] to nationalism with a complete and almost reckless abandon.

(Dawson, 1966, p. 51)

"Germany" did not actually exist at this time: West of the Rhine were several petty principalities, which, after 1806, Napoleon organized into a "confederation;" east was the dominant German-speaking monarchy, Prussia, now dominated by the French. The Prussian defeat caused Schleiermacher to lose his appointment at the University of Halle, and he fled to Berlin, the Prussian capital, where he lectured at the university and preached at various churches. His sermons urged political and military resistance against the French armies, developing a cultural concept of nationality based on the German language and legitimized with Protestant theology. In 1813, three months before his lecture on translation at the Berlin Akademieder Wissenschaften and eight months before Napoleon was finally defeated at the Battle of Leipzig, Schleiermacher delivered a sermon entitled "A Nation's Duty in a War for Freedom," in which he represented the war with France as a struggle against cultural and political domination. If victorious, he exhorted the congregation, "we shall be able to preserve for ourselves our own distinctive character, our laws, our constitution and our culture" (Schleiermacher, 1890, p. 73).

In June, the month of his lecture, Schleiermacher wrote a letter to Friedrich Schlegel in which his nationalism turned utopian:

My greatest wish after liberation, is for one true German Empire, powerfully representing the entire German folk and territory to the outside world, while internally allowing the various Länder and their princes a great deal of freedom to develop and rule according to their own particular needs.

(Sheehan, 1989, p. 379)

This vision of Germany as a union of relatively autonomous principalities was partly a compensation for the then prevailing international conflict, and it is somewhat backward-looking, traced with a nostalgia for the domestic political organization that prevailed before the French occupation. Napoleon had introduced social innovations achieved by the revolution, abolishing feudalism in Prussia and promoting "enlightened" despotism. Schleiermacher himself was a member of a bourgeois cultural elite, but his nationalist ideology is such that it admits aristocracy, monarchy, even an imperialist tendency—but only when they constitute a national unity resistant to foreign domination

Presented to the Prussian academic establishment on 24 June 1813, at the height of the conflict with France, Schleiermacher's lecture constructs a role for translation in a nationalist cultural politics. His theory of foreignizing translation should be seen as anti-French because it opposes the translation method that dominated France since neoclassicism, viz. domestication, making the foreign author travel abroad to the target-language reader. When surveying the limited acceptance of foreignizing translation in Western culture, Schleiermacher reserves his most withering sarcasm for France:

> The ancients obviously translated little in that most real sense and most moderns, deterred by the difficulties of true translation, also seem to be satisfied with imitation and paraphrase. Who would want to contend that nothing has ever been translated into French from the classical languages or from the Germanic languages! But even though we Germans are perfectly willing to listen to this advice, we should not follow it.
>
> (Lefevere, 1977, p. 88)

French exemplifies those languages that are "captives of too strict a bond of classical expression outside of which all is reprehensible," especially the innovations and deviations introduced by foreignizing translation. In a satiric dialogue from 1798, A. W. Schlegel had already made explicit the nationalist ideology at work in identifying French culture with a domesticating translation method.

> Frenchman: The Germans translate every literary, Tom, Dick, and Harry. We either do not translate at all, or else we translate according to our own taste.
>
> German: Which is to say, you paraphrase and you disguise.
>
> Frenchman: We look on a foreign author as a stranger in our company, who has to dress and behave according to our customs, if he desires to please.
>
> German: How narrow-minded of you to be pleased only by what is native.
>
> Frenchman: Such is our nature and our education. Did the Greeks not hellenize everything as well?
>
> German: In your case it goes back to a narrow-minded nature and a conventional education. In ours education is our nature.
>
> (ibid., p. 50)

Schlegel's dialogue indicates the metaphysical underpinnings of German nationalism, its assumption of a biological or racial essence from which the national culture issues: "Education is our nature." This agrees both with Schleiermacher's view that "our nation" possesses a "mediating nature" and with the organic metaphor he uses to describe the effect of foreignizing translation on German.

Just as our soil itself has no doubt become richer and more fertile and our climate milder and more pleasant only after much transplantation of foreign flora, just so we sense that our language, because we exercise it less owing to our Nordic sluggishness, can thrive in all its freshness and completely develop its own power only through the most many-sided contacts with what is foreign.

(ibid., p. 88)

Schleiermacher's nationalist theory of foreignizing translation aims to challenge French hegemony not only by enriching German culture, but by contributing to the formation of a liberal public sphere, an area of social life in which private individuals exchange rational discourse and exercise political influence.

If ever the time should come in which we have a public life out of which develops a sociability of greater merit and truer to language, and in which free space is gained for the talent of the orator, we shall be less in need of translation for the development of language.

(ibid., p. 89)

Yet Schleiermacher's public sphere manifests the contradiction that characterized the concept from its emergence in eighteenth century aesthetics. As Peter Uwe Hohendahl puts it, "although in principle the capacity to form an accurate opinion is considered present in everyone, in practice it is limited to the educated"(Hohendahl, 1982, p. 51). So in Schleiermacher: Although the work of foreignizing translation on the German language is seen as creating a national culture free of French political domination, this public space is open explicitly for "the talent of the orator," a literary elite.

Because this is a strongly nationalist elite, it employs foreignizing translation in a remarkable project of German cultural imperialism, through which the linguistic community "destined" for global domination achieves it. Here nationalism is equivalent to universalism:

An inner necessity, in which a peculiar calling of our people expresses itself clearly enough, has driven us to translating en masse; we cannot go back and we must go on. [...] And coincidentally our nation may be destined, because of its respect for what is foreign and its mediating nature, to carry all the treasures of foreign arts and scholarship, together with its own, in its language, to unite them into a great historical whole, so to speak, which would be preserved in the centre and heart of Europe, so that with the help of our language, whatever beauty the most different times have brought forth can be enjoyed by all people, as purely and perfectly as is possible for a foreigner. This appears indeed to be the real historical aim of translation in general, as we are used to it now.

(Lefevere, 1977, p. 88)

Thus, readers of the canon of world literature would experience the linguistic and cultural difference of foreign texts, but only as a difference that is Eurocentric, mediated by a German bourgeois elite. Ultimately, it would seem that foreignizing translation does not so much introduce the foreign into German culture as use the foreign to confirm and develop a sameness, a process of fashioning an ideal cultural self on the basis of an other, a cultural narcissism, which is endowed, moreover, with historical necessity. This method of translation "makes sense and is of value only to a nation that has the definite inclination to appropriate what is foreign"(ibid., p. 80).

The ideological ensemble in Schleiermacher's cultural politics precipitates contradictory permutations (elite literature / national culture, bourgeois minority / "Germany," foreignizing / Germanizing), so we should not be surprised to find him speaking for and against foreign imports in German culture—in that same turbulent year, 1813. His bourgeois nationalism shapes both his advocacy of "many-sided contacts with the foreign" in the translation lecture and his xenophobic condescension in the patriotic sermon: "Every nation, my dear friends, which has developed a particular, or clearly defined height is degraded also by receiving into it a foreign element" (Schleiermacher, 1890, pp. 73 – 74). This assumes, contrary to the lecture, that German culture has already attained a significant level of development, presumably in classical and romantic literature, which must be protected from foreign contamination and imposed universally, through a specifically German foreignization of world literature. Schleiermacher's translation theory intervenes in "die gesammte Geistesentwikkelung," a phrase that may seem restricted nationally in Lefevere's English, "the whole evolution of a culture"(Lefevere, 1977, p. 81), but is shown to have worldwide application in Berman's French: "le processus global de la formation de l'esprit" (Berman, 1985, p. 333). And only Berman discloses the idealist metaphysics at work in the German text by choosing "esprit" for "Geist."

Schleiermacher's theory is shaky ground on which to build a translation ethics to combat ethnocentrism: His lecture does not recognize any contradiction in asserting that "our nation" is distinguished by "respect for what is foreign" while envisioning the geopolitical domination of a German bourgeois cultural elite. It also does not recognize antinomies in its thinking about language and human subjectivity which are likewise determined by a bourgeois nationalism. Schleiermacher evinces an extraordinarily clear sense of the constitutive properties of language, those that make representation always an appropriative activity, never transparent or merely adequate to its object, active in the construction of subjectivity by establishing forms for consciousness. The "proper field" of the translator, Schleiermacher states, consists of

> those mental products of scholarship and art in which the free idiosyncratic combinatory powers of the author and the spirit of the language which is the repository of a system of observations and shades of moods are everything, in which the object no longer dominates in any way, but is dominated by thoughts and emotions, in which, indeed, the object has become object only through speech and is present only in conjunction with speech.
>
> (Lefevere, 1977, pp. 69 – 70)

At the same time, however, Schleiermacher's concept of "free idiosyncratic combinatory powers" signals a move toward an autonomous subject whose "thoughts and emotions" transcend linguistic determinations. "On the one hand," Schleiermacher asserts,

> every man is in the power of the language he speaks, and all his thinking is a product thereof. [...] Yet on the other hand every freely thinking, mentally self-employed human being shapes his own language. [...] Therefore each free and higher speech needs to be understood twice, once out of the spirit of the language of whose elements it is composed, as a living representation bound and defined by that spirit and conceived out of it in the speaker, and once out of the speaker's emotions, as his action, as produced and explicable only out of his own being.
>
> (ibid., p. 71)

The "spirit of the language" determines every speech act, is binding on every subject, but part of that action nevertheless answers only to an individual "being." At one point, the priority of language over subject is tellingly reversed, with the author becoming the sole origin of the "spirit:" the readers of a foreignizing translation are said to "understand" when they "perceive the spirit of the language which was the author's own and [are] able to see his peculiar way of thinking and feeling" (ibid., p. 72). As Berman points out, Schleiermacher's lecture manifests the late eighteenth century shift from representation to expression as the conceptual paradigm for language, and hence subject displaces object as the basis of interpretation (Berman, 1984, p. 233). Schleiermacher's thinking about language is informed by romantic expressive theory, grounded in the concept of free, unified consciousness that characterizes bourgeois individualism.

As his exposition proceeds, it turns to metaphor and illustration, defining the "spirit of the language" in ethnic terms, yet without abandoning the transcendental subject:

> We understand the spoken word as an act of the speaker only when we feel at the same time where and how the power of language has taken hold of him, where in its current the lightning of thought has uncoiled, snake-like, where and how the roving imagination has been held firm in its forms. We understand the spoken word as a product of language and as an expression of its spirit only when we feel that only a Greek, for instance, could think and speak in that way, that only this particular language could operate in a human mind this way, and when we feel at the same time that only this man could think and speak in the Greek fashion in this way, that only he could seize and shape the language in this manner, that only his living possession of the riches of language reveals itself like this, an alert sense for measure and euphony which belongs to him alone, a power of thinking and shaping which is peculiarly his.
>
> (Lefevere, 1977, p. 72)

The metaphors—"lightning," "snake-like," "roving"—continue the individualistic strain by depicting the subject as a coherent essence, radically independent of language, given to serpentine, potentially subversive "thought," possessing a free "imagination" that takes on various accidental "forms" (obviously, "lightning" and "snake-like" also resonate with mythological and theological allusions, especially in a lecture by a classical scholar and Protestant minister—but these possibilities will not be pursued here). The most striking move in this passage may well be Schleiermacher's example, which initiates a discontinuous series of specifications and revisions, putting the individual in command, first, of a national culture with a literary canon ["the riches of language;" cf. the international "treasures of foreign arts and scholarship" (ibid, p. 88)], then a specifically literary, even scholarly appreciation of the Greek language ("measure and euphony"), and finally a cognitive "power" that is "peculiarly his," self-expressive and fundamentally self-determining.

The passage is a reminder that Schleiermacher is setting up the understanding of language associated with a particular national cultural elite as the standard by which language use is made intelligible and judged. Hence, in the case of foreignizing translation, "the reader of the translation will become the equal of the better reader of the original only when he is able first to acquire an impression of the particular spirit of the author as well as that of the language in the work" (Lefevere, 1977, p. 80). Yet the author-orientation in Schleiermacher's theory, his anthropomorphosis of translation from an intertextual to an intersubjective relationship, psychologizes the translated text and thus masks its cultural and social determinations. This is the much criticized move in Schleiermacher's hermeneutics: He tends to evaporate the determinate nature of the text by articulating a two-fold interpretive process, both "grammatical" and "technical or psychological." A grammatical explanation of the objective "connection between the work and the language" combines with a psychological explanation of the subjective "connection between the work and the thought involved in it" (Szondi, 1986, p. 103). Schleiermacher, however, sometimes collapses this distinction, as in his aphorisms on hermeneutics from 1809 to 1810, which refer to "combining the objective and subjective so that the interpreter can put himself 'inside' the author" (Schleiermacher, 1977, p. 64). In the case of German foreignizing translation, then, the translator enables the German-language reader to understand the individuality of the foreign author so as to identify with him, thereby concealing the transindividual, German-language ideologies—cultural (literary elitism), class (bourgeois minority), national ("German")—that mediate the foreignized representation of the foreign author. Such thinking about language and subjectivity is clearly more consistent with domesticating translation, oriented toward conformity with target-language cultural values, and so can do little to question the dominance of transparent discourse in translation today. On the contrary, Schleiermacher's psychologization of the text assumes transparency, the illusory presence of the foreign author in the translation.

There is another kind of thinking in his lecture that runs counter to this idealist strain, even if impossibly caught in its tangles: a recognition of the cultural and social conditions of language and a projection of a translation practice that takes them into account instead of working to conceal them. Schleiermacher sees translation as an everyday fact of life, not merely an activity performed on literary and philosophical texts, but necessary for intersubjective understanding, active in the very process of communication, because language is determined by various differences cultural, social, historical:

> For not only are the dialects spoken by different tribes belonging to the same nation, and the different stages of the same language or dialect in different centuries, different languages in the strict sense of the word; moreover even contemporaries who are not separated by dialects, but merely belong to different classes, which are not often linked through social intercourse and are far apart in education, often can understand each other only by means of a similar mediation.
>
> (Lefevere, 1977, p. 68)

This observation clearly requires Schleiermacher to revise his nationalist concept of "the spirit of the language:" he understands it as "the repository of a system of observations and shades of mood," but this is too monolithic and too psychologistic to admit the concept of "different classes," a social hierarchy of cultural discourses, each so distinctively class-coded as to impede communication. Schleiermacher even finds it "inevitable that different opinions should develop as to" foreignizing translation strategies, "different schools, so to speak, will arise among the masters, and different parties among the audience as followers of those schools," but he ultimately individualizes the "different points of view," reducing them to the translator's consciousness, transforming cultural practices with social implications into self-centered eccentricities: "Each one in itself will always be of relative and subjective value only" (ibid., p. 81).

It is cultural difference, however, that guides Schleiermacher's prescriptions for the foreignizing translator, for the invention of discursive peculiarities to signify the foreignness of the foreign text. The translator must reject the discourse that is used most widely in the target-language culture, what he calls the "colloquial" (p. 78); "alltäglich" (p. 227), refusing "the most universally appealing beauty each genre is capable of" in the language and instead risking the compassionate smile of "the greatest experts and masters who could not understand his laborious and ill-considered German if they did not supplement it with their Greek and Latin" (p. 79). Once again, the cultural difference marked by Schleiermacher's foreignizing translator runs between an educated elite and the uneducated majority: When the translator bends his language to a foreign likeness, he is not doing it with "each genre," "universally," but with literary and scholarly texts in Greek and Latin, so that only "experts and masters" will be able to "understand" his deviant use of language. Schleiermacher's translator avoids the "colloquial," unlearned language use, popular literary forms.

And yet, despite the questionable ideological determinations of Schleiermacher's lecture—its bourgeois individualism and cultural elitism, its Prussian nationalism and

German universalism—it does contain the (inadvertent) suggestion that foreignizing translation can alter the social divisions figured in these ideologies, can promote cultural change through its work on the target language:

> Every freely thinking, mentally self-employed human being shapes his own language. For in what other way—except precisely by means of these influences—would it have developed and grown from its first raw state to its more perfect elaboration in scholarship and art? In this sense, therefore, it is the living power of the individual which creates new forms by means of the plastic material of language, at first only for the immediate purpose of communicating a passing consciousness; yet now more, now less of it remains behind in the language, is taken up by others, and reaches out, a shaping force.
>
> (Lefevere, 1977, p. 71)

This passage reverses its logic. At first language is taken to exist in an unmediated "raw state," worked by a transcendental subject who "shapes his own language," who is the origin of linguistic and cultural innovation and development. By the end, however, the determinate nature of language emerges as the "shaping force" of subjects. In the interval, the materiality of language is socialized: No longer "raw," it contains "new forms" invented by "the individual," but exceeding the function they were intended to serve, the communication of "consciousness," because they have been derived from pre-existing forms used by "others." This indicates that subjectivity is neither self-originating nor the origin of language and culture, that its cultural values (e. g. "scholarship and art") are pre-given and constantly reworked ("elaboration"), and that therefore the subject can be considered self-determining only insofar as it ranks these values—or revises them and alters an established ranking. The discursive innovations and deviations introduced by foreignizing translation are thus a potential threat to target-language cultural values, but they perform their revisionary work only from within, developing translation strategies from the diverse discourses that circulate in the target language.

Schleiermacher's concept of foreignizing translation constitutes a resistance to dominant cultural values in German at the turn of the nineteenth century. The foreign in foreignizing translation then meant a specific selection of foreign texts (literary, philosophical, scholarly) and a development of discursive peculiarities that opposed both French cultural hegemony, especially among the aristocracy, and the literary discourses favored by the largest segment of readers, both middle-and working-class. Schleiermacher's translation project depends on an idealist concept of literature that is at once elitist and nationalist, individualistic yet socially determinate, defined in opposition to capitalist economic practices: "The interpreter plies his trade in the field of commerce; the translator proper operates mainly in the fields of art and scholarship" (Lefevere, 1977, p. 68).

It is this ideological ensemble that must be jettisoned in any revival of foreignizing translation to intervene against the contemporary ascendancy of transparent discourse. Today, transparency is the dominant discourse in poetry and prose, fiction and non-fiction, bestsellers and print journalism. Even if the electronic media have weakened the economic, political, and cultural hegemony of print in the post-World War II period, the idealist concept of literature that underwrites that discourse continues to enjoy considerable institutional power, housed not only in the academy and in the literary cultures of various educated elites, but in the publishing industry and the mass-audience periodical press. The distinction that Schleiermacher perceived between the field of commerce and the fields of art and scholarship has been eroded—if it ever existed as more than a fiction designed to consolidate literature as a transcendental cultural concept. Transparent discourse is eminently consumable in the contemporary cultural marketplace, which in turn influences publishing decisions to exclude foreign texts that preempt transparency.

Schleiermacher shows that the first opportunity to foreignize translation occurs in the choice of foreign text, wherein the translator can resist the dominant discourse in Anglo-American culture by restoring excluded texts and possibly reforming the canon of foreign literatures in English. Schleiermacher also suggests that foreignizing translation puts to work a specific discursive strategy. He opposes the foregrounding of the signified by which fluent translation produces the effect of transparency; for him a translation can be foreignized only by approximating the play of signifiers in the foreign text: "The more closely the translation follows the turns taken by the original, the more foreign it will seem to the reader" (Lefevere, 1977, p. 78).

Schleiermacher's lecture provides the tools for conceptualizing a revolt against the dominance of transparent discourse in current English-language translation. Yet the effects of this dominance have included, not only the widespread implementation of fluent strategies, but the marginalization of texts in the history of translation that can yield alternative theories and practices—like Schleiermacher's lecture. With rare exceptions, English-language theorists and practitioners of English-language translation have neglected Schleiermacher. His lecture has been recognized as a key "modern" statement in translation theory only recently, and it was not translated into English until 1977. And even its translator, André Lefevere, felt compelled to question Schleiermacher's value: "His requirement that the translation should 'give the feel' of the source language must [...] strike us increasingly as odd" (Lefevere, 1977, p. 67). Lefevere argued that translation should be domesticating, as "most theoreticians" recommended, and he specifically referred to Eugene Nida's version of this theory, quoting Nida to criticize Schleiermacher.

In effect, we are faced here with a not-illogical and very spirited defence of what we know now as "translationese" or, with another phrase: "static equivalence," and which is still very much with us, in spite of the fact that most theoreticians would now subscribe to the concept of dynamic equivalence, which "aims at complete natural-ness of expression and tries to relate the receptor to modes of behavior relevant within the context of his own culture. "

(Lefevere, 1981, p. 11)

Schleiermacher's concept of foreignizing translation seems odd to Lefevere only because the latter prefers to submit to the contemporary regime of fluency—in Nida's words, "complete naturalness of expression." The canonicity of fluent translation during the post-World War II period coincides with the emergence of the term "translationese" to designate unidiomatic language in a translated text (OED). Lefevere approves of Nida's "dynamic equivalence," a concept that now, with the increasing recognition of Schleiermacher's contemporary importance, must be viewed as an egregious euphemism for the domesticating translation method and the cultural political agendas it conceals. Because this method is so entrenched in English-language translation, Lefevere is unable to see that the detection of unidiomatic language, especially in literary texts, is culturally specific: What is unidiomatic in one cultural formation can be aesthetically effective in another. Any dismissive treatment of Schleiermacher maintains the forms of domestication in English-language translation today, hindering reflection on how different methods of translating can resist the questionable values that dominate Anglo-American culture.

Schleiermacher can indeed offer a way out.

【延伸阅读】

[1] Schleiermacher,F. (1992). On the Different Methods of Translating. In R. Schulte and J. Biguener(eds.), *Theories of Translation*. Chicago and London: University of Chicago Press.

[2] Venuti, L. (1995). *The Translator's Invisibility: A History of Translation*. London and New York: Routledge.

【问题与思考】

1. 本文原标题为"民族"(Nation)，探讨的却是异化和归化,如何理解作者的意图？
2. 施莱尔马赫支持异化翻译方法是为了阻抗他所处时代德国的德语文化吗？ 为什么？
3. 按照施莱尔马赫的观点,异化翻译应该如何操作？ 为什么？
4. 施莱尔马赫的翻译思想对韦努蒂有何影响？ 请说出理由。

选文三　重新解读韦努蒂的异化翻译理论
——兼与郭建中教授商榷

蒋骁华　张景华

导　言

本文发表于《中国翻译》2007 年第 3 期。

韦努蒂的异化翻译理论自 20 世纪末被引进国内后,许多学者对它进行了进一步的研究或阐发,但尚有一些基本问题需要澄清。本文着重围绕以下三个问题展开讨论,力图追本溯源,探赜索隐,准确解读韦努蒂异化翻译理论:① 韦努蒂异化翻译理论的内涵;② 韦努蒂的译者著作权思想与其异化翻译理论的内在联系;③ 韦努蒂的异化翻译理论是否属于解构主义翻译理论。

"异化翻译"(foreignizing translation)概念是劳伦斯·韦努蒂(Lawrence Venuti)于 1995 年在其名著《译者的隐形——翻译史论》(*The Translator's Invisibility—A History of Translation*)中提出来的①。郭建中教授在 1998 年《外国语》第 2 期的《翻译中的文化因素:归化与异化》一文中对它的介绍大约是国内译界最早的。2000 年郭先生在《中国翻译》第 1 期上发表《韦努蒂及其解构主义的翻译策略》,较系统地阐发了韦努蒂的异化翻译理论;同年稍晚,他在其专著《当代美国翻译理论》中专辟一节(第八章第二节),更系统地阐述了韦努蒂异化翻译理论的来源、内容及其影响。至此,韦努蒂的"异化翻译"理论被基本完整地引进国内。郭先生在引介和阐发中始终持有一个非常鲜明的观点,即韦努蒂异化翻译理论是典型的解构主义翻译理论。后来持相同观点的还有不少学者,如邓红风(2003)、任淑坤(2004)、封一函(2006)等。两年前,我们应邀翻译韦努蒂的 *The Translator's Invisibility—A History of Translation*,因此而查阅了不少西方有关文献,意外的"收获"之一是,迄今尚未找到与郭先生对应或相同的观点。这是什么原因呢? 另外,韦努蒂异化翻译理论引进后,我国译界出现了一场不大不小的对异化和归化的讨论。据我们不完全统计,仅 2000 年到 2005 年我国学术刊物上有关

---

① 　其实韦努蒂早在 1986 年在其发表于 *Criticism* 28(Spring)的一篇名为"The Translator's Invisibility"的论文中已经明确提出了"异化翻译"的概念(参见 Robinson,1997:97),但这个概念真正产生国际影响是在其名作 *The Translator's Invisibility—A History of Translation* 于 1995 年出版之后。另外,补充一点,我国传统译论中虽然没有明确、具体的"异化翻译"概念或提法,但其中并不缺乏"异化翻译"思想。追溯起来,唐玄奘的"五不翻"之说已经有明显的"异化翻译"思想雏形。玄奘可以说是世界上第一个对"异化翻译"进行归纳和理论总结的人。宋初高僧赞宁的"六例"说(详见王宏印,2003:78;陈福康,2000:38 - 42),则"大大地推进了玄奘的'五不翻'理论"(王宏印,2003:80),可以说,赞宁发展了玄奘的古典"异化翻译"思想。鲁迅的"宁信而不顺"之说(详见王秉钦,2004:110 - 127)在现代意义上与"异化翻译"理论有诸多类似。概括起来,我国传统译论中的异化翻译思想有如下内涵:a. 作为翻译方法,其内容包括 i. 音译,ii. 直译,iii. 保存句法形式;b. 作为文化策略,其内容包括 i. 保证佛典的准确、庄严和神秘,ii. 丰富汉语语汇,引进新的表达法,iii. 医治"脑筋糊涂"的病(即"改造国民性");c. 作为文化理念它含有一定的文化"精英主义"意识(参看本文注释 2)。

归化异化的论文多达 300 余篇。我们研读了 1998 年以来所有知名学者的和我们认为重要的有关论文,概括起来,大约有以下两种情况:① 认为异化翻译基本上相当于直译,如谭惠娟(1998)、刘重德(1999)、郑海凌(2001)、孙致礼(2002)等;② 认为异化翻译是直译的延伸,其内涵比后者丰富,如朱志瑜(2001)、王东风(2002)、葛校琴(2002)、尹衍桐(2005)等。从理论上讲,上述两种认识都是可行的。可问题是,既然异化翻译与直译不完全相等,或者,异化翻译比直译内涵丰富,那异化翻译的内涵究竟有哪些方面呢? 这些问题萦绕心中,挥之不去。殷然索之于上述诸文等,竟渺渺然语焉不详。笔者不揣浅陋,欲追问到底,探个究竟。本文将探讨几个关键问题:① 韦努蒂异化翻译理论的内涵;② 韦努蒂的译者著作权思想与其异化理论的内在联系;③ 韦努蒂的异化翻译理论是否属于解构主义翻译理论。我们谨呈一孔之见,盼同仁方家指教。

一、韦努蒂异化翻译理论的内涵

韦努蒂的异化翻译理论源于德国思想家施莱尔马赫(Schleiermacher)的启发。1813 年,施莱尔马赫在就不同的翻译方法发表演讲时指出:"只有两种翻译方法:要么译者尽可能让作者安居不动,让读者去接近作者;要么译者尽可能让读者安居不动,让作者去接近读者"(Lefevere,1977:74)。韦努蒂由此认为,"译者可以选择归化或异化的译法,前者以民族主义为中心,把外国的价值观归化到译语文化中,把原作者请到国内来;后者则离经叛道,把外国文本中的语言和文化差异表现出来,把读者送到国外去"(Venuti,1995:20)。韦努蒂进一步指出,异化翻译策略有利于民族文化的重构,有利于构造以异化为基础的文化身份。当然,异化翻译策略也会破坏目的语的民族文化概念,挑战民族文化典律和民族价值观(ibid)。

韦努蒂批判地继承了施莱尔马赫的思想,因为韦努蒂认为:一方面,施莱尔马赫对翻译的本质有了非常清醒的认识,翻译作为一种语言表征手段,不可能透明地和绝对充分地反映原作;另一方面,施莱尔马赫提倡异化的翻译策略只是针对受过教育的文化精英而提出的翻译话语。他对于这一社会群体的倚重主要是因为他们的文化权威,希望借此发展本民族语言,推动民族文化的演变。施莱尔马赫把他提倡的翻译策略纳入文化政治的议程之中,企望文化精英通过异化翻译来改进民族语言,进而影响本民族文化的形成。所以,韦努蒂批评施莱尔马赫不敢理直气壮地提倡异化翻译,有时甚至陷入自相矛盾的境地,他既在其演讲中提倡与"异域文化的全面接触",又在其言论中表达出对异域文化的恐惧心理(参看 Venuti,1995:106)。此外,韦努蒂与施莱尔马赫不同的是,他认为异化翻译不应该仅仅理解为单纯的逐字对应或在译文中保留外语词,尽管这两种方法都很有效(韦努蒂,2006:172)。

韦努蒂认为对"异化翻译"不能简单地定义,只有把译文与生成译文的文化话语联系起来,只有把特定的翻译理论和实践与价值取向联系起来,才能对这一概念作明确的定义:

> 异化翻译是一种另类文化实践,它发展在本土处于边缘地位的语言和文学价值观,包括因抵抗本土价值观而被排斥的异域文化。一方面,异化翻译时原文进行以我族为中心的挪用,将翻译作为再现另类文化的场点,从而把翻译提上了本土的文化政治议程;另一方面,正是这种另类的文化姿态使异化翻译能够彰显原文的语言和文化差异,发挥文化重构的作用,并使那些偏离我族中心主义的译文得到认可,并有可能修正本土的文学经典。(Venuti,1995:148)

异化翻译旨在彰显原文的差异,这种差异只有通过打破目的语中现行的文化准则才能得以保存(Venuti,1995:20)。异化翻译通常会偏离本土的文学规范,让读者感受一种异样的阅读体验——例如,选材可能是非文学经典,译文的话语可能会显得有些另类。韦努蒂的"异化"比我们经常讨论的类似直译的"异化"内涵丰富得多。首先,从 foreignizing 这个词本身来看,它既具有动词性质,也具有名词性质,因此既可以理解为一种倾向,也可以理解为一种状态。我们认为,韦努蒂异化翻译理论的内涵至少包含以下七个方面。

第一,异化翻译之"异"表现为翻译的"选材之异"(Venuti,1995:117),这是针对目的语翻译文学经典和翻译文化经典而言的。韦努蒂在《译者的隐形》第二章中重点强调了翻译选材的重要性和策略性。韦努蒂这一观点其实也源于施莱尔马赫思想的启发。施莱尔马赫认为异化翻译的出现首先表现为翻译的文本选择,译者可以通过翻译那些被主体文化排斥的文本,重构外国文学的经典,从而抵抗主体文化中的主流话语。在翻译过程中,选择与目的语主流文化风格迥异的异域文本,其价值在于不仅能打破目的语的文化准则,而且能改变目的语的文化构成,使翻译成为异质性的话语实践,从而把翻译作为研究和实践"差异性"的场所,而不是盲目地认同目的语的主流文化。所以,翻译的"选材之异"实际上不仅暗含了翻译话语的演变,还对目的语的主流话语有一种修正作用。另外,如果那些"通顺"的译文在原文选择和意识形态上挑战主流文化,那么这样的译文也只能算是一定程度的"异化",或者说是不彻底的"异化"。在《译者的隐形》第四章中韦努蒂引用 Tarchetti(1839—1869)把哥特式小说译入意大利文学的例子说明了这一点。韦努蒂认为 Tarchetti 用标准语言(即通顺语言)翻译与主流文学不相宜的小说,这一点是可取的。但他并不赞成当今译者采用 Tarchetti 那种剽窃式(Plagiarism)的翻译方法。

第二,异化翻译之"异"表现为翻译的"语言之异"和"文化之异"。韦努蒂在《译者的隐形》第一章中认为,译文越接近原文的措辞,对读者来说就越显得异化,就越有可能起到修正主流话语的作用;"语言之异"和"文化之异"能改变读者阅读译文的方式,让读者的主体性发挥更大的作用;异化翻译是不透明的,它不强调通顺,倾向于在译文中融入异质性话语;异化翻译是反抗透明话语在当代英语翻译中占主导地位的有效手段。透明话语不仅导致通顺策略大行其道,而且在翻译史上造成了许多重要文本的地位边缘化和价值扭曲(Venuti,1995:117)。韦努蒂反对奈达所提倡的动态对等,因为它实质上是一种归化翻译。

第三,异化翻译之"异"表现为译文的"文体之异"(详见《译者的隐形》第五章)。这主要指译者采用"陌生化"(disfamiliarization)的翻译策略,不仅在语言结构和用词上注重传达原文的"异国情调"(foreignism),还冒险在译文中采用非常用或非标准语汇,如采用不符合语言习惯或晦涩难懂的表达法,或者俚语、新词或古词混用在一起。例如,韦努蒂在《译者的隐形》第五章中通过庞德(Pound)的翻译,说明"文体之异"有时是以英语的古语体形式出现的。庞德的译诗《水手》(Seafarer)在语体上与现代英语差异很大,他的翻译贴近盎格鲁-撒克逊时期文体,模仿其复合词、头韵、音律,甚至模拟盎格鲁-撒克逊音位仿造新词。韦努蒂认为庞德的翻译彰显了异域文本的差异,但这并不是因为他的译文忠实而准确,而是因为译文偏离了美国的本土英语文学典范。

第四,异化翻译之"异"只是一个度的问题,韦努蒂在《译者的隐形》第一章中提醒我们,任何翻译都包含一个归化过程,即由源语的可理解性向目的语可理解性的转变过程。但是,"归化"并不等同于"透明"或"同化","同化"是根据本土的主流价值观对异域文本进行极其保守的

"简约"(reduction)。韦努蒂还提醒我们,异化策略有可能导致"妄用忠实"(abusive fidelity),但异化翻译并不等于忠实翻译,我们不能将异化翻译中的阻抗策略看做使译作更忠实于原文的策略。

第五,异化翻译作为一种文化策略,具有一定的文化干预功能。它强调语言差异和文化差异,这有利于发展多元文化,抵制欧美文化霸权,保护文化生态。

第六,异化翻译作为一种文化理念,含有"精英主义意识"(elitism)①(Robinson,1997:99 - 101)。韦努蒂认为,"受过良好教育的精英分子可以通过异化翻译来调控其民族的文化构成"(Venuti,1995:102),换言之,文化精英可以通过异化翻译来影响其社会主流价值观。韦努蒂心目中异化翻译的译者和读者都是"文化精英",而不是普通读者,因而异化翻译也被他称为"少数化翻译"或"小众化翻译"(minoritizing translation)(Venuti,1998)。异化翻译是不太适合普通大众的,因为"大众的审美意趣是追求文学中所表现的现实主义错觉,抹杀艺术与生活的区别;他们喜欢的译文明白易懂,看上去不像是翻译"(Venuti,1995:19)。

第七,异化翻译有提升译者和译文文化地位的企图。韦努蒂在《译者的隐形》第一章中从法律的角度,即通过批判英美现行版权法,试图论证译者拥有著作权的合法性或合理性(这一点在下一节中我们有进一步探讨)。后来韦努蒂在其 1998 年出版的《翻译之耻——为存异伦理的最终确立鼓与呼》(*The Scandals of Tranlation—Toward an Ethics of Difference*)一书中,试图从伦理的角度论证译者拥有著作权的合情性(即合乎伦理道德规范)。从"情"与"理"的角度多维论证,韦努蒂为提升译者和译文的文化地位可谓不遗余力。

总之,异化翻译是与归化翻译迥然不同的"另类翻译"(dissident translation);韦努蒂异化翻译理论比我们通常理解的"异化翻译基本上相当于直译"的理念复杂得多。在欧美语境中,译者一般通过以下方式彰显原文的异域特色:一是采用偏离当今盛行的归化话语的文体策略,如大量运用古词和外来词与通顺透明对抗;二是选择翻译那些可以挑战目的语中当代外国文学经典的文本。异化翻译的特色在于其"他异性",韦努蒂认为,异域文本的他异性只有在与目的语中的主流文化相比较才能显现出来。文化他异性可能会使目的语的文化价值体系发生改变,甚至重构。

韦努蒂提倡异化翻译,原因主要有三:第一,异化翻译可以促成目的语中外国文学经典的重构,推动目的语本土文学的变革。第二,异化翻译是一种干预策略,即对英语国家的文化霸权和不平等的文化交流进行文化干预;它的干预作用还表现在维护世界民主和地缘政治关系方面,它是一种遏制我族中心主义、种族歧视、文化自恋和文化霸权主义的文化措施。第三,传统的通顺翻译事实上造成了译者的隐形(invisible),导致了译者地位的边缘化。译者的隐形主要体现在以下两个方面:① 译者倾向于"通顺",努力使译文语言地道,可读性强,有一种透明的感觉;② 出版商、评论家和读者因喜欢通顺译文而要求译文读起来不像是翻译。韦努蒂

---

① 其实鲁迅的"异化翻译"思想中也含有一定的文化"精英主义"意识,如他在《关于翻译的通信》(1931)中将中国的译文读者分为三类,并主张对不同的读者要有不同的译文:"甲,有很受了教育的;乙,有略能识字的;丙,有识字无几的。而其中的丙,则在'读者'范围之外……至于供给甲类的读者的译本,无论什么,我是主张'宁信而不顺'的……我还以为即使为乙类读者而译的书,也应该时常加些新的字眼、新的语法在里面,但自然不宜太多,以偶尔遇见,而想一想,或问一问就能懂得为度。必须这样,群众的言语才能丰富起来。"鲁迅的主张是正确的,但其中还是难免有些文化"精英主义"意识,即异化翻译的读者主要是少数文化精英。这与韦努蒂异化翻译理论中的文化"精英主义"意识有些类似。但韦努蒂比较极端,而鲁迅则灵活、现实得多,因为他完全注意到了"乙类"读者的重要性。

认为，浑然天成的归化和通顺给人以"透明"的错觉，这实际上掩盖了生成译文的种种复杂因素，尤其是掩盖了译者对原文的关键性干预和复杂的思维过程，从而遮蔽了译者的工作价值。韦努蒂坚持译文作为译文的独立性和自足性。为使译者工作的价值和译者的文化地位在更大程度上真正得到承认，韦努蒂进一步提出了自己的译作著作权思想。

二、韦努蒂的译者著作权思想与其异化翻译理论的内在联系

韦努蒂对现行英美版权法中有关译作著作权的规定提出了质疑和挑战。韦努蒂认为现行版权法完全建立在"个人主义著作权思想"（individualist conception of authorship）之上，在很大程度上贬损了译文的价值（Venuti，1995：6，9）；它从心理上影响了译者的自我文化定位，迫使译者像影子一样生存在原作和原作者的光辉里。现行版权法把对翻译不利的法律身份固定和维持下来，将翻译定义为基于原作著作权的"改编"或"派生作品"（Venuti，1995：9）。这样，译者受制于作者，作者在原作版权有效期内对其翻译的出版拥有决定性的控制权。目前这种有效期是作者的有生之年再加50年。韦努蒂认为版权法既然把著作权定义为一种表达形式，而不是理念的创造，是语言的原创，而不是思想的原创；既然允许翻译作品以译者的名字登记版权，那么实际上也承认译者针对原文使用了另一种语言，重新创造了原作。这样，我们看到现行版权法不仅把译者置于非常尴尬的地位，而且还制造了一个悖论：译者似乎既是作者，又不是作者。现行版权法在解释译作著作权上运用了"双重标准"：一方面它把译作定义为派生作品，强调译作与原作的区别；另一方面为控制译作"越权"出版，它又强调译作与原作的相似性（Venuti，1995：8－11）。所以，现行版权法是以著作权的个人主义观为基础的，它把翻译排斥在原创作品之外。

韦努蒂认为，从历史发展的角度看，在出版行业形成之前，文学和各种形式的作品都是口头上的，作品并不属于某一特定的作者。在欧洲中世纪时代，人们认为作者并不是单一的概念，民间故事和神话传说等许多作品并非个人的创造，其中必然掺入集体的创作成分，人们认为作品其实是作者的语言与读者的解释相互交错形成的。出版行业兴起之后，著作权正式为个人所有，文本也就相应地成为作者的个人财产，剽窃的概念也逐渐形成。所以莫陇说："作家，这一新的职业是由机器所创造的，他的资产和身份处于危险之中"（Mallon，1990：4）。韦努蒂还批评了"浪漫主义的著作权思想"（Romantic concept of authorship），因为它把文本视为作者独有的思想和感觉，是一种自由统一的意识（Venuti，1995：165），认为这种思想在抬高作者地位的同时，实际上把作者这一称谓神圣化和荣誉化了；浪漫主义把作者定义为有创作天才的个体，作者具有非同常人的灵感，是作者给作品赋予了荣誉，从而进一步把作者的劳动固化为创造性的工作。事实上，许多作者，如柯勒律治（Coleridge），常在阅读时以笔记的形式把别人的思想记录下来，作一些加工整理，然后出版。柯勒律治在其诗歌中并没有区分哪些是自己的思想，哪些是别人的思想。

韦努蒂对现行版权法的批判与后现代哲学对作者原创性的质疑有一定的联系。韦努蒂认为，现行版权法承认作者对文本的所有权，即承认作者是文本的原创者，也就是说，作品是作者唯一的、排他的、个性的智力创造，但从总的文化发展趋势看，新的哲学思潮和文学研究方法，如新批评、接受美学、读者反应论等，正在逐渐削弱文本与作者的联系，从哲学思想上弱化作者对作品的著作权（Venuti，1995：8－11）。所以，韦努蒂认为，译者应该与作者"共享著作权"

(collective authorship)(Venuti,1998:61-65)。为做到这一点,译者可以通过异化翻译让自己"显形",在译作上标明译者的"著者"身份,并且利用译作的前言、后记及相关文章、讲座、访谈等,阐明实践异化翻译的依据,强调译者在翻译过程中的"劳动投资"(labor investment)。只有这样我们才有可能真正修正著作权的个人主义观,并改变译作屈居文化边缘的现状(Venuti,1995:311)。

仔细阅读《译者的隐形》,我们很容易意识到韦努蒂的译者著作权思想不是孤立地就事论事,而是其异化翻译思想的延伸,即通过让译者在法律意义上"现形"(visible),提升译者及其译文的文化和社会地位。为进一步实现这一目的,韦努蒂后来还从另一角度,即伦理的角度,详细论证译者拥有著作权是合乎伦理道德规范的(Ventui,1995;刘亚猛,2005)。

三、韦努蒂异化翻译理论是否属于解构主义翻译理论

阅读韦努蒂的代表作《译者的隐形——翻译史论》,我们不难发现韦努蒂的异化翻译理论受到了解构主义哲学思想的影响,也具有解构主义翻译理论的某些特征,如反主流、反传统,对一些翻译研究命题不断进行质疑,甚至试图颠覆等。但它是否应该属于解构主义翻译理论呢?如果说解构主义是一种思维方式,而非一些具体的观点,那么,韦努蒂的异化翻译理论与解构主义翻译理论有一些类似或相通之处。换言之,本文引言中提到的郭建中教授的观点有一定依据。但进一步追问下去,我们发现韦努蒂的异化翻译理论与解构主义翻译理论至少有以下五点本质区别:

第一,对待作者方面,解构主义强调的是互文性,而不是作者,宣布上帝已死,力图从根本上颠覆作者作为意义来源的理念。因而解构主义翻译理论否定作者的原创性,甚至否定作者的著作权;而韦努蒂的异化翻译理论承认作者的原创性和作者的著作权。

第二,在对待译者方面,解构主义翻译理论也否定译者的创造性和著作权;而韦努蒂的异化翻译理论从法律角度和伦理角度多维论证,反复强调译者的创造性和著作权也应该被承认。

第三,在对待原作方面,解构主义翻译理论"强调原文意义的相对性和不稳定性"(蒋晓华,1995),借助"互文性"否定原作的原创性;解构主义翻译理论认为,翻译与原作是一个连续体,任何文本(包括原作)都是互文本,它与其他文本有着无法割断的互文关系,后来的文本与先前的文本是一种继承与发展的关系。翻译是我们认识这种互文关系的一种简便而有效的方式:"文本大量涌现,每一个文本与先前的文本略有不同:它们都是翻译的翻译的翻译。每一个文本都有它的独特性,同时也是另一个文本的译作。任何文本都不可能是绝对的原作,因为语言本身就是一种翻译:首先是对非言语世界的翻译,其次每一个符号和每一个短语都是对另一个符号和另一个短语的翻译"(Bassnett,1990:12)。与此不同,韦努蒂的异化翻译理论承认原作的原创性(Venuti,1995:8-11)。

第四,在对待译文方面,解构主义翻译理论强调译文与原文平起平坐,认为原文因为有了译文才得以延续生命,才有了"后半生"(afterlife);译作使原作进一步超越了时空限制,扩大了原作的影响,原作对译作的依附性丝毫不亚于译作对原作的依附性。而韦努蒂的异化翻译理论在"描述译作的相对独立性的同时,仍不忘原作对它的决定性联系"(韦努蒂,2006:168)。换言之,译文有相当的独立性、创造性,但不能与原文平起平坐。

第五,在"存异"方面,解构主义翻译理论强调"存异",是因为只有"存异"才可以体现语言

符号意义的"差延"①,而体现"差延"是翻译的主要目的和意义所在(蒋晓华,1995)。换言之,译文体现了"差延",原文才能延续生命,才有"后半生"。而韦努蒂的异化翻译理论强调"存异",主要是为了消除"译者的隐形",抵制英美文化霸权,保护文化生态。

如果上述五点"本质区别"可以成立,那么,将韦努蒂的异化翻译理论归于解构主义翻译理论是不妥的。而且,从目前我们掌握的国外翻译研究文献来看,西方学者中还没有把韦努蒂的翻译异化理论归于解构主义翻译理论的。例如,根茨勒(Gentzler)在其《当代翻译理论(第二版修订本)》中认为,从翻译的政治来看,韦努蒂的"贡献是非常巨大的,因为他掀起了翻译的大辩论"(Gentzler,2001:38),但他并没将韦努蒂的异化翻译理论划归解构主义翻译理论,而只在该书的"解构主义与后殖民翻译"一节中提及韦努蒂的异化翻译理论与后殖民翻译理论的联系;在第六章中,根茨勒对解构主义翻译流派作了专门介绍,探讨了福柯(M. Foucault)、海德格尔(M. Heidegger)、

德里达(J. Derrida)等人的解构主义翻译思想,其中没有韦努蒂及其异化翻译理论。杰瑞米·曼迪(J. Munday)在其《介绍翻译研究:理论与应用》(*Introducing Translation Studies: Theories and Applications*)一书中单辟一章讨论韦努蒂的异化翻译理论,也没有将它归为解构主义流派。

因此,从总体上看,韦努蒂的异化翻译理论应该归于翻译的文化研究学派。这样归类,除了上述原因,还因为韦努蒂的异化翻译理论采用了文化研究学派在探讨翻译时所用的多维视角或"多种话语"(multiple discourses)。我们试考察以下事实:① 韦努蒂异化翻译理论之代表作《译者的隐形》主要从翻译文化史角度对 17 世纪以来的欧美翻译进行了批评性探讨,揭示了"译者隐形"的不合理性,本书涉及历史、文学、法律、语言学、政治学、翻译学等许多学科,运用了后结构主义话语(见第一、二、三、四章),西方马克思主义话语(见第一章),女性主义话语(见第四章)等。研读《译者的隐形》,我们会明显感觉到它既是翻译研究,也是文化研究。② 他的异化翻译理论与后殖民主义也有一定的联系,巴斯奈特(Bassnett,2006:158)认为韦努蒂把他的翻译理论融入后殖民语境,揭示了殖民地和宗主国之间在翻译上的不平等关系。另外,我国一些知名学者,如胡庚申(2004:33)、刘亚猛(2005)等,事实上已经将韦努蒂的异化翻译理论归于翻译的文化研究学派,刘亚猛甚至称韦努蒂是翻译的"文化研究学派的旗手"(同上)。

四、结语

应该说,韦努蒂对异化翻译的提倡和对现行著作权思想的批判,在反对欧美文化霸权,保护文化生态,提高译者和译文的文化地位方面有一定的积极意义:韦努蒂不仅把异化翻译和归化翻译作为翻译方法来研究,而且还将它们置于政治、历史和文化的大语境中来考察,这加深

---

① "差延"是德里达(Jacques Derrida)解构主义思想的核心概念。解构主义认为,任何符号都有一种基本的不完备性,即其所指意义并不能被直接把握,而且,一个符号的意义总需要别的符号形式来解释,而解释本身依靠的也是符号形式,这便又引起另一重解释。以此类推,就产生了德里达所谓的"差延"(differance),即"差异"和"延宕"现象。也就是说,符号的意义总是在拖延之中,并不存在一个终极的或原始完满的解释时刻。德里达把符号看做是"印记"(trace),符号的意义只能存在于自我差异之中,即永远的"差延"之中。"差延"是符号意义的存在方式,是"自性"(identitie)与"他性"(alteritie)的结合。例如,"僧敲月下门","敲"的含义只有在"推"、"开"、"撞"、"踢"等可能符号的意义差异中被我们基本感知到。也就是说,"敲"这个字不过是个"印记"而已,它既是自己,又不是自己,在这里,出现的和没有出现的意义,都表现在同一符号里。

了我们对翻译本质的认识;他对当今版权法压制译者与译文的现实进行批判,使我们对造成译者和译文边缘文化地位的根本原因有了更深刻的认识。但是,我们也应该警惕其负面影响:韦努蒂的异化翻译思想具有一定的反主流和反传统特征,如果译者选择在价值观或意识形态上异于主流文化的文本进行翻译,其译文可能被其社会所排斥。就我国的情况而言,语言过于异化或陌生化的译文肯定会造成大量读者的阅读和理解困难,因为现在已远非鲁迅的时代,尽管读者依然可分为“三类”,但比例已大大不同了。道格拉斯·罗宾逊曾对韦努蒂的异化翻译理论有过比较严厉的批判,认为异化翻译其实只能局限于狭小的学术圈子,并没有真正考虑普通读者的需要,韦努蒂的理论是典型的“精英主义理论”(Robinson,1997:99)。我们认为,总体上看,韦努蒂异化翻译理论的积极意义是主要的,消极影响是次要的;它的异军突起,不仅是一种文化现象,也是一种国际政治现象。

【延伸阅读】

[1] 陈小慰.韦努蒂“异化”理论话语的修辞分析.中国翻译,2010(4):5-10.
[2] 蒋童.韦努蒂的异化翻译与翻译伦理的神韵.外国语(上海外国语大学学报),2010(1):80-85.
[3] 贺显斌.韦努蒂翻译理论的局限性.外国语(上海外国语大学学报),2007(3):76-80.
[4] 刘亚猛.韦努蒂的“翻译伦理”及其自我解构.中国翻译,2005(5):10-15.
[5] 王东风.帝国的翻译暴力与翻译的文化抵抗:韦努蒂抵抗式翻译观解读.中国比较文学,2007(4):69-85.

【问题与思考】

1. 本文作者是如何从别人关于西方翻译理论的研究成果中找到研究课题的?
2. 韦努蒂异化翻译理论的内涵是什么? 本文是如何揭示的?
3. 本文作者是如何证明韦努蒂异化理论不是解构主义翻译理论的?

第八章　文化研究与翻译

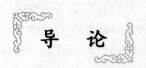

导 论

　　从 20 世纪 70 年代和 80 年代开始,翻译研究和文化研究蓬勃开展。正是翻译研究和文化研究的同时开展,使得这两股思潮相辅相成,形成合力,促使了西方翻译研究的文化转向。1990 年,翻译理论家巴斯奈特和列费维尔在其论文集《翻译、历史和文化》里,批评了各种语言学派的翻译研究,认为这些研究从以词为单位进步到以语篇为单位,但仅仅到此为止(Bass-nett & Lefevere, 1990:4)。他们还批评了那种将译本与源语文本进行费力的对比的做法,因为这种对比没有考虑文本所处的文化环境。巴斯奈特和列费维尔的研究超越了语言的界限,着重研究翻译与文化的互动、文化影响和制约翻译的方式,以及有关语境、历史和习俗的较重要的问题。他们检视由文选、评论、电影改编和翻译创造出来的文学的形象和这一创造过程所牵涉的机构。从作为语篇的翻译到作为文化和政治的翻译的转移,霍恩比(Hornby, 1990)在该论文集里称之为"文化转向"(cultural turn)。巴斯奈特和列费维尔援引"文化转向"这个术语作为文化转移的隐喻,并用它把论文集里的各种案例研究捏合在一起。《翻译、历史和文化》是一本重要的集子,标志着翻译研究的文化转向时代的开始。文化研究在多个领域都对翻译研究产生了影响,其中最重要的有三:改写式翻译、性别与翻译、后殖民主义与翻译。

　　列费维尔曾在比利时鲁文大学的比较文学系工作,后来到美国得克萨斯大学任教。他的研究受多元系统理论和操纵学派影响较大。他后期关于翻译和文化的著作在许多方面都代表着文化转向的一个连接点。他的观点在其专著《翻译、改写和文学名声的操控》里面得到最为充分的阐发。列费维尔特别检视了系统地制约文学文本的接收、接受或拒绝的"很具体的因素",研究了诸如权力、意识形态、制度和操控等问题。在他看来,身处这些权力位置的人们改写了文学,并制约了文学的大众消费。改写的动力有意识形态方面的或诗学方面的。列费维尔认为,在翻译、史料编纂、选集编纂、批评和编辑领域,相同的改写过程正在进行当中。翻译是最明显的、最容易辨识的一种改写。它具有最大的潜在的影响力,因为它能够把作者及其作品的形象投射到源语文化的界限之外(Lefevere, 1992a:9)。在文学系统内部,翻译受到三种主要因素的控制:文学系统内部的专业人士、文学系统外部的赞助和主流诗学。

　　翻译的文化研究不可避免地使翻译研究脱离了纯粹的语言分析,转而与其他学科有了接触。但是这种学科杂合化的过程不总是直截了当的。西蒙(Sherry Simon)在其专著《翻译中的性别:文化身份和传播的政治》(1996)中批评翻译研究常常使用"文化"这个术语就好像该术语指的是明显的、毫无问题的现实。比如列费维尔(1985:226)就曾简单地把"文化"定义为"文学系统的环境"。西蒙从性别研究的角度研究翻译。她观察到翻译研究中反映性别歧视的语言。典型的例子是 17 世纪的美而不忠实的法语译本被称为"忠实的美人"。女性主义理论家们注意到,翻译常常被视为低原文一等,其地位与在社会上和文学里面受压制的女性的地位相同。试图识别和批判把妇女和翻译降到社会和文学阶梯的最底层的混乱概念正是女性主义翻译理论的核心。西蒙十分强调翻译的文化转向的重要性,她认为,文化转向给翻译带来的是对性别和文化的复杂性的理解,它使我们得以把语言转换放置在当今多种带"后"字的现实中:后结构主义、后殖民主义和后现代主义(1996:136)。

后殖民主义翻译理论的代表人物之一是斯皮瓦克(Chakravorty Spivak),她的名著《翻译的政治》表明了文化研究尤其是后殖民主义是如何关注翻译和殖民等问题的。她认为,在殖民过程中,在散播有意识形态动机的被殖民民族的形象的过程中,翻译发挥了积极作用。翻译研究与后殖民主义理论的主要交集在于对权力关系的研究。后殖民主义翻译理论的另一代表人物尼兰贾纳(Niranjana),在其专著 *Siting Translation:History,Poststructurism,and the Colonial Context* 中指出,语言、种族之间的不平等体现了权力关系的不平等。殖民的主体历史是权力与知识实践的历史,翻译作为话语实践,是帝国权力控制和生产的场所。翻译为殖民者所用,为其支撑起一个话语系统、概念体系,并强化了殖民的霸权行径。

本章共选四篇文章。第一篇是 André Lefevere 撰写的"On Translation, Rewriting and the Manipulation of Literary Fame",以著名的《安妮日记》为个案,分析阐述了意识形态对改写的制约。第二篇"The Politics of Translation",作者是 Gayatri Chakravorty Spivak,该文从后结构主义、女性主义、后殖民主义三方面引导读者思考语言内部结构张力与语际文化张力、导致翻译的政治发生的机制等问题。第三篇是 Sherry Simon 著的"Gender in Translation",文章研究了性别意识在翻译研究中的应用,探讨了性别角色的差异及其在语言中的体现和表达方式。第四篇是李红玉撰写的《斯皮瓦克翻译思想探究》,该文全面考察了斯皮瓦克有关翻译的论述,从多个方面展现了斯皮瓦克翻译思想的丰富内涵。

 选 文

选文一 On Translation，Rewriting and the Manipulation of Literary Fame（Excerpt）

André Lefevere

导 言

本文选自列费维尔著《翻译、改写以及对文学名声的控制》(*On Translation，Rewriting and the Manipulation of Literary Fame*)第五章"Translation:Ideology——On the Construction of Different Anne Franks"。

比利时翻译理论家安德烈·列费维尔(1945—1996)是文化学派的代表人物之一,他著述

丰厚，涉及比较文学和翻译理论。他把翻译置于文化的大背景下进行考察，关注文化语境、历史、规范等更为宏大的课题，指出翻译不仅仅是语言层面上的转换，更是译者对原作进行的文化层面的改写。本文选自其代表作《翻译、改写以及对文学名声的控制》第五章。本文阐述的是意识形态对改写的制约，所举例子是著名的《安妮日记》。《安妮日记》是一位出生在德国的犹太少女安妮·弗兰克在荷兰被德国占领的两年期间写下的自我经历和其成长过程。这本书由于涉及历史政治原因，在不同时代、不同国家出版就有一些不同的变化。书中给出了大量实例，重点讨论了德文版翻译的诸多问题，以此论证了翻译受到的限制，包括译者本人的观点、意识形态以及赞助者。这些例子都具有相当浓厚的文化色彩和时代代表性，令读者在学习理论的同时，能够领略国与国之间文化差异的独特魅力。

There are all kinds of statements in Anne Frank's diary that make it obvious that she wanted to be a writer and that she wanted her diary published after World War Two, long before Bolkestein, a minister in the Dutch cabinet in exile in London, broadcast a message to the occupied Netherlands over the BBC, urging his countrymen "to make a collection of diaries and letters after the war" (Paape 162). That collection was made, and it has since grown into the "Rijksinstituut voor Oorlogsdocumentatie," or State Institute for War Documentation, which published the most complete edition of the *Dagboeken van Anne Frank* (*Anne Frank's Diaries*) forty-four years after the Bolkestein broadcast.

A comparison between the original, 1947 Dutch edition of the diary and the material collected in the 1986 edition gives us insight into the process of "construction" of an image of the writer, both by herself and by others. A further comparison between the Dutch original and the German translation sheds light on the "construction" of the image of a writer who belongs to one culture in—and especially for—another.

I shall quote only one of the many statements in the diary attesting Anne Frank's ambition to become a writer or, at least, a journalist: "I have other ideas as well, besides *Het Achterhuis*. But I will write more fully about them some other time, when they have taken a clearer form in my mind" (Mooyaart-Doubleday 194). This, at least, is in the English translation of the Dutch text as published in 1947. The corresponding entry (for May 11, 1944) in the original diaries, first published in the 1986 Dutch edition, also contains a detailed plot for a short story entitled "Cady's Life" and based on the life of Anne's father, Otto Frank (Paape 661). The short story had already "taken a clearer form" in Anne Frank's mind and was probably suppressed by Otto, or by Contact, the publisher of the 1947 Dutch edition.

When it became clear to Anne that the diary could, and should be published, she began to rewrite it. The original entries were made in notebooks; the rewritten version was produced on loose-leaf paper. Anne Frank was unable to finish the rewriting. Both the notebooks and the loose-leaf version were recovered by Miep, one of the Dutch employees of the Frank firm who helped the Franks and others to hide out in the *Achterhuis*. Miep discovered the material after the German Sicherheitsdienst had arrested the Franks and their friends, and taken them away (see Paape 69 – 88).

Anne Frank's own rewriting of the entries in the original diary amounts to a kind of "auto-editing." In editing herself she seems to have had two objectives in mind, one personal and the other literary. On the personal level, she disclaims earlier statements, especially about her mother, "Anne, is it really you who mentioned hate? Oh, Anne, how could you?" (Mooyaart-Doubleday 112), and about more intimate subjects: "I am really ashamed when I read those pages that deal with subjects I prefer to imagine more beautiful" (Paape 321). The entry for January 2, 1944, signals a turning away from the personal and toward the literary: "This diary is of great value to me, because it has become a book of memoirs in many places, but on a good many pages I could certainly put 'past and done with'" (Mooyaart-Doubleday 112). What is "past and done with" on the personal level becomes material for the literary rewrite.

An obvious example of "literary" editing is the description of one of Anne's encounters with Peter, the boy whose parents share the Franks' hiding place and who becomes Anne's first real love. The original entry reads: "As I sat almost in front of his feet" (Paape 504). The rewritten entry (for February 14, 1944) reads: "I ... went and sat on a cushion on the floor, put my arms around my bent knees and looked at him attentively" (Mooyaart-Doubleday132). The "edited" pose is much more in keeping with what Anne must have seen in the movie magazines she so avidly read. It is a very close approximation of the pose her culture expects the young heroine (in the theatre or film version of *The Life of Anne Frank*, for instance) to assume. It is a Universe-of-Discourse element (one might even say cliché) consciously inserted into the text.

An example of more consciously literary editing occurs in the entry for May 13, 1944. The original entry mentions a tree "stuck full of leaves" (Paape 662); the rewritten entry has the phrase, which amounts to a literary cliché in Dutch, "loaded down with leaves" (Paape 662). The most obvious example of literary editing is represented by the decision to change the names of all those who have, since January 2, 1944, become "characters" in a "story." Anne Frank obviously thought this a necessary strategy for the "book entitled *Het Achterhuis*" (she is most definitely not referring to it as a "diary") she "wanted to publish ... after the war" (Mooyaart-Doubleday 194). Consequently, Anne Frank appears as "Anne Robin" in the loose-leaf version.

Anne Frank was not the only editor of Anne Frank's diary, however. When Otto Frank, her father, came back to Amsterdam after the war, he was given both the notebook and the loose-leaf versions of the diary. He produced a typescript of the material in German, and sent it to his mother in Switzerland, who could not read Dutch. This typescript apparently vanished later on, but Otto Frank produced a second typescript which was to become the textual basis of the 1947 Dutch edition of the diary, and of the translations made into many languages since. A comparison between the original material now available in the

1986 *Dagboeken* and the 1947 Dutch edition merely shows that editing has taken place. It does not show who actually edited what over and beyond Anne Frank's own "auto-edits," which stop when the family was arrested and taken away.

Otto Frank tried to get his daughter's diary published after the war, both in the Netherlands and in Germany. He tried a few Dutch publishers and was eventually successful. Contact, one of the Dutch publishing houses, agreed to publish the typescript, but on condition that changes be made. Since Otto Frank had already made some changes of his own, and since Anne Frank had rewritten most of the original entries, the difference between the original material and the published version is like a palimpsest. It is pointless to speculate as to who changed what, but it is possible, and enlightening, to draw up a topology of the changes made. These can be said to belong to three categories: Some changes are of a personal nature, some are ideological, and some belong in the sphere of patronage.

On the "personal" level, details of no possible importance to anyone are omitted. Also on that level, "unflattering" references to friends, acquaintances, or indeed members of the family are omitted as well. The description of all of Anne's classmates (Paape 207) has disappeared from the 1947 edition, as have references to her mother and "Mrs Van Daan." Anne tells her father that she loves him much more than she loves her mother (Paape 284), and Mrs Van Daan, whose real name, preserved in the first draft of the diary, was "Van Pels," is accused of greed (Paape 240) and overeating (Paape 282). Yet many unflattering references to both women remain in the 1947 edition, which leaves the reader a litter puzzled as to the criteria for editing that were followed. There may well not have been any, except for the desire to protect people's reputations. This desire continues to manifest itself in the 1986 Dutch edition, which is still not complete.

On page 449 of the 1986 edition, for instance, we are told in a footnote that "Anne Frank gives a very unfriendly and partly inaccurate description of her parents' marriage in the 47 lines that have been omitted here. This passage has been deleted at the request of the Frank family." The personal obviously interferes with the literary. Or, if you wish, the editors decide to bend to one kind of ideological constraint.

Lines that may have been important for the (auto-) construction of the character "Anne Robin" have been omitted so as not to give the impression that the writer Anne Frank did not entirely correspond to the ideologically sanctioned image of what a fourteen-year-old should be—at the time she was writing the diary. Similarly, unflattering references to the personal life of "M. K.," an acquaintance of the Franks who seems to have collaborated with the Germans and given promiscuously of her person, are omitted: "24 words have been deleted at the request of the person in question" (Paape 647). Moreover, as we are informed on the same page, the initials M. K. were chosen at random because the person did not want her own initials used.

References to bodily functions of all kinds have also been omitted, as has a rather graphic description of a case of hemorrhoids (Paape 282). Like many persons her age, Anne

Frank appears to have been more than somewhat interested in bodily functions, especially defecation, because defecation was for a while associated in her mind with the birth of children, witness the description of defecation in a children's book called Eva's *jeugd*, which she quotes at some length (Paape 285).

In the original version of the diary, Anne Frank keeps addressing (imaginary) letters to various friends left behind in the "real" world for a few weeks after the Frank family went into hiding. The letters are "imaginary" in that they were written, but could never be sent. These letters represent a marked deviation from the original intention of the diary as Anne Frank herself conceived it. Originally the diary was to take the place of the "really good girl friend" Anne Frank never had. This is also the reason why (nearly) all entries in the diary were written in the form of letters and addressed to "Kitty," the name Anne Frank had given her diary/imaginary friend. The letters that have been omitted suggest that Kitty was not enough, at least not initially, and that Anne Frank/Robin found it much more difficult to adapt to the sudden cataclysmic change in her life than is implied by the 1947 edition. In these letters she continues to act as if communication between herself and the real friends she had left behind in the world outside is still possible, much as it was before the Franks went into hiding. She even writes to a friend called "Conny" that "you are welcome to stay with me for a while" (Paape 267). Fantasies about life after the war (Paape 301) and, especially, a trip to Switzerland with her father, which point in the same "escapist" direction, have also been omitted from the Dutch 1947 edition.

The topic of sex acts as a link between the "personal" and the "ideological" edits. Meulenhoff, the first Dutch publisher to evaluate the manuscript of Anne Frank's diary for publication, refused to publish it because of "the very personal nature of the diary and the sexual musings it contains" (Paape 78). Similarly, De Neve, an editor at Contact, told Otto Frank that "spiritual advisers objected to the printing of certain passages (about masturbation, for instance)" (Paape 80). As may be expected, the "sexual musings," referred to are mainly concerned with Anne Frank's own awakening sexuality. They consist of a description of a discharge in her underwear preceding the onset of menstruation (Paape 286), of menstruation itself (Paape 304, 598), of her genitals (Paape 294, 583 – 584), of different strategies used to find out about sex without having to ask grown-ups (Paape 562, 576)—of all the elements, in short, that would fit the "heroine" of any "Life of Anne Frank" published from the sixties onwards, but not the heroine of the diary published in 1947.

It is of course also possible that the person Anne Frank may indeed have been "really ashamed" when she (re-) "read those pages" (Paape 321) , and that she herself may have omitted them in the loose-leaf version. They have been omitted in any case, as has Bep/Elli's story about an unwed mother (Paape 305) and the "dirty words" like "bordeel" (brothel) and "cocotte" Anne picked up from her reading (Paape 305). Finally, in the original diary Pfeffer (whose name is changed to "Dussel" in the loose-leaf version) "lives together with a Gentile woman, much younger than he is, and nice, and he is probably not married to her"

(Paape 320). In the first published version of the diary, Dussel's wife "was fortunate enough to be out of the country when war broke out" (Mooyaart-Doubleday 51).

Another edit involving both the personal and the ideological concerns the Goldsmith/Goudsmit affair. Goldsmith was a lodger in the Franks' house in Amsterdam. After the Frank family went into hiding, they left him more or less in charge of their possessions. In the passages that have been omitted from the 1947 edition (Paape 256, 309). Anne Frank hints heavily at the probability that Goldsmith sold or otherwise disposed of the Frank possessions to his own advantage. These passages may have been omitted out of an unwillingness on the part of the Frank family to admit that they had been deceived, or out of a sense of solidarity, even piety, among the victims of the Holocaust.

The most obviously ideological omissions are those of the passages Anne Frank wrote on the problem of the emancipation of women. The longest passage, introduced by the question "Why woman occupies a position so much lower than man's among the nations" (Paape 692), is deleted in its entirety, and further passing references to the topic are either weakened or deleted.

Finally, it is obvious that Otto Frank bowed to constraints in the sphere of patronage, and it is also obvious that he had no other choice. The typescript of Anne Frank's diary had to conform to the specifications laid down by Contact, the publishing house, for its "Proloog" series, of which the diary would be a part. As a result, Contact's editor (s?) "proposed 26 deletions, 18 of which were indeed carried out in the typescript" (Paape 82).

Anne Frank (perhaps the time has come to call her "Anne Frank") is subjected to further transformations in the German translation of her diary. That translation, based on Otto Frank's (second) typescript, was made early on by Anneliese Schütz, a friend of the Frank family. Anneliese Schütz was a journalist who had emigrated to the Netherlands to escape from the Nazis, just as the Franks had. Since Otto Frank was trying to publish the composite material labeled with his daughter's name, either in the Netherlands or in Germany, it stood to reason that he would allow a friend to translate his typescript into German, so that it could be offered to publishers in Germany. Anneliese Schütz translated from a typescript that had not yet been edited by the Contact editor(s), which is why the German translation contains references to sexuality which had been removed from the Dutch 1947 edition, and which were later inserted back into the English translation.

The "notorious" passage in which "Anne Frank" asks a girl friend (identified by name in the original entry) "whether, as proof of our friendship, we should feel one another's breasts" (Mooyaart-Doubleday 114) therefore appears in both the German and the English translations, but not in the Dutch 1947 original, nor in the French translation, which is entirely based on that original.

Otto Frank's evaluation of Anneliese Schütz's translation is, unfortunately, accurate. He states that she was "too old to do it, many expressions are schoolmarmish and not in the tone of youth. She has also misunderstood many Dutch expressions" (Paape 84). Among the most obvious are: "ogenschijnlijk" (Paape 201) [seemingly], which is translated as "eigentlich" [really] (Schütz 10); "daar zit hem de knoop" [something like "there's the rub," literally, "there sits the knot"] (Paape 201) becomes "ich bin wie zugeknöpft [I feel as if I'm buttoned up] (Schütz 10)." Zulke uilen"[such idiots] (Paape 215)is turned into" solche Faulpelze [such lazy people] (Schütz 12); "Ongerust" [worried] (Paape 307) becomes "unruhig" [restless] (Schütz 39). "Rot" [rotten] (Paape 372) is rendered by "rötlich" [reddish] (Schütz 64), a typical elementary classroom howler. "Rataplan" [the whole kit and caboodle] (Paape 402) becomes "Rattennest" [rat's nest] (Schütz 78). "Ik zat op springen" [I was about to explode] (Paape 529)is turned into "Ich wäre ihr am liebsten ins Gesicht gesprungen" [I would have loved to have jumped into her face] (Schütz 90). *Springen* can mean both "explode" and "jump" in Dutch, as it can in German too. Schütz opted for the homonym that does not fit the context. "Wat los en vastzit" [what is loose and what is secured] (Paape 595) turns into "Was nicht niet-und nagelfest ist" [what is not secured and fastened down] (Schütz 147), and "de landen die aan Duitsland grenzen" [the countries bordering on Germany—"grenzen" is a verb] (Paape 669) becomes "die an Deutschlands Grenzen" [those at Germany's borders—"Grenzen" is a plural noun] (Schütz 180).

As if more proof were needed, the Schütz translation once again illustrates the fact that publishers rarely care overmuch about the quality of the translation of any manuscript that either might not sell (as the Lambert Schneider Verlag, which published the *Tagebuch* in hardcover in 1950, may have thought) or sells very well (as the same publisher and, especially, the Fischer Verlag, which published the first paperback edition, must have thought after 1955). The fact that the Schütz translation was and is reprinted time and again also points to another institutional constraint: the pernicious influence of copyright laws which, in this case, even embarrasses the publisher. The most recent editions of the *Tagebuch* contain a note in which the publisher apologizes in veiled terms for the inferior quality of the translation and promises to issue a better translation as soon as legally possible.

The most famous of Schütz's "mistranslations" is that of the Dutch "er bestaat geen groter vijandschap op de wereld dan tussen Duitsers en Joden" [there is no greater enmity in the world than between Germans and Jews] (Paape 292), which is translated as: "eine grössere Feindschaft als zwischen *diesen* Deutschen und den Juden gibt es nicht auf der Welt !" [there is no greater enmity in the world than between *these* Germans and the Jews] (Schütz 37). The editors of the 1986 Dutch edition comment: "Otto Frank discussed this sentence with Anneliese Schütz and they came to the conclusion that '*diesen* Deutschen' corresponded more closely to what Anne had wanted to say" (Paape 85). This "mistranslation" is only one among many that have been made for reasons best described as ideological—a mixture of a more old-fashioned "ideology" based on a certain view of the world, and the more contemporary "ideology" of profit pure and simple. In Anneliese Schütz's own words: "A book you want to sell well in Germany ... should not contain any insults directed at Germans" (Paape 86).

Schütz translates accordingly and tones down all instances of descriptions of Germans in Anne Frank's diary that could be construed as "insulting." As a result, the plight of the Jews in the Netherlands is, correspondingly, made to appear less harsh than it actually was. "Jodenwet volgde op Jodenwet" [one Jewish law followed the other] (Paape 203) is turned into "ein diktatorisches Gesetz folgte dem anderen" [one dictatorial law followed another] (Schütz 11), as if these laws had little or nothing to do with the Jews. The details of these laws, the terminology they were expressed in, are also hushed up. Where Anne Frank says her family had to leave Germany because they were "volbloed Joden" [full-blooded Jews] (Paape 202), Schütz translates simply: "Als Juden" [as Jews] (10).

When Otto Frank has given his wife's bicycle "bij Christen mensen in bewaring" [to Gentiles for safekeeping] (Paape 218), Schütz simply writes: "bei Bekannten" [to acquaintances] (14), thus obscuring the very distinct boundaries the Nazis wanted to draw between Jews and Gentiles all over Europe. When Mrs Van Daan "keerde terug en begon te kijven, hard, Duits, gemeen en onbeschaafd" [came back and began to scold, harsh, German, mean and uncivilized] (Paape 274), "German," used here as an adjective to convey a further insult, is left out in Schütz (34).

Anne Frank's description (based on hearsay) of Westerbork, the German concentration camp in the Netherlands from where Jews were shipped "East," as the current euphemism would have it, is weakened in a similar way. Anne Frank writes: "voor honderden mensen I wasruimte en er zijn veel te weinig WC's. De slaapplaatsen zijn alle door elkaar gegooid" [I washroom for hundreds of people, and there are far too few toilets. The sleeping spaces have all been thrown together] (Paape 290). Schütz has: "viel zu wenig Waschgelegenheiten und WC's vorhanden. Es wird erzählt, dass in den Baracken alles durcheinander schläft" [far too few washing facilities and toilets available. It is said that they all sleep together in the barracks] (36 – 37). The translation suggests that there are more washrooms than just the one of the original, and the impact of the "sleeping together" in a disorderly fashion is weakened by the addition of "it is said."

The rest of the description, concerning the consequences of the state of affairs just mentioned, is simply omitted in the translation. Anne Frank writes on: "men hoort daardoor van verre-gaande zedeloosheid, vele vrouwen en meisjes, die er wat langer verblijf houden, zijn in verwachting" [therefore you hear of far-reaching immorality; many women and girls who stay there for a longer period of time are pregnant] (Paape 290). If this fact is not mentioned in the translation, the Germans, whose families and descendants are supposed to read the *Tagebuch*, also, quite logically, did not gas any pregnant women or girls in Auschwitz.

In the diary, Anne Frank is very upset by the German policy of shooting hostages, which she describes as follows: "zet de Gestapo doodgewoon een stuk of 5 gijzelaars tegen de muur" [the Gestapo simply puts 5 hostages or so against the wall] (Paape 292). The translation weakens this to "dann hat man einen Grund, eine Anzahl dieser Geiseln zu erschiessen" [they then have a reason to shoot a number of these hostages] (Schütz 37). "[T] hey" instead of the dreaded "Gestapo" makes the description seem somewhat less terrible, and "shoot" instead of "puts against the wall" "elevates" the act to a more abstract level.

Similarly, the person who might discover the secret entrance to the place where Anne and her family are hiding, grows in Anne's imagination into "een reus en hij was zo'n fascist als er geen ergere bestaat" [a giant, and he was such a fascist, no worse exists] (Paape 298). In German, the person has simply become "einen unüberwindlichen Riesen" [an unconquerable giant] (Schütz 39). The "fascist" has disappeared from the German text so as not to depress its sales. An analogous omission occurs in the translation of Anne Frank's statement on the languages spoken in the hideout: "toegestaan zijn alle cultuurtalen, dus geen Duits" [all civilized languages are allowed, so no German] (Paape 330). The German translation reads: "alle Kultursprachen, aber leise" [all civilized languages, but softly] (Schütz 46).

Anneliese Schütz uses omission to further political (and economic) advantage. Where Anne Frank writes: "de Moffen niet ter ore komen" [not come to the ears of the Krauts] (Paape 490), the German translation reads: "den 'Moffen' nicht zu Ohren kommen" [not to come to the ears of the "Moffen"] (Schütz 114). A footnote explains "Moffen" as a Spottname für die Deutschen [abusive name for the Germans] (Schütz 114). "Mof," plural "Moffen," was indeed the wartime "abusive name" for the Germans. In the Dutch text, therefore, "Moffen" has quite an impact on the reader. That impact is undercut in German simply by the non-translation of the term. To a German reader, "Moffen" tends to sound "exotic," even when supplemented by a footnote, and not really insulting.

Not coincidentally the mean, aggressive cat in the warehouse is called "Moffi" by the inhabitants of the hideout. German readers, who either do not know what a "Mof" is until they reach page 114, and/or think of "Mof" as exotic after they have been enlightened, are likely to miss the point of the insult. Logically, the "moffen" live in "Moffrika" (Paape 695), which Schütz leaves untranslated. It becomes "Bocheland" in English (Mooyaart-Doubleday 210) and "les Boches" in French (Carenand Lombard 269). The cat duly becomes "Bochi" in French (Caren and Lombard 91) and "Boche" in English (Mooyaart-Doubleday 68).

The English translation sometimes tries to convey the fact that the Franks and the others in hiding with them, all being German refugees, did not really speak standard Dutch but rather a mixture of Dutch and German, more Dutch than German in the case of the children, more German than Dutch where the parents are concerned. This mixture of languages helps to highlight the fact that the "characters" in the diary are people who have already been uprooted once and are now hiding from their former countrymen in mortal fear of their lives. None of this is conveyed by the German translation. Dussel, for instance, says in the original: "*Du kannst dies* toch van mij aannemen. Het kan mij natuurlijk niets schelen, *aber Du musst* het zelf weten" [(German italicized) *You can* take *this* from me. It does not matter to me, of course, *but you must* know for yourself] (Paape 412). Mooyaart-Doubleday, the English translator, tries: "But d*u kannst* take this from me. Naturally I don't care a bit, *aber du* must know for yourself" (94).

Neither the German nor the French translator makes any attempt at all to render the mixture of languages. In fact, Schütz scales the heights of absurdity by "translating" Dussel's next "macaronic" statement, "ich mach das schon" [I'll take care of it] (Paape 502) as "Ich weiss schon was ich tue" [I know what I'm doing] (118).

Yet political, or politico-economic features are responsible for one set of changes only. There is another set of changes in the German text, also caused by ideological motivations, but of a less obvious, more insidious nature. Schütz consciously or unconsciously turns Anne Frank into the cultural stereotype of the "proper" young adolescent girl of a time that had not yet invented the teenager, "properly educated" as befits her social status, presumably to make her more acceptable to a fifties audience.

First, Schütz "cleans up" Anne Frank's language. Her friend Harry, for instance, will not be allowed to say in German what he says in Dutch. Whereas the Dutch Harry says: "Het is daar ook zo'n rommelzootje" [it's such a mess there] (Paape 221), the German Harry "echoes": "gefiel es mir da nicht" [I did not like it there] (Schütz 15). People who complain about their defecation ("ontlasting" [Paape 269]) in Dutch complain about their digestion ("Verdauung" [Schütz 32]) in German.

After a bombing raid on Amsterdam, Anne Frank writes that it will take days before all the victims have been dug up ("opgegraven" [Paape 389]). In German, the victims are "geborgen" [recovered] (Schütz 72) in a much more decorous way, which also takes the sting out of the horror. The chamber pot Anne Frank takes with her to the bathroom in the Dutch original (Paape 339) vanishes in German. It remains quite sensibly "pot de nuit" in French (Caren and Lombard 116) and becomes "pottie" in English (Mooyaart-Doubleday 88). When Dussel begins "vrouwen-verlangens te krijgen" in Dutch [get a desire for women] (Paape 679), he gets much more decorous "Frühlingsgefühle" [Spring feelings] (Schütz 184) in German. The German translation also completely leaves out Anne Frank's rather elaborate description of the way Mouschi, Peter's cat, urinates in the attic.

Second, Anne Frank has to behave "properly" for a child her age. She has to conform to what is considered proper cultural behavior for the upper-middle-class fourteen-year-old, even if that kind of "proper behavior" has been made less than a little ridiculous by the war and the living conditions in the hideout. When the Dutch Anne Frank is allowed to "lachen tot ik er buikpijn van krijg" [laugh until I get a bellyache] (Paape 446), the German Anne Frank is only allowed to do what German children do when they laugh, at least according to Anneliese Schütz: "unbeschwert und glücklich lachen" [laugh without a care and happily] (98).

The Dutch Anne Frank successfully accomplishes the following task: "uit een lichtblauwe onderjurk met kant van Mansa heb ik een hypermoderne dansjurk vervaardigd" [from one of Mansa's (mother's) light-blue slips with lace I made a hypermodern dancing dress] (Paape 469). The German Anne Frank has her mother do the same thing for her: "aus einem hellblauen Spitzenkleid hat Mansa mir ein hypermodernes Tanzkleid gemacht" [Mansa made me a hypermodern dance dress from a light-blue slip with lace of hers] (Schütz 107).

There are other things a young girl, German or not, of Anne Frank's age and social status is not supposed to know or do. When Anne Frank describes the flowers she gets for her birthday as "de kinderen van Flora" [the children of Flora] (Paape 198), thereby displaying her knowledge of mythology, which is one of her hobbies, Schütz will have none of this precocious namedropping; in German, Anne Frank gets "Blumengrüsse" [flower greetings] (Schütz 19).

No effort is made to reproduce in German any of the stylistic effects Anne Frank tries to achieve in Dutch, as she does in the following example by means of the repetition of the word "koud" (cold). In Dutch, children walk "van hun koude woning weg naar de koude straat en komen op school in een nog koudere klas" [from their cold home to the cold street to end up in an even colder classroom at school] (Paape 349). In German, the children walk "aus der kalten Wohnung auf die nasse, windige Strasse und kommen in die Schule, in eine feuchte, ungeheizte Klasse" [from their cold home to the wet, windy street and they arrive at school in a damp, unheated classroom] (Schütz 54).

Fourteen-year-old girls are also not allowed to sit in judgment on their mothers or elder sisters. Anne Frank writes in Dutch that she would never be satisfied with "zo'n bekrompen leventje" [such a limited life] (Paape 650) as her mother and Margot, her elder sister, seem willing to settle for. The German Anne Frank, on the other hand writes "so ein einfaches Leben" [such a simple life] (Schütz 172). Finally, with a relentless logic that borders on the grotesque and should, properly speaking, render the whole of Anne Frank's endeavor useless or, at best, superfluous, the girls Anneliese Schütz models her Anne Frank on are not even supposed to keep diaries. Anne Frank writes in Dutch that there are certain things she does not intend "aan iemand anders mee te delen dan aan mijn dagboek, en een enkele keer aan Margot" [to communicate to anyone else but my diary, and once in a while to Margot] (Paape 705). In German, Anne Frank writes that she has things she is determined to "niemals jemandem mitzuteilen, höchstens einmal Margot" [never communicate to anyone, at the most once in a while to Margot] (Schütz 196). The diary, the object of the exercise, the text read all over the world, simply vanishes from the translation, sacrificed to the "image" of Anne Frank the German translator wishes to project.

"Proper" girls also write in a "proper" style. Creativity is actively discouraged in the German translation. When Anne Frank writes, "we zijn zo stil als babymuisjes" [we are as quiet as baby mice] (Paape 279), the German translation reads "wirverhalten uns sehr ruhig" [we are very quiet] (Schütz 35). When a bag of beans suspended against the door of the attic bursts, spilling its contents and leaving Anne standing "als een eilandje tussen de bonengolven" [like a small island among waves of beans] (Paape 318), the translation simply describes her as "berieselt von braunen Bohnen" [bedrizzled by brown beans] (Schütz 43).

When the Jews are led to "onzindelijke slachtplaatsen" [dirty slaughterhouses] (Paape 368), the "dirty" obviously has to disappear from the German translation, in which the Jews are simply "zur Schlachtbank geführt" [led to the slaughter bench] (Schütz 62). Finally, when the inhabitants of the hideout "kijken met bange voorgevoelens tegen het grote rotsblok, dat Winter heer, op" [look up at the big rock called Winter with fearful apprehension] (Paape 422), they simply "sehen mit grosser Sorge dem Winter entgegen" [look ahead at Winter with great worry] (Schütz 90).

The girl Anne Frank writing her diary has become the author Anne Frank because she herself and others were constrained by ideological, poetological, and patronage considerations. Once Anne Frank took the decision to rewrite for publication what Anne Frank had written, the person Anne Frank split up into a person and an author, and the author began to rewrite in a more literary manner what the person had written. Others responded to the constraints of ideology and patronage in her stead, and they did so as they saw fit. She had no say in the matter. That is why part of her experience, very definitely a formative part, is missing from the 1947 Dutch text, and why she has been made to conform, in German, to a cultural stereotype and made to water down the description of the very atrocities which destroyed her as a person.

【延伸阅读】

[1] Lefevere, A. (1985). Why Waste Our Time on Rewrites?: The Trouble with Interpretation and the Role of Rewriting in an Alternative Paradigm. In T. Hermans (ed.), *The Manipulation of Literature: Studies in Literary Translation*. Beckengan: Croom Helm.

[2] Lefevere, A. (1992). *Translation, Rewriting and the Manipulation of Literary Fame*. London and New York: Routledge.

[3] Lefevere, A. (1993). *Translating Literature: Practice and Theory in a Comparative Literature Context*. New York: The Modern Language Association of America.

【问题与思考】

1. 影响《安妮日记》的翻译的主要文化因素是什么？
2. 意识形态在《安妮日记》出版和翻译过程中起了怎样的作用？
3. 《安妮日记》的德文版与英文版有何差异？如何看待这些差异？
4. 如何通过学习本文来正确理解列费维尔的改写理论？

选文二　The Politics of Translation

Gayatri Chakravorty Spivak

导　言

《翻译的政治》一文以"翻译就是阅读"、"广义翻译"、"阅读就是翻译"三段式论述构建全文,从后结构主义、女性主义、后殖民主义三方面引导读者思考语言内部结构张力与语际文化张力、导致翻译的政治发生的机制、狭义的与广义的翻译的政治等问题。

斯皮瓦克从后结构主义出发,总结出语言内部存在"三层结构"——"修辞"、"逻辑"、"静默"。殖民、经济差异等导致的文化政治也是催生翻译的政治的重要因素,"翻译腔"现象就是语言理解不足、盲目迎合强势文化的典型印证。就译者而言,她们应"完全服帖于原文"和"具备对源语言场地的鉴别能力"来穷尽修辞的目的义和探索文本的"静默"的实现过程。在广义翻译方面,斯皮瓦克暗示了它与狭义翻译的区别主要在于,广义翻译所涉及的文本不存在另一个对等的传达对象。转换的两种语言中的一种凭借文化或民族影响力的优势压制了另一种语言,殖民暴力以及单纯的逻辑转化引发翻译的政治。在这里,某种绝对的语言权威导致了翻译的不可能性、修辞的偶发性相对较高,涉及的文化翻译背景也相对较多。

翻译的政治关注更多的是文化、权力层面差异所引起的语言间的不平等地位。从斯皮瓦克的论述中可以领悟到:不同语言文化具有差异,翻译行为会使源语与目标语两种语言文化在碰撞、交融的过程中产生一种或明或暗的、不对等的关系。

The idea for this title comes from Michèle Barrett's feeling that the politics of translation takes on a massive life of its own if you see language as the process of meaning construction. [①]

In my view, language may be one of many elements that allow us to make sense of things, of ourselves. I am thinking, of course, of gestures, pauses, but also of chance, of the sub-individual force-fields of being which click into place in different situations, swerve from the straight or true line of language-in-thought. Making sense of ourselves is what produces identity. If one feels that the production of identity as self-meaning, not just meaning, is as pluralized as a drop of water under a microscope, one is not always satisfied, outside of the ethicopolitical arena as such, with "generating" thoughts on one's own. (Assuming identity as origin may be unsatisfactory in the ethico-political arena as well, but consideration of that now would take us too far afield.) One of the ways to get around the confines of one's "identity" as one produces expository prose is to work at someone else's title, as one works

---

① The first part of this essay is based on a conversation with Michèle Barrett in the summer of 1990.

with a language that belongs to many others. This, after all, is one of the seductions of translating. It is a simple miming of the responsibility to the trace of the other in the self.

Responding, therefore, to Michèle with that freeing sense of responsibility, I can agree that it is not bodies of meaning that are transferred in translation. And from the ground of that agreement I want to consider the role played by language for the *agent*, the person who acts, even though intention is not fully present to itself. The task of the feminist translator is to consider language as a clue to the workings of gendered agency. The writer is written by her language, of course. But the writing of the writer writes agency in a way that might be different from that of the British woman/citizen with the history of British feminism, focused on the task of freeing herself from Britain's imperial past, its often racist present, as well as its "made in Britain" history of male domination.

Translation as reading

How does the translator attend to the specificity of the language she translates? There is a way in which the rhetorical nature of every language disrupts its logical systematicity. If we emphasize the logical at the expense of these rhetorical interferences, we remain safe. "Safety" *is* the appropriate term here, because we are talking of risks, of violence to the translating medium.

I felt that I was taking those risks when I recently translated some late eighteenth-century Bengali poetry. I quote a bit from my "Translator's Preface:"

> I must overcome what I was taught in school: the highest mark for the most accurate collection of synonyms, strung together in the most proximate syntax. I must resist both the solemnity of chaste Victorian poetic prose and the forced simplicity of "plain English," that have imposed themselves as the norm ... Translation is the most intimate act of reading. I surrender to the text when I translate. These songs, sung day after day in family chorus before clear memory began, have a peculiar intimacy for me. Reading and surrendering take on new meanings in such a case. The translator earns permission to transgress from the trace of the other— before memory—in the closest places of the self. [1]

Language is not everything. It is only a vital clue to where the self loses its boundaries. The ways in which rhetoric or figuration disrupt logic themselves point at the possibility of random contingency, beside language, around language. Such a dissemination cannot be under our control. Yet in translation, where meaning hops into the spacy emptiness between two named historical languages, we get perilously close to it. By juggling the disruptive rhetoricity that breaks the surface in not necessarily connected ways, we feel the selvedges of

---

[1] Forthcoming from Seagull Press, Calcutta.

the language-textile give way, fray into *frayages* or facilitations.① Although every act of reading or communication is a bit of this risky fraying which scrambles together somehow, our stake in agency keeps the fraying down to a minimum except in the communication and reading of and in love. (What is the place of "love" in the ethical?) The task of the translator is to facilitate this love between the original and its shadow, a love that permits fraying, holds the agency of the translator and the demands of her imagined or actual audience at bay. The politics of translation from a non-European woman's text too often suppresses this possibility because the translator cannot engage with, or cares insufficiently for, the rhetoricity of the original.

The simple possibility that something might not be meaningful is contained by the rhetorical system as the always possible menace of a space outside language. This is most eerily staged (and challenged) in the effort to communicate with other possible intelligent beings in space. (Absolute alterity or otherness is thus differed-deferred into an other self who resembles us, however minimally, and with whom we can communicate.) But a more homely staging of it occurs across two earthly languages. The experience of contained alterity in an unknown language spoken in a different cultural milieu is uncanny.

Let us now think that, in that other language, rhetoric may be disrupting logic in the matter of the production of an agent, and indicating the founding violence of the silence at work within rhetoric. Logic allows us to jump from word to word by means of clearly indicated connections. Rhetoric must work in the silence between and around words in order to see what works and how much. The jagged relationship between rhetoric and logic, condition and effect of knowing, is a relationship by which a world is made for the agent, so that the agent can act in an ethical way, a political way, a day-to-day way; so that the agent can be alive, in a human way, in the world. Unless one can at least construct a model of this for the other language, there is no real translation.

Unfortunately it is only too easy to produce translations if this task is completely ignored. I myself see no choice between the quick and easy and slapdash way, and translating well and with difficulty. There is no reason why a responsible translation should take more time in the doing. The translator's preparation might take more time, and her love for the text might be a matter of a reading skill that takes patience. But the sheer material production of the text need not be slow.

---

① "Facilitation" is the English translation of a Freudian term which is translated *frayage* in French. The dictionary meaning is:

 Term used by Freud at a time when he was putting forward a neurological model of the functioning of the psychical apparatus (1895): the excitation, in passing from one neurone to another, runs into a certain resistance; where its passage results in a permanent reduction in this resistance, there is said to be facilitation; excitation will opt for a facilitated pathway in preference to one where no facilitation has occurred.

 [J. Laplanche and J.-B. Pontalis, *The Language of Psycho*-Analysis (Hogarth Press, London, 1973), p. 157]

Without a sense of the rhetoricity of language, a species of neo-colonialist construction of the non-western scene is afoot. No argument for convenience can be persuasive here. That is always the argument, it seems. This is where I travel from Michèle Barrett's enabling notion of the question of language in poststructuralism. Post-structuralism has shown some of us a staging of the agent within a three-tiered notion of language (as rhetoric, logic, silence). We must attempt to enter or direct that staging, as one directs a play, as an actor interprets a script. That takes a different kind of effort from taking translation to be a matter of synonym, syntax and local colour.

To be only critical, to defer action until the production of the utopian translator, is impractical. Yet, when I hear Derrida, quite justifiably, point out the difficulties between French and English, even when he agrees to speak in English—"I must speak in a language that is not my own because that will be more just"—I want to claim the right to the same dignified complaint for a woman's text in Arabic or Vietnamese. [1]

It is more just to give access to the largest number of feminists. Therefore these texts must be made to speak English. It is more just to speak the language of the majority when through hospitality a large number of feminists give the foreign feminists the right to speak, in English. In the case of the Third World foreigner, is the law of the majority that of decorum, the equitable law of democracy, or the "law" of the strongest? We might focus on this confusion. There is nothing necessarily meretricious about the western feminist gaze. (The "naturalizing" of Jacques Lacan's sketching out of the psychic structure of the gaze in terms of group political behaviour has always seemed to me a bit shaky.) On the other hand, there is nothing essentially noble about the law of the majority either. It is merely the easiest way of being "democratic" with minorities. In the act of wholesale translation into English there can be a betrayal of the democratic ideal into the law of the strongest. This happens when all the literature of the Third World gets translated into a sort of with-it translatese, so that the literature by a woman in Palestine begins to resemble, in the feel of its prose, something by a man in Taiwan. The rhetoricity of Chinese and Arabic! The cultural politics of high-growth, capitalist Asia-Pacific, and devastated West Asia! Gender difference inscribed and inscribing in these differences!

For the student, this tedious translatese cannot compete with the spectacular stylistic experiments of a Monique Witting or an Alice Walker.

Let us consider an example where attending to the author's stylistic experiments can produce a different text. Mahasweta Devi's "Stanadāyini" is available in two versions. [2] Devi has expressed approval for the attention to her signature style in the version entitled

---

① Jacques Derrida, "Force of Law: The 'Mystical Foundation of Authority'," trans. Mary Quaintance, *Deconstruction and the Possibility of Justice: Cardozo Law Review*, XI (July—Aug. 1990), p. 923.

② "The Wet-nurse," in Kali for Women (eds.), *Truth Tales: Stories by Indian Women* (The Women's Press, London, 1987), pp. 1 – 50 (first published by Kali for Women, Delhi, 1986), and "Breast-giver," in Gayatri Chakravorty Spivak, *In Other Worlds: Essays in Cultural Politics* (Methuen/Routledge, New York, 1987), pp. 222 – 240.

"Breastgiver." The alternative translation gives the title as "The Wet-nurse," and thus neutralizes the author's irony in constructing an uncanny word; enough like "wet-nurse" to make that sense, and enough unlike to shock. It is as if the translator should decide to translate Dylan Thomas's famous title and opening line as "Do not go gently into that good night." The theme of treating the breast as organ of labour-power-as-commodity and the breast as metonymie part-object standing in for other-as-object—the way in which the story plays with Marx and Freud on the occasion of the woman's body—is lost even before you enter the story. In the text Mahasweta uses proverbs that are startling even in the Bengali. The translator of "The Wet-nurse" leaves them out. She decides not to try to translate these hard bits of earthy wisdom, contrasting with class-specific access to modernity, also represented in the story. In fact, if the two translations are read side by side, the loss of the rhetorical silences of the original can be felt from one to the other.

First, then, the translator must surrender to the text. She must solicit the text to show the limits of its language, because that rhetorical aspect will point at the silence of the absolute fraying of language that the text wards off, in its special manner. Some think this is just an ethereal way of talking about literature or philosophy. But no amount of tough talk can get around the fact that translation is the most intimate act of reading. Unless the translator has earned the right to become the intimate reader, she cannot surrender to the text, cannot respond to the special call of the text.

The presupposition that women have a natural or narrative-historical solidarity, that there is something in a woman or an undifferentiated women's story that speaks to another woman without benefit of language-learning, might stand against the translator's task of surrender. Paradoxically, it is not possible for us as ethical agents to imagine otherness or alterity maximally. We have to turn the other into something like the self in order to be ethical. To surrender in translation is more erotic than ethical. ① In that situation the good-willing attitude "she is just like me" is not very helpful. In so far as Michèle Barrett is not like Gayatri Spivak, their friendship is more effective as a translation. In order to earn that right of friendship or surrender of identity, of knowing that the rhetoric of the text indicates the limits of language for you as long as you are with the text, you have to be in a different relationship with the language, not even only with the specific text.

Learning about translation on the job, I came to think that it would be a practical help if one's relationship with the language being translated was such that sometimes one preferred to speak in it about intimate things. This is no more than a practical suggestion, not a theoretical requirement, useful especially because a woman writer who is wittingly or unwittingly a "feminist"—and of course all woman writers are not "feminist" even in this broad sense—

---

① Luce Irigaray argues persuasively that, Emmanuel Levinas to the contrary, within the ethics of sexual difference the erotic is ethical. "The Fecundity of the Caress," in her *Ethics of Sexual Difference*, trans. Carolyn Burke and G. C. Gill [Cornell University Press, Ithaca, N. Y. (1993)], p. 6.

will relate to the three-part staging of (agency in) language in ways defined out as "private," since they might question the more public linguistic manoeuvres.

Let us consider an example of lack of intimacy with the medium. In Sudhir Kakar's *The Inner World*, a song about Kāli written by the late nineteenth-century monk Vivekananda is cited as part of the proof of the "archaic narcissism" of the Indian [sic] male. [1](Devi makes the same point with a light touch, with reference to Krsna and Siva, tying it to sexism rather than narcissim and without psychoanalytic patter.)

From Kakar's description, it would not be possible to glimpse that "the disciple" who gives the account of the singular circumstances of Vivekananda's composition of the song was an Irishwoman who became a Ramakrishna nun, a white woman among male Indian monks and devotees. In the account Kakar reads, the song is translated by this woman, whose training in intimacy with the original language is as painstaking as one can hope for. There is a strong identification between Indian and Irish nationalists at this period; and Nivedita, as she was called, also embraced what she understood to be the Indian philosophical way of life as explained by Vivekananda, itself a peculiar, resistant consequence of the culture of imperialism, as has been pointed out by many. For a psychoanalyst like Kakar, this historical, philosophical and indeed sexual text of translation should be the textile to weave with. Instead, the English version, "given" by the anonymous "disciple," serves as no more than the opaque exhibit providing evidence of the alien fact of narcissism. It is not the site of the exchange of language.

At the beginning of the passage quoted by Kakar, there is a reference to Ram Prasad (or Ram Proshad). Kakar provides a footnote: "Eighteenth century singer and poet whose songs of longing for the Mother are very popular in Bengal. " I believe this footnote is also an indication of what I am calling the absence of intimacy.

Vivekananda is, among other things, an example of the peculiar reactive construction of a glorious "India" under the provocation of imperialism. The rejection of "patriotism" in favour of "Kāli" reported in Kakar's passage is played out in this historical theatre, as a choice of the cultural female sphere rather than the colonial male sphere. [2]It is undoubtedly "true" that for such a figure, Ram Proshad Sen provides a kind of ideal self. Sen had travelled back from a clerk's job in colonial Calcutta before the Permanent Settlement of land in 1793 to be the court poet of one of the great rural landowners whose social type, and whose connection to native culture, would be transformed by the Settlement. In other words, Vivekananda

---

① Sudhir Kakar, *The Inner World: A Psycho-Analytic Study of Childhood and Society in India*, 2nd edn (Oxford University Press, Delhi, 1981), pp. 171ff. Part of this discussion in a slightly different form is included in my "Psychoanalysis in Left Field; and Fieldworking: Examples to fit the Title," in Michael Munchow and Sonu Shamdasani (eds.), *PsychoAnalyis, Philosophy and Culture* (Routledge, London, 1994), pp. 41 – 75.

② See Partha Chatterjee, "Nationalism and the Woman Question," in Kumkum Sangari and Sudesh Vaid (eds.), *Recasting Women* (Rutgers University Press, New Brunswick, NJ, 1990), pp. 233 – 253, for a detailed discussion of this gendering of Indian nationalism.

and Ram Proshad are two moments of colonial discursivity translating the figure of Kāli. The dynamic intricacy of that discursive textile is mocked by the useless footnote.

It would be idle here to enter the debate about the "identity" of Kāli or indeed other goddesses in Hindu "polytheism." But simply to contextualize, let me add that it is Ram Proshad about whose poetry I wrote the "Translator's Preface" quoted earlier. He is by no means simply an archaic stage-prop in the disciple's account of Vivekananda's "crisis." Some more lines from my "Preface:" "Ram Proshad played with his mother tongue, transvaluing the words that are heaviest with Sanskrit meaning. I have been unable to catch the utterly new but utterly gendered tone of affectionate banter"—not only, not even largely, "longing"—"between the poet and Kāli." Unless Nivedita mistranslated, it is the difference in tone between Ram Proshad's innovating playfulness and Vivekananda's high nationalist solemnity that, in spite of the turn from nationalism to the Mother, is historically significant. The politics of the translation of the culture of imperialism by the colonial subject has changed noticeably. And that change is expressed in the gendering of the poet's voice.

How do women in contemporary polytheism relate to this peculiar mother, certainly not the psychoanalytic bad mother whom Kakar derives from Max Weber's misreading, not even an organized punishing mother, but a child-mother who punishes with astringent violence and is also a moral and affective monitor?[1] Ordinary women, not saintly women. Why take it for granted that the invocation of goddesses in a historically masculist polytheist sphere is necessarily feminist? I think it is a western and male-gendered suggestion that powerful women in the Sākta (Sakti or Kāli-worshipping) tradition take Kāli as a role model. [2] Mahasweta's Jashoda tells me more about the relationship between goddesses and strong ordinary women than the psychoanalyst. And here too the example of an intimate translation that goes respectfully "wrong" can be offered. The French wife of a Bengali artist translated some of Ram Proshad Sen's songs in the twenties to accompany her husband's paintings based on the songs. Her translations are marred by the pervasive orientalism ready at hand as a discursive system. Compare two passages, both translating the "same" Bengali. I have at least tried, if failed, to catch the unrelenting mockery of self and Kāli in the original:

> Mind, why footloose from Mother?
> Mind mine, think power, for freedom's dower, bind bower with love-rope
> In time, mind, you minded not your blasted lot.
> And Mother, daughter-like, bound up house-fence to dupe her dense and de-
>   voted fellow.
> Oh you'll see at death how much Mum loves you
> A couple minutes' tears, and lashings of water, cowdung-pure.

---

[1] Max Weber, *The Religion of India: The Sociology of Hinduism and Buddhism*, trans. Hans H. Gerth and Don Martindale (Free Press, Glencoe, Ill., 1958).

[2] More on this in a more personal context in Spivak, "Stagings of the Origin," in *Third Text*.

Here is the French, translated by me into an English comparable in tone and vocabulary:

> Pourquoi as-tu, monâme, délaissé les pieds de Mâ?
> O esprit, médite Shokti, tu obtiendras la délivrance.
> Attache-les ces pieds saints avec la corde de la dévotion.
> Au bon moment tu n'as rien vu, c'est bien là ton malheur.
> Pour se jouer de son fidèle, Elle m'est apparue
> Sous la forme de ma fille et m'a aidé à réparer ma clôture.
>
> C'est à la mort que tu comprendras l'amour de Mâ
> Ici, on versera quelques larmes, puis on purifiera le lieu.

> Why have you, my soul [*mo nâme* is, admittedly, less heavy in French], left
> Ma's feet?
> O mind, meditate upon Shokti, you will obtain deliverance.
> Bind those holy feet with the rope of devotion.
> In good time you saw nothing, that is indeed your sorrow.
> To play with her faithful one, She appeared to me
> In the form of my daughter and helped me to repair my enclosure.
> It is at death that you will understand Ma's love.
> Here, they will shed a few tears, then purify the place.

And here the Bengali:

মন কেন মার চরণ-ছাড়া ।
ও মন, তার শক্তি, গাযে ধুরিত, বাঁধ দিযেয জিত -দযা ॥
সময় থাকতে, না দেখলে মন, কেমন তোমার কন্নাগোড়া ।
আ তক্ত চুলিযে, তমযা মাযেনযে বাঁধন আমি ধারের বেড়া ॥
মাযে মত তানাযেয, মুযান মাযের ছেত্যেশেষ,
তোমেন দুত -মুচের কন্নাবগাঁযৈ, শেযে দিবে তোযারচূযা ।

I hope these examples demonstrate that depth of commitment to correct cultural politics, felt in the details of personal life, is sometimes not enough. The history of the language, the history of the author's moment, the history of the language-in-and-as-translation, must figure in the weaving as well.

By logical analysis, we don't just mean what the philosopher does, but also reasonableness—that which will allow rhetoricity to be appropriated, put in its place, situated, seen as only nice. Rhetoricity is put in its place that way because it disrupts. Women within male-dominated society, when they internalize sexism as normality, act out a scenario against feminism that is formally analogical to this. The relationship between logic and rhetoric, between grammar and rhetoric, is also a relationship between social logic, social reasonableness and the disruptiveness of figuration in social practice. These are the first two parts of our three-part model. But then, rhetoric points at the possibility of randomness, of contingency as such, dissemination, the falling apart of language, the possibility that things might not always be semiotically organized. (My problem with Kristeva and the "pre-semiotic" is that she seems to want to expand the empire of the meaningful by grasping at what language can only point at.) Cultures that might not have this specific three-part model will still have a dominant sphere in its traffic with language and contingency. Writers like Ifi Amadiume show us that, without thinking of this sphere as biologically determined, one still has to think in terms of a sphere determined by definitions of secondary and primary sexual characteristics in such a way that the inhabitants of the other sphere are para-subjective, not fully subject.[①] The dominant groups' way of handling the three-part ontology of language has to be learnt as well—if the subordinate ways of rusing with rhetoric are to be disclosed.

To decide whether you are prepared enough to start translating, then, it might help if you have graduated into speaking, by choice or preference, of intimate matters in the language of the original. I have worked my way back to my earlier point: I cannot see why the publishers' convenience or classroom convenience or time convenience for people who do not have the time to learn should organize the construction of the rest of the world for western feminism. Five years ago, berated as unsisterly, I would think, "Well, you know one ought to be a bit more giving etc.", but then I asked myself again, "What am I giving, or giving up? To whom am I giving by assuring that you don't have to work that hard, just come and get it? What am I trying to promote?" People would say, you who have succeeded should not pretend to be a marginal. But surely by demanding higher standards of translation, I am not marginalizing myself or the language of the original?

I have learnt through translating Devi how this three-part structure works differently from English in my native language. And here another historical irony has become personally apparent to me. In the old days, it was most important for a colonial or post-colonial student of English to be as "indistinguishable" as possible from the native speaker of English. I think it is necessary for people in the Third World translation trade now to accept that the wheel has come around, that the genuinely bilingual post-colonial now has a bit of an advantage. But she does not have a real advantage as a translator if she is not strictly bilingual, if she merely speaks her native language. Her own native space is, after all, also class organized. And that organization still often carries the traces of access to imperialism, often relates inversely to access to the vernacular as a public language. So here the requirement for intimacy brings a recognition of the public sphere as well. If we were thinking of translating Marianne Moore or Emily Dickinson, the standard for the translator could not be "anyone who can conduct a conversation in the language of the original (in this case English)." When applied to a Third World language, the position is inherently ethnocentric. And then to present

---

① Ifi Amadiume, *Male Daughters Female Husbands* (Zed Books, London, 1987).

these translations to our unprepared students so that they can learn about women writing!

In my view, the translator from a Third World language should be sufficiently in touch with what is going on in literary production in that language to be capable of distinguishing between good and bad writing by women, resistant and conformist writing by women.

She must be able to confront the idea that what seems resistant in the space of English may be reactionary in the space of the original language. Farida Akhter has argued that, in Bangladesh, the real work of the women's movement and of feminism is being undermined by talk of "gendering," mostly deployed by the women's development wings of transnational non-government organizations, in conjunction with some local academic feminist theorists. [1] One of her intuitions was that "gendering" could not be translated into Bengali. "Gendering" is an awkward new word in English as well. Akhter is profoundly involved in international feminism. And her base is Third World. I could not translate "gender" into the U. S. feminist context for her. This misfiring of translation, between a superlative reader of the social text such as Akhter, and a careful translator like myself, speaking as friends, has added to my sense of the task of the translator.

Good and bad is a flexible standard, like all standards. Here another lesson of post-structuralism helps: These decisions of standards are made anyway. It is the attempt to justify them adequately that polices. That is why disciplinary preparation in school requires that you write examinations to prove these standards. Publishing houses routinely engage in materialist confusion of those standards. The translator must be able to fight that metropolitan materialism with a special kind of specialist's knowledge, not mere philosophical convictions.

In other words, the person who is translating must have a tough sense of the specific terrain of the original, so that she can fight the racist assumption that all Third World women's writing is good. I am often approached by women who would like to put Devi in with just Indian women writers. I am troubled by this, because "Indian women" is not a feminist category. (Elsewhere I have argued that "epistemes"—ways of constructing objects of knowledge—should not have national names either.)[2] Sometimes Indian women writing means American women writing or British women writing, except for national *origin*. There is an ethno-cultural agenda, an obliteration of Third World specificity as well as a denial of cultural citizenship, in calling them merely "Indian."

My initial point was that the task of the translator is to surrender herself to the linguistic rhetoricity of the original text. Although this point has larger political implications, we can say that the not unimportant minimal consequence of ignoring this task is the loss of "the literary and textuality and sensuality of the writing" (Michèle's words). I have worked my

---

[1] For background on Akhter, already somewhat dated for this interventionist in the history of the present, see Yayori Matsui (ed.), *Women's Asia* (Zed Books, London, 1989), ch. 1.

[2] "More on Power/Knowledge," in Thomas E. Wartenberg (ed.), *Re-Thinking Power* (State University of New York Press, Albany, NY, 1992).

way to a second point, that the translator must be able to discriminate on the terrain of the original. Let us dwell on it a bit longer.

I choose Devi because she is unlike her scene. I have heard an English Shakespearean suggest that every bit of Shakespeare criticism coming from the subcontinent was by that virtue resistant. By such a judgement, we are also denied the right to be critical. It was of course bad to have put the place under subjugation, to have tried to make the place over with calculated restrictions. But that does not mean that everything that is coming out of that place after a negotiated independence nearly fifty years ago is necessarily right. The old anthropological supposition (and that is bad anthropology) that every person from a culture is nothing but a whole example of that culture is acted out in my colleague's suggestion. I remain interested in writers who are against the current, against the mainstream. I remain convinced that the interesting literary text might be precisely the text where you do not learn what the majority view of majority cultural representation or self-representation of a nation state might be. The translator has to make herself, in the case of Third World women writing, almost better equipped than the translator who is dealing with the western European languages, because of the fact that there is so much of the old colonial attitude, slightly displaced, at work in the translation racket. Post-structuralism *can* radicalize the field of preparation so that simply boning up on the language is not enough; there is also that special relationship to the staging of language as the production of agency that one must attend to. But the agenda of poststructuralism is mostly elsewhere, and the resistance to theory among metropolitan feminists would lead us into yet another narrative.

The understanding of the task of the translator and the practice of the craft are related but different. Let me summarize how I work. At first, I translate at speed. If I stop to think about what is happening to the English, if I assume an audience, if I take the intending subject as more than a springboard, I cannot jump in, I cannot surrender. My relationship with Devi is easygoing. I am able to say to her: I surrender to you in your writing, not you as intending subject. There, in friendship, is another kind of surrender. Surrendering to the text in this way means, most of the time, being literal. When I have produced a version this way, I revise. I revise not in terms of a possible audience, but by the protocols of the thing in front of me, in a sort of English. And I keep hoping that the student in the classroom will not be able to think that the text is just a purveyor of social realism if it is translated with an eye toward the dynamic staging of language mimed in the revision by the rules of the in-between discourse produced by a literalist surrender.

Vain hope, perhaps, for the accountability is different. When I translated Jacques Derrida's *De la grammatologie*, I was reviewed in a major journal for the first and last time. In the case of my translations of Devi, I have almost no fear of being accurately judged by my readership here. It makes the task more dangerous and more risky. And that for me is the real difference between translating Derrida and translating Mahasweta Devi, not merely the rather more artificial difference between deconstructive philosophy and political fiction.

The opposite argument is not neatly true. There is a large number of people in the Third World who read the old imperial languages. People reading current feminist fiction in the European languages would probably read it in the appropriate imperial language. And the same goes for European philosophy. The act of translating into the Third World language is often a political exercise of a different sort. I am looking forward, as of this writing, to lecturing in Bengali on deconstruction in front of a highly sophisticated audience, knowledgeable both in Bengali and in deconstruction (which they read in English and French and sometimes write about in Bengali), at Jadavpur University in Calcutta. It will be a kind of testing of the post-colonial translator, I think.

Democracy changes into the law of force in the case of translation from the Third World and women even more because of their peculiar relationship to whatever you call the public/private divide. A neatly reversible argument would be possible if the particular Third World country had cornered the Industrial Revolution first and embarked on monopoly imperialist territorial capitalism as one of its consequences, and thus been able to impose a language as international norm. Something like that idiotic joke: If the Second World War had gone differently, the United States would be speaking Japanese. Such egalitarian reversible judgements are appropriate to counter-factual fantasy. Translation remains dependent upon the language skill of the majority. A prominent Belgian translation theorist solves the problem by suggesting that, rather than talk about the Third World, where a lot of passion is involved, one should speak about the European Renaissance, since a great deal of wholesale cross-cultural translation from Graeco-Roman antiquity was undertaken then. What one overlooks is the sheer authority ascribed to the originals in that historical phenomenon. The status of a language in the world is what one must consider when teasing out the politics of translation. Translatese in Bengali can be derided and criticized by large groups of anglophone and anglograph Bengalis. It is only in the hegemonic languages that the benevolent do not take the limits of their own often uninstructed good will into account. That phenomenon becomes hardest to fight because the individuals involved in it are genuinely benevolent and you are identified as a trouble-maker. This becomes particularly difficult when the metropolitan feminist, who is sometimes the assimilated post-colonial, invokes, indeed translates, a too quickly shared feminist notion of accessibility.

If you want to make the translated text accessible, try doing it for the person who wrote it. The problem comes clear then, for she is not within the same history of style. What is it that you are making accessible? The accessible level is the level of abstraction where the individual is already formed, where one can speak individual rights. When you hang out and with a language away from your own (*Mitwegsein*) so that you want to use that language by preference, sometimes, when you discuss something complicated, then you are on the way to making a dimension of the text accessible to the reader, with a light and easy touch, to which she does not accede in her everyday. If you are making anything else accessible, through a language quickly learnt with an idea that you transfer content, then you are betraying the text and showing rather dubious politics.

How will women's solidarity be measured here? How will their common experience be reckoned if one cannot imagine the traffic in accessibility going both ways? I think that idea should be given a decent burial as ground of knowledge, together with the idea of humanist universality. It is good to think that women have something in common, when one is approaching women with whom a relationship would not otherwise be possible. It is a great first step. But, if your interest is in learning if there *is* women's solidarity, how about leaving this assumption, appropriate as a means to an end like local or global social work, and trying a second step? Rather than imagining that women automatically have something identifiable in common, why not say, humbly and practically, my first obligation in understanding solidarity is to learn her mother-tongue. You will see immediately what the differences are. You will also feel the solidarity every day as you make the attempt to learn the language in which the other woman learnt to recognize reality at her mother's knee. This is preparation for the intimacy of cultural translation. If you are going to bludgeon someone else by insisting on your version of solidarity, you have the obligation to try out this experiment and see how far your solidarity goes.

In other words, if you are interested in talking about the other, and/or in making a claim to be the other, it is crucial to learn other languages. This should be distinguished from the learned tradition of language acquisition for academic work. I am talking about the importance of language acquisition for the woman from a hegemonic monolinguist culture who makes everybody's life miserable by insisting on women's solidarity at her price. I am uncomfortable with notions of feminist solidarity which are celebrated when everybody involved is similarly produced. There are countless languages in which women all over the world have grown up and been female or feminist, and yet the languages we keep on learning by rote are the powerful European ones, sometimes the powerful Asian ones, least often the chief African ones. The "other" languages are learnt only by anthropologists who *must* produce knowledge across an epistemic divide. They are generally (though not invariably) not interested in the three-part structure we are discussing.

If we are discussing solidarity as a theoretical position, we must also remember that not all the world's women are literate. There are traditions and situations that remain obscure because we cannot share their linguistic constitution. It is from this angle that I have felt that learning languages might sharpen our own presuppositions about what it means to use the sign "woman." If we say that things should be accessible to us, who is this "us?" What does that sign mean?

Although I have used the examples of women all along, the arguments apply across the board. It is just that women's rhetoricity may be doubly obscured. I do not see the advantage of being completely focused on a single issue, although one must establish practical priorities. In this book, we are concerned with poststructuralism and its effect on feminist theory. Where some post-structuralist thinking can be applied to the constitution of the agent in terms of the literary operations of language, women's texts might be operating differently because of the social differentiation between the sexes. Of course the point applies generally to the colonial context as well. When Ngugi decided to write in Kikuyu, some thought he was bringing a private language into the public sphere. But what makes a language shared by many people in a community private? I was thinking about those so-called private languages when I was talking about language learning. But even within those private languages it is my conviction that there is a difference in the way in which the staging of language produces not only the sexed subject but the gendered agent, by a version of centring, persistently disrupted by rhetoricity, indicating contingency. Unless demonstrated otherwise, this for me remains the condition and effect of dominant and subordinate gendering. If that is so, then we have some reason to focus on women's texts. Let us use the word "woman" to name that space of para-subjects defined as such by the social inscription of primary and secondary sexual characteristics. Then we can cautiously begin to track a sort of commonality in being set apart, within the different rhetorical strategies of different languages. But even here, historical superiorities of class must be kept in mind. Bharati Mukherjee, Anita Desai and Gayatri Spivak do not have the same rhetorical figuration of agency as an illiterate domestic servant.

Tracking commonality through responsible translation can lead us into areas of difference and different differentiations. This may also be important because, in the heritage of imperialism, the female legal subject bears the mark of a failure of Europeanization, by contrast with the female anthropological or literary subject from the area. For example, the division between the French and Islamic codes in modern Algeria is in terms of family, marriage, inheritance, legitimacy and female social agency. These are differences that we must keep in mind. And we must honour the difference between ethnic minorities in the First World and majority populations of the Third.

In conversation, Barrett had asked me if I now inclined more toward Foucault. This is indeed the case. In "Can the Subaltern Speak?", I took a rather strong critical line on Foucault's work, as part of a general critique of imperialism. [①] I do, however, find, his concept of *pouvoir-savoir* immensely useful. Foucault has contributed to French this or dinary-language doublet (the ability to know [as]) to take its place quietly beside *vouloir-dire* (the wish to say—meaning to mean).

On the most mundane level, *pouvoir-savoir* is the shared skill which allows us to make (common) sense of things. It is certainly not only power/knowledge in the sense of *puissance/connaissance*. Those are aggregative institutions. The common way in which one makes sense of things, on the other hand, loses itself in the sub-individual.

Looking at *pouvoir-savoir* in terms of women, one of my focuses has been new immigrants and the change of mother-tongue and *pouvoir-savoir* between mother and daughter.

---

① Spivak, "Can the Subaltern Speak?", in Cary Nelson and Lawrence Grossberg (eds.), *Marxism and the Interpretation of Culture* (University of Illinois Press, Urbana, 111., 1988), pp. 271 - 313.

When the daughter talks reproductive rights and the mother talks protecting honour, is this the birth or death of translation?

Foucault is also interesting in his new notion of the ethics of the care for the self. In order to be able to get to the subject of ethics it may be necessary to look at the ways in which an individual in that culture is instructed to care for the self rather than the imperialism-specific secularist notion that the ethical subject is given as human. In a secularism which is structurally identical with Christianity laundered in the bleach of moral philosophy, the subject of ethics is faceless. Breaking out, Foucault was investigating other ways of making sense of how the subject becomes ethical. This is of interest because, given the connection between imperialism and secularism, there is almost no way of getting to alternative general voices except through religion. And if one does not look at religion as mechanisms of producing the ethical subject, one gets various kinds of "fundamentalism." Workers in cultural politics and its connections to a new ethical philosophy have to be interested in religion in the production of ethical subjects. There is much room for feminist work here because western feminists have not so far been aware of religion as a cultural instrument rather than a mark of cultural difference. I am currently working on Hindu performative ethics with Professor B. K. Matilal. He is an enlightened male feminist. I am an active feminist. Helped by his learning and his openness I am learning to distinguish between ethical catalysts and ethical motors even as I learn to translate bits of the Sanskrit epic in a way different from all the accepted translations, because I rely not only on learning, not only on "good English," but on that three-part scheme of which I have so lengthily spoken. I hope the results will please readers. If we are going to look at an ethics that emerges from something other than the historically secularist ideal—at an ethics of sexual differences, at an ethics that can confront the emergence of fundamentalisms without apology or dismissal in the name of the Enlightenment—then *pouvoir-savoir* and the care for the self in Foucault can be illuminating. And these "other ways" bring us back to translation, in the general sense.

Translation in general

I want now to add two sections to what was generated from the initial conversation with Barrett. I will dwell on the politics of translation in a general sense, by way of three examples of "cultural translation" in English. I want to make the point that the lessons of translation in the narrow sense can reach much further.

First, J. M. Coetzee's *Foe*. [1] This book represents the impropriety of the dominant's desire to give voice to the native. When Susan Barton, the eighteenth-century Englishwoman

---

① For an extended consideration of these and related points, see my "Versions of the Margin: Coetzee's *Foe* reading Defoe's *Crusoe/Roxana*," in Jonathan Arac (ed.), *Theory and Its Consequences* (Johns Hopkins University Press, Baltimore, 1990).

from *Roxana*, attempts to teach a muted Friday (from *Robinson Crusoe*) to read and write English, he draws an incomprehensible rebus on his slate and wipes it out, withholds it. You cannot translate from a position of monolinguist superiority. Coetzee as white creole translates *Robinson Crusoe* by representing Friday as the agent of a withholding.

Second, Toni Morrison's *Beloved*. [①] Let us look at the scene of the change of the mother-tongue from mother to daughter. Strictly speaking, it is not a change, but a loss, for the narrative is not of immigration but of slavery. Sethe, the central character of the novel, remembers: "What Nan"—her mother's fellow-slave and friend—"told her she had forgotten, along with the language she told it in. The same language her ma'am spoke, and which would never come back. But the message—that was—that was and had been there all along" (p. 62). The representation of this message, as it passes through the forgetfulness of death to Sethe's ghostly daughter Beloved, is of a withholding: "This is not a story to pass on" (p. 275).

Between mother and daughter, a certain historical withholding intervenes. If the situation between the new immigrant mother and daughter provokes the question as to whether it is the birth or death of translation (see. above, p. 409), here the author represents with violence a certain birth-in—death, a death-in-birth of a story that is not to translate or pass on, strictly speaking, therefore, an aporia, and yet it is passed on, with the mark of *un*translatability on it, in the bound book, *Beloved*, that we hold in our hands. Contrast this to the confidence in accessibility in the house of power, where history is waiting to be restored.

The scene of violence between mother and daughter (reported and passed on by the daughter Sethe to her daughter Denver, who carries the name of a white trash girl, in partial acknowledgement of women's solidarity in birthing) is, then, the condition of (im)possibility of *Beloved*: [②]

> She picked me up and carried me behind the smokehouse. Back there she opened up her dress front and lifted her breast and pointed under it. Right on her rib was a circle and a cross burnt right in the skin. She said, "This is your ma'am. This," and she pointed ... "Yes, Ma'am," I said ... "But how will you know me? ... Mark me, too," I said ... "Did she?" asked Denver. "She slapped my face." "What for?" "I didn't understand it then. Not till I had a mark of my own."
>
> (p. 61)

This scene, of claiming the brand of the owner as "my own," to create, in this broken chain of marks owned by separate white male agents of property, an unbroken chain of re-memory in (enslaved) daughters as agents of a history not to be passed on, is of necessity more poignant than Friday's scene of withheld writing from the white woman wanting to

① Toni Morrison, *Beloved* (Plume Books, New York, 1987). Page numbers are included in my text.

② For (im)possibility, see my "Literary Representation of the Subaltern," in my *In Other Worlds*, pp. 241-268.

create history by giving her "own" language. And the lesson is the (im)possibility of translation in the general sense. Rhetoric points at absolute contingency, not the sequentiality of time, not even the cycle of seasons, but only "weather." "By and by all trace is gone, and what is forgotten is not only the footprints but the water and what it is down there. The rest is weather. Not the breath of the disremembered and unaccounted for"—after the effacement of the trace, no project for restoring (women's?) history—"but wind in the eaves, or spring ice thawing too quickly. Just weather" (p. 275).

With this invocation of contingency, where nature may be "the great body without organs of woman," we can align ourselves with Wilson Harris, the author of *The Guyana Quartet*, for whom trees are "the lungs of the globe."[1] Harris hails the (re)birth of the native imagination as not merely the translation but the transsubstantiation of the species. What in more workaday language I have called the obligation of the translator to be able to juggle the rhetorical silences in the two languages, Harris puts this way, pointing at the need for translating the Carib's English:

> The Caribbean bone flute, made of human bone, is a seed in the soul of the Caribbean. It is a primitive technology that we can turn around [trans-version?]. Consuming our biases and prejudices in ourselves we can let the bone flute help us open ourselves rather than read it the other way—as a metonymic devouring of a bit of flesh.[2] The link of music with cannibalism is a sublime paradox. When the music of the bone flute opens the doors, absences flow in, and the native imagination puts together the ingredients for quantum immediacy out of unpredictable resources.

The bone flute has been neglected by Caribbean writers, says Wilson Harris, because progressive realism is a charismatic way of writing prize-winning fiction. Progressive realism measures the bone. Progressive realism is the too-easy accessibility of translation as transfer of substance.

The progressive realism of the west dismissed the native imagination as the place of the fetish. Hegel was perhaps the greatest systematizer of this dismissal. And psychoanalytic cultural criticism in its present charismatic incarnation sometimes measures the bone with uncanny precision. It is perhaps not fortuitous that the passage below gives us an account of Hegel that is the exact opposite of Harris's vision. The paradox of the sublime and the bone

---

① Karl Marx, "Economic and Philosophical Manuscripts," in Rodney Living-stone and George Benton trans., *Early Writings* (Vintage, New York, 1975), pp. 279 – 400; Wilson Harris, *The Guyana Quartet* (Faber, London, 1985). These quotations are from Wilson Harris, "Cross-cultural Crisis: Imagery, Language, and the Intuitive Imagination," Commonwealth Lectures, 1990, Lecture no. 2, 31 Oct. 1990, University of Cambridge.

② Derrida traces the trajectory of the Hegelian and pre-Hegelian discourse of the fetish [Jacques Derrida, *Glas*, trans. Richard Rand and John P. Leavey, Jr. (University of Nebraska Press, Lincoln, Nebr., 1986)]. The worshipper of the fetish eats human flesh. The worshipper of God feasts on the Eucharist. Harris transverses the fetish here through the native imagination.

here lead to non-language seen as inertia, where the structure of passage is mere logic. The authority of the supreme language makes translation impossible:

> The Sublime is therefore the paradox of an object which, in the very field of representation, provides a view, in a negative way, of the dimension of what is unpresentable ... The bone, the skull, is thus an object which, by means of its *presence*, fills out the void, the impossibility of the signifying *representation* of the subject ... The proposition "Wealth is the Self" repeats at this level the proposition "The Spirit is a bone" [both propositions are Hegel's]: In both cases we are dealing with a proposition which is at first sight absurd, nonsensical, with an equation the terms of which are incompatible; in both cases we encounter the same logical structure of passage—the subject, totally lost in the medium of language (language of gesture and grimaces; language of flattery), finds its objective counterpart in the inertia of a non-language object (skull, money). [1]

Wilson Harris's vision is abstract, translating Morrison's "weather" into an oceanic version of quantum physics. But all three cultural translators cited in this section ask us to attend to the rhetoric which points to the limits of translation, in the creole's, the slave-daughter's, the Carib's use of "English." Let us learn the lesson of translation from these brilliant inside/outsiders and translate it into the situation of other languages.

Reading as translation

In conclusion, I want to show how the post-colonial as the outside/insider translates white theory as she reads, so that she can discriminate on the terrain of the original. She wants to use what is useful. Again, I hope this can pass on a lesson to the translator in the narrow sense.

"The link of music with cannibalism is a sublime paradox." I believe Wilson Harris is using "sublime" here with some degree of precision, indicating the undoing of the progressive western subject as realist interpreter of history. Can a theoretical account of the aesthetic sublime in English discourse, ostensibly far from the bone flute, be of use? By way of answer, I will use my reading of Peter de Bolla's superb scholarly account of *The Discourse of the Sublime* as an example of sympathetic reading as translation, precisely not a surrender but a friendly learning by taking a distance. [2]

P. 4: "What was it to be a subject in the eighteenth century?" The reader-as-translator (RAT) is excited. The long eighteenth century in Britain is the account of the constitution and transformation of nation into empire. Shall we read that story? The book will least touch

---

① Slavoj Zizek, *The Sublime Object of Ideology*, trans. Jon Barnes (Verso, London, 1989), pp. 203, 208, 212.

② Peter de Bolla, *The Discourse of the Sublime: Readings in History, Aesthetics and the Subject* (Blackwell, Oxford, 1989). Page numbers are given in my text.

on that issue, if only to swerve. And women will not be seen as touched in their agency formation by that change. The book's strong feminist sympathies relate to the Englishwoman only as gender victim. But the erudition of the text allows us to think that this sort of rhetorical reading might be the method to open up the question "What is it to be a post-colonial reader of English in the twentieth century?" The representative reader of *The Discourse of the Sublime* will be post-colonial. Has that law of the majority been observed, or the law of the strong?

On p. 72 RAT comes to a discussion of Burke on the sublime:

> The internal resistance of Burke's text ... restricts the full play of this trope [power ... as a trope articulating the technologies of the sublime], thereby defeating a description of the sublime experience uniquely in terms of the enpowered [sic] subject. Put briefly, Burke, for a number of reasons, among which we must include political aims and ends, stops short of a discourse on the sublime, and in so doing he reinstates the ultimate power of an adjacent discourse, theology, which locates its own self-authenticating power grimly within the boundaries of godhead. Was it also because Burke was deeply implicated in searching out the recesses of the mental theatre of the English master in the colonies that he had some notion of different kinds of subject and therefore, like some Kurtz before Conrad, recoiled in horror before the sublimely empowered subject? Was it because, like some Kristeva before *Chinese Women*, Burke had tried to imagine the Begums of Oudh as legal subjects that he had put self-authentication elsewhere? [①]*The Discourse of the Sublime*, in noticing Burke's difference from the other discoursers on the sublime, opens doors for other RATs to engage in such scholarly speculations and thus exceed and expand the book.

Pp. 106, 111 – 112, 131: RAT comes to the English National Debt. British colonialism was a violent deconstruction of the hyphen between nation and state. [②] In imperialism the nation was subl(im)ated into empire. Of this, no clue in *The Discourse*. The Bank of England is discussed. Its founding in 1696, and the transformation of letters of credit to the ancestor of the modern cheque, had something like a relationship with the fortunes of the East India Company and the founding of Calcutta in 1690. The *national* debt is in fact the site of a crisis management, where the nation, sublime object as miraculating subject of ideology, changes the sign "debtor" into a catachresis or false metaphor by way of "an acceptance of a permanent discrepancy between the total circulating specie and the debt." The French War, certainly

---

① References and discussion of "The Begums of Oudh," and "The Impeachment of Warren Hastings" are to be found in *The Writings and Speeches of Edmund Burke*, ed. P. J. Marshall (Clarendon Press, Oxford, 1981), vol. 5: *India: Madras and Bengal*, pp. 410 – 412, pp. 465 – 466, p. 470; and in vol. 6: *India: Launching of the Hastings Impeachment* respectively.

② See my "Reading the Archives: the Rani of Sirmur." In Francis Barker (ed.), *Europe and Its Others* (University of Essex, Colchester, 1985), pp. 128 – 151.

the immediate efficient cause, is soon woven into the vaster textile of crisis. *The Discourse* cannot see the nation covering for the colonial economy. As on the occasion of the race-speci-ficity of gendering, so on the discourse of multinational capital, the argument is kept domes-tic, within England, European. [①] RAT snuffles off, disgruntled. She finds a kind of comfort in Mahasweta's livid figuration of the woman's body as body rather than attend to this history of the English body "as a disfigurative device in order to return to [it] its lost literality." Reading as translation has misfired here.

On p. 140 RAT comes to the elder Pitt. Although his functionality is initially seen as "demanded ... by the incorporation of nation," it is not possible not at least to mention empire when speaking of Pitt's voice:

> The voice of Pitt ... works its doubled intervention into the spirit and character
> of the times; at once the supreme example of the private individual in the service of
> the state, and the private individual eradicated by the needs of a public, nationalist,
> commercial empire. In this sense the voice of Pitt becomes the most extreme exam-
> ple of the textualization of the body for the rest of the century.
>
> (p. 182)

We have seen a literal case of the textualization of the surface of the body between slave mother and slave daughter in *Beloved*, where mother hits daughter to stop her thinking that the signs of that text can be passed on, a lesson learnt *après-coup*, literally after the blow of the daughter's own branding. Should RAT expect an account of the passing on of the textua-lization of the interior of the body through the voice, a metonym for consciousness, from master father to master son? The younger Pitt took the first step to change the nationalist empire to the imperial nation with the India Act of 1784. Can *The Discourse of the Sublime* plot that sublime relay? Not yet. But here, too, an exceeding and expanding translation is possible.

Predictably, RAT finds a foothold in the rhetoricity of *The Discourse*. Chapter 10 be-gins: "The second part of this study has steadily examined how 'theory' sets out to legislate and control a practice, how it produces the excess which it cannot legislate, and removes from the centre to the boundary its limit, limiting case" (p. 230). This passage reads to a de-constructive RAT as an enabling self-description of the text, although within the limits of the book, it describes, not itself but the object of its investigation. By the time the end of the book is reached, RAT feels that she has been written into the text:

> As a history of that refusal and resistance [this book] presents a record of its
> own coming into being as history, the history of the thought it wants to think dif-
> ferently, over there. It is therefore, only appropriate that its conclusion should
> gesture towards the limit, risk the reinversion of the boundary by speaking from

---

① See my "Reading the Archives: the Rani of Sirmur." In Francis Barker (ed.), *Europe and Its Others* (University of Essex, Colchester, 1985), pp. 128 – 151.

the other, refusing silence to what is unsaid.

Beyond this "clamour for a kiss" of the other space, it is "just weather."

Under the figure of RAT (reader-as-translator), I have tried to limn the politics of a certain kind of clandestine post-colonial reading, using the master marks to put together a history. Thus we find out what books we can forage, and what we must set aside. I can use Peter de Bella's *The Discourse on the Sublime* to open up dull histories of the colonial eighteenth century. Was Toni Morrison, a writer well-versed in contemporary literary theory, obliged to set aside Paul de Man's "The Purloined Ribbon?"[①]

> Eighteen seventy-four and white folks were still on the loose ... Human blood cooked in a lynch fire was a whole other thing ... But none of that had worn out his marrow ... It was the ribbon ... He thought it was a cardinal feather stuck to his boat. He tugged and what came loose in his hand was a red ribbon knotted around a curl of wet woolly hair, clinging still to its bit of scalp ... He kept the ribbon; the skin smell nagged him.

(pp. 180 – 181)

Morrison next invokes a language whose selvedge is so frayed that no *frayage* can facilitate full passage: "This time, although he couldn't cipher but one word, he believed he knew who spoke them. The people of the broken necks, of fire-cooked blood and black girls who had lost their ribbons" (p. 181). Did the explanation of promises and excuses in eighteenth-century Geneva not make it across into this "roar?" I will not check it out and measure the bone flute. I will simply dedicate these pages to the author of *Beloved*, in the name of translation.

【延伸阅读】

[1] Bhabha, H. (1994). *The Location of Culture*. London and New York: Routledge.
[2] Cheyditz, E. (1991). *The Poetics of Imperialism: Translation and Colonization from the Tempest to Tarzan*. New York and Oxford: Oxford University Press.
[3] Robinson, D. (1997). *Translaiton and Empire: Postcolonial Theories Explained*. Manchester: St Jerome.
[4] Said, E. (1978). *Orientalism*. London: Penguin.

【问题与思考】

1. 斯皮瓦克的后殖民主义思想与德里达的解构主义思想有何关联?
2. 语言的修辞与逻辑之间有何关系? 探讨这一关系有何意义?
3. 斯皮瓦克是如何看待西方世界的第三世界女性文学作品翻译的? 为什么?
4. 学习这篇文献对我们的翻译研究有何指导意义?

---

① Paul de Man, "The Purloined Ribbon," reprinted as "Excuses (*Confessions*) in de Man," *Allegories of Reading* (Yale University Press, New Haven, 1979), pp. 278 – 301.

选文三 Gender in Translation（Excerpt）

Sherry Simon

导　言

　　谢莉·西蒙是加拿大著名翻译理论家、文化专家。她十分看重文化研究对翻译研究的重要意义，认为"文化研究给翻译带来的是对性别和文化的复杂性的理解"。她的专著《翻译的性别：文化身份和传播的政治》（*Gender in Translation：Cultural Identity and the Politics of Transmission*）是女性主义翻译理论最广为阅读的著作。本论文节选自该书的第一章"Taking Gendered Positions in Translation Theory"，是对全书主要思想精髓的概述。

　　文章研究了性别意识在翻译研究中的应用，探讨了性别角色的差异、这些差异在语言中是如何体现和表达的以及如何通过翻译将这些表达植入不同译本。文章认为，传统的翻译理论要求译文在内容、形式和风格上忠实于原文，而女性主义译者在翻译实践中为彰显自己的女性身份，认定自己有权对原文产生质疑，如果原文与女权主义观点相悖，她们有权对原文进行干涉并做出修改。忠实的对象既不是作者也不是译者，而是由作者与译者共同参与的写作方案。

Because they are necessarily "defective," all translations are "reputed females." In this neat equation, John Florio (1603) summarizes a heritage of double inferiority. Translators and women have historically been the weaker figures in their respective hierarchies: Translators are handmaidens to authors, women inferior to men. This forced partnership finds contemporary resonance in Nicole Ward Jouve's statement that the translator occupies a "(culturally speaking) female position" (Jouve, 1991, p. 47). And Susanne de Lotbinière-Harwood's echoing self-definition: "I am a translation because I am a woman" (de Lotbinière-Harwood, 1991, p. 95).

Whether affirmed or denounced, the femininity of translation is a persistent historical trope. "Woman" and "translator" have been relegated to the same position of discursive inferiority. The hierarchical authority of the original over the reproduction is linked with imagery of masculine and feminine; the original is considered the strong generative male, the translation the weaker and derivative female. We are not surprised to learn that the language used to describe translating dips liberally into the vocabulary of sexism, drawing on images of dominance and inferiority, fidelity and libertinage. The most persistent of these expressions, "les belles infidèles," has for centuries encouraged an attitude of suspicion toward the seemly but wayward translation.

Feminist translation theory aims to identify and critique the tangle of concepts which relegates both women and translation to the bottom of the social and literary ladder. To do so, it must investigate the processes through which translation has come to be "feminized," and attempt to trouble the structures of authority which have maintained this association.

What indeed are the processes through which translation maintains and activates gender constructs? To begin to answer this question, I have chosen to move along a number of planes. First, conceptual: How have the sites of translation theory been implicitly gendered and how can this theory be transformed? This is the task of the introductory chapter, which brings together the work of theorists who seek to disturb the clichèd language used to describe translation, and to replace it with terms which convey the active play of identities within translation practice. They do so through their understanding of the performative, and not simply representational, nature of language. Feminist translation thus reframes the question of "fidelity," which has played like a stultifying refrain through the history of translation. For feminist translation, fidelity is to be directed toward neither the author nor the reader, but toward the writing project—a project in which both writer and translator participate.

Gender difference has been played out not only in the metaphors describing translation, but in actual practices of translation, in the specific social and historical forms through which women have understood and enacted their writing activities. How has this relationship between social and writing roles been articulated (Chapter Two)? On the one hand, translation was the means through which women, beginning in the European Middle Ages, particularly, were able to gain access to the world of letters. Long excluded from the privileges of authorship, women turned to translation as a permissible form of public expression. Translation continued to serve as a kind of writer's apprenticeship for women into the nineteenth and twentieth centuries. (George Eliot was first known as the "translatress of Strauss," before she was known as a novelist.) In addition, translation was an important part of the social movements in which women participated, such as the fight against slavery. First-wave feminism was closely associated with this movement. Women have translated in order to build communication networks in the service of progressive political agendas and in the creative renewal of literary traditions. The great works of nineteenth and twentieth century French, Russian and German modernism were translated in part by women who made translation an expression of their political convictions. They believed, as Madame de Staël had so clearly stated, that movements of literary exchange are vital to the democratic life of any nation.

There is an intrinsic interest in unearthing the neglected intellectual and literary work of women: in bringing to light the strong figure of the "translatress" Aphra Behn, in making heard Madame de Staël's ringing appeal to translation as a cure for the ills of sclerotic literatures, in remembering the remarkable creative accomplishments of Constance Garnett and Jean Starr Untermeyer. The goal of this initial survey, however, is not so much to construct an archive as to suggest the kinds of interrelations upon which such genealogies might be built. Rather than provide a simple listing of women translators, this overview seeks to highlight a number of moments when translation became a strong mode of expression for women. These moments show to what extent the role of the translator meshes with social values, and how positions in the social hierarchy are reflected in the literary field.

"The location and organization of difference are crucial to a culture's self-representation and its distribution of power," observes Mary Poovey (Poovey, 1988, p. 199). A mapping of some of the points of interdependence between the literary and social fields illustrates indeed how differences are "organized" through various levels of society. One particularly striking example of such literary and social imbrication is the way translation offered itself as a means of expression for women during the English Renaissance, when the world of letters was otherwise closed to them. Women were encouraged to translate religious texts when they were forbidden from undertaking any other kind of public writing activity. Women were able to use this very limited point of entry for significant ends (Krontiris, 1992). This example highlights the way in which the social values of writing roles are intensely contextual, expressing the very specific lines of tension which traverse gendered positions at a given moment.

In what ways have women interpreted their role as translators? Feelings of aggressive rivalry or affectionate fusion have often been evoked to describe the closeness which translators feel for the texts they are working on—and, by extension, their authors. These feelings can be exacerbated when differences of gender are also involved, and when the translation work involves contact between the two writers. While some feminist translators have suggested that they might best deal with the discomforts of a negative legacy by ensuring that women's texts are translated only by women translators, men's by men, this solution could not be a long-term one. As Lori Chamberlain argues,

> one of the challenges for feminist translators is to move beyond questions of the sex of the author and translator. Working within the conventional hierarchies ... the female translator of a female author's text and the male translator of a male author's text will be bound by the same power relations: What must be subverted is the process by which translation complies with gender constructs.
>
> (Chamberlain, 1992, p. 72)

The creative discomforts of working relationships have been described with considerable wit by major translators of the twentieth century, Jean Starr Untermeyer, Willa Muir, Helen Lowe-Porter and Suzanne Levine. Beyond their anecdotal interest, and their value as chronicles of the translation process, these accounts show in what ways gender difference has been present—in sometimes productive, sometimes insidious, ways—in the activity of language transfer.

Two especially important areas involving feminist theory and translation are reserved for special examination in this book. The first is the transatlantic displacement of the writings of the French feminists, Luce Irigaray, Julia Kristeva and Hélène Cixous, into the

Anglo-American intellectual world (Chapter Three). This exchange brings into light the network of tensions which are so characteristic of our current intellectual context: the conflictual pulls between internationalist feminist solidarity and national affiliations, the deconstructive drive toward attenuation of authorship and the continuing structures of textual authority, the fading of disciplinary borders and their continual reappearance. The "taming" of French feminist theory in the Anglo-American context came about through the gradual interpenetration of philosophical systems, on the one hand the speculative Continental tradition and on the other the more empirical Anglo-American tradition; this process of accommodation was facilitated by various levels and procedures of mediation: commentary, interpretation and translation.

The transatlantic passage of French feminist thought brought about effects of distortion and appropriation. These effects inevitably accompany any important movement of ideas; they result from the diversity of interests and desires which commands the exchange, and from the reformulation and renewals demanded of the target language. The distortion effects of the exchange are perhaps best witnessed in the reception given to the work of Hélène Cixous, which was until recently interpreted on the basis of a very narrow sampling.

The second case study examines contemporary feminist biblical translation (Chapter Four). What is particularly striking about the feminist intervention in this area is that it does not consider itself, nor is it often considered to be, an aberration in a seamless tradition. Rather, feminism appears as yet another social and ideological stance from which Bible translation can be undertaken—a new face in a long line of competing figures going back to the Septuagint. The debates over feminist and inclusive-language interpretations of the Bible enhance our understanding of translation as a substantial interpretative move, at the same time as they draw attention to the conflictual implications of gendered language. While there are strong and powerful voices calling for inclusive-language versions of the Bible (resulting in the 1995 publication by Oxford University Press of an inclusive-language version of the New Testament and Psalms), there are equally insistent voices—among feminists—calling for more historically anchored versions. As is often the case with the Bible, the interaction between dogma and meaning becomes particularly intense. The long history of the Bible magnifies the importance of translation issues, showing them to be ideologically saturated. In contrast to most other areas of cultural transmission, where translation is so often treated as a mechanical act, biblical scholarship has always recognized that translation carries with it both the dangers and the promises of interpretation.

In both the transportation of French feminism and new projects of Bible translation there is a particularly revealing conjunction of gender and language issues. Consciously feminist principles are invoked in the choice and manner of the texts translated. These connections allow us to see how translation frames and directs ongoing processes of intellectual transmission. The links of mediation are not automatic; they are not imposed or organized by some dispassionate cultural authority. Rather, translators are involved in the materials through which they work; they are fully invested in the process of transfer.

The final chapter explores the forms which an alliance between translation studies and cultural studies could take. Following recent feminist theory, this section projects gender onto the larger canvas of cultural identity issues. Gender is an element of identity and experience which, like other cultural identities, takes form through social consciousness. The work of theorist Gayatri Spivak, in particular, works as a pivot, engaging the practice of translation with postcolonial theory. Like Homi Bhabha, Gayatri Spivak challenges the meaning of translation within a universe of shifting borders, emphasizing the powers of translation to define and articulate otherness. Postcolonial theory, like the writing of women who invoke the transformatory potential of translation (such as Nicole Brossard, Eva Hoffman, Christine Brooke-Rose), questions the borders between nations and languages.

Each of the chapters investigates one area of the interplay between gender and translation, but makes no claim to exhaust this area. That most of the transators discussed wrote in English is a sign of the preliminary nature of this research. While the first and last chapters are largely theoretical in nature, the three middle chapters are intended as case studies which will hopefully provide material useful for continued research in these areas. Whether the complicities between gender and translation become the basis of a consciously transformative project (as in feminist translation theory and practice) or whether they emerge out of social positions and networks, investigation of the interplay between them leads to unexpected views of otherwise familiar terrain.

A final preliminary remark must be made concerning the meaning of the term gender. Judith Butler opens her attempt to "trouble" the meaning of gender in something of an irreverent tone:

> Contemporary feminist debates over the meanings of gender lead time and again to a certain sense of trouble, as if the indeterminacy of gender might eventually culminate in the failure of feminism. Perhaps trouble need not carry such a negative Valence.
>
> (Butler, 1990, p. ix)

She argues that the search for definition should be abandoned in favor of genealogical critique:

> A genealogical critique refuses to search for the origins of gender, the inner truth of female desire, a genuine or authentic sexual identity that repression has kept from view; rather, genealogy investigates the political stakes in designating as an *origin* and *cause* those identity categories that are in fact the *effects* of institutions, practices, discourses with multiple and diffuse points of origin ... Precisely because "female" no longer appears to be a stable notion, its meaning as troubled and unfixed as "woman,"and because both terms gain their troubled significations only as relational terms, this inquiry takes as its focus gender and the relational

analysis it suggests.

(ibid. , p. xi)

Gender, therefore, is never a primary identity emerging out of the depths of the self, but a discursive construction enunciated at multiple sites. In the context of this particular study, the historical variability of discourses of gender must be emphasized. Although Aphra Behn and Barbara Godard both use prefaces to draw attention to their identity as women translators, the import of that identity is vastly different in each case. While Behn points to her gender to apologize for her lack of a classical education and her ignorance in scientific matters, Barbara Godard emphasizes the ways in which her understanding of the creative project of the author animates her own work.

The ways in which translators draw attention to their identities as women—or more specifically as feminists—are highlighted here in order to explain the affinities or frustrations they feel in their translation work, and in order to elucidate texts which themselves exploit the resources of grammatical gender for imaginative or political purposes. Gender is not always a relevant factor in translation. There are no *a priori* characteristics which would make women either more or less competent at their task. Where identity enters into play is the point at which the translator transforms the fact of gender into a social or literary project.

Gender in translation studies

Some of the most exciting developments in translation studies since the 1980s have been part of what has been called "the cultural turn. " The turn to culture implies adding an important dimension to translation studies. Instead of asking the traditional question which has preoccupied translation theorists—"how should we translate, what is a correct translation?"—the emphasis is placed on a descriptive approach: "What do translations do, how do they circulate in the world and elicit response?" This shift emphasizes the reality of translations as documents which exist materially and move about, add to our store of knowledge, and contribute to ongoing changes in esthetics.

More importantly, it allows us to understand translations as being related in organic ways to other modes of communication, and to see translations as writing practices fully informed by the tensions that traverse all cultural representation. That is, it defines translation as a process of mediation which does not stand above ideology but works through it.

This turn in translation studies prepared the terrain for a fruitful encounter with feminist thought. Feminism has been one of the most potent forms of cultural identity to take on linguistic and social expression over the last decades. "*La libé ration des femmes passe par le langage*" was a familiar rallying call of the 1970s: Women's liberation must first be a liberation of/from language. Through the work of feminist scholars over the last twenty to thirty years, there has emerged a clear sense of language as a site of contested meanings, as an arena in which subjects test and prove themselves. And so it is hardly uprising that translation studies should be nourished in important ways by feminist thought.

The consequences for translation have been various and decisive. Over the years, the critique of sexism in language has moved from a largely corrective and action-oriented attention to vocabulary (as we see in the work of Louky Bersianik or Mary Daly) to a broader examination of the symbolic power of the feminine in language. Attention has shifted from critical analysis of a single linguistic code (English, French) to the conceptual terms regulating the intervention of individual and collective subjects within speech and writing.

The alliance between translation studies and feminism therefore emerged out of a common intellectual and institutional context. As fields of inquiry which emerged during the 1970s' and gained increasing institutional recognition through the 1980s, translation studies and feminist thought are similarly grounded in the dynamics of a period which gave strong prominence to language. Translation studies have been impelled by many of the concerns central to feminism: the distrust of traditional hierarchies and gendered roles, deep suspicion of rules defining fidelity, and the questioning of universal standards of meaning and value. Both feminism and translation are concerned by the way "secondariness" comes to be defined and canonized; both are tools for a critical understanding of difference as it is represented in language. The most compelling questions for both fields remain: How are social, sexual and historical differences expressed in language and how can these differences be transferred across languages? What kinds of fidelities are expected of women and translators—in relation to the more powerful terms of their respective hierarchies?

For these fields of study, language intervenes actively in the creation of meaning. Like other forms of representation, language does not simply "mirror" reality; it contributes to it. Translation, we know, refers to a process of interlinguistic transfer. Translators communicate, re-write, manipulate a text in order to make it available to a second language public. Thus they can use language as cultural intervention, as part of an effort to alter expressions of domination, whether at the level of concepts, of syntax or of terminology.

Engendered theory

Le traducteur subit, soumis, subjugué. Femelle, même s'il est parfois amazone. Pris, prisonnier, enferré, enserré. Ne s'appartient plus. Aliené, absorbé, ravi et dépossdé de sa parole propre. Parole de l'autre, l'auteur, la hauteur. Le traducteur est inférieur, postérieur, postsynchronisé. Le traducteur rend en son langage l'auteur publiable, mais il est oubliable.

(Albert Bensoussan, quoted in Levine, 1991, p. 183)

Although presented in humorous mode, as a parody of the wordplay fashionable in French writing during the 1970s, Albert Bensoussan's description of the translator as female is consonant with a long tradition. Translation is often explained in metaphorical terms, some figures—including the sexist tropes mentioned earlier(p. 1)—assuming extraordinary longevity. Two other popular figures are the "property" and the "clothing" metaphors. Translation is consistently represented as an unequal struggle for authority over the text: The author is the landlord, the translator simply a tenant. Even more persistent is the clothing metaphor, which presents the foreign author as now clothed in new garb (Woodsworth, 1986).

Recent discussions of the use of metaphors to describe translation point to the real hermeneutical value of metaphor. It is suggested that there is something about the translating experience that calls for metaphorical language (D'hulst, 1992). If this is indeed the case, we can wonder at the persistence of sexist language to describe translation. If metaphor is to be considered proto-theoretical language, then the language of translation theory has indeed been profoundly marked by gender.

John Florio's reference to translations as "female" has spawned a rich progeny. In numerous prefaces and critical texts, including work as recent as George Steiner's *After Babel* (1975), the relation between author and translator, original and translation, is frequently sexualized. Lori Chamberlain suggests that these figures point to a frustrated struggle for mastery of meaning and for paternity rights over the bastard product of interlinguistic transfer. As Lori Chamberlain's discussion makes clear, the metaphorics of translation are a symptom of larger issues of Western culture and in particular of the anxieties involved in establishing and maintaining borders.

> What proclaims itself to be an aesthetic problem is represented in terms of sex, family, and the state, and what is consistently at issue is power ... I would argue that the reason translation is so overcoded, so overregulated, is that it threatens to erase the difference between production and reproduction which is essential to the establishment of power.
>
> (Chamberlain, 1992, p. 66)

The historical continuity of gendered theorizing of translation is remarkable. Chamberlain refers to a particularly violent image taken from Deuteronomy 21, pp. 12 - 14 and used by Thomas Drant, the sixteenth-century English translator of Horace, to explain his method of translating the satirist. He refers to God's command to the Israelites to shave the heads and pare the nails of captive women they wish to make their wives in order to remove all signs of beauty from them. Elizabeth Castelli has pointed out that this reference goes back in fact to Jerome, the father of biblical translation, who makes reference to the same scriptural citation to explain his work with secular texts (Fiorenza, 1993, p. 195). This example points to the remarkable continuity of the Western tradition of gendered theorizing of translation.

The extraordinarily long career of the term "Les belles infidèles" is another case in point. Introduced by the French rhetorician Ménage (1613—1692), the adage declares that, like women, translations must be either beautiful or faithful. Its success is due in some measure to the way it positions fidelity as the opposite of beauty, ethics as the opposite of elegance, the drudgery of moral obligation as incompatible with stylistic (or marital) felicity. It is certainly not fortuitous that the expression was coined at a time when translations were considered as the principal means by which French was to be legitimated as a national language. The strategy used by Nicolas Perrot d'Ablancourt and his school of translators (which was known as the School of "Les belies infidèles") was in fact a notoriously blatant policy of infidelity. He and his fellow-translators, many of them members of the Académie francaise, sought to enhance the prestige of French literature by providing translations of the Ancients, yet they wished at the same time to consolidate the norms of elegance of a nascent prose style (Zuber, 1995; Cary, 1963). Their program called therefore for systematically unfaithful translations. This stylistic infidelity has become something of a permanent feature of the French tradition of translation, according to Antoine Berman (Berman, 1992). But correcting this cultural bias involves a reconceptualization of the relation between word and meaning, letter and spirit; it also involves a revaluation of the power of the receiving culture to mold imported works according to its own image.

The conflict between beauty and infidelity, between letter and spirit, reaches far back into the memory of Western culture. The terms which we use to divide production from reproduction include some of the most fundamental concepts of our philosophical vocabulary. Derrida has shown how these recurrent oppositions stem from a complicity between gender conceptions and writing, mimesis and fidelity. The conventional view of translation supposes an active original and a passive translation, creation followed by a passive act of transmission. But what if writing and translation are understood as interdependent, each bound to the other in the recognition that representation is always an active process, that the original is also at a distance from its originating intention, that there is never a total presence of the speaking subject in discourse (Derrida, 1979)?

If there is no primary meaning to be discovered, if translation is not in thrall to a deep and distant truth, where is fidelity to be grounded? It is appropriate that "fidelity," this vexed and much disputed term in the history of translation, should also have strong resonances in the history of gender politics. The crisis in marriage and the crisis in translation are identical, if considered from the point of view of their initial contract, according to Barbara Johnson.

> For while both translators and spouses were once bound by contracts to love, honor, and obey, and while both inevitably betray, the current questioning of the possibility and desirability of conscious mastery makes that contract seem deluded and exploitative from the start.
>
> (Johnson, 1985, p. 143)

Absolute fidelity, in this age of electronic reproduction, is reserved to the technologies of the photocopier and the sound system—although even these technologies are constantly confronted with the disappearing horizon of the absolute. When the indeterminations of consciousness are involved, can there be any standard by which fidelity is measured?

Fidelity reconstrued

The poverty of our conventional understanding of fidelity lies in its reliance on numerous sets of rigid binary oppositions which reciprocally validate one another. Translation is considered to be an act of reproduction, through which the meaning of a text is transferred from one language to another. Each polar element in the translating process is construed as an absolute, and meaning is transposed from one pole to the other. But the fixity implied in the oppositions between languages, between original/copy, author/translator, and, by analogy, male/female, cannot be absolute; these terms are rather to be placed on a continuum where each can be considered in relative terms. As Susan Bassnett points out, contemporary translation studies are struggling against "the old binary concept of translation [which] saw original and translated text as two poles," seeking in contrast to conceptualize translation as a dynamic activity fully engaged with cultural systems (Bassnett, 1992, p. 66). Barbara Godard emphasizes the ways in which this view of translation eliminates "cultural traces and self-reflexive elements," depriving the translated text of its "foundation in events." "The translator is understood to be a servant, an invisible hand mechanically turning the word of one language into another" (Godard, 1990, p. 91). It is by destroying the absolutes of polarity that we can advance in our understanding of social and literary relations. Attention must shift to those areas of identity where the indeterminate comes into play. Equivalence in translation, as contemporary translation theory emphasizes, cannot be a one-to-one proposition. The process of translation must be seen as a fluid production of meaning, similar to other kinds of writing. The hierarchy of writing roles, like gender identities, is increasingly to be recognized as mobile and performatire. The interstitial now becomes the focus of investigation, the polarized extremes abandoned.

Because it is an activity which has long been theorized in terms of a hierarchy of gendered positions, the rethinking of translation will necessarily upset traditional vocabularies of domination. In particular, the rethinking of translation involves a widening of the definition of the translating subject. Who translates? Fidelity can only be understood if we take a new look at the identity of translating subjects, and their enlarged area of responsibility as signatories of "doubly authored" documents. At the same time, a whole nexus of assumptions around issues of authority and agency come to be challenged. When meaning is no longer a hidden truth to be "discovered," but a set of discursive conditions to be "re-created," the work of the translator acquires added dimensions.

It is in the context of the need for new vocabularies to describe translation that Barbara Godard argues for women "writing their way into subjective agency" through a poetics of identity which might be called "transformance" (Godard, 1990, p. 89, p. 90). Feminist writing and translation meet in their common desire to foreground female subjectivity in the production of meaning. "The feminist translator, affirming her critical difference, her delight in interminable re-reading and re-writing, flaunts the signs of her manipulation of the text. *Woman handling* the text in translation would involve the replacement of the modest-self-effacing translator. [...] Feminist discourse presents transformation as performance as a model for translation ... This is at odds with the long dominant theory of translation as equivalence grounded in a poetics of transparence" (ibid., p. 91). Susan Bassnett argues for an "orgasmic" theory of translation, the result of "elements [that] are fused into a new whole in an encounter that is mutual, pleasurable and respectful" (Bassnett, 1992, p. 72).

Faced with texts which themselves challenge the way in which meaning is made, the translator is increasingly aware of her role in *determining* meaning, and of her responsibility in rendering it. Susanne de Lotbinière-Harwood (1991) and Suzanne Jill Levine (1991), in different ways, explain how their creative interaction with the work will provoke the emergence of new meanings. De Lotbinière-Harwood puts special emphasis on re-gendering the English language, in response to the provocative gender-consciousness of French-language writers; Levine is attentive to the marks which a conflictual "close laboration" with text, author or cultural context will leave in the translation.

【延伸阅读】

[1] Chamberlain, L. (1992). Gender and the Metaphorics of Translation. In L. Venuti (eds.), *Rethinking Translation: Discourse, Subjectivity, Ideology*. London and New York: Routledge.

[2] Simon, S. (1996). *Gender in Translation: Cultural Identity and the Politics of Transmission*. London and New York: Routledge.

[3] von Flotow, L. (1997). *Translation and Gender*. Manchester: St. Jerome Publishing Ltd.

【问题与思考】

1. 如何理解西蒙的"忠实的对象应该是由作者与译者共同参与的写作方案"这一观点？
2. 女性主义译者在翻译过程中通常采取什么样的翻译策略？为什么？
3. 女性作家的作品是否只应由女性译者翻译？如果你是西蒙，你会如何看待这个问题？
4. 文化研究对翻译研究有何积极意义？为什么？

选文四　斯皮瓦克翻译思想探究

李红玉

导　言

本文发表于《中国翻译》2009 年第 2 期。

斯皮瓦克是当今世界著名的文学理论家和文化批评家。随着翻译研究文化转向的发生，她的翻译思想和实践逐渐引起国际译学界的重视。在我国，翻译研究者对斯皮瓦克还缺乏足够关注，认识上也存在一定局限。为弥补这一缺憾，本文全面考察了斯皮瓦克有关翻译的论述，从翻译的本质、作为暴力的翻译、作为阅读的翻译和普遍意义上的翻译四个方面展现斯皮瓦克翻译思想的丰富内涵。

一、引言

盖亚特里·查克拉沃蒂·斯皮瓦克（Gayatri Chakravorty Spivak），1942 年生于印度，1963 年定居美国，现为哥伦比亚大学"社会和文学比较研究中心"负责人。她早年师承保罗·德曼（Paul de Man），是当今世界著名的文学理论家和文化批评家，与爱德华德·萨义德（Edward Said）、霍米·巴巴（Homi Barbar）并称为后殖民理论"神圣的三剑客"（罗伯特·扬语），是女性主义理论的代表人物之一，著名的马克思主义者和解构主义者。她与翻译有着不解之缘：1976 年，她凭借对德里达《论文字学》（De la grammatologie）的翻译，蜚声美国；之后，便在其深邃的理论探讨中不时引用翻译例证，穿插翻译问题。她还将翻译作为实践其后殖民女性主义理论的试验田，翻译了印度著名女作家马哈斯薇塔·德维（Mahasweta Devi）的多部作品，如《想象的地图》（Imaginary Maps）（1994）、《乳房的故事》（Breast Stories）（1997）、《老妇人》（Old Women）（1999）等，其中《想象的地图》获得 1998 年印度国家文学学会翻译奖。近十余年来，随着翻译研究文化转向的发生，她的翻译思想和实践已引起国际译学界的重视，日益成为女性主义翻译研究和后殖民翻译研究的重要内容（参见 Simon，1996：145 - 147；Gentzler，2004：182 - 186；Munday，2001：133 - 134 等）。在我国，学者们对其翻译思想的关注还非常有限，直到 2005 年才出现相关探讨（陈永国，2005：37 - 43），到目前为止相应研究仍较为匮乏。为数不多的几篇论述也还存在以下不足：首先，学者们对斯皮瓦克翻译思想的了解大都局限于她的《翻译的政治》（"The Politics of Translation"）（1992/1993）一文，对其他与翻译相关的论述涉及较少。第二，学者们对其翻译思想的认识还存在偏差，有的学者对斯皮瓦克翻译思想中的语言三重结构、翻译的政治等关键概念理解较为粗糙，或生搬斯皮瓦克佶屈聱牙的某几句原文，或将其思想作简单化的理解（参见袁晓亮，2007：24 - 25；张宁，2007：50 - 52）；有的则将斯皮瓦克提出的"作为阅读的翻译"和"作为翻译的阅读"混为一谈，认为"翻译就是阅读，阅读就是翻译"(关熔珍,2008:63),无视两者在语境、内涵和目的上的差异等。为弥补这些不足,本文全面考察了斯皮瓦克与翻译相关的论述,以展现其翻译思想的丰富内涵。

二、斯皮瓦克的翻译思想

斯皮瓦克有关翻译的探讨主要集中在德里达《论文字学》的"译者前言"(1976/2007)、《翻译的政治》("The Politics of Translation")(1992/1993)、《作为文化的翻译》("Translation as culture")(2000)、《被问及翻译:游移》("Questioned on Translation:Adrift")(2001)和《后殖民理性批评》("A Critique of Postcolonial Reason:Towards a History of the Vanishing Present")(1999)中。她的论述互文性极强,包括大量解构主义、马克思主义、女性主义和精神分析的理论资源,行文晦涩难懂。任何试图全面介绍其理论并进行本质化解读的尝试都必定是一种失败,因而本文对其翻译思想的考察只能是遵循其文本的印记,在文本的播散(dissemination)中进行阐述的一种尝试。

1. 关于翻译的本质

斯皮瓦克对翻译的思考始于对德里达《论文字学》的翻译,因而从一开始,她对翻译的理解就跳出了传统翻译观念的樊篱,体现出鲜明的解构主义特征。在德里达《论文字学》"译者前言"(1976/2007)中,斯皮瓦克从译者的角度诘问传统翻译观念:为什么翻译就该受到怀疑,译者就该处于次要地位?(斯皮瓦克,2007:80)她否认翻译是对意义的传达,"质疑源初绝对特权"(同上:79),认为"文本没有稳固的同一性,没有稳固的原文"(同上:5),文本是开放的,一直处于播散(dissemination)①之中。"翻译是互文性的一个版本"(同上:79),它非但不次等于原文、依赖原文,反而是对原文的"替补行为"(同上:80)。她援引德里达的翻译哲学思想,指出"翻译实现了所指和能指之间的差异"(同上:80);翻译是必要的,但又是不可能完全实现的,因为"我们从不会、事实上也从没有让纯粹所指(能指工具——或'载体'——保持完整无缺的处子之身)从一种语言'转移'到另一种语言中去,或在一种或同一语言中做这样的转移"(同上:80)。

在《翻译的政治》(1992/1993)中,她同样质疑了文本的同一性,突出了文本的播散。不过在这篇文章中,斯皮瓦克更多借鉴的是德曼关于逻辑、语法和修辞的论述。西方传统哲学认为逻辑、语法和修辞是人文学科的基础,其中"逻辑处于无可争议的优势地位,它使语言成为一个稳定的实体,并确保概念把握现实;语法作为逻辑的同盟,被认为能够正确表达逻辑推理和修辞形式,以便维护语言的严谨性和规范性";而"修辞是对语法的越轨,有可能造成意义含混的危险"(周颖,2001:48)。受此观念影响,传统翻译理论重视逻辑和语法,强调发现并传达原文所蕴含的真理,即作者意图,忽略文本中的修辞。德曼则对这种思想提出质疑,认为修辞不应处于逻辑和语法的对立面,而应与之形成共生关系,使文本在三者间的张力中存在。秉承德曼的这一思想,斯皮瓦克消解了逻辑、语法和修辞之间的等级,主张语言具有修辞本质(rhetorical nature)。她指出语言的"三重结构"包括逻辑、修辞和静默(silence),"逻辑通过清晰的指示

---

① 播散是德里达解构主义思想的一个重要概念,它包含播撒种子、精子和语义的意味,形象地表明意指活动就像播种一样,是散异的。意义不是在场的,始终处于时间和空间上的"延异"(différance)之中。

关联让我们从一个词跳到另一个词",它指明关系,指涉意义;而修辞扰乱逻辑的系统性,它悬置意义;静默则是修辞运作的方式,它存在于词与词之间,存在于语言之外(Spivak,1993:181)。这一三重结构让人们关注语言和文本的散异,即在修辞的干扰下,文本的意义并不能通过逻辑和语法被固定下来,意义是不确定的;它还让人们超越语言的局限,关注语言之外的静默,即"在语言的旁边和周围可能存在的任意偶然性"(同上:180)。斯皮瓦克将修辞扰乱逻辑而使语言和文本解除疆界、在差异中播散的状况,比喻为"语言织物的织边已经让位,磨损成易化(frayages or facilitation)"(同上:180)。易化是弗洛伊德的术语,指的是兴奋在传播通路中阻抗减小的这一现象①。斯皮瓦克借用这样一个术语表明,在翻译中,跨越疆界的播散必定遭遇阻抗,磨损不可避免,但这种播散也是一种易化的过程,是阻抗减小的过程,它体现的是"作为同一性的差异的政治"(politics as difference-as-identity)(Spivak,2001:22)。翻译不应试图将文本封闭起来,限定意义的播散,而应正视差异,允许文本在磨损中散播。译者的责任也不应是消除阻抗,将原文中所谓的同一性,即固定的意义,搬运到译入语中去,而应关注在原文中具有颠覆性的修辞(Spivak,1993:181),在翻译中用一种"中间话语"(in-between discourse)对这种修辞进行合理的挪用。

2. 作为暴力的翻译(translation as violence)

既然翻译不是对"一堆一堆的意义的转移"(同上:179),而是意义播散和建构的过程,那么翻译就无可避免地涉及权力和政治。作为一名女性主义者和后殖民理论家,翻译中的权力和政治正是斯皮瓦克关注的中心。当翻译中所体现的权力和政治涉及对她/他者的简化、贬低甚至压迫时,翻译就成为一种暴力工具。

这种暴力可能出现在出于"姐妹情谊"的全球女性主义阵营之中。在1993年《翻译的政治》一文中,斯皮瓦克考察了第三世界妇女文本被译成英文的情况。她发现第一世界女性翻译这些作品本是出于好意,希望这些文本被更多女性主义者阅读,使第三世界女性发出声音。但在翻译时,民主的法则却被强者的法则所取代。在不了解构建第三世界女性主体的"历史框架、知识-权力(pouvoir-savoir)机制"的情况下,第一世界女性将自己的历史和美国第二次女性主义浪潮中所主张的女性普遍模式强加于第三世界女性之上,以此来理解她们和她们的文本(Spivak,1999:164)。第三世界文学被译成了一种"流行的翻译腔"(with-it translatese),巴勒斯坦女性的作品读起来就像台湾男作家的作品(Spivak,1993:182)。文本中的修辞性、文化政治性和其中所铭刻的性别差异都被抹去(同上:182)。这让第三世界女性文本的文学性大打折扣,使它们对于说英语的学生而言根本无法和欧美本土女作家莫妮克·维蒂格(Monique Wittig)、艾丽斯·沃克(Alice Walker)等媲美(同上:181)。更重要的是,在第一世界女性的自我面前第三世界女性(文本)失去了她性。全球"姐妹情谊"(sisterhood)的好意成了对第三世界她者的暴力,成了一种"新殖民主义的构建"(neocolonialist construction)(同上:181)。

当帝国主义将暴力施加在屈从的语言之上时,翻译的暴力更为明显。斯皮瓦克曾在《后殖

---

① 易化是弗洛伊德用以描述神经机构功能的一种神经学术语,即"从一个神经元到另一个神经元的兴奋要克服某些抵抗"。当兴奋反复通过,导致通道中的抵抗持久降低,人们就说这里存在易化。"同时,兴奋总是偏向于选择易化了的通道而非没有易化的通道"(转引自Spivak,1993:314)。参见Psychoanalysis:Facilitation[OL]. http://www. answers. com/topic/facilitation. 上网日期:2008年8月20日;Clymour, Clark. Freud's androids[A]. In Jerome Neu eds. The Cambridge Companion to Freud[C]. Cambridge: Cambridge University Press. 1991: 44-85.

民理性批评》中分析过英国作家卢迪亚·吉卜林(Rudyard Kipling)的短篇小说《征服者威廉》("William the Conqueror")所隐含的帝国主义暴力。在这篇小说中,吉卜林大量运用了英国人在印度殖民地所使用的印度斯坦语的混杂语(pidgin Hindusthani)。这种语言毫无语法可言,在印度本族人看来是非常落后、不恰当也不正确的,但吉卜林的叙述行为却认可了这种语言使用,并将之塑造成合理的、不用翻译就可以直接使用的语言。斯皮瓦克认为这样的语言使用背后暗含了一种殖民主义的观点,即印度斯坦语是一种仆人使用的语言,十分卑劣,根本不值得英国人正确掌握(Spivak,1999:162)。而在描述印度仆人的印度斯坦语时,作者却费尽心思甚至通过音译,将印度斯坦语翻译成古的、笨拙的英语。这更加突出地为英语读者塑造了印度斯坦语的劣等形象。斯皮瓦克将这种译与不译的决定称为"作为暴力的翻译",因为它们在效果上标示了"将某一语言看成次等的想法"(同上:162)。

3. 作为阅读的翻译

为了抵制作为暴力的翻译,避免将她/他者按照自我进行同化和简化,避免帝国主义对她/他者的鄙夷和贬低,保持她/他者的独立性、完整性和平等性,斯皮瓦克站在第三世界的立场上,针对第一世界的译者,提出了"作为阅读的翻译"(translation as reading)(Spivak,1993:179)。她认为"翻译是最亲密的阅读行为"(同上:180)。这种阅读不是为了理解意义的普通浏览,而是在阅读中关注语言的特殊性(specificity)(同上:180),即修辞性;"引诱文本展露其语言的局限"(同上:183),即静默;并根据语言的线索,揭示写作主体/能动者如何被语言和语言背后的社会、历史所书写。

在这种阅读中,译者服帖于(surrender to)她/他所译的文本(同上:180),"成为最亲密(intimate)的读者"(同上:183)。只有这样,译者才能将她/他者看做在自我之前就存在的独立体:"译者获得许可,在自我最亲近的地方,从记忆之前的他者踪迹越界"(同上:180)。斯皮瓦克用爱(love)和爱欲(erotic)取代了翻译中的伦理关系。因为作为伦理的能动者,译者"无法最大限度地想象她/他性(otherness, alterity)",为了符合伦理我们只能"把她/他者变成像自我的东西"。(同上:183)这就可能涉及对第三世界她/他者出于"好意"的归化。而只有"在爱和关于爱的交流与阅读中",我们才能允许"她/他"的存在。"译者的责任就是易化原文和其影子之间的爱,这种允许磨损、限定译者能动性和她/他想象中或实际读者要求的爱"(同上:181)。在这种爱和爱欲中,译者克制自我,克制译入语读者需求,让"她/他"以"他/她"而非以"我"的形象出现,完全体现了对她/他者的尊重。

斯皮瓦克认为真正的翻译必须为她/他者在语言中创造逻辑和修辞"参差不齐的关系",这样才能为能动的她/他者构成一片天地,能动者才"可以用道德的方式、政治的方式、日常生活的方式行动;因此能动者用人的方式在世界上活着"(同上:181)。为了实现这种真正的翻译,译者必须在译文中重现原文中逻辑、修辞和静默的张力,再现原文的文体试验(stylistic experiences)。她以德维的作品 Stanadāyini 的标题英译为例说明了关注文体试验的重要性。德维的这部作品讲述的是一个印度妇女迫于生计成为奶娘,靠不断怀孕来为上层权贵的孩子们哺乳,最后罹患乳腺癌的故事。该文标题 Stanadāyini 修辞风格非常怪异,意为奶妈。在两个译文中,斯皮瓦克的翻译注意到了作者的风格特色,生造了一个词,将之译做 Breast-Giver(乳房给予者),再现了原文中修辞的静默(rhetorical silences);而另一个译本忽略了原文的试验性文体特征,用人人熟悉的 Wet Nurse(奶娘)作为译文标题,虽然也传达了原文的意思,但却压抑了原文怪异标题所包含的讽刺意味,同时也无法营造让人震撼的效果,原文中修辞的静默被丢失(同上:182-183)。除了关注文体试验之外,斯皮瓦克还指出,在翻译中"语言的历史、作者所处的历史时代、翻译中和作为翻译的语言的历史(the history of the language-in-and-as-translation),也必须在编织(weaving)中出现"(同上:186)。也就是说,译者还必须详细考察源语的历史和作者所处的社会、历史和文化语境,在当时、当地的背景下更加亲密地理解原文,服帖于原文,并将这些背景中的因素编织到翻译中去。斯皮瓦克对德维作品的翻译就生动地为这一点提供了注释。在翻译中,斯皮瓦克拒绝将德维仅仅看成是印度女作家,她认为这样的简化和抽象包含着"民主文化议程、对第三世界特殊性的消除和对其文化公民的拒绝"(同上:189)。她也拒绝为德维的文本和印度的本土生活作"元小说"的建构。相反,她在译文集中提供译者序、作者访谈和前言,通过她和作者的共同叙述,为读者重现了作者和文本的具体语境,帮助读者想象真正具有文化差异的她者。

斯皮瓦克还为第三世界女性文本的译者如何在翻译中成为最亲密的读者提出了专门的建议。她认为首先,由于女性主义作者也许会质疑那些更加公众化的语言使用,而用一种私人化的语言进行写作,所以译者在日常生活中可以尝试用她者语言讲一些私事,以培养与该语言的亲密感(同上:183)。第二,"译者必须能够在源语领域(terrain)的基础上进行甄别"(同上:189),以区分女性创作中好的和坏的、抵抗的和屈服的作品(同上:188)。因为并不是所有第三世界女性的写作都是好的(同上:188)。当然,好与坏也是一个具有弹性的标准,是在特定语境下被建构起来的。所以,译者必须充分了解源语中文学创作的现状,以便能独立地,而不是依赖第一世界的已有标准,作出这种区分。她/他必须认识到,在英语空间中看起来具有抵抗性的作品也许在源语空间中是反动的(同上:188)。斯皮瓦克主张译者挑选一些不符合潮流和主流的作家作品进行翻译,因为有意思的文本恰好是那些"你无法从中了解一个民族国家主流文化再现或自我再现的主流观点"的文本(同上:189)。最后,也是最重要的一点,斯皮瓦克认为应该埋葬出于"姐妹情谊"而将妇女看成无差别的统一体的观点。她重申了她的"策略本质主义",指出在最开始接触其他女性的时候,认为女性之间有共同的东西,这样很好,因为这可以在女性间形成一种否则就无法形成的关系。但第二步要做的就是谦虚地学习她的母语,在这一过程中你就会立刻发现差异,你也会同时日以继日地感受到你们的团结(同上:191)。这就是对文化翻译的亲密性的准备(同上:192)。

在操作层面上,斯皮瓦克认为服帖于原文主要是一种直译。译者首先全速翻译,如果停下来思考翻译给英语带来哪些影响,如果心中装着读者,如果无法将意图主体(intending subject)即作者,仅仅当成一块跳板,她/他就无法服帖(同上:189)。这样快速翻译完第一个版本之后,译者再根据草稿的语言特点用一种"中间话语"进行修改(同上:190)。在修改中,译者也不应考虑可能的读者需求。她/他必须摒弃在学校所学的对等原则,必须抵制英语中的标准文体。

4. 普遍意义上的翻译

除了探讨狭隘意义上的翻译,斯皮瓦克还关注作为跨界和转换的普遍意义上的翻译,并将之同狭隘意义上的翻译一起看做是构建后殖民主体的重要途径。

在她看来,阅读也是一种翻译。这里的阅读既包括对真正意义上的文本的阅读,也包括对普遍意义上的文本,即任何形式的,包括图像的、声音的、社会的、历史的、政治的文本的阅读。

斯皮瓦克曾探讨过后殖民女性如何阅读白人理论的问题：表面上看起来和第三世界女性相距甚远的英语话语中的理论对第三世界女性有用吗？她以自己对彼得·德·保拉（Peter de Bolla）的《雄浑的话语》（*The Discourse of the Sublime*）的解读为例，说明在阅读这些理论时，应采取"作为翻译的移情阅读（sympathetic reading as translation），恰恰不是服帖，而是保持距离的友好学习"（同上：197）。在这种情况下，读者成为"作为译者的读者（reader as translator，即 RAT）"（同上：197）。"作为译者的读者"绝不盲从文本，而是站在第三世界的立场上独立思考，当文本中的观点能够启发"作为译者的读者"时，他/她欣然接受，并在阐释中"超越和扩展该书"（同上：198）；当文本中的观点暴露了第一世界的局限时，"作为译者的读者"则嗤之以鼻，不屑一顾，此时作为翻译的阅读就失效了（同上：199）。在这种作为翻译的阅读中，自我与他/她者保持了友好的距离，第三世界的读者不会在阅读第一世界作者的作品中失去自我，而第一世界的她/他者也得到了尊重，不会因为自我的抵制而被拒之门外，或失去独立性。斯皮瓦克指出，"所有阅读都是翻译，错误和偏差是阅读游戏的一部分……当我们忘记这一点，并为了认同而阅读，最糟糕的是为了在文本的镜子中看到我们自己的脸而阅读的时候，我们失去了对作为原文占位符的他者的尊重"（Spivak，2001：14）。

　　普遍意义上的翻译还可以作为一种文化的穿梭运动而存在。在《作为文化的翻译》（2000）中，斯皮瓦克注意到后殖民主体实际上生活在本土文化和帝国主义文化的翻译之中。她借用精神分析学家梅兰妮·克莱茵（Melanie Klein）的"穿梭中的主体"（the subject in the shuttling）所涉及的翻译概念，探讨了作为编码的翻译（transcoding as translation）所构成的文化运作。克莱茵认为人类婴儿总是抓取/掠夺（grab）某一样东西，然后是许多其他东西。"这种抓取/掠夺一个与内部（an inside）无法区分的'外部'（an outside）构建了一个内部，这种抓取/掠夺来来回回不断进行，通过所抓取/掠夺的东西将一切编码进一个符号系统。这种天然的/粗鲁的（crude）编码可以被称为'翻译'"（2000：13）。"在这一永无止境的编织中，主体在穿梭的翻译中形成"，作为自然的人成为文化中具有不稳固主体的人（同上：13）。在这一理论的基础上，斯皮瓦克探讨了澳洲土著在后殖民语境下的生存状态。她指出，在西方文明入侵后土著和他们的传统文化开始疏远，书写土著主体的旧文化符号系统也随之坍塌。在殖民压迫下，土著人只能要求得到主流教育，学习英语的文化符号系统，获得"插入文明社会"的机会；同时他们也要求在课程中纳入对土著文化的描述和评说，以便让他们自己的符号在英语符号系统中作为文化习语（cultural idioms）在戏剧、艺术、文学、主流文化甚至理论等表演形式中再现（同上：16）。土著人就生活在这种私人习语与公共英语符号间的编码转换的翻译之中。在此翻译中，他们形成了既不同于传统文化，也不同于西方文化的，具有抵抗性质的杂合文化。这表明土著并不是在对帝国主义文化毫无抵抗的情况下就丧失了文化特色，这种反抗恰好体现在他们对西方文化的翻译之中。斯皮瓦克还探索了通过翻译让属下（subaltern）发出声音的可能性。"属下"这一概念源于意大利马克思主义者安东尼·葛兰西（Antonio Gramsci），指的是处于资产阶级宏大叙事和知识权力系统边缘的人和群体，在斯皮瓦克这里指的是"没有文化流动性的人"（同上：18）。属下用他/她们自己的习语说话，但他/她们具有独特性的言说却并不能被主流所听到。而"如果没有被听到，就不算真正的发言"（No speech is speech if it is not heard）（Spivak，2000：22）；只有当说和听都充分实现时，只有当回应来自谈话双方时，言说才能真正实现，否则即便属下是在说话，那也是无效的自说自话罢了。斯皮瓦克认为，"正是这种听到-以便-回应的行为（this act of hearing-to-respond）也许可以被称为翻译的当务之急（the imperative to translate)"(同上:22)。也就是说,要想倾听属下的声音,让属下获得文化流动性,就必须想办法将属下具有独特性的习语翻译到具有普遍性的标准话语中去。但这种翻译不能被认为是出于好心、帮助遇到麻烦的人,也不能认为是对他/她者的代表。相反,"这种人与人之间创建的翻译是在他/她者的常态中,充满关爱和耐心的倾听,足以注意他/她者已经默默地作出了(发言的——笔者加)努力"(同上:22)。这就意味着,在这种翻译中,我们不能用标准的语言——不管这种语言多么本土化——来取消属下语言中的习语,而应保持属下语言的特殊性。斯皮瓦克建议编写"同语字典"(same-language dictionary),将属下的习语译入标准语言中去,供属下使用。只有这样,"属下性才能痛苦地将它自己(itself)翻译到一种霸权之中,这种霸权可以利用并超越一切我们从高处能组织的援助和抵制"(同上:22)。

三、结语

从"翻译的本质"、"作为暴力的翻译"、"作为阅读的翻译"和"普遍意义上的翻译"四个方面,我们可以发现斯皮瓦克的翻译思想以解构主义为基础,以后殖民主义理论和女性主义理论为视角,揭示了翻译作为暴力工具和抵抗工具的两面性,探索了在翻译中尊重差异、构建女性/后殖民主体的途径,对翻译研究的许多方面都具有极大的启示作用。尤其在全球化的今天,随着新殖民形态的出现,中国这一历史上未真正沦为殖民地的国家,如今也被卷入文化殖民的危险之中。在这种背景下探究斯皮瓦克的翻译思想,并以此为基础深入后殖民和后殖民女性主义翻译研究就具有非常现实的意义了。

【延伸阅读】

[1] 陈义华.斯皮瓦克后殖民批评的后殖民性.山东大学学报:哲学社会科学版,2011(3):25 - 29.

[2] 陈永国.从解构到翻译:斯皮瓦克的属下研究.外国文学,2005(5):37 - 42.

[3] 关熔珍.翻译政治之比较:斯皮瓦克与鲁迅.鲁迅研究月刊,2007(9):44 - 48.

[4] 孙景尧."垂死"之由、"新生"之路——评斯皮瓦克的《学科之死》.中国比较文学,2007 (3):1 - 10.

[5] 王晓路.文化政治与文化批评——斯皮瓦克文学观的解读.外国文学,2004(5):37 - 43.

【问题与思考】

1. 本文作者为何选择"翻译的本质"、"作为暴力的翻译"、"作为阅读的翻译"和"普遍意义上的翻译"四个方面来展现斯皮瓦克翻译思想的内涵?

2. 本文作者是怎样遵循斯皮瓦克文本的印记,在文本的播散中阐述斯皮瓦克的翻译思想的?

3. 本文作者在论文结语部分为何要提到中国?

第九章 哲学与翻译

导 论

在西方,从柏拉图、亚里士多德开始,哲人们就开始关注有关人、语言、符号和世界的关系。柏拉图的模仿论、亚里士多德的再现论、奥古斯丁的符号论、洛克的指称论给翻译理论提供了无尽的理论源泉。直到现代,随着语言的转向,语言哲学与翻译的关系联系得更紧了。维特根斯坦的语言游戏、奎因(William van Orman Quine)的翻译不确定性、海德格尔的现象学翻译观、德里达的解构主义以及戴维森(Donald Davidson)的不可通约性,都从不同的角度或解释翻译活动的现象,或给翻译研究以形而上的启迪。因此,任何完整的翻译理论都离不开哲学的途径。没有哲学这个"钢筋骨架"做支撑,翻译学这幢大厦会像"巴别塔"一样轰然倒塌。在西方翻译理论史上,不少哲学大家要么把翻译作为研究哲学的一种媒介,要么直接通过翻译而"思",研究语言和哲学问题,翻译既是他们研究的手段,又是目的(刘军平,2009:247)。20世纪下半叶以来,有多种哲学理论对翻译研究产生巨大影响,其中尤以阐释学理论和解构主义理论最引人注目。

阐释学起源于德国浪漫主义时期的施莱尔马赫和20世纪的海德格尔,但翻译的阐释学研究要数斯坦纳(George Steiner)的《通天塔之后》(*After Babel*)影响最大。他把阐释学方法定义为"研究理解口语或书面文本的意义,并试图按照意义的一般模式判断理解过程"。《通天塔之后》初版于1975年,后来于1992年和1998年再版,据称是"自18世纪以来对翻译理论和过程的首次系统研究"。该书首先重点探讨译者的心理和智力活动,接下来讨论翻译过程中意义产生和理解的过程,然后提出他自己的以阐释学为导向的理论模式。他的著名的阐释学翻译四步骤包括信任、侵入、吸收和补偿。他结合文学翻译的例子对四步骤模式作了仔细分析。

斯坦纳认为,如果真正的理解和翻译发生在两种语言相互弥散之处,那么超越自我的能力就变得十分重要。他说,"这种自我朝向他者的影射是译者技艺的最终机密",并援引庞德的翻译为例。庞德把汉语译成英语,而他汉语懂得并不多。斯坦纳认为这是一种优势,因为对源语文本和文化不熟悉,译者得以从事翻译,而不受两种语言文化相互接触而产生的前见和复杂性的影响。

斯坦纳的著作在初版30年后仍在再版重印,由此可知其受欢迎程度。《通天塔之后》文献征引范围很广,是一部里程碑式的著作。它吸引了许多非专业人士去了解翻译理论。诸如贝尔曼和韦努蒂这样的翻译理论家更是受其影响至深。和斯坦纳一样,贝尔曼和韦努蒂也非常重视将异质文化引入目标语文化,他们从来不把好的翻译等同于通顺的归化翻译。

本雅明(Walter Benjamin)1923年发表的论文《译者的任务》("The Task of the Translator")

提出了一种关于翻译的实验性的观点。它原先是本雅明翻译的波德莱尔《巴黎塑像》德语译本的序言,后来成为非常重要的一篇关于文学翻译的哲学文献。本雅明论文的中心思想是,译本的存在并不是为了让读者理解原文的语义或信息内容。译本虽然单独存在,但与原文休戚相关,它产生于原文之后,从原文"来世"中出现,并赋予原文"延续的生命"。此外,本雅明还提出"纯语言"理论。他的思想深深影响了解构主义哲学的代表人物、法国翻译理论家德里达。

德里达创制的一套术语复杂而且不断改变,其中最重要的当数"延异"(differance)。该术语巧妙地利用了动词 differ 的两个语义 defer 和 differ,其中任一个都不能包含该词的全部语义,其拼写形式 differance 从 difference 演化而来,在视觉效果上表示能指的模糊和意义的延宕。德里达的解构主义理论从索绪尔的所指、能指等一些能定义、捕获和稳定意义的概念入手,解构了语言学得以存在的一些重要前提。索绪尔的符号代表着概念,他的语言学建立在独特的语言系统基础之上,德里达的延异却表示差异和延宕之间的时空里的某个不确定的位置。

德里达认为,自柏拉图以来的西方理性主义有一个根本的错误,即都在寻找某些"超验所指"(在任何语言中的任何时间都表达同样概念的所指),并以它们为中心,建构起具有等级秩序的逻各斯中心主义。要解构逻各斯中心主义,必须先解构其赖以生存的"可译性"基础。这样,解构问题转化为翻译问题。翻译,特别是语际翻译,见证、展现和诠释了能指与所指的分裂、所指/概念/意义自身的分裂、语言的(内部的和外部的)分裂以及文本的(内部的和外部的)分裂。在这一切发生的同时,翻译也撕裂了自身。它不再担"翻译"的名,而蜕化为无限暧昧的"变形"(transformation)概念,德里达用莎士比亚名剧《威尼斯商人》中的一句话"when mercy seasons justice"(情理兼顾)揭示了其内涵。德里达的相关翻译理论可见于他的两篇论文:"Des tours de Babel"(1985)和"What is a Relevant Translation?"(2001)。

本章共选三篇文章。第一篇是 Walter Benjamin 撰写的"The Task of the Translator",该文是解构主义翻译理论的重要奠基性文献。第二篇"After Babel",为 George Steiner 所著,文章阐述了以阐释学为基础的翻译活动的四个步骤。第三篇是袁伟著的《本雅明说的是啥?》,对本雅明的"可译性"、"余生"和"纯语言"等概念的内涵作了初步梳理。

 选 文

选文一　The Task of the Translator

Walter Benjamin

导　言

本文选自韦努蒂编《翻译研究读本》。

瓦尔特·本雅明(Walter Benjamin, 1892—1940)是 20 世纪前半期德国著名思想家、哲

学家、文艺理论家。他出身富有的犹太人家庭，早年攻读哲学，1920年定居柏林，从事文学评论及翻译工作。1933年纳粹上台，他离开德国，定居巴黎。法国沦陷后，他在逃亡美国的途中自杀。本雅明的思想植根于犹太教神学传统，并受马克思主义、超现实主义等思潮影响。《译者的任务》是1923年本雅明为所译的波德莱尔的《巴黎塑像》写的序，文章被奉为解构主义翻译理论的重要奠基性文献。

　　本雅明在文中首先提出顾及受众无益的观点，接着谈到支配翻译的法则，也即原作的可译性。他认为原作的可译性取决于是否有合适的译者以及原作本质是否有翻译的需求，其中第二点尤其重要。在探讨语言间亲缘关系的出处时，本雅明引入了一个重要而抽象的"纯语言"概念。在"纯语言"这个总体集合里，每种语言的意指方式相辅相成，相互补充，臻于完满。而翻译则是指向通往这种难以企及的最高境界的途径。文章结尾处，本雅明极力推崇《圣经》翻译中所用的隔行对照式的极端直译法。这是因为尽管翻译突显了语言的差异，但同时也催生新的表达方法。通过翻译的途径可以使现存的语言最终迈向"纯语言"的理想境界。翻译的价值就在于它对语言差异的反映和强调程度。本文的许多观点在一定程度上破解了人们对传统译论中忠实原则的盲目追求，对后来20世纪后期兴起的解构主义翻译理论产生了很大影响。（参见谢天振《当代国外翻译理论导读》：319-320）

In the appreciation of a work of art or an art form, consideration of the receiver never proves fruitful. Not only is any reference to a certain public or its representatives misleading, but even the concept of an "ideal" receiver is detrimental in the theoretical consideration of art, since all it posits is the existence and nature of man as such. Art, in the same way, posits man's physical and spiritual existence, but in none of its works is it concerned with his response. No poem is intended for the reader, no picture for the beholder, no symphony for the listener.

Is a translation meant for readers who do not understand the original? This would seem to explain adequately the divergence of their standing in the realm of art. Moreover, it seems to be the only conceivable reason for saying "the same thing" repeatedly. For what does a literary work "say?" What does it communicate? It "tells" very little to those who understand it. Its essential quality is not statement or the imparting of information. Yet any translation which intends to perform a transmitting function cannot transmit anything but information—hence, something inessential. This is the hallmark of bad translations. But do we not generally regard as the essential substance of a literary work what it contains in addition to information—as even a poor translator will admit—the unfathomable, the mysterious, the "poetic," something that a translator can reproduce only if he is also a poet? This, actually, is the cause of another characteristic of inferior translation, which consequently we may define as the inaccurate transmission of an inessential content. This will be true whenever a translation undertakes to serve the reader. However, if it were intended for the reader, the same would have to apply to the original. If the original does not exist for the reader's sake, how could the translation be understood on the basis of this premise?

Translation is a mode. To comprehend it as mode one must go back to the original, for that contains the law governing the translation: its translatability. The question of whether a work is translatable has a dual meaning. Either: Will an adequate translator ever be found among the totality of its readers? Or, more pertinently: Does its nature lend itself to translation and, therefore, in view of the significance of the mode, call for it? In principle, the first question can be decided only contingently; the second, however, apodictically. Only superficial thinking will deny the independent meaning of the latter and declare both questions to be of equal significance ... It should be pointed out that certain correlative concepts retain their meaning, and possibly their foremost significance, if they are referred exclusively to man. One might, for example, speak of an unforgettable life or moment even if all men had forgotten it. If the nature of such a life or moment required that it be unforgotten, that predicate would not imply a falsehood but merely a claim not fulfilled by men, and probably also a reference to a realm in which it *is* fulfilled: God's remembrance. Analogously, the translatability of linguistic creations ought to be considered even if men should prove unable to translate them. Given a strict concept of translation, would they not really be translatable to some degree? The question as to whether the translation of certain linguistic creations is called for ought to be posed in this sense. For this thought is valid here: If translation is a mode, translatability must be an essential feature of certain works.

Translatability is an essential quality of certain works, which is not to say that it is essential that they be translated; it means rather that a specific significance inherent in the original manifests itself in its translatability. It is plausible that no translation, however good it may be, can have any significance as regards the original. Yet, by virtue of its translatability the original is closely connected with the translation; in fact, this connection is all the closer since it is no longer of importance to the original. We may call this connection a natural one, or, more specifically, a vital connection. Just as the manifestations of life are intimately connected with the phenomenon of life without being of importance to it, a translation issues from the original—not so much from its life as from its afterlife. For a translation comes later than the original, and since the important works of world literature never find their chosen translators at the time of their origin, their translation marks their stage of continued life. The idea of life and afterlife in works of art should be regarded with an entirely unmetaphorical objectivity. Even in times of narrowly prejudiced thought there was an inkling that life was not limited to organic corporeality. But it cannot be a matter of extending its dominion under the feeble scepter of the soul, as Fechner tried to do, or, conversely, of basing its definition on the even less conclusive factors of animality, such as sensation, which characterize life only occasionally. The concept of life is given its due only if everything that has a history of its own, and is not merely the setting for history, is credited with life. In the final analysis, the range of life must be determined by history rather than by nature, least of all by such tenuous factors as sensation and soul. The philosopher's task consists in comprehending all of natural life through the more encompassing life of history. And indeed, is not the continued life of works of art far easier to recognize than the continual life of animal species? The history of the great works of art tells us about their antecedents, their realization in the age of the artist, their potentially eternal afterlife in succeeding generations. Where this last manifests itself, it is called fame. Translations that are more than transmissions of subject matter come into being when in the course of its survival a work has reached the age of its fame. Contrary, therefore, to the claims of bad translators, such translations do not so much serve the work as owe their existence to it. The life of the originals attains in them to its ever-renewed latest and most abundant flowering.

Being a special and high form of life, this flowering is governed by a special, high purposiveness. The relationship between life and purposefulness, seemingly obvious yet almost beyond the grasp of the intellect, reveals itself only if the ultimate purpose toward which all single functions tend is sought not in its own sphere but in a higher one. All puposeful manifestations of life, including their very purposiveness, in the final analysis have their end not in life, but in the expression of its nature, in the representation of its significance. Translation thus ultimately serves the purpose of expressing the central reciprocal relationship between languages. It cannot possibly reveal or establish this hidden relationship itself; but it can represent it by realizing it in embryonic or intensive form. This representation of hidden significance through an embryonic attempt at making it visible is of so singular a nature that it is rarely met with in the sphere of nonlinguistic life. This, in its analogies and symbols, can draw on other ways of suggesting meaning than intensive—that is, anticipative, intimating—realization. As for the posited central kinship of languages, it is marked by a distinctive convergence. Languages are not strangers to one another, but are, *a priori* and apart from all historical relationships, interrelated in what they want to express.

With this attempt at an explication our study appears to rejoin, after futile detours, the traditional theory of translation. If the kinship of languages is to be demonstrated by translations, how else can this be done but by conveying the form and meaning of the original as accurately as possible? To be sure, that theory would be hard put to define the nature of this accuracy and therefore could shed no light on what is important in a translation. Actually, however, the kinship of languages is brought out by a translation far more profoundly and clearly than in the superficial and indefinable similarity of two works of literature. To grasp the genuine relationship between an original and a translation requires an investigation analogous to the argumentation by which a critique of cognition would have to prove the impossibility of an image theory. There it is a matter of showing that in cognition there could be no objectivity, not even a claim to it, if it dealt with images of reality; here it can be demonstrated that no translation would be possible if in its ultimate essence it strove for likeness to the original. For in its afterlife—which could not be called that if it were not a transformation and a renewal of something living—the original undergoes a change. Even words with fixed meaning can undergo a maturing process. The obvious tendency of a writer's literary style may in time wither away, only to give rise to immanent tendencies in the literary creation. What sounded fresh once may sound hackneyed later; what was once current may someday sound quaint. To seek the essence of such changes, as well as the equally constant changes in meaning, in the subjectivity of posterity rather than in the very life of language and its works, would mean—even allowing for the crudest psychologism—to confuse the root cause of a thing with its essence. More pertinently, it would mean denying, by an impotence of thought, one of the most powerful and fruitful historical processes. And even if one tried to turn an author's last stroke of the pen into the *coup de gröce* of his work, this still would not save that dead theory of translation. For just as the tenor and the significance of the great works of literature undergo a complete transformation over the centuries, the mother tongue of the translator is transformed as well. While a poet's words endure in his own language, even the greatest translation is destined to become part of the growth of its own language and eventually to be absorbed by its renewal. Translation is so far removed from being the sterile equation of two dead languages that of all literary forms it is the one charged with the special mission of watching over the maturing process of the original language and the birth pangs of its own.

If the kinship of languages manifests itself in translations, this is not accomplished through a vague alikeness between adaptation and original. It stands to reason that kinship does not necessarily involve likeness. The concept of kinship as used here is in accord with its more restricted common usage: In both cases, it cannot be defined adequately by identity of origin, although in defining the more restricted usage the concept of origin remains indispensable. Wherein resides the relatedness of two languages, apart from historical considerations? Certainly not in the similarity between works of literature or words. Rather, all suprahistorical kinship of languages rests in the intention underlying each language as a whole—an intention, however, which no single language can attain by itself but which is realized only by the totality of their intentions supplementing each other: pure language. While all individual elements of foreign languages—words, sentences, structure—are mutually exclusive, these languages supplement one another in their intentions. Without distinguishing the intended object from the mode of intention, no firm grasp of this basic law of a philosophy of language can be achieved. The words *Brot* and *pain* "intend" the same object, but the modes of this intention are not the same. It is owing to these modes that the word *Brot* means something different to a German than the word *pain* to a Frenchman, that these words are not interchangeable for them, that, in fact, they strive to exclude each other. As to the intended object, however, the two words mean the very same thing. While the modes of intention in these two words are in conflict, intention and object of intention complement each of the two languages from which they are derived; there the object is complementary to the intention. In the individual, unsupplemented languages, meaning is never found in relative independence, as in individual words or sentences; rather, it is in a constant state of flux—until it is able to emerge as pure language from the harmony of all the various modes of intention. Until then, it remains hidden in the languages. If, however, these languages continue to grow in this manner until the end of their time, it is translation which catches fire on the eternal life of the works and the perpetual renewal of language. Translation keeps putting the hallowed growth of languages to the test: How far removed is their hidden meaning from revelation, how close can it be brought by the knowledge of this remoteness?

This, to be sure, is to admit that all translation is only a somewhat provisional way of coming to terms with the foreignness of languages. An instant and final rather than a temporary and provisional solution of this foreignness remains out of the reach of mankind; at any rate, it eludes any direct attempt. Indirectly, however, the growth of religions ripens the hidden seed into a higher development of language. Although translation, unlike art, cannot claim permanence for its products, its goal is undeniably a final, conclusive, decisive stage of all linguistic creation. In translation the original rises into a higher and purer linguistic air, as it were. It cannot live there permanently, to be sure, and it certainly does not reach it in its entirety. Yet, in a singularly impressive manner, at least it points the way to this region: the predestined, hitherto inaccessible realm of reconciliation and fulfillment of languages. The transfer can never be total, but what reaches this region is that element in a translation which goes beyond transmittal of subject matter. This nucleus is best defined as the element that does not lend itself to translation. Even when all the surface content has been extracted and transmitted, the primary concern of the genuine translator remains elusive. Unlike the words of the original, it is not translatable, because the relationship between content and language is quite different in the original and the translation. While content and language form a certain unity in the original, like a fruit and its skin, the language of the translation envelops its content like a royal robe with ample folds. For it signifies a more exalted language than its own and thus remains unsuited to its content, overpowering and alien. This disjunction prevents translation and at the same time makes it superfluous. For any translation of a work originating in a specific stage of linguistic history represents, in regard to a specific aspect of its content, translation into all other languages. Thus translation, ironically, transplants the original into a more definitive linguistic realm since it can no longer be displaced by a secondary rendering. The original can only be raised there anew and at other points of time. It is no mere coincidence that the word "ironic" here brings the Romanticists to mind. They, more than any others, were gifted with an insight into the life of literary works which has its highest testimony in translation. To be sure, they hardly recognized translation in this sense, but devoted their entire attention to criticism, another, if a lesser, factor in the continued life of literary works. But even though the Romanticists virtually ignored translation in their theoretical writings, their own great translations testify to their sense of the essential nature and the dignity of this literary mode. There is abundant evidence that this sense is not necessarily most pronounced in a poet; in fact, he may be least open to it. Not even literary history suggests the traditional notion that great poets have been eminent translators and lesser poets have been indifferent translators. A number of the most eminent ones, such as Luther, Voss, and Schlegel, are incomparably more important as translators than as creative writers; some of the great among them, such as Hölderlin and Stefan George, cannot be simply subsumed as poets, and quite particularly not if we consider them as translators. As translation is a mode of its own, the task of the translator, too, may be regarded as distinct and clearly differentiated from the task of the poet.

The task of the translator consists in finding that intended effect [*Intention*] upon the language into which he is translating which produces in it the echo of the original. This is a feature of translation which basically differentiates it from the poet's work, because the effort of the latter is never directed at the language as such, at its totality, but solely and immediately at specific linguistic contextual aspects. Unlike a work of literature, translation does not find itself in the center of the language forest but on the outside facing the wooded ridge; it calls into it without entering, aiming at that single spot where the echo is able to give, in its own language, the reverberation of the work in the alien one. Not only does the aim of translation differ from that of a literary work—it intends language as a whole, taking an individual work in an alien language as a point of departure—but it is a different effort altogether. The intention of the poet is spontaneous, primary, graphic; that of the translator is derivative, ultimate, ideational. For the great motif of integrating many tongues into one true language is at work. This language is one in which the independent sentences, works of literature, critical judgments, will never communicate—for they remain dependent on translation; but in it the languages themselves, supplemented and reconciled in their mode of signification, harmonize. If there is such a thing as a language of truth, the tensionless and even silent depository of the ultimate truth which all thought strives for, then this language of truth is—the true language. And this very language, whose divination and description is the only perfection a philosopher can hope for, is concealed in concentrated fashion in translations. There is no muse of philosophy, nor is there one of translation. But despite the claims of sentimental artists, these two are not banausic. For there is a philosophical genius that is characterized by a yearning for that language which manifests itself in translations. "*Les langues imparfaites en cela que plusieurs, manque la suprême: penser étant écrire sans accessoires, ni chuchotement mais tacite encore l'immortelle parole, la diversité, sur terre, des idiomes empêche personne de proférer les mots qui, sinon se trouveraient, par une frappe unique, elle-même matériellement la vérité.*"[①] If what Mallarmé evokes here is fully fathomable to a philosopher, translation, with its rudiments of such a language, is midway between poetry and doctrine. Its products are less sharply defined, but it leaves no less of a mark on history.

If the task of the translator is viewed in this light, the roads toward a solution seem to

---

①　"The imperfection of languages consists in their plurality, the supreme one is lacking: Thinking is writing without accessories or even whispering, the immortal word still remains silent; the diversity of idioms on earth prevents everybody from uttering the words which otherwise, at one single stroke, would materialize as truth."

be all the more obscure and impenetrable. Indeed, the problem of ripening the seed of pure language in a translation seems to be insoluble, determinable in no solution. For is not the ground cut from under such a solution if the reproduction of the sense ceases to be decisive? Viewed negatively, this is actually the meaning of all the foregoing. The traditional concepts in any discussion of translations are fidelity and license—the freedom of faithful reproduction and, in its service, fidelity to the word. These ideas seem to be no longer serviceable to a theory that looks for other things in a translation than reproduction of meaning. To be sure, traditional usage makes these terms appear as if in constant conflict with each other. What can fidelity really do for the rendering of meaning? Fidelity in the translation of individual words can almost never fully reproduce the meaning they have in the original. For sense in its poetic significance is not limited to meaning, but derives from the connotations conveyed by the word chosen to express it. We say of words that they have emotional connotations. A literal rendering of the syntax completely demolishes the theory of reproduction of meaning and is a direct threat to comprehensibility. The nineteenth century considered Hölderlin's translations of Sophocles as monstrous examples of such literalness. Finally, it is self-evident how greatly fidelity in reproducing the form impedes the rendering of the sense. Thus no case for literalness can be based on a desire to retain the meaning. Meaning is served far better—and literature and language far worse—by the unrestrained license of bad translators. Of necessity, therefore, the demand for literalness, whose justification is obvious, whose legitimate ground is quite obscure, must be understood in a more meaningful context. Fragments of a vessel which are to be glued together must match one another in the smallest details, although they need not be like one another. In the same way a translation, instead of resembling the meaning of the original, must lovingly and in detail incorporate the original's mode of signification, thus making both the original and the translation recognizable as fragments of a greater language, just as fragments are part of a vessel. For this very reason translation must in large measure refrain from wanting to communicate something, from rendering the sense, and in this the original is important to it only insofar as it has already relieved the translator and his translation of the effort of assembling and expressing what is to be conveyed. In the realm of translation, too, the words [in the beginning was the word] apply. On the other hand, as regards the meaning, the language of a translation can—in fact, must—let itself go, so that it gives voice to the *intentio* of the original not as reproduction but as harmony, as a supplement to the language in which it expresses itself, as its own kind of *intentio*. Therefore it is not the highest praise of a translation, particularly in the age of its origin, to say that it reads as if it had originally been written in that language. Rather, the significance of fidelity as ensured by literalness is that the work reflects the great longing for linguistic complementation. A real translation is transpa- rent; it does not cover the original, does not black its light, but allows the pure language, as though reinforced by its own medium to shine upon the original all the more fully. This may be achieved, above all, by a literal rendering of the syntax which proves words rather than sentences to be the primary element of the translator. For if the sentence is the wall before the language of the original, literalness is the arcade.

Fidelity and freedom in translation have traditionally been regarded as conflicting tendencies. This deeper interpretation of the one apparently does not serve to reconcile the two; in fact, it seems to deny the other all justification. For what is meant by freedom but that the rendering of the sense is no longer to be regarded as all-important? Only if the sense of a linguistic creation may be equated with the information it conveys does some ultimate, decisive element remain beyond all communication—quite close and yet infinitely remote, concealed or distinguishable, fragmented or powerful. In all language and linguistic creations there remains in addition to what can be conveyed something that cannot be communicated; depending on the context in which it appears, it is something that symbolizes or something symbolized. It is the former only in the finite products of language, the latter in the evolving of the languages themselves. And that which seeks to represent, to produce itself in the evolving of languages, is that very nucleus of pure language. Though concealed and fragmentary, it is an active force in life as the symbolized thing itself, whereas it inhabits linguistic creations only in symbolized form. While that ultimate essence, pure language, in the various tongues is tied only to linguistic elements and their changes, in linguistic creations it is weighted with a heavy, alien meaning. To relieve it of this, to turn the symbolizing into the symbolized, to regain pure language fully formed in the linguistic flux, is the tremendous and only capacity of translation. In this pure language—which no longer means or expresses anything but is, as expressionless and creative Word, that which is meant in all languages—all information, all sense, and all intention finally encounter a stratum in which they are destined to be extinguished. This very stratum furnishes a new and higher justification for free translation; this justification does not derive from the sense of what is to be conveyed, for the emancipation from this sense is the task of fidelity. Rather, for the sake of pure language, a free translation bases the test on its own language. It is the task of the translator to release in his own language that pure language which is under the spell of another, to liberate the language imprisoned in a work in his re-creation of that work. For the sake of pure language he breaks through decayed barriers of his own language. Luther, Voss, Hölderlin, and George have extended the boundaries of the German language. And what of the sense in its importance for the relationship between translation and original? A simile may help here. Just as a tangent touches a circle lightly and at but one point, with this touch rather than with the point setting the law according to which it is to continue on its straight path to infinity, a translation touches the original lightly and only at the infinitely small point of the sense, thereupon pursuing its own course according to the laws of fidelity in the freedom of linguistic flux. Without explicitly naming or substantiating it, Rudolf Pannwitz has characterized the true significance of this freedom. His observations are contained in *Die Krisis der europäischen Kultur* and rank with Goethe's Notes to the *Westöstlicher Divan* as the best comment on the theory of translation that has been published in Germany. Pannwitz writes: "Our translations, even the best ones, proceed from a wrong premise. They want to turn Hindi, Greek, English into German instead of turning German into Hindi, Greek, English. Our translators have a far greater reverence for the usage of their own language than for the spirit of the foreign works ... The basic error of the translator is that he preserves the state in which his own language happens to be instead of allowing his language to be powerfully affected by the foreign tongue. Particularly when translating from a language very remote from his own he must go back to the primal elements of language itself and penetrate to the point where work, image, and tone converge. He must expand and deepen his language by means of the foreign language. It is not generally realized to what extent this is possible, to what extent any language can be transformed, how language differs from language almost the way dialect differs from dialect; however, this last is true only if one takes language seriously enough, not if one takes it lightly."

The extent to which a translation manages to be in keeping with the nature of this mode is determined objectively by the translatability of the original. The lower the quality and distinction of its language, the larger the extent to which it is information, the less fertile a field is it for translation, until the utter pre-ponderance of content, far from being the lever for a translation of distinctive mode, renders it impossible. The higher the level of a work, the more does it remain translatable even if its meaning is touched upon only fleetingly. This, of course, applies to originals only. Translations, on the other hand, prove to be untranslatable not because of any inherent difficulty, but because of the looseness with which meaning attaches to them. Confirmation of this as well as of every other important aspect is supplied by Hölderlin's translations, particularly those of the two tragedies by Sophocles. In them the harmony of the languages is so profound that sense is touched by language only the way an aeolian harp is touched by the wind. Hölderlin's translations are prototypes of their kind; they are to even the most perfect renderings of their texts as a prototype is to a model. This can be demonstrated by comparing Hölderlin's and Rudolf Borchardt's translations of Pindar's "Third Pythian Ode." For this very reason Hölderlin's translations in particular are subject to the enormous danger inherent in all translations: The gates of a language thus expanded and modified may slam shut and enclose the translator with silence. Hölderlin's translations from Sophocles were his last work; in them meaning plunges from abyss to abyss until it threatens to become lost in the bottomless depths of language. There is, however, a stop. It is vouchsafed to Holy Writ alone, in which meaning has ceased to be the watershed for the flow of language and the flow of revelation. Where a text is identical with truth or dogma, where it is supposed to be "the true language" in all its literalness and without the mediation of meaning, this text is unconditionally translatable. In such case translations are called for only because of the plurality of languages. Just as, in the original, language and revelation are one without any tension, so the translation must be one with the original in the form of the interlinear version, in which literalness and freedom are united. For to some degree all great texts contain their potential translation between the lines; this is true to the highest degree of sacred writings. The interlinear version of the Scriptures is the prototype or ideal of all translation.

A note on Harry Zohn's translation
Steven Rendall

In 1968 Harry Zohn published a pioneering translation of Walter Benjamin's "Die Aufgabe des Übersetzers," entitled "The Task of the Translator." Because of copyright restrictions, Zohn's version continues to be the main form in which Benjamin's famous essay is known to English-language readers. These notes examine certain problems raised by Zohn's version.

The most obvious are four glaring omissions. One of these has been noted by a number of critics:

> gewisse Relationsbegriffe ihren guten, ja vielleicht besten Sinn behalten, wenn sie nicht von vorne herein ausschliesslich auf den Menschen bezogen werden.
> (Benjamin, 1980, p. 10)
> Certain correlative concepts retain their meaning, and possibly their foremost significance, if they are referred exclusively to man.
> (Benjamin, 1968, p. 70)

Here the omission of the negative completely inverts Benjamin's meaning and makes it impossible to follow the logic of his argument at this point. Paul de Man, in his commentary on Zohn's translation, regarded this omission as particularly crucial because it conceals what de Man saw as Benjamin's assertion of the inhuman, mechanical operation of language, of the essential *inhumanity* of language (de Man, 1986).

A second omission I have not seen mentioned by critics occurs later in the essay:

> Wenn aber diese derart bis ans messianische Ende ihrer Geschichte wachsen ...
> (Benjamin, 1980, p. 14)
> If, however, these languages continue to grow in this manner until the end of their time ...
> (Benjamin, 1968, p. 74)

Here Zohn neglects to translate the word "messianisch," and this again cannot be considered insignificant, particularly with regard to the intense debates about the role of messianism in Benjamin's thought in general and in this essay in particular.

The third omission, which also seems to have passed unnoticed, occurs in the crucial passage where Benjamin is discussing the "wesenhafte Kern" that is the true translator's chief concern, and whose ripening points towards the (messianic) "realm of reconciliation and fulfillment of languages" without ever quite reaching or realizing it:

> Den erreicht es nicht mit Stumpf und Stiel, aber in ihm steht dasjenige, was an

einer Übersetzung mehr ist als Mitteilung. Genauer lässt sich dieser wesenhafte Kern als dasjenige bestimmen, was an ihr selbst nicht wiederum übersetzbar is.

(Benjamin, 1980, p. 15)

The transfer can never be total, but what reaches this region is that element in a translation which goes beyond transmittal of subject matter. This nucleus is best defined as the element that does not lend itself to translation.

(Benjamin, 1968, p. 75)

In this case, Zohn fails to translate the words "an ihr" and "wiederum" in the second sentence, with the result that it seems Benjamin is suggesting that the object of the translator's chief concern lies completely outside his reach. Although in one sense this may be true (as Paul de Man has argued), the point here is surely that whatever aspect of the "wesenhafte Kern" is echoed in a translation ("an ihr" clearly refers back to "dieÜbersetzung" in the preceding sentence) cannot be translated again. This presupposes, of course, that the "wesenhafte Kern" can be translated a first time. The reason it cannot be translated again—that is, the reason a translation of a translation gives no access to this essential nucleus of language—is as Rodolphe Gasché's reading of the essay suggests, that this "wesenhafte Kern" of language consists of communicability or translatability itself, that which within language exceeds any given use, situation—or "language" (Gasché, 1988). A translation of the kind Benjamin is defining makes perceptible the element of "pure language" simultaneously hidden and designated in the text to be translated—and which is precisely its translatability. One may find Benjamin's explanation of this point in the rest of this paragraph less than wholly clear, but the problem is not solved by merely eliding the words that cause it.

A fourth omission, which also seems to have gone unnoticed, occurs in a passage where Benjamin is discussing the traditional concepts of freedom and fidelity in translation:

Treue and Freiheit—Freiheit der sinngemässen Wiedergabe und in ihrem Dienst Treue gegen das Wort—sind die althergebrachten Begriffe in jeder Diskussion von Übersetzungen.

(Benjamin, 1980, p. 17)

The traditional concepts in any discussion of translations are fidelity and license—the freedom of faithful reproduction, and in its service, fidelity to the word.

(Benjamin, 1968, p. 79)

Zohn's translation omits the words *sinngemässen Wiedergarbe* ("rendering in accord with the meaning"), thus making it hard for the reader to see that the "freedom" Benjamin refers to is the freedom-demanded by translation theorists from Horace to Dryden and beyond—to deviate from the letter of the text in order to render its spirit.

The omission is apparently connected with a fundamental misunderstanding of Benjamin's text reflected in Zohn's translation of the following passage:

Wenn Treue und Freiheit der Übersetzung seit jeher als widerstrebende

Tendenzen betrachtet wurden, so scheint auch diese tiefere Deutung der einen beide nicht zu versöhnen, sondern im Gegenteil alles Recht der andern abzusprechen. Denn worauf bezieht Freiheit sich, wenn nicht auf die Wiedergabe des Sinnes, die aufhören soil, gesetzgegebend zu heissen?

(Benjamin, 1980, pp. 18 - 19)

Fidelity and freedom have traditionally been regarded as conflicting tendencies. This deeper interpretation of the one apparently does not serve to reconcile the two; in fact, it seems to deny the other all justification. For what is meant by freedom but that the rendering of the sense is no longer to be regarded as all important?

(Benjamin, 1968, p. 79)

Zohn's rendering makes it appear that the reinterpreted concept is freedom, and that the re-interpretation deprives the concept of fidelity of any justification. This is precisely the reverse of what Benjamin's text says. The preceding passage has offered a reinterpretation of fidelity to the word (*Wörtlichkeit*) that disconnects it from the translation of meaning, and it is clearly this reinterpretation to which Benjamin is referring here. Thus the concept that is deprived of any justification by this reinterpretation is freedom, and the last sentence should read: "For what can the point of freedom be, if not the reproduction of meaning, whch is no longer to be regarded as normative?"

【延伸阅读】

[1] de Man, P. (1986). *The Resistance to Theory*. Minneapolis: University of Minnesota Press.

[2] Derrida, J. (1985). *The Ear of the Other*. Avital Ronell, trans. New York: Schokens books Inc.

[3] 约瑟夫·F. 格拉海姆. 围绕巴别塔的争论//陈永国主编. 翻译与后现代性. 北京:中国人民大学出版社,2005:76.

【问题与思考】

1. 翻译的任务是什么？是翻译信息还是翻译语言？抑或两者都是,抑或两者都不是？为什么？

2. 如何理解本雅明的"纯语言"概念？

3. 如何理解本雅明的"再生"(afterlife)概念？

4. 如何理解本雅明文中的两个明喻:花瓶和切线？

5. 本雅明的翻译理论对我们的翻译研究有何指导意义？

6. 本雅明的翻译理论对德里达有何影响？

选文二　After Babel (Excerpt)

George Steiner

导　言

　　斯坦纳是西方对翻译过程进行深入研究的著名学者。他在 1975 年出版的《通天塔之后》(After Babel)被称为"里程碑式的著作"。作者指出"语言处在永远的变化过程中"。在语言的共时与历时的研究进行中,阐释与翻译活动始终贯穿其中,即一切交际或交流活动都是形式地或语用地隐含着翻译活动的,都是通过解释或翻译来实现的。"阐释学运作"("The Hermeneutic Motion")正是《通天塔之后》一书的第五章内容。斯坦纳在该章中着重阐述了以阐释学为基础的翻译活动的四个步骤:信赖、侵入、吸收和补偿。斯坦纳著作语言艰涩,内容深僻,因此也有人在无法充分理解其理论之后,转而批评他故弄玄虚。所以在理解这篇文章时我们需要从以下几个方面加以注意:

　　首先,要认识到这篇文章的价值意义何在。斯坦纳以阐释学为基础对翻译划分的四个步骤有利于我们更加清楚地认识到什么是翻译——翻译的本质问题。其次,要深刻地认识到这四者之间的关系。它们是彼此孤立的步骤,还是彼此包含、相互联系、难以分割的整体的关系? 对这个问题模模糊糊,就会对整篇文章的真正内涵有所偏离,难以把这个思想很好地应用到实践中去。再次,在实际运用过程中,不能把翻译现象与这四个步骤一一对应进行匹配,最后的研究结果不能只局限于对翻译过程的简单划分,不应忽略这四个步骤中所蕴含的其他价值,比如译者主体性在这四个步骤中的具体体现。

The hermeneutic motion, the act of elicitation and appropriative transfer of meaning, is fourfold. There is initiative trust, an investment of belief, underwritten by previous experience but epistemologically exposed and psychologically hazardous, in the meaningfulness, in the "seriousness" of the facing or, strictly speaking, adverse text. We venture a leap: We grant *ab initio* that there is "something there" to be understood, that the transfer will not be void. All understanding, and the demonstrative statement of understanding which is translation, starts with an act of trust. This confiding will, ordinarily, be instantaneous and unexamined, but it has a complex base. It is an operative convention which derives from a sequence of phenomenological assumptions about the coherence of the world, about the presence of meaning in very different, perhaps formally antithetical semantic systems, about the validity of analogy and parallel. The radical generosity of the translator ("I grant beforehand that there must be something there"), his trust in the "other," as yet untried, unmapped alternity of statement, concentrates to a philosophically dramatic degree the human bias towards seeing the world as symbolic, as constituted of relations in which "this" can stand for "that," and must in fact be able to do so if there are to be meanings and structures.

But the trust can never be final. It is betrayed, trivially, by nonsense, by the discovery that "there is nothing there" to elicit and translate. Nonsense rhymes, *poésie concrète*, glossolalia are untranslatable because they are lexically non-communicative or deliberately insignificant. The commitment of trust will, however, be tested, more or less severely, also in the common run and process of language acquisition and translation (the two being intimately connected). "This means nothing" asserts the exasperated child in front of his Latin reader or the beginner at Berlitz. The sensation comes very close to being tactile, as of a blank, sloping surface which gives no purchase. Social incentive, the officious evidence of precedent—"others have managed to translate this bit before you"—keeps one at the task. But the donation of trust remains ontologically spontaneous and anticipates proof, often by a long, arduous gap (there are texts, says Walter Benjamin, which will be translated only "after us"). As he sets out, the translator must gamble on the coherence, on the symbolic plenitude of the world. Concomitantly he leaves himself vulnerable, though only in extremity and at the theoretical edge, to two dialectically related, mutually determined metaphysical risks. He may find that "anything" or "almost anything" can mean "everything." This is the vertigo of self-sustaining metaphoric or analogic enchainment experienced by medieval exegetists. Or he may find that there is "nothing there" which can be divorced from its formal autonomy, that every meaning worth expressing is monadic and will not enter into any alternative mould. There is Kabbalistic speculation, to which I will return, about a day on which words will shake off "the burden of having to mean" and will be only themselves, blank and replete as stone.

After trust comes aggression. The second move of the translator is incursive and extractive. The relevant analysis is that of Heidegger when he focuses our attention on understanding as an act, on the access, inherently appropriative and therefore violent, of *Erkenntnis* to *Dasein*. *Da-sein*, the "thing there," "the thing that is because it is there," only comes into authentic being when it is comprehended, i. e. translated.[①] The postulate that all cognition is aggressive, that every proposition is an inroad on the world, is, of course, Hegelian. It is Heidegger's contribution to have shown that understanding, recognition, interpretation are a compacted, unavoidable mode of attack. We can modulate Heidegger's insistence that understanding is not a matter of method but of primary being, that "being consists in the understanding of other being" into the more naive, limited axiom that each act of comprehension must appropriate another entity (we translate *into*). Comprehension, as its etymology shows, "comprehends" not only cognitively but by encirclement and ingestion. In the event of interlingual translation this manoeuvre of comprehension is explicitly invasive and exhaustive. Saint Jerome uses his famous image of meaning brought home captive by the translator. We "break" a code: Decipherment is dissective, leaving the shell smashed and the vital layers

---

① Cf. Paul Ricœur, "Existence et herméneutique" in *Le Conflit des interprétations* (Paris, 1969).

stripped. Every schoolchild, but also the eminent translator, will note the shift in substantive presence which follows on a protracted or difficult exercise in translation: The text in the other language has become almost materially thinner, the light seems to pass unhindered through its loosened fibres. For a spell the density of hostile or seductive "otherness" is dissipated. Ortega y Gasset speaks of the sadness of the translator after failure. There is also a sadness after success; the Augustinian *tristitia* which follows on the cognate acts of erotic and of intellectual possession.

The translator invades, extracts, and brings home. The simile is that of the open-cast mine left an empty scar in the landscape. As we shall see, this despoliation is illusory or is a mark of false translation. But again, as in the case of the translator's trust, there are genuine borderline cases. Certain texts or genres have been exhausted by translation. Far more interestingly, others have been negated by transfiguration, by an act of appropriative penetration and transfer in excess of the original, more ordered, more aesthetically pleasing.

There are originals we no longer turn to because the translation is of a higher magnitude (the sonnets of Louise Labé after Rilke's *Umdichtung*). I will come back to this paradox of betrayal by augment.

The third movement is incorporative, in the strong sense of the word. The import, of meaning and of form, the embodiment, is not made in or into a vacuum. The native semantic field is already extant and crowded. There are innumerable shadings of assimilation and placement of the newly-acquired, ranging from a complete domestication, an at-homeness at the core of the kind which cultural history ascribes to, say, Luther's Bible or North's Plutarch, all the way to the permanent strangeness and marginality of an artifact such as Nabokov's "English-language" *Onegin*. But whatever the degree of "naturalization," the act of importation can potentially dislocate or relocate the whole of the native structure. The Heideggerian "we are what we understand to be" entails that our own being is modified by each occurrence of comprehensive appropriation. No language, no traditional symbolic set or cultural ensemble imports without risk of being transformed. Here two families of metaphor, probably related, offer themselves, that of sacramental intake or incarnation and that of infection. The incremental values of communion pivot on the moral, spiritual state of the recipient. Though all decipherment is aggressive and, at one level, destructive, there are differences in the motive of appropriation and in the context of "the bringing back." Where the native matrix is disoriented or immature, the importation will not enrich, it will not find a proper locale. It will generate not an integral response but a wash of mimicry (French neo-classicism in its north-European, German, and Russian versions). There can be contagions of facility triggered by the antique or foreign import. After a time, the native organism will react, endeavouring to neutralize or expel the foreign body. Much of European romanticism can be seen as a riposte to this sort of infection, as an attempt to put an embargo on a plethora of foreign, mainly French eighteenth-century goods. In every pidgin we see an attempt to preserve a zone of native speech and a failure of that attempt in the face of politically and economically enforced linguistic invasion. The dialectic of embodiment entails the possibility that we may be consumed.

This dialectic can be seen at the level of individual sensibility. Acts of translation add to our means; we come to incarnate alternative energies and resources of feeling. But we may be mastered and made lame by what we have imported. There are translators in whom the vein of personal, original creation goes dry. MacKenna speaks of Plotinus literally submerging his own being. Writers have ceased from translation, sometimes too late, because the inhaled voice of the foreign text had come to choke their own. Societies with ancient but eroded epistemologies of ritual and symbol can be knocked off balance and made to lose belief in their own identity under the voracious impact of premature or indigestible assimilation. The cargocults of New Guinea, in which the natives worship what airplanes bring in, provide an uncannily exact, ramified image of the risks of translation.

This is only another way of saying that the hermeneutic motion is dangerously incomplete, that it is dangerous because it is incomplete, if it lacks its fourth stage, the piston-stroke, as it were, which completes the cycle. The a-prioristic movement of trust puts us off balance. We "lean towards" the confronting text (every translator has experienced this palpable bending towards and launching at his target). We encircle and invade cognitively. We come home laden, thus again offbalance, having caused disequilibrium throughout the system by taking away from "the other" and by adding, though possibly with ambiguous consequence, to our own. The system is now off-tilt. The hermeneutic act must compensate. If it is to be authentic, it must mediate into exchange and restored parity.

The enactment of reciprocity in order to restore balance is the crux of the métier and morals of translation. But it is very difficult to put abstractly. The appropriative "rapture" of the translator—the word has in it, of course, the root and meaning of violent transport—leaves the original with a dialectically enigmatic residue. Unquestionably there is a dimension of loss, of breakage—hence, as we have seen, the fear of translation, the taboos on revelatory export which hedge sacred texts, ritual nominations, and formulas in many cultures. But the residue is also, and decisively, positive. The work translated is enhanced. This is so at a number of fairly obvious levels. Being methodical, penetrative, analytic, enumerative, the process of translation, like all modes of focused understanding, will detail, illumine, and generally body forth its object. The over-determination of the interpretative act is inherently inflationary: It proclaims that "there is more here than meets the eye," that "the accord between content and executive form is closer, more delicate than had been observed hitherto." To class a source-text as worth translating is to dignify it immediately and to involve it in a dynamic of magnification (subject, naturally, to later review and even, perhaps, dismissal). The motion of transfer and paraphrase enlarges the stature of the original. Historically, in terms of cultural context, of the public it can reach, the latter is left more prestigious. But this increase has a more important, existential perspective. The relations of a text to its translations, imitations, thematic variants, even parodies, are too diverse to allow of any single theoretic, definitional scheme. They categorize the entire question of the meaning of meaning in time, of the existence and effects of the linguistic fact outside its specific, initial form. But there can be no doubt that echo enriches, that it is more than shadow and inert simulacrum. We are back at the problem of the mirror which not only reflects but also generates light. The original text gains from the orders of diverse relationship and distance established between itself and the translations. The reciprocity is dialectic: New "formats" of significance are initiated by distance and by contiguity. Some translations edge us away from the canvas, others bring us up close.

This is so even where, perhaps especially where, the translation is only partly adequate. The failings of the translator (I will give common examples) localize, they project as on to a screen, the resistant vitalities, the opaque centres of specific genius in the original. Hegel and Heidegger posit that being must engage other being in order to achieve self-definition. This is true only in part of language which, at the phonetic and grammatical levels, can function inside its own limits of diacritical differentiation. But it is pragmatically true of all but the most rudimentary acts of form and expression. Existence in history, the claim to recognizable identity (style), are based on relations to other articulate constructs. Of such relations, translation is the most graphic.

Nevertheless, there is unbalance. The translator has taken too much—he has padded, embroidered, "read into"—or too little—he has skimped, elided, cut out awkward corners. There has been an outflow of energy from the source and an inflow into the receptor altering both and altering the harmonics of the whole system. Péguy puts the matter of inevitable damage definitively in his critique of Leconte de Lisle's translations of Sophocles: "ce que la réalité nous enseigne impitoyablement et sans aucune exception, c'est que toute opération de cet ordre, toute opération de déplacement, sans aucune exception, entraîne impitoyablement et irrévocablement une déperdition, une altération, et que cette déperdition, cette altération est toujours considérable."[1] Genuine translation will, therefore, seek to equalize, though the mediating steps may be lengthy and oblique. Where it falls short of the original, the authentic translation makes the autonomous virtues of the original more precisely visible (Voss is weak at characteristic focal points in his Homer, but the lucid honesty of his momentary lack brings out the appropriate strengths of the Greek). Where it surpasses the original, the real translation infers that the source-text possesses potentialities, elemental reserves as yet unrealized by itself. This is Schleiermacher's notion of a hermeneutic which "knows better than the author did" (Paul Celan translating Apollinaire's *Salomé*). The ideal, never accomplished, is one of total counterpart or repetition—an asking again—which is not, however, a tautology. No such perfect "double" exists. But the ideal makes explicit the demand for

---

[1] Charles Péguy, "Les Suppliants parallèles" in *Oeuvres en prose* 1898—1908 (Paris, 1959), I, p. 890. This analysis of the art of poetic translation first appeared in December 1905. Cf. Simone Fraisse, *Péguy et le monde antique* (Paris, 1973), pp. 146 - 159.

equity in the hermeneutic process.

Only in this way, I think, can we assign substantive meaning to the key notion of "fidelity." Fidelity is not literalism or any technical device for rendering "spirit." The whole formulation, as we have found it over and over again in discussions of translation, is hopelessly vague. The translator, the exegetist, the reader is *faithful to* his text, makes his response responsible, only when he endeavours to restore the balance of forces, of integral presence, which his appropriative comprehension has disrupted. Fidelity is ethical, but also, in the full sense, economic. By virtue of tact, and tact intensified is moral vision, the translator-interpreter creates a condition of significant exchange. The arrows of meaning, of cultural, psychological benefaction, move both ways. There is, ideally, exchange without loss. In this respect, translation can be pictured as a negation of entropy; order is preserved at both ends of the cycle, source and receptor. The general model here is that of Lévi-Strauss's *Anthropologie structurale* which regards social structures as attempts at dynamic equilibrium achieved through an exchange of words, women, and material goods. All capture calls for subsequent compensation; utterance solicits response, exogamy and endogamy are mechanisms of equalizing transfer. Within the class of semantic exchanges, translation is again the most graphic, the most radically equitable. A translator is accountable to the diachronic and synchronic mobility and conservation of the energies of meaning. A translation is, more than figuratively, an act of double entry; both formally and morally the books must balance.

This view of translation as a hermeneutic of trust (*élancement*), of penetration, of embodiment, and of restitution, will allow us to overcome the sterile triadic model which has dominated the history and theory of the subject. The perennial distinction between literalism, paraphrase and free imitation, turns out to be wholly contingent. It has no precision or philosophic basis. It overlooks the key fact that a fourfold *hermeneia*, Aristotle's term for discourse which signifies because it interprets, is conceptually and practically inherent in even the rudiments of translation.

【延伸阅读】

[1] Steiner, G. (1998). *After Babel: Aspects of Language and Translation*. London & Oxford: Oxford University Press.

【问题与思考】

1. 斯坦纳所谓对文本意义的信任到底是指什么？发生在翻译过程中的什么时候？
2. 译者究竟是如何侵入源语文本并掳掠意义的？
3. 译者将源语文本吸纳进译入语文化受了哪些因素的制约？
4. 到底什么是补偿？怎样补偿？怎样才能达到斯坦纳所说的"平衡"？
5. 译者主体性在这四个步骤中是如何具体体现的？
6. 斯坦纳翻译四步骤理论有何缺陷？如何进一步完善该理论？

选文三　本雅明说的是啥？

袁　伟

导　言

本文发表于《国外文学》2007年第4期。

本文认为《译者的任务》是本雅明的一篇影响重大的翻译理论文章，迷人却也令人迷惑；艰深晦涩，似乎尤难译：非常的思想往往不是化为常识，就是沦为乱语。本文通过比较中英文译本与德文原文的异同，对本雅明的"可译性"、"余生"和"纯语言"等概念的内涵作了初步梳理。

关于本雅明的《译者的任务》，保罗·德曼说过这样一句话：此文大大的有名，行业中人若未曾对它说三道四，无足轻重也。① 德曼本人即就本雅明的这篇名文狠狠说过一气，也自成名文一篇，其结论当然不过一家之言，少不了可以商榷质疑处。但就我们而言，德曼起手给自己限定的那个所谓针对本雅明这篇文章能够提出的问题里"最简单、最幼稚、最实际"的问题，似乎倒可以为我们拿来，一问再问，也成为当下我们的问题：[w]hat does Benjamin say?② ——本雅明说的是啥？

本雅明的文章原以德文写就，取名"Die Aufgabe des bersetzers"。坊间广为学人引用的本子，还有佐恩（Harry Zohn）的英译本"The Task of the Translator"以及冈迪亚克（Maurice de Gandillac）的法译本"La tâche du traducteur"。不过，在德曼看来，西方世界能够识文断字的人，面对本雅明的这篇文章，彼此间已难寻可资深入探讨的前提共识。而祸根正是翻译：对文本最熟、最近的译者竟"似乎全然不知本雅明在说什么"。③ 于是德曼才要问那个貌似"荒谬"的问题：本雅明白纸黑字说的是啥？

我们不禁也为中文译本担心起来。因为中文世界通行的三个译本——① 张旭东译《译作者的任务》（见《启迪》，牛津大学出版社1998年版）；② 乔向东译《翻译者的任务》（见《中国比较文学》1999年第1期）；③ 陈永国译《翻译者的任务》（见《本雅明文选》，中国社会科学出版社1999版）——无一不是由佐恩的英译派生而来。如果德曼所言不差，如果英译者确有昏昏然，那么中文译者可得昭昭乎？纵使英译者昭昭然，中文译者会不会又昏昏然仍也不知本雅明在说什么呢？中文世界能对本雅明白纸黑字说的是啥取得起码的共识吗？

以下我们就围绕本雅明文中的若干重要概念，依据德文原文，对中英文译本作一考察。要言之，由译例入手，梳理概念；以概念梳理，反照译例。如此初探一回。

---

① Paul de Man, *The Resistance to Theory* (Minneapolis: University of Minnesota Press, 1986), p. 73.

② Ibid.

③ Ibid.

一、可译性

本雅明认为,文学作品的翻译不是传达意义,而是一种独特的表现形式(Form)。决定这种形式的法则在于原文的可译性。可译性有两层含义:① 在一部作品的全体读者里能否找到称职的译者;② 作品的本质是否容许翻译,而且,按照这种表现形式所具有的意蕴,也要求翻译。对这两层含义,本雅明有如下申说:

> Nur das oberflachliche Denken wird, indem es
>
> den selbstandigen Sinn der letzten leugnet,
>
> beide für gleichbedeutend erklaren. Ihm
>
> gegenüber ist darauf hinzuweisen, daβgewisse
>
> Relationsbegriffe ihren guten, ja vielleicht
>
> besten Sinn behalten, wenn sie nicht von vorne
>
> herein ausschlieβlich auf den Menschen
>
> bezogen werden. (Gesammelte SchriftenI:10,以下简称 GS)

本雅明在这里强调的是可译性有与人无涉的一面,也是其更为重要的含义。人不能译,不等于作品没有可译性。进一步说,本雅明所谓的可译性,其实是独立于人的主观经验之外而寄寓在语言之内的一个客观法则,是语言自身的渴望与诉求。把握这一层至关重要,因为可译性堪称本雅明翻译理论的基石。明乎此,我们才能理解,何以英译者单单漏掉一个否定词 nicht,便引来了德曼等一些明眼人的苛责。因为意思完全相反,而且后果很严重:

> It should be pointed out that certain correlative concepts retain their meaning, and possibly their foremost significance, **if they are referred exclusively to man.**
> (IlluminationsⅢ70,以下简称Ⅲ。黑体为笔者所加,本文所有译例均如此)

后果确实很严重,因为两位中文译者跟着佐恩,也非常无辜地犯了大错:

> 我们应该指出某些相关的概念只有同人联系起来时才有意义,有时或许竟获得其终极的蕴涵。(张译 64 页)

> 应该指出的是:相互关联的概念如果它们被用来专指人则仍然具有各自的含意,而且可能是最重要的含意。(乔译 72 页)

佐恩的英译,最早见于 1968 年版的英译本雅明文集 *Illuminations*。以今天本雅明在英语世界的影响论,佐恩自然功不可没。但"The Task of the Translator"这篇译文却日渐为人诟病,德曼虽然没挑他几个错,话却说得最为刻薄。于是,当 1996 年哈佛大学出版社开始推出多卷本英译本雅明文选时,"The Task of the Translator"已然是被佐恩重新修订后的面目,只是书中未作交代。万幸的是,陈译跟从的恰是改过自新后的佐恩,终于大节不亏:

> It should be pointed out in refutation of such thinking that certain correlative concepts ... if they are not from the outset used exclusively with reference to man.
> (Selected WritingsI:254,以下简称 SW)

> 应该指出,在对这种思考的拒绝中,某些对应概念,如果从一开始就没有专门用

于人的指涉的话……（陈译 280 页）

为进一步理解本雅明的"可译性"，我们不妨再看一例，而这一次，虽然前后两个英译本均无太大差池，但中文译者却看不懂佐恩了。

先看德文：

> bersetzbarkeit eignet gewissen Werken wesentlich—das heiβt nicht, ihre bersetzung ist wesentlich für sie selbst, sondern will besagen, daβeine bestimmte Bedeutung, die den Originalen innewohnt, sich in ihrer bersetzbarkeitauβere. (GSI：10)

再看前后两个英译：

> Translatability is an essential quality of certain works, which is not to say that it is essential that they be translated; it means rather that a specific significance inherent in the original manifests itself in its translatability. (Ill71) Translatability is an essential quality of certain works, which is not to say that it is essential for the works themselves that they be translated ... (SWI：254)

佐恩的修订本，比照德文 für sie selbst，在 it is essential 后补上了 for the works themselves，意思自然更见完备。然而，他的这番明白计较却让中文译者犯了糊涂：

> 可译性是某些作品的一种本质特征，这不是说对于正在被翻译的作品本身是本质的……（陈译 280 页）

陈译显然是误把一个主语从句看做了定语从句。虽然可以说，陈译在拐弯抹角地说着"不是能被翻译的作品才有可译性的本质"，就绝对意义而言，也是"可译性"的题中之意，但这与本雅明的论述层次显然不同：中译本的表述在原地迁延循环，而本雅明实际已然更进一步，触及可译性与人无涉的实质意味了。

如果说陈译错得有些刁诡，那么追随佐恩旧译的两位译者则有"指鹿为马"的嫌疑：

> 可译性是特定作品的一个基本特征……不如说，原作的某些内在的特殊意蕴通过译作而显露出来。（张译 65 页）可译性是某些作品的一个本质特征……这意味着原作中某种固有的特定意义在译作中会自然流露出来。（乔译 72 - 73 页）

与上一回的盲目紧跟不同，两位译者这一次似乎没再那么死心眼。在本雅明说 bersetzbarkeit，在佐恩也说 translatability 的地方，张译和乔译通通换成了"译作"。或许是认错了字，也可能就是以为两者意义相同，换个说法更通俗易懂些。但上一回是无辜而错，罪在 Zohn；这一次却睁眼失察，难辞其咎。因为本雅明这里的意思恰是可译性与翻译或译作不是一回事。我们已经知道，可译性是原作语言的固有属性，严格地说，与具体的译作无关，与人的主观欲望和努力无关。

关于语言的这种与人无涉的根本属性，本雅明在后文论及原文与译文关系时，曾有一段明确告白。我们不妨在这里引出，以与他的"可译性"相互发明。本雅明说，译文无法近似于原文，因为原文在变：作家一时的文风后来会式微，文学创作的内在趋势可能重新抬头。曾经新鲜的，后来会腐朽；曾经流行的，后来会陈旧。这便是所谓语言的"后熟"（Nachreife：原指在丰收时尚未完全成熟的水果之类在储存期间的成熟）。紧接下来，就是那段告白。鉴于英译本前后差别甚微,无关宏旨,且都准确传递了原文的信息,我们在此只需引出其一,而不必再搬来德文,毕竟英译本就是我们汉译本的原文:

> To seek the essence of such changes, as well as the equally constant changes in meaning, in the subjectivity of posterity rather than in the very life of language and its works would mean—even allowing for the crudest psychologism—confusing the root cause of a thing with its essence. More precisely, it would mean denying, by an impotence of thought, one of the most powerful and fruitful historical processes. (SWI:256)

本雅明说得很明白:语言及意义变化的实质不在使用语言的人,而在语言及作品本身。语言及作品自有其生命。这是违背常识的一个见解。联系他对可译性作为原文语言之客观诉求的论说,我们当知道那与他的独特语言观原是一脉相承,同时也更意识到,领会这一点,对理解本雅明的翻译理论是何等重要。然而,中文译本里的本雅明说的却是一番令人困惑的话:

> 可是如果我们不在语言及其作品的生命本身之中,而是在其后世繁衍的主观性中寻找这种变化的本质,我们就不仅陷入幼稚的心理主义,而且混淆了事物的起因和事物的本质。更重要的是,这意味着以思想的无能去否定一个最有力、最富于成果的历史过程。(张译67页)

> 去探求这些变化的实质,同时去探求在意义、后世读者的主观性而不是现有语言及其作品上一样发生着的不断变化的实质,即使顾及最不成熟的心理因素,也将意味着混淆事情的根本原因和事情的本质。更确切地说,这意味着因为思想的贫弱而否认最强有力和最富有成果的历史进程。(乔译75页)

> 要探讨这些变化的本质,以及在意义、后代的主体性方面而非在语言及其作品的生命中发生的同样经常的变化,就意味着——甚至允许用最粗糙的心理主义——把事物的根由与本质混为一谈。更确切地说,这意味着由于思想的无能而否认一个最有力和最有成果的历史进程。(陈译282-283页)

显然,除了张译靠点谱(可什么又叫"后世繁衍的主观性"呢?),乔译和陈译里的本雅明完全就是别样的逻辑。说中文的本雅明更加晦涩,越发深不可测了。这意味着——我们不妨借来本雅明的语言观,套改一下三段译文里唯一还算完整正确的那个句子——因为汉语的贫弱加无能而否定了本雅明的一个极其重要的思想。

二、原文·译文·余生

说到本雅明的翻译理论,恐怕最常为人念叨的就是他对原文与译文关系的界说,什么"来世",什么"现世",什么"后来的生命"等。看看本雅明的原话怎么说:

> Daßeine bersetzung niemals, so gut sie auch sei, etwas für das Original zu bedeuten vermag, leuchtet ein. Dennoch steht sie mit diesem kraft seiner bersetzbarkeit imnachsten Zusammenhang. Ja, dieser Zusammenhang ist umso inniger, alserfür das Original selbst nichts mehr bedeutet. Er darf ein natürlicher ge-

nannt werden und zwar genauer ein Zusammenhang des Lebens. So wie die
ußerungen des Lebens innigst mit dem lebendigen zusammenhangen, ohne ihm etwas zu bedeuten, geht die bersetzung aus dem Original hervor. Zwar nicht aus sei-
nem Leben so sehr denn aus seinem>berleben<. Ist doch die bersetzung spater als
das Original und bezeichnet sie doch bei den bedeutenden Werken, die da ihre er-
wahlten bersetzer niemals im Zeitalter ihrer Entstehung finden, das Stadium ihres
Fortlebens. In v lliger unmetaphorischer Sachlichkeit ist der Gedanke vom Leben und
Fortleben der Kunstwerke zu erfassen. (GSI: 10－11)

佐恩修订后的译文自然较前完善些：以 evident 译 leuchtet ein,在这里当然比 plausible 更
见准确。

It is plausible that no translation, however good it may be, can have any significance as regards the original. Yet, by virtue of its translatability the original is
closely connected with the translation; in fact, this connection is all the closer since
it is no longer of importance to the original. We may call this connection a natural
one, or, more specifically, a vital connection. Just as the manifestations of life are
intimately connected with the phenomenon of life without being of importance to it,
a translation issues from the original—not so much from its life as from its
afterlife ... The idea of life and afterlife in works of art should be regarded with an
entirely unmetaphorical objectivity. (Ⅲ: 71)

It is evident that no translation, however good it may be, can have any significance as regards the original. Nonetheless, it does stand in the closest relationship
to the original by virtue of the original's translatability ... (SWI: 254)

那么,中文译者对这段极其重要的文字是如何传达的呢?

可以说,译作无论多么完善,也无法取代原作的重要性,但原作却可以通过可译性
而同译作紧密地联系在一起。事实上,正因为译作对于原作是无足轻重的,它才更为紧
密地同原作联系起来。我们不妨把这种联系视为天然的,或者更进一步,把它视为译作
同原作间的生命线。正如生活的表象虽与生活的现象密切相关却对之不构成任何重要
性,译作也以原作为依据。不过它依据的不是原作的生命,而是原作的来世……对于艺
术作品的现世和来世之观念,我们应从一个全然客观而非隐喻的角度去看。(张译 65 页)

任何译文,不管多好,都不能跟原作相提并论,这种说法貌似有理……事实上,当
译文对于原作不再重要时,这种联系就更加紧密。我们可以……更确切地将之称做
不可或缺的联系。就像生活的表象和对它并不重要的生活现象有着紧密的联系一样,
译文是从原作衍生出来的——更多地来自于原作的"来世"(afterlife),而不是"现世"
(life)……艺术作品的"现世"和"来世"观念具有完全非隐喻性的客观性。(乔译 73 页)

显而易见,任何译文,不管多么优秀,与原文相比都不具有任何意味。然而,它确
实由于原文本质的可译性而最接近于原文;事实上,这种关联更加紧密,因为它不再
对原文具有任何重要的意义……是一种必不可少的关联。正如生命的各种显示与生
命的现象紧密关联而对生命没有什么意义一样,译文缘出于原文——与其说缘自其

生命,毋宁说缘自其来世的生命……艺术作品中生命和来世生命的观点应该以完全无隐喻的客观性来看待。(陈译 280 - 281 页)

我们首先看到的是:在本雅明说译作对于原文无甚意义、无关紧要(niemals … etwas für das Original zu bedeuten vermag),在英译(as regards)也无误的地方,三位中文译者措辞虽有不同,但意思如一:译作再好,与原文相比,定也有所不及。这种很常识的论断,虽然听来合情合理,却也像拿"译作"换称"可译性"一样,与本雅明的要旨大异其趣。因为它的另一面正是传统译论里被奉为圭臬的要求:译作当尽可能准确地传达原文的形式和意义。本雅明要否定的正是追求这种"准确性"的模仿论。他在后文明确指出,要把握原文与译文间的真实关系,必须借鉴认识论里对模仿论的批判思路,证明如果译作以与原作近似为鹄的,那么一切翻译皆无可能。当然,这里的关键还是本雅明的那个为人津津乐道的命题:译作源于原文的余生(berleben),标志着原文的生命延续(Fortleben)。英译本以 afterlife 译 berleben,当是取其 later life 或 continued existence 之义,因为 berleben 并无 afterlife 的另一义:life after death。然而,中文译本以"来世"、"现世"这样的字眼对译 after life 和 life,虽然用来简洁顺手,却有令本雅明皈依佛门之嫌。至于时而"生命"、时而"生活"的译法,似乎只能说明译者不太明了本雅明的 life,尽管接下来作者就有明示:所谓艺术品的生命及生命延续的概念完全不是什么比喻性的说法;生命非仅限于有机体,而是有历史即谓之有生命。哲学家的任务恰是从宽广的历史生命看自然生命。德里达在这里看到了他所说的"隐喻的逆转"(la catastrophe metapho-rique)。他的解释对我们把握本雅明的要旨不无裨益:当我们用"生命"之类熟悉的字眼谈论语言和翻译时,我们不是了解"生命"之意在先,而是要从语言及其在翻译中的"余生"观点出发,进而把握"生命"之意。[①] 显然,当本雅明说原文与译作之间的关联是"生命的关联"(ein Zusammenhang des Lebens)时,他并不是在打比方。虽然我们无法断定佐恩的 vital 是本义还是引申隐喻义,但中文译本里的"生命线"或"不可或缺"或"必不可少",却分明是把本雅明的"隐喻的逆转"又给反正了过来。一反一正,自是两样境界。那么,这种"生命的关联"到底是如何建立的呢? 何以译作与原文血脉相连却对原文无甚意义? 何以又因可译性而与原文关系最近(注意:是关系的紧密而非陈译的"最接近原文")? 何以这种关联(注意:是原文与译作的关联,而非张译与乔译里的"译作"),唯因于原文无甚意义,却更加地密切?

按本雅明的申说,伟大艺术品的生命史分为三个阶段:上承起源—成形问世时—永恒传世期。最后这个生命延续的阶段也叫作品的"名声"(Ruhm)。名声起,则翻译生——超越达意功能的翻译。故而,译作非为原文服务,而是因原文的名声生出:

> Sie [bersetzungen] dienen daher nicht sowohl diesem, wie schletchte bersetzer es für ihre Arbeit zu beanspruchen pflegen, als dass sie ihm ihr Dasein verdanken. (GSI:11)

英译者对这句话的传达虽欠周到明晰,但大意不差:

> Contrary, therefore, to the claims of bad translators, such translations do not so much serve the works as owe their existence to it. (SWI:255)

---

① Jacques Derrida, "Des Tours des Babel," in Joseph Graham ed., *Difference in Translation* (Ithaca and London: Cornell University Press, 1985), p. 222, p. 224.

遗憾的是中文译者一时眼花,竟给出了一个颇具通俗解构主义意味的解读:

因此……这种译文与其说符合作品的需要,毋宁说作品由于译文而得以存在。(陈译 281 页)

《译者的任务》虽然颇得解构大师们的青睐,但本雅明的"解构"似乎尚未至此。在他那里,译作当然是由原文作品来,唯生于原文的"余生",却不为模仿原文;生于原文永恒传世时的"名声",却不为再现原文。何以如此?因为原文的余生已然是其语言文字的"后熟"期,原文随之亦变,原文已非"原"文。而原文的"生命延续",则必然意味着原文生命的变化与更新,译作已成原文生命的更新扩展(Entfaltung)之场。这种生命的扩展,本雅明强调,是有着更高目的性的,所谓一切有目的的生命现象,归根结底,为的不是这生命本身,而是要表达其本质,再现那高于其自身的意蕴来。这个意蕴也就是作为翻译法则的可译性所表达的寄寓在原文身上的那个"特定的意蕴"。其实,上一例关于可译性的最后一句话之后,紧跟而来的便是我们当下例子的第一句。两相结合,我们对于可译性的认识又可再进一步:原文本质上对于翻译的渴望,并非为了原文本身的再现,而是为了一个高于原文的意蕴。可这个说来道去的意蕴到底是什么呢?本雅明现在终于给我们明白道出:"所以,翻译的目的,归根结底,为的是表达语言彼此间的至亲关系。"由此当知陈译何以不当,因为所谓译作"由于原文本质的可译性而最接近于原文"的说法,不仅遮蔽了这层关系,而且在他的行文语境里,似有译作与原文面目相像的强烈意味。本雅明解释说,这个至亲关系乃是不同语言间除却历史纽带之外在表意上的一种先验的关联。它比译作因模仿再现原文而来的那种表面的相似所意味的关系要"深刻得多也明确得多"。等他后来完全亮出底牌时,我们可知这个至亲关系,指向的便是不再意谓什么也不再表达什么的"纯语言"。故而,唯因其于原文无甚意义,反而更加紧密。张译与乔译以"译作"换易其实指代 this connection 的 it,则是不察本雅明论说层次的递进,又在原地迁延了。

那么译作将如何表现语言间的这种至亲关系呢?本雅明说得有些玄,不过表述倒还清晰:以萌芽或集约形态再现之。

Sie kann dieses verborgene Verhaltnis selbst unm glich offenbaren, unm glich herstellen; aber darstellen, indem sie es keimhaft oder intensiv verwirklicht, kann sie es. Und zwar ist diese Darstellung eines Bedeuteten durch den Versuch, den Keim seiner Herstellung ein ganz eigentümlicher Darstellungsmodus, wie er im Bereich des nicht sprachlichenLebens kaum angetroffenwerden mag. Denn dieses kennt in Analogien und Zeichen andere Typen der Hindeutung, als die intensive, d. h. vorgreifende, andeutende Verwirklichung. —Jenes gedachte, innerste Verhaltnis der Sprachen ist aber das einer eigentümlichen Konvergenz. (GSI: 12)

试译:这种隐秘的关系其本身,翻译无法揭示之,无法创立之;但通过赋予其萌芽或集约的形态,翻译可以再现之。确切地说,这种通过尝试,通过其萌芽形态来再现一种意味,是一种完全独特的再现方式,在非语言生命的领域里,几乎难得一见。因为,与这种集约的,也即预示性的、暗示性的赋型不同,非语言生命是以其他指涉方式作为类比结构和符号的。但语言间的这种想象的至亲关系却是一种独特的聚合。

佐恩的两个译本大意无别,唯词句略有不同。虽然 This 和 it 的指代,不能如德文里那般一目了然,但在上下文里,顺其语义,所指也算不言而喻:

It cannot possibly reveal or establish this hidden relationship itself; but it can represent it by realizing it in embryonic or intensive form. This representation of hidden significance through an embryonic attempt at making it visible is of so singular a nature that it is rarely met with in the sphere of nonlinguistic life. This, in its analogies and symbols, can draw on other ways of suggesting meaning than intensive—that is, anticipative, intimating—realization. As for the posited central kinship of languages, it is marked by a distinctive convergence. (Ⅲ: 72)

It cannot possibly reveal … This representing of something signified through an attempt at establishing it in embryo is of so singular a nature … In its analogies and symbols, it can draw on other ways of … As for the posited innermost kinship of languages … (SWⅠ: 255)

然而,英译本的不言而喻,却令中文译者胡乱抓狂:

翻译不可能自己提示或建立这一暗藏的关系,但它却可以通过把它实现于初级的或强烈的形式之中而显现这一关系。这种赋予暗藏的意义以可感性的初级尝试旨在再现这种意义,其本质是如此独特乃至它几乎从未同非语言的生命领域遭遇。这一特性以其中类比和象征带来了暗示意义的其他方式,它们不像意义的强有力的实现方式那样充满预言性和提示性。至于诸语言间的预设的亲族关系,其特征在于一种明显的重合性。(张译 66 页)

翻译本身不大可能揭示或者确立这种潜隐的关系;可是却能通过对处在初始或集中状态下的这种关系的认识,将它表达出来。通过最初的使其再现的努力,对潜藏意义的表现具有其独特的本质,这在非语言生命的领域内几乎不曾遇到过。通过比喻和象征,这可以依靠暗示意义的方法,而不是依靠强化的,也就是预想的、提示性的认识来达到。至于语言之间假定的亲属关系(kinship),一种明显的趋同性就是其标志。(乔译 74 页)

它不可能揭示或确立这种隐藏的关系本身;但却可以通过胚胎的或强化的形式实现这种关系而将其再现。试图在胚胎中加以确立的尝试意指某事物,对这种事物的再现具有如此独特的性质以致在非语言生活领域极少遭遇得到。在其类比和象征中,它可以依赖其他方式暗示意义,而非强化的——即预见性的、暗示的——实现。至于假定的语言间的内在亲缘性,则以一种特殊的趋同性为标志。(陈译 282 页)

如果说每段译文的头尾两句,尚能令人读出些许意思,那么三段译文的中间部分,却无一不是对读者智力和耐心的绝对挑战:两个不同领域的再现方式及特点已经不可理喻地绞在了一起。更为糟糕的还是,在本雅明那响亮的艰涩名头下,在一头一尾尚能读通的情形下,你抓破头皮依然不解后,首先怀疑的很可能就是自己的智力。

三、纯语言:表意·意指·意指方式·救赎

“纯语言”大概是本雅明翻译理论里玄而又玄的一个概念。虽然对这“众妙之门”作者早早地埋下伏笔,从论述可译性开始,便一路以原文身上的 Bedeutung(意蕴)不断地戳戳点点,临

了还以语言间的亲缘关系进一步地铺垫过渡,但图穷匕首见的时候,我们似乎并没有豁然顿悟的感觉。且看纯语言的原始出场:

Vielmehr beruht alleüberhistorische Verwandschaft derSprachen darin, daβin ihrer jeder als ganzer jeweilseines und zwar dasselbe gemeintist, das dennoch keiner einzelnen von ihnen, sondern nur der Allheit ihrer einander erganzendenIntentionen erreichbar ist: die reine Sprache. Wahrend namlich alle einzelnen Elemente, die Wrter, Satze, Zusammenhange von fremden Sprachen sich ausschlieβen, erganzen diese Sprachen sich in ihren Intentionen selbst. DiesesGesetz, eines der grundlegenden der Sprachphilosophie, genau zu fassen, ist in der Intention vom Gemeinten die Art des Meinens zu unterscheiden. In Brot und pain ist das Gemeinte zwar dasselbe, die Art, es zu meinen, dagegen nicht ... Wahrend dergestalt die Art des Meinens in diesen beiden Wrtern einander widerstrebt, erganzt sie sich in den beiden Sprachen, denen sie entstammen. Und zwar erganzt sich in ihnen die Art des Meinens zum Gemeinten. Bei den einzelnen, den unerganzten Sprachen namlich ist ihrGemeintes niemals in relativerSelbstandigkeit anzutreffen, wie bei den einzelnen Wrtern oder Satzen, sondern vielmehr in stetem Wandel begriffen, bis es aus der Harmonie all jener Arten des Meinens als die reine Sprache herauszutreten vermag. So lange bleibt es in den Sprachen verbogen. Wenn aber diese derart bis ans messianische End ihrer Geschichte wachsen ... (GSI: 13 - 14)

试译:相反,语言间超越历史的一切关联都在于,每一种语言其整体的意指虽然同一,但单个的语言无一能够企及,唯有集合众语言间彼此互补的表意方能达到。这个同一的意指就是纯语言……

上一例的最后一句说,语言间的亲缘关系是一种独特的聚合关联。本例则可谓在进一步地申说如何殊途同归。行文的逻辑就在其间所谓语言哲学的一个基本原则上:语言的表意包含必须区分的两面——意指与意指方式。不同的语言,意指方式固有不同,如德语里说 Brot,而法语里说 pain,但意指如一,都是"面包"。唯不同语言的同一意指——纯语言,却不似单个字词如 Brot 或 pain 的意指——"面包"——这样相对独立、确凿,藏于众语言之中,变化不居,必待一切不同意指方式聚合协调后方能见出。故从纯语言看,不同意指方式互补而已,不同语言的表意互补而已。这便是体现语言间亲缘关系的独特聚合之所在。虽然这个纯语言依然让人匪夷所思,但本雅明对于如何聚合倒也说得分明。奇怪的是,尽管他在这里一词一字地说了必须在表意里区分出意指与意指方式,但英译者似乎就是视而不见,上来便把三个概念混为一谈。佐恩的旧译是这样的:

Rather, all suprahistorical kinship of languages rests in the intention underlying each language as a whole—an intention, however, which no single language can attain by itself but which is realized only by the totality of their intentions supplementing each other: pure language ... While the modes of intention in these two words are in conflict, intention and the object of intention complement each of the two languages from which they are derived; there the object is complementary to the intention … If, however, these languages continue to grow in this manner until the end of their time … (Ⅲ：74)

对照德文，差别立见：在本雅明说"意指"意思（eines und zwar dasselbe gemeint ist）的地方，他说表意（intention）；在本雅明说意指方式（die Art des Meinens）互补的地方，他说表意与意指（intention and the object of intention）让语言互补；在本雅明说意指方式互补以趋意指（die Art des Meinens zum Gemeinten）的地方，他说意指（the object）与表意（intention）互补。这种张冠李戴的译文成为中文的"原文"后，倒是在张译和乔译那里获得了相当忠实的再现：

> 相反，任何超历史的语言间的亲族关系都依赖于每一种语言各自的整体性意图。不过这种意图并不是任何语言单独能够实现，而是实现于所有这些意图的互补的总体之中。这个总体不妨叫做纯粹语言……这两个词的意向性样式之间有冲突，然而意向性和意向性对象却使这两个词变得互补，它们自己也正来自两种互补的语言中，只有在这里，意向性和它的对象间才是相辅相成的……要是诸语言以这种方式继续成长，直到它们寿命的尽头……（张译 68 页）

> 相反，所有超历史的语言之间的亲属关系存在于每种语言各自的整体意图（intention）中……这两个词语……然而其意图及意图的对象却使两种语言互补，它们自身来自这两种互补的语言。恰恰在这里对象和意图之间是相互补充的……这些语言就以这样的方式继续发展着直到其生命的最后关头。（乔译 76 页）

结果也自然与它们的"原文"一样：本雅明由清晰的晦涩变成了清晰的混乱，走向纯语言的聚合之路模糊了。佐恩后来严格比照德文，大幅修正了这段英文旧译，虽然基本还原了本雅明的意向，却仍未能尽善。对照以他的新译为原文的汉译，这一点可以看个分明：

> Rather, all suprahistorical kinship of languages consists in this … Even though the way of meaning in these two words is in such conflict, it supplements itself in each of the two languages from which the words are derived; to be more specific, the way of meaning in them is supplemented in its relation to what is meant … (SWI：257)

> 相反，语言间一切超历史的亲缘性都包括这一点：在作为整体的每一种语言中，所指的事物都是同一个。然而，这同一个事物却不是单独一种语言所能表达的，而只能借助语言间相互补充的总体意念（intention）：纯语言……即便这两个词的意指方式处于这种冲突之中，但却从这两个词所衍生的每一种语言中得以补充自身；确切说，这些词的意指方式与这种方式与所意指的东西的关系构成了互补。（陈译 283－284 页）

首先，照陈译的意思，语言间超历史的亲缘性，除了"这一点"之外，还有其他的那一点或别的什么点：亲缘性的内涵发生了有违本雅明原意的悄然扩张。这一疏忽显然又是译者一时眼花所致：误将 consists in 看成 consists of。至于何以偏用"意念"一词换称意为"表意"的 intention，外人实难意会。当然，这些都是汉译者的问题。但下面的问题，英译者恐怕亦有与焉。本雅明的原意是，Brot 和 pain 这两个词的意指方式虽然不同，意味有别，但法德两种语言的意指方式却是互补的。这其实还是在解释开头不久那句话的意思：不同语言虽然在字词等单个成分上相互排斥，但在表意上却呈互补关系。英译者虽然基本照搬了德文的句式结构，但表达出来的意思却像陈译所示，与原意相去甚远（当然，说法德两种语言分别由各自的"面包"派生,则又是陈译的临场发挥):两种语言在意指方式上的互补变成了其意指方式在各自语言内得到补充(在陈译那里,则变为两个词的意指方式)。而以 in its relation 企图传达这里含有"趋向"之意的德文介词 zu,未免太过含混,不仅意指方式互补以趋意指之意不明,还给误解误读留下了足够的想象空间。

这段英文旧译的第二个问题则是业已被人指出的漏译 messianische 一词。原本一个深具犹太神秘主义意味的表述,变成了一个简单的修辞——the end of their time,继而在张译和乔译那里又带上了些许伤感的意味——所谓"寿命的尽头",所谓"生命的最后关头"。虽然不过一词之差,其后果却堪比界定可译性时漏译了那个 nicht。因为,如果说纯语言在大半场基本陷于技术性语汇的包裹中,令人难窥真容,那么,临近终场时的 messianische 一词,则好比掀开了帷幔的一角。诚如乔治·斯坦纳所说,一切翻译理论必然都是关于语言的理论。[1] 本雅明的纯语言其实就是浸透了卡巴拉神秘主义语言观的一个假说。在本雅明看来,人类因原罪的堕落,首先是语言精神的堕落,人语诞生了:不再是纯粹而具魔力的命名语言,而是成为表达外在虚妄知识的工具;不再是伊甸园语言的普世同一,而是分裂成混乱不通的多言多语。[2] 虽然如此,那完美单一的纯语言却似一股潜流,分散在这众声喧哗的背后,推动着人语向原初的和谐一体回归。抵达终点即回到起点,此即卡巴拉所谓之救赎。[3] 而翻译,因其能克服语言的多杂和封闭,在差异的勾连中现出纯语言的萌芽,遂成救赎之道。其实,救赎、纯语言以及在文中多次出现的和谐等字眼,属于一个完整的概念体。其源头就在卡巴拉的 Tikkun 教义上(Tikkun,希伯来语,清除污渍、恢复和谐之意[4])。可以说,如果对犹太神秘主义与本雅明学说之间的脉络不清不楚,那么,面对本雅明的翻译理论,我们就难以摆脱雾里看花的隔膜。遗憾的是,即便生在西方的犹太人,大多也不明自家的这个"传统",英译者先前的失察,似乎也是情有可原的事,而我们因为无辜失足,当然更没有不能释然的理由。何况陈译随了修订后的英译本,也把那"救赎"二字给救赎了回来。

结语

《译者的任务》要义何在? 德里达曾有一精炼的概述:翻译一不为读者,二不为达意,三不为再现原文。[5] 可是,我们此番却拿来本雅明这篇文章的原文与各色译文横比竖量地斤斤计较,又为读者又为达意又为原文再现,说来也算是本雅明文章的一段非常刁诡的"余生"。尤其刁诡的还是,我们这里品评的译者,竟仿佛像本雅明翻译学说的忠实实践者,还透着以其人之道还治其人之身的高明。这意味着什么? 意味着本雅明的翻译理论其实无用? 不如"信达雅"对翻译实践有着切实的指导意义? 站在传统译论观上,怕也只能得出这样的结论。但是,当我们津津乐道他的诸多新颖概念的时候,我们每每忽略了,本雅明所谓译者的任务在文中往往是

① George Steiner, *After Babel* (Oxford and New York: Oxford University Press, 1998), p. 436, p. 67.

② Walter Benjamin, "ber Spracheüberhaupt undüber die Sprache desMenschen," in GS, Ⅱ, p. 153, p. 151.

③ Gershom Scholem, *Major Trends in Jewish Mysticism* (New York: Schocken Books, 1995), pp. 245 - 246, p. 233.

④ Ibid.

⑤ Jacques Derrida, "Des Tours des Babel," in Joseph Graham ed., *Difference in Translation* (Ithaca and London: Cornell University Press, 1985), p. 222, p. 224.

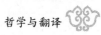

与哲学家的任务相提并论的,具有"深刻的哲学的、伦理的和神秘的意味"。① 而这又意味着什么呢? 至少有一点是明确的:以所谓理论指导实践的观点看本雅明的翻译理论,那是误读了本雅明,狭隘化了本雅明。因为,翻译在本雅明这里绝非一个技术问题。当他说翻译是有别于文学创作的一种形式,针对的是语言整体时,当他把翻译定位在文学与哲学之间时,他实际上已给翻译赋予了某种本体的地位。翻译由此超越技术层面,已然成为一个语言哲学的问题,甚至显露出更大的潜能。早在其第一篇语言哲学论文里,本雅明就明确有言:"翻译这个概念必须建立在语言理论的最深层面上,因为它的影响深远,能量太大,无法像人们有时候以为的那样,可以放在事后这样或那样来处理。"②这就在提醒我们,要深入理解本雅明的这篇译论,必须联系他那独特的语言哲学乃至历史哲学来看。不过,那是另外一篇文章的内容了。我们当下关注的还是他的几个形而上概念的形而下问题,是本雅明在中文里白纸黑字说些个什么的问题。从 1998 年至 1999 年,短短一年之内,《译者的任务》就有三个中文译本面世,足见中国学者对本雅明的学术思想何等看重。然而,一而再、再而三的翻译,本雅明依然面目浑浊,又足见把握本雅明的思想何其不易。纵观当代译入中土的外国理论家,本雅明即便不算最难参透的,至少也在最难啃动之列,晦涩之名,近于狼藉。中文读者嚼着诘屈聱牙的文字,每每叹其奥义艰深,然为名声所诱,遂强打起精神,要在那人称闪光的段片思维和汪洋恣肆的哲性诗文间理出个头绪,却每每又发现如乱码般整齐排列的方块字队列密不可透,几番近身肉搏,大多还是败下阵来,乃至摔书叹息,只怪自己资质驽钝,这似乎倒佐证了尼采刻薄世人的那句话:泥腿子就不该踏地毯,撞破脑袋也无益。③ 然而,一个并非无端自扰的担心是:当我们在中文里穷追热捧本雅明的时候,真正的本雅明或许已然消失在了以方块字的实在狂欢所虚构出来的天书中。再过十年,我们会不会依旧摔书兴叹:本雅明说的是啥?

【延伸阅读】

[1] 蔡新乐.本雅明:翻译的终结与灵韵的在场.解放军外国语学院学报,2011(3):64-68.

[2] 曹明伦.揭开"纯语言"的神学面纱——重读本雅明的《译者的任务》.四川大学学报:哲学社会科学版,2007(6):79-86.

[3] 黄海容.本雅明翻译观述评.中国翻译,2007(4):19-24.

[4] 袁文彬.本雅明的语言观.外语学刊,2006(1):12-22.

[5] 袁筱一.从翻译的时代到直译的时代——基于贝尔曼视域之上的本雅明.外语教学理论与实践,2011(1):89-95.

【问题与思考】

1. 本文是如何研究本雅明的翻译理论的? 其研究有何特点?

2. 本文是如何进行多种文本比较的? 多文本比较的优势何在?

3. 本文作者是如何理解"可译性"、"余生"和"纯语言"这三个概念的?

---

① George Steiner, *After Babel* (Oxford and New York: Oxford University Press, 1998), p. 436, p. 67.

② Walter Benjamin, "ber Spracheüberhaupt undüber die Sprache desMenschen," in GS, Ⅱ, p. 153, p. 151.

③ Friedrich Nietzsche, *Jenseits von Gut und B se* (München: Dtv/de Gruyter, 1999), KSA, Band 5, p. 148.

第十章　翻译研究的跨学科性

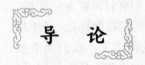

导　论

　　翻译研究为什么具有跨学科性？一是由于翻译作为研究对象具有高度复杂性和综合性，任何单学科都难以完成研究任务，而必须依靠多学科的交汇、融合才能揭示翻译的本质；二是研究主体运用的翻译研究方法必须具有较高的集成性和相互借鉴渗透的特征；三是尽管20世纪80年代和90年代外语和翻译界对翻译研究的兴趣迅猛增长，在西方学术界依然有些机构和个人不愿意把翻译研究与那些建立时间较早的学科同等对待（Munday，2001：182）。学者们就试图将翻译研究学科与其他学科结合，打破学科之间的壁垒，加速不同学科间的信息交流，促进本学科的更好发展。

　　翻译研究的跨学科性表现在语言学研究的最新成果应用于研究翻译和翻译教学上面。西方的学者自20世纪50年代便开始将语言学领域的研究成果引入翻译研究之中；斯内尔-霍恩比于1987年发表的《翻译研究：综合法》的博士论文被认为是"自20世纪70年代末翻译研究作为一门独立的学科兴起以来，第一本系统地借鉴语言学理论，尝试提出一种适用于各种翻译类型的综合理论的原创性极强的著作"（李德超、朱志瑜，2006）。奈达和卡特福德试图创立翻译语言学，但他们不是简单地将两者融合，而是使其相互借鉴，彼此受益。20世纪70—80年代语言学对翻译的影响主要是文体学、篇章分析和篇章语言学，比如一些德国翻译理论家对篇章语言学的运用（Anderman，2007）。近年来与翻译研究结合比较多的是社会语言学和语料库语言学。

　　翻译研究的跨学科性也表现在翻译研究与其他社会科学甚至自然科学学科的交融结合。1991年，Sonja Tirkkonen Condit主编了一部论文集《翻译的实证研究与跨文化研究》，其书名就已表明翻译学科已与非语言学科建立了基本联系。斯内尔-霍恩比与人合编了几部论文集，其中包括《翻译即跨文化交际》（*Translation as Intercultural Communication*，Snell-Hornby，1996）和《跨学科的翻译研究》（*Translation Studies：An Interdiscipline*，1994）。后一部论文集收入了1992年维也纳翻译会议的论文，内容涉及范围宽泛：历史、跨国文化、后现代主义、解释学、互文性、哲学、专门术语、医学、法学、语言学和翻译理论。

　　近些年，翻译研究突破了纯语言学方法的局限，开始发展本学科的研究模式，例如图里的描述性翻译研究（Toury，1995）。哈蒂姆和梅森从话语分析的框架入手，把语言选择与文本中主流意识形态结合起来，从而在研究中加入了文化考量（Hatim & Mason，1997：15-24）。皮姆（Pym，1998）在描述翻译史的编写工作时采用了跨学科（interdisciplinary）和跨文化（intercultural）两个术语，并对霍尔姆斯（Derek Holmes）规划翻译学科的方式提出了质疑。他描述了同时进行研究的两个项目,这两个项目研究过程中综合利用了多种跨学科方法,因此都是跨学科研究。皮姆(2007)认为,翻译理论家从哲学家那里借鉴了许多理论,如美国的韦努蒂等人借用哲学理论使 20 世纪 90 年代的翻译研究更为关注道德伦理问题而不是忠实和对等。

从文化视角入手研究翻译的学者也开始使用跨学科的研究方法。尼兰贾纳(Niranjana,1992)从后结构主义视角研究后殖民。韦努蒂(Venuti,1995,1998)吸收了后结构主义、文学理论与批评、史料编纂、哲学和法国话语分析的研究方法。铁木志科(Tymoczko,1999b)将文学研究、语言学研究和翻译研究的一些概念融合在一起,把从事文学翻译的译者等同于用殖民者的语言为国际读者写作的后殖民作家。在她看来,文学翻译译者和后殖民作家都面临着跨过文化和语言鸿沟传输文化的任务,都面临着一些不可避免地受意识形态驱动的选择。哈维(Harvey,1998/2000)的研究则是语言学分析与文化批评理论的有机结合。

翻译研究的跨学科性还表现在新兴学科的研究成果应用于翻译研究。模糊集合(fuzzy set)、熵(entxopy)、配价理论(valency theory)均已在语义分析、定位、转换和搭配研究中得到应用,并产生了积极影响。控制论(cybemetics)、接受美学、格式塔心理学、现代传媒技术的成果又对翻译信息的传输、反馈、控制以及如何防止信息丢失和失真产生了深刻的启示。埃斯尼·奥康奈尔(Eithne O'Connell,2007)讨论了现代技术对翻译的影响,回顾了应用于视听媒体的配音翻译、字幕翻译等的历史,分析了它们各自的特点。奥康奈尔强调指出,不能只关注科技进步对屏幕翻译的影响而忽视政治、经济、文化等在其中发挥的重要作用。

本章共选三篇文章。第一篇是 Mary Snell-Hornby 撰写的"Translation Studies:An Integrated Approach",该文以格式塔整体理论和原型学为基础提出翻译研究的综合方法。第二篇"Translating Camp Talk:Gay Identities and Cultural Transfer",作者是 Keith Harvey,该文把文学分析的语言学方法与文化理论视角相结合,通过研究同性恋语言及其翻译,从而丰富、发展了跨学科体系下的翻译理论研究。第三篇《当代翻译研究的跨学科性及理论融合——评〈翻译研究指南〉》是王宏和刘伟合写的书评,评析了一部总结当代西方翻译跨学科研究成就的论文集《翻译研究指南》(A Companion to Translation Studies)。

选文一 Translation Studies：An Integrated Approach（Excerpt）

Mary Snell-Hornby

导 言

玛丽·斯内尔-霍恩比(Mary Snell-Hornby)是英国著名翻译理论家。她创建了以格式塔原理为基础的综合研究法,试图借鉴文学、语言学和其他学科的知识原理研究翻译问题。

本文节选自她的专著《翻译研究：综合法》(*Translation Studies：An Integrated Approach*)第一章"An Integrated Approach"。

　　本文在回顾、分析翻译研究的历史与现状，着重对欧洲翻译研究的两个主要流派——莱比锡学派和操纵学派——进行比较研究的基础上，认为语言学和比较文学都不能涵盖翻译研究，进而以格式塔整体理论和原型学为基础提出翻译研究的综合方法。格式塔整体原理是心理学的一个范畴，它强调整体不等于各部分的总和，而是各部分的有机关联，所以不能仅仅通过对部分的分析来理解整体。同样，原型学注重的是聚焦和细微的差异。斯内尔-霍恩比运用原型框架，强调各种翻译文本是不可分割的连续体。实际上，原型学的构架就是一种综合方法，它要求翻译研究必须注重语言在较大的文本、情景和文化语境中的关联，并通过这种关联来确定字和词的确切含义。译者的文本分析应该从确定文本的文化和情境出发，下一步是分析文本的结构，从宏观结构开始，直至词汇衔接层面，包括文本题目和文本内容的关系，最后总结出文本翻译所用的策略。她强调，文本分析并不只限于深入地研究孤立的现象或词项，而是要追溯一种由关系组成的网络。在这个网络里，每个词项的重要性由它们与文本的相关性和在文本中的功能决定。

The ideas discussed so far will now be presented in concrete form as a basis for an integrated concept of translation studies. In the diagram on the following page a system of relationships is established between basic text-types—as prototypes—and the crucial aspects of translation. On the horizontal plane the diagram represents a spectrum or cline, where sharp divisions have been replaced by the notion of gradual transition, hence no demarcation lines have been drawn in. At the same time, on the vertical plane, the diagram represents a *stratificational model* which, in accordance with the gestalt-principle, proceeds from the most general level (A) at the top, downwards to the most particular level (F) at the bottom—or, in other words, from the macro-to the micro-level.

Level A presents the conventional areas of translation which up to now have been kept all too separate: on the left literary translation, traditionally the province of poets and scholars and once the only area thought worthy of the theorist, and on the right special language translation, traditionally inferior and the main concern of the translation schools. "General language translation" is still a vague concept which up to now has only been negatively defined as "not literary" and "not technical," but which is nonetheless implicitly the concern of the linguistically oriented *Übersetzungswissenschaft*. In this concept the historical dichotomy has been replaced by a fluid spectrum, whereby, for example, prototypically literary devices such as word-play and alliteration can be accommodated both in "general" newspaper texts (cf. 2.4.1 below) and in the language of advertising, and conversely prototypically technical terms from the language of science or culture-bound items from the "general" area of politics or everyday living can be explained and interpreted as literary devices (cf. 4.2 below).

Level B presents a prototypology of the basic text-types, from the Bible to the language of modern technology, which are the main concern of the translator. While traditional theory concentrated on the items situated at the extreme left of the spectrum, the Bible, the monuments of Classical Antiquity and the great works of the European tradition, particularly Shakespeare's plays, only a few of these areas have been given detailed attention in modern theory, and even then the focus has been limited to specific aspects (for Bible translation see Nida & Taber, 1969, for lyric poetry Levy, 1969 and Beaugrande, 1978). The special problems of children's literature and stage-translation until recently only received scant attention (cf. Verch, 1976, Reiss, 1982 on children's literature and Snell-Hornby, 1984, Bassnett-McGuire, 1985 and Schultze, 1986 on the translation of drama). At the other end of the scale are the special language text-types, the main fare of the modern professional translator, in the training institutes the major areas are law, economics, medicine, science and technology, and these are now being dealt with intensively in academic studies (cf. Schmitt, 1986; Stellbrink, 1984a, 1985; Gerzymisch-Arbogast, 1986, 1987). On the diagram limited space permitted only a narrow selection of basic text-types; there are of course many others, along with numerous blend forms (cf. 4. 1 below).

Level C shows the non-linguistic disciplines—or areas of so-called "extralinguistic reality"—which are inseparably bound up with translation. The terms are placed at the point of the cline where they are thought to apply most, but again, we are concerned here with the dynamic concept of focus and not with grid-like compartments involving rigid classification; the arrows indicate the range of application or, where they overlap, interaction. Essential for special language translation, for example, is specialized factual knowledge of the subject concerned, while literary translation presupposes a background in literary studies and cultural history. A necessary precondition for all translation is knowledge of the sociocultural background (see 2. 1 below), both of the source culture and the target culture concerned.

Level D names important aspects and criteria governing the translation process itself, an extremely complex area which at this point is dealt with only briefly, as most of them form the main topic of chapters to follow. D(i) focuses on the source text: Crucial here is the *understanding* of the text (see 2. 1 and 4. 1 below), which does not simply involve familiarity with words and structures, but presupposes the ability to penetrate the sense of the text, both as a complex multidimensional whole and at the same time in its relationship to the cultural background (see 3. 3 below). With certain special language texts involving standardized concepts (particularly in science and technology) the scope of interpretation is narrowed down considerably. D(ii) names focal criteria for the envisaged translation: The notion of invariance can only apply in cases of conceptual identity (standardized terminology), while the concept of equivalence is here still considered to be of some relevance for certain types of special language translation where the focus is on isolatable lexical items (see 3. 5. 1 below). Basically however, our conception of translation supports the more dynamic approach pioneered by Hönig and Kussmaul (1982), whose dominant criterion is the *communicative function* of the target text [the stage indicated in D(iii)], which governs what they call the "notwendigen Grad der Differenzierung" (the necessary degree of precision) (see Hönig and Kussmaul, 1982, p. 58ff. and 2. 2 below). With texts involving the *creative extension* of the language norm (2. 3 below)—this applies mainly but not exclusively to literary texts—translation involves *recreating* language *dimensions* and results in a shift of *perspective* in the target text (2. 4 below).

Level E names those areas of linguistics which are relevant for translation. Of basic importance is text-linguistics in all its aspects, from the analysis of the macrostructure (see 3. 2 below),thematic progression and sentence perspective (cf. Gerzymisch-Arbogast, 1986) to coherence and cohesion. Older literature requires knowledge of Historical Linguistics, while special language translation presupposes familiarity with work in terminology and access to data-banks. Contrastive Linguistics, both in syntax and lexicology, has great potential for translation theory, although up to now its results in this respect have been meagre (cf. 3. 5 below). Other disciplines of relevance for translation as an act of communication within a specific situational context would be sociolinguistics (as the study of language varieties), pragmalinguistics (in particular the speech act theory, cf. 3. 4 below), and psycholinguistics (as regards the interdependence of language, experience and thought, cf. 2. 1 below). And finally, the lowest level F names phonological aspects of specific relevance for certain areas of translation, as for example, speakability in stage translation, alliteration and rhythm in advertising language.

With this prototypological framework the foundations have been laid for our conception of translation studies as an integrated and independent discipline that covers all kind of translation, from literary to technical. In this view, translation draws on many disciplines, but is not equal to the sum total of their overlapping areas and is not dependent on any one of them. As a discipline in its own right, translation studies needs to develop its own methods based, not on outside models and conventions from other disciplines, but on the complexities of translation. The present study is intended as a step in that direction.

At this stage I should like to summarize, in four briefly worded hypotheses, the results of what has been established so far.

(1) Translation studies should not be considered a mere offshoot of another discipline or sub-discipline (whether Applied Linguistics or Comparative Literature): Both the translator and the translation theorist are rather concerned with a world between disciplines, languages and cultures.

(2) Whereas linguistics has gradually widened its field of interest from the micro-to the macro-level, translation studies, which is concerned essentially with texts against their situational and cultural background, should adopt the reverse perspective: As maintained by the gestalt psychologists, an analysis of parts cannot provide an understanding of the whole, which must be analyzed from "the top down. "

(3) Translation studies has been hampered by classical modes of categorization, which operate with rigid dividing-lines, binary opposites, antitheses and dichotomies. Frequently

these are mere academic constructs which paralyze the finer differentiation required in all aspects of translation studies. In our approach the typology is replaced by the prototypology, admitting blends and blurred edges, and the dichotomy gives way to the concept of a spectrum or cline against which phenomena are situated and focused.

(4) While the classic approach to the study of language and translation has been to isolate phenomena (mainly words) and study them in depth, translation studies is essentially concerned with a web of relationships, the importance of individual items being decided by their relevance in the larger context of text, situation and culture.

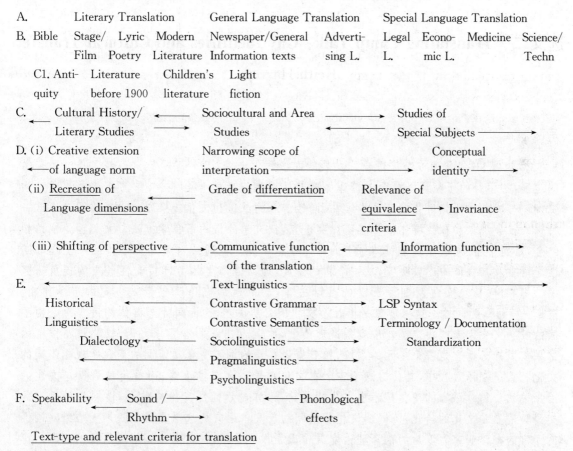

Text-type and relevant criteria for translation

【延伸阅读】

[1] Pym, A. (1998). *Method in Translation History*. Manchester: St Jerome.

[2] Snell-Hornby, M. (1988). *Translation Studies: An Integrated Approach*. Amsterdam and Philadelphia, PA: John Benjamins.

[3] Tirkkonnen-Condit, S. (1991). *Empirical Research in Translation and Intercultural Studies*. Tübingen: Gunter Narr.

【问题与思考】

1. 为什么说霍恩比的翻译研究综合法是以格式塔理论为基础的？
2. 为什么说霍恩比的翻译研究综合法借鉴了原型学理论？
3. 霍恩比的翻译研究综合法如何实施？其具体步骤是什么？
4. 霍恩比的翻译研究综合法对我们作翻译研究有何指导意义？

选文二　Translating Camp Talk：Gay Identities and Cultural Transfer

Keith Harvey

导　言

20 世纪 90 年代西方翻译理论的发展转向多元化进程，翻译研究已经超越了单纯语言学的范围，跨学科的研究已经在西方翻译界掀起了浪潮。英国著名学者、曼彻斯特大学理工学院翻译与跨文化研究讲师凯斯·哈维在《同性恋者的身份和文化转换》一文中，将同性恋这一特殊的社会现象和社会群体作为其研究突破点，把文学分析的语言学方法与文化理论视角相结合，从而丰富、发展了跨学科体系下的翻译理论研究。他通过对英法文学作品中出现的同性恋语言及其翻译的比较研究，从一个新的角度，即同性恋者的男性持女性气质的视角研究了性别身份、社会文化及翻译三者的互动关系，为以后的翻译研究带来一定的启示作用。凯斯·哈维认为同性恋这一现象是由社会文化因素所决定，因而同性恋群体的语言也是由不同的社会文化因素所决定。对应到翻译理论上，他认为翻译是语篇与文化、权势相互作用的结果。同性恋语言是一个多元的系统，随着言语篇章的词汇变化及语调的变化呈现出不同的文化特点。翻译过程中，其关键点不在于在文化背景下去定位语篇，而是定位语篇与文化的因果关系。篇章语言的变化显示出文化的差异，语言显示性别身份的差异，性别身份语言的交错运用显示文化的转化，不同的文化背景制约着文本语言的选择。虽然凯斯·哈维对同性恋语言的翻译研究为以后的翻译理论发展作出了很大贡献，但仍有一些值得商榷的问题。比如他所研究的主要是文学作品中的文本语言，与现实语言之间存有差距；另外他认为同性恋只是由社会因素造成的，忽视了其他造成同性恋现象的可能性。不难看出，凯斯·哈维以同性恋语言作为突破点所作的跨学科翻译研究，仍有可以改进和发展之处。

Camp is regularly attested in fictional representations of homosexual men's speech in French-and English-language texts from the 1940s to the present. What is more, camp talk is associated with a whole range of homosexual identities in French and English fiction，from the marginalized transvestite (Genet，1948)，through to middle class "arty" types (Vidal，

1948/1965; Wilson, 1952; Bory, 1969), the post-Stonewall hedonistic "faggot" (Navarre, 1976; Kramer, 1978) and the politicized AIDS-aware "queer" (Kushner, 1992). It could be assumed from this that when translating such fiction translators need merely to be aware of the comparable resources of camp in source and target language cultures. However, while the formal aspects of camp might appear constant, the functions that camp performs in its diverse contexts are far from uniform. I will argue later that one of the chief variables determining these functional differences is the conception of homosexuality as a defining property of identity. For the moment it is important to note that the functions of camp are intimately bound up with the question of its *evaluation*.

1　Formal and functional dimensions of camp

In order to open up the factor of evaluation to scrutiny, the functions of camp talk can usefully be broken down into two distinct (micro and macro) dimensions. First, the immediate fictional context of camp talk will often suggest whether it is to be given a positive or negative evaluative load. For example, a character such as Clarence in Jean-Louis Bory's novel *La Peau des Zèbres* (1969) is presented to the reader as a cynical, self-absorbed, emotionally-stunted individual. His camp talk (he is the only homosexual character in the book to employ camp) is read in the novel as a key symptom of his limited affective potential. In contrast, Belize in Tony Kushner's play *Angels In America*, *Part One: Millennium Approaches* (1992) is presented as the main source of emotional and practical support for Prior, a young gay man dying of an AIDS-related illness. His camp is positively viewed in the play as a source of strength and much-needed humour. In both of these cases, the evaluation is located at a micro-functional fictional level. The macrofunctional dimension taps into the wider (sub)cultural values that homosexual/gay identity has established for itself and within which the fictional text operates and develops its meanings. Bory's novel works hard to promote the notion of homosexual ordinariness. His characters love, suffer and live their lives just as heterosexual characters do in countless other love stories. They just happen to love people of the same sex. In this context, Clarence's camp talk is a macrocultural trace of difference and marginality which it is deemed desirable to overcome. In contrast, Kushner's representations of camp at the micro level are instrumental in the elaboration of subcultural difference as a desirable goal. *Angels In America* presents camp as a sign of gay resistance and solidarity in the face of a whole array of threats to the gay individual and his community, from AIDS to the discriminations and hypocrises of the dominant culture. In Kushner's text, camp is invested with a political charge predicated upon an irreducible and subversive gay difference. Camp here, then, receives a positive evaluative load in both functional dimensions.

It is with this recognition of the double-layered nature of the evaluation of camp that the work of a translator reaches a key point of difficulty. For, while the micro-functional dimension of evaluation in a given source text might arguably be apparent to a translator, as to any attentive reader, recognition of the macro-functional dimension of camp will depend on a cluster of factors that go beyond close attention to the source text and involve cultural and even autobiographical issues for the translator. These issues include: (1) the existence, nature and visibility of *identities* and *communities* predicated upon same-sex object choice in the target culture; (2) the existence or absence of an established *gay literature* in the target culture; (3) the stated *gay objectives* (if retrievable) inherent in the undertaking of the translation and publication of the translation (for example, whether the text is to be part of a gay list of novels); (4) the *sexual identity* of the translator and his or her relation to a gay subcultural group, its identities, codes and political project. In what follows I wish above all to focus on the questions of homosexual/gay identities, communities and writing in source and target cultures and to attempt to link the existence of such pressures with the translated textual product.

I will begin by analysing an example of verbal camp in a contemporary English-language text, relating this to a general description of verbal camp. I will then outline some major accounts of camp as a cultural phenomenon by straight and gay-identified commentators before discussing two specific examples of camp and its translation, one from English to French and the other from French to English.

2 Verbal camp

A couple of related points need to be made briefly before looking at the example. The first concerns the specificity to the repertoire of camp talk of the features I identify. The second relates to the nature of the evidence I am considering. Rusty Barrett's (1995, 1997) enquiries into gay men's language practice are valuable in order to think through these issues. His use of Pratt's (1987) linguistics of contact is particularly useful.

In a contact model of language use, speakers "constitute each other relationally and in difference" (Pratt, 1987, p. 60). This model contrasts with the more familiar "linguistics of community" present in dialectology, according to which essentially homogeneous language practices result from a consensual process of socialization of the individual by a community. As Barrett notes wryly, "Generally, people do not raise their children to talk like homosexuals" (1997, p. 191). A linguistics of contact would recognize the fact that gay men and lesbians work within and appropriate prevailing straight (and homophobic) discourses. Specifically, it would be able to account for gay speakers' frequent use of language practices associated with a whole range of communities "defined in terms of ethnicity, class, age, or regional background" (ibid.). For example, Barrett suggests that while white middle-class gay men may draw upon lexis identified with African-American vernacular speech (for example *girlfriend* and *Miss Thang*, often employed as vocatives) and upon the ritual insults associated with black speech events (see also Murray, 1979; Leap, 1996, p. 10). African American gay men might make use of those features of white woman's English that Lakoff (1975) suggested were typical, for example the careful discrimination of colour terms and the use of tag questions. This account points to a powerful citational fluidity in language styles that is consonant with Pratt's contact model.

As Pratt herself notes: "A linguistics of contact will be deeply interested in processes of appropriation, penetration or co-optation of one group's language by another" (1987, p. 61).

This notion of "contact" in language practice is also useful in addressing the question of the status of the evidence in my description of camp talk. I am chiefly interested in literary representations, but occasionally reference is also made to work done in the sociolinguistics of actual language practice. There seems, however, to be little justification for mixing the two types of language. The evidence from each field of study appears, strictly speaking, to be inadmissible in the other. This conclusion itself turns out to rest upon an assumption that can be challenged, namely that whereas fictional representations of talk are *constructed* deliberately by an author for the purposes of character development and narrative advancement, real language use is a *reflection* of the sociolinguistic group(s) to which speakers belong. Barrett's account of the inherently citational nature of gay camp talk undermines the clear distinction between fictional representations of talk and real talk. Both, in this account, draw on a stock of language features that are invested with cultural (and stereotypical) values in order to achieve the *effect* of a specific communal identity: "For speakers who wish to use language in a way that will index a gay identity ... the form of language often reflects a stereotype of gay men's speech" (Barrett, 1997, p. 192). What counts, then, is not the empirically verifiable truth of the relation between a language feature and a speaker's identity, but the fact that these language features have come to stand for certain gendered and subcultural differences. Camp talk enlists these stereotypical differences in order to index a distinct sexual identity.

2. 1 On the surface of camp

Tony Kushner's *Angels In America*, *Part One*: *Millennium Approaches* (1992; Act Two, Scene Five, p. 44) features a verbal exchange between two gay male characters, Belize and Prior. Belize is black and Prior white. They were once lovers. Belize used to be a drag queen. He is visiting Prior in hospital, where the latter is receiving care for an AIDS-related illness. Prior is referring to the fact that the drug he is being given causes him to hear "a voice." Belize has threatened to tell the doctor unless Prior does so himself:

> *Prior*: ... You know what happens? When I hear it, I get hard.
> *Belize*: Oh my.
> *Prior*: Comme ça. (He uses his arm to demonstrate.) And you know I am
> slow to rise.
> *Belize*: My jaw aches at the memory.
> *Prior*: And would you deny me this little solace—betray my concupiscence to
> Florence Nightingale's stormtroopers?

Belize: Perish the thought, ma bébé.

Prior: They'd change the drug just to spoil the fun.

Belize: You and your boner can depend on me.

Prior: Je t'adore, ma belle Nègre.

Belize: All this girl-talk shit is politically incorrect, you know. We should have dropped it back when we gave up drag.

Prior: I'm sick, I get to be politically incorrect if it makes me feel better.

We can begin by noting that in this passage there are certain prepositional features that are typical of gay camp talk. The preoccupation with sexual activity (the erection, fellatio) is often associated, as here, with references to extinct passion and a tragi-comic awareness of the ephemeral nature of sexual desire. Furthermore, in camp the talk of sex contrasts with an attentiveness to conventional moral codes of behaviour, with speakers often alluding to the principles of decency and rectitude to which they feign to adhere (for example Prior's suggestion that Belize could not possibly "betray" him). The incongruity inherent in the juxtaposition of a detailed interest in the mechanics of sex with a trumpeted adherence to traditional moral codes is one of the chief sources of irony in camp.

Turning to the formal level, this passage is rich with camp traits. The most obvious is the inversion of gender-specific terms, the "girl-talk" that Belize refers to. The practice of girl-talk overlaps with the camp strategy of renaming that includes the adoption of male names marked as "queer"—Quentin Crisp's name was *Denis* before he "dyed" it (Crisp, 1968, p. 15)—and the disturbance of the arbitrary practice of attributing proper names—for example, Rechy's *Whorina* (Rechy, 1963, p. 304) and *Miss Ogynist* (ibid. , p. 336). Lucas (1994, p. 132) gives evidence of how such queer renaming has a history that dates back at least to the 18th century in Britain, while Pastre (1997, p. 372) shows how similar practices are at work in contemporary queer France. In the Kushner extract, the female terms combine with the use of French and are realized by feminine adjectives in vocative expressions (*ma bébé*, *ma belle* Nègre). The effect of such renaming is to signal the speaker's critical distance from the processes that produce and naturalize categories of identity. Because this opens up disjunctures between appearance and reality, the effect is also to undermine the schemata with which the addressee is operating. Thus, even a gay man has his perception of the world disturbed by a man who introduces himself as *Vicky* (Navarre, 1976), or *Miss Rollarette* (Kramer, 1978).

However, femininity is not only signalled in the text by such obvious lexical devices as names. The exclamative sentence *Oh my* is multiply determined as camp style and constitutes an example of what I would call the emphatics of camp, all of which contributes to camp's construction of the theatricalized woman. Alongside exclamations, these emphatics include a taste for hyperbole as well as the use of the "uninvolved" or "out of power" adjectives (*marvellous*, *adorable*) that Lakoff (1975, pp. 11 – 14) claimed were typical of women's language. The imitative nature of emphatics is made clear by Crisp when describing a Mrs

Longhurst he knew as a child: "This woman did not fly to extremes: She lived there. I also became an adept at this mode of talk and, with the passing of the years, came to speak in this way unconsciously" (Crisp, 1968, p. 24). In this connection King (1994), citing the polemical book *The Phoenix of Sodom* (1813), notes how "talking like a woman" has been a feature of homosexual camp at least since London's eighteenth-century Molly Houses (where homosexual men met in secret to have sex). Once arrived in a Molly House, men affected "to speak, walk, talk, tattle, curtsy, cry, scold & mimick all manner of effeminacy" (quoted in King, 1994, p. 42). Furthermore, "every one was to talk of their Husbands & Children, one estolling [sic] the Virtues of her Husband, another the genius & wit of their Children: Whilst a Third would express himself sorrowfully under the character of a Widow" (ibid.). The construction of a "woman" is clearly achieved through the parodic accumulation of stereotypical language features, such as those I term "emphatics."

However, the form of the exclamation "Oh my" in the Kushner extract does more than just suggest a generalized femininity. For a gay reader, it evokes a specific culturally-situated and theatricalized type of femininity, namely the "Southern Belle" made famous by Vivien Leigh in *Gone with the Wind*—see also John Rechy's queens in *City of Night* (1963, p. 48, p. 287, p. 328), who often affect Southern accents. As such, the phrase builds into the text the type of inter textual reference to a major example of popular culture that is typical of gay talk. Leap (1996, p. 15), for example, traces a reference to film star Mae West's famous line "Why don't ya come up and see me some time" in an overheard discussion between a maitre d' and a potential customer, both of whom Leap assumes to be gay. In another reference to a famous film heroine, Maupin's (1980) novel *Tales of the City* includes this exchange between lovers Michael and Jon (Maupin, 1980, p. 119):

> Michael shrugged. "I want to deceive him just long enough to make him want me."
>
> "What's that from?"
>
> "Blanche Dubois. In *Streetcar*."

Such intertextualities have at least two effects. First, they create ironic distance around all semiotic practice, constituting devices of "defamiliarization" (Fowler, 1986, pp. 40 – 52) and, in particular, signal a suspicion of all encodings of sincerity. Second, they reinforce gay solidarity between interlocutors. To understand the slang or catch on to the allusion is also to feel that one belongs to the community. (Note how Jon immediately identifies Michael's sentence as a quote in the extract above.)

Prior's lines "Comme ça" and "Je t'adore ma belle Nègre" draw on another of verbal camp's most consistent devices in English, the use of French. Clearly, this accomplishes a humorous nod to sophistication and cosmopolitanism, French language and culture being saturated for the Anglo-Saxon world with the qualities of style and urbanity. What is more, France is popularly known first and foremost for its consummate skills in the arts of *surface* refinement (fashion, perfume). The use of French, then, does not just decorate the text linguistically. Rather, it alludes to a complex of cultural values and stereotypes that carry decorativeness as an attribute. It is interesting to note that French camp, in a parallel gesture, resorts to the use of English words and phrases: *"Well, thank you very much, kind Sir ... "* (Camus, 1988, p. 64; italics in original); "C'est exciting!" (Navarre, 1976, p. 177). While the English use of French signalled a kind of tongue-in-cheek sophistication, the French use of English here points (perhaps with equal ironic distance) to the spread of English-language popular culture across the world in the late 20th century. Indeed, a phrase like *"Well, thank you very much, kind Sir"* suggests the inter textual reference to Hollywood heroines already noted. In other words. English in French camp also functions principally as a cultural, rather than merely linguistic sign.

Language games such as these may be characteristic of a type of critical semiotic awareness that is especially heightened in gay people, resulting from a long exclusion from mainstream signifying practices. But they may also signal a more defiant attitude to cultural norms, as Sullivan has suggested when noting that gay people show "in their ironic games with the dominant culture that something in them is ultimately immune to its control" (Sullivan, 1996, pp. 71 – 72). Comparable in its effect is the formal aspect of register-mixing that verbal gay camp typically delights in. Camp likes to expose the mechanisms at work in the choices speakers make with regard to appropriateness. Camp speakers, for example, will typically use levels of formality/informality that are incongruous in a particular context, or juxtapose different levels of formality in a way that creates linguistic incongruity. In Kramer's *Faggots*, a character (re-)named *Yootha* juxtaposes mock-literary and low registers to describe a sexual encounter with another man in a toilet: "He immediately inquires, 'how much?' I, *not expecting such bountiful tidings*, because I would have *done him for free* ... I am saying 'My pleasure'" (Kramer, 1978, p. 179; my italics). And Prior's rhetorical flourish ("And would you deny me this little solace—betray my concupiscence to Florence Nightingale's stormtroopers?") contrasts with his next utterance, an informal and unadorned expression of potential displeasure ("They'd change the drug just to spoil the fun"). Indeed, the whole exchange, based around sexual innuendo and wordplay, could be construed as highly inappropriate given Prior's rapidly declining health. However, as the last lines suggest, this inappropriateness also accomplishes an act of critical resistance.

2.2 Ambivalent solidarity and politeness theory

It is important to add to our description of this passage a consideration of a microfunctional feature that I would term *ambivalent solidarity*. This is a crucial interactive aspect of gay camp that can be obscured by an exclusively formal and taxonomic approach. Broadly, ambivalent solidarity revolves around the mechanisms of attack and support, either of which can be covert or on-record. Thus, two characters might feign support for each other by surface prepositional and formal means while in fact attacking the other's sexual prowess or probity through innuendo and double-entendre, as in the conversation between the transvestites Divine and Mimosa in *Notre-Dame des Fleurs* (Genet, 1948, pp. 177 - 178). Crisp describes the stylized cattiness that was characteristic of gay get-togethers when he was younger as "a formal game of innuendoes about other people being older than they said, about their teeth being false and their hair being a wig. Such conversation was thought to be smart and very feminine" (Crisp, 1968, p. 29). In the Kushner passage, there are elements of covert attack (e. g. Belize's mock complaint at Prior's slowness at getting an erection) alongside numerous on-record assurances of support and trustworthiness (e. g. Belize's "Perish the thought"). In contrast, gay characters might deploy the put-down as an on-record attack. White (1988, p. 42) gives the following example:

> We were all smiling. I was mute and ponderous beside my new companions. I assumed each bit of repartee had been coined on the spot. Only later did I recognise that the routines made up a repertory, a sort of folk wisdom common to "queens," for hadn't Morris recklessly announced, "Grab your tiaras, girls, we're all royalty tonight, why I haven't seen so many crowned heads since Westminster Abbey—" "I know you *give* head, Abbie, but the only crowns you've seen are on those few molars you've got left."

Here, the parting shot, though vicious, is in fact part of an elaborate game used to hone the tools of queer verbal self-defence and to reassert, albeit paradoxically, a communal belonging (see the pioneering work on gay insults by Murray, 1979).

The pragmatic theory of politeness (Brown & Levinson, 1987), with its key notion of the "face-threatening act," could usefully be brought to bear on this aspect of camp talk. According to politeness theory, all speakers have both negative and positive face-wants which they strive mutually to respect. Negative face-wants are based upon a desire not to be restricted in one's freedom of action.

As a result, a speaker will mitigate the imposition implicit in the formulation of a request (the "face threat") by the encoding of an utterance that fronts deference. Camp talk threatens an addressee's negative face-wants with its on-record requests for solidarity and support. Positive face-wants, in contrast, are based upon the desire to be appreciated and approved of. In Brown and Levinson's terms, camp can often be seen to involve threats to an addressee's positive face-wants by indicating that the speaker does not care about the addressee's positive self-image, hence, the insults, ridicule, put-downs etc. One small example will suffice to show the potential of this approach to the analysis and its usefulness in describing translations. After a nocturnal sexual encounter in a public garden, the narrator of Camus' *Tricks* (1988, p. 70) meets an acquaintance on the cruising ground. This man comments:

> —Tiens, Renaud, mais vous vous dévergondez! Qu'est-ce que vous faites là?
> [Hey, Renaud, but you are getting into bad ways! What are you doing here?]

This remark constitutes a clear threat to the addressee's positive face-wants by casting aspersions on his behaviour. Yet it is overloaded with the ironies of ambivalent solidarity: First, the speaker could just as easily address the remark to himself (he, too, is on the cruising ground); second, the notion of "getting into bad ways" is one which both addressor and addressee know belongs to the moral code of the dominant culture. Through such a comment, this code is thus being mocked for the benefit of both addressor and addressee. Interestingly, the English translation (Howard, 1996, p. 30) exaggerates the threat to the positive face-wants of the addressee:

> "Hey, Renaud, you whore! What are you doing here?"

Here the face-threatening act is intensified by several means: Whereas the source text encoded a comment on the moral behaviour of the addressee, the speech act here is a clear (grammatically moodless) insult. In the French, the speaker ironically affects moral superiority through the use of a term (*se dévergonder*) more usually associated with formal registers, while in the English the vulgarity of *whore* diminishes the speaker's claims to a superior moral stance. Further, the use of *whore* exemplifies the typical camp move of employing a term usually reserved for women. The target text, then, amplifies the camp in several ways, but in doing so arguably loses some of the irony present in the source text's (feigned) encoding of moral censure. Politeness theory can be used to help identify exactly how shifts of this type might occur.

3 Camp, gay sensibility and queer radicalism

From Sontag (1964) to queer theorists of the 1990s, much of the work on camp has taken place within cultural studies, film studies and gay and lesbian studies. It has not, therefore, paid much attention to the detailed mechanisms of language.

However, its insights are relevant to our purposes.

In "Notes on Camp," Sontag conceives of camp as a type of aesthetic sensibility that is characterized by a delight in "failed seriousness" and the "theatricalization of experience" (1964, p. 287). In order to explain the link between camp and homosexuals, Sontag suggests that the camp sensibility serves a propagandistic agenda for the homosexual cause: "Homosexuals have *pinned their integration* into society on promoting the aesthetic sense. Camp is a *solvent* of morality. It *neutralizes* moral indignation, sponsors playfulness" (ibid.; my emphases). It would seem reasonable to suggest that a bid for social integration by a minority group was political by nature. However, by insisting that camp is first and foremost "an aesthetic phenomenon" (ibid.), Sontag makes her view of it as "disengaged, depoliticized or at least apolitical" (ibid.) prevail to the detriment of any political potential. While also downplaying its political potential, Booth (1983, p. 17) nonetheless breaks with Sontag by asserting that "Camp is primarily a matter of self-presentation." He is thereby able to include a characterization of the verbal style of camp people in his account, noting characteristics that extend from the level of topic (marriage, "manly" sporting activities, etc.) to a specific manner of vocal delivery (ibid., p. 67).

> A camp quality of voice may also express lassitude: the typical diction is slow almost to the point of expiration, with heavy emphasis on inappropriate words (lots of capital letters and italics) rising painfully to a climax, to be followed by a series of swift cadences—a sort of rollercoaster effect, which in Regency times was known as the "drawing room drawl."

The reference to "capital letters and italics" is interesting here. Booth is ostensibly talking about non-written camp "performance," yet the literary quality of this style suggests the presence of written-textual devices of emphasis. This confusion of different linguistic channels is in itself a testimony to the success of camp's deconstruction of the binarism "spoken/written" as an analogy of "natural/constructed."

As far back as the 1970s, gay-identified commentators argued that there were limitations to an exclusively aesthetic and depoliticized reading of camp practice (Dyer, 1977; Babuscio, 1977/1993). Babuscio, a historian, suggests that camp emerged as a gay response to contemporary society's penchant for "a method of labeling [that] ensures that individual types become polarized" (Babuscio, reprinted in Bergman, 1993, pp. 20 – 21). Thus, camp's critical mechanisms are specifically developed to mock, dodge and deconstruct the multiple binarisms in our society that stem from the postulation of the categories natural/unnatural. Using film texts for his examples, Babuscio suggests that gay camp deploys four linked strategies: irony; aestheticism; theatricality; humour. Irony is based upon the principle of "incongruous contrast between an individual or thing and its context or association." Babuscio suggests various examples of gender crossing through masquerade (e.g. Garbo in *Queen Christina*). In order to be effective, irony must be shaped. This is where the strategy of aestheticism comes into play. The camp emphasis on style deliberately "signifies performance rather than existence" (ibid., p. 23). What is more, it leads typically to a deliberately exaggerated reliance on questions of (self-) presentation: "The emphasis shifts from what a thing or person *is* to what it *looks* like; from *what* is being done to *how* it is being done" (ibid., p. 24). Theatricality in camp develops inevitably from its aestheticism. Babuscio's explanation for the gay deployment of theatricality takes its place in a long line of feminist critiques of the constructedness of gender roles (e.g. Millet, 1971; Butler, 1990):

> If "role" is defined as the appropriate behaviour associated with a given position in society, then gays do not conform to socially expected ways of behaving as men and women. Camp, by focusing on the outward appearances of role, implies that roles, and, in particular, sex roles, are superficial—a matter of style.
>
> (Babuscio, 1993, p. 24)

Humour, born of the ironic appreciation of incongruity, is the fourth of the features Babuscio mentions. Interestingly, it is with humour that Babuscio explicitly points up the political potential of camp. He writes of camp humour "undercutting rage by its derision of concentrated bitterness" (ibid., p. 28). Calling camp a "protopolitical phenomenon," he notes more- over that it "steadfastly refuses to repudiate our long heritage of gay ghetto life" (ibid.). This gives rise to the typical inversion of values that camp revels in "even when this takes the form of finding beauty in the seemingly bizarre and outrageous, or discovering the worthiness in a thing or person that is supposedly without value" (ibid.).

If Babuscio recognized camp's political potential, then 1990s' queer Camp—written with an upper-case "C" when "conceptualized as a politicized, solely queer discourse" (Meyer 1994, p. 21, p. n. 2)—has gone much further. Not only has queer criticism redefined Camp as a central strategy in its exposure of the functioning of "straight" institutions and values, queer thinkers have used it to found the wider "ontological challenge" (ibid., p. 2) of queer: "Queerness can be seen as an oppositional stance not simply to essentialist formations of gay and lesbian identities, but to a much wider application of the depth model of identity" (ibid., p. 3). Queer's radical indeterminacy resides in its conception of identity as a pure effect of performance: "At some time, the actor must *do* something in order to produce the social visibility by which the identity is manifested" (ibid., p. 4). Language contributes actively to this elaboration of the effect of identity. Furthermore, the "performance paradigm" that Meyer inherits from Judith Butler's theory of gender means that contemporary sexual identities ultimately depend on "*extrasexual* performative gestures" (ibid., p. 4; my emphasis). This is an important insight for understanding the way "gay" functions semiotically in contemporary culture. For, if the fact of sexual activity itself between people of the same gender appears to be the *sine qua non* for the (self-) attribution of the labels "gay" or "lesbian," it is also true that such activity is actually absent from view and only present through the work of other extrasexual signifying practices which thereby become linked to it metonymically.

In this play of surfaces feigning substance, it is hardly surprising that Camp should occupy a central place as the total body of performative practices and strategies used to enact a queer identity. Meyer's reading of Camp and its political potency is achieved through a deployment of Hutcheon's conception of parody as "an extended repetition with critical difference" (Hutcheon, 1985, p. 7). Thus, parody (and, for Meyer, Camp) emerges as an essentially intertextual operation on the value that is invested in an original text. The traditional denigration of parody stems from an ideological position that endows the original with supreme cultural importance and suppresses any suggestion that the source is itself the outcome of an intertextual process. A re-evaluation of parody as a primary and pervasive cultural operation entails a reconsideration of the hierarchy of values that have hitherto marginalized it. Meyer suggests that Hutcheon's work is particularly useful for theorists of Camp if the factor of process rather than form is highlighted: "By employing a performance-oriented methodology that privileges process, we can restore a knowledgeable *queer* social agent to the discourse of Camp parody" (1994, p. 10). In other words, a focus on the doer and the doing, and not the finished textual product, allows the queer theorist to highlight the neglected potential for cultural agency in the parodie moment: "The relationship between texts becomes simply an indicator of the power relationships between social agents who wield those texts, one who possesses the 'original,' the other who possesses the parodie alternative" (ibid.).

Meyer's Camp is thus a kind of Trojan Horse penetrating the otherwise unbreachable preserve of straight semiotic practice, a necessarily parasitic enterprise that manages nonetheless to endow the voiceless queer with cultural agency. The required link to dominant practices is also helpful in explaining how different evaluations of Camp can be adhered to within the gay community: "Camp appears, on the one hand, to offer a transgressive vehicle yet, on the other, simultaneously invokes the specter of a dominant ideology" (ibid.). For some, the "specter of dominant ideology" embedded in Camp blocks its potential as an instrument of cultural critique and political action. Penelope and Wolfe (1979, p. 10, cited in Jacobs, 1996, p. 62), for example, castigate the use of derogatory terms for women in the camp put-down becaus it endorses "the politics of patriarchy." In contrast, for Meyer himself the transgression inherent in Camp founds queer's suspicion of identity categories and constitutes the necessary backdrop for queer cultural agency.

4　Translations, transformations

I will now examine two extracts from novels that contain fictionalized camp talk and set them alongside their published translations. The first novel is Gore Vidal's *The City and the Pillar* (1948/1965), translated into French as *Un Garçon près de la Rivière* (1981) by Philippe Mikriammos. The second is Tony Duvert's *Paysage de Fantaisie* (1973), translated into English as *Strange Landscape* (1975) by Sam Flores. I will seek to show that in the first translation the camp is either minimized or deprived of its gay communal values. In contrast, the second translation fronts the gay camp elements and transforms the passage into one with a clear homosexual message. These textual facts will be related to the cultural contexts in which they were produced.

4.1　Vidal and Mikriammos: coming out in New York and Paris

In Vidal's 1965 Afterword to *The City and the Pillar* we are told that homosexual behaviour is entirely natural since "All human beings are bisexual" (Vidal, 1948/1965, p. 157). However, Vidal insists that "of course there is no such thing as a homosexual;" the word is "not a noun describing a recognizable type" (ibid.). He thus deprives homosexuality of its claim to constitute a key element of identity in the same gesture as he legitimizes it. In one sense, Vidal's view is consistent with the description of the hero, Jim, an ordinary American male who can, and often does, pass as heterosexual. Nonetheless, the novel contains a portrait of well-established communities of men who certainly do identify as homosexuals.

While it is true that the picture of these communities that emerges is far from positive (the men Jim meets at gay parties are often bitchy, jealous and small-minded), they do exist as a distinct social group. And their use of verbal camp is presented as one of their defining traits: Vidal notes that "their conversation was often cryptic," a "suggestive ritual" (ibid., p. 46). Jim, the hero, does not contribute to camp, and is sometimes bored or made to feel uneasy by it. On the microcontextual level, then, camp receives a negative evaluation. However, one of the key features of camp is that it has irony at its own expense built into it. Through this irony, camp is often able to subvert the negative evaluation that might be loaded on to it. As a result, I contend, camp emerges in Vidal's novel—and despite its author's avowed intentions—as a macro-contextual sign of an established homosexual identity and community.

The extract I wish to examine is from a passage describing a party held in New York by Nicholas J. Rolloson (Roily), a minor character. Jim has been taken to the party by his ex-lover, a film star called Shaw. By this time in the novel, Jim has had two important homosexual affairs and gay social life is not unfamiliar to him. Mikriammos' translation of the passage is reproduced immediately after Vidal's text.

> "You know, I loathe these screaming pansies," said Roily, twisting an emerald and ruby ring. "I have a perfect weakness for men who are butch. I mean, after all, why be a queen if you like other queens, if you follow me? Luckily, nowadays everybody's *gay*, if you know what I mean ... *literally* everybody! So different when I was a girl. Why, just a few days ago a friend of mine ... well, I wouldn't go so far as to say *a friend*, actually I think he's rather *sinister*, but anyway this acquaintance was actually keeping Will Jepson, the *boxer*! Now, I mean, really, when things get that far, things have really gone far!" Jim agreed that things had indeed gone far. Roily rather revolted him but he recognized that he meant to be kind and that was a good deal. "My, isn't it crowded in here? I love for people to enjoy themselves!"
>
> "I mean the right kind of people who appreciate this sort of thing. You see, I've become a Catholic."
>
> (Vidal, 1948/65, p. 120)
>
> —Je déteste ces tantes si voyantes, s'exclama Rolloson en tournant la grosse bague de rubis et d'émeraudes qu'il portait à son doigt. J'ai un faible pour les garçons qui sont costauds. Je ne vois pas l'intérêt qu'il y a, pour . nous autres tantes, à aimer les tantes! Vous me suivez? Heureusement, aujourd'hui, tout le monde en est: absolument tout le monde ... Tellement différent du temps où j'étais une fille! Mon cher, il y a quleques jours un de mes amis, je ne devais pas dire un ami car je le trouve assez sinistre, mais enfin ... cet ami m'a appris donc qu'il entretenait Will Jepson le boxeur! Quand les choses en sont là, c'est qu'elles sont déjà avancées!

Jim dit qu'en effet la situation avait évolué. Rolloson le révoltait un peu mais il se disait que le bonhomme avait de bonnes intentions et que c'était très bien comme ça.

—Quelle foule j'ai ce soir! J'adore voir les gens qui s'amusent ... Enfin, je veux dire les gens qui vibrent comme nous ... Vous savez que je viens de me convertir au catholicisme?

(Mikriammos，1981，pp. 152 – 153)

I will examine two groups of features in these texts: first, lexical and prosodic; second, textual and pragmatic.

In the English text, the lexis of Roily's camp is rich with subcultural value, both at the level of individual items and that of collocation. For example, Roily (he remains the more formal "Rolloson" throughout the translation) employs *pansies* with a pejorative meaning to describe other homosexuals and *queen* as an elected (albeit ironic) term to describe himself. Such uses concord with the values that gay men would still invest in these items today. The distinction, however, is flattened in the translation, where both terms are translated by *tante/s* (literally "aunt/s"), a pejorative term, even amongst French homosexuals. Roily's ironic reflection on the vogue for *gay* is historically intriguing. Vidal could not have known in 1948 that this term was to play a crucial role as a definer of a distinct identity. However, *gay* in the translation (published, let us remind ourselves, in 1981) becomes the largely pejorative *en être* (literally, "to be of it/them"), a term which also effectively erases the sense of an emerging identity by employing a phrase that is void of lexical content, functioning entirely through implication. For French readers, *en être* is also likely to carry a Proustian resonance, being employed in *la recherche du temps perdu* to designate homosexual characters (e. g. Proust, 1924, pp. 17 – 18). This literary echo, far from reinforcing the idea of an identity/community across time, brings with it Proust's fundamental ambivalence with regard to homosexuality: In *La recherche* homosexual characters might be increasingly omnipresent, but they are nonetheless judged to be unfortunate victims of a moral flaw. Roily's stock of subcultural signs is further impoverished by the translation of *butch* as *costauds* (literally, "stocky, well-built"). *Butch* is a long-standing member of the gay lexicon, usually employed (ironically) to designate the surface features of desirable masculinity, either of another gay man (who is not a "queen") or of a heterosexual male. In contrast, *costauds* is a mainstream French term that fails to connote the irony accruing to the gay awareness of gender performativity.

The source text also features collocations that are gay-marked. For example, *screaming pansies* is gay camp not primarily because of the noun (which could be employed as abuse by heterosexuals), but because of its collocation with *screaming*, an ironic/pejorative term indicating how out and flamboyant a particular gay man is. Despite its potential force as criticism, *screaming* also contains an element of approval when used by a gay man, suggesting as it does unmistakable gay visibility. The translation, *ces tantes si voyantes* [literally, "these (such) showy aunts"] uses a term, *voyantes* ("showy") that, again, is mainstream French and unambiguously pejorative. Another collocation, *perfect weakness*, also functions as camp in Roily's talk. The use of *perfect* with *weakness* is marked hyperbole in general English, its quasi-oxymoronic quality suggesting the self-conscious intensity of the feeling being expressed. The translator makes no attempt to capture this and translates it simply as *faible* ("weakness"). Five other lexical items in this passage are realized in italics (*gay*, *literally*, *friend*, *sinister*, *boxer*), thereby contributing to the emphatics in which the collocation *perfect weakness* plays a part. This typographical feature is typical of representations of verbal camp in English. It exaggerates (and thereby renders susceptible to irony) the speaker's own investment in the propositional content of his speech, and helps to take the addressee—willingly or not—into his confidence. It thus binds together speaker and addressee in discoursal and subcultural solidarity. The stress patterns of French, as a syllable-timed language, do not allow this prosodic feature (and its written encoding) to the same degree. The translator, therefore, has not used italics in this passage; neither does he attempt to compensate for the loss of this stylistic feature. As a result, Roily's camp is diminished, as is the passage's construction of a clear type of homosexual identity.

It is also important to note the textual and pragmatic functions that the many co-operative discourse markers have in the text, for example: *You know*; *if you know what I mean*; *actually*; *now*, *I mean*, *really*... As well as furthering the speaker's propositional stream, such terms act as a constant "involving" mechanism directed at the addressee. They are devices that crucially contribute to the gossipy tone of Roily's talk. None of those co-operative markers just cited is translated in Mikriammos' text. With one notable exception, the French text downplays the verbal links that Roily attempts to make with his fellow homosexual Jim. The exception is the translation of Roily's exclamatory use of *Why* by *Mon cher* (literally, "My dear"), which might constitute an attempt at compensation. A final important example of the way a discourse marker such as *You see* can function is in Roily's last comment: "I love for people to enjoy themselves! I mean the right kind of people who appreciate this sort of thing. You see, I've become a Catholic." The joke is excellent, Roily suggesting that there is a causal link between his conversaion to Catholicism and his desire for people to enjoy themselves at parties. The latter becomes thereby transformed into an act of Christian charity, with *You see* making the link. As is typical with camp, we cannot be entirely sure whether the speaker is intentionally sending himself up or whether the joke is at his expense. At any rate, it manages to ridicule and trivialize piety and the Church, a frequent butt of gay jokes. Mikriammos changes *You see* to "You know" and precedes it with suspension marks. The combined effect is not to suggest a causal link between Roily's propositions, but rather to mark a topic change. The camp joke is thus missed.

How can the changes noted in the translation be explained? I would like to suggest that the translator has (inevitably, one might say) produced a text that harmonizes with the prevailing view of human subjectivity that obtains in his—the target—culture. Edmund White's

(1997) suggestion that gayness—construed as a defining property of a distinct group of human beings—conflicts in France with the philosophy of the universal subject inherited from the Enlightenment can be useful here. Thus, in France there is a suspicion (even amongst those who practise "homosexual activity") of the validity of a subcultural label such as "gay." Indeed, the very imported nature of the term makes its use unstable, as is clear from a comment such as the following: "We can use the English spelling 'gay' *to stress its cultural meaning imported from the USA*, or the French spelling 'gai,' with the same meaning" (Gais et Lesbiennes Branchés, Website 1995, English-language version; my italics). We are reminded here of Mikriammos' suppression of the item *gay* from his translation. This lack of a comfortable, home-grown label for the category reflects a more general reluctance in France to recognize the usefulness of identity categories as the springboard for political action. In his Preface to Camus' *Tricks* (1988), Barthes critiques the self-categorizing speech act predicated on "I am" for its implicit submission to the demands of the Other.

> Yet to proclaim yourself something is always to speak at the behest of a vengeful Other, to enter into his discourse, to argue with him, to seek from him a scrap of identity: "You are ... " "Yes, I am ... " Ultimately, the attribute is of no importance; what society should not tolerate is that I should be ... *nothing*, or to be more exact, that the *something* that I am should be openly expressed as provisional, revocable, insignificant, inessential, in a word: irrelevant. Just say "I am," and you will be socially saved.
>
> (Barthes, in Howard, 1996, p. vii)

Advocates of Anglo-American attempts to theorize and promote gay and lesbian visibility would no doubt respond that *nothing* precisely identifies the dominant culture's goal with regard to homosexual self-articulation; "nothing" and "irrelevance" have long been the nullifying conditions against which we struggle. The relative reluctance of French homosexuals to selfidentify according to the variable of sexuality has direct implications for the construction of a subcultural community based on sexual difference. It leads to scepticism of "la tentation communautaire" ("the temptation of the community," Martel, 1996, p. 404), a symptom of the fear that the construction of a distinct gay community would constitute a regrettable retreat into separatism.

Edmund White attributes a view such as Martel's to a specific Gallic conception of the relationship between the individual and the collective:

> The French believe that a society is not a federation of special interest groups but rather an impartial state that treats each citizen regardless of his or her gender, sexual orientation, religion or colour as an abstract, universal individual.
>
> (White, 1997, p. 343)

Thus, although some early French theoretical work in the field (e. g. Hocquenghem, 1972) may still strike a chord today in Anglo-American queer thinking, there is relative absence of radical gay (male) theorizing in contemporary France. Merrick and Ragan (1996, p. 4) have noted the consequences this has had for research within the French academy:

> [L]ess work has been done on the history of homosexuality in France than in some other Western countries ... The emphasis on national identity has led to the downplaying of differences in race, sex, and sexual orientation ... Figures like Gide and Yourcenar have been treated more as French writers, who happened to have sex with people of the same sex, than as homosexual writers per se.

The resulting consensus appears grounded in the view that, even if one were to construe homosexuality as a key factor of identity, homosexuals would be well advised to lay their hopes in the general progress of human rights that find their origin in the universalizing Republican texts and events of 1789. This has led to an attitude to issues of gay identity, history and community that appears conservative from the perspective of Britain and the USA. Camp, I have argued throughout this paper, can be seen as a typical (indeed, perhaps as the key) semiotic resource of gay men in their critique of straight society and in their attempt to carve out a space for their difference. I would like to suggest that we see a significant textual consequence/realization of the French resistance to this view in Mikriammos' decision to avoid reproducing the gay verbal camp in Vidal's text.

4.2 Duvert and Flores: polymorphous perversity or gay sex?

If the identity category "gay" is problematic in France, it follows that the notions of gay writing and gay literature are also disabled in the French cultural polysystem by a universalizing tendency in the Gallic conception of subjectivity. White recalls an interview he gave in the early 1980s to a French gay magazine during which he "astonished" the journalist by telling him that "of course" he considered himself a "gay writer." He also remembers how in the mid-1980s all the male French writers who had been invited to an international gay literary conference in London "indignantly refused" to attend (White, 1994, pp. 277 – 278). This is put down to a resistance on the part of French writers to the perceived limitation that would be imposed upon their subjectivity, as well as their literary activity, by such a label. Instructive in this respect is Renaud Camus' rejection of the term "homosexual writer" in *Notes Achriennes* (1982; translated and quoted in Vercier, 1996, p. 7):

> Nothing is so ridiculous as this concept of "homosexual writer," unless it's "Catholic writer," "Breton writer," "avant-garde writer." I already have trouble being a "writer." I'd rather be two or three of them or more than agree to being a "homosexual writer."

As a consequence, it could be argued that there is indeed no gay fiction in France: The immediate cultural and political identity necessary to give it momentum (both in terms of production and reception) is undermined by the resistance inherent in larger social and cultural factors. French fiction that treats aspects of homosexuality and "the homosexual condition" exists, of course. Of this, twentieth-century French literature has many examples (see Robinson, 1995). However, this literature tends not to contribute to the articulation of a culture, identity and sensibility that is differently gay. In this context, it is not surprising that the figures, say, of the transvestite and the queen continue to be marginalized or down-played in contemporary French writing and that their characteristic linguistic register, camp, fails to accrue the positive values it has gained in much Anglo-American work.

The work of Tony Duvert, though little commented upon in France (and barely read or translated outside France), gives us an insight into the vision of non-mainstream sexualities that has long existed amongst French "homosexual" writers such as Gide and Peyrefitte. No one could dispute that homosexuality is one of Duvert's chief preoccupations. However, in Duvert's novels and theoretical works (1974, 1980), homosexual activity takes place in the context of a larger interest in pre-pubescent and adolescent sexualities. Ultimately, Duvert's texts seek to explore and extend the human experience of sex and sexuality per se. He re-peatedly returns to the theme of sexual relations between children and between children and adults. Although much of this activity is same-sex based, there is a clear sense in which it is the openness, polymorphousness and (to use a Duvertian word) "innocence" of children's in-terest in physical and sexual activity that is his central theme. It is important when consider-ing Duvert that the distinct universe of modern French writing on sexual diversity is attended to. Thus, so-called "pederastic literature" (Robinson, 1995, pp. 144 - 173) in French letters should not be conflated with the existence of a gay literature as this is understood in both British and American literary polysystems. Indeed, many Anglo-American writers would probably resist having their work on adult same-sex relations conflated with explorations of pederasty.

The passage from Duvert's work that I have chosen to comment upon here comes from *Paysage de Fantaisie* (1973), a strange visionary text which employs many of the tech-niques of the high *nouveau roman* to suggest fragmentary consciousness, shifting narrative points of view, and problematized identity. The action, such as it is, appears to take place in and around a boarding school / correction centre / hideaway for children and adolescents. Sexual games and activity are a central concern. In the following passage, a group of boys are role-playing the visit to a heterosexual brothel by several adult men who first have to negotiate with the Madam of the establishment before they can enjoy one of the girls for sale. This scene is interesting for its role-playing of sexual commerce, and also because it gives us a literary representation of male parody of women's talk, one of the key aspects of camp. (I have edited the source and target texts, reproduced here one after the other, so as to concen-trate on the representations of direct speech. I have also italicized the speech of the Madam to facilitate readability. The lack of standard punctuation and the use of space between portions of text is, however, an original feature of source and target texts.)

　　... la maquerelle un petit bavard comme une pie a chapeau de paille défoncé leur

dit

hélas mes beaux messieurs avez-vous quelque argent?

c'est combien? demandent les garçons

oh là là c'est cher cher! ...

...

He la p'tite dame z'avez une putain qui met les bouts!

oh la garce eh Jacky pourquoi tu joues plus?

c'est la merde avec vos conneries j'vais dehors moi

...

c'fille-là elle a des couilles madame dit un client ...

nos demoiselles des couilles pas du tout! proteste la gérante et elle

courait de gamin en gamin soulevant les jupes

...

baisez celle du milieu seulement hein il me montrait ...

(Duvert, 1973, pp. 102 - 103)

... the madam one of the smaller kids as gossipy as a magpie pinned to some old
dame's bashed in gay nineties straw boater says

alas my good sirs have you enough money?

how much is it? asks one of the boys

dearie dearie me it's not cheap oh no not for any of my darling girls! ...

...

Hey madame you've a whore here who's cutting out!

oh that bitch hey there Simon why aren't you playing with us anymore?

you're all full of shit that's what you are with all your stupid asshole
fairy games I'm going out for a walk

...

hey this floozy here has got balls says one of the clients to the twittering
madam

*one of my young lovelies sporting balls really sir you must cease this
vulgarity instantly*! the madam gives a toss to her head then runs from
lady to lady lifting skirts

...

then I'll fuck that one lying there in the middle he pointed at me

(Flores, 1975, pp. 111 - 112)

There is evident camp here in the source text Madam's utterances. Three main camp
features can be mentioned: (1) A readiness with feigned outrage, expressed through exclamations (*oh*) and the presence of exclamation marks. (2) A playfulness with archaic linguistic register, as in *hélas mes beaux messieurs* (literally, "alas my handsome sirs"), the interrogative inversion of *avez-vous* and the use of *quelque*, instead of the partitive article, to

modify *argent* ("money"). This contrasts with the coarseness of *la garce* ("the bitch") and the sexual explicitness of *des couilles* ("balls"). (3) The self-conscious teasing and seductiveness of the dispreferred response to the boys' direct question *c'est combien* ("how much is it?"): *oh là là c'est cher cher*! (literally, "oh la la it's expensive expensive"). This response only in fact replies to the question by pre-empting the outraged response that the men will probably have when told how expensive it is. It is an acute comment on the differential power factor at work in a dialogue that is part business deal, part sexual politics.

Flores' translation transfers much of the camp. It also significantly transforms Duvert's text in two ways: First, the Madam's camp is intensified and made still more theatrical; second, the scene becomes one of homosexual seduction and less a playing out of childish curiosity with sexual roles and boundaries. In short, Flores' text is "gayed." How is this achieved textually? The main strategy is that of additions to source text material. For example, the Madam is introduced in the French text as wearing *un chapeau de paille défoncé* (literally, "a bashed-in straw hat"). The translation carries out a transformation here by suggesting that the source text's "pie" ("magpie") is itself "pinned to ... [a] straw boater." More significant is the presence in this sentence of two added details, neither of which appears motivated by the source text: (1) *Some old dame* (modifying *straw boater*) functions metonymically to reinforce the element of gender parody; (2) *gay nineties*, through the presence of the dangerously homonymie *gay*, sets off a sub theme that becomes explicit by the end of the passage. The gender roles parody is further reinforced by the addition of *oh no not for any of my darling girls* to the Madam's *dearie dearie me it's not cheap*. Later additions include, *really sir you must cease this vulgarity instantly*, further developing the feigned outrage of the "woman," and *the madam gives a toss of her head* (for *proteste la gérante*: literally "protests the manageress") before *then runs from lady to lady* (for *elle courait de gamin en gamin*: literally, "she ran from boy to boy"). The cumulative effect of these additions is to heighten the factor of performance in the gender roles and to intensify the theatricality of the Madam.

The other trend I mentioned is that of the fronting of homosexual seduction. This is contextualized and facilitated by the intensified theatricalization of the Madam's drag. Indeed, in this connection the addition to the target text of the adjective *twittering* to describe the Madam is significant, as the metaphor of bird (and other animal) noises is often applied to the speech of homosexual men—especially camp ones—in both source and target cultures (cf. Crisp, 1968, p. 84; Duvert, 1969, p. 52, Green, 1974, p. 45). The presence of *twittering*, like that of *gay*, sets off suggestive resonances of homosexual identity that are not present in the source text. The manifestation of this identity becomes explicit when one of the boys refuses to play, complaining: *You're all full of shit that's what you are with your stupid asshole fairy games* (for *c'est la merde avec vos canneries*: literally, "it's shit with your cunt-stupidities"). The addition of *stupid asshole fairy games* makes clear Flores' homosexual reading of the source text. The references to anality and to sexual deviance suddenly transform the scene into an elaborate excuse for male-male intercourse, and thereby deflect from a reading that prioritizes the polymorphous explorations of children. This gaying of the text culminates in a decisive transformation:

> then I'll fuck that one lying there in the middle he pointed at me.

Here, a crucial element of agency is attributed to the boy who utters the phrase (beginning "I") and then points at the narrator (another boy). This rewrites the source text's:

> baisez celle du milieu seulement hein il me montrait
> (lit.: just fuck the one [female] in the middle hey? he pointed at me)

In the source text it is the Madam who gives an imperative and maintains the fiction of the heterosexual role-playing with *celle* ("the one" [female]). Later in this scene, when two boys actually do sneak off for gay sex, their activity appears in the source text to be yet another experiment in pre-adult sexual activity. In the target text, their same-sex activity is already contextualized and prepared for by the homo-eroticism in Flores' reading of the role-playing.

In the light of the transformations in Flores' text, it may be considered unlikely that Duvert himself played any role in producing the translation. However, in a Translator's Note at the front of the book, Flores writes: "I would like to thank the author, Tony Duvert, for his Job-like patience in dealing with my many queries concerning his text, and also for replying so lengthily to them." Although this does not prove that Duvert read (or understood) the whole of the translation, it certainly puts us on our guard against concluding that Flores was able to take unwarranted and unsanctioned liberties with the text. We are permitted then to surmise that perhaps Duvert both understood and approved of the English version. One might suggest that this is because Duvert, as a relatively marginalized and untranslated author, would be pleased with any translation into another language of his work, whatever the quality. Perhaps a more serious suggestion would be that Duvert was aware of the emerging movement of homosexual liberation in the USA in the mid-1970s, and also of the contribution that a gay literature could make to such a movement. Through gay liberation Duvert may have hoped that the message in his books with regard to child sexuality would receive a better reception in the USA by becoming caught up in the general sweep of a sexual revolution that was led by adult homosexuals. In this context, it may be argued that he was willing for his work to undergo the textual interventions deemed suitable in order for it to join this incipient social, cultural and literary movement (to be "gayed", in short). It is also worth noting that Grove Press, who published *Strange Landscape*, has consistently championed gay writing over the years (Pulsifer, 1994, p. 216). By 1975 their gay list may already have been taking shape. A gay text, in the American sense, would have been just what they were looking for from Duvert's writing. Flores, in short, was responding to these combined (sub)cultural and commercial pressures.

5 Concluding remarks: texts and contexts in translation studies

I have sought to establish how a verbal style, camp, is linked with the delineation of homosexual male characters in French-and English-language fiction and, further, how the translation of this style in its fictional settings reveals the effects of constraints and priorities of differing cultural settings. Specifically, I have suggested that the changes, omissions and additions present in two translated texts can be illuminated by recourse to debates on sexual identity and to the literary systems operational in French and Anglo-American contexts.

It would be disingenuous of me to say at this point that any uncertainty discernible in my conclusions (the hedges, *mights* and *maybes* of the preceding paragraphs) is due primarily to the "work-in-progress" nature of this paper. The problems this uncertainty raises are much more fundamental and threaten to disable attempts to *explain* (as opposed to merely *describe*) the data offered. They are a consequence, I believe, of crucial theoretical and methodological issues currently confronting translation studies, namely the need to make explicit the imbrication of texts and contexts. Translation is not just about texts: Nor is it only about cultures and power. It is about the relation of the one to the other. In this respect, translation studies is not unlike critical linguistics, the branch of contemporary language study that has grown out of the fusion of functional-systemic linguistics and critical theory. Critical linguistics is also struggling to produce paradigms that will allow it to relate the minutiae of textual analysis to the interactional, social and political contexts that produce language forms and upon which those language forms operate. As Fowler has recently put it, it is now time for the critical linguist "to take a professionally responsible attitude towards the analysis of context" in order to avoid an over-reliance on "intersubjective intuitions" and on "informal accounts of relevant contexts and institutions" (Fowler, 1996, p. 10; see also Fairclough, 1992, pp. 62 – 100). Much the same could be said to the scholar of translation.

What is required, then, in translation studies is a methodology that neither prioritizes broad concerns with power, ideology and patronage to the detriment of the need to examine representative examples of text, nor contents itself with detailed text-linguistic analysis while making do with sketchy and generalized notions of context. Specifically with regard to my work, many more instances of camp talk call for description in order to bring out the trends not only between French, British and American texts, but also between texts from different periods (e. g. pre-and post-the AIDS crisis), between texts that fictionally represent different social strata, and also texts that demonstrate different literary aspirations. It is important, in other words, to maintain the notion of camp as a potentially plural one, remaining alert to its textual inflections and variations. This is the close text-linguistic branch of the work. However, macro-cultural trends also crucially need to be kept in view and related to the textual descriptions in a heuristically satisfying manner. Ultimately, these trends alone are able to offer us convincing explanations of how a text comes to mean in its context, of what value a text accrues as a sign, be it of a postulated universal subjectivity or an irreducible subcultural difference. The challenge is to find a way not just to *situate* discourse in its interactional and cultural settings, but to give the relationship between setting and discourse the force of causality.

Acknowledgements

I am very grateful to the following people for their encouragement and criticism during the writing of this paper, as well as for opportunities to discuss the material in workshops and seminars: Mona Baker, Jean Boase-Beier, Peter Bush, Roger Fowler, Lawrence Venuti. I would like to thank Christopher Robinson for pointing out the Proustian resonance of *en être*, discussed on page 458.

【延伸阅读】

[1] Brown, P. and Levinson, S. (1987). *Politeness: Some Universals in Language Usage*. Cambridge: Cambridge University Press.

[2] Chamberlain, L. (1988). *Gender and the Metaphorics of Translation*. In L. Venuti (ed.), *The Translation Studies Reader*. London and New York: Routledge.

[3] Nida, E. A. (2001). *Language and Culture: Contexts in Translating*. Shanghai: Shanghai Foreign Language Education Press.

【问题与思考】

1. 本论文主要运用了哪些学科的研究方法？哈维是如何把这些方法结合在一起的？
2. 哈维是如何研究性别身份、社会文化和翻译三者之间的相互关系的？
3. 本论文对今后的跨学科翻译研究有何启示？

选文三 当代翻译研究的跨学科性及理论融合
——评《翻译研究指南》

王 宏 刘 伟

导 言

本文发表于《外语研究》2008 年第 2 期。

20 世纪 90 年代以来，翻译的跨学科研究在西方开展得比较多，取得了丰硕成果。《翻译研究指南》(*A Companion to Translation Studies*)一书较为全面地总结了当代西方翻译跨学科研究的成就。本文以书评方式把《翻译研究指南》介绍给跨学科研究尚属冷门的中国翻译研究界，是非常及时的。本文首先介绍了《翻译研究指南》一书各章的主要内容，然后分析了该书"充分体现了翻译研究的跨学科性"等三大优点，最后指出了该书存在的些许不足之处。

1 引言

当代翻译研究正不断吸取人文学科和自然学科的最新成果,丰富、扩大其研究范围和领域。翻译研究作为一门独立学科已不容置疑,翻译研究的跨学科性质也变得越来越明显。2007年4月,多语言事物出版公司(Multilingual Matters Ltd.)出版了由英国华威大学翻译与比较文化研究中心皮尔特·库赫乌茨扎克博士(Piotr Kuhiwczak)和艾塞克斯大学卡琳·里陶博士(Karin Littau)主编的《翻译研究指南》(A Companion to Translation Studies)一书。该书系统总结了当代翻译理论的发展,尤其关注翻译研究与诸多相关学科的关系。笔者认为,该书对于厘清翻译研究的学科渊源、展望未来的发展方向颇具参考价值。

2 内容简介

本书"导论"由两位主编撰写。作者指出,自20世纪90年代以来,翻译研究已在西欧、北美、亚洲、东欧、南美等地区普及,出现了许多专业学会和期刊,各种有关翻译的辞典、百科全书、选集和教科书也相继出版。这标志着翻译研究时代的真正到来。埃德温·根茨勒曾把翻译研究迅猛发展的原因归结于冷战结束、发展中国家尤其是中国的崛起、自我意识的增长。本书主编又增加了两条:全球化及其综合作用以及各种理论的相互融合。

第一章"文化与翻译"由英国沃里克大学比较文学教授苏珊·巴斯奈特(Susan Bassnett)撰写。作者指出,由法国社会学家皮埃尔·布迪厄(Pierre Bourdieu)提出的文化资本(cultural capital)和文本格栅(textual grid)是翻译研究的重要工具;西方文化引入非西方文化的过程往往是扭曲的;翻译研究的文化转向能使我们更为深刻地了解文本转换的复杂性以及我们生活的这个世界急速变化的文化互动模式。

第二章"哲学与翻译"由西班牙洛维拉维吉利大学高级翻译系主任安东尼·皮姆(Anthony Pym)教授撰写。他从三个方面阐述了翻译研究和哲学的相互关系:哲学家视翻译为隐喻,翻译研究者用哲学话语研究翻译,哲学话语的翻译又促进了翻译研究的发展。皮姆还介绍了美国分析哲学家奎因关于翻译不确定性的思想,论述了德里达的解构主义对翻译研究的影响。皮姆认为,翻译理论家从哲学家那里借鉴了许多理论,如美国的韦努蒂等人借用哲学理论使20世纪90年代的翻译研究更为关注道德伦理问题而不是忠实和对等。

第三章"语言学与翻译"的撰写者是英国萨里大学教授冈尼腊·安德曼(Gunnila Anderman)。作者分析了翻译研究和语言学的关系,指出奈达和卡特福德试图创立翻译语言学,但他们不是简单地将两者融合,而是使其相互借鉴,彼此受益。20世纪70—80年代影响翻译的语言学派主要是文体学、篇章分析和篇章语言学,比如一些德国翻译理论家对篇章语言学的运用。作者还论述了社会语言学对翻译的影响、最新的研究范式、迅速发展的语料库语言学等。

第四章"历史与翻译"由英国沃里克大学翻译与比较文化研究中心主任林恩·朗(Lynne Long)博士撰写。她指出研究翻译史能给我们两种启示:一是不能把翻译规则等同于科学规则,因为它和语言一样是灵活多变的;二是对翻译史的思考与确立当代的翻译策略密切相关。

第五章题为"文学翻译",由伦敦大学比较文学教授西奥·赫曼斯(Theo Hermans)撰写。作者分语言学、功能主义、后结构主义三部分说明文学翻译研究的最新发展。语言学方面,早年是语义学对文学的影响,最近 10 年语料库语言学和批评语言学进入了文学翻译研究。功能主义方面,作者论述了目的论、描述翻译研究、多元系统理论对文学翻译研究的指导作用。最后,作者用相当篇幅论述了后结构主义、解构主义、后现代主义翻译研究的特点。

第六章"性别与翻译"由加拿大渥太华大学教授路易斯·冯·费洛托(Luise von Flotow)撰写,主要介绍了性别研究的两个范式及其对于翻译研究的意义。

第七章"戏剧翻译"由奥地利维也纳大学玛丽·斯内尔-霍恩比(Mary Snell-Hornby)教授撰写。她指出,从前的翻译研究把戏剧翻译视为文学翻译,强调翻译文本与原文本的对等和忠实。20 世纪 70 年代,翻译研究者开始重视戏剧翻译的时空感和共时性,20 世纪 80—90 年代开始关注舞台剧本翻译的特点,尤其是其中人物对话的翻译。戏剧翻译有两个侧重,一是重视戏剧符号的翻译,如戏剧人物的言谈风格和行为举止,二是强调译本的整体演出效果。

第八章"影视屏幕翻译"由爱尔兰都柏林城市大学翻译和文本研究中心高级讲师埃斯尼·奥康奈尔(Eithne O'Connell)撰写。她讨论了现代技术对翻译的影响,回顾了应用于视听媒体的配音翻译、字幕翻译等的历史,分析了它们各自的特点。奥康奈尔强调指出,不能只关注科技进步对屏幕翻译的影响而忽视政治、经济、文化等在其中发挥的重要作用。

第九章"政治与翻译"由英国阿斯顿大学克里斯蒂娜·沙夫纳(Christina Schäffner)教授撰写。沙夫纳从翻译的政治、政治文本的翻译和翻译文本的政治化三个方面探讨了翻译与政治的关系。她指出,20 世纪 80 年代中期出现的描述性翻译研究和翻译研究文化转向揭示了翻译现象的复杂性,人们认识到,任何鼓励、推动、阻碍或妨碍翻译的行为实际上都是政治行为,而对政治题材的不同文本的翻译往往会体现不同的政治目的。

3 主要特点

作为一本总结性、指导性的学术著作,本书具有以下特点。

首先是它的总体线索比较独特。现有的翻译理论总结性著作主要有两种,一种以时间为线,另一种以流派为线。两种各有利弊。以时间为线,可以清楚地展现整个学科在不同时期的发展状况,但容易切断理论发展的脉络,模糊理论发展的连续性;以流派为线,可以比较清晰、连贯地展示某一具体理论发展和成熟的过程,但各种理论本身的性质及其相互之间的关系容易模糊。本书的线索是翻译研究与各相关学科的关系,既涉及时间又涉及流派,可以兼顾两者的特点。

其次是充分体现了翻译研究的跨学科性。本书选择的九个相关学科或领域,既与翻译研究关系密切,它们彼此之间也相互交叉、融合。

再就是本书提供了大量参考文献信息,书后所列参考文献近 30 页,从多学科、多角度反映了西方翻译研究的历程,集中体现了本学科已取得的成果及最新的发展动态。最近几年的如 M. 欧勒翰 2004 年的《翻译研究语料库介绍》(*Introducing Corpora in Translation Studies*),G. 安德曼和 M. 罗杰斯 2007 年的《语料库运用:语言学者和译者》(*Incorporating Corpora: The Linguist and the Translator*),A. 阿姆斯特朗 2005 年的《翻译,语言学,文化》(*Translation, Linguistics, Culture*),G. 安德曼 2005 年的《舞台上的欧洲:翻译与戏剧》(*Europe on Stage: Translation and Theatre*),P. 奥雷罗 2004 年的《视听翻译论题》(*Topics in Audiovisual Translation*)等。

4　简评

　　本书各章由国际知名翻译研究学者分别撰写,既有对过去的总结又有对当代翻译研究的评述和展望,集各家之长,从多学科角度展现了翻译研究的全貌,然而也有一些不足之处:

　　一是专业术语过多。这本书的本意是为了给初涉翻译研究的学生和研究者提供入门指南,但是使用过多术语又不加以解释,会妨碍读者理解,达不到编者的意图。

　　二是没有涉及非西方的翻译理论。该书作者主要来自欧美国家,所介绍的翻译理论都是以欧美文化为背景。翻译是人类共有的语言活动,翻译理论也理应具有全球性特点。该书没有专门提到中国乃至亚洲和非洲翻译界在译学建设中所作出的成就和努力,这从另一方面提醒我国翻译界同仁须加倍努力,拿出有分量的研究成果与国际翻译界同行分享。

【延伸阅读】

[1] Kuhiwczak, P. and Littau, K. (2007). *A Companion to Translation Studies*. Clevedon: Multilingual Matters Ltd.

[2] 李红玉. 一幅翻译研究的地图——《翻译研究指南》评述. 东方翻译,2009(1):92-95.

[3] 邢杰. 历史、现在与未来:翻译研究在世纪初的思考——《翻译研究指南》述评. 中国翻译,2008(2):33-36.

[4] 熊兵. 透视当代西方翻译研究的一扇窗户——《翻译研究指南》评介. 上海翻译,2009(1):78-80.

【问题与思考】

　　1. 写西方翻译理论著作的述评应从哪几个方面入手?

　　2. 在述评中简介著作主要内容应注意什么? 为什么?

　　3. 在述评中应如何分析著作优点? 为什么?

　　4. 在述评中指出著作之不足时应注意什么? 为什么?

参考文献

[1] Anderman, G. (2007). *Voices in Translation: Bridging Cultural Divides*. Clevedon: Multilingual Matters Ltd.

[2] Anderson, B. (1991). *Imagined Communities: Reflections on the Origin and Spread of Nationalism* (revised edition). London and New York: Verso.

[3] Arnold, M. (1861/1978). *On Translating Homer*. London: AMS Press.

[4] Baker, M. and Saldanha, G. (2004). *Routledge Encyclopedia of Translation Studies*. New York: Routledge.

[5] Bartsh, R. (1987). *Norms of Language*. London: Longman. (104)

[6] Bassnett (-McGuire), S. (1985). Ways Through the Labyrinth Strategies and Methods for Translating Theatre Texts. In T. Hermans (ed.), *The Manipulation of Literature: Studies in Literature Translation* (pp. 87 - 102). London & Sydney: Croom Helm.

[7] ——and Lefevere, A. (eds.). (1990). *Translation, History and Culture*. London: Pinter.

[8] ——(1992). Writing in No Man's Land: Questions of Gender and Translation. *Ilha do Desterro*, 28,63-73.

[9] Berman, A. (1984). *L'Epreuve de l'étranger: Culture et traduction dans l'Allemagne romantique*. Paris: Gallimard.

[10] ——(1985). La traduction et la lettre, ou l'auberge du lointain. In *Les Tours de Babel: Essais sur la traduction*. Mauvezin: Trans-Europ-Repress.

[11] ——(1988). De la translation a la traduction. *TTR*, I, (1),23-40.

[12] ——(1992). *The Experience of the Foreign: Culture and Translation in Romantic Germany*. trans. S. Heyvaert. Albany: State University of New York Press.

[13] ——(1995). *Pour une critique des traductions: John Donne*. Paris: Gallimard.

[14] Blom, T. (1997). *Complexiteit en contigentie. Een kritische inleiding tot de sociologie van Niklas Luhmann*. Kampen: Kok Agora. (70ff)

[15] Butler, J. (1990). *Gender Trouble: Feminism and the Subversion of Identity*. New York and London: Routledge.

[16] Caren, T. and Lombard, S. (trans.) (1950). *Le Journal d'Anne Frank*. Paris: Calmann-lévy. (269)

[17] Cary, E. (1963). *Les Grands Traducteurs français*. Geneva: George et Cie.

[18] Catford, J. C. (1965). *A Linguistic Theory of Translation*. London: OUP.

[19] Chamberlain, L. (1992). Gender and the Metaphorics of Translation. In L. Venuti (ed.), *Rethinking Translation: Discourse, Subjectivity, Ideology*. London and New York: Routledge.

[20] Chesterman, A. (1993). From "Is" to "Ought": Translation Laws, Norms and Strategies. *Target*, 5(1),1-20.

[21] Dancette, J. (1994). Comprehension in the Translation Process: An Analysis of Think-aloud Protocols. In Dollerup and Lindegaard(eds.), *Teaching Translation and Interpreting* 2 (pp. 113 - 120). Philadelphia: John Benjamins Publishing Co.

[22] Dawson, J. (1966). *Friedrich Schleiermacher: The Evolution of a Nationalist*. Austin and London: University of Texas Press.

[23] de Beaugrande, R. (1978). *Factors in a Theory of Poetic Translating*. Assen: Van Gorcum.

[24] de Berg, H. and Prangel, M. (eds.). (1995). *Differenzen: Systemtheorie zwischen Dekonstruktion und Konstruktivismus*. Tübingen: Francke.

[25] de Lotbinière-Harwood, S. (1986). La Grammaire intérieure. *La Vie en Rose*, September, 34-35.

[26] ——(1991). *Re-belle et infidèle: La traduction comme pratique de réécriture au féminin/The Body Bilingual: Translation as a Rewriting in the Feminine*. Montreal and Toronto: Les Éditions du remue-ménage and Women's Press.

[27] ——(1995). Geo-graphies of Why. In S. Simon (ed.), *Culture in Transit: Translating the Literature of Quebec*, Montreal: Véhicule Press. *Target*, 4(1),33-51.

[28] Derrida, J. (1974). White Mythology. trans. P. E. Lewis, *New Literary History*, 4 (11),5-74.

[29] ——(1979). Living On/Border Lines. trans. J. Hulbert. In H. Bloom (ed.), *Deconstruction and Criticism*. New York: Seabury Press.

[30] —— (1985). Des tours de Babel. In J. F. Graham (ed.), *Difference in Franslation* (French original pp. 209 - 248, translation in the same volume by J. F. Graham, pp. 165 - 207).

[31] ——(2001). What Is a Relevant Translation? *Critical Inquiry*, Vol. 27, No. 2.

[32] D'hulst, L. (1992). Sur le role des métaphores en traductologie contemporaine. *Target*, 4(1),33-51.

[33] Even-Zohar, I. (1975). Decisions in Translating Poetry. *Ha-sifrut/Literature*, 21, 32-45 (Hebrew).

[34] Fiorenza, E. S. (1992). Charting the Field of Feminist Bible Interpretation. In *But She Said: Feminist Practices of Bible Interpretation*. Boston: Beacon Press.

[35] ——(ed.). (1993). *Searching the Scriptures Vol. 1: A Feminist Introduction*. New York: Crossroad.

[36] Florio, J. (1603). Translator's Preface to *Montaigne's Essayes*. London.

[37] Fokkema, D. (1991). Changing the Canon: A Systems-Theoretical Approach. In

Ibsch et al. , pp. 363 - 370.

[38] Folkart，B. (1991). *Le Conflict des enonciations. Traduction et discours rapporte*. Candiac: Editions Balzac.

[39] Gentzler，E. (1993). *Contemporary Translation Theories*. London and New York: Routledge.

[40] Gerzymisch-Arbogast，H. (1986). Zur Relevanz der Thema-Rhema-Gliederung für den Übersetzungsprozeß. In M. Snell-Hornby (ed.)，*Übersetzungswissenschaft: Eine Neuorientierung* (pp. 160 - 183). Tüblingen: Francke.

[41] Godard，B. (1990). Theorizing Feminist Theory/Translation. In S. Bassnett and A. Lefevere (eds.)，*Translation: History and Culture*. London: Frances Pinter.

[42] Göhring，H. (1978). Interkulturelle Kommunikation: Die Überwindung der Trennung von Fremdsprachen-und Landeskundeunterricht durch einen integrierten Fremdverhalt-ensunterricht. In M. Hartig (ed.)，*Soziolinguistik，Psycholinguistik. Kongreßberichte der Jahrestagung der Gesellschaft für Angewandter Lingistik，Vol*. 4 (pp. 9 - 14). Stuttgart: Hochschulverlag.

[43] Gregory，M. (1980). Perspectives on Translation from the Firthian Tradition. *Meta*，25 (4)，455-466.

[44] Halliday，M. (1973). *Explorations in the Functions of Language*. London: Edward Arnold.

[45] ——，McIntosh，A. and Strevens，P. (1964). *The Linguistic Sciences and Language Teaching*. London: Longman.

[46] Harris，B. (1990). Norms in Interpretation. *Target*，2(1)，115-119.

[47] Hatim，B. and Mason，I. (1997). *The Translator as Communicator*. London and New York: Routledge.

[48] Hermans，T. (ed.). (1985). *The Manipulation of Literature: Studies in Literary Translation*. London: Croom Helm.

[49] ——(1991). Translation Norms and Correct Translations. In Leuven-Zwart and Naai-jkens (eds.)，*Translation Studies: The State of the Art* (pp. 155 - 169). Amsterdam and Atlanta，GA: Rodopi.

[50] ——(1996a). *Norms and the Determination of Translation*. Clevedon : Multilingual Matters Ltd.

[51] ——(1996b). The Translator's Voice in Translated Narrative. *Target*，(8)，23-48.

[52] ——(1999). *Translation in Systems: Descriptive and System-Oriented Approaches Explained*. Manchester: St Jerome.

[53] Hohendahl，P. E. (1982). Literary Criticism and the Public Sphere. trans. R. L. Smith and H. J. Schmidt. In P. Hohendahl (ed.)，*The Institution of Criticism*. Ithaca，New York: Cornell University Press.

[54] Hönig，H. G. and Kußmaul，P. (1982). Strategie der Übersetzung: Ein Lehr-und Arbeitsbuch. Tübingen: Narr.

[55] Jakobson, R. (1959). On Linguistic Aspects of Translation. In Brower (ed.), *On Translation* (pp. 232 – 239). New York: Oxford University Press.

[56] ——(1960). Closing Statement: Linguistics and Poetics. In T. Sebeok (ed.), *Style in Language* (pp. 350 – 377). Cambridge, MA: MIT Press.

[57] Johnson, B. (1985). Taking Fidelity Philosophically. In J. F. Graham (ed.), *Difference in Translation*. Ithaca, NY, and London: Cornell University Press.

[58] Jouve, N. W. (1991). *White Woman Speaks with Forked Tongue: Criticism as Autobiography*. London and New York: Routledge.

[59] Koller, W. (1995). The Concept of Equivalence and the Object of Tranlation Studies. *Targer*, 7(2),191-222.

[60] Krontiris, T. (1992). *Oppositional Voices: Women as Writers and Translators in the English Renaissance*. London and New York: Routledge.

[61] Kussmaul, P. (1995). *Translating the Tranlator*. Amesterdam & Philadelphia: Benjamins.

[62] Laermans, R. (1997). Communication on Art, or the Work of Art as Communication? Bourdieu's Field Analysis Compared with Luhmann's Systems Theory. *Canadian Review of Comparative Literature*, 24(1),103-113.

[63] Lefevere, A. (ed. and trans.). (1977). *Translating Literature: The German Tradition from Luther to Rosenzweig*. Assen: Van Gorcum.

[64] ——(1981). German Translation Theory: Legacy and Relevance. *Journal of European Studies*, (11),9-17.

[65] —— (1983). Poetics (Today) and Translation (Studies). In D. Weissbort (ed.), *Modern Poetry in Translation: 1983*. London and Manchester: MPT and Carcanet.

[66] ——(1985). Why Waste Our Time on Rewrites?: The Trouble with Interprepation and the Role of Rewriting in an Alternative Paradigm. In T. Hermans (ed.), *The Manipulation of Literature: Studies in Literary Translation*. London and Sydney: Croom Helm.

[67] ——(ed. and trans.). (1992). *Translation, Rewriting, and the Manipulation of Literary Fame*. London and New York: Routledge.

[68] Levine, S. J. (1991). *The Subversive Scribe: Translating Latin American Fiction*. Saint Paul, MN: Graywolf Press.

[69] Levý, J. (1967/2000). Translation as a Decision Process. In *To Honor Roman Jakobson II* (pp. 1171 – 1182). The Hague: Mouton.

[70] ——(1969). *Die literarische Übersetzung: Theorie einer Kunstgattung*. trans. W. Schamschula. Frankfurt: Athenäum.

[71] Luhmann, N. (1984). *Soziale Systeme. Grundriss einer allgemeinen Theorie*. frankfurt: Suhrkamp. (191ff).

[72] ——(1986). Das Kunstwerk und die Selbesreproduktion der Kunst. In H. U. Gumpert and K. L. Pfeiffer (eds.), Stil. *Geschichte und Funktionen eines kulturwissenschaflichen*

Diskurs elements (p. 632). Frankfurt: Suhrkamp.

[73] ——(1986a). Systeme verstehen Systeme. In N. Luhmann and K. E. Schor (eds.), *Zwischen Intransparanz und Verstehen. Fragen an die Padagogik* (pp. 72 – 117). Frankfurt: Suhrkamp. (85ff).

[74] ——(1990). *Essays on Self-Reference*. New York: Columbia University Press. (196-197).

[75] ——(1995a). *Social Systems*. Trans. J. Bednarz. Stanford: Stanford University Press (English).

[76] Mooyaart-Doubleday, B. M. (trans.). (1954). *The Diary of Anne Frank*. London: Pan Books. (194)

[77] Munday, J. (2001). *Introducing Translation Studies*. New York: Routledge.

[78] New German Critique (1994). Special Issue on Niklas Luhmann.

[79] Newman, F. W. (ed. and trans.). (1856). *The Illiad of Homer*. London: Walton and Maberly.

[80] Nida, E. A. and Taber, C. R. (1969). *The Theory and Practice of Translation*. Leiden: Brill.

[81] Niranjana, T. (1992). *Siting Translation: History, Poststructuralism, and the Colonial Context*. Berkeley and Los Angeles: University of California Press.

[82] Nord, C. (1988a). *Textanalyse und Übersetzen: Theoretische Grundlagen, Methode und didaktische Anwendung einer ü-bersetzungsrelevanten Textanalyse* (Revised edition). Heidelberg: Groos.

[83] ——(1991). *Text Analysis in Translation*. Amsterdam and Atlanta: Rodopi.

[84] ——(1992). The Relationship between Text Function and Meaning in Translation. In B. Lewandowska-Tomaszcyk and M. Thelen (eds.), *Translation and Meaning*, Part 2 (pp. 91 – 96). Maastricht: Rijkshogeschool Maastricht, Faculty of Translation and Interpreting.

[85] ——(1996). Revisiting the Classics—Text Type and Translation Method. An Objective Approach to Translation Criticism. Review of Katharina Reiss's Möglichkeiten und Grenzen der Übersetzungskritik. *The Translator*, 2(1),81-88.

[86] ——(1997). *Translation as a Purposeful Activity: Functionalist Approaches Explained*. Manchester: St Jerome.

[87] O'Connell, E. (2007). Screen Translation. In P. Kuhlwczak and K. Litau (eds.), *A Companion to Translation Studies*. Clevedon: Multilingual Matters.

[88] Paage, H. et al (eds.). (1986). *Dedagboekenvon Anne Frank*. Gravenhage and Amsterdam: Staatsuitgeverij and Bert Bakker. (162)

[89] Pöchhacker, F. (1995). Simultaneous Interpretation: A Functionalist Perspective. *Hermes, Journal of Linguistics*, (14),31-53.

[90] Poltermann, A. (1992). Normen des literarischen Ubersetzens im system der Literatur. *Kittel*, 5-31.

[91] Poovey，M. (1988). *Uneven Developments：The Ideological Work of Gender in Mid-Victorian England*. Chicago：University of Chicago Press.

[92] Pym，A. (1992). Discursive Persons and the Limits of Translation. In B. Lewandows-ka-Tomasczyk and M. Thelen (eds.), *Translation and Meaning*, Part 2, (pp. 159 – 168). Maastricht：Rijkscogeschool Maastricht.

[93] ——(1998). *Method in Translation History*. Manchester：St Jerome.

[94] ——(2007). Translation and Philosophy. In P. Kuhlwczak and K. Litau (eds.), *A Companion to Translation Studies* (pp. 24 – 44). Clevedon：Multilingual Matters.

[95] Reiss，K. (1971). *Möglichkeiten und Grenzen der Übersetzungskritik：Kategorien und Kriterien für eine sachgerechte Beurteilung von Übersetzungskritik*. Munich：Hueber.

[96] ——(1976). Texttyp und Übersetzungstypen und die Beurteilung von Übersetzungen. *Lebende Sprachen*, 22 (3), 97-100.

[97] ——(1977). Texttypen，Übersetzungstypen und die Beurteilung vom Übersetzungen. *Lebende Sprachen*, 22(3), 97-100.

[98] ——(1982). Zur übersetzung von Kinder-und Jügendbuchern：Theorie und Praxis. *Lebende Sprachen*, (1),7-13.

[99] ——(1983). Adequacy and Equivalence in Translation. *The Bible Translator* (Technical Papers), (3),301-208.

[100] ——and Vermeer，H. J. (1984). *Grundlegung einer allgemeinen Translationstheorie，Translationstheorie*. Tubingen：Niemeyer.

[101] Roberts，R. (1992). The Concept of Function in Translation and Its Application to Literary Texts. *Target*, 4 (1), 1-16.

[102] Schleiermacher，F. (1838). *Sämmitliche Werke. Dritte abteilung：Zur Philosophie，Zweiter Band*. Berlin：Reimer.

[103] ——(1890). *Selected Sermons*. ed. and trans. M. F. Wilson. New York：Funk and Wagnalls.

[104] ——(1977). *Hermeneutics：The Handwritten Manuscripts*. ed. H. Kimmerle, trans. J. Duke and J. Forstman. Missoula, Montana：Scholars Press.

[105] Schmidt，S. (1989). *Die Selbstorganisation des Sozialsystems Literatur im Jahrhundert*. Frankfurt：Suhrkamp.

[106] ——(1991). Literary Systems as Self-Organizing Systems. In Ibsch et al. pp. 413 – 424.

[107] ——(1992). Conventions and Literary Systems. In Hjort, pp. 215 – 249.

[108] ——(1997). A Systems-Oriented Approach to Literary Studies. *Canadian Review of Comparative Literature*, 24(1),19-36.

[109] Schmitt，P. A. (1986). Die Eindeutigkeit von Fachtexten：Bemerkungen zu einer Fiktion. In Snell-Hornby (1986) (Hrsg.), *Übersetzungs wissenschaft-Eine Neuorientierung. Zur Integrierung von Theorie und Praxis*. Tübingen：Francke UTB.

[110] Schuttze, B. (1986). Theorie der Dramenübersetzung-1960 bis heute: Ein Bericht zur Forschungslage, unpubl. ms.

[111] Schütz, A. (trans.) (1995). *Das Tagebuch der Anne Frank*. Frankfury am Main: Fischer. (10)

[112] Sheehan, J. J. (1989). *German History, 1770—1866*. Oxford: Oxford University Press.

[113] Simon, S. (1996). *Gender in Translation: Cultural Identity and the Politics of Transmission*. London and New York: Routledge.

[114] Snell-Hornby, M. (1984). Sprechbare Sprache-Spielbarer Text: Zur Problematik der Buhneniibersetzung. In R. Watts and U. Weidmann (eds.), *Modes of Interpretation* (pp. 101 – 116). Essays Presented to Ernst Leisi, Tubingen: Narr.

[115] ——(1990). Linguistic Transcoding or Cultural Transfer: A Critique of Translation Theory in Germany. In S. Bassnett and A. Lefevere (eds.), *Translation, History and Culture* (pp. 79 – 86). London: Pinter.

[116] Steubrink, H. J. (1984a). Die Aufgaben eines Frenadsprachendienstes beim Abschlu? von fremdsprachigen Vertragen. Guest Lecture Hildesheim 12.11.1984, unpuble. ms.

[117] Szondi, P. (1986). Schleiermacher's Hermeneutics Today. In *On Textual Understanding and Other Essays*. trans. H. Mendelsohn. Minneapolis: University of Minnesota Press.

[118] Toury, G. (1980). *In Search of a Theory of Translation*. Tel Aviv: Porter Institute for Poetics and Semiotics.

[119] ——(1985). A Rationale for Descriptive Translation Studies. In Hermans (ed.), *The Manipulation of Literature: Studies in Literary Translation* (pp. 16 – 41). Lodon: Croom Helm.

[120] ——(1995). *Descriptive Translation Studies—And Beyond*. Amsterdam: Benjamins.

[121] Tymoczko, M. (1999). Post-Colonial Writing and Literary Translation. In S. Bassnett and H. Trivedi (eds.), *Postcolonial Traslation: Theory and Practice*. London: Routledge.

[122] UUmann-Margalit, E. (1977). *The Emergence of Norms*. Oxford: Oxford University Press. (9)

[123] Venuti, L. (1995). *The Translator's Invisibility: A History of Translation*. London and New York: Routledge.

[124] ——(1998). *The Scandals of Translation: Towards an Ethics of Difference*. London and New York: Routledge.

[125] ——(2000). *The Translation Studies Reader*. London: Routledge.

[126] Verch, M. (1976). Zum Problem english-deutscher übersetzungen von Jugendliteratur. *Revue d'Allemagne* Ⅷ,3,466-473.

[127] Vermeer, H. J. (1978). Ein Rahmen fur eine allgemeine Translationstheirie.

Lebende Sprachen, 23 (1), 99-102. Reprinted in Vermeer 1983, pp. 48 – 88. [*A Framework for a General Theory of Translation*] *First publication of the basic principles and rules of "Skopostheorie:" translation as a subcategory of intercultural interaction, "Spopos" rule, coherence rule, fidelity rule in a hierarchical order.*

[128] ——(1982). Translation als Informationsangebot. *Lebende Sprachen*, 27 (2), 97-101.

[129] ——(1983). Translation Theory and Linguistics. In Pauli Roinila, Ritva Orfanos, and Sonja Tirkkonen-Condit (eds.), *Näkökohtia käänämisen tutkimuksesta. Joensuu* (=*Joensuun kokeakoulu, kielten oasston ulkaisuja* (10) (pp. 1 – 10).

[130] ——(1986). *voraus-setzungen fur eine translationstheorie: Einige kapitel kultur- und sprachtheorie*. Heidelberg: Vermeer.

[131] ——(1987a). What Does It Mean to Translate? *Indian Journal of Applied Linguistics*, 13(2), 25-33.

[132] ——(1987b). Literarische Übersetzung als Versuch interkultureller Kommunikation. In A. Wierlacher (ed.), *Perspektiven und Verfahren interkultureller Germanistik* (pp. 541 – 549). München: Indicium (= Publikationen der Gesellschaft für interkulturelle Germanistik 3). [*Literary Translation as an Attempt at Intercultural Communication*]

[133] ——(1989a). *Skopos und Translationsauftrag-Aufsätze*. Heidelberg: Universitä (thw- translatorisches handeln wissenschaft 2), Second edition 1990.

[134] ——(1989b). Skopos and Commission in Translational Action. In Chesterman (ed.), *Readings in Translation Theory* (pp. 173 – 187). Helsinlci: Oy Finn Lectura Ab. [*Article specially written for the volume, outlining two central concepts in the theory of translational cation: the "Skopos" and the commission or translation brief (see chapter 3).*]

[135] ——(1990). Quality in Translation—A Social Task. The CERA Lectures 1990. The CERA Chair for Translation, Comunication and Cultures. Katholieke Universiteit Leuven, Belgium, June/July 1990[ms.]

[136] ——and Writte, H. (1990). Mögen Sie Zistrosen? Scenes &-frames &-channels im translatorischen Handeln. Heidelberg: Groos (=TEXTTconTEXT Beiheft 3). [*Application of the concepts "scene," "frame" and "channel" to translation.*]

[137] Ward, A. (1974). *Book Production, Fiction and the German Reading Public, 1740—1800*. Oxford: Oxford University Press.

[138] Witte, H. (1987). Die Kulturkompetenz des Translators—Theoretisch-abstrakter Begriff oder realisierbares Konzept. TEXTconTEXT2(2)Z, 109-137.

[139] Woodsworth, J. (1988). Metaphor and Theory: Describing the Translation Process. In P. N. Chaffey, A. G. Rydning and S. S. Ulriksen (eds.), *Theory in Scandinavia: Proceedings from the Scandinavian Symposium on Translation Theory*. Oslo: University of Oslo.

［140］Zuber，R.（1995）（1968）. *Les "Belles Infidèles" et la formation du goût classique*. Paris：Albin Michel.

［141］蔡毅. 关于国外翻译理论的三大核心概念——翻译的实质、可译性和等值. 中国翻译,1995(6).

［142］黄海容. 本雅明翻译观述评. 中国翻译,2007(4).

［143］蒋骁华,张景华. 重新解读韦努蒂的异化翻译理论——兼与郭建中教授商榷. 中国翻译,2007(3).

［144］李德超. 鲁文-兹瓦特论翻译转移的比较. 外国语言文学,2004(4).

［145］李德超,朱志瑜译. 翻译研究:综合法. 北京:外语教学与研究出版社,2006.

［146］李红玉. 斯皮瓦克翻译思想探究. 中国翻译,2009(2).

［147］廖七一. 当代英国翻译理论. 武汉:湖北教育出版社,2001:312-319.

［148］廖七一. 翻译规范及其研究途径. 外语教学,2009(1).

［149］刘军平. 西方翻译理论通史. 武汉:武汉大学出版社,2009.

［150］潘平亮. 翻译目的论及其文本意识的弱化倾向. 上海翻译,2006(1).

［151］司显柱. 朱莉安·豪斯的"翻译质量评估模式"批评. 外语教学,2005(3).

［152］王宏,刘伟. 当代翻译研究的跨学科性及理论融合——评《翻译研究指南》. 外语研究,2008(2).

［153］吴耀武,张建青. 佐哈尔多元系统翻译理论的批评性阐释. 外语教学,2010(5).

［154］谢天振. 当代国外翻译理论导读. 天津:南开大学出版社,2008.

图书在版编目(CIP)数据

当代西方翻译理论研究导引 / 韩江洪编著. — 南京：
南京大学出版社，2012.8
大学翻译学研究型系列教材 / 张柏然总主编
ISBN 978 - 7 - 305 - 09834 - 5

Ⅰ. ①当…　Ⅱ. ①韩…　Ⅲ. ①翻译理论－西方国家－
高等学校－教学参考资料　Ⅳ. ①H059

中国版本图书馆 CIP 数据核字(2012)第 068718 号

出版发行　南京大学出版社
社　　址　南京市汉口路 22 号　　　　邮　编　210093
网　　址　http://www. NjupCo. com
出 版 人　左　健
丛 书 名　大学翻译学研究型系列教材
总 主 编　张柏然
书　　名　当代西方翻译理论研究导引
编　　著　韩江洪
责任编辑　张　静　　　　　　　　编辑热线　025 - 83592123
照　　排　南京南琳图文制作有限公司
印　　刷　南京京新印刷厂
开　　本　787×1092　1/16　印张 24　字数 633 千
版　　次　2012 年 8 月第 1 版　2012 年 8 月第 1 次印刷
ISBN 978 - 7 - 305 - 09834 - 5
定　　价　48.00 元

发行热线　025 - 83594756　83686452
电子邮箱　Press@NjupCo. com
　　　　　Sales@NjupCo. com(市场部)